Soldier

Soldier

Anthony B. Herbert, Lt. Col., Ret.
with James T. Wooten

Holt, Rinehart and Winston

New York   Chicago   San Francisco

Published simultaneously in Canada by Holt, Rinehart
and Winston of Canada, Limited.

ISBN: 0-03-091456-6
Library of Congress Catalog Card Number: 72-78121

FIRST EDITION

Designer: Mary M. Ahern
Printed in the United States of America

For our wives

Soldier

1

Both my brothers were born well before me, Charles fifteen years earlier and Jules Paul eleven years, almost of a different generation— a fact of life for which I never really forgave them, because when World War II came along they both packed up and marched off, leaving me standing on the front porch cursing the irrevocable fact that in America in 1941, there wasn't a great demand for ten-year-old fighting men. I cried, too, when they left, not because they were going to war and might not come back, but because I couldn't go with them. My mother tried to comfort me. "The Army doesn't want you now, Tony," she said. "You've just got to learn to understand, rules are rules." But I neither could nor would. All I really knew for certain was that I wanted above all other things to be a soldier and that somebody or something was ruining my dream.

Now, three decades and two wars later, I can't see that much has changed—except that I don't cry any more. The dream remains, nourished over the years by a partial fulfillment, but still unrealized, still frustrated. The Army still doesn't want me and I still cannot or will not understand why. The difference between now and then is that, when I was a boy on the front porch, there was a chance of making it come true. Now there isn't.

I don't know whether an account of the way it happened holds deep significance for anyone except me, but looking back on it all now, I know I learned a few lessons, and perhaps there are some left for somebody else. On the other hand, perhaps my dream, like all dreams, was meant to be punctured ultimately, leaving behind only a whiff of hope for the next dreamer.

I didn't dream the night before it ended. I was exhausted and my sleep was little more than a lapse into utter unconsciousness. When I was awakened by my wife that morning, it was as though I hadn't even been to bed. My mind was dulled by the grim promise of the day. I knew that it would be one I would want to forget but would always remember. This time it wasn't just another mark on the calendar. In the first place, it was February 29, that bonus of an extra twenty-four hours added to the solar cycle every four times around; but more importantly, it was to be the day I would retire from the United States Army. The fact that the two coincided seemed entirely appropriate, because I knew, and those who knew me best realized, that the day I left the Army would have to be one hell of a special occasion. Not that the brass gave a damn. It was simply that I was about to do what I'd never thought I'd do: leave the Army before I was ready or willing to leave the Army, retire while I was still young enough and strong enough to continue making the kind of contributions I wanted to make and receiving in return the level of personal satisfaction that had attracted me to the Army and kept me there over twenty-three and a half years. For God's sake, I couldn't even remember the last time I'd given a passing thought to doing anything other than serving in the U.S. Army. It had almost always been a part of me—a basic, essential part of me from the moment my brothers left me standing on the front porch. If I knew one thing for certain, it was that I had been most fortunate in my choice of a career. There had been for me little of the quiet desperation Thoreau sensed in the mass of men; instead, there had been only the pure joy of living the way I wanted to live and doing those things in which I found the greatest pleasure. I had spent nearly a quarter of a century in the Army because nothing, absolutely nothing, interested me more. There had never been even the slightest trace of personal sacrifice, because it had always been exactly what I'd had in mind. I had begun as a teenage dropout from the Pennsylvania coal mines, a kid who could barely tell the difference between a mortar and a machine gun, and over the years and the miles and the mud, I had become a lieutenant colonel. It hadn't been a dull climb, either. I had been one of the youngest master sergeants in the Army and the most decorated enlisted man to fight in Korea—at least, that's what the Army said, and who would want to argue with the Army? I had returned to high school and then gone on to college, and I had earned a bachelor's degree and a master's degree and completed the major portion of the requirements for a doctorate. I had seen combat of all kinds and I had killed in battle and been wounded in battle, and I had won medals and awards and citations and commendations and decorations from my own country and several others, and I had seen and served in the best and worst places on the globe. I had met heroes and scum, kings and cowards, generals and presidents, and I had enjoyed the hell out of every single minute, and on the morning of February 29, 1972, I didn't have any apologies and only one regret: I didn't want out—not then, not the next day, and not until I knew I had nothing else to offer the Army and the Army had nothing else to offer me.

That day, all they were offering me officially was retirement, and even though it was their idea, it wasn't going to be easy. Nothing ever is in the Army, which may have been one reason I loved it so much. The day before, the brass at Ft. McPherson, a sprawling post on the outskirts of Atlanta, Georgia, had curtly asked me if I wanted the usual retirement formation and drill or if I would prefer to just sort of sneak out the back way. I chose the latter. There were a lot of other men retiring the next day, and I didn't want to create any possibility of spoiling it for them. I knew that for most of them, retirement was a blessed event, and just because I had my ass in a sling was no reason for them to suffer, too. The brass agreed with my choice and suggested that, as an alternative to the traditional retirement parade, I could simply stop by my office, pick up the retirement forms from my mailbox, sign them, put them back in the mailbox, get my pay, and get the hell out. That was all right with me. I was tired of all the bloody screwing around. But that morning, as I was finishing breakfast with my wife and daughter in our home in an Atlanta suburb, they called again and told me that the original plan had been scrapped and that I would report to the post headquarters where the officer in charge of personnel at Ft. McPherson would personally present me with my retirement papers and personally oversee my last few moments on duty. Sure, I told them again, why not? By that time, I was resigned to the order of things. I was retiring, I knew, and how I retired didn't matter. Hell, I told myself, I was pretty damned lucky I hadn't been court-martialed or just sacked outright with a dishonorable discharge and no retirement benefits. At least this way I could take care of my family and know that officially there were no black marks on my little report card at the Pentagon. But God, it hurt. I was forty-one years old, in the best physical condition of my life, and I had the kind of combat and peacetime experience I knew was valuable to the Army and to my country—to all of us—and I just did not want to leave.

When I parked my car outside Building 65 later that morning, it had never looked more bleakly military. It is a three-story structure that houses the complete headquarters complex of the entire post, and in the years I had been in the military, I had seen a thousand buildings like it: the light paint, slightly peeling and flaking; the darker trim around the windows; the flagpole outside with the chain clanking in the breeze and the banners flapping smartly. Just as the brass had promised, Lt. Colonel Robert Schneider was waiting. He ushered me into a vacant office where the retirement papers lay on a neat desk in the middle of the room. When the door closed behind me, I took a deep breath and tried to settle once and for all the seething inside me. It was the way it had to be, I told myself. All the options had been run and all of them had proved abortive for one reason or another, and there was really, honest to God, nothing left but those papers on that desk and the ball-point pen Schneider was taking from the pocket of his shirt. Still, even in those last few seconds, I wanted desperately to fix in my mind the precise reasons. What the hell had happened? Who did it to me? Did I do it to myself? When did it begin? Maybe I could trace it quickly back to Vietnam, back to that verdantly beautiful country that had somehow done such miserable hurt to my own land, back to that place that had cost us nearly 50,000 young American lives and well over 300,000 more casualties and billions and billions of dollars. But then it dawned on me there in the office that what was happening to me that day probably had its origins in some moment long before I had ever heard of Vietnam, at some forgotten point in time and space where one event, trivial and insignificant, had produced another and then another and then another, until the weight and mass of cause-and-effect history was moving me inevitably and inexorably toward that scrubby little office at Ft. McPherson and those papers and that pen.

"Uh, Colonel Herbert," Schneider was saying softly, "uh, I just want you to know that I didn't volunteer for this job." I nodded and smiled and he seemed relieved. "And I'd like for you to understand that I think it's a pretty goddamned lousy deal for you," he added.

"Thanks," I said. "But don't sweat it."

He wasn't finished. "And you probably already know it anyway, but I want to tell you that there are a hell of a lot of guys here and all over the Army who feel the same way," he said, handing me the pen and pointing to the blank line.

I smiled again, took the ball-point from him and leaned over the desk.

The pen broke in my hand. Maybe the pressures on me were greater than I realized that day, and maybe I was trying to ease them a bit by bearing down a little harder. On the other hand, not that I believed in such things, perhaps it was a sign, an omen of darker, drearier days ahead should I affix my signature to the little sheaf of documents there on the desk. Anyway, when I leaned over and pressed it to the paper, the cheap little plastic pen chose to end its functional existence and broke, sending its tiny spring flying across the room.

It wasn't the first time anything had ever disintegrated in my hands. The very first weapon I ever owned did it every time I squeezed the trigger. It was an old 12-gauge Fox with one of its two barrels spiked. My father, Charles Edward Herbert, Sr., gave it to me in the autumn of 1937 when I was a second-grader. Actually, it was the second time he had given me the gun. The year before, he had made a great ceremony of handing it over, but on my first hunt with him in the hills around our home in western Pennsylvania, I crawled through a fence carelessly dragging it behind me and it discharged. He took it away and refused to give it back—refused to even talk about it. All through that long winter, as I walked through the snowy woods with him, the only shooting I did was with a crooked stick. I'd kick out a rabbit and with great imaginary skill take aim down the stick and shout "Bang! Bang!" There are probably ten thousand rabbits scampering around in the brush there today whose great-grandfathers and great-grandmothers owe their very existence to my father's stern insistence that a careless kid should have nothing more lethal to shoot than a crooked stick. But the next fall, I got the gun back. "You mess up again, and I take it back again," my father said. I vowed I wouldn't, and I didn't, but every time I squeezed off a shot, the damned old thing would fly apart in my hands. The stock would go one way and the barrels another, and I'd be left with the handguard in my fist. But it shot straight and true and, best of all, it was mine.

Guns were always an integral part of life in the Herbert family, not because we were great sportsmen or anything like that, but simply because we liked to eat, and eating wasn't a simple matter for a coal miner and his family in those days. The mines were all my father had ever known: the day-after-day regimen of dust and dirt and darkness and penny-pinching poverty, with never enough pennies to pinch. Up until John L. Lewis and the United Mine Workers came along in 1939, the most cash my father ever saw for one week's work was $2.00. The rest of his compensation came in the form of credit at the Eureka Store, where Mr. Stahls, the manager and dutiful employe of the mine, would carefully match the amount of purchases against the amount of credits. It inevitably worked out at the end of the year that my father and every other miner in town had bought more than their credit allowed. All my life, I heard my father and mother worry about paying off the company store before they died. Their chief aim was to leave without passing that particular debt on to their children. They lived in a company-owned house in a company-owned town in a company-owned county. Neither my father nor any other man who worked in the mines could quit. How could they? The mines owned them. But none of us ever really felt poor. There were so many other families just like us that we had no standard of comparison. Everybody had to struggle to make it—at least, everybody with whom we had any contact—and for all we knew the whole world lived precisely as we did there in Herminie, forty miles from Pittsburgh, deep in the black heart of the bituminous coal-mine country.

To make ends almost meet, my father provided a guide service for hunters from Pittsburgh. My father sneered at their expensive weapons and their clumsy manners in the field, and there was nothing worse he could call you than a "Pittsburgh hunter." A part of his antagonism probably came from the fact that he was, as a matter of necessity, giving himself to them; but it had another facet, too. He distrusted them because they carried multi-fire weapons—pumps— and he was persuaded that this availability of repetitive fire was bound to produce a rather bloodthirsty carelessness. "Listen, Tony, the day you see me miss my first shot and have to take a second, that's the day you take over," he would say, stroking his double-barrel, 12-gauge Ithaca. I never saw that happen. He was the finest marksman I ever knew. I remember one afternoon in the summer of 1935—I think it was that year—he and my Uncle Joe Gracan were whiling away a Saturday beneath a cherry tree a few dozen yards from our house,

6

doing their dead-level best to empty a keg of homemade whiskey. Actually, they were supposed to be taking down a radio aerial strung between two tall thin posts, about sixty feet above the ground. My mother had asked them to get it down and restring it so that she could hear her programs that night, but both of them found the lounging and the liquor much more to their liking. Finally, though, my father must have felt a couple of pangs of conscience, because he haled me from the backyard where I was playing and asked me to bring him the 22-caliber rifle that was stacked with our other weapons behind a closet door in the house. Uncle Joe and he were both drunk as lords, but my father lifted the rifle to his shoulder and clipped the tiny wire off one insulator with one shot. He reloaded and did the same at the other end. Then, with great dignity, he and Uncle Joe reeled off toward the house to inform my mother that the job had been done. She shook her head and made one rather timid inquiry about the rest of the task—putting it up again in a better location—but they pretended not to hear her and wandered outside and went to sleep on the porch. I learned two lessons that afternoon: first, that my father was one hell of a shot, drunk or sober, and second—well, the keg they left at the cherry tree was so irresistible, I began to drink from it, in short, measured sips at first, and then, as I became increasingly numb, in longer, bolder swigs. An hour later the keg was empty and I was an extremely plastered five-year-old with an insatiable desire to visit the candy store, with not a penny to my name. Once there, I fell through a glass showcase and had to be carted home. It was my first and final toot. I don't have to be taught important lessons more than once.

My father's marksmanship never failed to amaze the Pittsburgh hunters. They were happy to pay him $2.50 a day for his help in finding pheasants, ruffled grouse, wild turkey, quail, snowshoe rabbits, or squirrels. As a part of the deal, we provided the dogs for the hunt as well, rounding up two or three from our ever-present pack of blue-tick hounds and beagles. During the deer season, my father would charge them a flat season fee of $12.00 that guaranteed them a buck. They always went back to the city satisfied with his services. I usually went along on those jaunts, lugging my Fox and waiting, as I had been instructed, until the Pittsburgh hunters missed before aiming my gun. With my father as a teacher, I learned quickly how to hit whatever I picked out as a target, and the guys from Pittsburgh made a big thing about how well I could shoot, even with an antique weapon that flew apart every time it was fired. I never thought much about it because, just as with our poverty, everybody I knew back then could handle a gun. It was no big deal. The big deal came when we found someone who didn't know how, like the Pittsburgh hunters. They made a joke of my gun, and one day some of our regular customers chipped in and bought me a new one. It was another 12-gauge Fox, and it didn't disintegrate when I fired it, and I loved it. But my father's lessons, taught with the old one, were already firmly implanted in my mind. "Your old gun is good for you," he would say. "It makes you shoot like you should the first time because you know you won't get a second time." He was damned sure right about that. Of course, I didn't realize it at the time, but it was probably one of the most valuable lessons I ever learned. I know now that it saved my life quite a few times as the years passed.

But while guns were always a part of our life, hunting was never really a sport for us. It was an income supplement and the guns were only a means toward that end. It was the same way with the game we killed. "It is only a matter of food and money," my father liked to explain. "If you ever kill just to be killing, you'll not hunt with me again." When I remember his rules now, I know with a great certainty that I was blessed among little boys. He was a simple, honest guy—one hell of a man.

His mother was pregnant with him when she and his father and his two older brothers and a sister came to this country from Lithuania in the fall of 1896. Like so many of their own countrymen and hordes of other Baltic immigrants, they settled in the coal fields of Pennsylvania because, in the life they had left behind, the mines had also been their way of life. My father was born in November of that year in Larmar, Pa., just a few miles from Herminie, but when his father became ill a year later, the entire family returned to Lithuania so that, as my father told it, his father "could put his bones into dirt he knew." The family's name then was Arbutus, and when my grandfather died in Europe in 1899, my grandmother married Nicholas Solkinus and the six of them returned to America as the century turned, this time to Herminie, a simple little town that was then, and has remained since, a community of about 2,000 people. There Grandpa Solkinus went to work in the mines, continuing the life he had known in Lithuania and establishing rhythms for himself and his stepsons that would remain constant into the next generation.

Although no one in Herminie ever concerned himself with genealogies, Grandpa Solkinus made me constantly aware of my heritage by always referring to me as Antinius Arbutus, roughly the Lithuanian equivalent of Anthony Herbert. I remember him well. He was the epitome of the East European miner, a grizzled man who puffed on a giant, curved pipe clenched between teeth worn down to stubs. Ever the story teller, he was always bursting with tales of his youth in the old country and jokes about my grandmother and terrifying predictions of what would happen to little boys who weren't especially kind to their grandfathers. "Antinius Arbutus," he would roar from his weathered rocking chair, "do you know what happened to me when I was a child?" "No," I would say. "Then stand close here and I'll tell you," Grandpa Solkinus would order. "My own grandfather, God rest his soul"—and here he would cross himself somberly—"my own grandfather once asked me for a hug around his neck and I did not want to give him a hug so I said, 'No hug today.' Do you know what he did? He threw me down the well and I was never heard from or ever seen again in my entire life." Then he would roar with delight and ask for a hug—and he always got one.

The family legends insist that when my teenage father began courting Mary Theibert, no one was more pleased than Grandpa Solkinus. She was the daughter of one of the most respected couples in Herminie, Mr. and Mrs. Jules Theibert. They had come to Pennsylvania from England and Mr. Theibert had quickly established himself as a talented artisan and a shrewd but fair-minded businessman. He was a master of glass cutting, and in addition to plying that trade he opened a livery stable, started a newspaper, and founded the town's first auto garage. The Theiberts lived in a large house on a high hill, and it was there that my father and mother were married in 1915. They were both quite young, and they seemed an unlikely match. He was from a coal miner's family and after only three years of formal schooling had dropped out and entered the mines himself. She was a girl who had grown up with fine linen and lace in a home where music and books were natural and money never a problem. But if the Theiberts ever objected to the marriage, they kept it a secret. They were gentle folks who seemed content with the fact that their daughter loved the man she married. They gave me the impression that one of the most important things was to live your own life and let others live theirs. Even when their rather sizable fortune was erased in 1929, they continued to live as genteel citizens. Mr. Theibert went to work as a time-keeper at the mine, but he was never bitter, and every night from their house on the hill came the sound of their piano or Mrs. Theibert's violin or her lilting voice. Grandpa Theibert may have lost his wealth but he never lost the respect of the people around him. Everyone in Herminie called him "Dad." I remember him as a man who seldom raised his voice and as one of two people who constantly encouraged me to take an interest in books. In fact, it was in his house that I first saw and touched and opened a book.

In contrast, the fortunes of my father's parents were on the rise during the 1920s and 1930s as a result of their manufacture and distribution of illegal whiskey. They moved out of the little company house to a better, larger one they bought for themselves, and it was there when I was five that I first saw a bathtub. It was a magnificent creation with large lion's paw feet—and the night I first caught a glimpse of it, it was brimming with homemade whiskey. Even though their business provided a more than adequate income for them, Grandpa and Grandma Solkinus continued to live in the style of European peasantry, preferring turnip tops grown out back to potatoes purchased at the grocery, and choosing not to install electricity in their house when it became available. They were strong, stubborn people who spent their money on property and believed that any change in their life style might bring about a change in their fortunes. I loved them both, just as I loved the Theiberts, but I continue to marvel even today that my parents' marriage survived the contrasts in their families.

While Grandpa was no wallflower, it was Grandma who held the Solkinus Distillery together. She came up with the recipes, manufacturing techniques, and price lists, and their business was not more than a few months old before it was well known throughout the community. There were few drinkers in town who did not know her face and her voice and her name and her front door, always open to the customer with cash. Both of my grandparents were very proud of their products. They handled a fairly broad line, including pick-handle whiskey, bathtub gin, and apple and elderberry brandies, and they never quite grasped the notion that what they were doing was wrong.

After all, in the old country what they were doing had been regarded as honorable and decent, and the better a man's whiskey the more respect he had in his community. The authorities in this country held a somewhat different view, however, and for some reason it was always my grandmother who was in trouble with them.

One afternoon when I was quite small, I inadvertently fingered her for a couple of revenuers. I was playing in her backyard when two gentlemen in pinch-back suits, bow ties, and straw skimmers approached and asked if I knew where they might find Mrs. Solkinus. Sure, I said, happy to cooperate. She was around in front. I pointed and followed them around the house. She was rocking away in her favorite chair and refused to go with them when they asked. She grabbed the arms of her chair and hung on for dear life, but they finally pried her loose and carried her away. This was not long after the kidnapping of Charles Lindbergh's son, and there had been a great deal of talk about that tragedy. I went running to my father, screaming that "the Lindbergh men" had kidnapped Grandma. She got six months to a year in the Greensburg jail. Months later when we drove by the place, I asked my father if that wasn't where Grandma lived. He never answered.

Grandma Solkinus was a strong woman, physically and emotionally. Although she seldom showed outward affection, she managed to maintain a steady, close relationship with her grandchildren. But she never forgot the day I squealed on her, and she pretended never to forgive me, even when she lay dying. My father came out of her room that day to tell me she wanted to see her Antinius and that she planned to put an eternal curse on me. I was a grown man by then, but I approached her bedside with some trepidation. It was all her idea of a joke, she said, but I was still relieved when I left the room without hearing her pronounce the Solkinus Distillery's Hex.

If my father ever complained about the grim cycles in his life, I never heard him. He was as steady as a clock: up before dawn, walk to the mine, back home in the evening for a glass of beer or two before supper, and then to bed. But with a wife and four children— Charles and Jules, my two older brothers, plus our sister Irene, four years my senior, and me—there was never enough money, never near enough, and the income from his guide service couldn't bridge the

11

gap. He trapped muskrats and sold the pelts to Montgomery Ward and Sears, Roebuck (an average skin would bring about $1.75, with an exceptionally good one selling for $3.00 or so), and although he approached his trapping with the same skill and determination he devoted to his job at the mine and his hunting, it still wasn't enough. There were occasions when he would have to trudge down to the welfare office. It was painful for him, I knew. He dreaded every trip he ever made down there, and when he came back with the government commodities—a bag of rice, a bag of raisins, a bag of corn meal—he had the look of a man who had stood in a line of men going nowhere. He was unusually grim, and for days afterwards he would not be himself, but somehow quieter, more withdrawn. I suppose the only comfort he had was in knowing that he wasn't the only husband and father in Herminie who was having trouble taking care of his family. All of us went to whatever lengths were necessary to get the job done. We made wine at home and sold or traded it for essentials. Charles took on an ice route, delivering the twenty-five-pound and fifty-pound blocks up and down the steep streets. We "picked" coal at the slate dump, a smoking mountain of coal waste deposited by the mine just at the edge of town. It was about a quarter of a mile across and three quarters of a mile long. Of all the childhood images I have retained, one of the most vivid is of that ebony hump rising above the houses, steaming and hissing like a volcano. We would trudge up its crumbling sides, pick up pieces of slate, knock the coal off and put it in the burlap sacks we carried. At the end of the day, we piled our sacks into a wheelbarrow and went downtown to sell the coal for a dime a sack. The slate pile was never one of my favorite places. There were cavernous, hollow pockets beneath its contours, and we had all heard of the two people who had gone to the dump and disappeared forever into its black bowels. But somehow we survived.

I have met people whose Depression childhood is for them a mark of inherent virtue, as though anyone without that particular deprivation in his life has been severely handicapped. I don't remember it that way at all, and in the years since, I have come to understand the universality of such things. I have seen poverty all over the world. It has no redeeming virtues, and it does not necessarily build better men. All it does is confront people with the rudiments of survival at an earlier age.

I didn't realize it at the time, of course, but Herminie was like almost any other coal-mine community in Pennsylvania or eastern Kentucky or West Virginia. It had twenty-two bars, four churches, and eight drinking clubs, and being predominantly a town of ethnic Roman Catholics, business was brisk on both sides of the street. There was Galante's Bar and Ghion's Bar and Cassanelli's Bar and Puklavec's Bar and Harenski's Bar, to name but a few, and on the Sabbath, when St. Edward's did its best business of the week and the bars all closed down, the Sons of Labor Hall took up the slack.

Main Street, the only paved thoroughfare in town, was six blocks long. We had a theater, two poolrooms, a bank, a couple of candy stores, a butcher shop run by the Badanjaks, a drugstore, an ice cream shop, and several markets for dry goods and sundries. All of them were on the upper side of the street, facing row upon row of the company houses in which lived almost everyone we knew.

The town was one of several built around a collection of mines that had attracted not only the Baltic immigrants but a lot of Scots and Irishmen as well. Sulphur Creek, a bright red stream fed constantly with the drainoff from the mines, separated our town from Limerick Hill, the first of the others. The social systems that were premised on that creek were as rigid as though it were the Berlin Wall. Still, despite our differences—I never knew what they were—we shared one common bond: the mines and their wailing whistles that shrieked out the beginning and the end of the workers' days, sounding for miles and miles through the hills, and sometimes signalling the reality of death.

My Uncle Joe Shearer, my mother's oldest sister's husband, died in a cave-in at the nearby Barking Mine when I was about four years old. Three or four other miners were also killed in that cave-in, and I remember the sound of the whistles. It was always like that back then, always some accident or cave-in that killed one or two or three men—not any "major disaster," as the newspapers like to say—and so it was forgotten or ignored by those who had the kind of power that would have made some difference in the condition of the mines and the dangers faced by those who worked in them.

Uncle Joe was one of my favorite relatives, second only to Grandpa Solkinus and Grandpa Theibert. He was a marvelous whittler, and although I don't remember that I was especially deprived of playthings, I recall that it was Uncle Joe and only Uncle Joe who regularly brought me toys, including wooden guns and swords he had

13

fashioned with his knife. On the day of his funeral, my mother left me in a large chair in our living room with strict instructions not to leave the house until she returned. Through the graying window curtains, I watched her walk up the hill and join the crowd of mourners waiting at St. Edward's, the Roman Catholic church in which she was quite active. (In fact, I have great difficulty remembering her without her rosary beads. She and Mrs. Buffalini, a neighbor, were always cooking for the nuns or washing and ironing for the priests.) I watched the casket containing the body of my Uncle Joe carried on the shoulders of six men, including my father, up the steps and into the sanctuary, and I saw my mother and her widowed sister with white handkerchiefs in their hands follow it inside—and I recall how still and quiet the house and the street and the town seemed to be. Normally, I would have obeyed my mother's instructions only as long as she was in sight, but that day I remained in that chair, my eyes riveted on the church a half block away, and didn't move until she returned. Later that night, Father Bernard Kelley visited the house to offer his condolences to my mother. Then, almost as a sign that what was done was done and what was past was past, he and my father retired to the front porch and drank Fort Pitt beer from large brown bottles.

The fact that the priest was Irish never struck anyone as incongruous in those days. Now, of course, as ethnic groups strain to maintain separate identities, it would be unthinkable in some communities. But in those days we more or less expected our priests to be Irish and we never held it against them or the church. In return, they seemed not to mind that their parishioners were of East European vintage.

I always loved Father Kelley, but I was never sure about the church. He was a kind old man who had been a hero in World War I and had the medals to prove it, according to my father, and he had been gassed. At times he seemed very nervous about being a priest, and maybe that was why he drank a great deal. But the most important thing about him was that he did not preach fear from the pulpit of St. Edward's. Nevertheless, I approached his church with fear. To me it represented a tomb, perhaps because I associated it with Uncle Joe's sudden and mysterious departure from my life. There was a small hole in the ground out in back of St. Edward's through which trucks would pour coal into the basement of the church. But in my young mind, it was the entrance to a hell to which one was sentenced by God, the abstract, absolute judge. I avoided the area as religiously as others approached it.

I'm not sure what my father's problems with the church were, but he seldom attended except at my mother's insistence. Most Sundays he would end up down at the Sons of Labor Hall with the rest of the guys, spending his day off with some cool beer and the warmth of the men he knew and respected. I suspect that he regarded the men who went to church regularly either as sissies or simply as undesirable company. They were the superintendents and the bankers and the school teachers, and I think my father just couldn't bring himself to be one of them. So, when the others filed into St. Edward's or into the other churches on Sunday morning, my father and all the other hunters and trappers and fishermen gathered at the club for a few drinks and a few hands of euchre.

Although I became an altar boy at St. Edward's when I was eight, it was only because it was what my mother wanted. She told me it would please Father Kelley, who was getting old and would be leaving soon—as he did, dying about four years later. I always believed that he thought I would also be a priest. Like my Grandpa Theibert, he was continually pressing books on me and encouraging me to read. Whatever hopes he may have had, the chances for any kind of wholesome relationship between the church and me were dashed by an experience I had during the first Christmas Eve Mass after he died. One of the ladies who had come with the new priest to keep the rectory in shape was standing in the back of the church arguing with the collection plate handlers. She kept telling them to send the plates out again into the midnight-mass congregation—a congregation of poor miners who generally gave more to the church than they should have—explaining that no one would realize what was happening, since everyone was drunk. While it was no doubt true that many of the people who had come to worship that night had been nipping a bit earlier in the evening, that seemed irrelevant to me. I was kneeling close by in the candlelit sanctuary. I won't ever forget her face as she took the money and put it in her apron. She was for years the representative of a witch for me. Thereafter, throughout the years, there were few instances when I did not immediately associate greed with the mention of the institutional church. I know Father Kelley might have relieved me of that burden, but he wasn't around—and besides, everywhere I've been, it has been invariably reaffirmed.

Dr. Latimer's office was on Main Street just across from Cassanelli's Bar. The doctor delivered all of us Herbert children, and the price for each successive child was somewhat higher than the last. I think the cost of my birth was $8.00 as compared with my oldest brother's, which was around $2.00 or perhaps free. It really made no difference anyway, because Dr. Latimer was never paid and really never expected to be paid by my father nor any other miner in town whose wife bore a child he delivered. The Doc was a very gruff old geezer who, for some reason or another, took an interest in me when I was about seven or eight years old. He was different from all the other people who had good jobs with the mines. He lived on Main Street, in the same building with his office. All the bosses lived on the hill above, separated from the riff-raff. Doc would always appear surprised when I showed up at his office late in the afternoon, and when he gave me copies of *National Geographic* magazine he acted as if he was giving me the crown jewels. I would take a magazine and sit for a few moments in his office in a set ritual. The pictures fascinated me, but the Doc always refused to answer my questions immediately. "Go home and look at them and read what it says beneath the pictures and see if that answers your questions," he would say. "If you still have questions, come back tomorrow and I'll try to help you with them."

So I would do that, and I'd always end up the next day with more questions than when I had left his office. He'd take me back into his office and we'd talk about the pictures and anything else that happened to be on my mind or his. Sometimes he would let me take a peek into the microscope he kept on a table next to his desk, and he would explain that what I was seeing through its lens were tiny animals that could be bad or good, "just like everything else in the world." It was Doc, I think, who first started impressing me with the idea that wherever people live, they are essentially the same. "Look at these natives," he would say, pointing to some bare-breasted folks from Australia or Africa. "They hunt just like you hunt, Tony, and just like your father and your brothers. The only difference is that they use a bow and arrow. They bleed if they get cut, and the fathers and mothers worry about their children and they all worry about food and about dying, and they all want to live as long as they can, just like you, Tony." The Doc never went to church. Somehow that impressed me. Like my father, he seemed always to be what he was. Never any phoniness around him or about him.

But if I had to pick one fellow who had the most to do with the course of my life, I suppose I'd have to pass over Doc Latimer and Grandpa Theibert and even my father and go back to Father Kelley. He was a good priest—good in the sense that he deeply knew the people in his flock. He knew their poverty and their hopelessness and their frequent desperation and, above all, he knew how absolutely necessary it was that their individual family incomes be supplemented. That was why he showed no reservations at all about doctoring baptismal certificates. In 1942, when I was twelve years old, he changed mine to make it read that I was sixteen and thus allow me to get a work permit and start bringing home a little cash for the family. He had done the same for my brothers, I was told, and for almost everybody else in town who had sons who were willing to work. I had taken my first job when I was ten, along with Richard Natale, the brother of a pretty little girl named Marygrace. We worked on Muller's Farm right outside of town, and every morning at 4:30, rain or shine, Mr. Muller would come into town and pick us up in his little truck. We were paid $1.50 a week and a gallon of raw milk, and for that we both drove tractors, cut wheat, dug potatoes, fed his cattle, and milked his cows. He knew what he was doing. Obviously, that wasn't helping much with the family financial burdens, and Father Kelley's forgery was an absolute necessity. With my work permit in hand, I got a job at the local glass factory—the one my Grandpa Theibert had helped organize and build—and started earning $18.00 a week. With the overtime available at $.49 an hour, I often brought home as much as $28.00 in one week. At first, I simply carried glass from one part of the factory to another; but then, because I was a big kid even at that age, I graduated to the position of glazier. I wore an asbestos suit and worked in the near vicinity of the open molds, where the heat became so intense that we were allowed to work only ten minutes before taking a ten-minute break. In six months, I became an operator of the molds and got a sizable raise that allowed me to bring home as much as $30.00 in some weeks. I had taken the job in the summer, and when school began, I simply asked to have my hours changed to the night shift and kept right on working.

The next summer, 1944, I was thirteen years old, but my work permit and my phony birth certificate said seventeen, and I had grown considerably since the previous spring. I went to work on the Pennsylvania Railroad, where I had heard the pay was better. At first, I worked in the roundhouse for $.85 an hour, helping to repair the giant steam engines. It paid well, for it was relatively dangerous work, with an awful lot of things falling around all day and a hell of a lot of noise. You never could hear if someone was yelling at you to tell you that a 600-pound piston was dropping straight on your head. I soon worked up to $.92 an hour, and then one day a truck driver didn't show up, and they asked around if anybody had had any experience driving trucks and I said yes. The truth was that I'd never driven one alone, but from then on I drove the truck that carried the huge train springs from one part of the rail yards to another—and for better pay.

All the while, the Herbert family maintained its A–1 guide service for the Pittsburgh hunters my father so detested, and in my early teens I expanded our trapping enterprise with a few score runs of my own. That was when I was most happy as a boy, I think: out in the woods in the early morning darkness, the snow crunching beneath my shoes, my breath visible with every exhalation—the quiet, the stillness, the challenge, the danger, real or imagined, and every morning, the reward. But I must confess that my trapping occasionally did present some conflicts, not only with the railroad job I was trying to hold, but with the normal impulses of a young adolescent. My brothers had both played football at Sewickley Township school (my father had helped build part of it during WPA), and it was just naturally expected that I would play, too. I was big enough, and I sort of enjoyed the normal teenage satisfactions like playing football. But I had divided loyalties. Not only did I have the job to consider, but I soon learned that the practice time required for high school athletics ate into the time I could spend in the field with my hunting and my trapping. (During games on Saturday, I would tie the hunting dogs to the bench and stash my gun beneath it while I played.) As a freshman end, I had been permitted to play a great deal more than my attendance at practice sessions might have warranted. But the next year, in the tenth grade, I just didn't have my heart in it. From the hillside where I trained our dogs in September, I could look down on the practice field, and I recall that I felt nothing but smugness. I was up there with the dogs and a shotgun in my hand, and those guys were down there, huffing and puffing and taking orders. But my choices weren't easy ones. In the winter, for example, I had to be up at 3:30 every morning to check out the 200 traps I was running before going to school—but I made a hell of a lot of money for a kid in those days, and my family was better off because of it. And what's more, I liked it.

It was during one of those winters in my early teens that the Kousters lost four of their children in one swift stroke of fate, and once again the mine whistle told the story to the neighboring communities. One of the older brothers, Harry, was a friend of mine. His two younger brothers and two sisters were out late one afternoon, playing on one of the "frog" ponds in the area—ponds created by the still drainage of the mines. The near-zero temperatures had frozen the water to what the kids believed was a safe depth, but the ice broke beneath one of them, and one by one the others plunged through and drowned too, trying to effect a rescue with the courage so typical of the area. All four dead. I had never seen Harry cry before. I caught his eye at Stader's funeral home, and his tears moved me to cry myself.

Still, there was no one event related to death that had greater impact on me, I suppose, than the day we buried Joe Ricci. Joe was part of our gang—one of several in our town and others nearby that would frequently be caught up in the usual mischief of kids. There was Billy McAlpine and Sammy DelGreco and my cousin, Corky Gracan, and Joe Shagday and Vic Carosella, my best friend in those days. Vic and I had been buddies since the second or third grade, because out of all the guys our age we were most nearly the same when it came to physical strength and endurance.

Very often, all of us would take rifles out to the town dump and shoot rats—which was more of a sportsman-like hobby than it might seem, because the rats were ferocious—absolute tigers. After a while they sensed what was happening and frequently turned to the offense, attacking one or all of us, hurling their bodies at our legs with their sharp teeth snapping in the air and occasionally finding the flesh through the fabric. One afternoon when Vic and I were about thirteen we were coming up the hill into town, crossing a bridge above the tracks which lead to the dump, when we heard the crack of a .22

19

down below and saw Corky, DelGreco, and Shagday down there leaning over Joe Ricci. Joe was stretched out across the ties. "Antinius, Antinius," he cried to me. "I'm hit, I'm hit." Vic thought he was joking, but when we reached him, we both knew he wasn't. Someone—it was never determined who—had put a bullet into his side, off a rib and into his kidneys. Sammy and I ran to Stader's mortuary and then across and down the street to Doc Latimer's. Joe was taken to Greensburg in a hearse. He lived for some months, but then gangrene set in, and they brought his body back to Herminie. The funeral was set at St. Edward's, where I was an altar boy. The priest took the watershaker from me and began to sprinkle its contents on the casket, and I remember that I stood there before the altar trying to figure out at which end of that great metal box they had placed Joe's head and which end his feet. I never had really thought in terms of the dead being punished. It had always been a matter of the living getting their come-uppance. But that night, my mother asked me to pray for the soul of Joe and, for the first time in my life, I did offer prayers on behalf of another person.

Not all the kids in Herminie were as rough as we were. The Natales, for instance, who lived a few doors away, were much more strict about what their children could and could not do. Richard, with whom I had worked on Mr. Muller's farm, his brother Jimmie and his sister Marygrace didn't get out and roam the streets as we often did. Instead, they were called in at dark, did their studies, and went to bed. Meanwhile, the rest of us were out taking on the Boltontown Gang or the Station Gang or the Church Street Gang (who, thanks to the Smiths, the Altmans, and Snitzel Peters, invariably whipped our asses) or the Hilltop Gang (whose asses we regularly whipped, since they were the biggest pansies in town). I think I spent half of my early life throwing rocks, although I quickly learned the difference between valor and discretion. One night, we received a challenge from the Turtle Creek Gang that we turned down. The reason was that they supposedly had a big, gangling bastard who could throw rocks better and harder than anybody in western Pennsylvania. His name was Leon Hart. Like John Lujack, a stalwart rock-thrower from the South Huntingdon Area Gang, he went on to Notre Dame, where he continued hurting people.

I never picked individual fights, but I never seemed to have any trouble getting into them either. I guess because I was larger than most of the guys my age, a lot of them couldn't resist the challenge. I don't want to come off badly by saying this, but I just can't remember ever losing one. There was one guy, Lefty, who always wanted to fight me because he'd heard that I was supposedly undefeated. Lefty was about three years older than I and a little bit bigger. Hell, I must have fought him and whipped him at least ten times, and three weeks later he'd be back asking for more. One day, when we were about fourteen, Joe Klaus and I were hitchhiking back from swimming when we ran into Lefty. He decided on a different tack this time and started picking on Joe. I stepped in and, for once, I started getting the worst of it. Before I knew it, Lefty had his belt around my neck with my back against a utility pole. He kept squeezing the belt. I was seeing black and purple and trying to kick him in the balls backward around the pole. But I couldn't reach him. Suddenly, the belt broke, and I pulled myself together and beat the hell out of him. I think that was our last fight.

While I was getting started as an adolescent, my brothers were fighting the war. Chuck became an infantry officer and a company commander in Italy, and Bud, a Navy man, served as chief torpedoman aboard a destroyer that prowled the North Atlantic. Their letters were never any aid or comfort to me. Vicarious combat, like books and movies and teleplays, has never been my cup of tea. I hadn't quite recovered from their abrupt departure from Herminie and their subsequent location in places with exotic names when they came home with medals on their chests and stories to tell the old man on the front porch. In the spring of 1944, that was what I wanted, and I wanted it badly. I still wanted to be a soldier, and I knew exactly how I could do it, the military's rules be damned. The phony baptismal certificate Father Kelley had worked up for me was my key. Actually, I was already getting some advice from the people at work about registering for the draft. They thought I was eighteen years old, and I saw no reason to disappoint them. I went over to Irwin with my work permit in hand and told Mrs. Gongaware at the draft office that I'd just forgotten about the need to register. She looked at me as if I were a low-life son-of-a-bitch who was trying to sneak out of my duty as an eighteen-year-old American citizen. Actually, I was a fourteen-year-old American citizen about to do my best to sneak into my duty. I'd like to say that it was all my idea but I can't remember whether it was me or a friend, Tony Spizzali, who was working with me at the railroad yards at that time under the same type fraud, who mentioned it first. It was May—school was still in session—and since what we were about to do wasn't exactly unheard of in Herminie, we didn't have any apprehensions about whether or not we could pull it off.

"Maybe we ought to tell our mothers," Tony suggested. And I rejected that. They wouldn't understand, I said. Once we were in and wrote to them, everybody would understand. So, early one morning while it was still dark, I left the house to meet Tony down at the Eureka Store. There were twenty steps down from our front porch to the street, and I knew every one of them. I was the one who had carried the coal from the street to the house, after the truck had delivered it from the mine in five-ton loads. I would transfer the huge pile, bushel basket by bushel basket, up the twenty steps and into the cellar. I knew those steps well enough not to make any noise when I descended them that morning and headed off into the world. We walked from the store out to the highway and caught a ride with Charlie Czhiczeck, a Lithuanian from nearby Hutchinson who worked at one of the steel mills in and around Pittsburgh. He let us out on the fringes of the gray city and we walked the rest of the way to the U.S. Post Office in downtown Pittsburgh, where we both joined the U.S. Marines.

The next day, the train Tony and I were riding southward through Virginia toward Parris Island, S.C., was halted in some backwoods town and we were taken off by a man who identified himself only as a "federal officer." We were both impressed, if disappointed. When we arrived back at the Pittsburgh depot, Mr. Gressman, our high school principal, was waiting and took us home. My father only shook his head, but my mother was glad to see me and smothered me with forgiveness. I went back to my traps and my school and my job at the railroad the very next day. I wasn't finished, however. I was only waiting.

Three years later, when May rolled around and my eleventh-grade studies seemed interminable, I tried again. This time it was legal. I was seventeen, and with my parents' signature I could join. On May 2, I went to Pittsburgh, to the Post Office again, and walked into the Marine recruiting office again. Sorry, the sergeant said. Their

May quota was filled and it would be about a month before I could actually begin training. Nope, I said, that wasn't what I had in mind. I was deeply disappointed. I had heard about "President Truman's Professional Army" and how difficult it was to be accepted into its ranks, and I thought that for a seventeen-year-old kid it would be doubly difficult. At that moment, a man wearing the U.S. Army 11th Airborne patch on his shoulder sauntered into the Marine office and noticed my quandary. "Hey, kid, you wanna be a paratrooper?" he asked. "What's that?" I inquired. "You jump out of planes and fight," he said—and I joined.

A week later, in the early morning of May 9, 1947, I got up to say goodbye to my folks. My father, who rose at 4:30 every morning of his life except Sundays, was sitting at the kitchen table when I came downstairs, already dressed and ready to leave. My mother was puttering quietly around the stove and the large white enamel cabinet, preparing lunch for my father to take to the mine. I sat down and poured coffee into a metal cup. I suppose my father felt it was absolutely necessary that he give me some parting advice although he, like I, had no idea what being a paratrooper meant. But it was good advice. As I recall, it went something like this:

"The uniform doesn't mean you're a soldier.

"Whatever you do, don't get disgusted. Stick with it, like you stick with it here at home. Remember what your brothers did. Nobody ever quit. It won't be any harder than hunting—than wading in the creek in the winter. Nothing is as hard as just getting started.

"It's like in the coal mines. Every step takes care of itself."

Then we walked out together. My mother didn't cry. I wouldn't have expected her to. Stoicism is a virtue that a coal miner's wife develops. I never remember my mother as a young woman—not that day or any other—and when my wife is sixty years old, she will be younger than my mother was at thirty. My mother waved from the porch as my father and I descended the twenty steps to the road. His ride to the mine came by and they disappeared into the darkness. I walked to the Eureka Store, caught a bus to Irwin, took a train to Pittsburgh, and on the morning of May 10, 1947, I arrived at Ft. Dix, N.J.

I recall that moment as among the happiest in my life: the moment I stepped off that train, I knew I was on my way to my dream. I was going to be a soldier.

2

Nearly three and a half years later, I stood on the deck of the *Walker,* a troop transport, watching the shoreline of Korea rise ahead of me in the bright light of an October morning. I was still a teen-ager and damned if I still wasn't a private, but whatever it was that Mr. Truman had sent us there to fight, I was willing and eager to fight it. In fact, I was desperate to fight it—whatever it was—and the thumping and throbbing of the little ship's engines seemed to be moving us precisely nowhere. The Sea of Japan stretched on and on, and so did the morning, and the coast seemed not one kilometer closer that it had when I first caught sight of it. In *Guadalcanal Diary,* one of the classic combat journals, Richard Tregaskis writes about the waiting and how that aspect of combat is nearly as painful as the fighting itself. It is for everybody, though I suppose for different reasons. Some are measuring their manhood, which can be a painful experience. Some are gathering up memories in the face of extinction —and that's no pleasant experience, either. And then there are those dumb Lithuanians like me who just can't wait, just absolutely can't stand to wait until the boat reaches the shore. Years later, when the Army decided I wasn't exactly the kind of man they wanted in its uniform, one of the nifty little tales being passed around at the Pen-tagon and on several bases was that I had cracked up. Somehow, the story went, the years had taken their toll and I had gone over the edge. Too bad, the rumor consoled. Maybe it was the strain of the com-bat and all or maybe it was something else, but I had cracked up and that was what was behind the Army's push to get rid of me. Now that I look back on all those years, damned if they might not have had a point—except that it would have been more accurate in October, 1950, than twenty years later. Who else but a crazy, coal-mines kid would be so damned anxious to get into combat that he almost got into a fight with the Navy people running the ship because it was moving at a speed too slow to suit him? Crazy? Maybe so— but only crazy to the extent that I had grown up with the bloody myth that what I was headed for that morning was a virtue above all other virtues. Nobody in Herminie had ever said a discouraging word about the Army, or about being part of it. The Army and the rest of the military were highly respected all over the country in those days; after all, we had just come through an earth-shaking time in history and had it not been for our armed forces, we might not have survived. Might not—hell, we wouldn't have. That was the contemporary line of thought and nobody in Herminie, especially not the Herbert family, was questioning it. Jules and Charles, Jr., had come home from World War II, and Jules had liked the Navy so much he had decided to stay in. Frank Bobnar, an eighteen-year-old twenty-one-year-old (Father Kelley's magic ink again) had come back to Herminie and married my sister, Irene, and he didn't have anything bad to say about his experiences—and neither did anybody else. What I had done when I'd enlisted was as honorable as entering the priesthood or studying medicine.

Finally, in mid-afternoon, Inchon loomed over the bow and the primary thought in my mind—that I remember, anyway—was that the Marines had landed some days before and there probably wasn't going to be anything left for us to do. The Army had screwed around, I bitched to my colleagues, and now there was no more combat left for us. "You think so?" one of the other kids asked hopefully as we strode down the makeshift gangplank and planted our feet on the soil of Korea. "You really think so?"

Whether that kid was infantry or not, I don't know. But if he was, he clearly hadn't been trained at Ft. Dix. I regard the three months I spent at Dix as some of the most important in my life. The training processes were good and tough. They should have retained more of the spirit included in them instead of paying so much attention to the Doolittle Commission, which was appointed the next year by President Truman and charged with the responsibility for examining the military and making recommendations for improvement. Generally, the Doolittle Commission decided that America deserved a civilized Army. For one thing, it recommended that there be no more swearing by sergeants or anybody else at recruits, or at anyone of inferior rank. In fact, the Commission decided that it should be against Army regulations to swear at all. This is only an example, of course, but it serves the purpose. People in the Army swear. They always have and they always will, and it doesn't make any difference what kind of rules are handed down. General Doolittle was no piker, and I recognize the contributions he made to the American military during World War II and afterwards, but it was from his Commission that a most damaging concept developed in the American military: Cover Your Ass. It still exists. CYA is simply the process whereby men in the Army find themselves pledging allegiance to a system of proprieties and paperwork rather than a personally demanding creed or a consuming purpose. As a result, with careers and rules and promulgations and memos and directives all hanging in the balance, many a man chooses simply to cover his ass rather than to do the right thing.

CYA and paperwork go together, and paperwork and stagnant minds go together, too. There are things to be done and so men do them—but first, they stop to cover their asses. They write it down and get it signed so that, with that signature, there is some proof of legitimacy, and they themselves are off the hook. Once it's down in black and white, that's it. It's history—and in the process, souls are sold for "the good of the brigade." By the time a soldier reaches the upper ranks, he may have become a completely anonymous figure, which is far better for him in terms of finding and reaching that lush green place in the suburbs he's had his heart set on for so long. Over the past two decades the people who believed in such things have succeeded far beyond their wildest dreams. They have created an Army of organization men, in which one is easily replaced by another at no loss to the larger motion and movement of things. Caesar, Alexander, Genghis Khan, Tamerlane, Richard, Arthur, Napoleon, Mad Anthony Wayne, Jackson, Grant, Lee, Sheridan, Mitchell, Pershing, Patton (the real one, not the one who served in Vietnam), Montgomery, Gavin, MacArthur, Ridgway—and since then, no one. Not that we don't have them just as capable now. We do, and those of us who've given our humps to the Army know there are still quite a few great or potentially great ones around. But they are a part of the organization, destined to be swallowed and never receive their just due in history. It is "centralized control" and it is a marvelous thing to behold. Centralized control and ass-covering make a mighty comfortable combination. Responsibility is reduced to file cabinets and the promulgation of regulations and rules—and the human soul, with all its strength and all its grace, disappears.

But all of that came after my basic training, and even though I found it easy to see through the average-man syndrome, the routine and the regimen served its purpose as far as I was concerned. Gunderson and I ended up in the same platoon. I think it's fair to say that we were both the same kind of guys: in excellent physical condition, rather lean and hungry, and too dumb to be afraid of anything much. The physical training was not exactly easy, but it wasn't the most difficult task we'd ever faced either. The calisthenics, the hikes, the running, the obstacle courses—we'd both been doing things equally strenuous all our lives. What we had difficulty with was the rigid social order of things, and I confess that even now it is something I still have not really quite accepted. Both of us were hard-headed and strong-willed, and if we thought we were right about something, it made little difference to us who said we were wrong—sergeants, corporals, or anybody else. I think we were not among the most popular kids at Dix—at least among the noncoms.

New Jersey can be hot from May to the last of July, and the mosquitoes were as vicious as the rats we used to shoot at the city dump in Herminie. I learned about venereal disease—I hadn't had occasion to gather much information about that back in Herminie—and I learned about the importance of doing Army things the Army way.

Three days after I arrived at Dix, my training platoon received its first free time. I decided to visit the Post Exchange, just to see what it looked like. I had spent two days learning how to make a bed the Army way, and the idea of doing something my way seemed most attractive. "Be back at 1930 hours," Sergeant Shoulders had said, and I left the barracks. On the way to the PX, I was waylaid by a group of WACs playing softball. They needed an outfielder, and I spent the remainder of the afternoon in centerfield. Late in the evening I returned to the barracks, contemplating the fine job of bunk-making I was going to do the next morning.

"Herbert," Sergeant Shoulders said grimly when I walked in.

"Yes, Sergeant?"

"What time is it, boy?"

I looked at my watch. It was a little after nine o'clock. "Nine o-three, Sergeant," I said.

"What time, boy?"

"Three past nine."

"What time, boy?"

"I don't know, Sergeant." I was dumbfounded.

"It's twenty-one o-three, boy, and you report to me first thing in the morning after breakfast," he said.

The next day I did just that, leaving my bunk a little less immaculate than I'd planned. The sergeant assigned me to remove fly excrement from the giant screens around the officers' club. He called it bug-shellac. I had to punch out the little squares with a stiff piece of wire. For the next few days everything I looked at appeared to be behind one of those damned screens. "Kinda strains your eyes, don't it, boy?" the sergeant comforted.

Then there was one time out on the firing range when Sergeant Shoulders, an immense man, paused at my position to ask if there was any particular reason for the rather unorthodox way I was grasping my weapon. "No, sir," I replied. "It's just the way I've always shot, that's all." He did not seem really happy with the answer and asked if I would please, just to satisfy his whim, hold it and fire it the way he had been trying to teach us "for the last goddamn week!" He strode off and dealt with several other recruits, and I returned to the Herbert grip. When he returned and inquired again, I wised off to him about being able to shoot better that way than anybody else could his way. That was probably true because the weapons were the easiest part of it all for me. The fact that it was true seemed quite irrelevant to Sergeant Shoulders. The critical thing was that I had shot my mouth off, and with no great fanfare he knocked hell out of me. Then he asked with deep, feigned courtesy if I would: one, please keep my goddamn mouth shut; and two, please try firing the weapon his way. I did and found that both worked better that way.

I had very little contact with officers during those weeks at Dix, but I understood what they were. They were the guys who really knew what it was all about. In my mind, they were no tougher physically—in fact, I had an idea that they probably weren't anywhere near as bad-assed as some of us, and I knew there weren't any three of them together who could hold a candle to Shoulders—but I believed they were a hell of a lot smarter than any of us and that was why they were officers. I wasn't sure then how you became an officer, but it seemed unimportant anyway. Some guys are troops and some are officers and that's the way it is, I thought. What they did, I figured, was to add up the I.Q. scores or something like that, and then they took the smartest ones and made them officers and the rest of the dumb-asses they made enlisted men, and somehow it worked better that way. Besides, I knew that there was a place called West Point, a college of some sort for the Army, and that a lot of the officers had graduated from there—and since I'd never graduated from anything in Herminie, it seemed only natural that those who had should be the leaders of the rest of us. The concepts I developed at Dix were not really as naïve as they might seem; it was just that I believed in the Army. I believed in doing what it said to do. I believed that in the midst of all the confusion and the chaos that might crop up in any given day during basic training, there was a sure and certain direction to it all—and that was good enough for me. I was being fed and clothed and trained and armed. That was exactly what I'd thought the Army would do and they were doing it, so why should I doubt the Army? It worked. That was good enough for me. Besides, I was going to be a paratrooper.

In August, 1947, after a brief furlough back in Herminie, I caught a bus to Pittsburgh and then a train headed south toward Georgia and a vast military post called Ft. Benning, just on the outskirts of Columbus. At home, there had been none of the reactions I'd seen in the movies when the scrawny kid comes back from the Army for the first time and everybody says how much better or stronger or bigger he looks. I hadn't changed in any way that anybody could tell from the outside looking in, and I don't recall that I felt any different than when I left, except, of course, that I was proud to be in the Army. My father asked one night on the front porch if it had been hard on me, and I remember telling him that it had been no more difficult than picking coal on the slag dump or taking care of my traps in the dead of the Pennsylvania winter. It was just as he'd predicted. Everything is just a matter of getting started, he said—and

I agreed. For the first time in our lives we drank a beer together. It wasn't the first beer I'd ever had, but it was one of our first together on such a basis, and it was a good night for me. I think it was good for him, too.

Someone told me that if I thought Dix was hot in July, I would never survive Benning in August. I did though, and so did most everybody else who went there that late summer of 1947 with the serious intention of becoming a paratrooper. Benning was and is a hell of a fine jump-school, and back then it was involved in "paratrooper training," not "parachute training." The two are quite different. For one thing, paratrooper training took about two months. Parachute training, as it's called these days, is over in about three weeks. Paratrooper training then offered the works: hand-to-hand combat, the use of the bayonet, glider training, the use of breakdown weapons. It was, in fact, a complete infantryman's course augmented by the fine art of getting to the ground you're going to fight for by jumping from an airplane. Again, I didn't find it beyond my abilities and I was one of only two guys in our training outfit who scored a maximum on the physical training tests. But the first jump was yet to come, and in the evenings it was the major subject of the barracks conversations. To jump from an airplane and then count on a piece of rag to keep you from banging your ass into the ground—it was quite a vision, and there were plenty of bad dreams. But the training was excellent: tough and straight and no screwing around, and they cut out a hell of a lot of guys long before the first jump because they knew they'd never make it out the door. For me, the night before the jump was one of going over and over in my mind all that they'd been teaching me, including the all-important contingency plans. What if the main chute doesn't open? What do you do then? What's next? Then what's next? The next day when I left the plane it all went so well, I almost wanted a malfunction just to see if I'd remembered all the contingencies. It was really a disappointment. Bang! The rag had blossomed and there was nothing to do except watch the ground come up fast—faster than I could believe. The old T–7 chute was not parabolic and you fell at twenty-four feet per second with a lot of oscillation. We had had all that training about the liquid roll and how to stay healthy when you hit, but I hit like a sack of coal and, like everybody else, I got dragged along. Since then, I've jumped hundreds and hundreds of times and like anybody else who's ever served as a paratrooper, I've been asked what it's like. The usual answers are generally too romanticized for my money. It really is a flat event. It's the waiting that makes it unique—but the tensions at the last minute aren't so unique. Athletes get the same feeling in the pits of their stomachs just before the big game. Then you leap out and there's a snap and a tug at your shoulders and you're airborne—and there's nothing to it. It's a little tight around the shoulders and the crotch because the web-harness is digging in; and there is some pressure on your chest because of the weight of the gear you carry down, but otherwise, you can get the same feeling by just standing still. You have no sensation of falling. In a matter of seconds, you're at horizon level and then you're down, ass over tea-kettle, scrambling up and after the chute, tearing out of the harness. Of course, you may notice that your breathing is a little faster than usual, and when you talk, you may catch a slight quiver in your voice, but all of that settles down quickly enough and you can go about the business at hand as though you'd arrived in a Lincoln Continental.

Of course, jumping isn't everybody's cup of brew. Years later, when I was an instructor, we had a little overweight fellow in one of our classes who had made it through several weeks on nothing more than guts. But that day we were to give them their first real leap. On the first pass there were two refusals aboard, the little fat guy and another one. We talked the other one out on the second pass and now we were working on chubby. The guy was hanging onto the over-head cable in the plane with a grip that turned his knuckles white. He was shaking his head back and forth and muttering, "No, no, no, no." The six-minute buzzer sounded for our third and final pass over the drop-zone. "Hell, man, you came this far, didn't you?" I was shouting at him above the engine noise of the plane. "Don't give it all up now." He continued shaking his head. "Damn it, he did it," I was shouting, recalling the kid who'd decided to go ahead and get it over with on the second pass.

"He was different. He was different," our reluctant student said, still mumbling, still shaking his head.

"He was no different than you," I shouted.

"He was different. He was different."

"How?" I shouted. "How was he different?"

"Because he jumped and I'm not going to," he answered.

I signalled the pilot that we were finished and we landed. I could

31

never quite bring myself to lose my temper with the guy. He was booted out, of course, but I'll always remember him with affection because he told the truth precisely as he understood it at that moment in his life.

I don't remember that we had any refusals the day of my first jump. Like little sheep, we shuffled along the center of the plane, jammed our hands outside the door and off we went—and from then on, it always seemed to go just as smoothly around me. When I got my first stripe in late September and received orders for Ranger Creek Camp, out near Ft. Lewis, Washington, I was one happy seventeen-year-old. Not everybody who volunteered got in, and the Army had convinced me it was an honor to be selected.

One thing was certain. If ever we fought a war in the snow, I was, by God, going to be one of the ones who was ready. The mountains and the winters in Washington are a lovely combination, and although I had learned to use snowshoes back in Herminie, I had never seen a real pair of skis. I learned about them, though, at Ranger Creek, and I still consider it one of the loveliest diversions ever created by man—not to mention an excellent means of transportation. I was at Ranger Creek for about two months, acquiring what the Army called "basic winter survival skills." During my stay there, after a few of us had picked up the essentials, we were called to climb Mt. Rainier to see if we could bring down the bodies of a large group of Marines whose plane had crashed into the mountain about a year before. The winters being what they are there, it had been impossible to make it up and get the bodies down. They wanted people who were big and strong and dumb and so off we went. When we finally reached the plane, we found that during the winter the victims of the crash had been buried under tons and tons of ice. In the morning sun, their crypt was transparent. There beneath my feet—I don't know how far down he was buried—was a dead Marine. The weight and the pressure of the ice around him and on him had literally flattened his body until it was four or five times its original size—almost like those distortions in fun house mirrors. (Later, I saw the same thing again when a North Korean soldier was run over by one of our tanks and his body was smashed against the iron-hard snow. His weapon was across his chest, and it, too, was crushed flat.) I was curious but not maudlin, as I recall; I simply wondered about the immense pressures that could cause something like that. Death no longer bothered or worried me as an abstract mystery. When Joe Ricci died back in Herminie, I learned finally the lesson that my Uncle Joe Shearer's abrupt departure from my life had hinted: that the dead are dead and that's it, and no amount of hand-wringing or crying or excuses has any bearing on that fact. No matter what, they don't get up. After Ricci's death, I no longer laughed at some of the dangerous things the kids in our gang were doing. Death was real and final and from that day on, I never made light of it. Yet I had no fear during my parachute training; I trusted the riggers, because I trusted the Army. Who was I to be afraid when the Army told me there was no reason for fear?

I stayed at Ft. Lewis and Ranger Creek Camp for about two months and then received an assignment to the First Special Platoon, a group of about eighty men who were learning survival techniques up in Alaska. It sounded like the best thing I could possibly have been ordered to do, and I went with great joy and stepped off a plane at Ladd Air Force Base and met the man who was to become my very first hero in the U.S. Army. His name was Emil Joseph Stryker, and he was then a second lieutenant. He could do anything and everything I and anybody else in the group could do, and he could do it all better. In the next ten months, I learned the difference between an officer and a guy who has a commission—and there was never a better example of that distinction than Lieutenant Stryker. He ate what we ate. He slept where we slept. He walked when we walked, and he ran when we ran, and when that was over, he was always ready for more. He was always teaching, always sharing the wisdom he had gained from World War II. He was outspoken but never a loudmouth.

He was little—no more than five-seven or five-eight—and boyish-looking to boot, even more so than Audie Murphy. But he was hard and wiry and so instinctively savvy to all those things the soldier must know and feel that I feel safe in saying that, had I not met Emil Stryker in 1947, I would not be alive in 1972. He taught us all of it—surveying the land, laying in artillery, using foreign weapons—and in matters of discipline, he always made sense. He was not, by most Army standards, the perfect officer. For instance, in these days of public-relations puffing about allowing beer in the barracks, I like to remember that way the hell up north in Alaska twenty-five years ago,

Stryker made sure that we always had beer in the barracks. Why not, he would say. After all, these guys are not drunks. They're learning to be paratroopers, the finest fighters in the world. Why should they be treated like coeds in some Seven Sisters school? And so we had the beer whenever we wanted it, with the stipulation from Stryker that if there was ever a single instance of abuse, everybody would suffer and the beer would be gone. There was no such instance.

Emil used the same approach in everything. The unit, he said, was the key. He didn't allow stragglers during physical training. If somebody was slowing down on one of those God-awful marathon runs that Stryker used to lead through the snow—with all of us wearing only khaki shorts and jump boots—Emil slowed down the whole group. Nobody was left behind, but everybody realized that when one guy lagged, everybody slowed down, and if speed were important he would be hurting the group. It was good teaching. I recall a kid named Webb, whom we immediately nicknamed Spider, who fell out of our group after the first four miles of a twelve-mile run. We carried him the rest of the way. We all realized the weight of the unit was on Spider and vice versa.

Moreover, most of us quit smoking and drinking. We couldn't survive with that damned Stryker out there in front, pumping away and hardly breathing deeply. He taught us that we could do anything we set our minds to do. For instance, back in those days our unit was equipped with 75-millimeter pack howitzers. (They're gone now, replaced with recoilless rifles.) They weighed about 750 pounds. One day, Stryker calmly told us that we were going to take them up one of the nearby mountains and implant them there as a routine training exercise. We had dog-sleds but no dogs, and burro-packs but no donkeys—but we did it. We pushed and pulled and dragged, and damned those guns and cursed the Army and Stryker—but, by God, we did it, and there wasn't a man among us who didn't have a new conception of himself because of that, because of Stryker.

I recall that one day I hit an officer at the base with a snowball. He had urinated in the snow and all of us in the Special Platoon had learned that the snow was one key means of surviving up there. We used it for drinking and for cooking, and this dumb-ass just went and pissed in our survival kit. So I picked up a handful of snow and let him have it in the back of the head. He reported me for it and Stryker put me out in the cold, building a trench. Even in that instance, however, there was a teaching principle built into his discipline. The trench he asked me to build was for the obstacle course that would be used later in our training. What's more, every man in my squad came and helped me, and Stryker seemed not to mind.

Sergeant Charles Dupont was in the group, too. Although he was a loudmouthed guy, just the opposite of Stryker, he was just as tough. He was short and heavy-set, and his left arm and leg were a little out of whack because he had been run over by a German tank in Italy in 1944. I remember the first day we arrived to begin our training in the Special Platoon. As we stood in formation, Dupont shouted to us to run twice around the air base—a distance of ten miles. "The men who make it will go around again and when they come in the third time, they will have the makings of a paratrooper," Dupont shouted. Most, but not everybody made that third lap, I think because we were worried about what that loudmouth Dupont might do if we did fall out.

It was tough but it was good, all of it. I learned that, as tough as Dupont was, he could be a good friend, too. I learned that a leader doesn't have to be aloof—that when the time is right, a leader can sit down and have a beer with those he is leading and shoot the shit as comfortably as anyone else.

The weeks and months passed and we were all as hard as nails and there was nothing else for us to do in Alaska. We had trained and trained, and we had served at Big Delta, Fairbanks, Ladd, Eilson Field, and at Galena on the Arctic Circle. We had learned almost everything we could learn about fighting and survival in the Arctic—and in October, 1948, we were disbanded.

At Ft. Lewis, Washington, they needed big people to be military policemen and Stryker managed to wrangle a spot for me, but the MPs just weren't my bag. Ft. Lewis was important to me, though, because it was there that I had an unexpected insight. I had been an honor graduate of the basic training at Ft. Dix. I had been an honor graduate at jump-school at Benning, and I had been the runner-up to the top man in Stryker's little school in Alaska—but there I was, after eighteen months in the Army, still a private. I finally figured out, with some help from an older corporal, that because I didn't have a high school diploma, I wasn't ever going to make it any higher. I realized that unless I just wanted to have some fun, I'd better get a diploma.

Actually, it wasn't the first time I'd thought about the formal education I didn't have. Richard Natale's sister had written to me while I was in jump-school, and practical kid that she was, she had gently advised me to get into some kind of correspondence school. Marygrace was a bit older than I and a hell of a lot smarter, and I began to give her suggestion some consideration. I also began to think about her a lot, and in the early winter of 1948, when I was assigned to go from Lewis across the country to Governor's Island in New York harbor to pick up an AWOL prisoner, I managed to knock off a couple of days and nights for a trip home. Marygrace and I had our first date then. We took a bus to Irwin to the theater, came back to Herminie and sat around her house talking. She was quiet and reserved, and I knew she was not exactly what the sergeants called a "trooper's girl." It was then that she really persuaded me that what I needed more than anything was a high school diploma—and the more I thought about it, the more reasonable her views seemed. Besides, she was pretty.

I went back to Ft. Lewis and started the machinery working for my discharge. The Army was not greatly saddened by my leave-taking. In fact, they seemed pretty damned eager to get rid of me until the day I was supposed to go through the final discharge process. All of us who were getting out that day were standing around outside the personnel office waiting for the doors to open. We had made our decisions and now we were champing at the bit, waiting to get those papers in our hands and be on our way. Finally, the doors opened and out stepped a fat sergeant. "Pick up those butts," he said, pointing to the cigarette stubs on the doorstep.

"I don't smoke," I said as I leaned down to pick up the first butt. With that, my folder went to the bottom of the pile on his desk and I was not discharged until the next day, November 8, 1948.

Mr. Henry Good, the Sewickley Township High School principal, looked exactly like Abe Lincoln. At least, he looked like what I thought Abe Lincoln should look like, not having had the privilege of examining very many five-dollar bills. He said there were two ways I could tackle my latest project. First, he said he could give me a veteran's break and let me sort of scoot through the rest of my junior year credits (I had quit, you recall, before the end of my third high school year), breeze through the senior stuff, grab a diploma and be off. On the other hand, Mr. Good suggested, I might want to take the matter seriously, get a tutor, bite off as much education as I could swallow in less than one academic year, and still have a diploma at the end. "Besides," Mr. Good concluded, "you already have the best tutor in town."

"Who?"

"Marygrace Natale," he answered, looking more than ever like Honest Abe.

He was probably right about that. And even if he wasn't, she was exactly suited to my rather peculiar needs at that time in my life. She was working at a sporting goods store in Herminie for my oldest brother, Charles. He had bought it in 1947 when he decided to settle down in Herminie, a displaced vet. Marygrace had graduated in the spring of 1947 at the time I was hauling my ass and those 75-millimeter cannons to the top of a freezing mountain in Alaska, and now Chuck considered her his finest employee. That was nice, because she was his only employee.

Going back to high school after having served about a year and a half in the Army was no easy or simple matter, and I don't think I'd ever have had the guts to stick it out if it had not been for Marygrace and Miss Albright, my English instructor. Both of them had a quiet, mature way of explaining how absolutely necessary it was that I stay around—and both of them, however reluctantly, always tried to relate it to my military ambitions. Miss Albright, sometimes quite tenuously, tried to make all my reading connect in some way with matters of soldiering—everything from *Silas Marner* to *The Merchant of Venice*—and that wasn't easy, particularly since she didn't know a great deal about the military in the first place. Marygrace became my strongest critic and my biggest help. Every night after school, I'd zip down to the store and we'd go over the books and the lessons together, and the wonder of it all was that I could take my eyes off her long enough to get in any studying. She was adamant, however. She insisted that there would be time enough for romance and all other lovely things after I graduated, and she pulled it off with the tough perspicacity of a drill sergeant. In fact, Marygrace may have been the roughest person I ever served with because of her quiet confidence in herself—and finally in me. It's hard to buck a combination of piety, beauty, and coal-mine stubbornness—so I stopped fighting it and started studying and probably learned more than I realized.

Some of the high school girls flirted in the hallways at school, but I already had my mind made up. They were children, Marygrace was a woman. They giggled, she had a nice, low chuckle. They were kids, but she was an adult. Besides, the dating patterns in Herminie were rather stagnant. A girl's first time out was usually on the night of the junior prom, and her next date was the night of the senior prom. There were casual relationships in the halls, of course, and this guy somehow became that girl's fellow, but because everybody was so damned poor, there was never much formal dating—I mean the kind where you go over to the girl's house and say hello to her father and wait in the parlor with her mother until she's ready and then leave in the car and go somewhere. That took money, a car, and some place to go—and none of these things were plentiful in Herminie.

The next spring, 1949, I decided I wouldn't go through the commencement and graduation exercises along with everybody else. Miss Albright protested. She said I'd done my work with diligence and that I'd passed everything, including the junior courses I'd had to cram into the schedule, and I deserved the honor of putting on a cap and gown and being handed a diploma right along with the rest of the class. I did it for her and it wasn't as bad as I thought it would be. It was almost fun and, besides, it was the beginning of the evening I proposed to Marygrace. She accepted but with reservations, because I was still intent on returning to the Army. That was all my high school graduation really meant: a ticket back into uniform. But Marygrace had seen how difficult it had been for me to buy the dinky little one-eighth carat diamond ring for her for $180 from Levine's, and with her practical mind, she could not see how we could manage a marriage and the baby she wanted on the $51 a month an Army private made back then. The $35 a month extra jump pay didn't help the situation all that much. "Okay," I said. "I'll try it your way"—and I did. I went to work in a fluorescent light company. The whole country was craft-oriented back then, a World War II syndrome, and so I became a painter—a spray painter, to be exact—and in one week I knew exactly how many strokes up and back it required to paint a reflector for a fluorescent light to a 97 per cent brilliance-and-reflectability level. I was a damned robot. Up and back and back and up and over and back. The monotony was painful. In six weeks, though, I was a bona fide craftsman, and although everybody else, including Marygrace, was exuberant about that achievement, I was downcast. All I had to do then, I reasoned, was keep up the good work for another thirty or forty years until my immediate superior died. I couldn't buy it. I couldn't even imagine how that might be. So, just to break the monotony, I went to a steel mill as a stoker and by January of 1950, I had become a furnace-master, responsible for tending four or five of the giant furnaces. It was one hell of a place to work. A steel mill is much like the docks. I must have had a dozen fights with older mill hands who couldn't adjust to a nineteen-year-old kid doing better than they were doing. There was always somebody you had to take on—and by January, I'd had it.

I told Marygrace I was going back into the Army. She didn't seem surprised. "How are we going to make it married?" she asked.

"I'll make rank," I said.

I re-enlisted in the 82d Airborne and left Herminie again on February 3, 1950. It was the period of the Army's insistence that its people learn a civilian trade. "Any dumb-ass can be an infantryman," the recruiter told me after I'd taken a battery of tests that indicated I had some mechanical aptitude. But recruiters weren't infantrymen, and they didn't know what it meant to have that taste in your mouth and that burning in your gut to just be a soldier. I was sent first to Ft. Dix again, and I argued for three days before they sent me to Ft. Monmouth, New Jersey, just outside of Asbury Park, to a ten-month radio school. It was really one of the best the Army had in those days, but I hated the damned thing. Crap. I'd already learned two trades. If there was one thing I didn't need more of, it was civilian know-how. What I wanted was to be a soldier and, damn it all, everybody I ran into seemed dead set on keeping that from happening. It finally occurred to me that maybe if I flunked the radio course—hell, we were building radios and television receivers and tearing them down and building them again—I might be sent to an infantry unit. It seemed logical, since the Army was telling me every day that the infantryman was the lowest thing around and that anybody could be one if he didn't have any brains or aptitude for the finer things. But that wouldn't work either, because my pride wouldn't allow me to flunk the course purposely. They kept telling me that even if I had such a dumb idea as to be a real down-in-the-mud type, the radio skills would come in very handy. It was small compensation and very little comfort.

Then the world changed. In June, 1950, the Korean War broke out and I had a feeling that, if I worked it right, I'd finally get my wish. I talked to everybody about getting out of that chicken-school and getting to Korea. I finally wound up talking to the senior NCO at Monmouth, a grizzled old sergeant major. "Go see the chaplain," he said—at least I thought that's what he said. I went to see the chaplain, who kindly informed me that perhaps the sergeant major had been referring to another old sergeant on the post by the name of Chaplin. Chaplin, in turn, gave me the best advice I ever got in New Jersey. "The only way to Korea right now is to pass this course." I took the regular course for eight hours a day and then worked myself into a four-hour cram course every night and managed to get out in September instead of late December. I was still assigned to the 82d Airborne, so I had to waive my original assignment to Ft. Bragg to wangle the Korean orders—but it kept working out just as I had known it would. I took a thirty-day furlough, but in the middle of it, I realized it was getting more and more difficult for me to screw up the courage to leave Herminie. Marygrace and I had become so deeply attached to each other that she was starting to cry when the word "leaving" was mentioned—and there were times when I thought maybe she knew what she was crying about. So with two weeks still on my furlough, I left town and headed for Rockford, Illinois, to pick up Harry Knaus, who had been at Monmouth with me and, like me, had decided he wanted to go to Korea. I talked him into leaving his furlough early, too, and we both headed to California to put the same bite on another Monmouth classmate, Gary Blair. Blair lived in Los Angeles and, like Knaus and me, he was anxious to get moving. We reported early and told them we were ready to go. By the first day of October we were on our way to Japan on an old ship named the *Leroy Eltinge*. In Japan, we took a few days of rest and some training, and late on the night of October 14 we boarded the *Walker* and pushed out into the Sea of Japan.

I sensed quickly that even though the Marines had got there first, the area around Inchon might offer at least a few opportunities for a kid who wanted to fight. But I wondered if I'd ever even get to a spot where it would happen. As soon as we were off the ship, it pulled away and headed back to Japan, leaving us rather bewildered on the dock, waiting for someone to tell us what to do. Finally we were loaded on trucks and hauled to a place they had named ASCOM City, just outside of Yung Dung Po, south of Kimpo Air Base and north of Inchon. It was a tent city, built by the Army.

"Go find a place to sleep," I was told by a corporal. I had no assignment, no real identity—but I was tired and it seemed the logical thing to do. I tramped over sleeping forms for a while before I finally found an empty cot. All over ASCOM City, the guys were fighting with each other, arguing, moaning and groaning about not being able to find their units. It had been pretty damned rough over there in those first few months, and even though it was going to get one hell of a lot rougher, the guys at ASCOM were pretty well beat up. When I finally settled down on a cot and was almost asleep, a kid nearby began coughing like Camille. I shined a flashlight on him. There was perspiration all over his face and his cough had turned to a hack—a deep, chesty hack that didn't sound at all normal. I went out in the dark to try to find a doctor, and after an hour or more, I finally ran into one. He refused to help. He said to bring the sick guy in the next morning. So I went back and sat with him all night. He died before dawn. Gary Blair and I carried him to the morning sick-call. "Here he is, you son-of-a-bitch," I said to the doctor. "Make him better now." The doctor called an MP, and Blair and I were chased out of the area.

That afternoon, we were called into a half-assed formation and asked if anyone had training as medics, radio operators, or radio repairmen. I put up my hand for the last one, and I was immediately assigned all the way down to Pusan. It terrified me. Pusan was leagues away from the war. I had come there to go to war. What the hell was happening, anyway? Then it occurred to me that these guys had no way of telling what was going on there. Nobody knew who was who or who was where or who should be going where or what he should do when he got there or what difference it might make if he never got there. What we had there at ASCOM City that day was complete chaos. From behind me I heard somebody yell, "Second Division," and since I'd once been in the 2d (as an MP back at Ft. Lewis), I jumped on the truck that was moving out. I noticed that a lot of the soldiers on board were Korean—in fact all but me. We rolled on northward throughout the afternoon, stopping every once in a while to add some trucks and take on rations, until suddenly, I figured out that since we'd left ASCOM, we'd built a convoy. But I had no idea where it was headed or even where I was. I just sat there with my helmet pulled low over my forehead and my hands on my rifle. Late that night, the headlights fell across a small, improvised wooden sign with an arrow pointing to "2 Division," and when four Koreans jumped out of the truck and began walking in that direction, I jumped out, too, and followed them up the road. I didn't know it then, but I had just unofficially joined the Korean Army's 2d Division. They didn't seem to care.

The ROKs were a gregarious lot. Always yakking. And that was precisely what they were doing on October 18 when a whole lot of North Koreans attacked the little hill they called home and I had adopted. It was my first combat, and it was like shooting rabbits. The first guy was about 100 yards away. I shot him in the chest and I could see the dust fly off his uniform. He flipped to the left in a heap. There were more that morning, but then the ROKs high-tailed it down the hill, and even though I was a dumb-ass from Herminie, I could see there was no reason for me to defend their hill—alone. I didn't like the way they were fighting, anyway. I had no way of telling, of course, having never been in combat before, but there was a lack of ardor in them that disappointed me. I hitchhiked back to ASCOM City and arrived there late that night to find that Blair and Knaus were still around.

"Where the hell you been?" Gary asked.

"To the war," I said.

"Hell," he answered. "You've been AWOL."

The next morning we were herded like cattle onto boxcars and shipped south to Pusan. The only warmth in the cars was from oil heaters and the smoke produced a thick, black phlegm in your throat. At one stop we made, I went outside to urinate. There were Koreans frozen to the outside of the train. Trying to escape the invasion from the north, they had grabbed the train at one stop or another and now they were dead, frozen stiff. They gave us crowbars to pry the bodies loose. We stacked them at the siding and continued toward Pusan, where, when we got off the train, we had to do the same thing again.

After a night's sleep in Pusan, I picked up a tip on just how to get back to the front. I remembered that my outfit in Ft. Lewis had been C Company of the 23d Infantry of the 2d Division, and so I went to the Replacement Depot, "the repot-depot," and reported in as a wounded returnee for C Company of the 23d Infantry of the 2d Division. They said they were glad to see me and cut orders for me to join that unit which, at the time, was fighting in the Toback Mountains, north of the 38th parallel, and moving pretty steadily toward the Yalu River. There was a lot of talk all over the country then about reaching the Yalu and ending the damned thing and getting home before Christmas.

I had made a good choice. When I finally caught up with my adopted unit—still without papers, still without the kind of orders that would stand up in a court-martial—I found some guys I knew from Ft. Lewis, and for the next few weeks, things really went well. We were moving at quite a clip toward the Yalu, and it was like a shooting gallery at times. Those North Koreans we couldn't catch or kill, we left behind. It was a kind of tanker mentality that the 2d and 7th Divisions, under the command of General Bulldog Walker, came by naturally. Walker had been Patton's right-hand man in Europe, and there we were out ahead of everybody and everything, bypassing enemy pockets, bypassing whole communities, and every goddamned private knew what was happening. We were riding jeeps and trucks and making forty, fifty, or sixty miles a day, leaving our lines farther and farther behind, and everybody was talking about drinking from the Yalu and going home for Christmas.

But one sergeant I'd known from Ft. Lewis brought it all down to earth for me. "When we get to the Yalu, we better pray that China stays out, because with all those people behind us, we're going to have to fight our way back—and we're probably going to lose the war," he said. He was almost right. MacArthur had wanted a confrontation with China at the Yalu as a premise for an all-out war—his recommendations about not getting bogged down in an Asian land war notwithstanding. He knew who the enemy was, and he knew it wasn't North Korea.

On the night of November 26, we had moved to within about ten miles of the Yalu, right at the top of the country. The next morning, the Chinese entered the war. I was in a forward command post that day, listening to a young lieutenant report back to headquarters.

"Thousands of them, sir. Thousands in the valley below us, sir."

There was a pause. "Yes, sir, I said thousands." Another pause. "Sir, I'm not estimating." He hung up the phone and cursed the party on the other end. "They don't believe me," he said. I walked with him to the top of the hill and in the valley below, as far as you could see, were thousands upon thousands of Chinese—a real sea of life. Some were on horseback, some were marching in columns. All of them were headed straight for us. Nobody back at headquarters would believe it, and none of us could figure out what to do. By the time they got close enough to fight, it was dark and we were literally pushed off the hill. We fell back because there was no other choice. There was no re-supply and there were no reinforcements, and, finally, there was nobody on the other end of the phone. We tried to regroup and occasionally did, but there were so many of them they just kept pushing us backward. They kept moving right with us. We lost hundreds of people. My platoon leader was killed. Almost everybody I knew so briefly there got it one way or another—all the time we were running —and all because of an ill-planned advance. They had wanted the Yalu face-down, and they had almost got it, except that the Chinese didn't wait for us to make it quite all the way. They did it to us good, really good. It was one of the worst defeats in our history, and it was the result of paper planners and politicians—including MacArthur.

The next few days were a nightmare. There were no more units, not in the strict sense. There was only the snow and ice and slush and mud and cold—and small groups of Americans trying to make it back past all those North Koreans we'd been in too much of a hurry to take care of on the way up. But out of it came a new sense of urgency in the American soldier. All of us who survived those first few days realized that no organizational prowess was going to save our asses. We were reduced to individual survival—and we did it because when man is reduced to that, man can survive, perhaps better than in units of whatever size or designation. We were falling back and regrouping and each time we regrouped, the group was smaller than before, until finally, we were no larger than shrimpsquads, and ultimately some of us were alone. But it was good fighting. Good in this sense: it was simple squad action, the guts of the infantry's strength, a few hard folks doing what soldiers do best. What I was doing in those next few days was precisely what I would get medals for a little later in the war, yet because there was no concern with chains of command or with the Army's way of doing things, there were no medals that time, no commendations or unit citations or such crap as that. There was only survival, and every mother's son was interested just in that. Finally, there was a breather, and after a succession of days with one group and another, and with a succession of lieutenants, I was asked by the latest lieutenant if anybody in our little group knew anything about Turkey.

"Yeah," I said, remembering that Thanksgiving had passed and gone without the usual accoutrements. "I know I didn't get mine."

"No, jackass, I mean the country," the lieutenant said.

"Yeah," I said. "It's got mountains."

"Good, Herbert," he said. "You're the guide."

That's how I became attached to a group of Turks who had come to Korea as part of the United Nations "peace-keeping" force. I was sent immediately back to the rear to pick up the Turks, and I went with some apprehension. After all, I knew what kind of position I was in as far as administration was concerned. I was AWOL. I had never received any formal orders or a particular assignment in the six weeks since I'd landed at Inchon. One of the sergeants had asked me about my records when I'd hooked up with C Company of the 23d. "I guess I'm running ahead of them," I said—and it worked. He never even lifted his head, just kept writing and nodding, and I moved on. But now I had to go back to the rear—back to where the records probably were, back to where the MPs would have nothing better to do than run me in because I didn't have one paper or another—and I wasn't really very happy about the assignment. There wasn't much I could do about it, though; the lieutenant insisted. I was scared for nothing. It took only a couple of hours to go back, find the Turks, and get back to the front, but when I got back to the hill where my unit had been, they were gone, and the Turks and I discovered what it was like to have one entire Korean hill for our very own.

The Turks were of about a company size. We established a perimeter on our hill and sat back to wait for some further word. I didn't speak their language and nobody in their group spoke English, so we spent a cold, quiet night and the next morning found ourselves surrounded by Chinese. I was nervous. There I was with a unit that had never been in combat before, we were surrounded, and I couldn't even talk to them. They couldn't have been happier. They were having a picnic. Every way they looked, it was the front. They could fire in any direction and kill Chinese. They used up most of the morning

45

doing just that, while I sat around trying to figure out how I could get the hell out of there. By the time the sun was high, everybody's ammo was low, but the Turks were calm as hell about it. They formed a skirmish line, fixed their bayonets and faced the north with grins on their faces. I saw the direction they were facing and knew instantly it wasn't where I wanted to go. I jumped up and jammed my fist to the south. Their line whirled, and I suddenly found myself swept along in one of the most successful, old-fashioned bayonet charges of the entire Korean War. I learned a lesson from that. Turks are never trapped. It's the people who surround them who are in trouble. Watching them use their bayonets that day was a revelation. They were dervishes. They had a peculiar style—one I hadn't learned back at Benning. They lunged, drove the bayonet into the abdomen, whirled, struck down hard on top of the rifle with their left hand, and consequently disemboweled their victim. My most vivid memory of that charge is of my gratitude to God or the United Nations or whoever was responsible for putting the Turks on my side.

Once we broke through the ring, we established a perimeter just south of the village of Kuneri and again began to function as part of the big machine, the Eighth Army. A new supply of ammunition arrived, and the Turks' affection for me seemed to increase, along with their hospitality. One of the ways they expressed their friendship was to allow me to accompany them on their daily patrols outside of the perimeter. They were volunteer forays, and although I was most uncomfortable being in a foreign outfit—there was nobody to talk to, nobody to chew my ass, just nobody—I wasn't about to volunteer for anything. I didn't have to. In their view, going on one of the patrols was a privilege, and they believed that I was simply being courteous when I didn't raise my hand as a volunteer. Since they were also warmhearted folks, they "permitted" me to go out on each and every one. Two weeks of such hospitality damn near killed me. I really wanted out. I was going to get back to my own unit one way or another. I knew it wasn't going to be easy. I had picked up only one word of Turkish, *arkadush,* and I didn't have the slightest idea what it meant. All I knew was that every time I killed a Chinese, one of the Turks would rap me on the back and shout, "*Arkadush.*" While I was giving great thought to making an exit from their midst, the Chinese moved in strength into a position across a valley from our elevated perimeter. I lay in my hole and listened and realized that, unless the odds were

46

changed, the Turks and I were about to be overrun. I moved down the hill in the dark, hoping to catch the Chinese in the valley and do something about the odds before they reached our positions. When I reached the valley floor, they came out, rustling and jingling through the darkness. I found a small hole and buried myself as deeply as possible, and the Chinese moved past me and up toward the badly outnumbered Turks. They began their attack and I watched, firing occasionally. The Turks tossed enough back to discourage the Chinese on their first try, and as they turned to come back down into the valley, I opened up with the Browning Automatic Rifle. I poured it into them, knocking down one hell of a bunch before they even came close to understanding what was happening. They scattered in every direction. Most went straight back up the hill into the Turks, who opened up and drove them right back down to me. Men were running past me screaming and firing in all directions and, I suppose, not knowing where to shoot with me there in the middle of them, firing in any direction I pleased. When my own weapon emptied I scooped up one of theirs, adding to the confusion, and I repeated the process again and again, picking up another weapon and beginning again, until suddenly it fell still and silent. I grabbed another of their weapons, straightened up and suddenly realized that no one else was running or shooting or screaming. It was as quiet as a snow scene from Currier & Ives, except for some faint moaning and crying from somewhere out there. I sat down and took stock and then moved into some bushes down in a small ravine, and the next morning that's where the Turks found me when they sent down a patrol to check out the valley. They said they counted more than a hundred bodies around my little hole.

The President of Turkey, Celâ Bayar, later gave me the "Osminieh," the first and only time a foreigner ever received the highest military decoration the Turkish government has to offer. Much later, President Truman asked me at the White House what it had been like to take care of that many soldiers, and it was at that point that I began treating the episode lightly. It seemed so much more comfortable to tell the President that it had come about as an accident and that I had only been trying to get away from the Turks without hurting their feelings. That was why I'd gone down into the valley, I told him. It seemed just about the only way to tell it to the President of the United States. I didn't know how many people I'd killed that night, but I knew damned well I had intended to kill them, and somehow that just didn't seem like the kind of thing to be discussed at 1600 Pennsylvania Avenue.

After that night in the snow, I decided to leave the Turks and get back to C Company again—if I could. I stayed about a week and then, after the battle of Kuneri Pass, become a part of what was known as the Magnificent Retreat. I fell back and joined in the defense of a town called Taegu, and it was there that I was first wounded. I was hit three times in the lower left leg and spent some time in a hospital at a train station outside the town. Coincidentally, while I was hospitalized, I met Joey Marletto, an old friend from Herminie, who was working there as a cook, and when I got on my feet again after a couple of weeks, I ended up in E Company, 38th Infantry Regiment— still sans papers, records, orders, or assignment.

It was a good accident, E Company. I met Sergeant Pogue Calvin and David Feinstein, from New York City, and Bugs Sadler, who later was a prisoner of the Chinese for about three years, and Billy Joe Buchanan, from Atlanta, who was later a prisoner for more than two years—and, of course, Captain Allen, a very good officer. I think I noticed he was good when he had his first run-in with a Polish guy from Texas who had been in World War II and had been called back to active duty as a National Guardsman. Allen told him to do something one way and the Polish guy told him he preferred to do it his way. Allen asked him if he wanted to go on report. "Don't give me that stuff, Captain," the Polish Texan said. "I don't give a damn about the report or anything else except getting this war over and getting my ass back to Texas in one piece. I'm not going to let any dumb-assed, regular Army captain screw up my strategy." Allen walked away. He was smart—and that's what made him a good officer.

It was about this time that things began to change. We started to get in replacements, most of them from the Reserves or the National Guard, and there was definitely a difference. They were guys who didn't have to cover their asses at any time, because their careers weren't on the line. They were the real citizen-soldiers that have always been the strength of this country. (Later, in Vietnam, we would fight a war without them, depending only on the young draftees and the careerists as noncoms and officers. It would make a difference, a big

48

difference.) There was, for instance, Roy Malinowski, a guy who came to E Company from the 187th Airborne. His only concern was to get the job done. No reports, none of that crap. All he wanted to do was win the war and go home. That was the difference I observed in officers back then. There were two kinds: those who worried about their images and those who worried about doing the job.

Actually, a hell of a lot of things were changing. Ridgway replaced MacArthur and we began to get an unlimited supply of ammo. Up until then, it had been pretty skimpy and every new clip had to be accounted for in reports and other paperwork. But with General Ridgway running the show, we settled down to fight—and fight we did. I made corporal before long, and then, with the number of casualties we were taking, I became a sergeant and a squad leader. It was, I suppose, a matter of default. It finally got down to me and I was still alive. Lieutenant Malinowski was the platoon leader and we were getting along fine—and all of us were doing our jobs.

One day, a few of us, including a chaplain, were standing on a hilltop watching what seemed to be an endless caravan of refugees moving south toward what they hoped would be something better. It wasn't there, of course, but they didn't know that; all they knew was that they wanted not to be around when the Chinese swept through their villages.

"They're the ones who always suffer," Malinowski said. "The innocents always get it worst."

The chaplain agreed. "They're beasts of burden," he said, shaking his head, "and their burden is life."

We had taken a hell of a beating after the Chinese entered the war, and we had our asses shoved south for a long time, but we finally got it together again and things began to change. Of course, that's how it looked if you were glancing at the "big picture." For the doggies in the squads, things hadn't changed all that much.

I hadn't had very many dealings with the intelligence arm of the 38th Regiment of the 2d Division when, one April morning, a Chinese "volunteer prisoner" came scooting into our area, just jollier than old St. Nick about his capture and spilling his guts. He had information, and I believed him. A forty-man patrol of Chinese had been moving up a nearby riverbed every night, cutting up a few of our people and then getting back home before dawn. His story matched our casualties for the previous few evenings, and being a dumb-ass, I couldn't figure out why he would give himself up and then lie. But the intelligence people and my company commander wouldn't buy his story. Still, they couldn't quite ignore it, so they told me to drop four of my squad and a .30-caliber machine gun crew of three men down into the riverbed to wait that night. I argued that the job called for more than seven men. The intelligence people were adamant. It probably wasn't true, anyway, they said, and what if the prisoner was trying to set a trap? Would I want to send more people down there just to get chopped up? No, they insisted, a small crew made more sense. The Old Man agreed. So that night I sat there in the blackness with the rain beating down on a blanket around my shoulders, waiting outside a bunker for the buzz of the phone and listening to the automatic weapons crackling from the direction of the riverbed. I cursed the intelligence people and the Old Man. Why couldn't the bastards have listened, I moaned. Just this once. I had sent only a patrol down there, four men and the machine gun crew, and I knew the prisoner had been telling the truth. They were going against six times that many Chinese and all I could do was sit there waiting for the phone, getting wet. It buzzed at last. The Old Man said it seemed that perhaps the prisoner was telling the truth after all. The intelligence people had been trying unsuccessfully all day to crack his story. He asked if I would take a couple of men out and check the patrol. I asked for more and he hung up by saying curtly that I could have two and myself. "Go the back way, through our lines, and I'll notify our people you're coming that way. Shouldn't be too bad," he said. "Be daylight before you get there."

With only three men, it doesn't take long to get going. We started down the hill in the mud, crawling, sliding, slipping, and still puffing a bit when the guys in the mortar-section, our own fellow Americans, put several bullets into Dekkar, the third man on my patrol, and killed him. They hadn't got the word from the Old Man. Just a little slip-up in communications, that's all. We continued to move down toward the riverbed and finally slipped down into its mud. It could have been a nightmare. Both of us were pissed and both of us were numb, because of Dekkar and because of the rain. We tiptoed along, waiting for the dawn, shooting and bayoneting, listening for Oriental voices and opening up whenever and wherever we heard them in the darkness. I fell three or four times in the mud and smashed my face on a rock jutting out of the bank. We watched the grayness come and walked up on our machine gun crew. Two were dead, another man was wounded, but the four riflemen were okay. The Chinese patrol hadn't done very well, either. They had twenty-two dead, including one officer and one noncom. We pulled twelve others alive out of the riverbed, including the other noncom. I went back to the bunker white with cold and anger and realizing that I could not find one ounce of respect in my being for the intelligence people or the Old Man.

One of our replacements was a former world's championship boxer and a decorated veteran of World War II. A Korean volunteer, he came to Easy Company in a blaze of glory, but I sensed immediately that he was an alcoholic and I recognized fairly quickly that he wasn't capable of handling the squad he was given. He seemed intent on spending most of his time baiting the smallest guy in his outfit, and one day the little guy, so intimidated by the boxer, just put his carbine to his temple and pulled the trigger. The boxer was transferred to another unit in the battalion and wound up in a platoon with two of my friends who were squad leaders. The boxer became the platoon sergeant.

One morning we watched through binoculars from a piece of high ground called the Kansas Line as the boxer and his platoon, including my buddies, defended a small knoll at the head of a valley. Their ground controlled the northern entrance to that valley and the Chinese wanted it badly. We watched assault after assault beaten back, but it became clear that the Chinese wanted that piece of rock enough to throw in a sufficient number of men to overrun a mere platoon—and if they wanted it that much, then so did we. At least, that was the logic of the CO, who ordered us to go to the assistance of the boxer's platoon. In a few minutes, Easy Company was moving down the forward slope and into the valley toward the knoll.

When we arrived, we found the boxer at the base of the little piece of high ground, unscratched. He said he had held until all was lost. He said he had regrouped the men and fought until they were completely surrounded and then had fought through the Chinese ring so that he could come for help. He said he was glad we were there and would be happy then to join us. The CO said that wouldn't be necessary and the boxer shuffled off toward the south as we moved up the knoll.

We reached the top and joined the defense and we held, but we carried off a lot of bodies, including those of my two buddies—but not before they told their side of the story. The boxer was no hero. He had cut and run when it finally became too tough for him. It didn't matter, though, because the boxer's story was the one the brass believed. He got a medal for his heroic defense of the knoll and immediately was transferred back to the rear, where he worked for one of the general friends he had made as a famous athlete.

Once we were being cut up pretty bad by some little bastard who sat tight behind a machine gun and just played hell with us for about five hours, long after the rest of his Chinese friends had bugged out. It cost us a lot of men to get up behind him, and I know he knew exactly what we were doing and realized that the longer he stayed, the poorer his chances were of ever crossing the Yalu again. We finally had him dead-to-rights. He was all alone with his back to us, chocked in tight against his weapon, still firing long bursts. I had him covered and I shouted at him to surrender when MacCullough, one of the guys in our squad, ran up beside me and poured a full magazine of twenty rounds from his AR into the guy. I rapped Mac in the mouth and the lieutenant chewed my ass out for hitting one of our guys, but Chinese or no Chinese, the dead machine gunner had been one hell of a trooper. He deserved better than he got. If he'd fought like that for us, he would have been a hero. Since he fought like that for them, he was regarded as a fanatic. That, I suppose, is the difference between winning and losing. I would have been proud to have had that guy in my outfit.

By May of 1951, the weather was breaking, and as much of a spring as Korea gets was coming on. We were at a patrol base forward of the front lines and had been there about ten days with only a few casualties and no really sizable assaults on our position. It was, as the

British might say, a piece of cake. We were relaxing except for the routine patrols, mail was coming in daily, and I knew it was too good to last.

The phone buzzed beside me. Lieutenant Malinowski was on the other end. "Peckover's patrol just got back, Herbert," he said. "He picked up enemy movement about 500 yards forward of the first platoon. Get a patrol ready to go after dark and I'll see you at the CP before you leave, at about 1900 hours."

"Airborne, sir," I said.

Trockavitch walked up. "Hey, Herb," he said, smiling. "Just picked up a box of cigars from my mother."

"Get ready for patrol," I said, bending over to pick up a map from my jacket. "And tell Isaacs and the rest of them to get ready, too."

"Have a cigar, Herb," Trockavitch insisted, dropping one past me onto my jacket.

He walked over to the group sprawled around a fire. "Jesus Christ, doesn't anybody around here but us run night patrols?" Isaacs screamed.

"Have a cigar, Isaacs," I heard Trockavitch say.

But the patrol never came off, nor did my meeting with Malinowski. The Chinese came on us just before dusk, wave after wave of them—whistles, bugles, screaming, horses, swords, sabers, bayonets. They gave us the works. It lasted for at least two hours until we were called off the hill. The call came just about the time we would have lost it anyway, but it was nice to know we hadn't been kicked off. Down in the valley, I found out that all but one of the officers in the company were gone, including Roy Malinowski. He had seen a grenade come rolling down the hill toward him and a group of doggies and had picked it up to throw it back when it exploded, tearing his arm off. The only one left was Lieutenant McNanamy, one of the gutsiest men I ever served with. He was to win eight Silver Stars in Korea, but that day what he had won by default was the command of Easy Company, 38th Infantry Regiment, 2d Division, 8th Army. He got with a captain from Intelligence and they decided to send my men and me on a contact patrol—a patrol that would simply go out from our perimeter and try to make contact with the 3d Battalion. So about ten of us left, headed south. We immediately ran into a mine field we had no idea was there. Probably ours, too. We had four dead before we reached the other side. When we finally made it to the 3d Battalion and told them the situation with Easy Company, they gave us some chow and we sat down to catch our breath, planning on going back in the morning. But sometime during the night, Easy moved and the 3d Battalion adopted us. We couldn't technically be allowed to leave them until word of the location of Easy came through. We were theirs.

As a result of our adoption we became, as far as I know, the only troops from our battalion involved in what came to be known as the Battle of Bloody Ridge. It was no worse than any of the rest of the days and nights we had spent in combat, but what we did not know was that it was the beginning of an all-out Chinese offensive. Our squad was on a hill when the attack came, and when the right flank gave way, once again we found ourselves surrounded. The enemy was everywhere and there seemed to be no alternative but to try to break out. We waited until dark and then sneaked down into the valley. By nightfall, after hitching a ride on the Red Ball Express truck convoy, we had found our unit, or what was left of it. The next morning, Lieutenant McNanamy and ninety-four of us were ordered to replace a battalion of Dutch soldiers on a hill just north of a small village called Usuli. It was to become relatively famous as the scene of the May Massacre. I was carrying five fragmentation grenades, two white phosphorous grenades, and four bandoliers of ammunition as we trudged up the hill in the darkness that evening. For the first time in eight months of Korean combat, I knew I was going to get it. I told Bugs, one of my best buddies, to write Marygrace when it happened, and then we both realized we were repeating the dialogue from a second-rate movie and we ended up laughing. The Dutch troops, moving down the hill, looked at us curiously as they passed. Crazy Americans. Always laughing. We reached the top just about the same moment the Chinese did and we fought for hours, many times hand-to-hand. We held them to a standstill until, once again, they literally snowed us under and there was no longer any doubt as to whom the hill belonged. No one had to call us down that night. We were driven down into the valley. I had a chunk of shrapnel in my left arm and a bayonet slash across my right elbow. Bugs was gone—captured, I assumed—Isaacs was also missing, Doc McCoy, with whom I had become friends, was somewhere out there with our wounded, and the rest were scattered to hell and back. There couldn't have been more than fifteen or twenty of us who made it back down into the valley and into an empty streambed. Just before dawn, we captured a couple of Chinese, gagged and tied them and took them with us as we tried to move south. About daybreak, we thought we'd pulled another big trick when we found Lieutenant Bankowski and Major Wilkins, from our old battalion headquarters, along with several other people from our company, some remnants of the 1st Ranger Company, and a few other stragglers, all gathered in a little village called Kun-mun-gul. What we had done, in fact, was break into a trap. Kun-mun-gul was surrounded by Chinese. We were a bit disturbed by the news of our dubious achievement.

There were about ninety of us in the ring, and the Chinese kept attacking in a veritable fire-storm across the paddies. It was the kind of situation where you just pick your spot to make your stand. They were closing in. It didn't seem worth praying about. The idea seemed to be to die as expensively as you could, and I spent a moment wondering how they'd take it back in Herminie and then settled down to fight. We were losing man after man to a machine gun behind us to the south and more to the mortars dropping among us. Sweat soaked our fatigues. The night was sweltering. My mouth tasted like rubber. I was hit superficially again in my left arm. It went on all through the night, but the little beggars just couldn't take us. They tried and tried, but they couldn't come through. But daylight would be another matter, we knew. We were in a little cut, surrounded by high ground, and without the protection of darkness it was going to be hell to pay.

At dawn, we were informed by radio that help would arrive by noon—but all of us knew that would be too late. One man had the guts to say it for the rest of us: Lieutenant Bankowski. "We either surrender or we have to take care of that machine gun to the south," he said. "Which will it be?"

His words drummed into my brain. Surrender or machine gun. Surrender or machine gun. I don't know what happened, really. All I know is that I dropped my weapon and picked up one with a bayonet on it and started down the road to the south. Somebody else started with me, and we had covered only about thirty yards when I heard shrapnel thunk into his body. I was alone. I was a bit to the left of the gun's position. That and the early morning haze allowed me to get to within three or four yards of the gun before I was spotted. The barrel swung around toward me. I jerked the trigger of the M–1. One round kicked dust into the gunner's face. I pulled again. Nothing. It was empty, but it was too late to turn back. I leaped into the machine gun hole, pinning the gunner to the back of it with my bayonet. The others were crouched inside. I clubbed one and stuck the other, and as I pulled the bayonet from the third man, I caught a movement out of the corner of my eye to my right. I turned my withdrawal of the bayonet into a butt-smash, but at the moment I heard the skull of the fourth one crack, I felt the wind rush from my lungs. The force of my movement tore his rifle from his hands. It sailed past me onto the rim of the hole, but it left its bayonet sticking in my side. I pounded his head into pulp, not realizing what he had done to me. I had felt what I thought was a blow from a rifle muzzle. I was still pounding the poor bastard when one of the other men from the village caught up and started bayoneting one of the ones I'd already killed. Finally, I stopped him just as Yunk Malonick, of Duquesne, Pa., drove up in a jeep. "We did it, Herb, we broke out," he yelled. "Come on, get in the jeep and let's get the hell out of here." I got in, and noticed the look on his face. "For Christ's sake, Herb, what's that in your side?" he asked. I looked down and realized for the first time what had happened. Yunk started to pull it out. I yelled and he left it in and took me that way to the rear and a hospital. I was lucky, I knew, even though I could feel that damn thing all the way through me. The surgeons who took it out shined it up and a couple of weeks later gave it to Jennifer Jones, the actress, who in turn presented it to me on a piece of red velvet. She was visiting U.N. hospitals around Korea, and I suppose she and the medical people thought it was a good idea, especially since I was doing very well and expected to be out of the hospital in just a few days. But I didn't feel too impressed by it. I threw the thing in the waste can and spread some napkins over it. It wasn't until the next day that I found out that what had taken place at Usuli and Kun-mun-gul was said to have "broken the back of their spring offensive." The papers said more than 30,000 Chinese were killed up there in a thirty-six-hour period. It was the last major push they tried.

I found out in the hospital that when I returned to Easy Company we'd be heading north—and that suited me fine. But although the 8th Army was by then pretty much in command of things, the Chinese and the North Koreans were still fighting like hell. When I got back, replacements were still slow and so I became a platoon leader. In July, 1951, we halted and set up stationary lines just north of the Imjin River, slightly north of the 38th parallel. Then the real-estate game began, as possession see-sawed back and forth. Both sides were jockeying for key portions of the terrain—chips to be used in the dickering at the Panmunjom conference table. There was some respite, however, and it was during one of the breathers that they pinned a lot of medals and awards on me in a parade ceremony in a big field next to the town of Imjin. It wasn't until I got back home months later that I knew what most of them were for. Besides, I was a little frightened by the fact that so many people knew who I was by then. After all, I was still AWOL as far as Army regulations went, and I still hadn't received an official assignment to a particular unit.

With the peace talks going full swing, a rotation system was instituted, and with that, there came a chance that I might make it home. I had given up on the idea long before, and the possibility was like a new lease on life. Like others, I began to fight a little more cautiously, to take fewer chances than I had before. I wasn't proud of caution, but I adopted it as my own personal posture for war—that is, until the battle for Hill 868 in September, 1951.

The hill was just east of Heartbreak Ridge, and it had been a thorn in the side of the 38th Regiment for weeks. Its contours were peculiar: Z-shaped with each bar of the Z inclined about 30 degrees above the preceding one. The entire company was involved in an advance and Hill 868 was slowing it down. George Company had reached the first junction on the hill after more than a week's fighting, and time was running short. If it wasn't taken, then the other units on the flanks couldn't continue the advance. Easy Company had been cooling it for a few days. I suppose we were the logical choice.

We moved out in the early morning, just before dawn, leaving the hill we were defending, climbing down its back side and around into a narrow gully. Ahead lay a wide valley and a small creek which we crossed with no difficulty. We veered to the right and then up the first ridge into the vicinity of George Company—a tired looking lot of men. Some looked up as we trudged past, but most did not. Some were smoking, some were munching rations, and some were just sitting and staring. We moved up toward their lead platoon, keeping our column about ten feet below the ridgeline as we walked. It served as a barrier to the steady fire that was pouring in from the second bar of the Z. When we arrived at the juncture of the ridge, we discussed the situation with the platoon leader and George Company's commander while their troops strung out behind us and flopped down on the path we had used. The George Company CO wished us luck and moved out his people and his equipment lock, stock, and barrel. It wasn't too much, anyway. They had been there a long time and had taken a hell of a licking. McNanamy was the company commander, and he was still a lieutenant. He and Herb Bull, also a platoon leader, and I sat down to try to work out something. It was not going to be easy, and I think we all knew that at best we were going to lose an awful lot of people. The ridge was only wide enough to attack one platoon at a time, and even then it would be fighting on a very narrow front. Moreover, it would have to attack along the edge of the hill, always keeping the ridge to its right to keep from exposing itself to the Chinese who were entrenched along the third bar of the Z. Finally, the place was naked. There were no trees, no gullies—nothing available for cover. The only possible tactic was to keep moving forward. McNanamy picked the third platoon, under Peckover, to lead the first assault. Then he looked at me, and then picked Bull for the third slot. "Any questions?" he asked.

"When?" Bull said.

"When you're ready," the lieutenant said.

We moved back along the trail to where our individual platoons were waiting, and forty-five minutes later the third platoon moved out. They really went "over the top," the only time in my entire career the phrase ever seemed appropriate. They climbed into a wall of fire. Many of them didn't even clear the ridge before they were knocked back onto us. Then, God save the artillery. From C Battery of the 38th Field came six altogether perfect, on-target rounds of smoke half-way between where we were and where we were going. The smoke spread beautifully into one long, fat, solid screen just as my platoon cleared the ridge and started moving through what was left of the third platoon. Roy Kamien, of New York City, was leading my forward squad, and by the time the smoke had cleared, we were at the juncture of the second and third bars, with fire from an automatic weapon in a bunker pouring in on us and cutting the platoon to ribbons. We wouldn't have made it if it hadn't been for Corporal "Cotton" Nelson, who was from somewhere down South. The kid ripped

58

a white phosphorous grenade from his belt and threw it straight through the tiny aperture of the bunker, sending everything up in one huge cloud of white hell. Now the juncture was ours. There was only the last bar of the Z to go. The Chinese were moving up the bar toward the summit, and we deployed as best we could in the terrain and picked off several of them. By the time the Chinese made it to the top, McNanamy and the rest of the Company had caught up with us. They rapped us on the back and told us what a hell of a good job we had done—and then the mortars started dropping in on us and we started taking casualties again. We needed the top just to stay alive. I had about twenty men left in my platoon out of about fifty or so that had begun the assault. We started up the last of the bars and by the time we had made it to a group of boulders, about halfway up, I had eleven left, including me. We dug in there and waited for the night to fall and the inevitable counterattack. When it came, we lost five more, but we held. Sometime after midnight a full-strength platoon from Fox Company found us. The platoon leader, a young lieutenant, had been my friend for quite some time, and so we waited out the night, huddling among the rocks, waiting for the morning, when his platoon would attack. During the night, he talked of his wife and his children, and the more he talked the more I could see the score. Fox Company's platoon had come to take the last of the ground, but I had no choice—as I saw it then, anyway—but to lead the assault. When dawn slithered in, I watched him and waited for him to give the signal, and when he did, I slammed the young lieutenant into the rocks with the butt of my carbine and raced out in front of his platoon. We hit another wall of fire, and with ten yards to go, less than half of us were still standing. Some started back to the boulders. Grenades were bursting all around and white phosphorous was mushrooming into the gray sky. Bullets were splattering the dirt and the rocks, and sweat stung my eyes, but all I could think about was that I was being cheated out of Hill 868. I started running back and forth among the troops, kicking their asses. I picked up one slight kid and literally threw him toward the top of the hill. Somebody shouted, "Okay, okay, we're going!"—and we headed up and took the top. It had been expensive. Fox Company's platoon had fifty per cent casualties and only Roy Kamien and I were left from our platoon. But I felt good. The hill was ours and the two of us sat down on top when it was over and talked about the ass-chewing I was going to get from the young lieutenant with the bump on his head. Roy reached out with his hand and rolled over the body of a Chinese soldier. A grenade exploded in his face. I was the only one left.

A few weeks later, I was lolling outside a bunker near our company's command post when McNanamy approached and ordered me to report to regimental headquarters. I thought my mother or dad had died or that some other great catastrophe had befallen someone in my family. A sergeant standing nearby gave me a camouflage scarf just to make me look pretty, and I grabbed a passing jeep down to regimental. There I was told that General Ridgway and the rest of the high command were going to pick an outstanding soldier from each of the countries represented in Korea, and that I was the regiment's pick. I couldn't believe it. I still thought there was some kind of trick afoot to charge me with being AWOL, but I took another jeep to a small airstrip and boarded a light plane for the short flight down to Seoul. I was taken to a flashy villa on the edge of town, where Ridgway and the rest of the brass were in dress uniform, sitting around, smoking cigars and drinking coffee. I was still in my fatigues, and they were a hell of a mess: torn, dirty, stiff from the sweat of my body and the mud of Hill 868. And I knew one thing for sure: if it was sharp-soldier time, then I was out. I talked with the brass a while and then left and walked to the gate of the villa. I was going back to Easy Company. The MP at the end of the drive stopped me. "Your name Herbert?" he asked.

"Yes," I said. "Sergeant Herbert."

"They want you back up at the house," he said.

I returned and was told that I was the one they wanted. There was some handshaking, and before I knew what was happening, I had been flown to Japan, washed, scrubbed, deloused, deodorized, given shots and new clothes, and was on my way to Washington.

We landed secretly at Andrews Air Force Base on the morning of October 24, 1951. I got cleaned up again, along with Sergeant John Snyder, who had been chosen by the brass also, and then we took off again and landed later in the morning—at Andrews again. This time, the big brass was there with a band and it was hoopy-do time. Then before I knew it, I had an official invitation to sleep that night in Blair House, and that afternoon I was in the Oval office at the White House, shaking the very limp hand of Harry S Truman. I was quite surprised by his grip. I had always thought of him as a sort of hard-bitten farmer who had the calluses to prove it, but his hands were smooth, almost feminine, and his grip lacked any vitality. I remember that from the ceiling hung a giant ear of corn from Missouri and on the wall a copy of the famous front page of the *Chicago Tribune,* trumpeting a Dewey victory over him in 1948. The second or third day I was in Washington, after endless rounds of radio and newspaper interviews and flashbulbs popping in my face, Truman called me back to the White House.

"All of this doesn't really impress you, does it?" he said. "You seem to me to be the kind of boy who'd much rather just be a soldier."

I shrugged and said he was very close to being right. I happened to remember just then that I hadn't been paid the whole time I'd been in Korea. Then, for the first time since I'd left Easy Company about a week before, I found out what the celebration was all about. The Army had decided it would be good for the U.N. countries involved in Korea to get a glimpse of its most decorated enlisted soldier. Later, I learned that it was decided right from the first that he would be an American—none of the other contingents were even surveyed—and supposedly he would reflect in some way the depth of America's commitment to the war or to the U.N. or something. By the time the decision had been made, I had won something like twenty-two medals, including three Silver Stars, a Bronze Star, six battle stars, four Purple Hearts, a unit citation, the Syngman Rhee Citation, the "Osminieh," the "Ville de Paris," a Korean Service medal with six bronze campaign stars, a U.N. service medal, and the combat infantry badge. I have no idea whether that was more than other guys won or not, but there I was in Washington, D.C., in the White House with Harry S Truman, and he was telling me that that was the reason I'd been pulled out of my outfit.

"Now we're going to send you on a tour of Europe and sort of show you off," the President said. "Will you do that for us?"

What could I say? They gave me my back pay—about $3,000—and off we went.

London, Antwerp, Brussels, The Hague—it went on and on and

on through November and December, and I thought it would never stop, wishing sincerely on some occasions to be back with Easy Company. In London I found out that when I got back I'd begin a similar trip in the States. The trip was not a complete disaster, though, because on the last few weeks of the European leg Mrs. Eleanor Roosevelt joined the troupe. She was a remarkably spirited woman whose kindness and insights changed my life. She had an élan about her that I've seen in no other person since. In Paris, I was so tired I went to sleep and fell off a chair in the parlor of the American Ambassador's mansion, and later that day Mrs. Roosevelt suggested that we both drop off the tour for just a day or so. She showed me a Paris I'd never have known without her, including not only the Louvre but the Folies Bergère and a host of other clubs. The officers escorting her were nearly as dead as I when it was over, and I was almost happy to get back to the glad-handing and the endless plane rides from country to country and capital to capital.

On the plane from London back to the United States, Mrs. Roosevelt gave me the advice that changed my life. She urged me not to be carried away by the status I'd suddenly acquired. She said the Army would try to use me and she asked me not to let them. I should quit the Army right then and there, she suggested, and go to college. It was the kind of world, she said, in which a man like me would go to seed without an academic background. Then, without stopping the pace of her conversation, she offered me financial help for college. I was speechless. In the first place, she had suggested that I leave the Army—and I was right back to that wall I'd faced the first time I'd enlisted and then dropped out. Was she right? I wondered. At twenty-one, I was one of the youngest master sergeants in the U.S. Army. Where could I go in the Army? What could I do? Sit around the NCO club at some post and talk about Korea? I didn't want that, and despite my hesitation I took Mrs. Roosevelt's counsel and decided to give college a try when my enlistment would end in fourteen months.

When I came home from Korea, the people of Herminie had a "day" for me. I guess it was just about the biggest thing a town could do for anyone. And though I may have enjoyed the old Fourth of July celebrations more, when the firemen turned on the hoses and the water whomped hell out of all the kids, I've got to admit I liked what the town did for me. My folks were proud, and Marygrace, still quiet and still pretty, was proud, too. That was in March, 1952, and although we wanted to get married immediately, due to duty assignments it had to be put off until July.

I was assigned in late March as an ROTC instructor at East High School in Denver. The reason? I had told the Army that I'd enjoyed skiing when I was in Washington and Alaska on my first hitch. They were dying to please. Two months later, I found out that a new Ranger Department had just begun, and I decided that was what I wanted. Each separate Army command was supposed to send a fixed number of personnel, and when I asked for that assignment, once again, I got what I wanted. They were still trying to please. I was in the third Ranger class ever to graduate, and when I finished the two-month course in late June I was sent to an intelligence school in Ft. Holabird, Md., and finally out to Chicago on my very first intelligence mission.

Some documents had been missing from the 5th Army Headquarters there. Army Intelligence suspected that they had been taken by some, or one, of the secretaries. What they wanted was a young guy who might be able to strike up an acquaintance with the suspects and find out what was happening. Were they part of an espionage ring? Were they operating free-lance just for money? Was there any political ideology involved?

A James Bond I was not, but I swear that the prettiest girl in the office, a Puerto Rican beauty, was the one they wanted, and with all apologies to Marygrace, I noticed her the moment I walked in. One afternoon we went for a beer. She told me she had been dating an MP but was bored with him and ready for a change, and a few days later we went to her apartment, where she introduced me to two other girls and a man.

The direction of the conversation was so obvious I could have written the dialogue myself. They began talking about relative morality—I think that's what they called it—and about how everybody seemed to be able to pick up some pretty big money just by bending a few rules. They mentioned one Chicago police lieutenant they all knew who made less than $300 a month from his job but had a big Lake Shore apartment, fancy as hell, and a big car to drive, and a pocket full of money. I listened and even agreed that there was probably a lot of cash to be made selling things that were supposed to be secrets. A few days later, after one date on which I had told her that I had crypto-classification, she asked if she could see some copies of various messages moving through the communications center at 5th Army Headquarters. Sure, I said, I'd give her the copies. I did—and they picked her up, along with the two girls and the other guy.

I did some other work for the intelligence folks there in Chicago before taking some leave and driving back to Herminie to get married. Marygrace and I had settled on July 12 as the date, but neither of us had bothered to tell the priest at St. Edward's about our intentions. There were several other marriages scheduled in the church for that date, and although my leave was ending we just couldn't be crowded in. We drove down to Winchester, Virginia, and a justice of the peace married us. Later, on September 11, we decided to be married again in the church, and once again, there was a mix-up. The altar boys didn't show up, and I ended up serving mass at my own wedding. Father Kelley would have been pleased. I don't think I blew a single line, and Marygrace seemed very impressed that the man she had married—both times—was so proficient in Latin.

Marygrace stayed in Herminie and I went back to Chicago to continue playing spy. Abruptly, I was assigned to the Mountain and Cold-Weather Training Command at Camp Carson, Colorado, and just before Christmas of 1952 I was parachuted into the mountains to help find some missing hunters. I was ill from a combination of flu and recurring malaria when I boarded the plane, and by the time they opened the door for the jump I knew damned well I had no business being there. I never found the hunters—they were still in their hotel and just hadn't bothered to call their families—but I lay out there in the snow for nine days, bleeding from the rectum, too weak to do anything but survive. While I was waiting to be rescued from my rescue mission, I began to remember what Mrs. Roosevelt had told me. I started putting it all together. Where was I going? What could my future possibly be? And I decided then and there in that damned wilderness that I was going back to school, and then I would become an officer and spend the rest of my life in the Army. It was, after all, what I wanted. I would just go at it on a new tack.

I wrote to Marygrace. She was jubilant. I wrote to Ronnie Kaiser, a good friend in Herminie, and he pre-registered me at the University of Pittsburgh. On February 5, I caught a plane from Denver to Chicago and another from Chicago to Pittsburgh. I hitchhiked from Pittsburgh to Herminie and got home at about 6:30 a.m. Marygrace was waiting with my books and two hours later I started college.

My mother was happy, too. "I'm glad you're out of the Army," she said. "You never know when we might have another war."

"That's right, mum," I replied. "But just remember, I'm really just on leave." Marygrace stared at me quizzically. "I just gave myself a furlough, that's all," I said—and I wasn't laughing.

3

I was not what you would call a brilliant student at the University of Pittsburgh. I decided to major in English because I remembered Malinowski telling me often, during our little arguments in Korea, that I seemed to have difficulty with the language. Actually, I suppose, the impetus for that choice came from a few journalists I had met, who had urged me to write a book about what happened to me in Korea. I wrote the book. It was called *Conquest to Nowhere,* and it was not a good book. It was not a lousy book, either—it just didn't really say much about anything, and besides, the guy who helped me write it wasn't too careful about what were his ideas and what were mine. Nevertheless, I thought it was pretty nifty to be a student of English and an author simultaneously. None of my professors seemed very impressed. In fact, one of them called me aside one day and bluntly but kindly informed me that neither I nor my ghost-writer would pass his course unless I picked up the pace. I did and I passed—but I was never destined for *summa cum laude.*

For one thing, the disciplines of the campus are different from the disciplines of the U.S. Army, and the adjustment factor is substantial. I don't know what comparison figures are available on GI students just out of the service and civilians who simply matriculate from high school to college, but I'd be willing to wager that not many ex-servicemen have set the campus on fire. Vietnam's returnees are probably less able to make the adjustment than any Americans before them, simply because that war is so very damned peculiar and has had such a unique effect both on the men who fought it and the country that twisted its psyche around it.

But of course I wasn't thinking about adjustment while I was adjusting, and I doubt that I ever did adjust. I was working my butt off in the steel mill again at night, driving to Pittsburgh to the University every morning, studying every spare minute, and enjoying being with the girl I'd married. Marygrace and I were living with her parents, and once again she became my tutor. When I graduated in September, 1956, it should have been her Bachelor of Arts degree, not mine. But my name was on the diploma and, as with the one from Sewickley Township High School, it was for me merely a means of getting back into the Army. This time, there were no disagreements between Marygrace and me about my re-enlistment. I had come to know the U.S. Representative from our district, and he had made it clear that when I decided to go back in, he would do everything in his power to see that I got a commission. Now I was ready and he went to work. Regular Army commissions were pretty scarce then, so I was formally inducted into the Pennsylvania National Guard with a provisional rank of second lieutenant. It was another adjustment, and a hell of a one. I had become both an instant officer and an instant gentleman, neither of which I understood. But I was willing to learn. So Marygrace and I set out in September 1956 for Ft. Benning, Georgia, and the Basic Infantry Officer's Course (BIOC), the school to which all Army lieutenants had to go, even West Pointers. It was, in a sense, basic training for officers.

Columbus, Georgia, wasn't strange to me and neither was Benning. I'd been there twice before: first, just after I enlisted as a high-school drop-out, and again when I became a Ranger after Korea. We rented a room in the home of the Columbus chief of police. Another of his boarders was an old friend of mine from one of my earlier tours at Benning. He had been a sergeant back then and had since retired and joined the Columbus police force. He greeted me with a few words that were far from being a welcome. "You have just made the biggest mistake of your entire life," he said one night as Marygrace and I were sitting in the swing on the chief's front porch. "You have, number one, decided to come back into the Army, and that doesn't make sense because the Army is not what it was when you left," he said. "Number two, you have come back in as an officer, and the officer corps is changing in the worst way." I was stunned. Nobody could have been happier than I was then, and this dumb-ass was sitting there telling me I'd made a mistake. Why was it such an error, I asked. "Because what you're getting in the Army these days are the rejects—not only the ones from civilian society but the ones who stayed in the Army after World War II," he said. "What you got to remember, Herb, is that in

Korea we still had an officer corps of guys who were climbing at the end of the big one. But now they're all retiring and the promotions are going to the people who couldn't quite get them during wartime. That's the biggest difference and it's important. You'll see, Herb, you'll see. You've made a mistake. I got out at the right time. You got back in at just the wrong time—and someday you'll understand exactly what I mean." Of course, I couldn't see it then, and I don't really want to agree now, even though I do. But back then nobody could have persuaded me that what I'd decided to do with my life was anything but the smartest move anybody ever made. After all, it matched the whole thrust of all of the earlier years. I went into the BIOC with a vengeance. I was going to be the best damned officer the Army had ever seen. I owed it to too many people not to be, I thought, and that became one of the premises of my career. I was always surprised that I could even be considered for the next promotion, and I wanted always to please the Army and not make them regret that they had made the move in the first place. The psychiatrist could take that apart with ease, I think. What had I substituted the Army for? My mother? My father? Whatever was the case, I was an Army man, trying to learn, trying to please, trying to be the best they had.

One of the policies for the course at Benning was that each student had to take a one-week tour at being the student company commander or the student company first sergeant. Since I'd had military experience, the company commander of our training group asked me to be the first student first sergeant. He never let me leave the job.

Not all of the instructors appreciated the fact that, because of Korea, I enjoyed a certain kind of distinction at Benning. I didn't do much to ease that problem, I suppose. One day, for instance, I was dozing in the bleachers at the artillery range. I'd been up the entire night before studying for one of the written examinations, and try as I would I couldn't stay awake. The instructor was teaching the Army's "new" way of zeroing in on an artillery target. He called it "bracketing." It was a simple theory, as old as da Vinci. The first round is over the target and the distance is measured through binoculars. The second round is short of the target and that distance is also measured. Then, the process is simply one of splitting the difference between the longs and the shorts and finally ending up right on the target. It isn't a bad way—it just doesn't work well in combat, and I knew it. Maybe that was another reason I was unable to stay awake. The instructor, a captain, noticed my lack of interest and tried to make a point about the difference between the old and the new Army methods. "We got us an older soldier here," he said, looking up at me. I was twenty-six years old at the time, and I wasn't sure he was talking to me or about me. I did one of those theatrical takes, looking behind me to check on the possible target of his comments. There was nobody there. He was talking to me. "Lieutenant Herbert," he was saying, "we understand you don't exactly appreciate the bracketing method, even though our generals seem to all agree it's the best— no," he elaborated, "the very best," and they all laughed.

"That's right, sir," I said. "I don't know about that, I've never been a general, but if you try to use that bracket in combat against anything with legs it'll be gone before you get to it."

"Well, now, Herbert," he said, "let's just see if that little fact is a true one." He was not a bad guy, and he really believed in his method. What he was trying to do, I realized, was simply use me as a teaching point, and although he was going about it with a bit of a vengeance, it wasn't an invalid technique. "You take one piece, Herbert, and I'll take another, and each of us will use our methods in directing the fire at the targets on those hills, and we'll see who zeroes in faster," he said.

"Airborne, sir," I said and roused myself from the bleachers.

I picked up a pair of binoculars, sighted out across the valley to the targets on the hill, gave the crew some range and direction, and asked them to fire one smoke. In the meantime, the captain had already fired a long and a short at his targets on the other hill. I watched our explosions through the binoculars, made some quick computations—not computations, really, just the estimates that come from experience—and gave my crew a new set of range and direction and fired for effect. Just as I'd known we would, we blew the hell out of every last target on the hill. The captain was still firing long and short, long and short, long and short.

It didn't please him a whole hell of a lot. After the class was over, he called me down and asked if I'd tried to make an ass of him in front of the other students. No, I said, I was just following orders. He dismissed me rather curtly, but although we continued to learn the bracketing method, he never again brought up the subject of having an "old soldier" around as a teaching foil.

By late February, 1957, I had won nine of the ten awards given to members of the BIOC and stood eleventh academically in the group. The award I was proudest of was the leadership trophy. My fellow-students selected its recipient, and that meant more than leading in such departments as military law or gunnery. That same month, General Cook, the commandant of the school, asked if I'd like a direct Regular Army commission. I thought it over for about ten seconds and said yes. It was another beginning.

After graduating from Benning, I was assigned as an instructor to the Mountain Ranger Training Camp at Dahlonega, Georgia. Rangers were the elite of the Army then. I couldn't have been prouder. The assignment was the result, I was told, of my high scores in the BIOC, my being a graduate of the Ranger course, the Alpine training I'd had in Washington, Alaska, and after Korea, in Colorado.

Marygrace and I drove from Columbus up through Atlanta and on into the mountains of north Georgia to Dahlonega, where I reported to Colonel Byerly, the commanding officer of the Mountain Ranger Training Camp. He was not pleased to see me. "We don't accept second lieutenants as instructors here," he said. "Don't they realize that at Benning?" I told him I didn't realize that myself and asked if he would mind calling Colonel Dalton, the Ranger commander at Benning, who had made the assignment. He did and Dalton told him to keep me thirty days, and then if he still wanted to send me back to do so. Byerly came back from the phone and ordered me to send Marygrace back to Benning. "And don't unpack, Herbert," he said. "You're only going to be here a month." He changed his mind, though, and kept me almost two years, until his retirement.

Teaching young men the essentials of mountain climbing, combat, and survival was more of a learning experience for me than for them. I began discovering things about the resources in me as well as the way the Army was moving. I was an alternate instructor at first, assigned to teach cliff descents on suspension traverses. I took it seriously—it was dangerous business if you didn't. The ropes to be used for the traverses, which were one inch in diameter and 900 feet long, cost the Army about $300 each. I had set up two of the traverses on a sixty-foot cliff the day before a new class was to begin, and that afternoon I went out to inspect the ropes. One of the criteria for determining the quality of that kind of rope was the presence of a tiny colored strand running all the way through its core. I inspected the first traverse and found the strand. But the second rope didn't have it, which meant that I simply couldn't approve its use. The strand was an indication that the machines used to put the hemp together into a strong enough cord had worked the way they were supposed to. If the strand wasn't there, something had gone wrong and the rope might be faulty. I went back to my quarters and wrote an unsatisfactory report on the rope, and then went to the chief instructor and told him of my findings. "The Army paid good money for that rope and you want to throw it away?" he argued. "We're not going to do that, Herbert." I explained what I had found—or rather what I had not found. "Strand, schmand," he said. "You go out there and test it again by going down the traverse. If it holds you, it's okay." I returned to the cliff and went down the traverse. It held. It was supposed to be sturdy enough to support a jeep. I went back and told the captain, and he ordered me to conduct the class the next day, using the rope. I filed the unsatisfactory report anyway and went to bed.

The next morning as we stood at the top of the cliff, I ordered the class into two lines. The captain nodded his approval from nearby. One group would use the traverse made of rope I'd inspected and approved. The other would use the traverse made of rope I'd inspected and rejected. A young corporal in the second group stepped off. The rope snapped and he fell sixty feet to the rocks below. I went down quickly on the other traverse. His body was so broken it almost crumbled in my hands as I lifted him to a jeep and sent him to the hospital. The captain had seen what had happened. He left the scene, running up over the hill. The students were nervous. They said they weren't going through with it. I made them a little speech on courage and reminded them that they'd all known that Ranger training included risks. It seemed to work. We spent the rest of the morning learning how to use the traverse. There were no further accidents, and at lunch time I went back to the base, where Colonel Byerly and the captain asked me how the kid who fell was going to be.

"He'll be DOA," I said.

"Don't say that," the captain said. "You can't say that. How the hell do you know?"

"Because I'm the one who put him on that jeep for the hospital," I said. "He'll be DOA."

The phone rang. It was the hospital calling, and the captain came back to Byerly and me with a strange look on his face. "The hospital says he was DOA," he reported.

It was quiet in Byerly's office. Finally, the captain said I was responsible for the accident.

"I realize that, sir, and I'll stand whatever comes from it," I said.

"You're responsible, you know," he said. "You're the one who's responsible."

"I know, sir, I know," I answered.

He called the Criminal Investigation Division at Ft. McPherson in Atlanta, and they arrived later that day to begin their inquiry into whether it had been an accident or sabotage. Their findings were that the rope had been faulty.

The kid who died from the fall had had a new baby. I didn't see how the Army could just let it drop there. Somebody was at fault, but everybody I talked to about it in the Army counselled me to let it lie. The Army wanted to write it off, but I was damned if I was going to go that route. I kept writing to the Mountain Safety Council and to the New England company that manufactured the faulty rope. All the while, I kept receiving advice and then some stern suggestions to cease the correspondence. Two years later, though, no thanks to the U.S. Army, the company supposedly paid the family $150,000. It was an out-of-court settlement. I learned later that the Army had preferred it that way and had strongly urged the company to make the payment as quietly as possible. I could see why. My unsatisfactory report on the rope was still on file.

A Ranger is supposed to be the epitome of the American fighting man, able to survive and fight wherever he is and however many there are with him, if any at all. His physical conditioning is torturous, and he is trained in a wide variety of skills and techniques. He learns to kill with his hands as well as use them as a semi-skilled surgeon. He learns to live off the land and to make the terrain work to his advantage. He is, in short, supposed to be a super-soldier, a guy who is tougher, better equipped to survive, and more capable of being an effective infantryman than any other kind of soldier.

A class of men with the Ranger badge as their goal would begin with three weeks at Ft. Benning. Then there would come another two weeks at Eglin Air Force Base in Florida, where they would undergo swamp and jungle training, including the use of small water craft and survival techniques. Finally the class would head up to Dahlonega, where they were supposed to learn Alpine methods.

Each class was headed by a senior tactical officer called TAC, who ran the class, kept the score sheets, and decided who failed and who passed. He was its father-figure, its counselor, its dean. Guys like me in the mountain phase and the instructors at Eglin and Benning were only teachers on a campus; the TAC was the commander of the class.

Dan Folberg was one of the first TACs I ever knew. He had been an All-American fullback at West Point, but I doubt that he had ever had anything tougher than a certain class of Ranger students made up entirely of West Point graduates. It was the only class in Ranger history that ever quit en masse. They were on a survival exercise in the swamps, without food or water, without anything except their native intelligence and their weapons. They just threw down their rifles and walked out on the theory that, if they all did it together, nobody could do anything about it. They threw their rifles into the mud and the water. When I heard about it, I thought it was like striking God. I knew what a rifle meant or should mean to an infantryman. I had been taught by Sergeant Shoulders at Dix and by little Emil Stryker up in Alaska that if an infantryman had a choice between comfort for himself or a warm, clean place for his weapon, the weapon got the nod. A soldier could stand rain but his rifle couldn't. A soldier could stand not being fed, but his rifle needed cleaning and oiling—and the soldier, by God, took care of those matters or he didn't survive. Now these bastards just up and threw their rifles in the swamp.

It wasn't the first time American troops had ever revolted against the system, of course. There was the case of the 95th Division in Europe in World War II, which a lot of people believe was the only insurrection of a unit that size in the history of the American military. There was at least one other, however. During the Korean War, a division commander at Camp Atterbury, Indiana, promised his troops a Christmas at home before deployment overseas in return for a good training cycle. His promise was against regulations, of course, since no more than one-fourth of any division can ever be on leave at one time. But the commander, a state-appointed National Guard general, didn't know that. By parade time the troops were ready for their leave. With all 14,000 of them, finely honed from their marvelous training cycle, standing there in the snow, the general announced that it would be impossible to give them all leave. All of them gathered up snowballs and began throwing them at the general. They chased him back to his division headquarters, yelling and screaming their hatred, and the general put together a stenographic crew and issued 14,000 passes—and to hell with the regulations.

The Army covered up the West Pointers' failure and the class was allowed to continue, but when I heard about it, I drew my first distinction between West Point officers and the others. It was, perhaps, an unfair judgment based on only a smattering of evidence. But I made it and followed it for the rest of my life. West Pointers were different, I decided. You had to watch them. I wasn't always right about that, but I was right often enough to have made it worth my while to take that attitude.

Hell, in Ranger training we even developed two different sets of instructions and rules, one to be used for West Point students and another for those who weren't from the Academy. We found out that, as a rule, the West Pointers didn't want to listen. We tried to place the Ranger student in a stress situation by making him as hungry and as tired as we could, and then get him to react as a Ranger. On a survival exercise, we would instruct the non-West Point students simply not to take anything to eat with them. We'd say, "No candy or anything like that in your pockets." We learned that you couldn't do that with the West Pointers. They'd stash their food in their hats and then say we hadn't said not to put it there. Or they'd take along something other than candy and say we hadn't forbidden whatever specific item they'd secreted away. The sons of bitches were quibblers, Byerly said one day.

"What's a quibbler?" I asked.

"A West Pointer," Byerly said.

Not long after the Ranger class of West Point people had walked out of the Eglin swamp, Colonel Dalton called me at Dahlonega and told me that I would TAC the next West Point class. I didn't much like the idea at first. I was still a second lieutenant, I pointed out. I would need everybody's backing if I took on a class of that kind of people. It wasn't just new graduates of the Point who ended up in those classes; these were men who had served several years, had made some rank, and had now decided they wanted to be in the most elite group the Army had. Dalton said I'd get the backing, and I agreed. I'm glad now that I did, because in the experience I met a major named Lou Millet. It didn't start out well for us. On the first day of my TAC assignment, I was down at Benning getting introduced to my students. Millet kept referring to me as "Lieutenant," and he made it sound like "leper." When I had taken about as much as I could take, I went to him and told him that I didn't mind the tone of his voice and that I'd salute him all that day and do whatever it was he wanted me to do because he was my superior in rank.

"But tomorrow, Major Millet, you're going to be just Ranger Millet and I'll expect the same kind of courtesy from you," I said. He smiled and we shook hands. He's been a good friend ever since and one hell of a soldier. His class, my first as a TAC, scored the highest averages in every single department in the history of Ranger training. And they still stand.

In March, 1958, I was promoted to first lieutenant and Byerly decided I should become the senior mountain-climbing instructor at Dahlonega. It was a bit unusual. I would have men who were senior to me as my juniors in the classes, and that sort of arrangement took a Presidential order. Byerly got it through Dalton and I took the job. Once again, it was more education and training for me than for the students. I must have run at least 200 night patrols through those Georgia mountains—hikes of fifty miles or more from Dahlonega all the way up to the Blue Ridge power station. In addition to those duties, I was teaching hand-to-hand combat and river-crossing techniques.

I didn't develop any really sophisticated theories about teaching, and I still haven't. What seemed important was that the teacher know what he was talking about and be able to show as well as tell. One of the fallacies in Army training these days is that this kind of experience is no longer a part of the tradition. Kids are taught combat techniques by men who, through no fault of their own, of course, have never spent a moment in combat—and we wonder how it is that we turn out soldiers like Calley. What seemed most important then—and still does—was that the students realize that the Army and war are not really games at all, even though they might seem that way at times, especially when you hear some of the barroom tales of "the way it was at Inchon" or "that night in the Mekong Delta." I saw so many Army teachers who were trying to make up for the times when they had been down at the bottom of the heap, when they had been the ones taking the orders. They played games with their men, building their own egos with nitpicking orders that produced nothing but dissent and rancor among the men. So often I found it that way in the military: the rules and the regs and the juvenile cover-ups and the children's games. It had nothing to do with creating a system of discipline or building soldiers. It was simply an ego game.

In the summer of 1959, with the Ranger department going great guns and with me enjoying my assignment to the full, the Army replaced Dalton as the Ranger commander with Colonel John Corley, whom they were grooming for general. Because of the potential they saw in Corley, it seemed only right that he have larger responsibilities. It didn't seem to matter that they brought in a non-Ranger to command the Rangers. All that mattered was that it was an elite command. But it was also too small a command for a future general, so the Army expanded the Rangers, and when the expansion came in the eliteness went out. They began to give Ranger badges to people who didn't even begin, much less finish, Ranger training. They gave them to graduates of the BIOC at Benning. When they decided to give Corley one, without his having undergone anything like Ranger training, and asked me to present it, I knew my days with the Rangers were numbered.

It was all a part of the changing Army, where image was more important than anything else. Corley thought I was one of the hard-assed Rangers, so he asked that I pin on the badge he hadn't earned. I flatly refused, so they got another non-Ranger to pin it on him, and then Corley turned around and pinned one on him. It was like magic.

Presto, you're a Ranger. Nowadays, you never know when you see that badge exactly what it means. There was a time, though, when it symbolized one great soldier.

By the time Corley arrived to take over the Rangers, I had already taken some time out from my instructional duties to attend the Pathfinder school at Benning and a scuba-diving school at Little Creek, Va., Pensacola, Fla., and St. Thomas in the Virgin Islands. The Pathfinders are paratroopers specially trained in infiltration techniques and radio-and-communications skills. Their job is to establish security and terminal guidance at a drop-zone before the landing is made. They're either dropped in themselves or, in some cases, they swim to the shore and make their way to the designated area. I was one of two honor graduates in the Pathfinder school and the only Army officer of the eight who began who graduated from the Navy's scuba school.

Now, with what I could see happening to the Rangers in 1959, I wanted a change. I felt stagnant, and I thought I was ready for an Airborne command. Byerly wanted to keep me around Dahlonega, and he even offered to arrange for me to work on my master's degree at the University of Georgia in nearby Athens. But I wanted something different, and I went to Corley with my request for an Airborne command.

"Herbert, you're a good officer," he said. "But one of the things you're going to have to learn about the Army is that there are other units besides the Rangers and the Airborne. If you expect to go up in the Army, you're going to have to learn that every soldier isn't an elitist like you."

And with that, he got the Department of the Army to assign me to the 16th Infantry, 1st Battle Group, 8th Division, and ordered me to Baumholder, Germany. I would be a platoon leader, he said. The discussion was over.

It was the summer of 1959, and the U.S. Army was then substantially altering a structural pattern that had stood for several generations. Under the direction of President Eisenhower and General Maxwell D. Taylor, it abandoned its basic Triangular system and moved into the nuclear age with a sparkling new organizational idea called the Pentomic Concept. The Triangular concept had simply meant that in each division there were three regiments, two up front and one back under combat circumstances. In each regiment, there were three battalions, two up and one back. Each battalion contained three rifle companies, each company had three rifle platoons, and each platoon had three rifle squads. It was a three-three-three pattern all the way down the line. Of course, the battalions had an additional heavy weapons support company, the companies had a similar kind of platoon, and the platoons included a weapons squad, but the pattern held all the way down. It was a fine concept, because it worked, and one of its chief advantages was that the chain of command was the most efficient structure possible. Each link was but a bit behind or a bit ahead of its immediate superior or junior. For instance, platoons were commanded by lieutenants, companies by captains, battalions by lieutenant colonels (with majors as staff officers), regiments by colonels and some generals, and divisions, of course, by generals.

But General Taylor and the President came up with the idea that, in nuclear warfare, the troops must be dispersed on the battlefield more widely than seemed, in their view, to be possible with the Triangular concept. Thus the Pentomic concept was born. It was ridiculous. There would be no difference in a nuclear battle if troops were dispersed twenty yards or a thousand. But it was a good-sounding name, and it was implemented in the Army. What it meant was that for each division there would be five "battle groups" and to each of those battle groups, five rifle companies, and five rifle platoons to each company. The basic strategy of the Pentomic concept was to be able to marshal the kind of strength with which the enemy could be driven to a specific "kill-zone," onto which nuclear firepower could then be concentrated with no apparent risk to the friendly troops.

What the Pentomic concept produced was one of the chief evils in the U.S. Army. It isolated the links in the command chain by enlarging the space between them. By eliminating the regiment as a unit, the Army ended up with very junior officers and very senior officers commanding at extremely close levels; the lines of communication were broken and the concept of Cover Your Ass was nourished.

Another effect of the Pentomic concept was its destruction of the regimental tradition. Tradition is really what makes men fight. The Marines have always realized that and always maintained their traditions—sometimes even at the expense of weaponry and supplies. But the Army somehow could not understand that it was the regiment in which the yesterdays were honored, and some of the regiments obliterated by the Pentomic concept went back as far as the Indian wars.

The new way was creating larger problems than anyone realized. There were more command slots but the Army wasn't training for command. Those not trained for command were given command anyway because the slots were there and had to be filled. It was, I think, a disaster from which the entire Army is still suffering.

Six weeks before I was scheduled to depart for Germany and my new post as a platoon leader in the 16th Infantry (the old regimental name; it was now the 1st Battle Group of the 8th Division), Marygrace gave birth to a daughter, Toni-Junell, at the post hospital in Ft. Benning. It was perfect timing, but what else could I have expected of her? The Army doesn't allow travel by infants at military expense until they're six weeks old, and precisely six weeks to the day after Toni-Junell showed up was the day we were all supposed to leave for Baumholder.

Marygrace and I liked Germany almost immediately. We found the mountains, the forests, the rather primeval quality of the countryside delightful, and the cities had a blossoming vitality to them by then that perfectly complemented our rural tastes.

I had just about resigned myself to the wisdom of Corley's counsel and the inevitability of his assignment. Maybe he was right, I thought. Maybe it would do me good to serve in a non-elite outfit—to get away from all those crazy paratroopers and all those tough-assed Rangers. Maybe it would be a broadening experience to see what the rest of the Army was like. So I settled down and tried to do my job with the 16th as a platoon leader, but I'd no sooner made that resolution than I got involved in a sequence of events that finally stretched beyond my control.

The annual Army Training Tests (ATTs) came up, and as part of my responsibility as a platoon leader, I had to put my people through a series of field exercises, inspections, and examinations. I was being graded by a bunch of paratrooper types from the 1st Battle Group of the 505th Division, and among the graders were a great many of the friends that I had made in my years as a paratrooper and a

Ranger instructor. Some of them I had trained and taught at Dahlonega and Benning. They were surprised to see me in the 16th Infantry. "What the hell are you doing in a leg outfit?" they asked, and I told them that it was my assignment and that I was doing the best I could. They were incensed and vowed that they'd see to it, by hook or by crook, that I got out and back with my own kind of people. I must admit that I was all for that, but I had no idea that they could pull it off. But they did. They went back to the 505th and, with a little pressure here and there, engineered my appointment as an examiner in the Expert Infantryman's Badge test. The EIB was a prestigious achievement in the Army and still is. A series of arduous, and I mean really arduous, tests are given to the individual entrant, and he has to pass every single one of them. I had won the badge twice: first in 1947 and again in 1952. It was one of my most prized possessions. I accepted the job quickly because it meant getting away from the rather humdrum command of a leg platoon and being with some of my people again. We gave the EIB test to five battle groups. Out of all the entrants, only two paratroopers were awarded the badge, and out of all the losers, only the colonel who was running the 16th Infantry, my outfit, complained. The colonel called in one of the majors who was giving the EIB test around Germany and protested the fact that no one from the 16th had won the badge. He accused the major of having rigged the examinations and of being partial to Airborne groups. The major, himself an Airborne man, asked if he might reply to those allegations and the colonel told him to speak his piece.

"Come in here, Tony," the colonel called from his office. "I want you to be a witness."

I went in the room and the colonel explained the disagreement they had. I sat down and the major opened up.

"Colonel," he said, "you are a goddamned phoney. What you want from me is a bagful of EIBs and I just, by God, will not go along with that kind of pissy-assed routine."

The colonel blanched and looked at me. "Herbert," he said, his voice nearly cracking, "you're a witness. He insulted me. He insulted me and he is, by God, going to get a court-martial."

I didn't hesitate. "I won't be a witness to that, sir," I said. "You told him to speak his mind and I heard you say that. Whatever he said at that point seems to be beyond a court-martial, sir."

The colonel was unimpressed with my logic. "Goddamn it, Herbert, you may be working for this crazy major today, but when the EIBs are over, you're going to be back here in the 16th working for me—and by God, then you'll do what I say."

I agreed that would probably be the case, but I again refused to participate in the major's court-martial, should it come off. I realized I had no choice about appearing at a court-martial if I were called as a witness, but the colonel also realized he couldn't dictate the substance of my testimony. It was a stand-off, he thought; I thought the major and I had won.

The major went back to the 505th with the story of the probable peril that awaited me once the EIBs were finished, and after some more pressures and string-pulling, I got a transfer from the 16th Infantry to the 1st of the 505th—and I was happy. I was assigned to Easy Company and I felt at home. I'd been in an Easy Company in Korea. Two weeks later, I became the executive officer of the company, and I must say I felt like a stud. I was in the company of an elite bunch of officers—the cream of the Airborne—and I was a lieutenant serving as the XO of the whole damned company.

I have said I only needed one lesson about alcohol, but there are times when tradition seems more important than sweet reason, and the prop-blast parties were a tradition in the Airborne. You don't see them much anymore because most unit commanders try to delay them for as long as possible, realizing, I suppose, the risk to their career. A prop-blast is the Airborne's initiation rite, and when I went to the 1st of the 505th, even though I'd already been through one blast thirteen years before, I decided that for the sake of appearances and pride, I'd do it again.

The participant is known as a "blaster," and that night all of us blasters reported in fatigues after supper to the field outside the officers' club. Each blaster had a sponsor whose only duty was to see to it that his charge stayed alive until the prop-blast ended. We teamed up, shook hands, and were given our choice of a full fifth of either bourbon, gin, rum, or scotch, which was then consumed completely while doing push-ups. When the bottle was emptied, the push-ups were over. Then we donned our ponchos. There was no rain. They were to increase our body heat as we left on a five-mile trot. At the half-way point, we were handed a water glass full of, again, whatever we preferred—bourbon, gin, rum, or scotch—and then we went on. On the way in, we lost Captain Ollie Olson. (He was the only man I knew in the entire Army who had been urinated on by an elephant. He had gone out and bought a really snappy set of dress uniforms soon after his first promotion and then had gone to the circus. There an elephant, quite unimpressed by Ollie, did it to him. He thought it was quite a distinction.) About a mile from the end of the run, Ollie joined us again, coming in from a small embankment above us in a great slow power dive, screaming "Supermaaaaaaaan!" He was grinning when he hit the ground and the grin still hadn't left his face when his sponsor hauled him off. Soon afterward, I slipped in a pool of vomit and banged my elbow on the road.

Next came a flight of stairs up to the officers' club, inside and then out through a second-story window into a huge vat of mud, which kept us from killing ourselves from the fall but damned near choked all of us. Then we were up and out for the traditional silver-steel helmet full of vodka and champagne. Once it was empty, the final trick was to make it to the desk by the door of the club and sign in on the log.

I don't know how, but I did it. Ten minutes later, two of my friends were carrying me back to the BOQ, both of my big toes dragging. I remember insisting that it really wasn't necessary for them to help me. They got me in a sack but five minutes later I was in Ollie's room, kicking him out of his. We argued about who was tougher, and then I accused him of vomiting on the floor of my room, and then it occurred to me that if I didn't take a cold shower, I would most certainly die. I went in with my clothes on. Ollie came running in a moment later to ask my help in getting Mike Jessior, another of our blaster buddies, to the hospital, since he seemed to have stopped breathing. I hesitated long enough to change clothes. Then we packed Mike up and took him to the post hospital. Leaving Ollie to guard the body, I went in past the desk to the doctor on duty. He looked up.

"Yes?"

"Doc," I said. "I have the drunkest human being alive—I hope —outside and I wonder if you'd have a look at him."

We walked down the hall together and Ollie met us coming in the door.

"You're right," the doctor said. "This is the drunkest human being I've ever seen."

It took a moment or two to explain that Ollie was not the patient, during which Ollie, angered at the doctor's remarks, took a long, slow-motion wind-up and a long, slow-motion swing which, when the doctor stepped aside, carried Ollie past him and through the window, cutting a great gash in the side of his palm.

"Stitches," said the doctor, and while he took care of Jessior, an assistant came over and started treating Ollie. About that time, some of our own medical-supply people, who had been blasters themselves that evening, arrived and took over the operation on Ollie, pushing the young assistant aside and locking the door to the little room where he had been working.

I woke early the next day—about 3 p.m.—and went to rouse Ollie for breakfast. He waved me off and I noticed that he had no thumb.

"My God," I said, "they cut off your thumb."

"You're crazy," he said, sitting up with the hand in front of his face. "You're right. Damn! Damn! You're right." But I was wrong. They had merely stitched his thumb and his forefinger together.

We went to get the medics to make the slight adjustment in Ollie's stitches, and as we passed the officers' club, we noted that the battalion surgeon was buried up to his neck in the flower bed just next to the door.

"Christ, Doc, you're a pansy," Ollie chortled as we walked off to find the medics.

I finally came out of the euphoria and started doing my job—a job which gave me a great deal of time to think about logistics, strategy, and a lot of other aspects of the Army I hadn't had time to deal with before. I couldn't get the idea of being a Ranger out of my mind, and I began to study Ranger history. It finally occurred to me that, although the very nature of the Ranger's job would entail a high casualty rate, it still appeared to have been extraordinarily high both in World War II and in Korea. In the big war, the Rangers had been organized in battalion-size special units, used for specific operations. In most cases they had paid dearly for that misuse. A perfect example was in Italy when the 36th Texas National Guard Division had bogged down at the Rapido River. General Mark Clark called in the 3d Ranger Battalion and because they weren't his troops—that was the handicap of being a special unit; you didn't belong to anybody—he wasted them in repeated, desperate attempts to get across the Rapido. They were chewed all to hell. What did Clark care? They weren't his men. The concept held true in Korea, where the Rangers were organized into company-sized units attached to divisions. They still didn't belong to anybody and the casualties, as a result, were still inordinately high. Commanders would rather use a special unit like the Rangers in a particularly hairy operation than commit and risk two of their own companies.

One of the arguments I'd always heard against Ranger groups or other elite units was that, once you began that kind of organization, you necessarily had to drain the Army of its cream. I thought that one of the best ways to defeat that kind of logic and to avoid the kind of abuse and misuse of the Rangers that had occurred in World War II and Korea was to organize a Ranger unit within the unit. In that way, the Rangers for any particular operation would belong to the unit charged with the job and there would be less of a tendency for the commander to waste men who did not belong to his unit. I tried the idea on the battle group commander, Colonel Theodore Mataxis, and he bought it.

In a matter of weeks, I had become the commander of the Provisional Ranger Platoon of the 1st of the 505th. My job was to take 180 men, much larger than the normal platoon, and build them into a Ranger unit that would function as an arm of the battalion. I was happy again. I was a Ranger. I was teaching other men to be Rangers. It was great.

It was while I was running the new Ranger platoon for Mataxis that I got to meet a legendary man I had read about: Otto Skorzeny, who had been Hitler's ace commando and who had been written up in one of the books on commando warfare. I had taken the Ranger platoon to France to train with the French paratroopers, and as troops will do, all of us would gather frequently in our favorite bar in Pau to talk about our job. During these conversations, the subject of heroes was often raised, and I mentioned to my French friends that, while I did not really regard Skorzeny as one of my genuine heroes, I did think he was probably one of the finest commando fighters of this century and that he could probably teach us all a lot.

"Would you like to meet him and perhaps see if he can teach you something, Herbert?" one of them asked.

"Of course I would," I said.

"Well, that is not impossible," he said.

"How can it be arranged?"

"Just keep asking around."

"Asking who?"

"Why don't you ask the most powerful man you know in the United States Army?"

I could think only of Mataxis, the battle group commander. I went to him and bluntly said I'd like to meet Skorzeny.

"Perhaps that can be arranged, Tony," he said.

It wasn't arranged immediately and, in fact, I had to do a lot of the arranging myself. But on later trips down to Pau and on little excursions to the village of Lourdes, the contacts were made. Skorzeny was still being very careful. He was living in exile in Spain. He and a small group of former German troopers had formed a corporation whose service was the arming and training of groups of guerrillas. If you wanted to know how to blow up a bridge without blowing up yourself, Skorzeny could teach you. Whatever you thought you needed to know about an underground war, Otto was your man—for a price.

My motivations were simple. I was a Ranger. I was training Rangers. I wanted to talk to anybody and everybody who could help me do my job better, and Skorzeny seemed to be one man who could. When the arrangements were finally made, I made another trip to France as a cover for my first meeting with the famed Nazi. Our rendezvous was in the Basque section of Spain, in the mountains of the north. He was much taller than I, and although he must have been in his late fifties by then, he had a lean, rangy physique. There was nothing pudgy about him. He spoke English, although he did not do a great deal of talking.

Actually, I was quite disappointed with the Skorzeny School of Commando Tactics. His methods were good, but they were dated, and everything he and his men mentioned I'd already learned as an American Ranger. My only education from Skorzeny was in the fine art of arson. It is no simple thing, for instance, to burn down a large factory. There are anti-fire devices all over the place, especially in the more modern ones, and although you might severely damage one section or another with various kinds of explosives, the chances of actually levelling the place are very small. What I learned from Skorzeny was the tricky business of using all the dust in the factory as an explosive. You simply take, say, about a half-pound of fast explosive and another half-pound of slow explosive, gather about forty or fifty pounds of dust from the floor and bins, pack it around the explosives and ignite them. The fast one goes off and electrifies the dust particles. The slow one energizes the dust which then itself explodes . . . and you've got yourself one fine old level factory there.

I met with the Skorzeny group in the Basque country some ten or eleven times. He wasn't always there. "He has other students, you must understand," his aides explained.

I suppose it was Lieutenant Sands, my closest friend in the French Foreign Legion, who acquainted me first with the little country known as Vietnam. We were sitting in a small restaurant in Pau when the subject came up. He had fought there with the French, and it was among his favorite subjects. Indochina and Algiers.

"No matter what kind of fighting you bring to that place," the lieutenant said of Indochina, "there is no way of defeating them because their motivation is nationalism. No western nation is going to make the kind of psychological and physical commitment it would require to beat that kind of esprit."

I asked why he fought there, then, if it was such a losing proposition.

"Because, Tony, it is always fun to fight," he said. Then, growing serious: "But anyone who fights them is eventually destined for destruction. They must be destroyed completely—how do you say? Whoomph! with the big bomb—or they will destroy you."

After concluding that there wasn't really a hell of a lot to learn from Skorzeny's little academy—a fact which I relayed to Mataxis—I wondered about trying to pick up a few things from the modern Germans. I had heard of their *Fallschirmjäger,* their paratroopers, and I began making inquiries about getting in their school just for a little observation. It would be impossible, I was told, utterly impossible. I decided to visit the school anyway, and one afternoon I walked in and found three of the German troopers I'd helped train in a program at Dahlonega. There was Major Lewitska, an engineer, and Lieutenant Lemprecht, and tough old Sergeant Ray, a veteran of the German parachute drop on Crete in World War II. It was quite a fortunate turn of events.

"Okay, here I am," I said to them after the usual round of greetings and back-slapping. They stared at me blankly. "Don't you remember when you were in my country, you said that if ever I was in yours and you could do anything for me, just to look you up and ask?" They nodded. "Well, now I'm asking," I continued.

"What do you want?" the major asked.

"I want to come to your school for a while," I said.

"Impossible," the lieutenant blurted.

"Yes, just impossible," the major echoed.

"Goddamn it," I said, "I should have known better than to expect anything from anyone who would let a corporal command their army."

That did it. They agreed that they had promised, and they agreed to let me come and stay for a while.

"And I want to bring all my men," I added.

"Impossible," Lemprecht said again.

"Yes, just impossible," Lewitska repeated.

"How many men do you have?" Sergeant Ray asked.

"Nearly two hundred."

The little office was quiet. They were thinking—thinking about promises made and promises broken, I suppose. Finally, Lewitska cleared his throat. "Bring them," he said.

"All of them?" I asked.

"All of them."

I did, and the Provisional Ranger Platoon of the 1st Battalion of the 505th Airborne Battle Group of the U.S. Army enrolled in the *Fallschirmjäger* school, and then their *Einselkämpfer* course—their equivalent to Ranger school. We didn't learn a lot, except that, in comparison at least, we were already pretty damned good.

Bravo Company of the 1st had a bad reputation. There were letters from the people around Mainz complaining that the men of

Bravo were nothing but hoodlums, and there were stacks of formal reports on file showing missing weapons and equipment. In May, 1961, Mataxis came to me and gave me command of Bravo with instructions to make something happen in it "worthwhile, for a change." Now, I was a lieutenant commanding a company in a battle group where all the other company commanders were captains. In fact, I had two captains serving under me, one as an executive officer and another at the parachute school in Wiesbaden—and although it took another Presidential order to make it legal, Mataxis didn't have too much trouble arranging that, either.

What happened in the next thirteen months is one of the things I'm proudest of in my career. The ratings for Bravo in June were just average, but for the next twelve months, we were graded the best company in Germany. There were fourteen trophies for unit excellence given by the 8th Division over the next year. Bravo won all of them.

Soon afterward, I received a call from home that my father was dying of stomach cancer. I flew back immediately, leaving my wife and daughter in Mainz, and my father and I had several long talks before I had to go back. He died while I was on the plane from the States to Germany.

In May, 1962, I was promoted to captain. By that time the Army was starting to re-examine the Pentomic organizational concept and had begun to come back around to the Triangular. All over the Army, young officers were writing papers critical of the Pentomic system, and what they were saying was finally making some sense to the upper echelons. The only problem then was Congress. What would Congress say if the Army decided, after only a few years of being Pentomic— and spending millions of dollars in the reorganization process—that it now wanted to be Triangular again? The answer they hit upon was to continue the ban on regiments, since that had been a cardinal point in the Pentomic plan, and use brigades instead. But rather than have three battalions to a brigade, it was decided that the number could be unlimited. As a result, the new-old plan created a lot of command vacancies. There were a lot of guys promoted to captain early, just as I had been, and there were even some assignments of generals to brigade commands. The communications gap was still there, since the steps from company commander, usually a captain, to battalion commander, usually a lieutenant colonel, to the head of the brigade itself were small ones—and generals just don't talk very well with captains and lieutenant colonels.

There was a company commander on the base in Germany who, because of some shortages in personnel and some administrative foul-ups, had to hold down the additional responsibility of post coordinator for a couple of weeks. He finally climbed the wall. He would spend half the day as post coordinator, writing orders for his own company with dates of completion that were utterly impossible to meet. Then, in the afternoon, back in his own unit, he would read the orders he had written that morning, answering them with pleas to extend the mission time, offering alibis. The next morning, as post coordinator, he would turn down his own requests. A first sergeant tried to point out that it was all pretty silly, but the guy insisted that, because the two jobs were completely separate, a man had to be big enough to separate them in his mind. He was cracking. Nobody did anything. He amassed a file of correspondence against himself as thick as an encyclopedia and finally, as post coordinator, he turned himself in, as company commander, and scheduled a court-martial for negligence. While they were trying to untangle the mess at Battle Group Head-quarters, he left. Weeks later, they found him down in Ettlebrook, standing on a street corner drawing sketches of the tourists at a buck a head.

Sergeant Candiotti was about as tough an old buzzard as I'd ever seen in the Army. He was a true gentleman-soldier, and he looked to be in as good a physical condition as when he had been the inter-service middleweight boxing champ nearly twenty years before. He was a sky-soldier all the way, and one with whom any young para-trooper should have been proud to serve. Still, though, I remember Candiotti best for an incident that was most untypical of him.

We drank our beer together in a certain bar in Mainz, talking Army and sports in a warm gathering of older Airborne officers and older sergeants who had served together in several places. One night, the talk turned to Ripley's famous "Believe It or Not" column, and a Captain Stevens, new to the unit, mentioned that he had only recently read about a man who could jut out his jaw, fold down his face and, as a result, "swallow" his nose.

"That's nothing," Candiotti said, "I can bite my eye." There was an immediate wager from Stevens that he could not. We watched the expression on Stevens's face when Candiotti calmly plucked out his famous glass eye and placed it between his teeth. Stevens took it pretty well and paid off immediately. "Tell you what, sir," Candiotti continued. "I'll give you a chance to get even. Double or nothing, I can do it with the other eye, too."

"Well, now, goddamn," Stevens said, getting up the cash. "I know damned well they're not both glass. You came in the door by yourself." This time we watched his face while Candiotti took out both his uppers & lowers and closed them over the other eye.

In August, 1962, I was transferred back to the United States to attend the Advance Infantry Command School's first Reorganization Of the Army Division (ROAD) class. I left Germany and the friends Marygrace and I had made with deep regret. We had both been happy there, and Toni-Junell seemed to prosper even more than babies usually do. It had become home—but the orders came and it had to be done. We returned to Ft. Benning. The place was becoming like a vacation spot to me.

A few weeks after I arrived, I was called out of class and told to report to a briefing at the officers' club just off the golf course. The news of the day was the Cuban missile crisis. When I arrived, I found that the men already there were being briefed on an invasion of Cuba. I also learned that General Westmoreland, the invasion task force commander, had selected me to lead one of two Pathfinder teams that would be dropped on the island in advance of the main invasion force.

I had mixed emotions about the idea—not that anybody asked me what I thought of its merits. But before I could gather my thoughts and apply any logic to the thing, the entire operation was cancelled. Benning had been overrun with high-ranking brass during the planning phase of the operation. They had been immensely happy in their work. When the invasion was called off, I began to hear generals and colonels cursing President Kennedy as a weak-kneed, candy-assed, chicken-livered coward. I eventually figured out that they were angry because

JFK had taken away their chance for glory. It didn't seem to matter that there were international complications and considerations and that the civilian commander-in-chief had given an order. All they appeared to be concerned about was that they weren't going into Cuba and it would never be in their files. It was quite a lesson for me.

But the brass did like Kennedy's interest in the Special Forces, those fellows in the Green Berets who had caught his fancy after he'd read about Che Guevara and Castro whipping the Batista forces. A lot of the brass had developed the merit badge syndrome by then. For instance, when I started in the Rangers, the only designation available (or necessary, in my view) was the badge, but as the years passed, the badge grew larger and finally a patch was added, and damned if they didn't finally throw in a little black beret with some of the Ranger groups. Once more, image was being substituted for substance.

Nevertheless, for our times, I suppose, the Special Forces were a practical idea. Kennedy was no fool, and neither were most of the Army leaders. If the U.S. was going to protect its interests around the world without becoming involved in the serious risks of large military confrontations, then training guerrillas was just the thing. You first transform a soldier into the equivalent of a Ranger, and then you teach him to be a political warrior as well; you teach him the language and how to endear himself to the local populace, and you teach him the art of assassination. You can then introduce your point of view in the person of the Green Beret. He is your ambassador in the village or hamlet, and if diplomacy, friendship, medical supplies, and dandy little projects designed to show America's love and affection don't work, then he can always blow hell out of the place and leave.

Just before I finished the Advanced Infantry Officer's Course at Benning, I was selected for Special Forces and assigned to Ft. Bragg for training. But before I could leave, my orders were changed, and I ended up in the Defense Language Institute in California studying Portuguese. There were five of us in my class. One man was going to Portugal to serve as a military attaché in the American Embassy in Lisbon. Two were destined for similar plush assignments in the embassies in São Paulo and Rio. The fourth was going to Panama to be a Special Forces instructor. And me? Well, I found out they had Africa in mind for me. Angola and Mozambique, specifically.

Late in November, just after President Kennedy was killed, I graduated from the language school and headed back to Ft. Bragg to join the newly organized 3d Special Forces. Its specialty, I learned, would be Africa. I was supposed to be in another elite outfit—Kennedy had called them that and the Army had quickly picked it up—but everywhere I looked in the 3d Special Forces, I saw all the rejects I'd ever known in the service. They were the officers who had been passed over so many times, they had not a hope of promotion before retirement. They were Methuselah colonels such as the commander, Colonel "Blinky" Bartholomews, and sixteen of the eighteen second lieutenants who had been passed over for promotion that year. They were sergeants who had quit under me in the past. The same thing was happening to the Special Forces that had happened to the Rangers. Because Kennedy liked it so much, it had to be expanded, and once the expansion began, it became simply one more scrap-heap. Everybody started sending in their rejects, and for good reason: if you put a second lieutenant who isn't worth a damn in a regular unit, he's probably got forty or fifty men under his command. But not in SF. There he's on his own. The same thing applied to the higher-ranking officers. The SF assignment decreased command responsibility for the inept officer, and for many of them it was exactly what the doctor ordered. There were no risks. It was easier to Cover Your Ass. It was plush duty. They ate it up, running all over Ft. Bragg in their dandy little jungle suits.

I was pretty miserable, but I tried to stick it out and was finally assigned to attend the Special Forces Officers School and the Special Warfare School, both at Bragg, and both of which proved worthless. We sat around and talked and read and philosophized about this and that. We read Che's stuff and Bernard B. Fall's fine book *Street Without Joy,* but we never actually learned anything other than the trite little ideas that can emerge at any bull session or bar gathering.

It was at the SF Officers School and the Special Warfare School that I first heard U.S. Army officers discussing torture as a military tactic. The French had loved it in Indochina and it had rubbed off. I'm not talking about just the abstract discussion of whether torture is internationally ethical. I'm talking about downright advocacy on the part of teachers and students of specific forms of it: the water-torture, heel-hanging, the way to almost kill a man with your hands or a blunt instrument without leaving a single mark on him.

In February, 1964, two teams of twenty-four volunteers each

were called for from the men in the 3d Special Forces. Their mission would be to stand by in East Africa should anything go wrong on an upcoming Gemini space shot. Out of all those red-blooded men, there were only two volunteers: another officer and I. They tried to fill out the teams by sending over other men on orders, and I discovered as we trained for the mission that a substantial number of them couldn't run the proverbial mile, much less take the kind of physical regimen we had planned. Some of them had high blood pressure as well. It was from them that I learned why the SF people were all so hot to go over to Vietnam, volunteering by the dozens every day. The SF got a $35 per diem in Vietnam which wasn't available in East Africa.

While we were training for the Gemini shot, word came that a small contingent of the 3d SF would be going into the Belgian Congo to assist Colonel Joseph Mobutu, the military dictator who held sway in that country. The Congo had been the scene of bloody internal strife for several months. It was not the kind of fight I wanted to get into, but when the advance party of five men was selected, I was chosen to go along. There were two American doctors in the group, both of whom spoke French, and the very first day we arrived in Léopoldville, the doctors were asked by a local black leader to address a large group of native para-medics in a nearby auditorium. They refused.

I asked them why they couldn't help the guy. All he wanted was a little professional advice for the scores of men he'd brought in from all over the country on the premise that the Americans couldn't possibly refuse. The doctors were adamant. That wasn't their mission there, they said. They both outranked me. A couple of days later, the same guy who had tried to set up the medical seminar took me to a local hospital, where I noticed a huge stockpile of American medical supplies standing untouched in a corner of a storeroom. The hospital was using Czechoslovakian medicine, because the identification tags and directions—and the accompanying propaganda—were printed in French. The doctor asked me to request that the American doctors come over to the hospital and simply translate the various labels on the medicine from America so that it, too, could be used. The doctors refused again. Not their jobs, they said. Not in their orders.

For months and months the U.S. had been pouring supplies, military and otherwise, into the Congo. Much of it was earmarked for a large paracommando base Mobutu had established just outside

Léopoldville. It was here, he told the American ambassador, that he trained the people who kept the Congo from falling into the hands of Communists. We bought his story and poured in the merchandise.

One of the jobs I had as a member of the advance party was to inspect the paracommando base. I asked a resident U.S. Air Force colonel, the man responsible for the Congo end of the shipping process, to take me out. He made some excuse at first, and when I insisted day after day, not knowing exactly where the base was located, he finally gave me an absolute refusal. There were rebels all over, he said. It was better to just stay in the embassy and direct things from there. So what our advance party amounted to was a group of five Special Forces officers being wined and dined in Léopoldville's finest hotel. Occasionally we would be driven to the embassy, where the latest reports from troublesome Katanga province would be read to us. I finally became so exasperated that I rented a car and decided to set out on my own to find that damned base. It was the only specific part of my orders for the Congo: find the thing, take a look at it and see what was going on there, and write a report on my observations. That was what I intended to do.

I can't say that, as I set out on my search (I had only a general idea of the direction from Léopoldville), I felt easy about the trip. It wasn't the rebels I was worried about so much as Mobutu's own people. First, his army had no privates. Everybody had to be promoted to preserve even a semblance of loyalty, and even with that there were massive defections daily to the ranks of the rebels or just back home. Practically speaking, Mobutu didn't run his army. Instead, five regimental commanders made most of the decisions by vote at informal meetings. If the dissenters didn't feel like taking their troops into a particular operation, they just went home and sat it out. None of the Mobutu soldiers ever smiled. It was uncomfortable to be around them.

Nevertheless, I was determined to find that paracommando camp, and after two days of driving around the outskirts of the city, I did. Actually, I found out there was no camp. It had once existed, but had long since been abandoned and the only occupants of the little settlement were deserters from both sides and women and children. On the way back into town I ran into a British ex-sergeant who told me it had been shut down for three years. I noticed that a lot of the equipment which had found its way there had been turned into decor in the little huts around the camp. Radio wire had been strung through the noses and ears of the natives and tubes and transistors were planted in their front yards. But most of the equipment that had been shipped from our country to the Congo, to be used by Mobutu in his valiant fight against Communism, had never reached the camp at all, nor any fighting men, either. In fact, as I learned later from several English officers, most of it had been funneled directly to Mobutu, who promptly sold it to the highest outside bidder and stashed the cash. When I reported to the Air Force colonel at the embassy, he said I must have made a mistake. Then he finally admitted that in his eighteen months in Léopoldville, he had never visited the base. No checks were ever made, he conceded, and he had no idea where the equipment went once it was unloaded in Léopoldville. Since our relationship with Mobutu and his army was supposed to be a relatively secret proposition, I suppose that was his way of really keeping it a secret.

Another supposedly secret relationship with Mobutu that was hardly a secret at all in the Congo was the presence and involvement of the U.S. Central Intelligence Agency. In the few weeks I was in the Congo, I kept running into Cubans who had fled Castro and were now flying for the CIA, taking allegedly commercial planes with military supplies and personnel—mercenaries for Mobutu—wherever the CIA directed. Some of them told me they had even flown strafing missions into Katanga.

I was elated. I had uncovered a fairly large gap in the supply chain between Ft. Bragg, where much of the stuff was originating, and Léopoldville, where almost all of it was disappearing. I wrote my report on the plane back to North Carolina, filed it, and went back to my duties.

A couple of days later, I was running a jump exercise in the 3d Special Forces. It was a night operation, and since I judged that the winds were above the maximum level for the safety of the troopers, I called it off. A Captain Bowden, the safety officer, disputed my judgment. He said he had dropped a helmet and it had hit the ground within the designated drop zone.

"I'm telling you, the winds are okay," he insisted.

"And I'm telling you they're not and this operation is cancelled," I said.

"I'm the safety officer," he argued. "It's my decision."

"And I'm running the exercise and I've already made the decision."

He swung at me. I thought it was a joke at first and stepped away. His fist struck my right shoulder. I was still not certain what was happening when he swung again. I stepped back, grabbed his arm and cross-hawked him to the ground, where I pinned him and grabbed his throat.

"You swing at me again, Bowden, and I'll tear out your Adam's apple and feed it to you," I said. A Major Beatty came up quickly and grabbed me around the throat. I put my elbow to his temple—and it was all over. Unknown to any of us that night, a National Guard officer, at Ft. Bragg to receive some partial Special Forces training, had been standing next to a nearby tree. He saw the whole thing.

A couple of days later, I was told that I would be offered an Article 15, a nonjudicial punishment, for the incident with Bowden and Beatty over the jump-exercise cancellation. I refused the Article 15 and was told they would court-martial me for assault. I got a military lawyer, who began collecting the evidence, but two days before the court-martial was to begin, the Army assigned my lawyer, the counsel for the defense, to be the prosecutor. He wouldn't return the documents he had gathered for my defense. I decided to go ahead with the trial and serve as my own attorney. The day before the trial, General York, the division commander, gave me the Article 15 without my consent, which is, of course, illegal. He said I'd be fined $25 and the whole thing would be forgotten. I said no deal. General Rosson, commander of the Joint Task Force Exercise Group, called from Florida to try to persuade me to take the Article 15 and assured me that, once that formality was taken care of, it could be forgotten and my records would never show it. I said nothing doing. They gave me the Article 15 anyway, and a few days later, General York had me transferred to the 82d Airborne, whose quarters and area of operations were far on the other side of the base from the Special Forces. It was there that the National Guard officer, who had no ax to grind in the matter, finally spoke up and told General York and the others what had happened that night I cancelled the jump exercise. The matter was stricken from the record, but there were never any apologies. So what the hell? I didn't expect any.

York assigned me to become operations officer (S3) in the 2d Battalion of the 505th. The battalion commander, Major Rose, one of the finest soldiers I've ever known, was soon replaced by a lieutenant colonel. After a couple of field problems, it became pretty clear that the 2d Battalion wasn't looking too good, especially in night maneuvers. As operations officer, I decided to run a night exercise in the daytime so that the men of the battalion could accustom themselves to nocturnal techniques without the initial handicap of darkness. Then, after getting that down straight, we could run the maneuver at night. Among the most important things in any Army unit's life in those days were the Army Training Test, the Inspector General's inspection, and the Command Material and Maintenance Inspection, and everybody from the General on down to the last private was concentrating on scoring high on those exams. The training exercises were increased in number and intensity, and one afternoon, while I was leading a company on an exercise whose objective was to reach a road we had named the "probable line of demarcation," I was having so much trouble that I began to move them at a slow walk and teach as we went. The radio operator interrupted me with a call from Golden Knight—General York. "He wants to know when you reach the road," he said. "Tell him not for about another two hours," I answered. But General York, for some reason or another, wanted my company to get to that road immediately as part of the training exercise. "Okay, sir," I said. I turned to the men and told them to strip their packs and drop their weapons and run to the road, which they did.

General York was pleased. He was smiling. "See, Tony, you're such a hard-ass you didn't think these men could do it," he said, glancing around at my puffing company.

"Well, sir, if you'll look around, you'll see they're unarmed and completely stripped of equipment," I said.

Somehow he found it merely a curious sight. He had interrupted a training exercise and given an order that made no sense—and now he just thought it was funny.

"Tony, what we're worrying about these days, as you probably know, is the IG inspection and the CMMI," the General said. "What about this battalion? Can it make it with a good score?"

I looked around. There waiting for my answer was not only the General but the commander of the brigade, as well as my own battalion commander and his XO. I swallowed hard and decided to risk it.

"Sir," I said, "this battalion couldn't pass if the inspectors were nine-year-old kids."

The General was a bit shocked by my answer. He looked around at each of the company commanders in the battalion and asked them the condition of their units. All said they were in fine shape and would pass the exams with flying colors.

"What do you say to that, Tony?" the General asked.

"I'd say these are either the dumbest company commanders in the U.S. Army or the biggest liars," I said.

The battalion commander was livid. "You're relieved, Herbert," he shouted. But the General countermanded the order. There would be a pre-inspection inspection, he said. That would decide who was closer to the truth, me or the company commanders.

I jumped in the jeep with the battalion commander to ride back to the office. He was mad as hell. "You're finished here, Herbert," he said. "Don't come back to work again." I didn't. The next week, when the pre-inspection inspection was held, the companies of the 2d battalion did not have one of their brightest days. In order to pass the General's inspection, a mock-up of the real one that was to follow, the units needed to score a minimum of ninety points. The highest score in any of the companies was fourteen.

Rather than relieve the colonel who was commanding the battalion, they relieved the executive officer and appointed me to his spot. There was one week to go before the big exam. I scoured Ft. Bragg looking for every sergeant I'd ever known in the Army and, whatever he happened to be doing, dragged him away to help me. I ended up with twenty-eight people. We started with Company A and tried to get the units in shape. After one week, they scored the highest total ever compiled on the CMMI tests—a straight 100 across the board.

In early April, 1965, three 82d Airborne battalions were flown down to Vieques Island, near Puerto Rico, for a drop practice exercise which would include a live-fire problem. It wasn't a happy day. The commander of the 1st of the 508th broke his leg on the jump and his executive officer had to take over the unit. Their progress toward the objective, a command post on a hill, was slow and faulty. Had it been the real thing, the battalion would have been creamed. The 1st of the 505th was next and they weren't much better. Then came my unit's turn. Incredible as it may seem a complaint was raised by the 1st of the 508th that, since their exercise had been commanded by the unit's executive officer, then the 2d battalion of the 505th should be under the XO's command, as well. That meant me. I was in the hilltop command post when the news came that I would direct the battalion exercise. It was a snap. Just like moving little men around on a board. But my premise was different than the other commanders' that day. I decided that my men would move deliberately up the hill, not in storm-the-beach fashion as the others had done—and it worked successfully.

A few days after we returned from Puerto Rico, the Dominican Republic began to heat up with a bloody, if not broad-based insurrection. On the morning of April 29, President Johnson, on the basis of information forwarded to him, decided that should the rebels succeed, the U.S. would have another Cuba on its hands. He decided to intervene, and by mid-afternoon the standby Airborne battalion at Ft. Bragg was put on alert. At Bragg, one battalion is always ready for instant or near-instant deployment, and it just so happened that on April 29 that battalion was the 1st of the 508th, the one commanded by the fellow who had broken his leg at Vieques Island. My unit, the 2d of the 505th, was scheduled to come in later along with the 1st of the 505th, my old unit from Germany. About two hours before the 1st of the 508th was scheduled for take-off, General York decided that I would lead the initial assault. Just as had happened earlier, when the proposed Cuban invasion was announced, I didn't have time to think about the pros or cons of the DomRep intervention. In fact, as I recall, I don't think I felt anything in particular about my role in the operation. The basic plan was that first the San Isidro Air Base would be secured, then the Duarte Bridge, and then the Army would link up with the few Marines at the U.S. Embassy in downtown Santo Domingo. In the process, the Army would lend its assistance to the local police and the local intelligence organizations in an effort to put down the rebellion.

We spent the rest of the afternoon checking out equipment and poring over the maps—the final decision on go or no-go was being held off—and then at about 6:00 P.M. that evening, we boarded the C-130s and roared down the runway, headed southeast, down to the Caribbean.

We were stacked for a drop on San Isidro, but at about 11:00 P.M. that night, as we were just getting ready for the bail-out, we were told that the air base was supposedly in friendly hands. I had to decide quickly whether to begin breaking the bundles for a landing or go ahead with the drop. If the base was in friendly hands, the drop was unnecessary—but if the information was wrong or if the friends down below were involved in an active defense of the base, then we'd be in a hell of a position trying to land and get off the planes into some kind of functional posture. Once we broke down the gear for a landing, it would be impossible to pack it up again for a drop; it was a point-of-no-return decision. Our communications said the information on San Isidro being in friendly hands was thought to be "of a fairly reliable nature," which is not a great deal of help when you're trying to make a choice for more than 800 soldiers. I finally decided to go with the information on the rationale that if we were broken down completely inside the ships and already geared up for a deployment on touchdown, then unless all hell actually broke loose on the ground we would be in good shape. The packages and the packs were breached and the men geared up for a landing. It turned out that the base was indeed in friendly hands. All was quiet as we sat down about 11:30 P.M. that night, and all stayed quiet through the early morning hours as the other American units followed us in. The next morning, without much trouble we took the Duarte Bridge across the Ozama River from the rebels. Colonel Viney, the brigade commander, then relieved me of the command of the paratroopers and gave me a three-pronged special mission, which consisted of helping the Dominican police get organized to defend their own ground, cooperating with Dominican intelligence in its organization, and running some kind of counterintelligence operation that would negate the rebels' covert activities and perhaps bring a number of them into custody.

I spent most of the rest of that first day with the Dominican police, but late that evening, when it had been decided that it was time for the Army to link up with the U.S. Marines, who were trapped in the American Embassy, I was told of a master plan that involved the assignment of certain streets and sectors to certain American units whose responsibility would be to hold those sectors or streets and thereby bottle up any kind of resistance. It was a good plan, I agreed, but nobody in our outfit was familiar with the street patterns or the geography of Santo Domingo. Why not run the two missions simultaneously, I suggested. As the Army tried to link up with the Marines at the Embassy, it could also deploy units to seal off the streets and various sectors, one street after another with one unit after another. We would then know where we were and where we had been and where we still had to go. Otherwise, I argued, you'd have a lot of people running around in the dark looking for a lot of streets with Spanish names that they didn't know how to read—real chaos—and a lot of people would probably die needlessly. General York, who had come in early in the morning, bought my idea, but when the assault started off into the quiet darkness of the evening, he came to me and asked if I would take charge. The practical effect of his order was that I ended up being not just in the most forward recon patrol, but the point man in that patrol. It was an uneventful evening, however, a real bummer from the glory standpoint. Only a few shots were fired at us. At each street we passed, I assigned several troops to seal it off. The operation not only resulted in a link-up with the Marines, it also cut the rebels off from each other and thus effectively broke the back of any substantial resistance.

For the next few days, I spent most of my time in counter-intelligence and working with the local intelligence people, as well as walking into a whole horde of CIA people, who ended up talking General York into giving them my services. Lt. Felix Soca, the recon platoon leader, and I had picked up a young rebel whose pockets were jammed with counterfeit $10 bills, and the CIA was going out of its mind at the thought of the entire Caribbean being flooded with the bogus currency. I went with them to the prisoner's house, where we stripped the entire place from ceiling through walls to baseboards and cellar. What we came up with was most interesting and changed the immediate direction of my assignments. The CIA finally concluded that the counterfeiting was not the work of the man I'd taken into custody but was rather the product of a highly skilled, complexly organized espionage ring. Most of their conclusions were based on the fact that buried in the walls of the prisoner's house were photographs of pretty young American and British girls caught in embarrassing positions with young Dominicans. The girls' passports were attached to the pictures. In two days, the CIA determined that a majority of the girls caught in bed by the camera were employed in quasi-sensitive posts in the Middle East and elsewhere. They were embassy sec-retaries, clerks in shipping offices, or second-level employes of the

AID program. They had come to the Dominican Republic on vacation. Their presence had been anticipated and they had been compromised. None of them knew for what purpose, of course, but the passports attached to the pictures gave us a fairly good sense of direction.

It was none of my business, the CIA told me, and I was simply to forget about the whole thing—but in the second week of May, a few days after I had reported back to Ft. Bragg, I was ordered to move immediately down to Macdill Air Force Base near Tampa, the headquarters of the Army's STRIKE command, and report to no less than the CG Stricom himself, General Paul D. Adams.

Adams outlined my new mission. I would be going to the Middle East, he said. The first part of my assignment would be to visit as casually as possible some of the girls whose photographs we had found in the walls of the Dominican rebel's house. I would explain the compromising situation that had been forced upon them and ask that in exchange for their country's gratitude, and silence, they give up their jobs before they reached some really sensitive position that would make them especially vulnerable to blackmail. Secondly, I would become a STRIKE liaison officer with "The Little White Fleet," the United States' show of force in the Indian Ocean and the only U.S. Navy contingent whose commander, an admiral, reported directly to an Army general. I would take along my diving gear, General Adams said, because since the British were leaving the Middle East and the Russians were moving in there, it might become necessary, at some later date, for our country to know how to approach the offshore oil refueling stations of those countries for the purpose of destroying the wells and other petroleum equipment . . . "Should that sort of thing prove to be the right thing," Adams added.

That was the mission. Could I cut it? I said I could, and he ordered me to report to Washington before I left, to the Pentagon and the Department of Defense, for briefings on the state of affairs in the Middle East.

It was the Fourth of July week when I arrived in Washington and reported directly to the Defense Department. Secretary Robert McNamara entered the briefing room for a moment and said hello, and then one of his aides began telling me the way it really was over there. I read all of the top secret contingency plans for the Middle East, and when I started to leave the aide told me that I was to report only to the Department of Defense and write weekly reports on the condition and combat attitude of the STRIKE command as it existed in that part of the world, "from a combat officer's point of view."

"And by the way," he said, "they want you to check in with the Navy, before you sign off."

"Yes, sir," I said.

The Navy people told me that I'd be working exclusively for them rather than for the Department of Defense per se, that I'd be reporting on the relationship between the Department of Defense and STRIKE command personnel in the Middle East "at least once a week," and that I was a "Navy man now."

"Oh, by the way," the Navy captain said as I was leaving, "the Marines want to see you before you shove off."

"Sure thing, sir," I said.

The Marines told me I'd be working for a Marine colonel aboard ship and this in effect would be reporting on a priority basis to them. I left Washington that night, bound for Ft. Bragg and my packing chores. If I understood all I'd been told in the Pentagon and added it up with what General Adams had asked me to do, I would be working for the U.S. Army, the U.S. Navy, the U.S. Marines, and the U.S. Department of Defense—with separate assignments from all of them, yet with a super-priority responsibility to each of them. Which didn't add up at all. I was still Army. My first loyalty as far as I was concerned was to General Adams, and on that note I kissed Marygrace and Toni-Junell goodbye, sent them off to Herminie, and headed for Bahrain Island, a small oil-rich sheikdom located in the Persian Gulf just south of Kuwait, and a berth aboard the *Duxbury Bay*, a reconverted World War II seaplane tender sailing the Persian Gulf, Indian Ocean, and Red Sea, loaded to the gunwales with communications and radar equipment.

One of the first things that I learned about being a quasi-agent of the U.S. Government—that is, being called one thing, a liaison officer, and doing another, spying on everything that moved, including my fellow Americans—was that your job has a rather unlimited nature. Once you get into that kind of endeavor, there's no telling what you might be asked to do. Well, actually, they don't *ask* you. When you reach that point in the intelligence structure, you find yourself dealing with a lot of civilians—State Department types, ostensibly—and they don't ask or order. They just very quietly, in a soft voice and with a courteous smile, suggest that it might be in the interest of the country, or in your own interest, or in somebody's or something's interest, to take on such and such a "little project." That's the way they talk. They're all just tiny, infinitesimal little projects, and the profile, even among fellow Americans who know what's coming off, is very, very low. Which is necessary, of course, if they expect to continue their "little projects," but nonetheless it did seem odd to be invited to tea in the home or the office of some port liaison officer and then be asked to help in the escape of the assassin of some sheik or minor revolutionary in some North African country. "Just a little project," they would say. Righto, pip pip, I would answer, and off we'd go.

On one such little project, I was asked to assist in the recovery of a British subject from the sheikdom of Sharjah, formerly the baili-wick of one Sheik Shakbut. It seemed that the British subject had done nothing wrong there but had simply, through no fault of his own, incurred the unjustified wrath of the authorities and—you know how those Arabs are—faced a rather lengthy but altogether unde-served prison sentence, or worse, if he didn't leave the area.

The British had a Hunter Hawker aircraft waiting for me at Muharaq Air Base on Bahrain Island. It deposited me in the middle of the desert, where I waited at a designated position, the crossing of several desert roads, for nearly three days. Finally a jeep drove up bearing two people. The driver dropped off his passenger, a fat little man, and disappeared into the desert. My job at that point was to make sure that I was picking up the right man. I asked several coded questions and got the answers I had been told to get. If he had not answered correctly, it had been courteously suggested that I kill who-ever gave the wrong answers—as I would have. I called in the Hawker on the radio, the fat guy and I boarded, and he told me almost before we were airborne again that it had been he who had given the business to the sheik "ages before." Is that right? I asked. "You're jolly well right that's right," he said.

One of the other little projects I was given was to try to de-termine which of the Arabs in the ports we visited were pro-Russian, which were pro-American, and which were so nationalistic as to be beyond any expectation of cooperation with either nation. I noticed that, when I delivered the third judgment on any of the people we met, they invariably wound up dead in a matter of days or weeks. I started holding off.

Sometimes the Hunter Hawkers flew me into the interior on missions to photograph oil installations and the surrounding terrain, always with the cover of drafting evacuation plans for American residents of the area. The *Duxbury Bay* would tie up here and there, I would contact the port liaison officer and ask to see his evacuation plans, he would invite me to his office, and there I would find out about my next little project.

After I'd been there some time I was assigned by General Adams and the Department of Defense to begin rewriting the contingency plans for each of the countries. We were committed strategically to maintaining the status quo in that area. That is, if Jordan attacked Israel and thereby threatened to change the delicate balances of power there, we were, on paper at least, committed to coming down hard on the side of Israel. The same was true if it went the other way, I was told. I didn't believe it—but I wrote contingency plans for that situation anyway.

Late in November, 1965, I was told to take forty days off from my duties aboard the *Duxbury Bay*. "A Christmas furlough?" I asked. Well, yes, in a way. I was ordered to Torrejón, Spain. The day I arrived I was shoved aboard the Embassy Flight, the State Department courier plane that is continuously moving from embassy to embassy around the world. We landed at Bangkok and then, in the late evening, put down in Saigon. I was given a name and a place to report to, and suddenly I discovered that I was right back in Special Forces. They asked me to become a part of the Phoenix program, a CIA-run operation whose basic purpose was to identify Viet Cong and eliminate them. The first thing I learned about the operation was that although it amounted to political assassination, they called it "execution" because, I suppose, it gave the whole thing a more judicious ring, a sort of legal mantle. What they wanted me to do was to take charge of execution-teams that wiped out entire families and tried to make it appear as though the VC themselves had done the killing. The rationale was that the other Vietnamese would see that the VC had killed another VC and would be frightened away from becoming VC themselves. Of course, the villagers would then be inclined to some sort of allegiance to our side, otherwise known as the good guys.

It was obvious what they were doing. I said I wouldn't be a part of it. I agreed to some other kind of mission or assignment but not that. I asked just in passing, who identified the people to be killed. I was told there were Vietnamese people in the villages who were being paid to point the finger. I asked how they knew for certain that the informer might not have a more personal reason for pointing the execution-teams to a particular family. I suggested that some of their informers might be motivated, for instance, by revenge or personal monetary gain, and I also threw out the possibility—not that they hadn't already considered it—that some of their stool-pigeons could be double or triple agents. They had answers for all my questions. I suggested that they just hand the Vietnamese informer a rifle and let him take care of the victims—which, I suppose, would have been an early form of Vietnamization.

The fellow running Phoenix at that time was a Colonel Singlaub, now General, though I believe he used a cover-name. Everybody there seemed to have a pseudonym of some sort or another. I saw guys I'd known in Special Forces back at Bragg whose names were entirely different in Vietnam. Maybe that was one way of escaping any guilt feelings about their work. It was my first contact with the dreamlike quality of that war. Perhaps that is one of the factors contributing to our defeat there. The war was unreal. The SF people took on assumed names. The enemy became dinks and slopes and gooks. The plane that fired mini-guns was called Puff, the Magic Dragon, and areas designated for complete devastation were called free-fire zones. It was like going through the looking-glass and, after your tour was finished, you could step back through the mirror and leave all the horror and all the dead in another, unreal world.

When I refused Operation Phoenix, I was assigned to cross the border into Cambodia and monitor traffic on the Ho Chi Minh Trail. It was a simple mission, but I was bothered just a bit by the declaration of the SF when I left for Cambodia that, should I get caught, I was to say that my Cambodian colleagues and I had become lost.

A month later, I flew out of Saigon, landed the next evening at Torrejón, spent a few days there and was back aboard the *Duxbury Bay*—and no one knew that I'd been anywhere except on Christmas leave to Spain. In the next few months, I would get several more assignments to Vietnam, all on the sly and all on the fringes of that back-door, political warfare at which the Special Forces were supposed to be so adept. I never really thought killing required much adeptness, though. All it took was pulling the trigger and being able to walk away. I suppose I was lucky I didn't actually witness any war crimes; I probably would have been in trouble much earlier.

When the 1966 war between India and Pakistan broke out, the Little White Fleet sailed close to shore and served as a communications coordinator for the embassies in both countries. We had American military advisors with both the Indians and the Paks, who were relaying messages to us which we then relayed to the respective diplomatic missions. After we'd taken messages from the American advisors with the Indians—messages about positions and troop movements and other vital military data—we relayed the same information to the Paks. We did the same thing later in 1967 in the Six-Day War between Israel and Egypt. The *Columbia*, the American vessel attacked during that war, was the same kind of ship, performing the same kind of mission as the *Duxbury Bay*.

Of course, that kind of double-dealing doesn't always work. For instance, in 1966, the Indians agreed to help us evacuate Americans from threatened cities in their country, but the Paks refused to allow American planes to land. It was ironic. We were feeding them strategic information on Indian movements, but they wouldn't cooperate with us on the evacuation of Americans. It probably meant that the information relay was a pretty sensitive arrangement known only to a few people within Pakistan. Whatever was the truth of the matter, when the Paks refused to allow us to land planes at Lahore for the purpose of picking up American civilians, General Adams of STRIKE was notified and two battalions of paratroopers were immediately put on alert in Germany. The theory was that we would simply drop the soldiers and let them take over the air base there until we could land planes and get the Americans out, after which the paratroopers would pack up and leave. I doubt seriously if it would have worked that way. It's a hell of a lot easier to get into a war, regardless of the scale of the involvement, than it is to get out. All of that became moot, however, because a naval officer and I went ashore and contacted the port liaison officer—him again—and relayed the American threat. His job was then to relay it to the Pak officials, which he did. They promptly allowed us to evacuate the Americans.

The girls photographed in bed in the Dominican Republic all cooperated completely. They had to. My spiel was that, if they didn't leave their jobs and go home, I couldn't guarantee that something wouldn't happen to them—an accident, of course. One or two asked if I were offering a threat. No, I said, I was just offering a lack of assurance, that's all. They all quit their jobs and went home. I imagine they checked the mirrors in the next room in which they made love. Or maybe they over-reacted and decided not to fool around with Latins anymore.

On one of my trips to Vietnam, I had a few days of real, genuine leave, when I returned to Spain and holed up in the Bachelor Officers' Quarters for a little rest and relaxation. I went to the PX and bought a record player and some music, closed the door, and tried to gather myself together.

I answered a knock on the door later in the day.

"Yes?"

"Are those Joan Baez records you're playing, sir?"

"They are."

"Are you a fan?"

"How many records make a fan?"

"Three or four, I guess."

"I have five in here. I'm a fan."

"They're forbidden to be played in the BOQ, sir."

"Forbidden?"

"She's a Communist."

"So?"

"So, they're forbidden."

"Says who?"

"Says me."

"And just who the hell are you? The tax-collector, or the judge advocate general?"

"Neither. I'm Colonel Calhoun, the senior officer of the BOQ. Either the records go or you go."

I had made major the year before. I was still outranked.

I moved out the next day, downtown to the Hilton Castilian, where it cost a couple of pesetas more, but I could still feel like an American.

Because of the oil and because we had important intelligence bases and communications points in Ethiopia, we always were and still are very, very kind to that country. So are the Russians. In fact, when the Ethiopian Naval Academy graduates its handful of new ensigns in the spring every year, both the Russians and the Americans break their asses trying to make friends. One spring, the Russians sent several ballerinas over to entertain the class of young sailors. All we could do was dispatch a couple of admirals. The Russians won that one. The admirals were prettier but they couldn't dance worth a damn.

But it was serious business, I suppose. The British were leaving Aden and we had no really good refueling bases in the area. The Russians were coming in heavy with fertilizer plants all around, and even a Lithuanian like me knew that a fertilizer plant is the easiest thing in the world to convert into a munitions factory, especially when you just happen to have all that potassium nitrate around. The Russians built one plant at Masawa, in Ethiopia, and it almost drove the admiral up the wall. "Right in our sights," I heard him say once. "Right in our goddamned sights."

In July, 1966, I requested a transfer and asked that I be allowed to work toward a master's degree in psychology at the University of Georgia. I chose that school because, having taken about thirty hours of graduate work at Auburn University in Alabama while I was a Ranger instructor at Ft. Benning, I figured it would be easier to transfer the credits to another southern school. I also knew that the University of Georgia's psychology department was highly respected and that there were usually openings in the school's ROTC department. I was right on every count except the transfer of hours. I had to start all over again, but the university was kind enough to allow me to get in some teaching hours, teaching psychology to civilians.

It was while I was studying in Athens, Ga., that my sister Irene was stricken with cancer of the uterus. She died in November, 1967, swept out in the prime of life. Less than three months later, in January, 1968, my mother, who had lived in Herminie with Irene and her husband since the death of my father, also died.

My mother went willingly, which maybe seems strange to say but is true. My father, with whom she had lived for almost fifty years, was gone, and now my sister, her only daughter, was gone too. And besides, she was extra religious and didn't look at death as death but rather as the ultimate aim of all life: to be with God. I was there when she died, and for the funeral, and though again it's a strange thing to say, and possibly at first blush somewhat incongruous, I came back from that funeral feeling good instead of sad. She died at peace, looking forward to God, rather than striving to hang onto life. Then too, I had heard so much about other funerals, about the bickering of survivors and all, that I just couldn't help but feel proud of my brothers and their wives. No bickering, nothing except love and a deep feeling of concern for each other and stories about Mom and Dad and Irene, and a deep, deep love pervading it all. It was as a death should be— a part of life.

I received my degree in July, 1968. I had been bitten by the knowledge bug; I wanted more and more and more of the kind of study I'd had for the previous two academic years. I decided that later on in my career I'd go for a doctorate if the Army would permit it. In the meantime there were books.

The same month I received the degree, I was also told that I had been selected to attend the Command and General Staff School at Ft. Leavenworth, Kansas, one of the places where the career officer has to punch his ticket if he hopes to go any higher. In August, I was promoted to lieutenant colonel and told to report to Leavenworth. But it wasn't what I wanted.

I wanted a full tour of Vietnam, and I went to Washington to plead my case with the Department of the Army. I might have been a student for the past two years, and I might have spent quite a bit of time doing the CIA's dirty laundry in the Middle East, but I was still a U.S. Army officer and there was still a war going on over there. Sure, I'd been there, but I'd never served with Americans—always the Cambodians or specially selected Vietnamese. I wanted to see how American troops were operating and I wanted to know what had changed in tactics and equipment. I had heard of the entrance of the helicopter into that war and of the major role it was playing—and hell, I'd never operated in combat out of a helicopter. I wanted to know. I wanted to go. I wanted to see. I wanted to fight.

Politically, I was fairly naïve. I believed what President Johnson was telling us. For instance, there was no doubt in my mind that what the government said happened at the Gulf of Tonkin really happened at the Gulf of Tonkin. Anyway, I don't think I would have cared then what really had happened at the Gulf of Tonkin. I believed we were in Vietnam to do good—and like any good soldier, I let the Army define the terms.

But volunteering to go to Vietnam and getting there were two different things. I was told in Washington that the only slots available were those being filled by advisors. Hell, I wanted a command slot with an airborne unit. That was my game, my basic skill. I was desperate. I wrote to General Rosson. He wrote back and said half my wish had been granted. I could go to a paratrooper unit, but I'd have no command—at least not immediately. I accepted.

Marygrace and Toni went back to Herminie again, and I took off for the West Coast and finally, after several months of trying, I was on my way to Vietnam.

4

There were white streaks in the water a mile below, and as the big jet sliced through the last layer of clouds and screamed into its final approach, I leaned toward the window for a better look. Cam Ranh Bay's cobalt waters raised a lacy border against the beige beach, and beyond the sand the jungle glistened green in the afternoon sun. Further inland, the gray hills rose gently into smoky, darkening highlands. It was startlingly beautiful. Like a kid in a candy shop I pressed my face against the plastic porthole.

I noticed the white streaks again and thought at first that they were wakes from some fast little Navy craft out on maneuvers, but as the plane descended, I saw I was wrong. They were wakes, all right, but not from boats. Down there below me, on August 30, 1969, in the throes of America's most torturous military conflict, when casualties on both sides were reaching 5,000 or more per week, when the most powerful country in the world was being drained and torn apart—down there on Cam Ranh Bay, they were water-skiing. Water-skiing, by God—dozens of young men and women making zigzag patterns across the water, the cool spray in their tanned faces, their free arms raised in that classic salute to speed and grace.

"Okay, fellows, buckle up," the stewardess chimed over the intercom. "And may I be the first to welcome you to Vietnam."

Rosson had guaranteed me a paratrooper outfit, but not a command. My assignment turned out to be as Inspector General in the 173d Airborne Brigade which was operating in Phu My province in the central highlands. I arrived at An Khe, the 173d Airborne Brigade's rear-area headquarters, and opened my doors for business to no less a first customer than his honor "the Mayor of An Khe," as the troops referred to him—the commander of the Brigade's Support Battalion, Lieutenant Colonel Jack Angel. He had stopped by for a private chat, he said, so we left my sergeant in the outer room and retreated into the bedroom where, in a quiet voice, he told me that he had heard I was trying to proselyte one of his sergeants to work in my office. He didn't appreciate it at all, he said, especially since all I had to do if I wanted anything was to ask him and he would be happy to cooperate.

"Of course, I expect some cooperation from you in return," he added.

"Like what?" I asked.

"Well, like talking things over before they go to the General," he replied. "Most things never even have to reach his ears if you and I cooperate—you know, Herbert, sort of run things ourselves, trust each other, get along and keep it all in the family."

I stared at him and said he had to be joking. I realized almost instantly that he was not. "I'm supposed to be an IG!" I said.

He seemed not to have heard, launching instead into a lengthy recitation of his immense responsibilities as the man in charge of the Brigade's rear-area headquarters. Everything at An Khe was under his purview, he said; men slept where he told them to sleep and took their meals wherever he assigned them and enjoyed themselves in his clubs and theaters and bought from his post exchange. It suddenly dawned on me that here was a senior lieutenant colonel, supposedly a professional soldier, who was bragging about his job as a billeting officer, a task generally reserved for a second lieutenant in the States and usually for a not-too-keen second lieutenant at that. He rambled on and on about the scope of his influence and I tried hard to look interested and concerned. Finally, he stopped. It was my turn.

"Look, Colonel, I understand your position, and if you'll just assign me a room and a mess, I'll be glad to cooperate," I said.

He smiled and relaxed in the chair.

"But you have to understand my position, too," I added. Now, he was staring.

"First, I haven't tried to proselyte any of your men. In fact, I haven't seen any of them that I'd want even if they were offered to me," I said. "Second, I'm an IG so I work for the commander who, by the way, is General Allen, not you. Since I work for the General,

I'll report to the General, and if that isn't a satisfactory arrangement for you, well, then you can talk it over with the General and maybe the two of you can work out something more suitable." His jaw line straightened noticeably. "In the meantime, if you're finished, I have a lot of work to do," I concluded. He looked ill. "Is there anything wrong?" I asked, rising from the bed.

"No, not at all," he said rather glumly, also rising. "I have some things to do myself." I nodded, opened the door to the outer room, and he left.

The place was quiet until the sergeant spoke. "You just made an enemy, sir," he said from his desk. "A real dangerous enemy."

I walked into the outer room. "Real dangerous?"

"Real dangerous, sir."

"Real, real dangerous?" I repeated, smiling slightly.

"Yes, sir, he's—okay, sir," he said sheepishly when he noticed my grin. "But no kidding, sir, he's real bad news."

I took some papers from his desk and looked at him.

"So am I, Sarge," I said, "and I'm not kidding either." I walked across the room to my desk and sprawled in the chair. "By the way, Sarge . . ." I said.

"Sir?"

"You're fired."

"Fired, sir? You kidding?"

"Nope," I answered. "How many days until you leave for home?"

"Two, sir."

"Good. Then, for two days at least, have a good time. Get drunk or get laid or get whatever the hell else good sergeants get in their last two days in country when they're not salted away in an IG shop with nothing to do."

"I don't mind, sir," he said.

"Come on, Sarge, let's be honest. You can't type and even if you could, there's nothing to type yet. You know goddamned well you're not an IG sergeant and, more important, you're going home, so just get the hell out of here and be gone."

I spun the chair around toward the wall and stared at the map delineating the Brigade's area of operations and, in a moment, I heard him approaching my desk.

"Sir?" he said.

"Yes?" I turned the chair around again.

"Good luck, sir," he said.

"Well, you take care, Sarge." We shook hands and he turned toward the door. "And by the way, thanks for the tip on my real dangerous enemy."

"No sweat, sir," he said, waving over his shoulder, and then he was gone. I walked to the door and watched him disappear up over the hill, heading into An Khe for his last two days in the country.

It was a hell of a place, whether you were a sergeant on your way out, a private on your way in, or an older lieutenant colonel getting locked into a new assignment. It was, in fact, two communities: the military sector, which served as the supply point and rear-area headquarters for the Brigade, and An Khe itself, which, like so many other towns in Vietnam, had become almost completely dependent on the military. It wasn't hard to tell where the base ended and the town began. The prices were different.

On the post, almost everything was free, and what wasn't was cheaper than ice at the South Pole, including first-class whisky at twenty cents a slug and sixteen-ounce steak dinners with all the trimmings for $1.50 or less. Five nights a week there were free movies and on the other two evenings live entertainment was available, featuring real live American girls on the stage and in the audience. The women came in a variety of colors, uniforms, and vocations. Some were singers or dancers or strippers. Others were Red Cross employees, a few were in Special Services, and the rest were nurses. There were never enough of them to go around, but they were there in numbers sufficient to make you wonder whether General Sherman might not have changed his mind about war if he had pulled a tour in the 173d at An Khe.

After the shows, there were ample amusements elsewhere. There were the clubs for the officers and the clubs for the noncommissioned officers and the clubs for the enlisted men, all with wall-to-wall slot machines. There was the NCO Motel with its flower gardens, barbecue pit, showers, baths, recreation yard, and games of chance; and there were the Steakhouse and the Pizza Palace and the Esther Williams swimming pool and the library and the Special Services Club, a hangout for AWOL personnel, and the eighteen-hole miniature golf course and the Happy Hooch Hotel, an outfit run by the Red Cross—and all of it was in Angel's hands, as he had proudly informed me. It was, by God, a sizable city and he was, by God, its mayor, and few of its citizens complained about his administration. There were very few requests for transfers.

Many of Angel's constituents were the men who were responsible for the defense of An Khe. Most of the Brigade's supplies moved through the post. The town itself had some strategic value—more to us than to them, I suppose, but it nevertheless deserved some form of security, and this was ostensibly provided by Angel's Green Line. That was the Brigade's official designation. He called them "Angel's Band," but the soldiers from outside called them the "Marijuana Brass." Their function was to protect the post, and I doubt that in the history of the military there has ever been a sorrier lot. They were, for the most part, too piss-poor to have cut it anywhere else in the Brigade. They had drug problems or were just plain useless. Men who couldn't make it in the field and couldn't politic their way into any other rear-area slot ended up on the Green Line. It was a gathering of misfits. If a unit rejected a man, he went to the Green Line. If his buddies turned him out, he went to the Green Line. If he was downright yellow and had to get out of the field under any circumstances, he could agree to extend his Vietnam tour six months and wind up on the Green Line. In U.S. Army language, Green Line assignments were called "fitting the right man into the right slot," but in practical terms that simply amounted to a bringing together of a sick bunch of sad-assed rejects who spent most of their time smoking pot in filthy, sandbagged bunkers dug around the perimeter of An Khe. That was the Green Line.

Every hundred meters or so, in the open spaces between their quarters, spotlights stood on concrete towers—a real, honest-to-God, .22-caliber Clausewitz-Maginot Line. We never, never learned. For years we had been teaching the fallacy of the fixed defense. In military classrooms from West Point to Ft. Benning, we had been finding fault with every example of that concept from the Great Wall of China to the Siegfried installations—and then, by God, we went to Vietnam and built the same silly Mickey Mouse contraptions: the

McNamara Line, the Bien Hoa Line, and the Green Line around An Khe and around every damned base in the country.

It had lost for France, it had lost for Hitler, and it was losing for us. They were inflexible. They were places to hide in, rather than fight from. In Korea, some dumb bastard came up with the idea of providing cover from overhead projectiles, and so we went underground into bunkers there and it was utterly stupid. Rabbits hide, tigers stalk, and if the infantry is to win, it must be a tiger. The advocates of fixed defense argue that the bunker offers protection from overhead attack. That is precisely bullshit. If anyone can show me a bunker that took a hit from artillery or B-40 rockets and wasn't penetrated, I'll carry his ammunition from here to the Halls of Montezuma and kiss his ass when we get there.

The best a soldier can hope for is an old-fashioned foxhole. It's open. He can see up and down and around. He can be in touch. He can fire. He can lie in wait—but he can't hide, not as he can in a bunker. A bunker is a blanket. But although the advantages of a foxhole are numerous, it isn't built for winning either.

In terms of guerrilla warfare, which was the precise nature of the war in Vietnam, the absurdity of the fixed defense is magnified. The guerrilla is a free agent who moves about at will. If you don't move with him, he can pick his time and place of attack or he can simply decide not to attack at all. If you choose to defend, then you must defend every place and all places in strength, or the guerrilla will still outnumber you at the one place and the one time he chooses to fight. No military unit in the world today is big enough or powerful enough to simply defend, and no war in history was ever won from within four walls. Defense is, at best, only a temporary tactic: to delay, to rest, to regroup, to permit an economy of force, or to lay the groundwork for a ruse.

General James Gavin had the right idea: enclaves, or major bases staffed with mobile forces. They would be continuously prepared for attack, with their eyes and ears attuned to the surrounding terrain: looking, listening, and searching through ambushes, reconnaissance missions, and intelligence patrols, and once in a while finding something. Even guerrillas have to get together occasionally if they expect to make any military progress. From the enclaves the American military could strike, destroy, and return to the enclaves to wait for the next time—and thus deprive the guerrilla of his basic strength, his initiative. We could then utilize the major advantage we had over the guerrilla: mobile power, the ability to get there first with the most, anywhere in the country, anytime we decided to move, against any size enemy force.

Tactics and strategy were seldom the subject of conversations among Angel's Green Line troops. For them, it was pot, binoctal, and heroin, and life in the Army was a trip they heartily enjoyed, especially on their frequent visits to the post exchange. A PX in a combat zone is not usually one of the better places in the world to shop, but at An Khe it was something to behold. It was a stroll down Fifth Avenue, a gaudy combination of Saks, Bonwit Teller, Hammacher Schlemmer, and Abercrombie and Fitch. The shelves were crammed with sheer pantyhose, filmy lingerie, imported perfumes, diamonds and rubies, fine china, radios, portable and console television sets, liquor, mink stoles, sable wraps, and nearly everything the American soldier fighting a tough guerrilla war could possibly require, including Napoleon's favorite brandy, Courvoisier, at $1.80 for a fifth. In all honesty, however, it should be pointed out that the exotic array of merchandise at the PX in An Khe had very little to do with the combat performance of the Brigade, since the troops involved in combat seldom had a chance to spend their money there. Like most of the other post exchanges in Vietnam, the one at An Khe was created, constructed, and maintained by and for the officers' corps and the rear-area commandos, those candy-assed misfits who made up the Green Line. It was a veritable trinket palace, a house crammed full of favors and presents for the local lassies. It also served conveniently as a black-market warehouse where goods were safely stored until the prices were right. A few of the items sold there may have made it back to the States, but most of the stuff ended up in the bars, whorehouses, and steam room-massage parlors in An Khe. For Angel's citizenry, it was steak at the Steakhouse and pizza at the Palace and ten-cent beer anywhere, with free coffee and cookies at the Happy Hooch and booze for pennies at any of the clubs and a piece of American ass at the Special Services Club or the library or plenty of other places. It was free cigarettes, free candy, free soap, free pipe tobacco, free toothpaste—and it could all be hauled off to downtown An Khe to be swapped for a piece of local stuff. It was all free to the right people, which, of course, did not include the "grunt," the guy whose ass was in the grass in the field.

He got his downtown and he paid through the nose for it. A percentage of what he paid came back to the post to the right people. Girls were a couple of bucks, as were steam baths and massages. "Saigon tea," the watered-down whisky served in civilian bars all over Vietnam, was four dollars a shot, and if the grunt refused to pay, an MP promptly arrived and convinced him it was the only right thing to do. The one thing unavailable to the An Khe visitor with money was the opportunity to make money. His limit on what he could spend at the PX was $200 a month. But for privileged An Khe regulars there was no limit, and dealing was a simple formula, foolproof for profit: buy cheap at the PX, sell expensive in An Khe. The margin was high and the overhead low. Robert Hall would have loved it. Through the courtesy of the American taxpayer, the average officer and senior noncommissioned officer enjoyed a life style unique in military history.

A couple of days after I fired the homeward-bound sergeant, Angel was back in my office. He suggested that perhaps I had misunderstood him the first time, and assured me that the last thing he wanted was for me to get the wrong impression. He hadn't really been talking about me in particular, he said, when he had discussed billet assignments; I was welcome in any mess I chose and at any time. Moreover, he continued, my sleeping arrangements were my own affair. Wherever it best suited me was all right with him, and anyway, he added, An Khe was a big place with enough of everything and anything for everybody. What he had really tried to do on the first visit was simply make friends with a new member of the team and keep a little weight off General Allen's shoulders. "In fact, there are some things the General definitely doesn't even want to know," Angel confided.

"Like what?"

Hooch-girls, he replied. They were the local women who often came to the quarters of officers and noncoms to handle domestic chores and stayed around for other assignments. Ultimately, many just moved in. If the General knew about the hooch-girls, Angel ex-

119

plained, then the General would be responsible; but if the General did not know about the hooch-girls, then the General would in no way have any responsibility for their presence on the post.

"And, by the way," he chortled, "wait until you see the one you're getting. She is a doll, a real doll. She'll be in tomorrow."

He didn't give me a hell of a lot of credit. "Look, Colonel, I don't need you to get me a hooch-girl. In fact, I don't need a hooch-girl, so don't send her around," I said.

"Of course, of course, Herbert, if you say so."

"Well, that's what I say," I answered. "And, Colonel, I haven't changed my position about my relationship to the General either. I still work for him and I'll continue to report to him anything and everything, until he changes the system."

His face dropped. "Right, Herbert," he said and started to leave. "But if you change your mind about the girl, let me know. I'll still be around and so will she."

He left and I reached up on the wall behind me and drew my Randall from its scabbard on my web belt. I scanned the opposite wall, picked out a knot in the wood, aimed and threw. It missed the knot by a couple of inches. No matter, I thought, because it still would have been close enough to the center of somebody's back or chest.

"Angel, my friend, you lose," I muttered to myself. "Screw you, and An Khe."

A couple of days later, General Allen sent word that he wanted to see me, so I caught the next chopper to Landing Zone English up at Bong Son, the Tactical Operations Center of the Brigade. The General greeted me warmly in his screened-in office, motioned me to a chair and introduced me to the case of the missing letters. It was an education for me. The general told the story this way.

A young man—we'll call him Rose—enlisted in the Army against his parents' wishes and wound up in Vietnam. His parents wrote him faithfully—seventeen letters and three packages in all—and when he arrived home in a coffin a few months later they comforted themselves with the assurance that he had died knowing they loved him even though they had disagreed with his enlistment. That faith was about all the Roses had, besides their grief.

A few months after they had buried their son, they received a large package from the Army containing their letters, all undelivered and unopened. The young soldier had never read a single line of them. The parents appealed for some explanation to President Johnson, who responded by demanding an investigation of the incident in the outfit in which young Rose had served: the 173d Airborne Brigade.

Before I joined the Brigade the formal inquiry had already been completed and General Allen held the official report on the incident in his hands as he told me the story.

"Herbert," he said. "Do you figure the President of the United States to be a jackass?"

"No, sir, I don't."

"Well, neither do I, Herbert," he continued, waving the report in my direction. "This is the report and it smells, Herbert. It smells like rotten cabbage."

He slumped back in his chair and stared out the screen at his imported flower garden. He didn't like the plant life indigenous to the highlands of Vietnam, so each Thursday morning a helicopter from Saigon delivered some posies from the Mekong Delta, along with some of that region's darker, richer soil. Every Thursday afternoon, the Delta flowers were replanted in Delta soil just outside his window. It was a lovely garden, and the General took great pride in its care and maintenance. In fact, he spared no effort from several enlisted men to keep it in tip-top condition.

"This report really smells, Herbert," he began again. "I want it corrected—redone, rewritten—and I want it back by tomorrow."

I suggested that the deadline was a little fast, but General Allen brushed that aside. "Crouch is outside and he'll provide whatever administrative back-up you need, so just get to An Khe, get it done, and get it back here by tomorrow."

"If I can, sir," I said.

"You can, Herbert, it's all there," he said, handing over the papers. "It just needs to be reworked."

"I'll do my best, sir," I said, turning to leave.

"And Herbert," he said.

"Yes, sir?"

"Herbert, let the chips fall where they may," he said.

"I understand, sir."

"Good. Have you had lunch?"

"No, sir, but I'd better be on my way if I'm going to get this done," I said.

"Right, Herbert," he said and returned my salute.

Major James E. Crouch was indeed waiting outside, and as we walked away together toward the helicopter I noticed a duck waddling around the other side of the General's office. A pair of dog-tags jingled on a small chain around its slender neck.

"What's that?" I asked Crouch.

"That's the General's duck," he said.

"The General's—?"

"Yeah."

"Oh," I said. "The General's duck."

We boarded the helicopter and headed back to An Khe. The report in my lap had originally been Crouch's responsibility. He, as the Brigade's adjutant general, and Lieutenant Colonel Herbert Matsuo, the executive officer of the 4th battalion, had been given the job of explaining to President Johnson what the hell had happened to those letters to Rose. Crouch was quiet. If he was uncomfortable about the report, he didn't show it—but he damned well should have been. It was trash. It needed quite a bit more than just "reworking" or "rewriting," as the General had suggested. But he had also said that I was to "let the chips fall where they may," and so I wasn't worried about anything except the deadline.

The brown ridge was behind us as we banked over the library and touched down next to the building that housed the Headquarters Company of Angel's Support Battalion. We climbed out and walked to Crouch's office where he pointed to a desk, indicating that it was mine to use, and promptly disappeared, apparently for lunch.

By the time he returned, I had made a list of the men I needed to interview for the new report. I gave it to Crouch along with a request for a couple of typists, a recorder, and a sergeant.

"Sure, sir," he said. "Whatever you need."

So I began. It was clear that the Rose case had not been one of the 173d Brigade's finer moments. The young soldier had ended up in the Brigade by transfer from some other unit and after staying awhile in the 1st of the 50th, the mechanized infantry battalion, he had been transferred to the 4th battalion. A few days after his transfer, his mail came in and was sent to the 1st, and then returned to the mailroom at An Khe—a Brigade operation under Crouch's command—

where it should have been processed, corrected and shipped up to the kid in the 4th Battalion. But apparently nobody cared whether it got there or not. The mail clerk tossed the letters in a bag and the bag into an old wall locker, and they were forgotten until weeks and weeks later when they were found by the mail clerk's replacement. The letters were unopened but the packages had been looted. The new clerk reported his discovery to Major Crouch and the letters were forwarded up to the 4th battalion. In a few days they were right back at An Khe, marked: "Deceased, Return to Sender." Back they went, across the ocean to the Army Post Office in San Francisco and finally to Rose's parents, who had buried their son weeks before.

It had been a grand failure on the part of almost everyone involved—from the mail clerk to his immediate commander and on up to Crouch, who had the final authority for the operation of the mailroom at An Khe. It was a simple failure. That's how I wrote it, anyway.

The next day, in the General's office, I sensed that he didn't like the new report. The first one had managed to keep the blame off the Brigade, but its logic had been rather twisted and tenuous. Hence its odor. My report described the whole affair as a Brigade failure.

"Is this it?" the General said sharply.

"Yes, sir," I said.

He accepted it with my signature and I left feeling pretty smug. For my first time around as an IG, I thought I had performed pretty well.

I was feeling so good, as a matter of fact, that I managed not to lose my temper when a couple of officers came past the General's office and smartly saluted his duck. I'd been told by that time that, half-seriously, half-jokingly, the duck received salutes from the men around the TOC, but it hadn't occurred to me how really ridiculous it was. When I saw it, I burned, but only for a moment. I felt much too good about my first IG report to let something like that bother me.

Months later, I heard rumors that my report had been doctored so that when it finally reached the President's desk, the Brigade was again exonerated. Whether the report was changed, I don't know. I never saw it again. But I do know that the boy's parents were told by the U.S. government that the 173d Airborne Brigade wasn't at fault in the loss of the letters and packages.

Again, months later, Crouch swore under oath that I had recommended disciplinary action *against Rose* "if he was still on active duty." Incredible. Still on active duty? Rose was dead, it was he and his family that had been aggrieved in the whole affair—so why the hell would I suggest disciplinary action against him? He was the wrong man, not to mention a dead man. More importantly, why would Crouch insist under oath that I had made such a recommendation—unless my report on the incident was different from the one that had reached the President's desk.

Sergeant Major Charles T. Abbott arrived one morning like a gift from heaven. "Hey, hey, Colonel," he said, smiling broadly and pumping my hand. He hadn't changed. Everybody called him "Hey, Hey" because he stuttered. He had been carrying that name around with him years before I first came to know him, and that had been a long time back. He was a great man if for no other reason than that he had made sergeant major with a hell of a speech impediment. Abbott was a pro. He had come to the 173d to replace Angel's sergeant major in the Support Battalion. It never worked out, perhaps because Angel was unable to see beyond Abbott's speech impediment. At any rate, Angel persuaded his own man to stick around for another six months and therefore had no place for Abbott, who was probably the best sergeant major he had ever had an opportunity to get. "You can have him if you've got room, Herbert," Angel had said, and it was truly like manna from above.

With Abbott's cunning assistance, I soon had two first-class typists, a brand new jeep with the sharpest driver in the Brigade, and an option from Angel on any new building not already in use—and there were plenty of them. One afternoon a captain from Angel's office and I went office-hunting together.

I knew the general area I wanted: a collection of large, one-story, barracks-size buildings where military intelligence kept Vietnamese detainees. Although the dirt road into the area was slightly washed out, it could be easily repaired. The place was far enough from the Steakhouse that nobody would drop by unless he had business, but close enough to the mainstream of the post for anyone to come by if he did have a reason. It was ideal, I thought—but only for an office. I would continue living in my chalet. Jesus H., it was peculiar. I had served nearly twenty years, all over the world, and now

I could just up and say I had decided to maintain my residence in a goddamned chalet.

It was the monsoon season and the afternoon sky was slate gray as the captain and I scouted the buildings. I walked in front as we went from one to another and then to the next—and then I spotted what I wanted. The exterior was perfect. No boards had been torn away, the screens were in fine shape, there was plenty of parking space, and it was close to the main post road. It had one drawback: the doors were gone.

I walked to the open frame and peered inside. It was twilight inside with a burst of light around the open doorway at the other end. I could see two men down on their haunches. One was taking a deep drag on a cigarette, and while I watched he exhaled slowly and passed it to the other man. The captain and I stepped inside together and walked quietly across the concrete floor. When we were halfway down the long building, they spotted us, dropped everything, and bolted for the door. I drew my .45 and fired one shot through the roof. "Hold it!" I shouted and they fell over one another trying to stop. I kept the pistol on half-cock and moved between them and the door. I glanced down at the floor where they had been crouching. A half-filled Pall Mall package lay next to a wad of marijuana. I sent the captain for the MPs and motioned with the pistol for the two to sit down against the wall of the barracks.

"Just get comfy, my friends," I said. "It'll probably be a while."

They glanced at each other and stared at me. Finally, the bigger one spoke. "You wouldn't dare shoot," he said, nodding at the pistol.

"No?" I thumbed the hammer back to full-cock. "Who told you that?"

"You'd end up in Leavenworth for the rest of your life," he said.

"Maybe so, pal, but you'd never know about it," I said.

He stared at me and then glanced quickly at the door. I sat down against the other wall. "You'd never know a thing about it, my friend, because I'll tell you something: there ain't no other side, it's all black." I stood up. Both of them were eyeing the open doorway.

"Try me," I said, "or else set your asses down before I decide to do it just for the hell of it." We all sat down. When the MPs came, they read the pair their rights, treated them with dignity, gathered the evidence from the floor, tagged it, and took it away. They were damned impressive.

125

"Sir," one of the MPs said. "Would you and the captain mind coming with us while we book these people?"

"Not at all," I said, and Angel's captain nodded in assent. We all went to see the desk sergeant, who was of a slightly different cut than the fellows who had made the arrest.

"This is just a waste of time," he said. "Nobody's going to do anything about it."

"What the hell do you mean?" I asked.

"Sir, marijuana is preferred over tobacco two to one by officers, senior NCOs and all the rest, including the grunts," he said.

"Well, Sarge, I wouldn't know. I don't smoke either," I said. "Now, let's just get these papers in the works."

"Okay, sir, but it'll die," he said. "Sir, there ain't nobody here who gives a damn." I didn't answer. "But if you insist," he said after a while.

"Oh, I do, Sarge, I really damn well do."

He handed us paper and ball-point pens. We sat down to write our statements. "Sir," the desk sergeant said. I looked up from the paper. "If you make out that statement, you're a marked man," he said earnestly, glancing over at the two guys we had caught in the barracks. "The fucking riff-raff will get you one way or another. Why don't you think about it a while, sir, and then come back."

I stood up and reminded myself that patience really is a virtue, then walked over to his desk. "What's your rank?" I asked.

"Sergeant First Class, sir."

"Okay, Sergeant First Class, you pick up the fucking pen and you write." I turned to the captain. "Are you scared?"

He looked over at the two pot-smokers and back at me. "Not hardly," he laughed.

"Good," I said. "Let's just dictate our statements to this here Sergeant First Class." About an hour later, we were ready to leave. "When they're finished, Sergeant First Class, bring them over to the IG shop and we'll sign them," I said.

"Yes, sir, Colonel," the sergeant answered. "Colonel what, sir?"

"Herbert, Sergeant First Class. Colonel Herbert." I waved goodbye. "See you tomorrow—with the statements."

"Yes, sir."

Within a few weeks, I realized that the desk sergeant had been worth listening to. He had it pegged. Pound for pound, the Brigade was garbage. Discipline was lax, the troops were slovenly, disrespectful, and sluggish, mentally as well as physically. It was obvious that in An Khe at least they were no match for either the Viet Cong or the North Vietnamese regulars. As the sergeant had said, they preferred pot, two to one. But marijuana was only an expression of a deeper, more serious failure. At An Khe, the troops wore what they damn well wanted to wear, including beads and bracelets. They capped their teeth with different colors—red, blue, and gold—and they called the hierarchy "motherfuckers" and printed "Fuck the Green Machine" on their jackets and hats. Some of them wore earrings, a few sported noserings, and the battle flag of the Confederacy flew from many of the bunkers. The sergeant was right about nobody giving a damn, too. Almost everyone looked the other way.

An Khe was a staff-and-headquarters post, crammed with chairborne-commando types. In any other war, it would have been ridiculous, but not in Vietnam. Every careerist who could wheedle his way over was there, drawing combat pay, while the citizens back home were getting bled for the bill. The troops knew best what to call it: a humbug!

The 173d was the largest brigade in Vietnam, with over 10,000 men attached to it. It was, according to the manual, a combat brigade with absolutely no dead weight. But it was a humbug. There were five so-called combat battalions in the Brigade, and not one of them had more than 600 physically present for duty. Out of a total of 10,000 men, then, there were no more than 3,000 at the battalion level, which means that some 7,000 people were assigned to support roles: steakhouses, pizza huts, clubs, headquarters, the General's mess, artillery, engineers, etc. Even among the approximately 3,000 at the combat battalion level, not all were out looking with their rifles. Some were, of course, but the battalions had their "rear areas" just like the Brigade, with their own steakhouses, their own clubs. Each battalion was composed of five companies, one of them a makeshift outfit responsible for heavy weapons—which left four companies for walking. No company in any battalion in the Brigade had more than seventy-five men physically present and ready to go. Thus, each battalion fielded about 300 combat troopers, except that each battalion assigned one company to guard its base of operations each day. That left a maximum of 225 men available for the field, or 1,125 on a Brigade basis. And that would have been on a good day with everybody out and everybody with a rifle—but everybody didn't carry a rifle. Some toted radios, some stayed back and typed, some worked in company supply, some were "fireflies," the daily helicopter resupply lifts, and some just plain screwed off. So on an average day, the 173d Airborne Brigade could field appoximately 800 men—if all its battalions were out. In the year I was in the Brigade, all the battalions were never out simultaneously.

We fielded less than 800 of 10,000 troops, in the Brigade. On a countrywide basis, it meant that out of the 500,000 men we had there at the peak of our involvement, less than 50,000 were engaged in the business of fighting in the field—and that figure applies only if all the other outfits were doing as well as the 173d. As General Westmoreland liked to say, the 173d was the cream of the whole crop.

It wasn't that our kids didn't fight well in the field. It was just that so damned few of them ever got there. We had a 500,000-man Army fielding less than any one infantry division did in World War II or Korea. On paper, we were hell on wheels. The reports had a column for it: In the Field—and on paper it was 98 per cent or more every day. I've filled in those reports myself and they look truly magnificent. All the guys at the Steakhouse: In the Field; all the guys at the clubs: In the Field; the General's orderlies: In the Field; the life guards at the Esther Williams' pool: In the Field. Stunning, absolutely stunning —and from time to time I found myself inclined to go along with it. It was so mesmerizing that when I later took over a battalion myself, I had to add another column to my reporting procedure just to keep things straight. "Ass In the Grass," I called the new column. It was no joke. It was necessary.

"There's a killing, sir," the two GIs were shouting at the door of the chalet. It was late at night and the sound of their voices must have carried all the way across the post. "There's been a killing out in the street." I let them in and heard their story while I dressed and strapped on my .45. They had been sleeping, had heard a scuffle on the main road that ran through the post, and had gone to look. Two men were beating another while someone else was running up the hill screaming for the duty officer, the man who was in charge of the entire post until the next morning.

"Did he come?" I asked the two.

"Yes, sir, he came," one of them answered.

"It was some lieutenant," the other one volunteered. "Some young guy."

I began undressing again. "So, what happened?" I asked.

"Nothing, sir," they said, almost in unison.

"Nothing?"

"Well, sir, the lieutenant didn't do anything," one of them said. "He just didn't do a damned thing." The two of them looked at each other and shrugged.

"What the hell do you mean?" I said. "He must have done something—beat somebody, shot somebody or something."

They shook their heads. "No, sir, nothing," one of them continued. "One of the guys who was doing the beating threw up his hands like in a karate stance and told the lieutenant that if he drew his weapon he would chop him."

"And?"

"And the lieutenant said something—I couldn't hear it very well —and pointed to the guy on the ground, the one they had been kicking around, and one of them said they'd take care of him or something like that and the lieutenant just left and went back up the hill." He stopped his narrative and looked at his buddy who nodded. "The next thing we see is them two guys picking this guy up from the road and carrying him off into the bushes."

They led me to the spot and we found the guy. He wasn't quite dead, but he was a hell of a lot less alive than he had ever been. We took him to the hospital, where I wrote down both their names and then went to find the duty officer. Incredibly, he corroborated what they had said. What was even more remarkable was that he did so without a stammer or a blush.

"But what about the guy on the ground?" I asked.

"They said they would take care of him."

"They did, my friend, they really took care of him—and you could have stopped the goddamned thing." I was hot and getting hotter, and by then he was getting uncomfortable. "What the hell kind of duty officer are you?"

"I don't understand, sir."

I leaned close to him. "You better, because you are in very deep shit right now. Why the hell didn't you stop it? Why didn't you make an arrest? Why didn't you do something?"

"The guy said he would karate me."

"But you had a .45, man," I said.

"I guess I just didn't want to get involved," he said, shaking his head.

"Well, you're involved now, Lieutenant. You are up to your ass involved. I'll see you in the morning."

I went back to the chalet and wrote it up immediately. It was unbelievable. A United States Army lieutenant, the duty officer, armed with a .45-caliber automatic pistol (he had worn it low on his hip like a gunfighter), had allowed two freaks to bluff him with no more than the threat of a half-assed karate chop. I was learning. The lessons weren't pleasant. The people at home probably believed what they had been told about how the night in Vietnam belonged to the Viet Cong, but that wasn't true at An Khe. There, the night belonged to the riff-raff, the freaks of the Green Line. It was no secret any longer who really ran An Khe. It wasn't the mayor—at least not after the sun went down. It was those ragged-ass losers in their beads giving the finger to anybody and everybody. I gave my statement to Angel after breakfast the next morning and recommended that charges be filed against the lieutenant. I provided the names, ranks and serial numbers of the two witnesses who had banged on my door—and grabbed a helicopter for LZ English for an appointment with General Allen. It was the last I heard of the incident. There were no charges. The lieutenant kept his job and his rank and later became the manager of the officers' club at An Khe; Angel kept his job and his rank, and the kid we'd found in the bushes finally limped out of the hospital. Everything was as smooth as a cat's ass.

Major Paul H. Ray, the Staff Judge Advocate for the Brigade, felt as I did when I discussed it with him later.

"A damned shoddy affair," he said.

I liked Ray. He was sharp, friendly, and possessed a fine sense of humor. He was an organization man, and even though that created quite a gulf between us, I appreciated him for what he was and we spent a great deal of time together. It was a profitable relationship, at least for me, because from Ray I was able to keep abreast of the Brigade's crime scene. It was one hell of a scene, which had begun long before either Ray or I had arrived.

His files were grim. Once, fourteen troops from one of the battalions had taken a twelve-year-old Vietnamese girl from her family "for questioning." Her father had protested, and was rewarded with a stroke across the head with the butt of one of the soldier's rifles. The girl would be returned, they assured him—and she was. Two days later, after fourteen men had raped her, had anal intercourse with her, pumped her full of morphine ("She couldn't feel no pain," one of the All American boys later explained), punctured one of her intestines, slapped her and kicked her, she was brought home. She died. The Brigade's charges were for rape only. A false certificate from a Vietnamese doctor describing the girl as alive and healthy was bought with U.S. taxpayers' money and one, just one, of the fourteen men received a slap on the wrist in a court-martial—and it was all over. A few extra American dollars were magnanimously donated for the child's funeral. "The problem," said Paul Ray, "is that most of our people are incapable of lending any dignity to the Vietnamese. Take that kid's family, for instance. I don't believe anybody thought about their grief. They just said, 'What the hell? A dink's a dink.' "

His files held other goodies. The practice of taking trophies— ears, noses, and fingers—from a dead enemy was fairly common in Vietnam, but I doubt that any outfit collected more of them than the 1st Battalion of the 50th. One of its lieutenants reportedly had the largest collection in the country, and when the report was checked, the investigators found all the evidence they needed. They had the goods on an American soldier who was systematically mutilating the bodies of enemy soldiers. He was had, dead to rights, but he was permitted to go home "for personal reasons" and he never came back. The hardship discharge he received was based on "compassionate reasons," a dependent mother to support. The image of the Brigade was saved. The chips had fallen elsewhere again. There were dozens of other cases in Paul's files, all equally sickening, all equally disheartening, all closed and beyond recall or repair. "If there is such a thing as justice, it must exist in the hereafter, because it sure isn't here," Ray said once, and I agreed. We were powerless. His job was to prosecute and mine was to inspect and investigate. Neither had anything to do with cases already salted away in the files. The girl was raped and that was that. She died and that was that. The lieutenant had mutilated bodies and that was that.

"Pretty, isn't it?" Ray asked.

"Yeah," I answered. "Makes me glad to be a U.S. trooper. Fills my little heart with pride to be on the team."

I had decided that despite what might have happened in the past and regardless of all the shit that couldn't be corrected, being an IG just might turn out to be one hell of a fine job. The twenty infantry-rifle companies in the 173d would all have to be inspected, wouldn't they, and if I could work out a routine that would allow me to get in some combat along with my inspections, wouldn't that be grand? It wasn't really going to be such a chore after all. I could spend a night in the field with every company over a month's period. It would be a matter of taking the IG office to the troops rather than sitting back and waiting for them to come in. Most of their complaints could be dealt with right there in the field. I could deal with the others when I returned to An Khe. It was the right way, I decided, but there was one catch: I needed an assistant, someone to man the office during my field inspections. The General responded favorably to my plans and I got Captain Paul Coutre. It turned out to be a fortunate choice for the Brigade and for me. He was a Chemical Corps man, intelligent, mature, and diligent—and with his help and Abbott's procurement skills, we set up shop in the new building, and I went on tour, making the rounds.

The pattern was simple. First, a briefing with the General and then out to the battalion headquarters for my own briefing with the commander—both of them prefaces to the task of receiving complaints in the rear areas. Then I would be off to the companies with a crinkled notebook and ball-point pen in my pocket. The gripes were fairly standard: no pay for several months, family allotments not being received back home, new babies that hadn't been seen. Some of the men had legitimate complaints, a few expressed trivial dissatisfactions —but I soon discovered that almost all of the bitches at any level of the Brigade were either the direct or the indirect result of piss-poor leadership. Being an IG was an extremely educational experience. I was spending about twenty nights a month with ass-in-the-grass troops, blending in as well as I could, taking every opportunity afforded me to discuss tactics. I found that one of the best ways to get to know any particular outfit was to accompany its men on an ambush.

Generally they were a disgrace. The ambush teams were usually composed of from eight to eighteen men, and when they left their camps they made more noise than a platoon of cuckoo clocks in a morgue. It was intentional, too, based on the premise that if the enemy heard them coming, the enemy would leave. It was a theory that cost more than one life in Vietnam. The 173d's ambush disciplines were sloppy and dangerously stupid. Once the teams arrived at the bushwhack spot, their Claymore mines would be scattered in a rough perimeter and the troops would dig into position. The night would settle, the bugs would emerge for their darkling adventures, and the troops would creep into their ponchos. It was an incredible mess. Equipment would be strewn and scattered and even the "alert" man would be bundled up in his own security blanket, less than half awake, with his rifle somewhere off in the grass. If he needed it, it would take some reaching to get it. They snored and hacked and rustled their gear all night and slapped at the goddamned bugs. For many of them, an ambush was for sleeping. No one really intended to fight. Their plans were almost always the same: if the enemy came, the mines would be blown and everybody would run like hell.

The purpose of an ambush is, plainly and simply and precisely, to kill. It takes little skill, but it does require patience, good discipline, and courage. You must be silent, keep your weapon ready, and stay alert. When they come, you slide the safety off silently, blow the mines and open up with everything you have. You fire at every moving object until there is nothing left but dust, and then you break it off and sit and wait some more—just as quietly as before, just as patient, just as alert. At daylight, you search for the bodies, take care of your wounded, and move out. It's clean, simple, and efficiently effective. Any combat commander can get the concept across in ten minutes— but then, of course, he has to set the example, which is what I tried to do several times. Out on an ambush I never got any closer to rest than one knee on the ground and my rifle was always ready and my gear was on. Frequently I'd have the Claymore controls by late evening and the machine gun by midnight. By one o'clock, I'd have everything. I'd nudge a guy here and there, trying to get them to keep down the noise. Sometimes I'd move off twenty meters or so to get away from their sounds and lean up against a tree with my eyes turned to the clear patches between the brush. Once in a while the enemy came, moving in on the snoring and the coughing. I could feel them coming, so damned sure of themselves, every last one of them ready for easy pickings. I'd hold off until the last second, hoping someone else would open up first—but they never did. They were asleep. I'd blow the mines and all hell would break loose, with my firing and the enemy screaming and dying and my buddies on the ambush running like hell. When it was over, I'd sit back and wait, and at daylight, the ambushers would come back, looking for my body, and I'd tell them how easy it had been and try to drive home a few points about the principles of bushwhacking. "Maybe next time, we can get more if you just keep the noise down," I'd say, and then we'd call in the patrol's report and finally we'd part, usually on good terms.

The fault was obvious: poor leadership and, more specifically, absentee leadership. Few of the ambush patrols I accompanied included a senior noncom or officer. The enlisted men had humped it all day long and carried their load, and then at night they were expected to stay awake and cut it again the next day. They took their sleep where and when they could get it—on patrol—and for the most part the company commanders didn't know what the hell was going on, or worse, just didn't care. It was their fault, but the real culprits were at a higher level: battalion commanders who wrote out their procedures almost verbatim from the Ft. Benning Operations and Training Handbook, passed them down to their subordinates, and let it go at that. They were covered. The procedures had no relationship to the realities of combat.

Late one evening, I flew in to spend a night with Company B of the 4th Battalion. They had already called it a day when I jumped down from the chopper's skids into the deep grass. The captain presented himself, reported and watched the helicopter disappear into the dusk. A few men were sitting around picking at C rations, while others were lolling among the dozens of fallen trees. I asked the captain to get me any of his men who had complaints or problems, and then I strolled around the area by myself. It didn't take long to decide what kind of commander he was. His troops were shoddy, which is the kind of criticism traditionally uttered by some rear-area commando who insists on spit-shined shoes in the middle of the jungle monsoon. But it isn't, not necessarily. "Field standards," which apply to combat conditions, are important, and those were the criteria I applied as I walked through B Company's area. A good soldier wears even the most ragged gear well. Even in the field, he is trim, neat and tight, with pockets buttoned and no loose or hanging straps or webbing. He does not wear sunglasses. He keeps a clean face and a clean weapon and clean ammunition. These kids didn't cut it. The reason? I could only conclude it was poor leadership. It expressed itself in many ways. The captain had picked a miserable site for defense that night. It was buried deep in the grass, much too far from any crest, and there were no fields of fire and no overlapping coverage. The automatic weapons were placed in positions that made them nearly useless. The only way the site would have been militarily effective would have been for the enemy to have just blundered into it, and that possibility had been eliminated when the captain ordered the company to dig in. We always dug in, thereby applying another World War II tactic to the jungle. Brilliant. In the jungle, success depends on surprise and stealth. We understood this to some degree. We would tippy-toe into an area, but then we would blow the whole ball game by hacking out holes and cracking branches and cutting down trees. Moreover, it was a useless dissipation of human energies after a day of beating down elephant grass in 100-degree heat. The captain seemed essentially uninterested. Two of his men looked like survivors of the Bataan Death March. Their clothing was torn to shreds and both were shoeless.

It was strictly a matter of leadership. It always was. Take the contrast I found between B Company and C Company. It was the same battalion, same area of operations, with approximately the same number·of troops and the same kind of mission. Yet while B Company was a mess, C Company was STRAC: strategic, tough, and ready around the clock. They were airborne, man, all the way. One night I went along on a platoon-sized patrol commanded by a young lieutenant. It was like clockwork; like beautiful Swiss clockwork. We moved quietly, paused for a silent C-ration meal, and drifted off further into the brush to set up shop. Nobody smoked, nobody talked. Charlie Company and its Lieutenant Webster were hunters, and as I sat tight against a palm tree that night, I felt good about being out with them. They had a purpose. Just before dawn, Webster received orders to "drift" back to the base, about twelve miles away. Helicopters were unavailable, he was told, so the orders were to foot it back and bring along the "mermites," thermal food-containers that weighed about thirty pounds and were clumsy as hell to carry. Webster stared at me in the early morning light. "It's stupid," he said.

"But it's an order," I replied, playing it straight.

He looked at me steadily and then made up his mind. "Yeah," he said. "Well, fuck them. We're not carrying no goddamned cans back through bush." He turned to his radio man. "Pass the word to get rid of the garbage, cans and all. We're going to hike so keep it light and don't leave anything for Charlie." The radio man turned to leave, and Webster stopped him with a hand on his shoulder. "The first fucking noise, somebody gets it in the mouth," he warned, and then turned to me. "I'll take the gig and the ass-chewing." Webster had a real outfit because he was a real leader. He had a good reputation and he earned an even larger one by the time he left.

The captain in B Company and Webster in C Company both had the same raw material, yet one was running a sloppy, sad-assed show that couldn't cut it, and the other was commanding a tough, tight, combat-ready and combat-able outfit. The difference was leadership.

After every inspection, I'd have another briefing with the battalion commander, board the chopper for An Khe and prepare the report for General Allen. It was a good system. It was working. The IG shop was getting to where the troops were and I was getting to where the action was, and I was finding out more about the Brigade than I ever would have in any other way.

In my office one night, Paul Ray told me another nice story. Somebody had wanted a safe and a used one had been found in the An Khe salvage pile. It was a beauty, but when it was hauled to the guy's office and opened, they found it crammed with secret and top-secret documents. They were tactical papers that had supposedly been burned months before. They included battle plans, supply routes, and troop quantities, and the obvious question was whether they had been compromised. The obvious answer was that indeed they had been. The lock was meaningless. The standard procedure at the base was for personnel to simply open, read, photograph, and replace—a technique that insured against losses. Nothing would be disturbed so there would be nothing to report—ever.

The case had been investigated before my arrival. The Brigade had handled it strictly as a local matter, even though it had obviously involved more than just the Brigade; at the end of the inquiry, no one had been charged and no one was at fault. In case the matter ever came up, there was a report in the file. The Brigade had been covered.

That was the pattern. Another case that fitted it perfectly was the court-martial of a trooper nicknamed "Three Fingers." He had been charged with attempted rape after breaking into the quarters of one of the girls attached to a civilian entertainment group and allegedly inserting three of his fingers into her vagina, threatening to "tear her up to her throat" if she so much as made a sound. She was a statuesque woman, big and sturdy, and she up and whipped his ass, and after she'd done that, she filed charges. Unlike the General, she wasn't particularly concerned about where the chips fell. Since her charges couldn't be ignored, it was a time for finesse. A special court was appointed, the object of which was to make sure that the matter stayed within the Brigade—and it did. Three Fingers beat the rap. He was found guilty but he was never punished. He went right back on duty.

It was a funny story, and it was hard not to laugh about a paratrooper getting his duff drubbed by a blonde during an attempted rape. But what wasn't so funny was the fact that Three Fingers became an instant hero in the Brigade. Almost every officer I knew actually respected him for what he had done. Many of them saluted him when he walked by, and he was spoken of in almost reverent terms in the mess. Paul Ray liked the story and told it frequently, ending with the description of how the blonde had appeared at the court-martial sans panties. I met her later in Ray's office. I almost had to sympathize with old Three Fingers. I stared at her and, by God, she had forgotten them again. But it wasn't funny, not really. Attempted rape had taken place. The Brigade had screwed up again by making a hero of a criminal. Almost everyone seemed to have lost sight of the fact that rape is a damned serious allegation. An American girl in Vietnam, under our charge and the protection of the Brigade, had been physically assaulted by one of our own men and all the Brigade could think about was its own image.

It was clear that any investigation in the 173d Airborne Brigade served one primary purpose: to protect the 173d Airborne Brigade. If an irregularity appeared, an investigation was conducted, and if the investigation acquitted the Brigade it was forwarded to higher headquarters. If it did not, then it was written up in as positive language as possible and filed—within the Brigade. The odds were that no one would ever be called upon to produce it, and if the dice came up wrong, the investigation was there showing that action had been taken, along with the Letters of Reprimand, the general expression of disapproval for almost any irregularity or infringement. Whatever the offense, the punishment was seldom appropriate—like giving a five-dollar traffic ticket for hit-and-run—but it was action taken, and as far as the Brigade was concerned it met the requirements.

Nothing ever seemed to bother anyone in the 173d. For instance, as a matter of routine I personally inspected the Adjutant General's office. It was my job to do so. Like almost everything else, it was a failure. How so many men could do so little with so much for so long was a monumental achievement in itself. A warrant officer ran the whole show in shower clogs. "Clearing up the jungle rot," he explained, even though he knew that I knew the closest he had ever been to the bush was on the path to the latrine. The whole office was a humbug—sheer scrap—with the exception of a few enlisted clerks who strained their balls every day and night to keep it going. "The guys in the field deserve better than this," one of them told me. "We try to make up for all the shit. For them—not for Major Crouch." The major was directly responsible for the operation of the Adjutant General's office. He wasn't going to like my report, I knew, but it was plain that it had to be.

The AG records were a shambles. Men had been assigned to jobs far removed from their skills: radio technicians as machine gunners, machine gunners as wiremen, wiremen as riflemen, riflemen as radio technicians. Important personnel data sent up from the companies were seldom posted to individual records. Promotion orders were running at least eight weeks behind schedule, a failing that often required men who had been promoted in the field to give up those same promotions after rotating out of country, and to return "overpayments." Sometimes they were court-martialed for "impersonation."

Other men never received medals and decorations they had earned. Right now, there are men all over the world who honestly won Distinguished Service Crosses or Silver Stars or Bronze Stars or other awards who have never received so much as an official thank-you for their courage and gallantry. In some cases, a trooper's file would simply be missing and the man would go without pay or dependent checks for months. About the only thing running at all at the AG office was the Awards and Decorations Section, but like a lot of other things at An Khe, it was run mainly for the brass and the elite. One guy that I'd seen getting wretchedly airsick on a half-hour helicopter flight to LZ English had a string of Air Medals that would have embarrassed Billy Mitchell. Crouch himself had a Combat Infantryman's Badge and, in my final report, I not only criticized the AG office but demanded that Crouch's award be cancelled. He and Angel were furious. I simply did not understand the problems of the Adjutant General, they said, and they were right. As hard as I tried to understand the problems the report still came out "negligence." I had, without knowing it, dug one more shovel of dirt out of a hole which later, it was hoped, might become my grave.

I turned my attention to the "mayor." This was my job, and I was beginning to get with it. Angel had issued final clearance to an engineer unit transferred to another section of the highlands out of An Khe. His clearance, according to his report, was based on a complete and final inspection of the unit's former area. Abbott and I went to have a look, and found almost everything except the Viet Cong. They had probably come and gone and taken what they wanted by that time, anyway. There were weapons of every caliber, including machine guns. There were explosives, field gear, clothing, bedding, and drugs—everything an enemy unit might need to support itself for a long time. In fact, by our estimate, more than $150,000 worth of equipment had been left behind as scrap by the engineer unit, just sitting there waiting for anyone who wanted to take it. "We are our own worst enemy in Vietnam," I had read somewhere in Lederer, and it was true. Without us, the Viet Cong would have withered, shrivelled, and died. We were often supplying both sides. It turned my stomach—not because of the cost to the taxpayer; I was as indifferent to that as the next officer—but because of what it meant in lives. I was furious. It meant that the war was being unnecessarily prolonged and that kids were dying needlessly. Abbott and I gathered the evidence and turned it in along with a screaming report. General Allen "cautioned" Angel and a letter was forwarded to the engineers' outfit—all of which amounted to not a hell of a lot, but it was some headway at least. If nothing else, in the future Angel would see to it that he got around before we did. It was progress.

One of the inconvenient things about having to go up to LZ English was that it did not afford me the opportunity for combat as did my frequent inspection trips to field companies. To compensate, I generally spent my spare time at LZ English in the Brigade's Tactical Operations Center (TOC), listening to radio traffic and waiting for a chance to ride shotgun with the General or anybody else who went out. It was a pretty good technique. In Vietnam, the commanders liked to be on the scene of the action—in the choppers at 1,500 feet plus the actual elevation of the terrain. They cluttered up the radio networks with their incessant conversations, but they were right there, on the spot. Nothing ever happened of any scale that wasn't monitored from the air by one or more commanders. My Lai was as yet unreported, but for anyone to believe now that the brass were unaware of what happened there is utter stupidity. In any other war, the "hover and observe" tactics of the commanders would have been fatal, but this was the Indian War, as General Allen liked to call it. We had the Sharps rifles and they had the bows and arrows. Whatever happened at My Lai didn't happen without overhead observation.

One evening a call came into the TOC for a dust-off, a medical evacuation helicopter. I moved to the edge of my chair, and as I listened I checked my gear. Then the radio went silent. There was no request for artillery, no after-action report, nothing. It had either been a booby trap or a self-inflicted wound, I thought, or perhaps another goddamned accident—one of the most tragic products of the Vietnam War. If ever a legitimate study is made of that war, most Americans will be stunned to learn that we killed a hell of a lot of our own people, once again a failure directly traceable to poor leadership. All it took was the sound of a booby trap or the sighting of movement and we were prone to just open up, to fire into the jungle and brush in every direction without any idea of who might be on the right or left or behind or ahead. We did it over and over again—to ourselves.

The radio crackled.

"Kilo, this is Able. Over."

"Able, this is Kilo. Go ahead. Over."

"This is Able. Scratch dust-off. Change WIA to KIA on pick-up. Over."

"This is Kilo. Roger. Out."

Killed in Action. What action? The radio transmissions left one hell of a lot of unanswered questions. They would, no doubt, be answered later, I thought, unbuckling my gear. One for them and none for us. It was getting to be the whole story for the 173d. "If anything comes up, how about giving me a kick," I said to the radio-man.

"Roger that, sir," he replied.

I shuffled over to the corner of the TOC and sank into a heap against the wall. It was a hell of a lot better than what the ass-in-the-grass grunts had that night, I knew, and besides, I wasn't going to have to heat my own breakfast the next morning and eat it from a can. I slept well. At breakfast, the questions were unanswered. Once again, we had killed one of our own. In this particular case, he had caused his own death, it was said. He was a young lieutenant, out on his first patrol. According to the report, he had set up the ambush and then left its perimeter to establish security, which was completely ass-backwards, but neverthless the way he had been trained by the U.S. Army.

When I was in Ranger School at Ft. Benning, I had seen the example set dozens of times without any criticism. Training, bullshit. We had too damn many academics. We trained not only with blank ammunition but with blank attitudes as well, using instructors who had gone through the same kind of blank training—men who in their wildest dreams could not relate to a real combat patrol because it had never been a part of their own experience. The Army claimed the instructors were "combat veterans" and some, no doubt, were, but most had merely been in combat zones.

Because of that kind of training, the young lieutenant was dead. The report detailed how he had gone out from the patrol's main body to position the outpost people himself, just as he had been taught, and then headed back through deep jungle and at night, alone, toward his main group. In the daylight, moving through the brush is hard; at night, it's a formidable task. When his men heard movement to their rear, the report related, they called him on the radio. At least, he had had enough sense to take it along. He gave the order to "cream 'em" and they did. He was dropped in his tracks. Schooled, trained, Ranger, Airborne—and he had ordered his own execution. I tried to console myself by thinking that anybody so goddamned ignorant deserved to die, but it didn't work. I knew he had been trained by guys like me—not me personally, but by senior personnel like me. It was our fault. I tried to imagine myself doing what he had done, even several years earlier, and couldn't. He was worse than untrained; he was badly trained. He had no business being out there in charge on his first patrol, and his battalion commander couldn't be held blameless either. It was sickening. We were the healthiest, wealthiest, supposedly best-trained soldiers in the world. Our Army had the finest raw material of any country, we had the equipment and the experience to do better, and we fought like a bunch of amateurs. I shoved my coffee aside and looked around the TOC. There were white cloths and flowers on the tables and paintings on the walls. It was ludicrous. I grabbed a chopper back to An Khe and on the way constructed the rest of that night's pitiful drama. The dead lieutenant was from a little town in Pennsylvania, not far from where I had grown up. A telegram would soon arrive and the middle-aged mother would collapse on the couch in the living room while the father tried to console her through his own tears. I imagined myself walking into the room and standing at the end of the couch, looking down on them, and saying that I had killed their kid. The vision passed and I was grateful that he wasn't one of my men and I wouldn't have to explain it, even to myself.

It was some Christmas, thanks to the folks back home. There were literally tons of gifts in sacks and bundles from big cities and little towns all over the country. They had been collected by the kids and mothers and brothers and sisters and the fathers who were, in many cases, veterans themselves, remembering how lonely a holiday can be for a guy fighting halfway around the world. It nearly chokes me to say it, but all of those people were bamboozled—taken once again by the men of the U.S. Army. In the Brigade chaplain's tent, ransacked Christmas bundles were piled to the ceiling and letters were scattered around on the floor like so much holiday confetti. Nobody gave a damn. Much of what was sent ended up in the black market without ever getting near the grunts. Some of it provided season's greetings for the local prostitutes, and some of it was burned: piled up, gasoline poured on, and up it went.

We had too much—much, much too much. Whatever the reason was—the nature of the war, the differences in the attitudes of the personnel—the abundance was overwhelming. The Red Cross, for instance, came up with 15,000 individual Christmas packages for the 10,000 men of the 173d. Each package had an individual waterproof bag with a ball-point pen, windproof lighter and fluid, a pocket knife, a notebook, some instant beverages, and several other items. Some of us helped the Red Cross people get them to LZ English, where we saw the better part of them go up in smoke along with the rest of the trash. "Not enough time," the Brigade chaplains explained. Bullshit. They were too busy bickering among themselves over which of them would say the midnight mass. Christmas in the 173d was a farce, as far as the headquarters was concerned. But Christmas was only a minor matter, as I was learning in my role as an IG.

Master Sergeant Frank Booth arrived with a well-deserved reputation as one hell of an IG man. I had known him at Ft. Bragg, and I remembered him as an honest, tough, gutsy guy who worked hard. His specialty was funds; he was a holy terror on audits. I was out of my mind happy to see him, especially since I was responsible for the inspection of 104 separate funds within the Brigade. He was exactly what I needed. It was too good to be true. I recall thinking the first day Booth came to work that they better by God change their ways. We weren't amateurs anymore. We had Coutre and Hey, Hey Abbott and the two typists and the driver, and now we had Booth. With only a few exceptions, we had a good relationship within the Brigade. We were not out to nail anyone but rather to prevent wrongdoings if possible or correct them as best we could after they occurred. Generally, the run-of-the-mill irregularities were dealt with over the telephone. Commanders were usually happy to correct any situation before it went on the record, and that was fine with us. The troops began turning to us more and more and all of us began to feel substantial pride in what we were doing. In fact, Abbott and I joked frequently about "our team." But with our increased efficiency and the augmented number of complaints from individual soldiers, we were compiling information that seemed certain to lead to a major scandal: narcotics, the black market, grand larceny. In almost no time at all, we knew we were approaching a point at which we could finger the brains of the organizations responsible. A sergeant working out of Angel's Support Battalion Brigade Supply office came in and volunteered one juicy tidbit. His sworn testimony alleged that officers in Brigade Supply were trading thousands of dollars worth of equipment to the South Koreans for liquor and wine. The alcohol turned up later on the black market tables in downtown An Khe. The strategy was simple and ingenious: who would associate Korean merchandise on the black market with American personnel, especially when so much U.S. merchandise was available? The sergeant gave us names, dates, and places, and we added more of our own after a preliminary investigation. The pieces of the puzzle were soon complete and I took them to General Allen, who told us to handle the formal inquiry. Our work was leading us closer and closer to the guts of the system and word of what we were doing spread through the post. One morning Angel came by the office to inform me that Sergeant Major Abbott was "being considered" for charges—his charges. He explained by telling me about an early morning inspection he had made at the NCO Motel where Abbott was living at the time. He had found a Swiss-made submachine gun in Abbott's quarters as well as "an abundance of other unauthorized weapons in other rooms." He freely conceded that the weapons had all been discovered in the quarters of noncoms who had "done me a bad turn." Abbott, who did not even carry authorized weapons and did not collect souvenirs, was a bit surprised, to say the least. Almost every chairborne commando in the Brigade was carrying any kind of weapon they chose. Their choices included everything from .25-calibers to .357 Magnums. Abbott and I discussed Angel's threat and he decided to fight it. We found out that every last weapon discovered in the surprise inspection had come from a cache stored at the NCO Motel and used for trading purposes with the U.S. Air Force personnel at Tuy Hoa, according to Sergeant Roy Wren, the motel manager. Through the grapevine, Abbott and I heard that Angel was going to offer Article 15, a nonjudicial form of punishment, to all of the sergeants in whose rooms he had "found" unauthorized weapons. An Article 15 is usually the alternative other than court-martial given to a man accused of some infringement of regulations. It is very much like asking a man to accept a hundred lashes rather than take the chance of losing his head. In most cases, the guilty ones accept the Article 15s—and some of the innocent, too, particularly those who do not completely understand the system. An Article 15 can mean the end of a career. The court-martial usually proves less severe since many of the charges included in an Article 15 are dropped "for lack of evidence" before the matter moves into formal trial. The rule of thumb should be that a commander should not offer an Article 15 unless he is prepared to take the same charges to a court-martial, but as with so many other things, the Army went at it backwards. The Article 15 became a club, a weapon in the hands of commanders to be used on those too ignorant of the system to resist. Abbott was not ignorant. He decided not to accept the Article 15 should it be offered by Angel.

Booth and I were on our way to the mess-hall when Angel caught us and called me aside. "About this Abbott thing," he said. "How do you think we ought to handle it?"

"Why ask me?" I said, keeping my voice loud so that Booth could serve as a witness.

"He's your sergeant, isn't he?"

"If he's mine, why not just turn the whole thing over to me?"

"No, no, I can't do that," he said. "I'm responsible for the discipline back here. It wouldn't look right."

"Then why ask me?"

"Well, since you know the sergeant well, I thought maybe you'd have some recommendation," he continued. "I don't want to hurt Abbott's career, but I don't want my reputation damaged either. We could handle it together in a sort of friend-to-friend way."

He had spent too much time dealing with amateurs. If I accepted his terms for a private arrangement on Abbott, it would mean the end of any effective IG role in the Brigade. "I really can't accept that, Colonel," I answered. "The circumstances are all very vague—illegal search, no actual possession of the weapons and no real ownership of the weapons—and I believe you know where they all came from." Angel was really listening now. "I don't believe Abbott is going to accept any Article 15," I said. "In fact, I'm pretty sure he's going to go the court-martial route—but then that's a matter between you and Sergeant Abbott."

I moved away from him and he stopped me with a hand on my shoulder. "But I've already told General Allen," he said.

"Told him what?"

"That Abbott and the others have accepted Article 15s," he said. "What we can do is just keep the General pacified and when he's gone in a couple of weeks, I can just throw all of them out. There wouldn't be any record of it and no harm done."

I had already heard that General Allen was getting ready to leave the Brigade but I simply could not believe what Angel was saying.

"Talk to Abbott at least, okay?" he said.

"I'm sorry, I can't," I replied. "I just can't tell anybody to accept an Article 15, even as an interim measure." I picked his hand off my sleeve and left with Booth.

Later that day, Abbott said he was undecided about the Article 15 and told me that Angel wanted to see me at my convenience. After supper that evening I stopped by his office. We were alone. There were no witnesses and neither of us wasted any time or words. He was in a real bind, he said. He had counted on my good faith when he had told General Allen that the sergeants, including Abbott, were going to accept Article 15s. "Court-martials are sticky, Herbert," he said—and for once I agreed with him. They are indeed. Reputations suffer regardless of the verdict and even Abbott could not come out unscathed. He was in line for the Support Battalion Sergeant Major job again and it could hurt him badly. Angel asked me to tell Abbott that if he would accept the Article 15, he would only be fined and the fine would be delayed until after General Allen's departure from the Brigade. Then, Angel said, he would simply forget the whole thing. That his plan was illegal seemed of no concern to him. "It's up to Abbott, now," he said, "and will you do me the courtesy of relaying what I've said?"

Not only did I "relay" it to the sergeant, I gave it to him in writing in a sworn statement. He didn't want it that way, but I insisted that he have a memo for his records. After all, I told him, Angel could die or I could die and he needed some cover. "Fuck them," Abbott said. "I'm not taking no Article 15 for something I didn't do." But he did, to save the court-martial, and the Article 15 and the fine were dropped, just as he had been promised. Later, under oath, Angel verified that he had indeed used the Article 15 against Abbott, refunded the money, and declined to forward the record to higher headquarters, as the Uniform Code of Military Justice requires.

Sergeant Wren, the motel manager, once told me and Booth that the tab for the Brigade's entertainment ran close to $200,000 a month. That was probably too high, but with as many as eight entertainment groups working in the Brigade simultaneously, it had to be expensive. The groups worked a circuit from An Khe to LZ English to Tuy Hoa to LZ English North to LZ Uplift to Ban Me Thuot—a headquarters circuit that seldom reached the grunts. Nothing was too good for our guys as long as they were not ass-in-the-grass types. The good music and the broads were not fit consumption for grunts. The entertainers were wined and dined as guests of the big brass in their air-conditioned trailers and in the best rooms at the NCO Motel. The women in the troupes never knew such popularity as when they were in the 173d, while the fellows were busy arranging the kickback percentages. Some were whores, nothing more. Others were bona fide entertainers. "But none of them goes home unscrewed," Sergeant Wren remarked one day. Some of the kids who came to entertain worked hard and damned sure earned whatever was left after the kickbacks and the inflated expenses.

The Doughnut Dollies of the Red Cross had been asking for a jeep for several weeks. A complaint had been filed with us because the Red Cross was officially entitled to a vehicle and we were supposed to provide it. They needed it to get around An Khe and for making scheduled flights. It was not a luxury item, it was a necessity, and at An Khe it was no problem to get them one. Nearly every last rat's ass in the post had one for himself, yet Angel had refused to provide one for the Red Cross.

Until I went to the 173d, I had a pretty sour attitude toward the Red Cross, a holdover I suspect from my experiences with them in Korea. There they had been piss-poor and more interested in themselves than in their stated role. But at An Khe, they were the only straight outfit on the post and the Doughnut Dollies who manned the Happy Hooch were great girls. They couldn't be bought, and that was indeed a rarity in the 173d, where almost everyone and everything had a price. While most of the men understood this, Angel apparently could not, or at least he seldom displayed any appreciation for the role they were playing. His refusal to provide a jeep for the girls, as he had been ordered to do by higher headquarters, was but one expression of his hostility.

"They really need one," I told him that day over our coffee.

"Right now, I just can't do it," he said. "If they need transportation, all they have to do is call."

"Come on, Jack," I said. "I can't even get one when I call." I pulled a sheaf of papers from my pocket. "Besides, USARV says we're supposed to provide one."

"Maybe later."

I stood up. "Okay, Jack. You realize, of course, that they have filed a legitimate complaint against us and all the directives are on their side," I said, holding up the papers. "Maybe I ought to restate the bidding. They filed a complaint. They have every right to a jeep. I came to you. You cannot provide one. Correct?"

Once again, he was beginning to understand.

"I didn't say that," he replied. "I said that I could not provide one today."

"When?"

"Tomorrow," he said. "We have one coming out of maintenance."

"I'm sorry I misunderstood, Jack," I said. "That's why it's always best to restate the bidding, I guess. Thanks—for the girls as well as for me."

"They could have come direct to me," he said, pouting.

"I'll tell them that, Jack," I said. "In the heat of battle, we all make mistakes."

It was progress. A little bit at a time, I said to myself, just one thing at a time.

General Allen ordered us to inspect the clubs' funds. He would be leaving soon and he said he wanted to make sure everything was "up to snuff" before he moved out. Some of the 104 separate funds hadn't been dealt with by the IG for more than a year, and a few of them were in atrocious condition. For example, in the NCO officers' club complex at An Khe, Booth, the auditing terror, turned up deficits that ran into six figures. His initial report was stunning. I called in a certified public accountant from the Brigade's Finance Section to check him out. Booth checked out. The report was staggering in its implications. It was not some penny-ante party gone astray; it was big-time crime. General Allen read the report and refused to accept it. When he left, it was still in his "in" basket.

The operation centered on slot machine slugs. At least $500,000 worth of them were unaccounted for. No one had signed for them. They had simply disappeared. The slugs were ostensibly provided for the local members of the clubs. A soldier purchased them at the counter with military scrip, and if he won he cashed in his slugs for scrip. If he lost, then the slugs remained in the possession of the club. Periodically the machines were emptied and the slugs taken back to the counter to be sold again. It was, on the surface, plain and simple gambling profit, the way it works in Las Vegas or Monte Carlo or anywhere else. But the secret to the operation was that the slugs could be used in any slot machine in Vietnam, and there were one hell of a lot of the one-armed bandits in clubs from Saigon to Danang. The $500,000 worth of slugs had been sold at a considerable discount to men who used them in machines outside the Brigade's area of operations.

The records of the Steakhouse and the Pizza Hut were equally shocking. Tons of meat were unaccounted for, along with thousands of pre-fixed pizzas and truckloads of liquor and beer. Three years later Congress would be pulling the covers off what would become known as the "Club Scandals." It would involve generals and the very top sergeant of the whole Army, Sergeant Major Woolridge, whom General Westmoreland himself had hand-picked as the U.S. Army's first "top kick." Even then the Army would still be trying to sweep it under the rug.

It was in our Brigade that the investigation which led to the scandals started—our investigation, launched at General Allen's request. Thanks to Booth and the CPA from the Brigade Finance Section, the country finally got a whiff of the way things were.

The lines were being drawn and the IG shop was no longer sloughed off in dinner conversation. It had become a power and I had become, for some of my comrades-in-arms, the enemy.

The General called me to LZ English and commended me. He said he was more than satisfied with the IG shop's work and he thanked me for what he said was substantial progress. "The garbage can is starting to look good," he said.

It wasn't true, of course, but I suppose he believed it and it was no doubt a comforting thought for him. The truth was, of course, that the Brigade was still a garbage can. We hadn't even begun to scratch the surface. But I appreciated his commendation, and I listened as he talked about his aims and ideas for the Brigade. "But I'll be leaving soon," he said, standing and offering his hand. "As you know, Tony, I fully intended to give you a battalion command, and I still do."

It would be the 3d Battalion and I would get it in April, he said. This would necessitate an extension of my tour so that I could get in my six-months minimum of command time. But it would be worth the extension, he said. The present commander of the 3d Battalion would have his six months in by April, which was another anomaly of the Vietnam War. It mattered not that a commander was doing a great job or a crappy job. Six months was the magic number. Officers got their tickets punched in six months and got the hell out to some other assignment, to work on another credit and get another coupon certified. General Westmoreland had said a long time before, when I was still a major, that the Russians were very envious of the way our officers' corps was getting tremendous combat experience in Vietnam, and even then I knew it was bullshit. It takes a commander a couple of months to become acclimated to his responsibility, a couple more to get going, and then he's gone—it was crazy. Besides, we were losing in Vietnam, a fact which the U.S. Army officers' corps seemed not to want to recognize. It would have been better to have fought the whole goddamned war with a hundred honest-to-God commanders than the thousands of half-assed "combat leader" types we were producing. Whatever gave us the notion we could build a better mousetrap in six months? It was a pipe dream, and what was worse was that the "leaders" we were grinding out would be not an asset but a detriment in a big war, should one come; then they would be considered experts and the delusion would cost us plenty.

I waited until the General finished before I told him I couldn't take the 3d Battalion. "There isn't enough time, sir," I said. "Thanks a lot, but it's too late." I would be leaving in June, I explained. I had been notified that I would be attending the Command and General Staff College at Leavenworth, Kansas. "In fact, sir, even if I took a battalion today, I'd have a hard time making the minimum six, considering the time for processing and all."

"Well, Tony, maybe not six months, then," he countered, explaining that the commander of the 2d Battalion, a Colonel Nicholson, was scheduled to go out in late January. "I'll make it clear when I leave that you're to get the 2d, all right?"

"I understand, sir, and thanks," I said. "I'll be ready."

"And, Tony, if anything opens up sooner, it's yours," the General added, referring to the possible combat death of a commander. It was a remote chance, with action in our area as light as it was, but it could happen. The General then turned to more immediate matters. The Brigade Chemical Officer was leaving the country and he would have to move Captain Coutre from my shop into that slot. Major Walter J. Werner would be transferred from Company A of the 1st Battalion to the IG operations.

Like any other infantryman saddled with an office job, Werner came to An Khe reluctantly, very reluctantly. It was one of the paradoxes of the war that we sent combat leaders to our rear-area offices. They were quitting the service daily because they were shut off from combat commands. We were filling combat slots with ticket-punchers who were there to get one more credit on their record and then be on their way to greener pastures. They had little motivation except their career impulses. Generally they failed to understand their men and regarded them simply as things to be used. It was a stupid, utterly senseless policy that contributed to our loss of the war and to our losses of men.

I remembered Werner. I remembered him very well for his guts— not in the face of the enemy but in the face of his commander. It had occurred soon after I came to the Brigade. Werner had gone in and brought out the bodies of three of our guys who had been staked out on a hillside. The bodies had been spotted from the air, spread-eagled in the open on their backs. When Walt brought them in, it was clear to the men who saw the bodies that they had bought the farm the hard way. The three deaths, the torture, and the manner in which they had been found were logged and would have been forgotten, except that a few days later three more bodies were spotted from the air in precisely the same spot. They were from the other side. A note was pinned to one of them. It said that a court-martial would have been impossible under the circumstances, and so the three men who had tortured and executed the three Americans had been tortured and executed in a similar manner. The note was signed, "An NVA Major." Werner reported it exactly as it had occurred, but his battalion commander refused to accept it. What the hell was Werner trying to do,

151

he asked, credit the North Vietnamese Army with humane actions? The second trio of bodies were those of innocent civilians who had been murdered for propaganda purposes, Werner was told. He was encouraged to alter his report. He refused—and that took guts. It probably also meant that he was no longer on the team, and both of us suspected this as precisely the reason he was now a part of the IG office. "I'm sorry as hell, Walt," I said the first day he showed up. "But I have to level with you and say that I couldn't be happier about getting you here."

He smiled, but without much enthusiasm.

The face of the Brigade brass was changing pretty fast. A new executive officer, Lieutenant Colonel John D. Bethea, was already at his desk, and three new majors were coming aboard. "Get rid of them," Allen said. We had too many majors already, he suggested. That was no doubt true; at least we had too many in support roles. There was a standing joke: "I'll trade you one good major for two cases of blank ammunition and a case of C rations and if you're up tight, you can owe me the Cs and the blanks." If no one spoke up for a major, he generally was on his way, but when Master Sergeant Childers, with whom I had served many years, looked me up and told me one of the new men whom Allen wanted to get rid of was Ernie Webb, I knew I had to do something. Webb had been one of ours. He was Airborne all the way, and had gone to Germany soon after I left there for the States in 1962. He had been Childers' platoon leader. "Was he any good?" I asked.

"Come on, sir, I trained him," Childers grinned. That meant, as far as I was concerned, that Webb was good. But it was still a problem.

"Listen, Childers, do you know how many majors this Brigade has?"

"It doesn't matter, sir, he's good and the Brigade needs good men, doesn't it?" He was right there. The Brigade needed more than just one Ernie Webb, but he would do for a start. He had a sponsor. Me. The next night at the officers' club in An Khe I met Ken Accousti, one of the other new majors, and he sold himself to me as well. He had air assault experience, he said, and since that was the name of the game, I became a double sponsor, and later a triple sponsor when the other major was said to be top-notch, too. I went to the General with my recommendations. He seemed not to care much. He was leaving. He accepted all three men. Webb became commander of the Jungle School at An Khe, Accousti went to Brigade Operations, and the other major ended up in Brigade Civil Affairs.

Fragging, the deliberate attack on a noncom or officer by an enlisted man or men, was not unknown in the 173d. One sergeant over in the Signal section had made the mistake of raising hell with a trooper about the cleanliness of his area. The man wired a Claymore mine outside the sergeant's room, aimed it right through the wall at the switchboard, went to a phone and called his victim. The sergeant lost both legs. There was a fragging in the 2d Battalion, too, with seven wounded. They had tried to get Nicholson with explosives and on another occasion they had tried to blow up his Tactical Operations Center. One of the men in the 2d Battalion had reportedly blown himself to bits with a Claymore mine, but my investigation failed to corroborate this. It had been in his hands, that was cerain, but there were two men in a nearby bunker handling the controls to the mine when it went off. The victim had left the bunker to retrieve the mine at the request of the other two—and somehow, they said, the circuit had been completed. I wasn't a real detective, but even though two company commanders swore it was accidental, I did sign my report with a recommendation that the Criminal Investigation Division check into it. They never did.

The 4th Battalion had a genuine insurrection. Herb Matsuo, the battalion executive officer, told me about an old colonel living in an air-conditioned trailer who had become a sort of father figure for the riff-raff in the battalion. "No kidding, Tony," Herb said. "He's actually pulled all the freaks in around him and made them a personal bodyguard outfit with weapons and all—and the old geezer is dumb enough to believe they're responding to him." The colonel called the men his Mafioso, Herb said. "They're going to cause serious trouble, Tony. They're the worst kind of people we have over here. They're killers, and I'm not joking. You better get the word to Allen before it's too late."

"Is it that serious?" I asked.

"I'm telling you there's about to be some real shit in the fan," he insisted. "These bastards are going to turn things upside down."

153

"But is it the kind of thing to take to the General?" I asked, still a bit skeptical.

"Goddamn it, Tony, there's going to be big trouble here and nobody seems to give a damn, including you. Let me show you their records." The documents were persuasive. The old colonel had to be a fool. He was tinkering with out-and-out criminals. I promised Herb to get the information to General Allen as soon as possible, but while I was at English telling him about it, it blew up. The word came in that there had been a real honest-to-God uprising down at Tuy Hoa. The old colonel's bodyguard was holed up in a bunker with a machine gun, a couple of .45s, and some grenades. Allen hit the ceiling. He gave the assignment to me, Paul Ray, and the Provost Marshal. The object was, as the General explained it, to get them out of the bunker, into the brig, charged, convicted, and sealed away— quietly. Herb had it under control before we arrived, although Ray liked to tell a different story which detailed how we three had taken care of it. He had rolled a 106 recoilless rifle into position in front of the bunker. "All I need is the authority to fire this goddamned thing," he said, and whether I had that authority or not, I delegated it to him. "All right," he shouted to the bunker. "You stupid bastards have three seconds. You come out on your own or be blown out." End of message —and end of troubles. I flew back to LZ English and the old colonel's bodyguard rode back with Ray and the Provost Marshal. It was that simple except that Ray, who was an accomplished bullshit artist, liked to expand the story to include us in the capture.

It was about this time that the big prison riot occurred at the huge military stockade at USARU headquarters at Long Binh which broke into a national scandal—and it might be significant to note that this one too was started by the 173d, with one of the Brigade troopers murdering another. We stirred things up, man.

I had more business in the 4th Battalion. A couple of days after Herb had quelled the insurrection, the battalion's A Company was demolished by the Viet Cong. The company commander had been killed, as well as the commander of a 4th Division artillery battery. General Allen, Sergeant Major Bittorie, and I were on the first chopper after dawn. The entire area was a shambles. Two Conex containers, large metal bins used to ship furniture overseas, were still smoldering, and there was equipment scattered all over the scenery. The battalion commander, Sandy Wyand, hadn't arrived as yet. The dead lay uncovered and the survivors sat around in a virtual state of shock. The smell of cordite and marijuana hung in the air. The General asked a few questions and Bittorie identified a body. I kept quiet. It was another incredible turn for me. I noticed that although we had lost one hell of a lot of people, there were absolutely no enemy bodies, and I noticed also that neither the General nor Bittorie commented on that fact. I approached the subject twice but was cut short both times. "They put up one hell of a fight," the Sergeant Major said, and the General nodded in agreement.

"Aw, come on, John," I said—and I got two of the strangest looks of my career. I suppose I was some kind of nut or something because I recognized a defeat when I saw it. Paratroopers were apparently never defeated. They might be overrun by a numerically superior force, but they were never defeated. What I had said apparently bothered Allen, though, because he felt compelled to talk about it twice on the way back. Once he said it appeared to have been "one hell of a fight," and later on he said it was unfortunate that we couldn't have delayed our departure until a thorough search of the area had been completed. By ourselves back at English, Bittorie and I discussed it at length. We had known each other for a long, long time and had served together for several years. We had been talking things over for years, as friends. "There were no VC or NVA dead, John," I said. "There won't be, either, no matter how goddamned long or thoroughly they search."

"Damn it, sir, we don't know that yet."

"We know it and so does the General."

He threw up his hands. "What the hell are you going to make that kind of trouble for? We both know they carry off their dead. It could have happened there."

"Bullshit. There were no enemy dead. That unit was damn well overrun, probably caught sleeping," I said, reminding him about where we had found the dead CO and the artillery battery commander. "Both officers killed in their Conexes," I continued, "and by the way, those things have no place in the field." The Conex was made for shipping, not for fighting. They had their use, all right, as furniture crates. Unfortunately, they were just about the size of a cell, and they had steel doors. Military Intelligence and the Criminal Investigation

Division used them for precisely that: cells and interrogation cages. A scream didn't carry far through Conex walls. Then some cunning combat commanders found a way to hook them up under helicopters and fly them into the field for use as command posts. Once again, it was stupid; it was the security blanket syndrome all over again. From inside you could neither hear, see, nor fight. Moreover, an officer had no right to be inside a Conex when his men were living in the holes.

"John, every position laid in at that place was piss-poor," I continued. "There were no interlocking bands of fire, the machine gun wasn't laid in properly, and the goddamned troops were about as grubby as I've ever seen. Not one weapon in the lot was in good shape."

"Aw, come on, sir," he said. "They had been out a long time." There was no reason to answer. I just stared at him. "Okay," he conceded. "So they were piss-poor, but it's our fault." He poked a thumb into his chest. "It's our fault. These captains are young but we stick them out there and ask the impossible. We never bother to tell them how to do it." It was quiet in his quarters. He picked up a packet of papers and threw them across his bed. "We don't tell them because we're too damned busy with this paperwork." He turned to me. "You're a fucking commander and what do they have you doing?" He went to his cooler and pulled out a pair of beers. "I'm a fighter, too, and so is Childers and so is Abbott and what the hell do they have us doing?" Bittorie ranted, opening the beers and handing me one can. He sat back down on his bed. "Okay, sir, what do you think really happened to A Company last night?"

I looked at my watch. It was time to catch the flight to An Khe. "Well, for one thing," I said, standing up, "a lot of men were shot to hell and died needlessly—and for another thing, somebody was sure as hell responsible for that."

"Who?"

"Like you said, all of us, in a way. Maybe. I don't know yet, but if I find out, I'll clue you in. Take care and thanks for the beer."

I went back to An Khe and then down to the 4th Battalion for an inspection. According to the rotation I had established, it wasn't their turn for an official IG visit, but General Allen said it was their turn so it was their turn. Maybe something was bothering him about A Company, too. I flew into Tuy Hoa into a quagmire and then out to a makeshift, rear-area supply point. There were a couple of storage tents for supplies and two large hospital tents for personnel. A Company had a new commander by then, but one of the old members relayed word that he wanted to see me in private. We talked in one of the large hospital tents with the monsoon rains beating down. It was dark and dingy, and here and there drops of water were tap-tap-tapping down through seams in the roof. Canvas cots were aligned along the wall of mosquito net. The man sat on one of them facing me with his hands clasped between his legs. He was of Mexican descent, although a little tall by my past experience with Mexican-Americans, and not surprisingly, he was a Catholic. He began there. He was not as religious as he should be, he said. He did not like war, he said. He never wanted to harm anyone, he said. Then he looked up, pleadingly. "Sir," he said, "you must get me a transfer to a rear unit."

"I haven't got that kind of power," I said, shrugging my shoulders. I watched him wringing his hands. "Do you have a legitimate reason? Something valid that I can use?"

"No, sir," he said, in a barely audible voice. "No, sir, I just do not like war."

I stood up. "I'm sorry. Maybe you should talk to the priest."

He kept his head down and answered. "They're going to kill me."

"Who?"

"A Company."

"A Company?"

Now he looked back up at me. "I smoke marijuana."

I tried to help him along. "So?" I waited and waited. It was no use. I tried another tack. "You say you're a Catholic. Is that right?"

"Yes, sir."

"Then you must have something to say. You have a mother and a father and a God, and if it's bad and may cost you your life, then you must say it. You can't hide."

"Will it get me out?"

"I don't know. Try me."

We were both silent for what seemed like hours. Finally he looked at me, rubbed his hands together, and seemed to resign himself. He had been on outpost the night A Company was overrun, he said. Just before dusk there had been a big pot party in the unit and almost everybody was there. Almost everybody was stoned.

"Officers too?" I interrupted.

"Yes, sir, officers too," he replied.

"Was there anybody who didn't take part in the party?"

He said there were at least two sergeants for sure. "That's all I can vouch for," he said. "Four of us went out, down this trail to the listening post, and we strung in the wire and dug a sort of shallow hole and settled down for the night. We had both radio and wire contact with the line. I was on the first time from about seven to eight, and nothing happened. I went back on at about eleven, I guess, and about eleven thirty I saw these two dinks coming up on my left. They both had long poles with satchel charges on the ends." He held his hands apart in front of his face for a moment and then dropped them back down, clenching them between his knees.

"I tried to wake the other guys with my feet. I didn't want to make any noise. I could see the dinks going up the hill and placing their charges against the Conexes."

"Didn't you try to call the line?" I asked.

"Yes, but no one answered. I kept ringing the telephone." He looked me straight in the eyes. "The other guys were awake by then and we all tried to warn them and then the charges exploded just as the captain answered the phone. The VC started running up the hill all around us, shooting and screaming."

"What did you do? Did you fire back?"

He shook his head. "No one did, I told you. They were all stoned, crashed. No one fired a shot."

"But what did you do?"

"We crawled out of the hole and left everything. Crawled over into the bushes. Just in time, too. We saw two dinks walk up to the hole and start fishing stuff out." He stood up and pretended to be holding a weapon. "I got scared and started firing. Both guys went down."

"Then what?"

"We started running up the hill. The dinks were all running back down. Just then, one of us got a bullet in the back of the head and he fell." He rubbed his hand up along the back of his neck. "But it only tore his helmet. He got back up and made it with the rest of us. The whole damned hill was on fire. Both Conexes were burning. Nobody was doing anything. So we stayed by the Conexes until daylight."

"Where were the other platoons in the company?"

He stared at me. "On the back side of the hill."

"Didn't they come over? To help? To do something?"

"Not until after daylight, just before you and the General arrived."

That didn't sound right. It had been a long flight from English. "How long before we arrived?" I asked. He shrugged and I touched the back of his hand. "Had you been smoking marijuana?"

He shrugged again. "We all had."

"Then why is your life in danger?"

"Because they said they'd kill me if I told."

I stood up. "Get some breakfast. I'll see you later and I'll get you out of here at least. I can't promise to get you out of a line unit, but I'll try."

I took it directly to General Allen, and I did try. I don't know whether I succeeded. Later I heard two stories: one a report that the boy had been lifted all the way back to An Khe, and the other that he had been killed "accidentally" while out on patrol.

After talking with the General about the kid, I started my inquiry. I spoke with some of the others in the platoon—some were still in the hospital—and to the kid whose helmet had been ripped up when they were running from the hole up the hill. When I finished, there was no doubt. It had been marijuana. I took it back to Allen, and he didn't like it one bit. The company had been creamed and there wasn't a single dead enemy. I suggested that we write it up as a lesson learned, one that even a nitwit trooper could understand. No one individual had been at fault, I reasoned. It had been marijuana, and as bad as that was, it could serve a valuable purpose as a combat lesson for the living: marijuana and guns don't mix.

The General was staring at me when I finished. "You must be mad," he said.

"Sir?"

"Do you realize what you're asking?" he said, walking over to his window for another glance at those goddamned flowers. "Can you imagine what you've just suggested? Those were American kids. Two captains and one hell of a lot of American kids are dead." He threw up his hands in disgust and sat down at his desk. "And you want me to tell higher headquarters and their families that they were on dope?"

"Not dope, sir, marijuana—and we don't have to say that every-one was on it. Just point out that it was the reason they had their ass creamed."

He stood up again. "I'll have to think about it. For the time being, just keep it to yourself, understand?"

I stood up, too. "I understand, sir."

He sat down again. "And I will consider it."

Later, I read about A Company's fate in the *Stars and Stripes* and in our own Brigade newspaper, *The Sky Soldier*. The two accounts were nearly identical: the company had put up one hell of a fight but had been overrun by a numerically superior force at a substantial cost to the enemy. It was one more glorious chapter in the glorious history of the 173d Airborne Brigade. The official accounts of that night on that hill were a goddamned discredit to every mother's son who fought worth a lick in Vietnam. The General no doubt believed it saved some face. Bittorie never mentioned it again. Neither did I.

The story of A Company's heroism and gallantry was published about the same day that Lieutenant Colonel Joseph Ross Franklin joined the Brigade as a replacement for Colonel B. F. Delamater, the deputy commander. Franklin had graduated from West Point in 1949 and had won a Distinguished Service Cross in Korea. His head was completely hairless. He shaved it. He looked and talked like a bad-assed combat commander. He was impressive, no doubt about that, and his teeth sparkled. "They say he's a breath of fresh air," Abbott remarked.

Angel introduced us one day in the mess at An Khe. Franklin said he'd drop by the IG shop later, and just before closing time he did. I asked Abbott to get a couple of files before he and the others left, and Franklin and I began to discuss our backgrounds. He was certain we had served together somewhere before, and he mentioned that Angel had told him I was a mustang. "I prefer to call it a direct commission," I said.

"Any college?" he asked.

"I just finished my master's in psychology before coming over this time."

"Where'd you get your bachelor's?"

"University of Pittsburgh."

"And your master's?"

"University of Georgia."

"Have you started on your Ph.D.?"

"I've already finished the core program, but it takes more than just credits. I'll still need an internship."

"Then you're almost a doctor."

"Not quite, but maybe someday."

"Then you intend to finish?"

"Certainly. Why else start it?"

"Well, you know. Career. Promotion."

"Nope, that's not why I'm into it. I really want to be a psychologist. In fact," I laughed, "I am one."

He laughed, too. "Jack Angel tells me you've got quite a set of records here," he said, pointing toward the file cabinets. "Mind if I look through them?"

"They're IG files, sir."

He stared at me—very hard, very icy. "They're 173d files, Herbert," he said.

I got the message. No one, Delamater or anyone else, had even bothered to test me, but I had known that someday it might come to this, and thanks to my years I was prepared. I laughed and tried to make Franklin feel at ease. "Not quite, sir," I said. "My orders are cut out of First Field Force Victor and the IG files are restricted."

"You're denying me access to them?" Franklin asked.

"Not me, sir. Regulations."

He got up and walked over to one of the cabinets, leaned on it and flashed a beaming grin, the biggest, brightest one I'd seen in a long time. "Then how about a briefing," he finally suggested, "and don't pull any punches, Herbert."

When I finished, he had one question. "We're that bad, huh?"

"We're worse, sir, but you'll see for yourself—and it's not because of the caliber of the troopers, either. We have the finest top sergeants I have ever known in the Army and we have the healthiest, toughest privates you can find anywhere."

"But the worst general," he said.

"Not really," I said. "Allen is okay."

"Then?"

"Leadership, sir," I said, and then as he nodded I related every last error I had seen in the Brigade. When I was finished I attributed them all directly to a lack of leadership.

"How do you mean that, Herbert?" Franklin asked.

161

It was precisely what I wanted him to ask. "The troops are ragged-assed because they have no one to emulate that they respect. Men are dying because leaders don't care enough to lead. It isn't Allen in particular, although he's included. But the real problem is at a much lower level, at the level of the battalions and the companies. If I followed the regulations, I'd be recommending courts-martial for every last battalion commander I've seen in this Brigade and I've seen them all. They write 'policy' books, have their men initial them and then try to correct any violations after they occur. Nobody leads by example. They command from 1,500 feet up in a chopper and they wear spit-shined boots like they were on parade while their men hump through the bush with their asses half out of their trousers. Everybody plans—big—but nobody sees to it that their plans are carried out. Our lieutenant colonels fight their battalions on paper as if they were chess pieces on a board."

The office was deathly quiet until he spoke. "What do you recommend, Herbert?"

"Well, since you asked, kick a couple of battalion commanders in the ass. Get them out of their birds and onto the ground. Make them spend a few nights out with their units and don't permit them the right to transfer the men they consider bad news. Force them to get off their asses and lead—and we'll have a Brigade."

"That's exactly why I'm here, Herbert," he said.

"Sir?"

"To lead," he said. "That's why the Brigade is getting a new general: to lead. General Peers is damned sick of Allen and this entire hodge-podge." He walked to the door. "Things are about to change, Herbert—for the better." He stepped out into the darkness. I slipped the files back into the cabinet and sat down for a moment to think it through. Maybe he was going to make a difference, I mused. Maybe, as Abbott had told me, Franklin would be "a breath of fresh air." I hoped so.

A couple of days after I met Franklin, the 1st Battalion commander was injured when his helicopter was shot down. He broke some bones and had some internal injuries. Bethea, the new executive officer, called from LZ English: "The General wants you to come on down on the first flight with all your gear. Be prepared to go into the field. Report to me as soon as you get in." I was ready. Sergeant Major Bittorie had called me previously to tell me that Allen had decided it was time to fulfill his promise and give me command of the 1st Battalion. I already had a chopper laid on. I was primed.

It was a waste of time and effort—a dry run.

I was met at the airstrip by Bittorie who told me that I wasn't going to get the battalion after all. It wasn't Allen's fault, he said. The General had firmly decided to give me the command and had notified General Peers at First Field Force Victor. Peers, who had a guy from Washington who had been waiting over six months for command, had cancelled it. Allen, according to Bittorie, had argued for me and had got an ass-chewing for his trouble. Peers did guarantee, however, according to Bittorie, that I would get the next vacant battalion. "Sure, John, sure," I said. "Well, the least I can do is check in with Bethea and see how he handles it."

Bethea handled it this way: "The General wanted you to know that Colonel Henniger is coming in to take over the 1st Battalion," he said. Apparently, he lacked whatever it took to explain it fully.

"Is that why I needed all my gear?" I asked. He did not reply. I waited.

"Do you have anything else?" he finally asked.

"No, sir," I said. "Nothing at all."

That night, Bittorie and I drank beer into the wee hours. We laughed a lot and told lies to each other and remembered other days, but inside I was crying and he knew it. It was the first time in my career that I cursed the goddamned club, that elite clique that runs the Army in what I considered that night to be the worst possible way.

The next morning, back at An Khe, I met Henniger, the guy who was taking over the 1st Battalion. It was his first command, so I tried to tell him what I knew about the battalion as a result of my inspections. "I'm not going to say congratulations," I told him when I'd finished. "You edged me out." I thrust out my hand and he took it. "But good luck, anyway," I said. "If I can help, just call." I meant it. I knew it wasn't his fault. Besides, I thought, the 2d Battalion is a lot better area. Sure, Tony, sure. It has a better area, and besides, I still had a job to wind up.

The last item on the agenda was a receipt due from Saigon on some furniture purchased by the officers' club at An Khe. The young lieutenant who had been the duty officer the night the guy had been beaten up by the other two men—the lieutenant who wore his .45 low but backed down to a karate threat—was now running Angel's officers' club, and he had ordered $3,000 worth of barrel furniture from the States—*air mail*. When I heard about it, I didn't believe it and neither did anyone else, including General Allen. "You'll see. It must have been a slip in the carbon," he said. We were waiting for confirmation and I had been calling Saigon almost daily. Since I wasn't going to take over the 1st Battalion and since I had nothing better to do, I put in another call. Eureka! The furniture had arrived: $3,000 worth of barrel furniture and $7,000 worth of air mail postage. I caught Allen outside his trailer. "Got a minute, sir?" When I finished the story, he looked pale.

"Have any recommendations, Herbert?" he asked.

"No, sir, just one request."

"Which is?"

"When the stuff comes in, sir, can I have the stamp?" I was laughing so hard, tears were running down my cheeks. "I ain't never seen a $7,000 stamp." Allen burst into laughter, too, although it couldn't possibly have been as funny to him as it was to me. He was, after all, responsible.

It was our first and our next-to-last laugh together. He was leaving two days later and there was a going-away party for him the next night. We were out on the veranda of his mess, gathered around the bar, and it was the only time I ever heard him talk like a soldier. He must have been one hell of a sergeant, but he wasn't much of a drinker because by ten o'clock, he was smashed.

"Sing, sir," his aide, Ed Northington, urged. "You promised, sir. An Airborne song."

"Blood upon the Risers," somebody shouted.

"Beautiful Streamer," somebody else yelled.

"No, no," said somebody else. "Rendezvous with Destiny."

The General stood up, with one hand on the top of the bar. His drink was in the other hand and he waved his glass in a wide, sweeping motion. "Piss on all those five-jump Johnny songs," he said, lifting his glass. "I'm going to sing you a real one." He placed his glass on the bar, and most of us gathered around him. It was quiet on the veranda. "We were in Bastogne," he began. "It was cold and it was

164

Christmas and General McAuliffe called us all together and told us that the Germans had asked if we wanted to surrender or die." Allen looked around and waved his arm. "See, they wanted to know if we'd lay down for them or we'd fight and die. So, McAuliffe asked us what we wanted to do. You know what I said?" Allen asked us. "I said 'nuts,' that's what I said and then I said to McAuliffe, 'What do you want to say?' and then we all went back out into our holes and started to sing." The General began to sing then. The tune was *Tannenbaum*, but the words were: "Oh, go to hell, Oh, go to hell! Oh, go to hell, Oh, go to hell! Oh, go to hell, Oh, go to hell! Oh, go to hell, Oh, go to hell!" We began to sing along but he stopped us. "Maybe you didn't understand me, men. They said they'd wipe us out," he said, trying to put his foot on a bar rail that wasn't there. His foot came down with a thud. "I mean it was a sobering thought. Some of us prayed, some of us cried, and some of us cursed—but we all kept singing." He started again. It was the same tune with different words. "Oh, very well, Oh, very well! Oh, very well, Oh, very well! Oh, very well, Oh, very well! Oh, very well, Oh, very well!"

He picked up what was left of his drink and downed it. "And always remember it was good old General Allen that taught it to you," he said. We all laughed, including the General.

It was the last one we had. He was gone the next day.

Brigadier General John W. Barnes took over the 173d, thus making complete the change of command that, as Abbott had said, was supposed to bring a breath of fresh air to that part of Vietnam. The first breezes stirred a couple of days after Barnes arrived. Walt Werner came into the IG shop in An Khe and told me that General Allen was being investigated on the basis of complaints from two sergeants in the 1st Battalion. Their lives had been threatened, they had told the IG of First Field Force Victor, and Allen was to blame for the threats because the 173d lacked discipline. General Allen had been weak and had failed to back up his subordinates, the sergeants had alleged. A Colonel Wilson from higher headquarters was making an inquiry about Allen. His first stop was to see a major who had only recently been assigned to 1st Battalion.

"The major backed up what the sergeants said," Werner reported.

"Just how the hell would he know?" I asked. "He never served under Allen." I scratched my head. "But one thing you can say for the major: he's damned sure loyal."

I asked Walt what the visiting colonel had said after he'd talked with the major. "Well, he indicated that it was beginning to look pretty bad for General Allen," he replied. "You think maybe we ought to call this Colonel Wilson? I've got his number."

I thought about it for a while and then I called. Our discussion was brief and to the point. General Allen's policies were as strong as any other commander's, I said, but the sergeants were partly right, too. Discipline was indeed poor because nobody anywhere seemed to give a damn. That fault could be traced all the way down to the battalion commanders, I told him. The written policies were fine, and a strong commander could use them to good advantage while a weak one could make them excuses if he so desired. Then I told the colonel that the major he had spoken with in the 1st Battalion had never served under Allen except as an aide to the commander before him, which meant that he could only know what the other man had told him about Allen. The colonel asked if I had a copy of the written policies and if I would see that he got one.

"Sure," I said. "No trouble at all—and by the way, has General Allen been told he's being investigated?"

"Why, no, I don't think so," Colonel Wilson replied.

"Well, it seems only cricket that he know about it, don't you agree?" I said. "Would you mind if I let him know?"

"No, not at all," he said. "Go right ahead."

I called Ed Northington, who had been Allen's aide and who was now in his new job as Special Services Officer, and asked him if he had heard about the investigation.

"Is the General in trouble?" he asked.

"Hell, no, but it's a lousy way to run a railroad," I said. "How about calling him and giving him the good word?" He said that was all right with him and left. I forgot about it and told Werner to do the same thing. "It's a dead horse, Walt," I said. That was a mistake. The next day I was summoned to LZ English by Franklin, the new deputy commander of the Brigade.

"You are a no-good, disloyal son-of-a-bitch," he said, for openers.

"What are you talking about?" I asked.

166

"You insulted one of my battalion commanders."

"One of *your* battalion commanders?" I repeated.

"Yes, goddamn it, one of mine," he said. "No sense trying to lie out of it, either, because your ass is going to swing." I was dumbfounded until he finally explained that he had heard about the call from Northington to General Allen. "And Northington said you had suggested that he call," Franklin said. "You did that without permission."

"What do you think I should have done?" I asked.

"Come to me, that's what."

"For what reason?"

"Because I'm the commander, that's why," he said.

And all along I had thought General Barnes was the new top man in the Brigade. My eyes were wide but I tried to keep any emotion out of my voice. I knew damned well I was treading on very thin ice.

"You, sir, are not my commander," I said, "the General is."

He exploded, and the breath of fresh air was gone forever. I was, he said again, a no-good son-of-a-bitch and a disloyal liar. I had, he continued, tried to sink Angel and others in the Brigade for my personal gain as the IG. General Barnes stepped out of his trailer and Franklin hailed him. "General, do you know what this colonel of yours did?" he said, shoving his finger in my chest. "He illegally warned General Allen of that investigation we had talked about."

"That's a damned lie," I said. Barnes stared at me, hard, and I tried to explain as fast as possible. "Call Colonel Wilson at First Field Force Victor and he'll verify what I say," I said.

"Oh, we can call Wilson, can we?" Franklin said, smiling broadly. He turned to Barnes. "I'll take care of it, sir." He turned back to me. "Then let's just do that little chore, Herbert, let's just get on it right now."

When he got Wilson on the line he seemed to be trying to intimidate him. "This is Colonel Ross Franklin, deputy commanding officer of the 173d," he said. "I have a young lieutenant colonel standing here with me right now and he's lying like crazy and using your name. His name is Herbert. Yes, that's right, Herbert. The IG, yeah. What's he lying about? Well, for one thing he's used the good name of this Brigade to assassinate the good name of one of its commanders." I was angry. I wanted to reach out and grab the hand-set from Franklin and tell the colonel on the other end of the line what was happening. All I could hope was that the colonel wouldn't fall for Franklin's game—but I was worried. Why wouldn't he fall for it? He didn't know me from Alger Hiss. Franklin was still talking. "Yeah, right after you conducted your classified investigation he ups and notifies General Allen that it's taking place." There was a pause while Wilson spoke, and I watched Franklin's facial features realign themselves. He was blushing. Finally he spoke again. "Yeah, that's right, Franklin," he said and then he spelled his name for Wilson. "No, no, Colonel Wilson, no interference was intended. Well, it simply looked odd, you know, but if you say so I guess you know your job. No, no, I'm not registering a complaint. I was just checking up to see if he was telling the truth." I relaxed. I didn't have to hear what Wilson had told him. Franklin's side of the conversation was clear enough. He hung up and looked at me curiously.

"Well?" I said.

"Well what?" he answered. "He's a goddamned liar just like you," he said, and then launched into me on a different tack, telling me once again that I had been disloyal—but this time to General Barnes. "You don't work for Allen anymore," he said. "You're working for Barnes. You don't owe Allen anything." I explained that I would have done the same thing for Barnes if they had been investigating him.

"Oh, as a matter of fact, I'd have done the same thing for any private," I said. "According to military justice, any individual has the right to know when he is the subject of an investigation."

"Don't tell me what military justice is," he interrupted. "You're a goddamned, disloyal liar."

I was a little tired of his harangue. I interrupted him. "I can assure you, Colonel, that I am neither a goddamned, disloyal liar nor a son-of-a-bitch—and don't call me either again." He exploded. It was the first time I entertained the notion that he was prone to hysteria. I was still standing. He jammed a finger at the chair. "You sit down! You sit down! You sit down right there," he screamed. So I sat down. He did the same and continued his ranting. He was the one who wrote my efficiency report, he said. It was to him that I would report everything in the future and I would clear all future investigations and complaints with him, he said. "Oh, no I won't," I said. I tried to explain why but he was on his feet again, screaming and yelling. "Listen, you bastard," he said—at least I wasn't a son-of-a-bitch anymore—"I have more medals than you and more degrees."

It was so blatantly incongruous that I thought perhaps I hadn't heard him correctly. It made no sense. He was a deputy brigade commander and I was just an IG. He had a Distinguished Service Cross and the equivalent of a Ph.D., while all I had was a master's. He was strong, healthy, fit, tanned, and had over twenty years' service as a West Point-graduated officer. I had been commissioned less than eleven years. What the hell was this all about, I wondered.

I had heard some talk about Franklin having acquired a reputation for being ruthless with his subordinates during his stretch of duty in Germany, and I knew I had to be careful. But there still wasn't much logic to his explosion. It wasn't the first time I'd run into an officer who was eccentric—who shouted or stormed or had some silly habit or affectation—so I knew that the situation couldn't be treated lightly. It was going to require some measure of self-control on my part.

"What do degrees and medals have to do with General Allen's right to know about his investigation?" I asked.

Franklin bit his lip, appeared to get a grip on himself and then spoke, quite softly. "Don't ever expect to command in this Brigade," he said.

I leaned forward. "Don't worry, sir, I don't," I replied. "I know the score. The General has already clued me on that," and Barnes had indeed already done that. One night soon after he had taken over the Brigade he told me that it would be impossible for him to fit me in as a commander. "I understand, sir," I had told the General. "Besides, I don't have enough time left in country to serve a full tour anyway. I depart in early June or July at the latest."

"Oh," Barnes had replied. "I thought you had until September."

"No, sir. I've got orders for Command and General Staff School at Leavenworth," I had said. "And besides, sir, I kind of like being an IG."

"Good, Tony, very good," Barnes had said. "I only have one change in the way you've been doing it. Keeping in mind that I do understand the close relationship between you and General Allen"—where in hell did he get that?—"I want you to do all of your coordination through my Chief of Staff, Colonel Bethea—never to me, directly."

It had crossed my mind that brigades do not have chiefs of staff. They have executive officers. "Sir," I had argued. "The IG works for the commander and it can't work any other way if—"

"It will work," he had interrupted. "It will. You are my IG and we'll do it my way and it will work."

I had watched Barnes from across the desk, and decided he would never understand that I was not really his IG, so there was no reason to try to explain it to him. "Yes, sir, I understand," I had said.

I looked back at Franklin and decided that he would never understand, either. "I know not to expect to command in the 173d, sir," I said.

"Then there's nothing more to discuss. Good day, Colonel."

"Good night, sir."

It was already dark when I stepped outside. I stopped by Bittorie's quarters and told him how I had been assured of never commanding in the 173d.

"Sure, Tony, I expected that," he said.

"What do you mean?" I said. I couldn't recall telling anyone about my conversation with General Barnes.

"I mean that Franklin has somebody else in mind for the next command slot," Bittorie said. "An old friend of his from the West Point Protective Association."

"That's bullshit, John," I said, and then told him of my conversation with Barnes.

But Bittorie insisted that it was Franklin and not Barnes responsible for keeping me from a command. "I heard him talking on the phone to another lieutenant colonel and he was promising him that he would take care of getting him a command in this Brigade," Bittorie said. "He told the guy he'd handle you and for him not to worry about you and your commitment from General Allen. Then Franklin saw me standing there listening and he said over the phone that he'd have to stop talking about it because one of Herbert's friends was eavesdropping."

"But, John," I argued, "Barnes is the man who handles command assignment, not Franklin. What the hell does Franklin have to do with whether I get a battalion or not?"

Bittorie shook his head. "I'm telling you, Tony, it's Franklin, not Barnes, and you better watch it."

"I still say it's bullshit, John," I said, "but let's just drink to the whole goddamned mess. And then, let's just forget it, because it doesn't matter to me anymore."

"It matters, Tony, it matters," he said, squeezing his empty beer can into a wrinkled wad. "It matters and you know it and so do I, so just don't say it doesn't matter—Colonel, sir."

Of course it mattered, but I knew I had the slot in the Command and General Staff School and so I was rationalizing, I suppose. But Bittorie's account of the phone conversation between Franklin and one of his buddies was at least an insight into the kind of administration the Brigade was getting. I just wish to hell I'd known then what I found out a couple of years later: that Franklin had been a captain in Germany when I was a lieutenant and that he had asked to come on parachute duty and take over B Company of the 505th—the company they gave me. If I'd known that, I might have been able to read more of the ample handwriting being scribbled on the walls all around me.

Each evening after dinner, General Barnes and Colonel Franklin sat at the head table of the general's mess, smoking cigars paid for from the mess fund and sipping wine bought the same way. It was time for "dinging," a childish version of a kangaroo court. The junior officer present was asked to stand and read from the "record book" the "dings" of the day, and he would begin his reading amid much smiling and nodding around the tables. "Major John Doe, serial number 65479022, was observed today in the vicinity of the briefing room with unshined boots and grease-pencil blotches on his jacket," the young officer would recite and everyone would laugh because that was part of the game. They laughed because the game belonged to Franklin and Barnes and they wrote the efficiency reports. A sentence would be passed by either the General or Colonel Franklin. Generally, it included paying for a couple of rounds of brandy for the group or perhaps performing some somersaults or occasionally shoving a peanut across the floor with one's nose. "Hear, hear!" everyone would shout, and the brandy would be passed and the next ding would be read. All of this was taking place while there were men with their ass in the grass, waiting in ill-laid ambushes with ill-laid plans, forfeiting their lives, losing their legs, or just trying to get enough leeches off their bodies to get a halfway decent night's rest. Barnes later said that dinging was a morale booster.

I stayed away from the General's mess whenever I could because of the dinging. After my first time, I didn't need it again. Hell, I didn't like children's games even when I was a child.

The same evening Franklin told me not to expect a command, after commiserating with Sergeant Major Bittorie, I walked over to the mess for some coffee, knowing the dinging was over. Almost everyone except General Barnes and Colonel Franklin was still there, sitting around the tables, shooting the shit. I sat down with the Brigade engineer, a fellow named Schmidt. He was a damned fine engineer and had, in fact, built the General's mess. It was an elaborate structure, but Schmidt called it a waste of manpower and I agreed.

"By the way," Schmidt said. "Congratulations."

"For what?" I said.

"Well, I heard you're taking over the 2d Battalion."

"Not hardly, friend," I said and explained the events of the day.

"Aw, hell, you can forget all that," Schmidt said. "Franklin's a better man than that. He'll think it over and come around, and besides, I heard that Barnes has already approached higher headquarters with somebody else's name and been overruled. Allen's word still means something."

Schmidt and I were still talking when Franklin came back in and sat down.

"Herbert," he said. "I want you to put in for your R and R tonight so that you can be back before five February. You'll be taking over the 2d Battalion on the sixth day after you're back—or thereabouts." He was smiling broadly. "Any questions?" he asked. "None, sir," I said. "Thanks." Maybe I had misjudged him. Maybe Schmidt was right. Maybe he was a better man than what had been shown that evening in his tent—or maybe Allen's word really was still worth something.

The next morning I went back to An Khe, and got ready for my vacation.

5

There was only one word for the way I felt as I flew back to An Khe from English: happy. Maybe there were two words: deliriously happy. I was getting what I wanted, the command of a combat battalion, and almost as a bonus I was heading off to Hawaii to see my wife and daughter. You must be living right, I told myself as I climbed down from the helicopter. And what about that Franklin? I knew I still didn't like him, but I realized in all the years I'd spent in the Army I'd met plenty of men I didn't like who were still damned good soldiers. Maybe this was another case of two officers whose personalities clashed for some unexplained reason, but who were capable of mutually recognizing and respecting each other's skills. Well, whatever it is, I thought, as I walked toward the IG office, it's working out in your favor, Herbert. You've done an honest day's work as the Inspector General, Allen promised you a battalion, and you're getting it. And you're going to see Marygrace and Toni. Good deal.

"Good morning, sir," Abbott said when I walked in. "Jesus, you look like the cat that just swallowed a flock of canaries."

So it showed, did it? I told him the good news and asked him to get started on my R and R processing. When I got to my desk, I noticed nothing of interest so I decided to maintain my state of euphoria. I whirled the chair around and the map on the wall behind me brought me back to the real world. It was a chart of the 173d's area of operations and down in the corner, neatly printed, were the words AO ALLEN. The maps hadn't been changed to reflect the arrival of the new commander, but in a few days I knew they would all be called AO BARNES. I wondered what the Vietnamese made of such presumptuous designations as, AO ALLEN, AO BARNES, AO JONES, AO SMITH, AO WESTMORELAND. The Vietnamese had lived there for thousands of years on land they believed to be theirs, but woke up one morning to find out it wasn't really their hamlet or village or province after all but AO ALLEN or AO BARNES. It was like the Indians in our own country. They hunted the land for generations and then found out it was really not theirs at all. It was AO JIM BRIDGER or AO KIT CARSON and finally AO AMERICA. It bothered me to think about the impact of the war and of our own participation in it on the people whose land Vietnam really was. I tried not to give it much thought, as a matter of fact. It interfered. I spun the chair back around to face the desk just as Sergeant Booth strode through the door. I had only been back from English a couple of hours, feeling like a goddamned conquering hero, but Booth was about to personally involve me in a situation which would help to destroy my career in the U.S. Army.

He had been on his way back to the IG shop from lunch, he said, when he saw some American soldiers abusing Vietnamese detainees in the prisoner compound nearby.

"They're assaulting hell out of them, sir," Booth said. There was rage in his voice and tears in his eyes. He said he had seen our people forcing the detainees into what he called the dead-cockroach position, spread-eagled flat on their backs. Other detainees were being questioned while being forced to maintain "leaning rest," the push-up position, he said. "Then when they don't get the answers they want, they just grab them up by their hair and beat hell out of them," Booth reported.

"Was it still going on when you left?"

"Yes, sir, it was. That's why you better get up there before somebody gets killed."

There was no one in the yard when I arrived, so I identified myself to the guard at the gate and asked him to call the officer in charge. I remained at the gate while he disappeared inside. In a moment, he returned with an MP sergeant. I told him about Booth's report. "Well, sir, I believe the interrogators were maybe a little too exuberant today," he said, smiling a bit. "Military Intelligence has been putting on a lot of pressure lately." I said nothing, waiting for him to continue. "Besides, sir," he said, "it's all over and there'll be no more of it."

"You're damned right there won't, Sergeant," I said, and informed him that I would be submitting a report on the incident to

Brigade. I told him he would probably hear from me again and I reminded him of his rights under Article 31 of the Uniform Code of Military Justice: he could remain silent if he chose to remain silent; he could make a statement if he chose to do so and anything he said could be used in court; and he was entitled to counsel if he wished. "By whose orders did this so-called interrogation take place?" I asked. He chose not to answer. I headed back to my office, where Booth wrote his statement and swore to its authenticity. Abbott called Bethea, the new executive officer, and I told him what had happened. He heard the whole story and asked me to hold on for a moment. When he returned to the phone he told me to come to English on the first available aircraft with Booth's statement and as many facts as were already in my possession.

"Yes, sir, I understand," I replied.

He was waiting for me when I arrived at English, the first time he had ever met the aircraft. We rode in silence to his office. Outside his building we discussed the incident again and he asked for Booth's statement. I stood by while he read it. When he had finished, he folded it and said he would see what General Barnes had to say. "You wait here," he said and disappeared into the General's trailer. I started running the mechanics of the investigation over in my mind while he was gone. When he returned he no longer had Booth's statement. "I'll take care of this matter," he said. Apparently he noticed the look of surprise on my face. "The General wants me to handle it personally, Herbert. It's out of your hands."

"Well, sir, that's okay with me except that an IG complaint has been made," I said. "It's a matter of record and regulations require that a report to higher headquarters be made."

He seemed not to listen or hear. He knew his regulations and his directives, he said, which was why, he added smilingly, he was an executive officer while I was an IG. He made it sound like a dirty word. I flew back to An Khe. Booth filed the carbon of his statement. We'll see, I remember thinking. We'll see whether he knows his regs.

Later that evening, Walt Werner stopped by the IG shop and while he was there I received an anonymous call from a soldier. He knew his rights, the caller said. He had the privilege as an American trooper to register a formal complaint anonymously. I recognized the voice and began taking notes. The subject of the call was Major Crouch, the Adjutant General. The major, the caller said, was taking an "illegal leave," a second R and R to Hawaii. It was illegal, he explained, because Crouch was not eligible for R and R. It was also illegal because he was taking free leave time for which he was not authorized and was taking a free commercial flight at the government's expense—for which he was not authorized either. "And besides," the voice on the phone added, "he's taking up an R and R slot for the month which should be going to some grunt." I could check out his story at Special Services, he suggested. All I needed to do to verify that Major Crouch already had taken his authorized R and R was to look on a certain page in the records.

"And, sir, if you'll look under the door of your hooch, you'll find a copy of his new orders authorizing him for a second R and R," he said and then hung up. Had I not recognized the voice, I might have written the matter off as a crank call. But there was no doubt in my mind about who the man on the other end of the line had been. It was Administration's First Sergeant, "Machine Gun" Bryant, and if anything had happened in Administration, he would know about it. Werner and I talked it over briefly and then I wrote up the call in complaint form.

"I'll stop by Special Services and check it out," I told Walt. "If there's any substance to it, I'll brief you in the morning." Back at my hooch, the copies were there, precisely where the voice on the phone had said they would be—and at Special Services, I found precisely what he had said I would find. Page by page, it was all there. The Sergeant on duty made a duplicate set of the records for me and I walked back to my chalet and went to bed. The next morning, I turned the whole matter over to Walt. He grimaced. I said, "What the hell do you want me to do, Walt? Stick around and do this investigation and miss my R and R? Hell's bells, man, I've got a date with two beautiful girls at Waikiki—and you, my friend, are going to handle this one." He frowned again before I realized he was kidding me. Although he didn't say it, I suspected Werner was glad to get the job. "I have only one suggestion, Walt," I told him. "Contact Crouch immediately and if this whole thing is illegal, he'll think twice before he actually leaves. If it's not illegal, then just wish him a bon voyage for both of us."

"Will do," Walt said. "Now get the hell out of here."

It was the last I heard about the Crouch case until I came back from R and R.

I finished what I thought was the last of my duties as IG in Tuy Hoa. It was a miserable day—rain, fog, and a ceiling no higher than your ankles—but Michael S. Allison, one of the gutsiest and most skilled pilots I'd ever seen, got me down to Tan Son Nhut airport and I grabbed the first flight for Hawaii, getting an empty standby seat and leaving a couple of days early. As the jet lifted off the runway, the mist closed in behind it, concealing the airstrip, the base, the country, and the war. The plane leveled off above the cloud layers and I was in another world. The sky was a bright blue and the afternoon sun sparkled on the wings. I settled back in the seat and relaxed. Eventually, I went to sleep. An hour or so later, the stewardess awakened me with a gentle tap on the shoulder and announced it was time for dinner, and as I rubbed my eyes and looked around, I spied a sergeant just ahead of me who bore a striking resemblance to a kid I'd met not long before I left. "Excuse me," I said, reaching up to touch his arm. He turned full-face and I realized I'd made a mistake. "I'm sorry, Sergeant, I thought you were someone else." Jesus, he looked exactly like him from the side-rear, I thought—and I ran it all through my mind.

Bittorie had told me about a sergeant in the 2nd Battalion who was rumored to be in line for the Congressional Medal of Honor. That was great, because heroes were getting scarce in Vietnam. It would be great for the sergeant and it would be good for the Army. It seems that he had fallen on a live grenade, the story went, and had thereby saved the lives of several of his comrades. As Bittorie rambled on, it occurred to me that Vietnam was producing a hell of a lot of this falling-on-a-grenade type of heroism. In fact, there seemed to be more of it in Vietnam than in all the rest of our wars combined. I had seen Jimmie Cagney do it once in a movie, and John Wayne and Richard Widmark had pulled it off a couple of times, but it made little sense to me either in the theater or in the realities of the battlefield. I always came back to the question of why the man didn't just pick it up and fling it away, as infantrymen are taught. That kind of response takes less time and no one dies. In fact, it's pretty difficult to die from a grenade at all. A man has to be damn near on top of one to get killed. Still, Vietnam was spawning dozens of such acts of bravery—and for me at least, it was a curious phenomenon.

Bittorie said the sergeant's company had been on a night maneuver and was just bedding down to wait until first light. There had been no firing and no casualties on either side. Then came one grenade and the sergeant fell on it in the dark. He shouted and the rest of them gathered around. No one else had seen it come in. The sergeant drew it out from beneath his body and hurled it out into the darkness. It exploded in a paddy.

"Just in time, right, John?" I said. "A bit luckier than Malinowski, right?"

We had both known Roy Malinowski in Korea when the grenade went off in his hand and cost him his arm, an eye, and a lot of other vital parts.

"Maybe if Roy had yelled at us, we could all have gathered around to witness it and he might have had the CMH, too, huh, John?" I said to Bittorie.

"Come on, sir," he said. "It was legitimate. There were witnesses."

"Then what kept it from going off until he threw it, while he was shouting and everyone else was witnessing?" Once the pin on a grenade is pulled and the handle is released, there is a maximum of seven seconds before it goes off. The primer has been struck and there's no stopping it halfway by falling on it or by doing anything else. The powdertrain continues to burn. "You're getting old, John," I said.

"Maybe the sergeant won't get it."

"Get what?"

"The CMH," Bittorie said.

"Oh, he'll get it all right, John," I said, reaching out to touch his chest with my finger, "for the good of the Brigade, if nothing else." I shrugged. "Besides, John, don't pay any attention to me. I'm getting a little older myself—and much too cynical." Maybe I was, and maybe it was because Vietnam was such an easy war compared to the others, with so really few of us killed, considering the number of us there. It had been our war for nearly a decade and we had over a half million men in the country. With our rotation, almost as many had already served in our Army there as had served in World War II. It had cost us up to that point about 37,000 dead, compared to 290,000 in World War II. There was really no comparison with

Korea. There we had lost about 33,000 for three years' fighting. In 1968, our most costly year in Vietnam, we lost 14,592 out of a total of 536,100 men. That meant that the odds that a man would be killed there during that year were something like thirty-seven to one. But overall odds, from the beginning of our involvement until the middle of 1969, were much better, about sixty to one. Vietnam, folks, was a damned safe, comfortable war, all things considered. As a result, when one of ours got it in Vietnam, it was much more personal than in other wars. The survivors had more time to feel the loss because of the longer time between casualties, and death was a personal tragedy. Perhaps because of these pressures, there was an abundance of post-humous medals—as though something had to be done. Maybe it was the least we could do. Maybe, damn it, I *was* getting old and cynical. The sergeant that Bittorie had mentioned really looked like a hero and a fighter.

I first met him when Bittorie introduced us at the LZ English airstrip. I asked him if he had chopped the guy who had thrown the grenade.

"Well, no sir, it was dark," he said.

"But you saw the grenade."

"It fell right beside me."

"Lucky for your guys it was you instead of me," I said. "I would have shouted, 'Grenade!' and hit the dirt away from it."

"I never considered it," he said, and I noticed that the sergeant was getting angry. I put out my hand to him.

"Well, good luck, Sergeant," I said. "And next time, try to at least consider it." We shook hands and parted. Falling on a grenade is a very brave or a very foolish act, I thought. The sergeant did not appear to be a foolish man.

Later we met again at the NCO Motel in An Khe. Bittorie had invited me over for a beer with him, Abbott, Booth, Childers, and a Sergeant Wilbanks, and when I arrived, the sergeant who had fallen on the grenade was there, too. He had come back to An Khe to check his records, he said, but I had been bumping into him frequently around the rear areas. He was sleeping in the replacement center, he said, and just that morning he said he had been forced out of the sack very early along with the recruits by some "buck sergeant." If it happened again the next day, he vowed, he would clean the sergeant's clock.

"So do it," I said.

"You really mean that?" he said, glancing at me over the table. He was trying to look his toughest.

"Yeah, Sergeant, I really mean it," I told the hero. "Kick his ass good. You outrank him."

"And you'll take the responsibility? I have your permission?"

I ordered another beer. "Sergeant, you have my permission," I said. I turned to Wilbanks, the first sergeant over at the Replacement Center. "Will, if he kicks your buck sergeant's ass tomorrow, it's my fault." I looked back at the hero. "And vice-versa." I raised both eyebrows. It was his turn. He didn't say anything. "Okay? Need anything else?" I turned to Bittorie and Childers. "You're witnesses. If anyone tries to get this here sergeant out of his bed tomorrow, he has my permission to kick his ass, but good. Everyone understand?" I watched Childers. "And that applies to you, too."

Childers smiled. We had known each other for a long time and he was one of the three greatest soldiers I had ever known.

"Okay, sir," Childers answered. "If you say so." He laughed. Maybe he had the hero pegged, too. I was convinced the guy was a candy-ass, a pussy. I was utterly persuaded that he had never fallen on any grenade. I glanced over at Bittorie and he seemed to know, too. The sergeant had faked it—not that anybody really gave a damn, because medals were only in the official record at the Department of Army, and that meant very little. Bittorie had put it best. "There are two reputations," he had said once. "There's the one in the Department of Army files for the paper readers and there's the one that goes from mouth to mouth around the barrooms, and it's the barroom rep that counts." The sergeant might very well get a CMH, but in the barrooms he'd get his ass whipped. It was too bad, I thought, too bad, because he was about to be one of my men.

Honolulu lay dark and sleeping when we landed, but the airport was aglow with wives and children and sweethearts there to greet their men. Almost all of the women cried and some of the soldiers did too. I watched them and it felt good to see pure happiness. I was a couple of days early so Marygrace and Toni were surprised when the phone at the Ala Moana Hotel awakened them at 4 a.m. and I was on the other end of the line. They were Army women, and they were as accustomed as anyone can ever be to the separations and the reunions that are part and parcel of military life, but they cried, too, when I met them an hour later in front of their hotel. They were beautiful. Toni seemed a foot taller than when I had left but Marygrace was the same: quiet, steady, strong, and soft.

We checked them out of their hotel and moved to another down by the sea, and then went out to rent a car. After breakfast, we bought some Hawaiian clothes—strictly tourists all the way—and set out on a tour of Oahu. In the afternoon we found a hill, a high one, looking out over the Pacific, and we sat there in the deep grass laughing and talking and touching each other until long after that first day's sun went down. It was joy, pure joy: the three of us together again with no one else around—with nothing but the hill and the sky and the sun and sea.

We saw everything there was to see on the island—all the tourist attractions and as much of everything else as possible. We took the standard pictures and spent a lot of our time on the water in a catamaran or on surf boards or in outriggers. One afternoon, while we were lolling on the beach, Marygrace asked about Vietnam.

"A royal screw-up," I said.

"You're anti-war, Tony Herbert?"

"No, that's not what I mean. I mean I'm just disgusted by what I've seen happening to the Army," I said. She looked puzzled. I had already told her about getting a battalion command, and although she knew it meant that I would be more vulnerable to injury or death than I was as an IG, she took it as she'd always taken my career. She was proud, she said. But now she looked bewildered as I talked about some of the things I had seen. "This war is not only killing our people, it's ruining our Army. The whole damned show is run without leaders —and we're losing, really losing." We talked the rest of the afternoon and finally she asked about what would happen when my Vietnam tour was finished. "Wait'll you hear this," I said, grinning.

"You're going to quit," she said, throwing some sand my way. "Right, Colonel Herbert?"

"Wrong, Mrs. Herbert. I've got orders for the Command and General Staff School at Leavenworth."

"Oh, Tony, that's great."

"And after that, I'm going to try to finish the doctorate," I said. "Maybe then, I can really contribute something to the Army."

"More than you have already?"

"Well, I just mean that from what I've seen in Vietnam, the Army could stand to have some leaders and maybe I can teach leadership."

"Teach it?"

"That's right, teach it," I said. I knew it could be taught, and I believed I knew what leadership was better than anyone I knew in or out of the military. Why me? Because, for the most part, those who had tried it before were generally disadvantaged in one way or another. If they were trained psychologists, they had to guess about the other part—combat. If they were combat veterans, they were usually not trained psychologists. I had both combat and training, and with a doctorate in psychology I believed I could damned well contribute. I had taken men who had been discarded by other commanders and achieved some fine results with them. It was leadership, and I knew it could be taught. It had bedeviled me since I'd come to Vietnam and seen the caliber of our leadership there. I knew why it was lousy and I knew how it could be corrected, and I also knew that the only way to make any inroads was to have the kind of credentials—the doctorate—that would get the attention of the men at the senior echelons of the military. The alternative, I knew, was to spend the rest of my career spinning my wheels like everyone else—and when it was over, the Army would be the same or worse than what I had seen in Vietnam.

"That would be a waste," Marygrace agreed.

"There's already been a lot of waste," I said. We talked about friends who had died who might not have died if the Army had been different. Again that day until the sun went down we sat and talked, the three of us, about love and religion and the Army and how we just were not going to let it all go down the drain.

It was growing dark when I asked Toni, half jokingly, if she had decided what she would be when she grew up.

"An Army wife," she said.

"But what if you fall in love with a civilian?" Marygrace asked.

"Well, then, he'll just have to join up," she answered.

I think she meant it, and neither my wife nor I laughed. We had talked about it before and we agreed that for better or worse we all loved the Army. We wanted nothing else.

"Is that okay, Dad?" Toni asked.

"I wouldn't have it any other way, baby," I said. "Except, except—"

"Except what, Dad?"

"Except I'd like for you to get at least a bird colonel if possible."

We all laughed, gathered up our paraphernalia from the beach, and went back to the hotel.

One afternoon the three of us ran into the mortician from our home town back in Pennsylvania. It was, by God, a small world, and I was so glad to see him I almost hugged him. I didn't, though. Not dignified for Army colonels to go around embracing undertakers. We spent the afternoon talking with him and his wife about Herminie and how things were back there and what had changed and what hadn't and who was still there and who was gone. That night before we went to sleep, Toni asked from her bed if he had been my father's undertaker.

"Yes, baby, he was," I said. "Now go to sleep, we have another big day tomorrow."

"He really was?"

"Yes, baby, why?"

"I just wondered," she said, turning her face to the wall and sighing.

I kissed Marygrace and lay back in the bed, staring out at the ocean through the glass doors at the end of the room. Not only had he handled the arrangements for my father's funeral, but for my mother's and sister's as well.

I thought about all of them that night and about the years that had passed and the things that had happened to all of us.

Now it was 1968 and I was thirty-eight years old. I had a wife and a daughter and I had killed one hell of a lot of people and watched a lot more suffer and cry and die, and now Ma was gone, too, and Pa, and my sister, Irene.

You are what you are, you dumb-assed Lithuanian, I thought that night as the moon illuminated the far end of the room. You are what you are, what you always wanted to be: a soldier.

Then it was over. Five days and nights with Marygrace and Toni had raced by like seconds. We spent our last evening at the Cannon Club up on Diamond Head, out on the open terrace, dancing beneath the stars, while Toni sat at our table beaming in the flickering candlelight. At the airport the next morning, it was hard to part, even though we'd done it before, many times. I held them both in my arms until the last minute, waved from the gate, and then didn't look back again. As the jet lifted off, I could still hear Marygrace saying she was proud of me. For what? "For everything," she said. "I'm just proud of you for being you."

I returned to the Brigade on January 26, 1969, and Bethea immediately summoned me to his office.

"I want to talk to you about Crouch," he said.

"What about Crouch?"

"What the hell are you accusing him of, anyway?"

"I'm not accusing him of anything," I said. "If you're talking about his R and R, then I suggest that you talk to Walter Werner. It was his investigation."

"Why the hell did you order an investigation in the first place without consulting me?"

"It was a legitimate complaint," I said. "It wasn't up to you to decide whether or not to investigate. Army regs are pretty plain about that. You want me to get you a copy?"

"I don't need a copy, Herbert," Bethea said. "This matter of Crouch isn't over yet because I've got a captain down from An Khe and he is prepared to make a statement."

"Well, then, Colonel, I suggest you get Werner down, too, so he can take the captain's statement." My God, it was starting all over again. I hadn't been back one day from R and R, from those good days with Marygrace and Toni, and it was starting up all over again. "You'll need Werner to take any statements because he handled the Crouch investigation."

"That's not good enough," Bethea said. "The General wants you to take it and me to sit in as a witness."

"Like hell, you'll be a witness," I exploded. "IG statements are taken in confidence, and if I'm going to take this one it will be taken in confidence or else you can do it yourself." That raised the hair on

184

his neck. He began accusing me of having a vendetta going against Crouch. "Listen, Bethea," I interrupted. "I'm getting a little sick and tired of your shit. I have to take scrap like that off Franklin and the General, but from you? Not on your life." I tapped him on the chest with my index finger. "Go slow, Bethea," I watched him inhale and turn crimson.

"Wait here," he finally blurted, sweeping past me and around the corner toward the General's trailer. I don't know if he saw the General or not but when he returned he said he had and that he would take the statement from the captain in my presence. "After dinging," he said. "Make sure you're here."

"I wouldn't miss it," I said.

When I came back later and listened to the captain's statement, I knew what Bethea had meant when he said he had a man who was "prepared" to make one. The man's statement cleared Crouch of any wrongdoing or any wrong intentions, completely and entirely. It had all been a big misunderstanding, the captain said. He had misunderstood Crouch. The major had really asked for an official leave and the captain had misunderstood and typed out R and R papers by mistake. "As soon as Major Crouch found out about it, he came down and corrected it," the captain said.

"Any questions?" Bethea said, turning to me with a smile.

"Well, since you asked—" I turned to the captain. "Are you telling us that you signed Crouch's name to the request and he didn't?"

He looked at Bethea before he answered. "Well, yes, he wasn't there and I didn't think it was all that important, so I just called him and asked for permission."

"Then it was just one big error on your part?" I asked.

"That's what he said," Bethea chimed in.

I ignored him. "Is that what you said, Captain?"

"Yes, sir, it is."

"Well, then, there's no sweat," I said, standing up. "I'll just get it all typed out tonight and you can sign it in the morning and that will be the end of it." I glanced at Bethea. "Okay?" His face was blank. "See you at breakfast, Captain. Goodnight."

I knew what I thought about the whole affair, but it didn't really matter because my job was to get it typed up and ready for swearing in the morning. I was satisfied. We had prevented a wrong-doing, even if it was unintentional, and that was a major part of the game.

185

I spent the rest of the night pecking at the typewriter and was ready before breakfast. I contacted Paul Ray and asked him to make arrangements for the swearing.

"Do you know the story on this captain?" Ray asked.

"Nope, but I got a feeling you're going to tell me."

"You're damned right I am," he said, pulling a file from his drawers. The captain had taken an Article 15 and had been fined by General Allen. The charge, in simple language, had been lying. The captain had been caught walking down a road one morning very near one of the airbases and was stopped by no less a personage than the commanding general himself, who wanted to know just where in the hell an officer could be coming from at such an hour. The captain said he'd been to a party and was just getting in. Whose party, the General asked. One of the pilots, the captain answered. The General exploded. Pilots, you see, just did not party after midnight on his base. An investigation commenced immediately and the conclusion was the captain was a liar. The Air Force general turned it over to Allen and the result was the Article 15 and a pretty substantial fine.

"Then you think he's lying?" I asked Ray. He smiled.

When we set up the oath, I asked Ray to read the captain the article on perjury as well as the Article 31 before he was asked to sign the statement he had given the night before. Ray did both and the captain then refused to sign the statement. Ray had him sign on the back of the statement that he had, in accordance with his rights under the 5th Amendment and Article 31 of the Uniform Code of Military Justice, refused to put his signature on the statement.

The next step was to see Bethea. Ray explained the captain's refusal to sign. Bethea turned to me and accused me of trying to intimidate the captain.

"Bethea," I said. "You are a complete ass."

"Yeah, well, Herbert, you just remember who writes your efficiency report," he mumbled—and I knew then that I had him by the short hairs. That was always their last threat.

"Get off it, man," I said. "So you write it and Franklin endorses it. So what? You know what it means. It means nothing. It means crap, that's what. I've been in over twenty years. That's 240 months and every goddamned one of my efficiency reports is excellent and a whole hell of a lot of them are maximums, which means that your piddling little one-monther may count as one two-hundred-and-fortieth of the total. So, little man, go right ahead and give me the zero."

I knew he wasn't about to do that because he had no grounds for anything other than an "outstanding"—and he knew it, too. Ray and I went over to the mess for a cup of coffee and a laugh. "When you get to be Chief of Staff, sir, how about getting me for Staff Judge Advocate?"

I looked at him over the rim of the cup. "If ever I make it, Paul, I'll be sure to give that serious consideration."

But despite our laughter, it wasn't over yet. That evening, Bethea had Walt Werner and Crouch come to English for a meeting in the General's mess. Werner sat on my right, and Crouch sat across from me with Bethea on his left, directly facing Walt. Bethea went into the whole affair again and then began his old accusations about "the way Herbert has been trying to get Major Crouch." Once again, I explained that I did not have anything to do with the investigation and cared very little about its outcome.

"Walt here did it all by his lonesome," I said, "except for yours and the captain's little contribution." Crouch sat back in feigned shock.

"Sir," he said, looking at Bethea. "I am appalled at Colonel Herbert's methods and his hatred." Crouch went on to say that he knew that I had actually threatened physical violence in several instances in order to get statements. Walt grinned at me, but waited until Crouch was finished. I spoke first.

"What you ought to do then, Major, since you have this information, is file an IG complaint or any other kind of complaint that you see fit to file," I said. Then, leaning across the table toward him, I let him have it full. "Crouch, I think you're a rat's ass, but I have neither the time nor the reason to bother to prove it—yet. So don't get wild with your mouth." I turned to Bethea. "I didn't do the investigation, he did." I pointed to Werner and then looked back to Crouch. "If you have a bitch, address it to Walt, not me."

Bethea finally spoke, breaking a long silence. "Major Werner?" he said, very formally.

Walt was no candy-ass. He looked at both of the men across the table before he spoke. He was the kind of a man who spoke for himself and said what he wanted to say regardless of the consequences. He turned to Bethea. "I don't believe that this is either the time or place for the discussion we're having, but if you're ready, I'm ready to present it to the General." I could have kissed Walt, but Bethea turned the same color as he had when we had discussed my efficiency report. The three of them—Walt, Bethea, and Crouch—left the table and headed for the General's trailer. I stayed behind until Walt came back and reported on their visit with the head man. "Whew," he said. "You talk about cold days in January."

"What do you mean?"

"I mean I just don't think the old man liked too well what I had to report."

"Which was?"

"That although Crouch hadn't actually taken a second R and R, it looked an awful lot like he had tried."

"What did Barnes say?"

"Nothing, nothing. Absolutely nothing," Walt said, pouring a cup of coffee. "But it got to him, I could tell. Hell, it had to get to him. Crouch is the Adjutant General. He had signed the orders. I just laid it on like it was."

"And the General didn't say anything?"

"Right, nothing. He just said he'd take care of it and let me go. He did say that Crouch would not be our new S1."

"Thank God," I said.

Walt went back the next morning to An Khe and Paul Ray asked me to come over to his office to take a look at an investigation in progress in the 2d Battalion—the unit I was about to take over.

"Take a look at this and please read it all before you comment," Ray said, handing me a file folder. The investigation had been handled by Major Henry Boyer, the executive officer of the 2d Battalion.

I flipped the cover sheet and turned to the first page. A three-inch by five-inch color photograph stared out at me. It was a picture of a Vietnamese male lying on his back in what appeared to be a shell crater. His face had been blown away. In gilt beneath the picture was engraved: "Peace on Earth from the Peace Makers. C Company. 173d Airborne Brigade"—or something to that effect. I glanced at Ray.

"C Company of the 2d Battalion," he said.

I turned the page and read it through.

"Well?" he said.

I put it down on his desk. "It's a cover-up?"

"You're damned right it's a cover-up, and little old Paul here is not going to be caught in the middle. You know what Franklin wants?" he asked, and without waiting for an answer he continued, "Franklin wants it swept under the rug. There are exactly fifty cards out like that and he wants them gathered and covered."

"And what if that's not possible?"

"Well, then I guess we'll just put the burden on Christ," he said, referring to Captain Christ, the commanding officer of C Company.

A directive from Military Advisory Command-Vietnam (MAC-V) required that such things be reported. I looked at Ray. "Are you going to report it?"

He threw back his head and rolled his eyes. "Are you kidding? With Franklin himself handling it?" He picked up the so-called report and placed it back in his files. "Not on your ever-loving life." He slammed the drawer shut and turned the key. "But I sure don't intend to get caught short either."

I had a beer that evening with Ernie Webb. We were sitting in that $10,000 barrel furniture at the officers' club. "Well, old man, how's the famous Jungle School?" I joshed. "You guys training them as well as they trained that lieutenant who radioed his men to open fire on him?"

"Not a hell of a lot better," he said glumly. It was not the answer I'd expected. The talk around the area was that Ernie had transformed the Jungle School into a worthwhile enterprise.

"Tough going?" I asked. He said he'd had a better job offer and he was thinking of becoming a General's aide up at First Field Force Victor. I damn near spilled my beer.

"You're kidding," I said.

"No, I'm not," he answered. "I'm not cut out to be a schoolmaster. I came over here to fight."

"No shit," I said.

He ignored it.

"The last time I was here I was an advisor. This time I expected to at least have a chance with a U.S. unit."

"And so?"

"And so I'm leaving." He tilted his glass.

"Why? Too tough? Or maybe you just can't wait like the rest of us?"

"Tough? In this Brigade?"

"So then stay around and help correct it," I said, raising my voice. "But if it's too tough, candy-ass, then take off your wings and move out, and when you're a granddaddy and all the little kiddies sit around and talk about their granddaddy Rangers and paratroopers, yours can say their granddaddy was a general's aide." He tried to interrupt me but I wouldn't allow it. "No, no, just go on, man. Be a general's aide. It's great for the career." I lifted my own glass and gave him his chance.

"You mean like being an IG?"

"Touché, Ernie, touché," I said, lifting a toast in his direction. "But I'm not quitting." I don't think I ever met a bona fide trooper who could stand that word—and if ever there was a trooper it was Ernie Webb. I ignored him for a moment until he slammed down his glass and stood up.

"I'd better leave now," he said. "I don't think we have much else to talk about."

I looked up. "That's right, aide, you run along." He walked toward the door. "And don't forget to write home to the wife and kiddies about your big decision," I shouted to him. "They'll really be proud." He slammed the door and I sat there in the $10,000 barrel furniture and felt like crying for the whole damned Brigade and the whole damned Army. We needed all the Ernie Webbs we could get. He was one of the best, just as Master Sergeant Childers had said. He had built a lousy, half-assed, slough-off school into a valuable training device, and he had integrity, guts, and sense. Every last sergeant whose opinion I cared about said the same about Ernie Webb. He was the best.

"But not if he quits," I mumbled in my beer. "If he quits, they're wrong."

The next day I was called to English for my last official investigation as the Brigade IG. There had been a payroll robbery in the medical company. Ten thousand American dollars had disappeared right out of the safe and Bethea had recommended to Barnes that I handle it. I explained to Bethea that regulations specifically recommended that IG personnel not be involved in such investigations. That didn't seem to matter, and I did the investigation. It really wasn't that difficult. The lieutenant in charge of the funds had placed them in a safe. The combination lock had been broken previously, which left only the padlock for security. The lieutenant had failed to post a guard before leaving for the evening's entertainment. He was responsible and accountable for the entire amount. I took it back to Bethea.

"But let me tell you something before you turn it in," I said.

"Huh?"

"If this investigation is turned in with my signature, then the IG files must be opened to any defense counsel who wants to examine them—and that," I smiled at him, "means all of the IG files."

"What the hell are you talking about?"

"Just what I said. Here, read it for yourself," I said, pointing out Army Regulation 20–1. I stood by while he read it once and then again and then handed it back.

"You're misinterpreting it," Bethea said.

"Am I?" I pointed to the phone. "Then why don't you just ding-a-ling First Field Force Victor and get a clearer reading on it?"

He picked up the phone and called and when he was through, he turned to me quite calmly and took the entire report on the robbery out of my hands. "No sweat," he said. "I'll just get them retyped and sign them myself."

"But you didn't do the investigation," I protested.

"So what?"

When I left, he was already halfway through the process of signing statements he had neither taken nor witnessed.

Two nights before I was to take over the 2d Battalion, Franklin had me down for what he called a "commander-to-commander chat." Of course, neither of us was a commander; I wouldn't be for two more days and he wasn't about to be at all as long as Barnes was around. In his eyes, I suppose, it was just a matter of terminology because, as I was beginning to realize, Barnes was the commander-in-name of the 173d and Franklin was its commander-in-fact. Barnes had his elaborate mess and his bar and his staff, but Franklin seemed to be running the Brigade.

I wondered why we all put up with the system. Barnes was

supposed to be the commander but Franklin wrote the efficiency reports, and there I was on February 4, 1969, listening to my "boss," Lieutenant Colonel Joseph Ross Franklin. It had been over six weeks since the holidays, but those Christmas cards from C Company in my new battalion were still not completely accounted for, he said. "So if you come across any, I want you to bring them to me in person," Franklin said. "Every last one, Herbert. Understand?"

"What about the MAC-V directive 20–4 we all initialed?"

He leaned back in his chair and half closed his eyes, shaking his head. "Herbert, Herbert, Herbert," he said. "You'll always be an IG." He opened his eyes and leaned forward on his desk. "Forget it. You're a commander. We commanders clean our own linen. Until you get the feel, cooperate, man, just cooperate." He chuckled and then fell silent. He was still smiling except for his eyes. I tried to speak as softly as possible.

"Sure, sir," I said. "I'll forget it just as soon as I get back my copy of the MAC-V directive that I initialed."

The games were over. He stood up, turned sideways, cocked his head and spoke in a steel-cold voice. "Listen, Commander," he spit out the word, "I don't have all damned night to sit around and chit-chat, so I'll get to the point." He leaned toward me. "I'm not asking, I'm giving you an order to bring those cards to me in person. Understand?"

"I understand, sir."

"Good," he said and dropped back into his chair. "We'll get along."

Sure we will, I thought, just as long as I don't come across any of those cards. It wasn't likely that I would. Hell, it was already February and the cards had been printed early in December. Grunts don't make a habit of hanging onto junk. They had either mailed them or got rid of them. I could afford to be agreeable. "I know we will, sir," I said.

He relaxed, "Good, good." He was smiling again. "Because I have a couple of other small favors I'd like to discuss—some commander-to-commander advice, so to speak." Man, how he loved that crap. "I want you to can Grimshaw as soon as feasible," he said.

This was no Christmas card in February. Grimshaw was a captain and in two days I would be his commanding officer.

"I can't just walk in and start firing people," I said, but he seemed not to hear me. I had no intention of firing Jim Grimshaw. He had only recently been transferred from the Brigade Headquarters Supply Section to the 2d Battalion and he was every inch the fighter we needed in Vietnam. He was Ranger, Airborne, and Special Forces, and he was a young man with a fine sense of humor and a happy grasp of the ridiculous. What he wanted most was to get out in the field and tangle. Franklin called him flamboyant, but he had the same qualities that were described as "dash" in General Patton. I called it individuality, but the words weren't important because I thought I knew what Grimshaw was all about. Give him a mission and some lee-way for his own ingenuity and he would pull it off better than you hoped. That was all any commander could ask. Grimshaw was pre-cisely the kind of man for the independent Ranger-type operations I intended to organize in the battalion. They were the standard Brigade operations that would damned sure make the 2d change its ways, and Grimshaw could contribute one hell of a lot to those changes. I had been the one who had gone to Allen and pushed hard for his transfer out of Supply and into the field because I knew that he was being wasted in his rear-area job. I wondered then, as Franklin was bad-mouthing Grimshaw that night, if he knew that I had endorsed Grim-shaw for the job. At the time I had believed I was doing Grimshaw and Colonel Nicholson, the 2d Battalion's commander, a favor.

"Grimshaw's a real wise-ass," Franklin was saying. "He's im-mature and Nicholson doesn't have any use for him and, as a matter of fact, neither do I."

That was true enough. Nicholson, the man I was succeeding as commander of the 2d, had already talked about the battalion with me and had described the plans he had made and "just had not had time or opportunity to implement." So now he wanted to do it on my time. In a pig's ass, he would—but I did listen to him and found that he seemed to know less about his battalion as its commander than I did as the brigade IG. I had inspected it thoroughly, from top to bottom, and then had sent Coutre down to do it again so that he could pick up anything I had missed. I had spent more nights out in the grass with 2d Battalion troops than Nicholson had. General Allen had let it be known that he considered Nicholson to be his best combat com-mander. I had another choice, Lieutenant Colonel H. H. Burke in the

3d Battalion, but I had to admit that Nicholson looked, walked and talked like a leader. He had everything except the one trait which I considered most essential: the ability or the guts to lead by example. I think you've got to be there—not 1,500 feet up in a chopper on the radio—and I think you've got to produce. All the rest is eyewash. Ask any grunt. Nicholson's troops called him "Stage-Door Johnny." They had tried to get him at least twice—once with a Claymore in the door of the Battalion's Tactical Operations Center and another time with a grenade under a sandbag. His court-martial rate was high, as were his levels of malaria, AWOLs, desertions, and Article 15s. The achievement rate was low, while the battalion was suffering some of the heaviest casualties in the Brigade—and all of this with some of the best troops any commander could have assigned to him. Still and all, I liked him. I was on better terms with Nicholson than I was with any other battalion commander.

Not only did Nicholson dislike Jim Grimshaw, he also had an equally negative attitude toward another of his officers, a lieutenant named Shotwell. Like Grimshaw, Shotwell had come to the battalion from Brigade Headquarters. He had worked for Jay Stanton, the Brigade Headquarters Commandant. "I'm the General's flunky," Jay liked to say, which was probably true. It was the same type of job that Patton had parlayed into a program of self-aggrandizement in the Mexican Campaign and World War I under Pershing. The difference, I suppose, was that Jay Stanton was no Patton and General Barnes was no General Pershing. Jay did his job well, if reluctantly, and I liked him because he was a fair man and deeply involved with his men. We had many a friendly argument. Frequently Lieutenant Shotwell would join us and we three would sit in Jay's air-conditioned, bug-proof, out-of-the-mud, wood-frame office smoking cigars, eating candy bars, and drinking coffee or soft drinks. Jay and I would listen to Shotwell bleed his heart out about the way he was being shoved out of the war and about his own suggestions for improving the quality of the Brigade. Jay and I loved to shoot him down—not just for the hell of it, though I suppose we "commanders" do have to keep in practice—but because we both realized that good officers have to learn to defend their ideas. Logic was not enough—not in Vietnam, anyway. You not only had to be able to sell your ideas but you had to be able to defend them against all rebuttals. So every time Jay and Shotwell and I got together, Jay and I usually wound up chewing the lieutenant out for his views. "If you feel so damned strong about this war, why the hell are you sitting in a headquarters behind a desk?" we would ask. We both knew the answer. He was like Jay, like me, and like Grimshaw. We were all brothers with the same disease. We were shut off from what we wanted most as soldiers: to fight. One day, Shotwell finally made it out to the 2d Battalion. He left his desk behind him and finally got the war he thought he wanted—and now Nicholson wanted him and Grimshaw booted out.

Moreover, Nicholson wanted to install replacements of his own choosing. I balked. He could take his lameducks and shove them as far as I was concerned. I would listen to his suggestions and his recommendations, but I wasn't about to stand still for any actual appointments. For Christ's sake, he was suggesting that he, Nicholson, pick the guys who would command for me. Not hardly. Anyone who was already in the battalion would stay in until his tour was over, but brand new appointments that I would be stuck with for my entire tour were horses of a different smell. I told Nicholson we would go to General Barnes if necessary on that matter. "I know what I'm talking about, Nick," I told him. "It would be bad business. It's my position now and I have to do it my way."

"Well, what about making some changes after you're in?" Nicholson had asked.

"Maybe."

"Good enough," he said. "I have one last suggestion. We have a young lieutenant named Potter. Larry Potter the Third. He's got to have his ears pinned back." Potter was the leader of the medical platoon and was slightly involved, Nicholson said, in the civil affairs program. I had never heard of him before. "He's a spoiled brat," Nicholson continued. "His old man's a retired general who used to be the Surgeon General, which is maybe why it's too rough for him. He wants out. Wants to go to Qui Nhon."

That seemed like a sensible transfer for a medical man. Qui Nhon had the only really good hospital in the area, but Nicholson was determined to keep him around and, as he said, teach him a lesson. "The bastard stays right here," he said. "He'll sweat it out like everybody else." I made up my mind there and then, listening to Nicholson, that if Potter wanted out, out he would go. "This Potter kid is an

195

immature brat," Nicholson had concluded, and that was what Franklin was saying that night as well.

"He can't cut the mustard and he wants out," he said. "Probably heard about you and doesn't want to serve under you."

"I understand, sir," I said—and I did understand very well. I had made it a rule to allow guys who didn't want to serve under me to move on with no hard feelings. A couple had left me and both had later requested transfers back; but nobody had ever left after having given me the opportunity to lead them. Unfortunately, with Potter, I wouldn't get that opportunity. I wasn't even the commander yet and he was ready to go.

Potter was Franklin's final point. I left and stopped by to see Bittorie, who wasn't alone. He had the sergeant major of the 2d Battalion with him. The guy was in real deep shit. He had been charged with having an unauthorized Vietnamese female in his quarters after hours. In Vietnam, all twenty-four hours of every day were "after hours" for that kind of caper. They had been found together one night and both of them were stoned. He said it had been a set-up, a fix designed to get rid of him. He didn't seem too disturbed. He was persuaded that he'd beat the rap when the time came and that served his purposes for the moment at least. Nicholson, his boss, was leaving, I was coming in, and the sergeant major was getting out, too. It was okay with me because he was an office sergeant major and Nicholson ran the battalion the same way. What I needed was a field sergeant major, and Dick Childers was perfect. General Allen had promised that when I got a command, if ever, Childers would be my sergeant major, and that was the only reason Dick had held back from taking other slots when they opened up. Now the charges against Nicholson's sergeant major were saving a lot of trouble and confusion. He could go and Childers could come right on in and it wouldn't create any problems for me, except pulling it off. I went back to Franklin.

"Well, who does that leave you, Herbert?" he said.

"Well, sir, there's Sergeant Major Abbott or Childers," I said, moving carefully. "I know Abbott stutters, but he's good, and Childers drinks a lot, you know." That was the clincher. He had some knowledge of Abbott but he knew absolutely nothing about Childers now except that he drank.

"It will be Childers," he said.

Once again, I had played my cards right. I was shaking inside,

I felt so damned smart. "If you say so, sir." I wondered how long it would be before he found out that Dick Childers and I had been together for years, or that he was in fact one of the finest if not the finest sergeant major in the entire U.S. Army. My God, just by not asking for him, I got him. It was a great lesson, and it became my principal style in my relationships with Franklin and Bethea. If I wanted something badly, I left the impression that I did not want it at all and that to get it would be bad for me and the battalion. Presto! It was mine.

"Herbert, you're just like any other commander," Franklin told me once during a discussion about some transfers that I badly wanted but had said I didn't. "You've got to take your share of the scrap as well as the cream." Right, Colonel Franklin, I thought. Just keep the scrap coming. What he didn't realize was that I knew those sergeants well. After all, the Airborne included the 82d, the 101st, the 173d, the 509th, and the Special Forces, and most of us had served in all of them—except, of course, for the Pentagon guys who had been too busy building careers instead of combat units. With the relationships I had built over the years, I was able to shore up the weaknesses I knew about in the 2d Battalion, most of which were taken care of when Franklin thought he was shoving Childers off on me.

Dick Childers was one of the three best NCOs I had known in the Army. "Dad" Casella and Bill Pere were the other two, and the four of us had served together over and over throughout the course of our service, by choice, not chance. I knew their families and I numbered them among my very few close friends. Childers had worked with me first in Germany and then later in the Rangers, as well as in many other spots. He had been Ernie Webb's platoon sergeant in Germany after I left. Dick and I had arrived in the 173d almost simultaneously, and Webb had come in a couple of months later. Childers and Bittorie would see to it that we went in together. But all of that turned out to be unnecessary. Franklin had done it for us.

Dick had already won the Distinguished Service Cross in Vietnam while serving in the 4th Division under General Peers, and he was rumored to be in for the Congressional Medal of Honor. My God, I thought, things were going better than I had dreamed. Franklin and I were still discussing the assignment of Childers when a call came through to him that I would take over the battalion on February 6, rather than the 5th.

"You've a day to waste, Herbert," Franklin said.

"Right, sir. Good night."

"Good night, Herbert, and good luck."

"Thank you, sir," I said.

As I walked back to my sack that night, I decided to use the next twenty-four hours as prep time. I wanted to work out the 2d Battalion in my mind. I lay down and began.

In the States, you might be able to go in and take your time with changes, but not in Vietnam. In the States, you could look around for a bit and maybe take a couple of weeks before actually making a change, but in Vietnam it was a different story. Take your time in Vietnam and men died, or lost legs or arms or eyes. So I had already been looking, and thanks to my opportunities as an IG and Coutre's help, I knew about as much as anybody could know about the 2d Battalion—and it all boiled down to one primary conclusion: like the entire Brigade, the 2d Battalion was fat in every area except combat. The solution was to trim.

I would start in the headquarters section, I thought, right in the base camp. I would tear up the flower patch there and plant them back in the field where they belonged. Thanks to Coutre and Abbott, I already had the thing down to individuals. I knew that each rifle company in the battalion was accustomed to leaving both its executive officer and its first sergeant in the rear, and many of them had platoon sergeants in rear-area jobs along with the supply sergeant and the supply clerk. Then there were the fireflies, the men waiting to see the chaplain or the Red Cross representative or the IG or the social worker or the psychiatrist. There were a few just sitting back at headquarters awaiting charges or courts-martial. It was a farce. The combat blood of the battalion was being drained away in all that penny-ante crap. That was about to cease.

I had already taken care of a few things. In the future, the Red Cross representative, the chaplain, and the IG would come to the battalion periodically and be flown out to the field where they would do their work. If there were any ass-chewings, they would take place in the field, not back at headquarters. Each company would have only three men back: either the executive officer or the first sergeant, one on each end of the administrative chain, the supply sergeant or his clerk, one on each end of the supply chain, and one clerk-typist.

Any supply personnel in the rear area would double up and load the helicopters, thereby cancelling out the need for the "special" personnel pulled back to the rear for that purpose. And the guys who were awaiting charges could await them just as well in the field as in the rear.

I didn't like the way Nicholson had handled the men who were on the way home. Frequently, they would come back to the rear as much as thirty days before they were scheduled to depart. That was a bunch of crap. I had learned my lesson in Korea. Rotation had been established and tigers became pussies. They had hung back and played it safe until we wised up and came in with a new policy: he who fought up front went home up front. I didn't have the authority to establish that policy in Vietnam, but I did have the authority to decide who came back to the rear and when. I could make sure a man kept his ass in the grass until seven days before his departure date, and I was determined that the battalion would start rewarding achievement rather than failure. Under Nicholson, if a guy rapped a sergeant in the mouth or if he refused to fight, he came back to the rear, sat on his ass waiting, drinking, seeing shows, smoking pot, and screwing everything that wiggled downtown until he was court-martialed or given an Article 15, at which point he would pay a small fine for his vacation of several weeks or months. Then he went back to his unit and did it again. But not with me. Every mother's son was going to hump it, and carry his share of the load, just like the few already out there.

There were other things running through my mind that night. Tactics, for instance. The infantry maxim was just a slogan and I wanted it in practice: Find 'em, fix 'em, fight 'em, and finish 'em. But it simply wasn't being used. I wanted to change that. Find 'em. Use reconnaissance and intelligence. The reconnaissance platoon was being used as a special ambush unit rather than for reconnaissance. The battalion had to have eyes and ears. Its area of operations was bordered on the east by the South China Sea and on the west by a string of mountains running north and south. From those ridges, a trooper with binoculars could see, in most cases, all the way to the sea. But it wasn't being used. Fix them. Fire and maneuver. One pins them down with fire while the other runs up around the rocks and comes in from the flank or from behind. Fire and maneuver have always been the key to infantry success, but in Vietnam we were just calling in artillery and backing off to wait. The next day we would go in and pick up the pieces—and generally there weren't any except for the women and the kids who hadn't had the sense to make it out of the area. Fight 'em. Close with and destroy the enemy—the military enemy. Kill them or capture them, but emphasize prisoners because they give information that leads to more prisoners. Dead men are just dead men. Capture them if possible, but if not, finish them off for good. I lay there in my sack that night trying to put it all together in my mind: where I had been and what I had done and how I had got where I was at that very moment in time and space. I was alive, I decided, because of two things: sheer luck and not forgetting. I attributed it to nothing else, but I knew that presence of mind had a great deal to do with one's fortunes. I also knew that there were some things beyond anybody's control. They just happened, regardless of planning or preparation or skill or courage or cowardice.

I went to sleep thinking about all that. The next day, I pored over all my battalion plans again and when I hit the sack the next night I knew I was as ready as I had ever been. I slept well.

6

Brigadier General John W. Barnes presented Colonel Nicholson with his packet, that collection of automatic decorations and awards we were passing out to almost every man in uniform about to cross the international date line. He then took the battalion's colors from Nicholson and placed them in my hands. "Take good care of them," he said. There was not time for an answer. He had turned to the troops gathered for the change-of-command ceremony and started his speech, a traditional oration at such rites. It's like a sermon in church: everybody knows it's coming and most everybody would be disappointed if there weren't one, but damned few pay any attention.

Barnes talked at great length about the achievements of the battalion under Nicholson's guidance. There had been approximately 200 kills or captures during the six months he had been in charge, he said, presenting that statistic as though it were something akin to a .400 batting average in the National League. Actually, it amounted to about one kill or capture for every two-man-years of service in Vietnam. The math is simple: 800 men in the battalion, under his command for six months, amounts to 400 man-years; you divide by the total number kills or captures during that period and come up with one per two man-years. At that rate, we could end the Vietnam War in just 240 years, providing no more VC or NVA were born in the meantime.

"The Army and Colonel Nicholson's country are proud of the job he's done here," General Barnes was saying. "And we're proud of the way you men have served under him. I have every confidence that, in the true tradition of airborne infantry, you'll do the same under Colonel Herbert."

Just what the hell was he trying to do to me? In a pig's eye they'd be doing the same under me. They were about to undergo some pretty big-assed alterations in their lives and their attitudes as American fighting men.

"Would you like to say a few words, Colonel Herbert?" the General asked.

I stepped forward and smiled at him and Nicholson and turned to the men. "I'll be talking to each of you later," I said—and that was it. The entire ritual had taken only about ten minutes out of my life, the band had played well, Nicholson was leaving, and I was now the commander of a combat battalion. All in all, I couldn't bitch about things. As we disbanded, the General asked that the officers step over to the combination library-pool hall for coffee and cake.

The General and I were talking, like two old biddies at a tea party, when Jack Angel came over and said I could count on his support, one hundred per cent. "Thanks, Jack," I said.

Bethea moved toward us and mumbled something about luck. I recall trying to catch his eye as we stood there no more than a foot apart. I had already heard about the meeting he had called at Brigade Headquarters the night before, and much later Bethea himself testified about what had occurred.

> I called all the principal staff officers in and told them that I recognized Colonel Herbert was not the most popular man in the Brigade; however, it was our responsibility as staff officers to insure that he got every bit of the support that staff could provide.

That meant that Herbert was to receive support just as though he weren't a rat's ass and a no-good son-of-a-bitch. Good old Bethea. Duty, honor, country—he was a Super Cadet, and as I watched him avoid my eyes I was unable to build any hatred. Instead, something akin to sorrow or, perhaps, pity, settled in. He was, by God, what he was, and like all the rest of us, he was a product of all his yesterdays. So was Barnes and so was I and so was Franklin, who had not attended the change of command but had gone on R and R to Hawaii. What the hell! I thrust out my hand. "Thanks, sir," I said. He somehow missed seeing my outstretched palm, even though his eyes were set downward. I kept it there until he turned and walked away.

Major Harry Skeins, the operations officer in my new battalion, strode purposefully through the door of the library-pool hall and went directly to General Barnes to tell him that a village north of English was popping. An NVA rifle company was pinned down by helicopter gunships and a South Vietnamese company led by an American officer and an American NCO.

By all rights, Major Skeins should have reported to me. It was just a little error in the chain and Harry and I could straighten it out later.

"All we need is a company to go in and pick up the pieces," he said to Barnes.

"Are they using artillery?" the General asked.

"Yes, sir," answered Skeins. "The ARVNS are in the hills west of the village and they're calling it in."

Barnes did not respond. I turned to Skeins. "Do we have a unit ready?" I asked.

"I've already notified A Company. Captain Cording," he said.

"Good," I said, turning to the General. "Want to go along, sir?"

"No, no, Tony," he said. "Can you handle it?"

I struggled to keep a straight face. "I'll try, sir," I said and turned back to Skeins. "Get the birds—and I'll need a radio man."

"There's a radio in the C and C chopper," he said.

"No, I mean for on the ground. Get me an SOI and a bandolier of M–16. See you up on the pad." I turned back to the General. "We'll keep you posted, sir."

I picked up the M–16, adjusted its sights, whipped on my belt and harness, shoved the knife into its shoulder sheath, and with the map open settled down cross-legged on the pad to wait for them. The weapon was across my lap, beneath the map, and I felt good— comfortable, I suppose—with its bulk and heft. I was an M–16 man, unlike Colonel Nicholson and the other dashing commandos. They preferred the CAR–15, the glamorous carbine that became to soldiers in Vietnam what the Thompson submachine gun had been to GIs in World War II. It was short and sharp and looked good on television or in movies or in pictures for the old family album, but it was, in fact, one hell of a lousy weapon. It misfired, jammed, and just plain did not operate—but it did look good. Nicholson had offered me his one day.

"You ever fired it?" I had asked, and his face had turned crimson. He had walked over to the edge of the clearing where we were standing, swung it down-range, smiled and squeezed off four rounds. The gun jammed.

The M–16, which I preferred, was light enough, it fired well if you maintained it, and it was comparable to any small weapon in the world when used for the purposes for which it had been designed. All you had to do was clean it once in a while, use the proper lubricant, and open the bolt if it happened to get wet, giving the barrel a chance to drain. Moreover, the M–16 wasn't different, and that was one hell of a big advantage if you knew what combat was all about. One of the best ways to survive was to look and act no different than anyone else. To be dashing was to be different, and to be different was to become a target.

Major Skeins and the chopper crew arrived and we bundled in and lifted off. In addition to the two of us and the crew, we had aboard a radio operator for me and a Captain Benny, the artillery liaison officer. As we headed for the village, Skeins briefed me. A Company, under Captain Cording, was already in the air, he said, and the artillery would lift in five minutes.

"The best place to set down is southeast of the village," Harry said.

"Northwest," I said. "I don't want the ARVN and us firing into each other."

"Northwest is open," he nodded. "It's open and we can orbit counterclockwise and keep our eye on all of it."

"Not me, Harry, you," I said. "The radio man and I will go in after the first lift and everybody else will stay in the air, except you," I said, pointing to the acting sergeant major, who was sitting in until Childers returned from R and R. "You can take your choice."

Skeins glanced around at the others. "Sir, you don't have to off-load. You can see it better from up here."

"You do it, Harry, and then tell me about it." I turned to the door to study the terrain and Harry went back to the radio, telling Cording and the flight leader that I was coming down. I was the new guy on the block, and it was my day. I concentrated on the breath-taking scenery unwinding beneath us: low, flat, lush green paddies laced by ribbons of canals; little white and brown ducks paddling along on the mirror-like surfaces; a boy with a long, thin bamboo stick walking a herd of buffalo along a bank near a small village with thatched roofs; coconut palms dotting the landscape and, here and there, the hard walls and roof of a temple standing above the terrain; black-trousered peasants with their pants legs rolled to the thigh, knee-deep and folded over in the paddies, pretending to be planting— none of them daring to look up from beneath their coolie-hats, not even the kids. They knew about war, and more than likely they knew more about this one than I did. They knew not to look up. By then it had become almost instinct. Each had probably known someone who had looked up who was now dead. I had actually read it in one of our so-called manuals: "When they look up, they're VC." Stupid, but typical.

Harry tapped me and pointed to the mountains. I followed his hand down and across to the cascades of rocks and boulders descending in a long, narrow scar into the valley.

"The caves?" I shouted, trying to be heard above the chopper's clatter.

"Right," he yelled back.

Harry knew the situation, and he taught me a lot in the short time we rode north toward the besieged village. The hard-core NVA were in the caves and the VC cells were in the villages. They were linked by their lifeline, the patrols. First you had to sever that link. Then you went to the cells in the villages and finally to the caves and the hills. It was the only way, he said, and I agreed.

He tapped me again. "Village coming up, sir," he said.

The artillery had lifted and A Company, he said, was one minute away from touchdown. I pointed out the LZ on the map and almost simultaneously recognized it on the ground. Harry went back to the radio and I felt the ship tilt beneath me, banking around in a broad orbit, coming up behind A Company's last chopper. The first one was already at touchdown and Skeins tried one last time.

"Sir," he was shouting. "You can see it better from upstairs."

I shook my head and pointed down. I checked my rifle, tapped the magazine, making certain it was seated, and motioned to the radio man to get ready. We dropped out the door and the sergeant major followed, moving directly toward the captain and his command group. I stuck out my hand. "Colonel Herbert," I said.

"Cording, sir, Captain Cording," he replied. "Company commander of A Company." He was opening a map and starting to brief me on the situation, but I interrupted him.

"Not now," I said, smiling. "When it's over." I glanced back at the troops milling around the LZ, rather aimlessly, I thought. Bunches made me nervous. "Besides we've already wasted enough time."

"Yes, sir."

I dropped back alongside one of the platoons. Hell, maybe it was the fact that I was there. I knew the company commanders in the 2d Battalion were not accustomed to having the battalion commander down on the ground with them, and I thought perhaps Cording was waiting for instructions from me. I got out of the way but then discovered that the platoon leader was no more gainfully employed than the captain.

"How long before you move out?" I asked.

"In a couple of minutes, I guess, sir."

"You got problems?"

"No, sir," he said, looking around. "It's always like this." His radio crackled, and after a brief exchange he waved his arm, spoke to a couple of his sergeants, and started moving his platoon up over a bank and across one of the rice paddies toward the village. I fell in along with his point-squad, the men leading the march—and it was damned well just that: a march. Every last one of them was in single file, crossing the paddy on a dike, and there wasn't so much as one wet boot. They headed straight down into the village, keeping to the paths, and we were there in less than fifteen minutes.

There was nothing there and after a while the men flopped down and began to munch on C rations, waiting for a flight home. No security was posted. It was like a goddamned picnic. The only people still searching for something in the village were the sergeant major and the dumb-assed new commander of the battalion. I had said nothing to Cording, thinking that he would get the picture if he saw us continuing the search. No such luck. I had seen it before as the IG. He needed it drawn out for him. I finally walked over to where he was sitting, munching on a cracker.

"Not trying to disturb your dinner or anything, Cording, but would you please get these people off their asses and ready—and this time we move through the village south to north, and this time we search. You got any questions?"

"Sir?"

He needed a blueprint in three dimensions. I detailed it for him.

"Item one, I want security posted, not only right now but any time and every time anybody sits down to rest."

"Yes, sir."

"Item two, I want their gear on and that means everybody. They can loosen it and get comfortable, yes, but they don't take it off and they don't stack their arms. I don't want anyone moving around without their gear."

"Yes, sir."

"Now, item three, I want this search organized and I want these people to have specific instructions. I want them to have assigned sectors, and this time I want a real search like it should have been on the first go-round."

"Sir?"

"A search, Cording, a search. Underneath the fire-pits. Under the haystacks and inside the haystacks. Look for breathing reeds or bamboos. Probe down inside of the grain crocks. Look for false walls and false floors and false anything."

"Yes, sir."

"And get somebody beside the sergeant major and me off these goddamned paths and down inside the bunkers. Get them under the floors and inside the bamboos and into the thorn thickets."

"Sir, Colonel Nicholson—"

"Just left the battalion this morning," I finished for him. "Assigned to Saigon, you know." I didn't want to hurt him. I just wanted to get some results. "Now look, Cording, if you still want to argue, we can do it later over coffee, okay?"

"Yes, sir."

"Now, get them off their asses within five."

When they started again, it was obvious that they were quite capable. They knew damned well how to conduct a search, and this time they came up with about a dozen women and kids, a few trails of blood, about 150 five-gallon drums of cleaned rice, and some field gear. There were no weapons and no documents, but Cording seemed embarrassed nonetheless, as though the relative success of the second search were somehow an insult to him. He insisted that the rice was of no importance.

"It's just personal stock, sir," he said.

"For a dozen women and kids?"

"It doesn't matter," he continued to insist.

"Well, maybe so, Cording, but it's not up to us to decide whether it is or not. We report what we find and Brigade decides, right?"

"Right, sir."

"Now make the report," I said, motioning to his radioman, "and if you're right, then call for a flight home."

But he was wrong. The company had to hold for the National Police who came in and extracted about eighty barrels of the rice.

I was most concerned about the blood trails. Whose were they? I was pretty sure that there had been no entire rifle company in the village that day, Major Skeins's report notwithstanding, except ours. So who got chopped up when the gunships hit the place? I knelt over one of the trails, wondering. If the gunships had seen them dropping, then they must have seen wherever they went or they must have seen somebody dragging them off, but for some reason the gunships had been conspicuously absent from the operation ever since we had landed. I had not even heard them on the radio-net, not even when we tried to raise them.

Since Franklin was in Hawaii on his vacation, I reported directly to General Barnes, telling him about the gunships. Forget it, I was told, because they were not my responsibility. They operated independently of the battalions.

"Besides, there are blood trails, aren't there?"

"Yes, sir," I said.

"Then forget it."

That was as far as it went. I rationalized. If there had been a mistake at the village, it had been a legitimate one, I told myself, and if some civilians died, it was unfortunate but it was the price. They had died accidentally, I thought. After all, we had come to Vietnam to help the Vietnamese.

Sid Berry, who is now a general, wrote about the use of artillery in Vietnam and put down a fairly catchy phrase that I liked. "Waste ammunition like a millionaire," he wrote in his paper, *Brigade Operations in Vietnam*, "and lives like a miser." Sid knew what he was talking about. I had him as a student in Ranger School at Ft. Benning in 1957 when he was a major and I was a brand new second lieutenant and an instructor. He was good then—the best in his class, in fact—and had been supposedly as good in Vietnam when he commanded a brigade in the 1st Infantry Division, the Big Red One. His paper had contributed almost as much as his command skills to winning his first star. There was only one thing wrong with his theories about the use of artillery: he and almost everybody else seemed to overlook the fact that Vietnam was still an infantry war. They liked to back off, pour in the big ones, and then come in and pick up the pieces. Bullshit. Artillery in Vietnam was still a supporting weapon—something to go in under, not the ultimate weapon we were trying to make it. The fact is that artillery in Vietnam was more of a show than anything else—except for the civilians. The soldiers went underground with the first round. The civilians were the ones who generally got it.

Yet everybody seemed to love artillery, just dearly love it. So did I, as a matter of fact. The difference was the degree of affection. Skeins gave me a demonstration the day after we had shot up the village and found nothing but the trails, the rice, and the women and kids. It was impressive. They laid in preparation fire on and around the designated landing zone. It lasted seven devastating minutes. One minute before the flights were to touch down, they lifted and shifted the artillery fire, moving back in a broadening ring around the LZ, blowing hell out of the surrounding hilltops until the last chopper was in and out. It was beautiful, just like at Ft. Benning. Straight out of the book. The troops came in, made the search, returned to the LZ, loaded on the birds, and clattered out, and the artillery closed back in around them and under them, again inundating the LZ.

Harry sat back and removed his headset. He was visibly pleased. "Like it, sir?"

"Very impressive, Harry."

"Really, sir?"

"Yeah, Harry, it was beautiful—but where the hell was the enemy?"

"Well, sir, sometimes yes and sometimes no."

I remembered the Brigade's score sheets. Mostly it had been no. He would have to be told the truth some time. In Europe and Korea, big doses of artillery were probably quite functional and no doubt efficient, but in Vietnam they were a waste; and worse, they killed innocents. In our sector where there were no large concentrations of troops, all operations were battalion or smaller, and generally they were company-sized. Attacks were made in the open, in the brush, in the villages, in the jungles—never against fortified, dug-in positions. There were no Siegfried Lines, except the ones we were building, and there were no prolonged, sustained encounters. Action was sudden, swift and sporadic. There were infantry shoot-outs, not great artillery duels. The enemy had nothing worth mentioning on the plains of Bong Son, at best some mortars and mines and booby traps, and maybe a rifle company or two behind it all. So why the hell were we playing it the way they wanted us to play it? Why didn't we play our game with our own rules? We had the choppers, we had the weapons, we had the technology, and we had the best damned soldiers in the world. The object was still to get there first with the most. We could have overcome every advantage the enemy had, and we could have done it so suddenly, their heads would have been swimming. When you off-loaded from the birds 300 meters from the target, you still had to come in through the mines and the booby traps while they sat back and picked off a few more with small weapons. When you finally did close with them, they flat disappeared or became civilians, leaving you to spend the rest of the day probing and searching, blowing off another leg here, another arm there.

I knew my enemy there because I had been there myself. Despite all the publicity and all the fanfare, the Viet Cong and the North Vietnamese Army regulars still couldn't cut it against the U.S. Army paratroops. If you went in right on top of the bastards with every gun going, they had very little choice. They could fight and die, drop it and surrender, or cut out. They would not have time for anyone to make the decision for them. It was instantaneous: the whop-whop-whop-whopping of the chopper blades and they had to make up their minds. I knew it would work—not forever, of course, because nothing does in war—because of their unbelievably slow communications system. I would have to be alert to the day that they finally figured out what the hell was happening to them and laid the trap. Like everything else, tactics had to be as flexible as the enemy.

We had been teaching that for years. We called it field ingenuity —the ability of every individual to think for himself in combat and to adjust himself and his men as the situation dictated. We had been teaching it, all right, but damned if we practiced it in Vietnam. We were programmed into Westmoreland's "Roman plow" approach and now, by God, we were no longer saying what we felt or believed but what seemed to be the best public relations. The gap between truth and what we were telling the American people was immense, from Johnson and McNamara to Westmoreland and Abrams. Artillery, indiscriminate murder, blanket bombing, saturation annihilation were not working because they simply do not work—not because the Saigon government was either weak or strong, or because of the monsoons, or because some of our kids were smoking pot or a few more of them back home were raising hell and marching, or because some Senators wanted to end the war. They simply did not work because Vietnam was still a grunt's war and grunts have to be led and we had very little real, effective leadership, especially at the highest levels.

The fact of the matter was that we could have cleaned Charlie's clock anytime we chose by simply making use of what we had, without resorting to nuclears or anything else. We were thinking and talking like a bunch of losers. "The night belongs to Charlie," they liked to say down at Saigon and at Brigade H.Q. Bullshit. "It takes a ratio of about fifteen to one to defeat the guerrilla," they were moaning. More bullshit. "Even the kids carry grenades," they explained. True, but still bullshit. "Guerrillas are fish and the people are their sea," they quoted Mao. It was more of the same old crap. The people may have been their sea, but not ours. They were phrases, just empty phrases.

"Sir," Harry was saying, "artillery's a damned good thing if you learn to appreciate it."

"Sure, Harry, sure—but aren't you supposed to kill enemy soldiers with it, or at least deprive them of their defenses or supplies or something?"

"Yes, sir."

"Well, you just set up a demonstration that includes those little items and maybe I'll learn to appreciate it a bit more, huh?"

The next day, Harry told me that Franklin was transferring him immediately to the Brigade Headquarters.

"Why?" he asked.

I should have been asking him. I told him I didn't know why he was being transferred. He seemed not to believe me, and I couldn't blame him inasmuch as Franklin had told him, he said, that the transfer was being made at my request. That was about as far from the truth as it could possibly be. If I needed anybody right now, it was Major Harry Skeins. I needed him for continuity's sake, if nothing else. The battalion already had a new CO and was about to get a new sergeant major as soon as Childers came back from R and R, and there were two or three other new assignments imminent. Why the hell would I want to get rid of Harry?

"Don't worry about it," I told him. "I'm going down to talk to Franklin."

Franklin was behind his desk and he greeted me warmly. "He just doesn't want to work for you," he said. "You know Skeins and Colonel Nicholson were very close."

"I don't believe that, sir. I just talked to Skeins."

"Okay, okay," he laughed. "So I was trying to make it easy for you. We really need him here at Brigade and he's available and he's the best choice."

"Needed at Brigade? With so many damned officers in there now that they're stumbling over each other? Come on, sir, the battalion can't afford it and neither can I."

"I'm sorry, Herbert, but the General has decided."

"Can I talk to him?"

He leaned over his desk. "Are you calling me a liar, Herbert?"

It came so suddenly I almost said yes. "No, sir, I just thought maybe General Barnes would reconsider."

"He won't," he said, waving his hand, "and you can't."

"Well, who do I get in return for Skeins?"

He picked up a ball-point pen and tapped it against his teeth. "Well, I know you don't like Webb and I know the two of you can't get along, but Webb is the General's choice, so you'll just have to make out the best you can and try to get along."

I felt the blood drain from my face. At that moment I realized what he was trying to do, and I believe that at that point he realized that I knew. I was convinced that he was intent on sinking my ass, regardless of duty, honor, or country.

"Do we understand each other, Herbert?"

"We do, sir," I said.

He quickly changed his tone and his mood. "Unless you start trusting me, Herbert," he said, shaking his head like a father bewildered by his errant son's behavior, "I just don't know, I swear I just don't know."

"Oh, I'll get along with Webb, sir, don't worry," I said.

"Good, good," he said. "Try, Herbert, really give it a try." He smiled as though he had won some significant victory. "Now, good day, Herbert."

I left, so goddamned happy that I actually forgot my jeep and walked right up the road. He was right. It was a good day. It was a beautiful day. I was getting old Ernie Webb, and Franklin thought it would be just one more hole in my ship. He just knew it would never work out because he'd probably heard about the discussion Ernie and I had had at the officers' club when he had mentioned the job as a general's aide. Franklin may have been one fine cadet at the Point, but he had a lot to learn about men. I would have given my left arm for Ernie, if I had thought that would have brought him to the battalion; instead I was giving up Skeins. That was tough—tough on him and on me too because I believe we could have become good friends, and I know we could have been a much better combination than he and Nicholson. The best I could hope for was that Harry would figure things out for himself.

I walked along, humming, telling myself to keep quiet about Ernie coming over. Don't tell anybody, Herbert, or like the dumb-ass you are, you'll blow it.

So now Nicholson was gone from the battalion and with Skeins leaving along with the sergeant major, I wondered who was next. Maybe Grimshaw or Larry Potter III?

I found out the next day. It was Cording. I was sitting in the mess with Hank Boyer, the executive officer, having a cup of coffee after lunch, when Cording, the captain who had been in charge of the unsuccessful sweep through the village on February 6, approached us and sat down.

"Can I interrupt you, sir?" he asked.

"You already have," I joked. "What's on your mind?"

He let me know, without pulling any punches. He was my best commander, he said. Colonel Nicholson had said he was, and yet I had insulted him in the field.

"I know my business as well or better than anybody in the battalion," he said. "If you don't trust my judgment completely, you'll have to get a new commander for A Company."

"You quit?" I said.

"If necessary, sir."

I slid him a cup of coffee and leaned toward him. "In a pig's ass, you quit, Captain." He started to get up. "Sit down," I said, using the same tone. There was no need to shout. I had dealt with this situation before. He sat down. "Item one, Captain, I am not Nicholson. Item two, I'm going to tell you who I am and then what you are."

It took about five minutes. I was the commander, I said, and he was a subordinate commander and neither of us worked for Westinghouse or IBM. We were soldiers, and there was no such item as quitting. "And as far as who my best company commander is, I'll decide that for myself, based on results, not mouth. That ought to take me about thirty days and that's exactly how long you're going to stay before you can leave. If you still want to get out then, come back and see me—but until then, you're going to hump it just like the rest." I picked up my cup. "Anything else I can do for you?"

"I want out."

"In thirty days."

"Can I go on R and R?"

"Anytime," I said and he left. Boyer and I talked about him for a while and we both agreed that, despite Cording's initial response to me, he would work out fine and would change his mind in a week or two. In twenty years, I could not remember a subordinate who had quit, and I had never hurt any of them regardless of what they had done in return. I could always find a part of me in every man, and Captain Louis K. Cording was no exception. I thought I had hurt his pride, but I knew he would get over it. His pride had conflicted with the company's mission and I had chosen to hurt one rather than the other. It was something all of us had to learn and I felt confident that he would learn it, too.

Hank changed the subject. "You're supposed to talk to Davis today."

"Who's Davis?" I said. "Oh, yeah, the chaplain?"

"Right," Boyer said.

I had met Davis in An Khe one day when he and Major Crouch were taking physical training. He had joked about not seeing me at mass, and I had responded by saying that if I couldn't do more of any one exercise than he and the major put together, I would serve as his altar boy. He chose pull-ups. It was a smart pick because he was small and wiry and he looked strong. He and Crouch went to it: fourteen for him and eight for Crouch. I did twenty-three.

"What's the most you can do, sir?" Davis asked.

"Just one more than you and Crouch, Father," I said, and we all laughed.

Hank was telling me that he would send the chaplain around in a few minutes.

"I don't think it'll take long for you to see that he's got a pretty big chip on his shoulder," Boyer said, and left. I finished my coffee and walked to the office.

Chaplain Davis came in and reported—not with a salute, but with a casual question. "You wanted to see me?" he said.

"Well, sort of, Chaplain," I said, motioning to the only other chair in the room. "Have a seat." He sat down. "I understood rather that it was you who wanted to see me, or is that wrong?"

He leaned forward in his chair. "No, no, it's not," he said. "It's about the mass." He then launched into a torrent of complaints about his fate in the U.S. Army. It must have included every dissatisfaction he had ever felt since coming to Vietnam, from General Allen to Colonel Nicholson to the battalion to the Brigade to the war itself.

"But what can I do specifically to help?"

"Well, the services for one thing," he said. "The mass. You can bring the troops back every Sunday for mass."

He had to be joking, I thought, and I waited for him to smile. He didn't. He was seriously requesting that I pull the entire battalion out of the field every Sunday for mass. "No, Chaplain, it's impossible," I said. "There aren't enough choppers in the Brigade and even if there were, I would not be allowed to pull them back and even if it were permitted, I wouldn't do it." I stared at him, awaiting a reaction. He was wearing a "Go to Hell" rag around his neck—not the usual sweat towel the grunts wore but one of the commercial jobs that were peddled on the streets of the major cities. The rag was emblazoned with the 173d's patch and the inscription was embroidered. His hair was unkempt and he wore the stubble of a beard. His rosary beads were outside his collar.

"What do you mean, sir?" he finally said. "I'm not actually assigned to your battalion. I'm a Brigade chaplain and I have other things to do besides going out to your troops on Sunday. I have the library, the hospital, I have Tuy Hoa and all the rest, and I have confessions. I'm not available at every other trooper's beck and call, and I don't have the time to waste by staying out overnight."

"Look, Davis," I countered. "I don't want to argue the semantics of assignment. You'll either go out to the troops or I'll get someone who will and there'll be no hard feelings. It's that simple."

"So, I'm fired, huh?"

"I didn't say that. Like you said, you work for Brigade and I neither hire nor fire at that level. Besides, if you work for them, then so do other chaplains—and if you're too busy, maybe one of the others can handle it. I think the troops will understand." He said nothing and I tried to bring it into perspective. "Look, I need a chaplain in the field and it's you that the troops like and admire." I didn't know if they did or not, but that approach was worth a try. "Out there is where it is," I said, standing and offering my hand. "Get your gear together and tomorrow we'll make the rounds, okay?" He shook my hand, but the entire conversation was apparently a waste. The next day he was unavailable. He had gone to Ben Me Thuot, I was told. I was disappointed. I had hoped he would cooperate. I needed a chaplain but I didn't need him at headquarters. I needed him in the bush with the people. I had thought that was what being a chaplain was all about.

But if I didn't have a chaplain, I discovered that I was abundantly blessed otherwise. I had three—count 'em—three radio operators, and a "bat-man" who did nothing but clean my quarters and attend to my "personal wants," as he described his functions. I not only had two drivers, I also had a personal bodyguard. It was ridiculous. I reduced my sultan's staff to the radio men, who could double as drivers if I ever decided to go anywhere and had both my arms and one leg broken. Everybody else was sent back to the field, including the servers in the officers' and NCO messes. Any mother that couldn't pick up his own steak should have been in the hospital, or not eating at all. They left, the messes somehow struggled along without them, and I watched my "field strength" grow.

Actually, "field strength" is not the proper term, just the Brigade's way of putting it. It was a separate column on the daily strength report sheet and it was just one more of the big lies we were telling each other. Long ago, when the Pharaohs called their soothsayers in for a look at tomorrow, the pattern had been pretty consistent: if the sooth-sayer came up with a sooth that said the Pharaoh was going to have seven or eight bad years and cap them off by getting murdered, the Pharaoh would generally get himself a new soothsayer, a man who could be trusted to say some optimistic sooths. Over the years, very little had changed except the name. Now we called them statisticians, and "field strength" was one of their very best games. It designated that portion of any unit "serving in a combat role" and in Vietnam we had regulations which prevented it from ever dropping below 98 per cent. It wasn't easy to come up with that many Brigade people serving in combat roles, so we simply changed our policies at the local level and described anyone who was not in an assigned position at higher headquarters or working at brigade or lower command levels, and anyone who was drawing combat pay, as being on call in some ethereal "reaction force." He was therefore considered a part of the Brigade's "field strength." It was a fake, and I knew it. That was when I decided to create another column for myself, to protect against self-delusion—my "ass-in-the-grass" column, for the men carrying the load. I happily watched the "ass-in-the-grass" numbers grow with each passing day. Throughout the Brigade, the maximum complement of combat people in the companies was about 75, but in the 2d, it was reaching 150 for some operations and was averaging close to 125. I had always believed in that old saw about treating troops like men and having them respond like men. It had never failed for me.

In fact, I found one of the bravest, best combat sergeants in the U.S. Army struggling away on the scrap heap—cleaning latrines to be more specific. Sergeant Wally Warden was policing the toilets with the Vietnamese coolies because Colonel Nicholson had decided it was the only task fit for him. "He's a goddamn coward who refused to fight," Nicholson had said. "He's a yellow bastard."

"If he can't cut it, then why not just reduce him?" I had asked Nicholson.

"It's not that easy. You need statements."

Nicholson had his ideas about what was yellow and what wasn't —and I had mine, of course—but there was one damned thing for sure: no U.S. Army sergeant was going to clean latrines in any battalion I commanded. He would either cut it or lose his stripes. Warden was my first project. I pulled him off his detail immediately, sent for his records, and called him in.

"Tomorrow, Sergeant, you go back to the field."

"No, sir, I'm not," Warden said calmly.

"Why not?"

"Because, like Colonel Nicholson said, I'm a coward."

"Bullshit, Warden, I just read what you are: a U.S. paratrooper with combat experience and a damned fine record to boot."

"I'm a coward."

"Okay, so you cleaned a few shit-houses, so have I." I watched his eyes. He didn't believe me. "Yeah, that's right, Sergeant, at least one anyway. Damned near made a career out of it, too. Worked for my Grandmother Herbert. For fifteen bucks, me and my cousin, Junior Gracan. We tried, man. We really tried. One bucket at a time, hauled it all the way down to the damned sulphur creek in a wheelbarrow. That's how much that money meant to us." I shrugged. "Unfortunately, we never did get the money because they kept filling it up as fast as we could empty it. Well," I smiled, "the pay was lousy, but like my old man said, it was steady work." I looked at him and he was laughing. "At least, Sergeant, you got paid."

"That's true, sir," he said.

"Look, you're a damned fine soldier. I can't undo your yesterdays but I can have something to do with tomorrow, and I want you back in the field. If the latrines get too full, maybe I can handle it. I've had experience."

He laughed again. "Okay, sir, I'll be ready in the morning." He had a certain inner dignity that was breaking through to the surface.

"Sergeant, can I ask another question?"

"It's your battalion, Colonel."

"Why?" I asked.

"Why what?"

"Why were you cleaning shit-houses?"

"Simple, sir, I wouldn't stand for the torture-bit and the civilians."

It added up—his damned fine record and his assignment to the latrines. I nodded my head to let him know that I understood. "You'll not be asked for any of that, I assure you."

"I hope not, sir. Which squad do you want me in?"

"LeRay's platoon, Company B."

"Platoon?"

"You're a platoon sergeant, aren't you?"

"Yes, sir."

"Okay, that's what you are so that's what you are," I said, smiling again. "Besides, if nothing else, they could end up with the cleanest slit trenches in the Brigade."

He laughed again. "Or I can call on you, sir?"

"Anytime, sergeant, anytime."

It was one of the best moves I have ever made. He would save my life twice within the next two weeks.

The Berm was a permanent perimeter-defense around English, the Brigade headquarters, and the 2d Battalion was responsible for its operation and maintenance—except for that small portion of it manned by the South Vietnamese. The battalion's headquarters were also at English, a proximity that may have figured in my later problems. The Berm was a sizable responsibility, what with headquarters being there and the rest of the equipment and all, but it was no great task. In fact, in time we came to think of duty on the Berm as a kind of stand-down, a rest from the field. The bunkers were there with lights and wire and minefields, and it all worked well if it was kept up. Defense could be effective if it was aggressive.

That, unfortunately, had not been the case. The very first night I was at English, the Berm had been hit. The lights went out and I started down toward the sector that had been attacked—not because I was the commander, but because no one else was willing to go down in the dark to Bunker 14. "They'd as soon shoot you down as any of the VC," I was told, and I remembered Africa where I had met officers who were afraid of their own troops after dark. When I arrived with Childers, the people in Bunker 14 were already stoned. We lined them up outside, called their CO, and while Childers manned the parapet, I checked the perimeter. Like so many other cases, it went undealt with. Nor was Bunker 14 exceptional. The entire Berm was a quagmire. Guns were laid in poorly and the wire was in a poor state of repair. The bunkers were shoddy. Some of the Claymores were wired in; some of them weren't. There were no functional routes of supply and there was no usable plan for the evacuation of wounded. Ammunition was rusty, and not only was marijuana plentiful, the hard stuff was available in ample quantities, too.

Now, the Berm was mine and I knew damned well that any day or night it could turn into another Pleiku. I made it a special project. I ordered a rotation of companies in and out of the Berm, with one of the platoons locked and loaded around the clock, ready for use as an instant reaction force while the rest of the company worked. We built a new fire-plan from scratch, laid in the automatics and covered the gaps in between with big stuff. We tied all the weapons into one solid wall of steel and did the same with communications and the minefields. We built an outpost line and then went to the bunkers. They were rebuilt and fortified. Many were torn down because they lacked even a single decent firing port. It was a continuous project throughout the duration of my command of the 2d. It became so popular that some companies went as far as to volunteer for an extra week in the field to avoid having Berm duty. We worked their ass off, with highly satisfactory results.

"Doesn't anybody in this unit want to fight?" I asked Hank Boyer one afternoon. I was pushing anybody and everybody back into the field, and Hank had come to see me about a black lieutenant from C Company who did not want to go out.

"Come on, sir, we got a guy who's in for a CMH," Hank said, defensively.

"Yeah, I met him back at An Khe where he spends most of his time."

"Aw, come on, sir."

"Hank, someday you're just going to have to face it. We got a chaplain who doesn't want to chap, a medical platoon leader who, I understand, doesn't want to medical platoon, a company commander who doesn't want to command, a sergeant first class cleaning toilets—and now this guy. What the hell kind of outfit is this?" I dropped my shoulders in fake disgust and threw up my hands. "Send him in, Hank, send him right on in."

He was a handsome, articulate man who had been a teacher in civilian life. He bore a striking resemblance to Harry Belafonte. As Boyer had told me, he did not want to go back to the field.

"I can't go back," he said.

"But you will," I said. I was getting a little tired of that kind of crap from men who were supposed to be infantry officers. It turned out that he wasn't actually refusing to go back to the field but rather to rejoin the same company in which he had previously served.

"Mind telling me why?" I asked.

"No, sir, I don't mind," he said, and told me he didn't want to serve again under the same commander.

"Because you're both lieutenants?"

"No, not that. It's more personal."

"I can't buy that, Lieutenant. Hell, if I let every man pick his commander, we'd have only one company. If you've got some definite reason for not wanting to serve under him, then maybe I can listen."

"I have, sir."

"Then tell me."

"Only if I have to."

"Only if you don't want to go back to him."

He opened up. He had been a platoon leader, and his group had "policed up" a detainee from a village and had reported the details to his CO over the company radio net. The platoon had begun to tie up the detainee for extraction when the CO called back, the lieutenant told me. The CO said that what they had out there was a KIA, a dead dink, a body count of one, to which the lieutenant replied that he did not have a dead person but a detainee in reasonably good health. "So he says, no, what we have is a dead dink killed trying to get away," the lieutenant continued.

"So what did you say," I asked.

"Well, I told him the guy might be a civilian."

"And what did he say?"

"He said that wasn't hardly possible because once he's dead, he's a dink."

Which in fact was about the only way it was played in Vietnam. Regardless of what a person might have been before he was killed, afterwards he was a dink. Very damned few people ever reported killing a civilian, regardless of how unavoidable the death might have been, and very damned few dead civilians failed to be included in the body counts. It was time to stop the lieutenant, though, before his narrative went beyond the point of no return. I held up my hand. "Hold it," I cautioned him.

"Sir?"

"Look, before you get too far, there are some other questions. But first, you have to realize that if you say what I think you may be going to say, then I'm going to have to report it. Therefore, it's only fair, in fact it's required by the regulations and the UCMJ, that I make you aware of your rights. Do you understand?"

"Yes, sir."

"Well, then, let me ask you this. Do you understand your rights under Article 31?"

"Yes, sir, I do."

"Well, let me go over them for you again anyway. You don't have to say anything. Anything that you do say can be used in court. You can stop right now or you can continue, or you can have military counsel right here while you do talk, if you wish—and that's it in a nutshell. Now, do you want to go on?"

"Since I've gone this far—"

"For Christ's sake, Lieutenant, at least think before you answer my next question, okay?"

"Okay, sir."

"Was the execution in fact carried out?"

"Yes, sir, it was."

"Now, Lieutenant, here comes the big one, and let me state again that you neither have to answer nor are you expected to answer just because I'm your commander. If it's going to incriminate you, I want you to understand that part for sure. Do you?"

"Yes, sir, I do."

"All right, then, who actually did the killing?"

He started to answer and then stopped abruptly. "Sir, I prefer not to answer that one right now if it's okay with you."

"That's your prerogative. You keep this to yourself until I get back to you. Do you want to put it in writing?"

"I think I'd better do that."

"Good," I said, handing him a pad. "Bring it back when you've finished, and forget about going out with C Company right now. It can wait."

I called in Boyer immediately and asked him about the lieutenant that the man had accused. I knew that Nicholson and Franklin had described him as one of the best around and I had watched him in action once when I had been IG. "What about him, Hank?" I asked.

"Well, he was Nicholson's favorite," he answered, "and he's a close friend of Chaplain Davis. The sergeant who's up for the CMH is from his unit. He had an excellent record, gets along fine with the troops, and I think he's the son of a retired master sergeant or warrant officer. Why?"

I told him the story I'd just heard.

"It's a lie, sir," he said. "That black bastard just doesn't want to go to the field."

"Hank, he is not a black bastard, he's a U.S. lieutenant, airborne infantry, just like us, remember?"

"I didn't mean it like it sounded. It's just that I know the other guy."

"Well, I don't, and I don't know this guy either. But I've heard his side so now let's get this other lieutenant and hear what he has to say. Fair enough?"

"Fair enough," Hank said. "I'll get him."

While I waited I went over it all again in my head. I was no lawyer but I knew there was a right way and a wrong way to handle it, and it wasn't going to be simple. When Hank came back with the other guy, I felt that I was as prepared as I could be.

"Have a seat," I said to him as Boyer left. He was as handsome as the other lieutenant, and like his friend, Chaplain Davis, he had finely chiseled features and a small, wiry build.

"I'm going to tell you a story, Lieutenant, but first I want to tell you a couple of things about it. First, the story is supposed to be true, and it accuses you. Second, if it is true, you're in a bind and so am I, because if it is, then I'll have to pull you out of command of your company. If it's not true, then you stay. So when I finish, give me at least this much. If it's absolutely a lie, tell me, and you can stay in command. I'll have to investigate anyway, but until proven otherwise, your word is enough. If it's true or partially true, you have a couple of alternatives: to remain silent, to request counsel, to talk or whatever else you may decide, and, of course, anything you say may be used in court. And one last thing. If you choose to remain silent, I'll have to at least pull you out of the command until the investigation is completed, for your own good as well as mine—and it wouldn't be done with prejudice. You have an excellent report from Major Boyer and Colonel Nicholson and those will not be changed one iota. Now, do you understand what I've said?"

"May I ask you who made the statement?"

"That I can't tell you."

"If he made it against me, I'm at least entitled to know, I believe, sir."

"It wouldn't be fair to either of you. Ready?"

"Affirmative."

I told it to him exactly as the other lieutenant had told it to me and waited momentarily when I had finished to give him time to think over what he had heard. "Now, Lieutenant, would you like to make a statement?"

He wet his lips with his tongue and glanced over at Hank. "I think I'll take my chances by remaining silent, sir," he said. I nodded, dismissed him, and he left.

"I don't believe he did it," Boyer said.

"Well, until we find out for sure, we'll move Chris Dorney to take the company and switch this guy to headquarters."

"He's due for an R and R," Boyer said.

"Which one? Dorney or the lieutenant?"

"The lieutenant."

"Then let him take it. We'll straighten out his assignment when he comes back." I remembered my instructions from Barnes. "In fact, we'd better not move anything tonight until I discuss it with Franklin. He's really going to blow his cork on this one."

"You bet your ass, sir. The lieutenant is his guy."

I picked up my cap, slapped it on my head. "Well, like they say in Mother Russia, Hank, tough shitsky. See you in the morning."

Hank was right. The white lieutenant was indeed a favorite of Franklin, according to whom I was a liar, a troublemaker and a disloyal commander. The lieutenant was, Franklin said, my best company commander, but I was just too damned dumb to realize it. Someday the lieutenant would make three of me. "What the hell kind of a commander are you?" he asked. "It's none of your business what occurred before you assumed command. He stays."

"I've already taken him out," I said.

"You have, like hell."

"I already have."

"Then put him back in."

"I'll back it up with an investigation," I said, handing him the other lieutenant's statement. He didn't bother to read it. He threw it on his desk.

"All right, all right," he said. "If you can't get along with him, then move him—but I warn you, Herbert, it better be without prejudice."

"That's exactly the way it will be."

He picked up the statement and glanced at it. "You believe this crap?"

"I don't know," I said. "I guess no one will know for sure until the investigation is completed."

He slammed the papers down. "There'll be no investigation."

"It's required, sir, I—"

"Goddamn it, Herbert, I said I'll handle it and I will. If anything is done, it will be with the General's approval, and it will be done by me. Can you understand that much?"

"I understand, sir. Do you want a statement from Major Boyer?"

"I want nothing until I'm ready, which means I don't want anyone discussing it either."

I returned to the battalion and explained it all to Hank. "The way I understand it, Franklin is going to Qui Nhon next week and he'll get around to a statement when he comes back," I said.

"I still don't believe he did it, sir, but all I can say is what I know."

"That's all Franklin will want," I said. Later that day we discussed it again and the subject of the accused lieutenant's efficiency report came up.

"He did a damned fine job for us, sir," Boyer said.

"Then write it up accordingly."

"But you'll have to endorse it."

"And I will, Hank, I will," I said. "I told him in there that it had nothing to do with his efficiency and it was without prejudice and I meant it."

"And what if he comes out a murderer?"

"Then the next time we'll write him up as an efficient murderer. Fair enough?"

I heard that Bummer also wanted out of the battalion, and this worried me. He was something special, a real living, walking legend in the Brigade and probably everywhere else he'd served in the three years he'd been in Vietnam. Sergeant Roy E. Bumgarner, Jr., had been with the 1st Cavalry before coming to the 173d, and now he was running the 2d Battalion's reconnaissance platoon, a group dubbed the Wildcats. I had seen him in action once before and I had been duly impressed. Bittorie and I had been standing at the crap table, the main pad at LZ English, waiting for a chopper to An Khe, when we noticed two helicopters making passes at an old LZ a few meters out. The first ship, Bittorie told me, contained men from the recon platoon and the second was a trailer. "Why the hell are they screwing around with an old LZ?" I asked, and as he began to expound on its foolishness, we saw the lead ship burst into a ball of fire as it was about to touch down. The second ship followed it straight in and touched down almost on top of the flaming wreck just as the sound of an explosion reached us. I grabbed some binoculars from the floor of a nearby helicopter and trained them on the holocaust. I saw a figure jumping from the skids of the trail ship right into the fire. He dragged out one body after another and I watched him until the smoke obscured everything. I thought perhaps the trail ship had also caught fire. I kept the glasses on the smoke until finally the second chopper rose, banked around and clattered straight back toward us. Bittorie and I raced down the hill together, jumped in a jeep and careened to the medical evacuation center.

The Bummer was already standing in the doorway, leaning against the sand bags. "Good afternoon, sir," he said, lighting a cigarette as though he were in the lobby of the Plaza.

"Good afternoon, Sergeant Major."

"Anyone dead?" Bittorie asked.

"Pilot for sure. Couple of the guys. Maybe saved one." He flicked some ashes. "Damned bird just went up too fast."

As Bittorie introduced us, the Bummer came away from the wall and clicked his heels and bowed his head in the most courtly European style. Strangely enough, it didn't seem ludicrous to me—maybe because of what I'd just seen him do through the binoculars.

"Sir!" he barked.

"Sergeant Bumgarner," I answered.

Bittorie asked what exactly had happened.

"The LZ was rigged," the Bummer explained. "The whole place was booby-trapped—just like I told you it was." There was no sense of accusation in his words—just fact. The scene would have been unrealistic on any screen, but Sergeant Bumgarner seemed larger than life. For a couple of minutes I lost sight of the deep tragedy I had just witnessed. The LZ had been rigged with wires strung to explosives and the copter had hit them with its skids on the way in. It was an old trick, and one of the reasons you could not afford to let up on the pilots or the crewmen. Every man had a responsibility. A patrol began the moment a man was named to it and it did not end until after the debriefing. Somebody had screwed up royally by taking them into an old LZ.

I noticed that Bumgarner was himself carrying quite a few scorched places. A medic came to the door and called for him. He stripped his cigarette butt, scattered the leftover tobacco, and rolled the paper into a tiny lump before he walked inside for his own care.

Bittorie called for the jeep. "That, sir, is one brave son-of-a-bitch," he said.

"I think cool is the word, John. Cool." And that was the word. He was steel and ice. It was rumored that in his forty-two months in the country he had personally killed over 1,500 people.

Now word had come to me that the Bummer wanted out of the battalion. We were pulling one of the companies back from a hill northwest of English. The operation was on orders from Brigade and we were about to close it out. It was routine, I was told, but I flew out to take a look. There was one hell of a lot of scrap left behind. I called in two more choppers and had the area cleaned up as much as possible. I didn't intend to leave anything behind that the VC could use—not if I could help it. I did have to give a little, though, because the leftover C-rations had already been buried. The enemy would come in later, I knew, and clean house. It was a part of the war. We were supplying both sides. Hell, just let me clean up after any U.S. unit, and I could have scuffed up enough to last me a war.

Then and there I decided to use the habit to our best advantage. I laid in artillery on the spot as we left, making it look as though it were a normal, final extraction, and then told the artillery to keep the guns laid in on the area. Then I put a reconnaissance patrol on the next hill. I thought perhaps it would take a couple of days.

In less than twelve hours we struck pay dirt. The Bummer was on the radio, calling from the recon patrol. "It's Wildcat Two, sir," the radio man said.

"What does he have?" I asked.

"A patrol approaching the site."

"Alert the artillery."

"He wants to talk to you, sir."

I picked up one of the hand-sets. "This is Involved Six. Over."

"This is Wildcat Two. Fourteen of them on the site. Over."

"Involved Six. Are they carrying weapons? Over."

"Wildcat Two. Eight armed. Six carrying rucksacks. Over."

"Six. Good. Can you adjust fire from your position? Over."

"Wildcat," Bumgarner answered, almost whispering. "Cannot adjust. I say again: cannot adjust. Do not fire. Do you roger? Over."

"Six. Roger that transmission. Cannot adjust. Do not fire. How far are you from the target area? Over."

"Wildcat. Too close. I say again: too close. Do not fire. I say again: do not fire. Out."

It left a hell of a lot unsaid, but I had been out there enough myself to know better than to transmit under such circumstances. If he was anything like me, the Bummer would simply have shut down the radio until he was ready and able to talk and receive.

"He's off the net, sir," the radio man said.

"I know."

"Shall I try him?"

"No, it's up to him. Right now, it's time for coffee. Sit down and have a cup and stay off that damned net." I grinned to take the sting out of my words. "And pour me one, too, if you don't mind— and then get the artillery back on tap and have them hold."

"Airborne, sir."

We drank one cup and then another and finally poured the third one.

"Smoke, sir?" the radio man asked.

"No, thanks," I said.

In the middle of the fourth cup, the Bummer came back in. "Involved Six, this is Wildcat Two. Over." It was loud and clear.

"This is Six. Over."

"This is Wildcat. Send a bird and score fourteen. Four rifles and some other gear. No documents. Trying to find the other weapons in the grass. Over."

I glanced at the radio man. "How many on that patrol?" I asked.

"Just the Bummer and a radio man, sir."

I clicked the hand-set. "This is Six. Bird on the way. I say again: bird on the way. Out."

Bumgarner came down to the mess after dropping off the captured weapons and gear in the TOC. I shook his hand. "I thought you were leaving. Didn't want to serve around here anymore."

"That was before Stage Door Johnny left," he said.

"Who?"

"Colonel Nicholson, sir."

"And now?"

"Now it's a whole new ball game."

I grinned. "Good," I said. "Very good, Sergeant. Now sit down and let's talk."

I had called one staff meeting early in the first week of my command and told the officers that from then on, we would dispense with the nightly ritual of the "evening briefing," something that had come to be almost standard procedure at every level in Vietnam. Anybody who wanted to see me could come in and talk, I told them. We were all in it together. There was no need for a formal meeting as long as everybody was doing his job.

From Bernie Gifford, the S1 (Personnel), I wanted a complete roster daily, and I wanted it in the morning, I said, to show me where the people were and where they were scheduled to be that day. I didn't want a damned personnel report in the evening showing me where they had been. I wanted somebody up at An Khe to get copies of each man's 201 file, and I wanted a roster of every last trooper in the battalion—name, rank, serial number, and military occupation specialty.

From Jack R. Donovan, the S2 (Intelligence), I wanted an intelligence summary each night and a "guesstimation" of how best we could follow up on the information the following day or at some future time. I told Donovan that I knew it would be a rough guess at best, but a rough guess was better than nothing. Even if we hit on just one out of ten, it would still be an improvement over nothing, and we would chalk up the misses to practice. I told him to hound Brigade intelligence because I didn't want the information after it was processed. "Last night, the VC held a meeting," was of no value to me at this level. It might look important on the briefing charts at Brigade, but for combat purposes it was useless. I'd rather have a SWAG—Scientific Wild Assed Guess—that tomorrow night there was

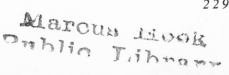

one chance in a thousand that the VC would have a meeting at a certain place.

I also stressed that we were changing the body count policy. There would be no more in-country R and Rs for "dead dinks." From now on, I said, the R and Rs would be for live prisoners and only for live prisoners. We needed intelligence badly, and you only got intelligence from live people. The trooper would get five days for a legitimate POW, with one day subtracted for each cut, bruise, or contusion on the prisoner. The better the condition of the merchandise, the more we were willing to pay for it.

From Ernie Webb, the S3 (Operations), I expected one hell of a lot. I wanted him to run his shop almost as though he were a commander, because that just about was what he would be in my absence. Operations was that kind of responsibility, and it was to be his exclusively with one exception: nothing went without my approval. I would lay down general guidelines and he would work out the details. If problems arose, I wanted to know about them immediately. I had been an S3; I knew how I had wanted the commander to let me operate then, and now I intended to let mine operate as he would like. On actual combat operations, there would be one additional rule: if I was on the ground, the S3 would be airborne, always, or else back in the TOC on the network. If I were up or back, then and only then the S3 could be on the ground.

From Captain Peter H. Quinn, the S4 (Supply), I wanted a really big job: a serial number by serial number check of every last item listed in the battalion. I wanted the supply Conexes cleaned up and ready for inspection by February 15. I wanted an order put in for survival knives and, regardless of how fast or slow the rate of supply, I wanted the knives issued from the lowest rank upwards. I didn't want to catch even one Spec/4 with a knife until every last private had one.

From Larry Potter, who in addition to being on the medical team was also the S5 (Civil Affairs), I wanted a list of civil affairs accomplishments, a list of projects underway, and a list of future projects, including some reasonable recommendations.

I told the battalion surgeon, Doc Tally, that all I expected from him each day was a verbal malaria report, by number and type, and any recommendations he might have as to how to keep the rate down. I had heard Tally at a briefing at Brigade while I was still the IG.

He had presented the only workable solution I had heard since I had been in Vietnam. The responsibility for malaria should be laid to the commanders, he said, all the way up and down the line.

"Get the word out, Bernie," I said to Gifford. "If I find a case of malaria, I want to see the company commander, the platoon leader, platoon sergeant, and squad leader, all together."

I turned back to Doc. "What about this Potter?"

"He's decided to stick around a couple of days," Doc answered.

"That's good," I said. "Damned good."

I turned to the others. "I want you all to come up with plans and recommendations," I told them—and I meant it. Hell, I didn't profess to be an expert in anything. I was the dumb son of a fine coal miner, and I could use all the help I could get. If anybody came up with a brainstorm, I damned sure wanted to hear about it. "And that includes suggestions for a commando raid on Hanoi from 'Doc' Tally," I concluded. I really wanted to listen to them because if a man makes a contribution to a plan, he has a material interest in making it succeed—so the trick is to forget about taking credit for ideas and to persuade others that they are their own. I thought out everything and tried not to waste words or time. Frequently it may have appeared to have been a spur-of-the-moment response, but it was generally prepared. The talks to the troops were good examples.

Even though they were volunteers, as all paratroopers are, the grunts were by nature different. They were not career men in the same sense that officers and most of the senior NCOs were career men, and they were not sensitive to opportunities for promotion or self-aggrandizement. But because individuals are aggressive and competitive by nature, the grunts did require an opportunity to express those instincts—or, in a word, a chance to operate. I knew the grunt. Hell, I was one of them—a promoted grunt, to be sure, but still a grunt. I had been an enlisted man over half of my entire career. I had fought as one and been wounded as one and I understood what made a grunt tick because I knew what made me tick. I had also been fortunate enough to gather enough psychological insight to comprehend them and myself even more deeply and thoroughly, at the same time gaining enough military experience to recognize that they were the best raw material in the world. They were bigger and healthier and more intelligent and better educated than any soldiers the U.S. Army had ever had the opportunity to use before, and they were superior to any soldier any other country was getting. Even with our training shortcomings—and they were, by God, plentiful—the grunts in Vietnam were still the best trained men around, as well as the best fed and the best equipped. Moreover, I think I recognized something that must have slipped by most of the brass, including Westmoreland and later Abrams: that the length of the hair on a man's head wasn't nearly as important as the caliber of the brain inside. I knew that the grunt was a man, just like me, and that he was entitled to the same respect I demanded for myself. His dignity was sacred. It could never be damaged. The commander could scream and rant and rage and curse like a sailor, but he could never encroach on the trooper's dignity. If the leader attacks his trooper's dignity, the trooper has but two alternatives: to fold up, roll over and die, or strike back. I was determined to follow the pattern that had worked for me in the past: to allow my men to make at least as many of the same kinds of mistakes as I had made, and God knows I had made my share and more; to deal with him honestly—to express admiration, respect, love, patriotism, and my own conviction that he represented, with all its faults, the greatest country in the history of civilization and the mightiest combat arm this universe ever assembled under a single power; to persuade him that it had not really been equipment and mass production that had won World War I, and II, and Korea, for us, but rather blood, guts, courage, know-how and a steadfast devotion to a cause. There had been battle after battle in those previous conflicts in which the U.S. had been outnumbered, outgunned, and out-equipped, and we still had cleaned their clocks. It was important, I thought, that the American soldier recognize that, and perhaps equally important that our enemies understand it as well—or the entire lesson would have to be learned again. Hitler spent years convincing the young people of Germany that in World War I their soldiers had really been the best in the world and but for a few unfortunate circumstances would have conquered Europe and perhaps England and America. Meanwhile, back home in the U.S., the veterans of the Argonne Forest were telling their children almost the same thing—embarrassed for the losers, always with a good word for the underdogs, preaching alibis for their own courage—and before long, their kids and ours were believing it. Germany was so convinced, in fact, that they had to try it again, and we had to kick their ass again.

I called some grunts together that first week and talked to them about it:

"Your grandfathers kicked their asses, your fathers and your older brothers kicked their children's asses, and now you can kick their grandchildren's asses," I said. "It is, my friends, the law of the jungle: the tiger's cubs are still tigers and the offspring of sheep are still lambs."

Then, quickly, I dealt with several points I felt they needed to start thinking about. I told them my views on the old myth that the night was somehow the property of the Viet Cong, and I explained in some detail why their superior diets gave them better night vision than Orientals whose nutrition had not been as good. I told them how convinced I was that they were bigger and better soldiers than any previous generation of Americans, and how persuaded I was that the war could be won in our area on our terms—and how that had very little to do with Washington or Hanoi or Saigon.

"It's plain and simple," I said. "Our objective is to kill him before he kills us. Out there, there are no international politics. It is a matter of dog eating dog, so you have to be the biggest and baddest dogs around, and you are—or at least I can help you to become that."

Then I laid out my strategy for the battalion. It was some lousy war when a piddling battalion commander had to lay out a master strategy, but that was the way it was. Hell, nobody else had laid anything out for those men, either from a national or an international perspective. I owed it to them to give them some kind of purpose and reason at the battalion level at least.

I told them that everybody in the battalion was going to fight. There were cheers and some laughter and a few jokes, and I knew that at least they had been challenged. I also told them that any problems they might have had with the battalion's previous administration were not my concern. "Yesterday is yesterday," I said. I told them that their slate was clean and that everyone was beginning again. "We have to trust each other," I said. "That is what war and infantry is all about. But there's another side to the coin: you screw up intentionally, and you've had the course."

I turned to strategy. I told them there'd be no more of the traditional backing off and calling in the big guns. I told them we would fire and maneuver and fire and maneuver, close with, kill, capture, and destroy the enemy, just like it says in the manual. "You people are going to be everything and more of what your daddies ever thought you could possibly be."

I had to get down to specifics with the company commanders, explaining that I believed the reason there had been blunders in the past was because they had been called on to do the impossible. It wasn't their fault or their troops' fault; it was the demand placed on them all to hump it both day and night: march and patrol all day, stay awake all night on ambush. It was not only impossible, it was also unrealistic. If I couldn't do it, neither could they, and I was damned sure ready to admit that I couldn't do it and therefore did not expect it of them.

"It's got to be one or the other, day or night—and I prefer the night," I told the company commanders. "But you have to have something for the daytime, too, so let's just take a look at the problem. What exactly are the problems in the field? Eating, which means cooking; sleeping, which means security; a chance to write letters home, sun away the sores, dry out the clothing and socks, and light up and bullshit with the buddies. I think there is a way to get it all done—and from now on, we're going to go at night."

I laid out the formation: every night, each of the companies would divide itself into three rifle platoons. The first platoon would divide itself into small, highly mobile ambush teams of no more than six men; each ambush team would have a starlight scope and a radio. The second platoon would divide itself in half, with one unit breaking down into small patrols like the first platoon and the other forming one large ambush, as well as acting as a reaction force for any of the smaller units that might happen to need assistance, including the ambush units from the first platoon. The third platoon would act as a platoon-sized reaction force for the entire company, as well as company-headquarters security, and along with the headquarters group they would never be more than a half hour's march from the most distant small ambush laid by the smaller units of the other two platoons. The third platoon would be on 25 per cent alert until called on, with 75 per cent of its men resting. In the morning the entire company would pull into a day "logger" as opposed to the standard practice of "loggering" at night; then everyone could sit around with minimum security out and read, write, or sleep, as well as take advantage of the sun to burn off the jungle rot and dry out clothing and socks, impossible at night. Just before dark, the platoons would rotate, with the first platoon becoming the second, the second becoming the third, and the third becoming the first.

The VC and NVA were operating at night, so we would do the same. It boiled down for the grunt to one night out of three with a 75 per cent rest, one with a 50 per cent rest, and one night with no rest—plus rest every day.

"As long as we obtain results with this, we'll abide by it. Okay with you guys?"

There were no objections, so I went to the next item. "We all know just whose side the locals are on, right? Well, then, we might as well take advantage of what we know about their allegiance and make it work for us rather than against us, okay? For starters, we're going to make use of the information the locals pass on to the enemy. Every patrol will move at least 200 meters after dark. Later we'll vary it. That's where the locals come in. They pass on the information as to where they last see our patrols—and the last time they really see them is just before dark. So after dark we move, and with our starlights and our radios, it's no big trick, even with sorry-assed bastards like us. Now, in addition, I want one ambush, under either the command of a platoon leader or platoon sergeant, to continue to roam throughout your area. That's our 'roving patrol,' guys, just like in Ranger School." All of them had been to Ft. Benning and it was worth reminding them once in a while that a few of the things they learned there were worth remembering. Nobody else in the Brigade seemed to care about the starlight scopes, so we had plenty.

"Now, in addition to all this, we've got a platoon back on the Berm, and they are on twenty-four-hour standby alert. We'll make changes later on because habits, as you guys know, are bad. Any tactics we adopt can only work for a limited time, and even then we're always going to have to be one step ahead mentally, or else be prepared to pay the price. Sooner or later, they'll catch on and adapt either by making use of our tactics against us—a trap—or by changing their own. But even there, we've got the advantage of communications. We can get the word out in a split-second—add the speed of radio transmission, and we can get it out to each and every unit down to the most remote individual. They have to depend on their grapevine, their runners, and their commercial nets, and that takes them days if not weeks, and sometimes it never reaches the ones still coming down the trails. That means we have a real edge because if and when they ever catch on, we can change in a day and start all over in a new direction which can fuck them up for a couple or more weeks."

They were listening and they seemed impressed.

"I think it's time to demonstrate just who the hell the night does belong to, them or us, and we already know that answer, right?"

I laid out the rest of it. When it was necessary to reinforce one unit with another, we would do it with the helicopters and leave the paraphernalia—the goodies and the rucksacks—behind. They could be brought in later. The mission would have priority. Bummer's recon platoon would be involved from now on in recon missions only and would operate mostly in the hills, and every company would stay in touch with them because they were to be the eyes and ears of the companies. "They can see one hell of a lot in your areas from up there that you just can't possibly see yourselves," I said. I expected results, especially if, as the General and all the score sheets said, the Bong Son plains were really better than 90 per cent VC. "But, mark this down, I want results with enemy soldiers, not civilians, not women or old men or kids. I want VC and NVA. Right?"

I watched their faces. I felt I was on solid ground. From that point on, it was my ball. They were five good company commanders. No battalion leader had a right to anything more than the guys who were standing around me there and then.

In Company A, I had Captain Noriega, Cording's R and R replacement. He had been both a platoon leader and the executive officer in the company and he was more than capable. He was no quitter. A Company was in good hands.

Bill Hill had Company B. He was one of Nicholson's lame-ducks. He knew it and so he paid his way. He was a huge, jovial man with the physique of an interior lineman, which I understood he had been at the University of Oklahoma. There would be no sweat in B Company.

Company C was led by Captain Christopher J. (Chris) Dorney, the replacement to the lieutenant accused of ordering the execution. Dorney, who had distinguished himself as a commanding officer in the 4th Division, where he served with Sergeant Major Childers, looked at me with a bit of a jaundiced eye because he did not agree with me on the subject of tactics. Nevertheless, he did what he was told to do, and no commander could expect more. Even with his own variations, he was destined to score regularly. What the hell if he didn't agree? Company C was in better hands than it had ever been.

Jim Grimshaw, the guy Franklin and Nicholson had warned me about, was the commander of D Company. He was an outright winner from start to finish, built and trained for precisely what I had in mind for the battalion. He was the kind of guy who could beat the VC and NVA at their own game, or at ours. It didn't matter to him, as long as it was war. It seemed a game to him, even as it had been to me many years ago, and he invited everyone to play, including Bill Hill. Within a week, Grimshaw was to challenge Hill to a contest to determine which had the better company and the two of them accounted for over 75 per cent of the battalion's body counts.

The mission of Company E differed from the others in that it served as a pool for the battalion's heavy weapons, the mortars and the 106s.

Headquarters company belonged to Captain Szabolcs M. de Gyurky. He liked to be called Mike but we all referred to him as the Count. Whether or not he was a real Hungarian count didn't matter. He walked, talked, ate, and lived like one. He was a displaced person, and if he wanted to come on like a count or a baron or whatever the hell else, he had every right to. He had paid the price. Anyway, I liked Mike. He had come into the battalion in a blaze of glory, with tiger fatigues sharply creased and all the rest. He had served in Special Forces and he was proud. I caught up with him the first time in the mess hall.

"Get rid of those damned tiger fatigues, lose twenty pounds in the next three weeks, and come see me as soon as you finish your itsy-bitsy cookie," I said, rattling him not at all.

He was a romantic from the old school, the kind the Army loved, because he would do anything for his country. He was good, so I put him in charge of headquarters company where there were some pretty deep difficulties.

"But I don't want to command a headquarters company, sir," he said.

"No shit, Dick Tracy," I replied. "And just what did you expect to command?"

"A rifle company, sir."

"Who came for the job, you or me?"

"I did, sir."

"Good. You're in headquarters company."

Then we would start the same argument all over. His father had been a division commander with the "Prussians," he said. He hated like hell to call them Germans.

"And did they win?" I would ask.

"No, sir."

"Good. You're in headquarters company."

His family had been warriors since time immemorial, he would say. They were known in Hungarian history as the Saracen Blades.

"And is Hungary one of the Big Three powers?"

"No, sir."

"Good. You're in headquarters company."

He said he had dreamed of commanding a unit in the "last of the airborne brigades."

"This is my last chance," he said.

I looked in his eyes and saw part of me. "Look, de Gyurky, in time we all get our chances, but right now I need a headquarters company commander, desperately, and I'm not joking."

"Headquarters company, sir, and I will do you a good job."

"For sure," I said, slapping him on the back. We shook hands on it. The Count was something of an enigma to me. He and his younger sister had been befriended as children during the Allied occupation following World War II. There had been candy bars and all the rest from some redheaded American sergeant. They never forgot him and decided early that they would come to America and he would become a U.S. trooper. If there was ever a higher compliment paid to U.S. forces in that war, I haven't heard it. The Count got his wish, the hard way, coming up from private. He and his sister had come to Ohio and started from scratch. She later died when a drunk driver struck her on a bridge in Akron. He still carried the scars of that trauma, and he still had the notion that the greatest feat for any man was to die for his country. He was brave, truly brave—perhaps to a fault.

I had been just as lucky with my staff. I had Gifford in S1, and while we all called him "Big Mouth" Bernie, he was extremely bright, and what he said, which was a lot, was good and valuable. In S2, I had Donovan—who else but a guy named Donovan in intelligence—and he was intelligence personified. In S3, operations, Skeins was leaving and Ernie was coming in. In S4, I had Quirin to handle supply and there was Doc Tally and Larry Potter III, and now I was getting Childers as Sergeant Major.

Tally and Potter were a perfect example of my good fortune. They were one hell of a medical team. Doc was the battalion surgeon and Potter was the medical platoon leader, but really almost like a second surgeon. Doc was too sensible to have believed in the Vietnamese War, but he was better than any battalion surgeon I had ever seen. Despite his fat little belly and a general air of joviality, he ran a tough, straight shop, and he cared about everybody, our kids and theirs. A wounded VC or NVA received as intensive and courteous care as I would have. It mattered not to him if they were wounded by them or us or merely sick or feeble. He cared for them, with his heart and his skills as a physician. I made it a point to take him along on the missions whenever possible, and sometimes he would make the big difference. If there was still a tick left in a man when he got to him, it usually turned out all right. He was that good. I used to kid him about being a good surgeon but a lousy ecologist. "You keep crowding up the scenery with people who, in the natural course of things, should have died a long time ago," I would say. His malaria program was far above the rest of the field battalions, but nobody at headquarters wanted to listen to his suggestions. Thus, while the Brigade as a whole had one of the highest malaria rates in Vietnam, the 2d Battalion had one of the lowest.

Potter was everything but a surgeon, and I was certain he could have done surgery, too, if given the chance. He was the son of a former Surgeon General of the United States and he had been around a doctor so long, the skills were almost second nature to him. Why he chose Medical Supply and Administration, I don't know, but that was Larry: a man who did his thing, not his father's. I used him frequently both as an auxiliary doctor and as the senior medical-aid man on operations. Because of his deep concern over the critical plight of the Vietnamese, I also made him Assistant S5, and later the S5.

Together, Potter and Doc ran a shop that was as neat, clean, complete, and competent as anything they had at the big hospitals at Cam Ranh Bay, Qui Nhon, or Saigon, and it was a damned sight better than the Brigade installation. In fact, when Brigade had an important visitor interested in medicine, they brought him up to see Doc and Larry.

I had had the luck of the draw. How the hell could I possibly lose with the staff and the commanders around me? I just had to do my share: lay down the laws and rules of the game, make sure they were understood by everyone, and provide some know-how. It would work, I knew it. I wondered why it hadn't before. It was strange; these were the same men with the same potential. Maybe the idea of letting Larry Potter transfer provided some insight. Who the hell would want to get rid of him? Nobody in their right mind, I decided. It was crazy.

In fact, the whole damned U.S. Army in Vietnam was crazy. The generals—Westmoreland, Abrams, Peers, Rosson, DePuy, Richardson, Ewell, Ramsey, and the rest—were all working on the premise that they were the best and that whatever problems we were having were the fault of the commanders at the lower levels. Bullshit. The major leadership problem in Vietnam was the generals, and the rest of the senior officers' corps—the colonels, the lieutenant colonels, and the majors. The captains, lieutenants, and enlisted men weren't to blame.

The generals were has-beens or never-beens of World War II vintage who had paper images built by the public information people.

Take a good look. Who and what did we have? Where were the Pattons or the Eisenhowers or the Terry Allens or the Darbys or the Marshalls, or the Bradleys or the Clarks or the MacArthurs? We had Westmoreland, true, but so what? He was an artilleryman whose chest was heavy with "meritorious awards" and conspicuously bare of combat decorations for valor or gallantry.

In World War II, bright young leaders rose rapidly because they could cut it, and those who couldn't quite do the job made major, lieutenant colonel, or perhaps colonel. When it all ended, the guys who could cut it either stayed in until retirement or got out and made it in civilian life. The rest saw they would have to compete and civilian ways were scary to them, so they stayed. Why not? The pay was good, there was a certain prestige after the big guys went home—and bang! Five years later there was Korea. Like the Pennsylvania Railroad, we did it all on seniority now, and the guys who stayed in after the war were senior. With the Korean War, they picked up another promotion or two, and ten years later there was Vietnam, a war with all the trimmings and none of the personal risks. Now they were the generals, but they were still the almost-rans they had been in World War II. They walked and talked like leaders, and wore the ribbons and the uniforms, so it was only reasonable that back in Washington they were regarded as leaders and were listened to.

At the next senior levels—the colonels, lieutenant colonels and majors—the problem was something else: time and investment. We had gone into World War I, World War II, and Korea with a Reserve and a National Guard. These were nonprofessionals, in the sense that they were noncareerists who came in to fight a war and get it over with so they could get back to their families and their ways of making a living. If somebody wrote them up or gave them an ass-chewing, who cared? Four or five years later they were going to be civilians again. But in Vietnam it was different. We went in with a completely professional officers' corps—careerists, men with investments. Our lieutenant colonels had somewhere between twelve and sixteen years of service. One bad report out of Vietnam and there would be no promotion. It was over, Charlie—out with less than twenty years, with $300,000 in retirement slipping down the drain. This was a hell of a club over any man, especially a man with a family. Who the hell would pay Johnny's way through college? So the name of the game became "Don't Make Waves," and that was why the My Lais weren't reported. You make a few waves, cause a few worries and wrinkle a few brows up there, and you're out. Who needs a troublemaker anyway? That's why, even years later, we are still sweeping things under the rug at home. The Army investigate itself? Crap. At what precise level was the criminality? I can see it now:

WESTMORELAND: Well, Mr. President, after a complete and thoroughly impartial investigation, we have concluded that the blame must be laid at the level of the commander of the U.S. Army in Vietnam.

THE PRESIDENT: And who might that be, General?

WESTMORELAND: Why me, sir. Yes, sir, that is correct, sir. I was responsible and I am now preferring formal charges against myself this very afternoon.

There were a few colonels and others who had their twenty years in already and spoke out, but damned few. Why? Because they also were professionals and careerists, who had a chance to make it big if they could come out of Vietnam with a great paper record. That was precisely why so many of them had emerged from their cubicles at the Pentagon to get that ticket punched. There's nothing like the old combat record and a chestful of ribbons when the promotion board meets five years later. Nobody remembers then that the medals were issued in a packet for just being there and not for heroism under fire. Hell, in Vietnam we issued medals for valor by roster! One big fat list of names with no specifics and no detailed descriptions of the actions for which they were being awarded. It got so bad in the 173d, it became necessary to write a special letter if a trooper wasn't up to rating even one of the packets—and documented evidence was necessary with the letter.

I dropped from the helicopter and walked over to the dike where Lieutenant Shotwell and his platoon were hunched down. The village lay just behind the paddy.

"Any in there?" I asked.

"Yes, sir," the lieutenant answered.

"How many?"

"Don't know, sir."

"Who's maneuvering?"

"No one."

"Why not?"

"We've been taking fire," he said. He looked strange, lying there talking while I was standing. There was a tinge of excitement in his voice. It seemed time to bring a little calm, and then some action. I changed the subject.

"I thought down at Brigade you just couldn't wait to get out here and demonstrate to one and all how it should best be done," I said. "Or maybe I misunderstood you." I shook my head and laughed. "Of course, they weren't shooting down there in that big, bad office, were they? In fact, they're not shooting one hell of a lot here, either." I held up my hands, palms upward to the sky, feeling for rain.

"You better get your ass down, sir. They're there all right," the platoon sergeant said. It was Sergeant Hubbard. Among the papers

Nicholson had left in his In box when he rotated was an unsigned battlefield promotion request for Hubbard.

"Are you sure?" I said.

"They were, anyways," Hubbard answered.

"Then get off your bellies and go get them," I said. "That's what you're being paid to do—so get a maneuver element out, and right now!"

They did it as well as anything they had ever done at Ft. Benning, and I was so goddamned proud I could have burst my buttons. I was seeing what I should have seen and it felt good, damned good. They laid down a base of fire under Shotwell's direction while Hubbard and I took one squad and moved off into the bush and came into the village from the south. It was over in three or four minutes. Hubbard and I reached the hut first. Inside were two dead VC, a rifle, and a bag of grenades. One grenade was still smoking in the center of the floor. I dove for it and wheeled it out the window where it hit a tree, bounced back, and exploded against the outside of the wall of the hut. Hubbard had joined me on the floor and his helmet rolled across it toward one of the bodies.

"Goddamnit, sir, do you expect to be with us long?"

I stood up and brushed myself off, keeping my rifle in my right hand, finger still on the trigger, barrel toward the bodies. "Not if you spend half of each working day down on your bellies, I don't," I said. "I'll just go out and get myself a battalion elsewhere." I looked down. "Two pissy little 98-pounders and one out-of-date rifle," I snorted. It was for his benefit, not mine. All I saw were two dead human beings. For what? For an idea? For whose idea?

The platoon handled the rest of the village in fine style, and although there was no other action, they moved well: carefully, quickly, and professionally. I wasn't sure about the rest of the battalion, but I knew I had one platoon for sure.

The next afternoon, I knew I had at least two. Lieutenant Larry LeRay's platoon, with Wally Warden aboard as its sergeant, was flying back from the beach near Bong Son—they had conducted a search there—and had drawn fire from the ground. A week before, it would have meant a report and some artillery, but that was when Warden was still cleaning the latrines. Now he had a platoon. He ordered the chopper around, radioed the message while he was banking, and had the pilot put them down close to the huts from which the fire had come.

Webb and I got there before they had cleared them—Ernie stayed airborne and I went down with Warden. We were moving up a hill toward the huts, through brush and neck-high thorn bushes. From the distance, it looked like grass. It was deceptive, ideal for the VC— the kind of place to dig in, with little holes here and there up under the thickest briars. They were rolling grenades down the hill toward us, and I knew right then that there were some tight ass-holes on that hill. If grenades were it, then we had them by the ying-yang; I could see some sick mother up there, kicking himself for firing those few rounds at the choppers. The grenades stopped and I pushed through the brush, concentrating on the holes ahead. Suddenly Warden shouted. Several men bounced from the hole just above the one I was watching and started firing rounds all around me. Warden let loose a burst of fire that tore at my eardrums and dropped one of them. A man appeared in the hole I had been watching and I saw the barrel of an AK–47 swinging around. I drilled him, saw his face disintegrate. Another one was running through the brush just above me and Warden shouted again and fired off another burst, dropping the man almost on top of me. Jesus, I thought, Warden could still be cleaning the toilets. It was picking up all over the hill as they started making a break for it. The radio man informed me that Bill Hill was coming in on the other side, and I knew it was all over but the shouting.

I never made it to the crest of the hill. We had wounded two of them, one so badly he didn't have to surrender. The other one had his hands locked above his head and was just coming out of that position when I arrived. Two troopers were covering him and a buck sergeant was moving toward him—and quickly, almost before I understood what I saw, he had his bayonet out and zeroed in on the prisoner's stomach. "You lousy bastard," the sergeant shouted—and I stuck out my foot, grabbed him around the throat and threw him to the ground.

"Hold it, Sarge," I soothed. "Take it easy."

"They're bastards," he shouted. "Dirty, stinking, dink, mother-fucking bastards."

Someone else had come over to help me. I pressed my knee down in his back. "Take it easy, Sarge, just nice and easy," I said. It was not the time for orders and commands. "Remember what I said about getting information from the living? Information!" I shouted and felt him go limp under my knee. After a couple of deep breaths, I let him stand and helped brush him off. "From this point on, Sarge, no killing of prisoners. Understand?"

He was much meeker and his voice was almost inaudible, but I heard his words: "I understand, sir."

"Good," I smiled. "Then, let's get on with it."

I had them move the wounded guy down the hillside and tie up the other one. "Call in the C and C and get this guy to a hospital," I said, pointing to the Viet on the ground. A medic was already working on him.

"I don't think he'll make it, sir," he said.

I had seen worse. "He'll make it." I turned back to the radio man. "Get that damned bird down here."

"He says he's not coming in for any wounded dink, sir," he said.

I reached over, grabbed the hand-set, and pressed the talk-switch. "Eagle, this is Six. Over."

"This is Eagle. Over."

"This is Six. Now listen close, 'cause I'm short on time and patience. I have a wounded soldier. I say again: a soldier. Bring that bird in. Over."

"This is Eagle. Is it U.S. wounded? Over."

I was finished pissing around. "This is Six. No, goddamnit, it is not. Now either bring that bird in or I'll have you shot out of the sky myself. Put Three on. Over." I needed to talk with Ernie. He crackled in on his own.

"This is Three. Was on another net to higher. Just monitored your last. On the way in. Out."

I watched the bird flare up and come in, had the guy loaded on, along with his healthy buddy, and shouted to Webb, "Get them back, Ernie. Let's see if we can save this one."

"Roger that," he shouted back.

I went back to the hill to observe the final clean-up. There were seven dead VC, maybe two of them NVA, with four rifles, one of them an AK–47, grenades, documents, a couple of radios, and a medical kit. I turned to Wally. "I wonder which one fired at the bird."

He glanced around at the bodies and gear and offered an expert opinion. "A loser, sir," he said. "A goddamned, dumb-ass, mother-fucking loser."

The spit of land was just one long, flat, narrow stretch of sand, and Lieutenant LeRay's platoon, still on standby alert at the Berm, had been ordered onto it for a probe. Brigade intelligence had come up with the idea that there was a hidden communications station there, so we had moved the men in for a look around. There wasn't a whole hell of a lot to do except line up at one end of the spit with a couple of mine detectors and start toward the other with the hope of running into something. I guessed that at best it might be buried equipment utilized at night and covered over at dawn, but a complete communications station could not absolutely be ruled out, so we went merrily on our way, probing and scanning and walking on the sand.

It was February 14, St. Valentine's Day, and I had been in command for one week. Things were looking up. Childers had come up with a new radio man, who had already served a full tour and was willing to stay on now that it looked as though there might be some action. He was a spanking new buck sergeant, a courageous, quiet, intelligent, and cool young man. He stayed with me for the rest of my command and left when I did. Gifford rotated out about the same time and Captain Preston A. Parrott replaced him as S1—but everything else was the same. Things were moving. The documents were panning out and each night we were getting as many as five kills or captures in our ambushes. Leads were starting to come in and, in fact, that was why we were out on the sand spit that morning. The Brigade had come up with the idea of the hidden station from some of the documents we had captured.

We worked on past noon with nothing to show for it except a platoon of sand-encrusted, sweaty faces. Ernie Webb showed up. "How goes?" he said.

"Wanna buy some sand, Ernie?"

"Not really."

"Then, it's going lousy."

"Well, let me give you some good news," he said, smiling.

It was the beginning of a chapter in the life of the 173d Airborne Brigade that the Army would still be denying four years later: Cu Loi.

Captain Striker, the operations officer for the Brigade Aviation Platoon, and another pilot had been out flying light observation helicopters (LOHs) that morning and had spotted four men running

Tony Herbert at nine with
niece Irene Wilps.

Jules Theibert, Tony's
maternal grandfather.

Right: 1932. Miners outside of Herminie Shaft.
Below: Fourth Street, Herminie. Company store is two-story structure at end of street; post office is on its right.
Below right: Madison Avenue, Herminie. Slate dump is in upper right-hand corner.

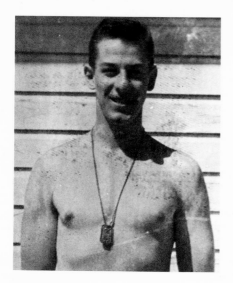

As a buck private—Ft. Dix, 1947.

Korea. Cpl. Herbert receives Silver
Star from Lt. Col. Frank T. Mildren,
who as MAC-V Commander in
April 1969 was responsible for the
initial investigation of Lt. Col.
Herbert's charges.

Pittsburgh, December 1951.
M/Sgt. Herbert and M/Sgt.
Ziya Burus of Turkey pose
on a UN-sponsored tour as
their countries' outstanding
soldiers of the Korean War.
The occasion was Tony
Herbert Day, as declared by
the governor of Pennsylvania;
Tony holds the key to the
city.

With Eleanor Roosevelt, in Paris on European tour.

1952. U.S. Army publicity photo for Ranger recruitment. Picture was used on posters and in numerous publications.

1962, Germany. B Company of the 505th Airborne Battle Group, Capt. Herbert commanding. Over a one-year period

1955. Herbert, actually a civilian at this time, was sent to Hollywood by the Army for publicity purposes. Here he exchanges books with World War II hero and movie actor Audie Murphy.

fourteen trophies for unit excellence were awarded in the 8th Division, and B Company won all of them.

1965, Ft. Bragg, North Carolina. Capt. Herbert discusses tactical exercises with 2d Airborne Division CO Maj. Gen. Robert York and Brigade Commander Col. Austin, just prior to the Dominican Republic intervention.

Execution in Santo Domingo by the rebels, many of them trained by the U.S.
Army to operate against Fidel Castro. Army denies that the incident ever occurred.
Doorway at left edge of top photo is on the right edge of bottom photo.

Muscat, Oman, 1966. Maj. Herbert stands with Arab leaders and British "liaison" officer, meeting to coordinate intelligence operations against local guerrillas.

The *Duxbury Bay,* flagship of the commander, Middle East Forces. A uniquely equipped electronic headquarters, it was responsible for the coordination of "all free-world intelligence in the Middle East and Africa south of the Sahara."

An Khe, Vietnam, 1968. Lt. Col. Herbert's IG hootch, within the steakhouse-swimming-pool-pizza-parlor-Officer-and-NCO-Club complex.

February 6, 1969. Brig. Gen. John Barnes presents the colors of the 2d Battalion, 503d Infantry, to Lt. Col. Herbert upon his assuming command of the unit.

Brigade Tactical Operations Center (TOC) at LZ English. Note transmission and receiving antennae for command and control of all field operations.

LZ English, Brigade Forward Headquarters, which according to Army policy should be able to operate out of two three-quarter ton trucks or one tent.

General Barnes presents Bronze Star for Valor to Sgt. First Class Wallace Warden for action during which he saved Lt. Col. Herbert's life.

Above left: Ernie Webb. *Right:* Lt. Col. Herbert's radio operator, Sgt. Potter, typically, "in the grass."

Enemy soldier staked out by North Vietnamese major for committing atrocities against Americans.

Water torture of Vietnamese detainee conducted by Military Intelligence sergeant from 173d Brigade Headquarters. Photo taken by Lt. Col. Herbert's pilot, Larry Pippen.

Col. Joseph Ross Franklin.
(Wide World Photos)

The Rockpile. In the foreground, VC suspects who later escaped.
Brigade Headquarters claimed they were released because they
were "old men and women."

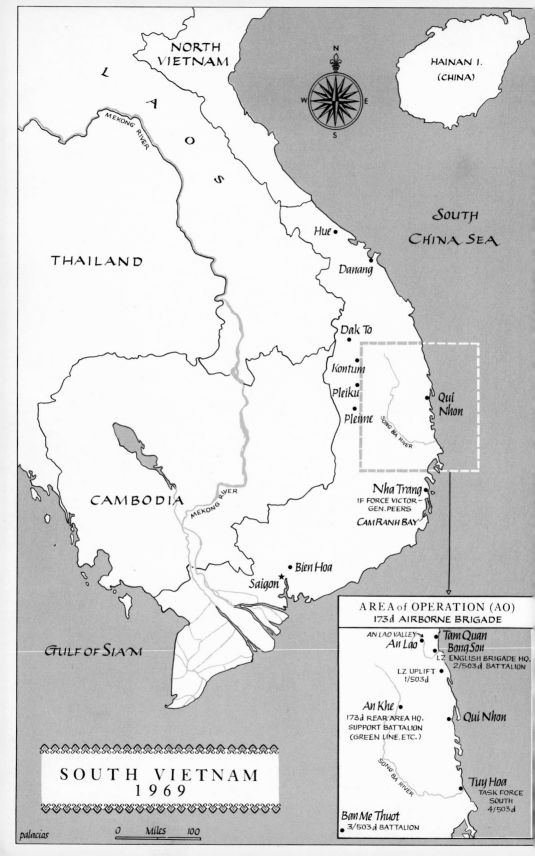

NORTH
VIETNAM

L A O S

MEKONG RIVER

THAILAND

HAINAN I.
(CHINA)

N
W   E
S

SOUTH

CHINA SEA

Hue •

Danang •

Dak To •

Kontum •

Pleiku •

Pleime •

Qui
Nhon •

SONG BA RIVER

CAMBODIA

MEKONG RIVER

Nha Trang •
IF FORCE VICTOR –
GEN. PEERS

CAM RANH BAY

Bien Hoa

Saigon ★

GULF of SIAM

SOUTH VIETNAM
1969

palacios

0   Miles   100

AREA of OPERATION (AO)
173d AIRBORNE BRIGADE

AN LAO VALLEY
An Lao

Tam Quan
Bong Son
LZ ENGLISH BRIGADE HQ.
2/503d BATTALION

LZ UPLIFT
1/503d

An Khe •
173d REAR AREA HQ.
SUPPORT BATTALION
(GREEN LINE, ETC.)

Qui Nhon

SONG BA RIVER

Tuy Hoa
TASK FORCE
SOUTH
4/503d

Ban Me Thuot •
3/503d BATTALION

through some palm trees along the beach near the village of Cu Loi. The men on the ground were obviously attempting to evade the eyes of the American pilots, but to no avail. Striker and the other pilot, with their LOHs equipped with light machine guns, went right in under the trees and killed all four. Striker landed and retrieved one weapon and a bundle of what he thought at the time were documents. They turned out to be a major payroll in gold certificates. It was quite a haul: a roster, a map, and the information that there would be a meeting that night in Cu Loi. The payroll was being delivered to the wheels of the Viet Cong, the infrastructure, as we called them. They ran the local cells and were the lifeblood of the guerrilla movement— not that they shed their blood very often, but in terms of providing the brains and the organization.

"What's Brigade planning to do about the meeting?" I asked Ernie.

He laughed. "You know Beacham and Accousti. It'll make a nice note at the evening briefing."

He was right. I did know Major Paul J. Beacham and Major Kenneth W. Accousti. The troops facetiously called them the Gold Dust Twins. Beacham was the Brigade's S2 while Accousti served as the S3.

"It would make a better note if we could get in on that meeting," I said. "Look, Ernie, I tell you what." I swept my hand toward LeRay's platoon, still poking around in the sand. "Get these guys loaded and in the air." I stood up and brushed off the sand. "Meanwhile, I'll get back and see what I can do about getting us invited to the meeting." I turned to my radio man, Sergeant Smith. "Get me the C and C, Smitty."

By the time the bird landed, Ernie had already explained things to LeRay, and joined me and Smitty on board for the short hop back to Brigade Headquarters at English. While Webb was on the network, I studied the map. Cu Loi was on a long peninsula. A narrow inlet widened down its western edge into a great, broad bay. On its eastern edge, long golden beaches ran down into the South China Sea. No wonder the VC liked it. It was typical of so many concentrations in the country. If we came from the west, we had to cross the bay while, in the meantime, the people in the village, the simple fisherfolk, moved quietly east and launched their little boats and went fishing. There was no overland way in from the north—the jungle on the other side of the inlet was thick and sturdy and did not lend itself to the portage of boats—and if we came in from the east, from the sea, they simply launched their craft into the bay and disappeared into the jungle on the other side. If we came in from the south, they had plenty of time to know we were there. The answer? Maybe a simultaneous attack from two directions, which sounded nice and looked even better on Brigade stationery. But out there the paper plans didn't matter very much. There was just too goddamned much jungle and too much water and too much land. They knew they were safe because they were just a small-fish target, except when they congregated as they were about to do that night. I intended to make certain that we didn't let the opportunity slip by us.

I went straight to Accousti myself, rather than sending Webb. Accousti didn't want to buy it. "The documents haven't even been processed yet, sir," he argued.

"When, Ken?"

"Late tonight. Tomorrow. I don't know."

"Then we can all sit around and talk about the meeting they had, right?"

"Come on, sir, lay off, will you?"

"Not hardly," I said, and kept boring in. I would take complete responsibility, I said. We already had the platoon in the air. Why not work them those last couple of minutes of the day? Hell, we could land, check it out, then fly back and go to bed. "At least the VC will know the Brigade cares enough to follow through, huh?"

He finally relented, but he cautioned that we would have no artillery and no air support except the two light observation helicopters that had turned up the information in the first place.

"You're wasting your time, sir. I can assure you, you're wasting your time," Accousti said.

"Well, it's our time, so if I want to make an ass out of myself—"

"All right, sir, but you'll have to come in at dusk, regardless. Okay?"

"Okay," I answered—and we were off. I could do without the artillery and the air support. I wouldn't have been able to figure out how to use it even if I'd had it. The two LOHs were just fine. We were already involved in too damned much indiscriminate use of artillery and air power against villages. I'd trade a whole damned flight of the best high-performance aircraft for one LOH in this type of operation, and if worst came to worst, I could still get my artillery.

I boarded the C and C with Ernie and we caught up with LeRay's flight enroute to the target. The instructions were given out over the net. There was no time to fool around or be cute. We told our people what to do in plain English, and if the enemy monitored us and got the message out and still had time to react—and whipped us to boot—then, hell, they deserved to win. While Ernie talked on the net, I made one last good study of the map, getting it all down in my head. When Webb had finished, I told him the operational order. "Smitty and I will take the ground. It'll be a while. I want you back at English on the net, and have one of the companies from the field locked and ready for pick-up."

"How about Dorney?" he asked.

"C Company is fine, just have them ready and keep the birds handy."

"That's a Roge," he said.

I got on the net with Kahila, my pilot. I wanted him to come in behind the last ship in LeRay's flight. "Touch down with them, okay?" I told him, and then settled down to study the terrain as we went in. I selected the LZ, gave the word to Ernie, leaned out of the bird and dropped a smoke canister right on target. The ship banked around and came up behind the last Huey. I checked my rifle, made sure of my knife, flicked the safety off the weapon with my index finger and tapped the magazine to ensure its seating.

Kahila wheeled in from over the sea and then clattered straight south. From my spot on the left side of the bird, all I could see was a small strip of that golden beach and a hell of a lot of the South China Sea. Ernie tapped me. "The LZ is red," he said. "Want to take it up?" I shook my head and gave him a thumbs-down. I felt my pulse accelerate a bit. Maybe I was getting old. Maybe I'd had too many wars. Just then I felt the flare-up from beneath my feet. I looked outside and leaped. I could hear the crack of the rifles even before the last bird was back up and off. I rolled to my feet. Smitty was up against a dune and I could see troops moving across the beach about seventy-five to one hundred meters away. Smitty got up, brushed himself off, and blew the sand out of the hand-set.

"Did you see LeRay?" I asked.

"Over there, sir," he said, pointing to a solitary figure moving southwest toward a group of troops down on their stomachs and knees, firing toward the south. "Get him on the net and have him hold until we get there. He's heading off wrong."

Smitty fell in behind me, talking all the while. I could see LeRay answering him on his mike. He stopped, turned around and saw us moving up. He dropped down on both knees. A couple of his men were still firing south and I saw two Viets running along the sand with the slugs digging at their heels. I told LeRay to tell them to forget it. They were too far away for M–16s. "Let's get it all back on the road northwest, Larry," I said, "toward the village—that's the mission." I figured the two running down the beach to be a diversion. It was old VC. LeRay was having some problems with his CAR–15. (Didn't they all?) I loaned him my .45 and we started back northwest. Warden and a machine gunner crossed the beach north of us and entered the jungle. Wally was giving the guy hell and he was saying, "Yes, Sergeant, yes, Sergeant." Smitty and I entered the jungle just south of where they had gone in while LeRay and the rest of his group went in just south of us. The two choppers were screaming in just above the branches, rapping in bursts of fire with their mini-guns, hanging there just above the trees, sliding sideways, back and forth. There was a hut just north of us and Smitty and I turned onto the trail leading to it. He picked up the LOH commander on the radio and learned that the birds had already creamed one guy with a rifle. The rest, he said, had gone inside. There were children with them, the pilot said. Did they have permission? I took the hand-set.

"This is Six. No. Permission denied. I say again: permission denied. Mark it with smoke. We'll take care of it and thanks. Over."

"Got it. Out."

I handed it back to Smitty. "Read LeRay in on the smoke," I said, keeping my eye on the canister as it dropped from the LOH and burst in a cloud, erupting up through the foliage. I could barely make out what looked like the corner of the hut. I stepped out on the path and Smitty fell in behind. When they could see us from above, one of the men in the chopper leaned out and gave us a wave and pointed down. I waved back and they wheeled off to the north. Someone fired on the other side of the hut. I dropped to one knee and Smitty hit the dirt behind me. Warden came running around the east side of the building. Smitty and I got back to our feet. Warden had been on the other side of the hut, trying to move up under cover of the choppers. As they had banked off, three men had broken from the edge of the building and over into a clump of brush from which they could cover the trail on which Smitty and I were walking. "I shouted for them to surrender once," Warden said. "One of them spun around and started up with his rifle so I dropped him. The other two grabbed him and all three dropped down into a bunker on the other side of the hut." Jesus, Warden had done it again. In one week, this former latrine orderly, Nicholson's coward, had saved my skin twice.

"Do they still have the rifle?" I asked.

"No, sir, but they've got an AK–47. The rifle's still in the brush where I dropped him."

"Okay, Wally, go back around the east side and Smitty and I will take the west. Take it slow and easy and we'll cover each other as much as possible."

"Right, sir," Warden said.

"Did you see anybody else?"

"Nope."

I flicked the safety off and stepped out.

It was a damned fine, solid hut. I knew immediately it didn't belong to a poor man nor to any little old rice farmer because there was no stall for the buffalo. It was a one-story structure built on a slab of concrete raised a couple of feet off the ground, much like a patio. It measured about forty feet square with its rear to the southeast. The porch was on the other side and a man was sprawled in the front yard, face down in the dust, dead. His rifle lay a few feet from his outstretched hands. I came around the porch and saw the entire family waiting there: a very old man—a real papa-san—an elderly woman, a young girl and two children. Over against the wall, a young man was sitting next to the doorway with his coolie hat pulled low over his face. He seemed to be working like hell to look old, and everybody else was trying very hard to make it all appear natural. That was a dead giveaway. Regardless of the circumstances, the locals always obeyed their instructions down to the letter. Act naturally, they were told, and they did exactly that regardless of what was happening to them or around them. The only ones looking anywhere but down were the girl and the children. They could not keep their eyes off the body sprawled before them in the dirt. I motioned for Smitty to keep them all covered and called for Wally to check out the body. The bunker was across the yard and I watched the entrance-hole, keeping the young stud by the doorway in the corner of my eye. We would get around to him in a second. Warden went up into one of the hut's two rooms, reappeared and passed by the young stud into the other room. Finally, he came out.

"Empty," he said.

"Good, Smitty, keep the group. Warden, you cover me." I crossed the yard to the bunker and nailed myself up against its outside edge. "Chieu Hoi!" I shouted, using the name of the program we had set up for leniency in return for immediate, unresisting surrender. "Chieu Hoi!" As always, there was no response. I waited, then stepped back and fired two quick rounds into the sandbags around the doorway. Then, stepping back against the wall, I lifted a grenade from my belt. The old woman on the porch screamed and there was one hell of a scuffling inside the bunker. They tripped all over each other coming out—hands first.

"Chieu Hoi! Chieu Hoi! Me Chieu Hoi! Chieu Hoi!" they were shouting.

"I figured you were," I mumbled to myself. There were three of them: two in khakis and the wounded guy stripped down to his shorts. I nudged them toward Warden. "Keep them covered," I said. "I'll get the bunker."

"I'll get it, sir," Smitty said, trotting across toward me.

"Goddamn it, keep that group covered," I shouted. "I'll get the damned bunker. We all get paid by the same people." I don't think it was bravado; it was just that I had learned years before that if you wanted to be followed, then you had to get your ass out and lead by setting the example. If I expected other people to go down inside bunkers and holes after the enemy, then I had better be ready to do it once in a while myself. This time it was my turn. I kept my rifle in front. It wasn't nearly as dangerous as everyone seems to think. After all, anybody in the bunker was trapped. He was finished one way or the other and he had but two choices: to live it out as a POW or give up the ghost. If anyone was in there and he fired, then I would get him or the guy after me would or the one after him—and he must have known that if we wanted to kill him, we would have gone in with a grenade in the first place. At Brigade, there was a consensus that these people were some sort of subhumans without any intelligence. But I had been out there before, and Buddhists, Taoists, and Confucians were a long way from subhuman.

It was wasted philosophy. The bunker was clean except for the AK–47, a couple of grenades, and about ten pounds of documents. I didn't take the time to go under the flooring as I would have if I had had more men with me. After all, there was still the young stud by the doorway, and if anybody there was hard-core VC, it was him. I kept my eye on him while Warden got on the net and called LeRay, requesting some assistance. While he was talking, other U.S. troops came into the clearing around the hut with another group of prisoners, all of them males. The new troops had a Kit Carson along, one of the hundreds of North Vietnamese who had surrendered and been re-indoctrinated and were now working for us. Their motivations were varied: some did it for money, a few for political rewards, some stayed a couple of days and then disappeared, but some were very good. The ones that stayed were very close to the American troopers. They became family, and the links between them and some of our guys were strong. I saw some of the toughest troopers in the country bawl their eyes out over a Kit Carson's body. I felt that way about Zin, the Kit along with us today. He was a soldier, and a damned good one, and I had never been able to hold back my respect for a good soldier, regardless of the colors he wore. Men who shared the possibility of death shared something quite indefinable.

The young stud by the doorway was that kind of a man, too. I watched him as some of the guys searched the brush, picking up pieces of equipment here and there. Zin was with them, turning up stuff as fast as he could: another rifle, another AK–47, more documents, more grenades, belts, packets, a radio, and a roster. It had been a headquarters-type unit and there had been a major payroll meeting. The choppers had picked off the paymaster of course—which had ended payday—but it had been too late for them to call off the meeting. They were all still around, scattered throughout the village. It had been a huge payroll with about forty paymasters. Zin said they would be carrying pistols and revolvers with maybe a couple of AKs and a couple of SKSs.

"Most all will have grenades, Colonel, sir," Zin added.

"You sure?"

"Very sure. They all do."

Zin moved over to the young girl and began asking questions, keeping his eye, as I was, on the hard-core stud. They said a couple of words in Vietnamese. The girl looked up and started to talk. The stud looked up. That was all: he just raised his head a fraction of an inch—and the girl fell silent. The stud dropped his head again. Zin grabbed the girl and shook her, shouting at her, but it was useless. He looked back at me and cut his eyes toward the corner of the porch where the young man was squatting against the wall. We both knew who was boss around there, as far as the VC were concerned.

Someone shouted, "Grenade!" and the others all hit the dirt. I dropped on one knee, holding my head down low in front of my shoulders. I saw the guy break out of the bush with another grenade in his hands. I squeezed twice on the trigger and watched the rounds slam into his chest, driving him up against one of the palms, bouncing him off into the bushes. I swung back around to the porch. The hard-core was already pushing himself up. I motioned him back down with the rifle barrel and this time our eyes met. There was no sense kidding each other any longer. Without any melodramatics, it was a little like a couple of gunfighters—one a little more experienced than the other, but no better; but for the luck of the draw and a little edge in experience, it might have been him with the rifle and me squatting on the porch holding up the doorway. I could see it in his eyes. He wouldn't make the same mistake the next time, if there were a next time. Jesus, I thought, give me a battalion of this type and I'd clean up Vietnam by myself.

Two of our men had been hit by the explosion. I didn't re-member even hearing the grenade detonate, except vaguely perhaps. That's how unimportant grenades were—for me, at least. I had seen them all over the world and had used them and had had them used against me, over and over. I did not respect them as a weapon. They were charges. They blew up and out. Lay one out at arms-length, stay down flat, and the worst it could do to you was give you a con-cussion. Run, and you got some shrapnel in your ass. I liked the grenade for its psychological impact, but not for the way it was used in the movies. Everybody has seen the same scene: the grenade goes in, the walls explode out, people catapult through the roof, and the entire building collapses. Crap. One day I'd probably lose my ass for not getting down all the way, but one thing was for sure: I still had the stud in my sights, and I wouldn't have if I'd hit the dirt along with everyone else.

Someone went over and yanked the body out of the bush. He had a radio, a pouch of documents, and about four or five more grenades. Someone shouted, "Grenade!" again, and this time we all hit it, including the stud. It came right off the porch and laid up against the cement and exploded between us. There were ricochets and I got a mouthful of sand, but nobody else was hurt. I bounced back up right behind the blast and the stud was still down on his stomach. It damn sure hadn't been his. LeRay went past me onto the porch and into the hut with Smitty right behind him. They emerged together.

"Nothing," said LeRay.

"It's empty," said Smitty.

The troops started rechecking the bush and Zin started questioning the stud. It was no use. He shook his head. "Not him, Colonel," he said.

"Watch him," I said and turned to LeRay. "That grenade came from the building. You take that side and I'll take this one." I turned the muzzle of the M–16 west and followed it around the building. I heard LeRay fire. Just then a grenade exploded and I got around the building just in time to see LeRay kicking away the reeds and dragging the body from between the false walls. The guy had been wedged into a section about the size of a bird cage. LeRay nudged the bloody body with his foot. "A loser, sir," he said quietly, gently, with that same catch in his voice that you hear in the movies just before the tears. "A goddamned loser-dink." He rolled it over gently. The guy had been a real trooper and he had tried just as he had been told, just as so many of our kids had been told and would have tried had they been in his place. Uncle Ho would never even know the poor bastard was dead, nor would he have given a shit had he known. Like those on our side, he was just another statistic. We left him there in the dirt.

When we returned to the yard, there were about fifteen detainees. Warden and two other men were tying them while two other troopers covered. A medic was tending the wounded. The right thing to do then would have been to have perched on the edge of the porch, ass propped up on one cheek, and to have pulled out a cigarette, a la John Wayne. Alas, I didn't smoke. I stood around watching, kicking up some more brush, ever the over-promoted private looking for one more belt, one more weapon, one more document, one more anything. I watched them tie up the last of them and stepped back into the clearing.

"Take them back to the LZ and get them on the first birds along with the wounded," I said, and turned back to the brush, still kicking around. There was no sense starting out in any other direction. LeRay had seen to it that we had men all through the village and it was getting close to dusk. Franklin wanted me on the net, so I moved back into the clearing and took the hand-set.

"This is Involved Six. Over."

"This is Speedster," he said. Damn it, he never used the correct call-signs. "What's the story? Over."

I gave it to him as best I could, and when I was done he told me a Vietnamese unit was coming in "just to make it legal." There would be a U.S. advisor with them, he said, and I was to turn over any detainees.

"Too late. Already out at the LZ ready for extraction."

He got nasty. He wanted them turned over to the advisor and the Vietnamese. If they were out on the LZ already, then I was to stop it and do as he said. "Over." Franklin switched.

"This is Six. Roger. Out."

It was too late. I could hear the birds coming in to the LZ. I'd have to explain later, I knew, but then those were the breaks of the game. I turned back to LeRay.

"Anything going?"

Before he could answer, firing broke out to the south and we were off and moving. "Get on the net and get the word out that we've got South Viets in the area," I shouted to him. Smitty came in on the path behind me just as Warden trotted breathlessly around the bend toward us. He was sweating like a coal miner the day after the strike, and I guessed that one of two things had happened: either our guys had opened up on the South Vietnamese accidentally or else the South Viets had been shooting indiscriminately, as they were so prone to do.

I was wrong on both counts.

Warden poured out the story. The U.S. advisor to the Viet police had met him enroute to the LZ and had, Warden said, "assumed responsibility" for the detainees.

"So I turned them over," he continued. "Then they just started questioning them and blowing their heads off, sir."

That was the firing I had heard to the south. We started back down the trail at a trot. An outright run was out of the question because, more than likely, if you broke out of the bush running, you were a dead-ass. Even at our speed, it was more than a few seconds before we reached a large, grassy clearing. The American lieutenant, the advisor, was on my left as we entered the clearing, and the rest were standing around in no particular formation. Across the clearing I saw one man, a Vietnamese, holding the young girl's hair with his left hand, bending her head back, baring her throat. His right arm was around her and a knife in his right hand was dug deeply in her flesh, beneath and to the left of her esophagus. All he had to do was pull and, click, she was gone. One of the children was hanging onto her pajamas, screaming, and the other child's face was being steadily squashed into the sand by the boot of another Vietnamese. The child was suffocating. I shoved the American lieutenant out of the way and shouted something, staring at the guy with the knife at the girl's throat. He was staring at me, too.

With great ease, he pulled the blade across. Her blood spurted and gushed down the front of her pajamas and she dropped to the darkening sand, pulling the child with her. It took no more than a second from the instant he moved the knife until she crumpled in a lifeless heap, her baby still screaming, still pawing at her legs. Her killer jumped back into the group of Vietnamese, pulling with him the guy who'd been suffocating the child. I should have shot them on the spot, while I could still identify them. The rest of the detainees were lined up against the bushes. Four of the men were already dead, lying in the grass off to my right with their heads blown away. A Vietnamese was parading up and down in front of the survivors, waving a pistol. I noticed that one of the four dead men was the stud we had captured at the hut. I felt myself go empty, something drained from me in that moment that I have yet to replace.

"You dumb son-of-a-bitch," I screamed, grabbing the American lieutenant by his shirt. In that instant, I was only a flick away from killing him. It passed. I calmed and turned him loose. "Just what the hell did you let happen here, Lieutenant?"

He was only an advisor, he said. They were only doing a job. They knew their business. Guerrillas weren't protected under the Geneva Accords. They were following orders.

Oh, God, I thought. A big, bad-assed American who had never

killed anyone in combat or captured a single prisoner legitimately had played hell with these poor devils. Big, bad-assed, All-American boy. God, I was frustrated. I raised my hand to slap him clear across the area. I lowered it.

"You get all your scrap together and then get the hell out of here," I screamed at him.

"Sir, I have a job."

I glanced down at the four dead men and over to the woman's body. "Not anymore you don't, Lieutenant." He was staring at me with what seemed to be disbelief. I moved as near to him as possible without touching. "Now, you get your people out of here—out of here," I said, quietly and calmly now. "You're finished here. The rest of this—like the charges—we'll take care of back at English."

I think I was steady by then, but there was great hatred inside me. I hadn't felt it with such intensity in years.

I turned to Wally Warden. "Get the rest of the detainees together and out to the LZ, and get on the radio and have your men guard the rest and make sure that none of these rats' asses get back to them." I went over and knelt down next to the girl's body. I looked at the children for a moment, wondering what was creeping through their young minds as they crawled and cried around their mother's bloody corpse. I picked up both of them and carried them over to the line of detainees against the bushes. I handed them to one of the men. "I'm sorry," I mumbled. "I'm sorry. Take care of them." I turned back to Warden. "Now get them out of here, Wally."

Smitty and I were left alone in the clearing—alone with the dead. "Smitty," I said, staring hard at the bodies of the men, "the hard-core stud there was a better man than that son-of-a-bitch of a lieutenant."

The radio crackled. "Speedster, sir," Smitty said, offering me the hand-set.

"This is Six. Over."

Franklin wanted to know whether or not I had given the detainees to the American advisor and the Vietnamese. I tried to tell him what had happened without using the word "murder" on the radio. "The lieutenant has overstepped his authority, sir, and had to be ordered out of the area," I said into the microphone.

"Let me talk to him," Franklin said.

"He's gone."

"You go get him and turn them over to him."

I tried to explain that that would be impossible under the circumstances, and for some reason I mentioned MAC-V Directive 20–4, the war-crime counsel from higher headquarters. He seemed not to be listening. I had been given a direct order, he said. Either I would obey it, or I would be guilty of violating direct orders under combat conditions. He made it sound very ominous.

"I'll explain it when I get back," I said.

"You bet your ass you will," he said. "You get back here right now."

"Roger that. Out."

I handed the set back to Smitty. There was some more firing off to the east. Dusk was settling fast. I bent down over the bodies of the four men. The flies were already gathering on their gaping wounds. I glanced back at the girl. The shadows were already reaching her form. In a couple of minutes, it would be black.

"Give them the word, Smitty," I said. "Out to the LZ."

We pushed off east while he was still talking into the set. The C and C came in in a swirl of loose sand. I looked back as we lifted off and banked away. There were a half dozen helicopters on the beach. Someone fired two rounds at the birds from the treeline. A door gunner blasted the area. Then it was still.

After berating me for disobeying combat orders, Franklin finally asked what had happened—and I told him every last sordid detail, right down to the blood leaping from the girl's throat.

"Herbert, you're a goddamned liar," he said.

I assured him I wasn't lying. "There were other witnesses, sir."

"Then you're exaggerating," he said. "Did the American, the lieutenant, take part?"

"Yes, sir, he was in charge. He had assumed responsibility for them from Sergeant Warden."

"But did you see him do any killing?"

"No, sir, I didn't."

"Then you're a goddamned liar. There were no U.S. personnel involved," he said. "Goddamn it, Herbert, you're always coming in with these wild-assed, exaggerated stories trying to make trouble. What the hell is wrong with you? You're getting carried away. Maybe you're getting old."

"Maybe, sir," I said, keeping my seat.

"What is it about you, Tony? For Christ's sake, we're not responsible for every last thing the Viets do. After all, it's their country and their war. All we can do is advise and assist. We don't have any operational control over them. That may be unfortunate, but that is a goddamned fact."

"Not this time, sir. That bastard was in charge. He supervised it and he watched it. He flew in on our birds under our orders, he was under our control, and he was in our General's area of operations."

"Are you calling General Barnes a war criminal?" he raged.

"No, sir, I'm not."

"Are you calling me a war criminal?"

"No, sir, I'm not calling you one either."

"Are you calling the lieutenant a war criminal?"

"Yes, sir."

He threw up his hands. "Goddamn it, Tony, what the hell am I going to do with you? You were a young lieutenant once yourself." He shook his head and laughed.

"Yes, sir, and before that, I was a sergeant and before that, a private—and I never murdered anyone, let alone women and prisoners."

"Murder? Did you see that lieutenant murder anyone?"

"No, sir, I did not."

"Then you better watch your ass," he said. "Maybe Bethea was right. Maybe you are getting soft, or maybe guerrilla warfare is too rough for you. I guess it's not quite as soft as a leg-outfit in Korea."

I had been around too long to let myself be baited. "Maybe so, sir."

"Or maybe you're not quite the hero everybody figures."

"Maybe not, sir," I said, standing up. "Sir, I'll get the statements for you and bring them in."

He stood up, too, and came right up against me. We were nose to nose. "No, Herbert, no, you won't do that," he said. "I'll get the statements and you, Lieutenant Colonel Herbert, will do exactly what I say. Understand?"

"I understand, sir."

"You're not the IG anymore. There are other investigators around and a hell of a lot more capable, too. They'll be around." He turned away and walked back behind his deck. "In the meantime," he continued, "you'll keep it all to yourself. Even you should be able to comprehend that much."

"I understand, sir."

"Anything else?"

"Yes, sir, there is. I don't ever want that son-of-a-bitch of a lieutenant or his goddamned scrap outfit out with any of my troops again."

"Don't worry about that, Herbert, the next time you can try it all alone."

He waved me off. I saluted, said my "Good evening, sir," and walked out. I had a crick in my neck and a pain in my back, but it was a waste of time to call for a jeep. I walked down the road to the battalion, checked by the TOC, and then dropped into the sack. I stared at the ceiling.

"Happy St. Valentine's Day to you, Mister Capone," I mumbled.

Two years later, Warden told the rest of the story:

August 24, 1970

I, Sergeant First Class Wallace A. Warden (224-38-3212), during the period of 14 February, 1969, was the platoon sergeant of the 1st Platoon, Company C, 2d Battalion of the 503d Airborne Infantry. We were on an operation that day looking for an underwater communications center which we could not locate. At approximately 1700 hours, helicopters picked us up to return the platoon to LZ English. While in flight, we were diverted to capture and destroy a VC meeting (in the) vicinity of Cu Loi. When we touched down, the LOHs and Cobras were firing. As soon as we landed, we received fire from the left flank and immediately assaulted the source of fire. We saw five VC running away from us. The LOHs called LTC Herbert and told him that they (LOHs) had some VC trapped in a general area. As we lined up to assault into the jungle, some men disappeared and did not come with me. After I moved in, only SP/4 Bunch and a machine gunner were . . . with me. After I moved up further and received fire from the VC, I found I was standing alone. I went forward, moved up to the building in front of me and saw three VC standing at one end of the building with weapons, so I went around to their flank and fired at them. This is when I ran into LTC Anthony B. Herbert, the Battalion CO, and his RTO [radio operator]. The VC ran into a hole. I told the Colonel that the VC had been waiting for him but now had gone into a hole. One had a submachine gun. Colonel Herbert went to the hole, hollered "Chieu Hoie" or something in Vietnamese, but no one came out.

He then fired into the hole and the man I had shot previously came out with his hands up, without his weapon. He said two or three more VC were in the hole. We hollered, but they would not come out. We said to the wounded man to go and tell them to come out. He did and six persons came out, all males from 19-30 years old. The radio operator and the Colonel stood guard while I tied up the prisoners. After I tied them up, I told the Colonel we needed help. At this time, my Kit Carson Scout came up and questioned the prisoners who said there were more VC around. We found one of their weapons hidden under a pile of wood with grenades, pistol-belt, poncho and khaki uniform. The rest of the platoon now caught up and secured the perimeter. We threw a hand grenade in the hole and the VC threw out two. Two of our troops were wounded. The Colonel told me to take the prisoners to the edge of the jungle so a helicopter could pick them up. I took one additional trooper with me for help. As I was taking the prisoners back, 25 meters from the edge of the woods, I ran into some Vietnamese (ARVN) soldiers in camouflage uniforms who tried to take the prisoners from me. I refused to give up the prisoners. At this time, an American lieutenant walked up and said it was his job to interrogate the prisoners. He was assigned to the Vietnamese (ARVN?) police. One of the Vietnamese walked up to a prisoner and said something in Vietnamese. The prisoner answered back and the Vietnamese gave him a vertical butt-stroke with his rifle. I then lost control of my prisoners because all of the Vietnamese police crowded around and pushed us out of the way, knocked the prisoners to the ground, put the muzzle of their weapons on them and spoke to them in Vietnamese. One of the Vietnamese police just plain shot and killed one of the prisoners by shooting him in the head and blowing the head apart. The lieutenant (American) told me that he would take charge of the prisoners. I did not, could not interfere because there were too many ARVN police with drawn weapons and only one trooper and myself there. I now ran back to the Colonel and told him that the ARVN Vietnamese were killing and beating up our prisoners. He took the radio telephone and called someone (and said) that he did not want anyone to shoot or beat up our prisoners because the prisoners would be going back to the rear by helicopter. At this time, one VC was killed in action and one wounded by the platoon (my platoon). I told LTC Herbert one was still alive so he told me to take them back to the edge of the jungle and turn them over to C Company, who had just landed for Med Evacuation. I took eight of my men to help me carry the wounded. When we arrived at the edge of the jungle, they (the ARVN police) had killed four of them, the hands of the prisoners were still tied behind their backs. I did not have a chance to give my additional prisoners to Charlie Company because the ARVN mobbed us and took them away. I went back and told the Colonel what happened and he told me to take all the ladies, children and old men to the edge of the woods and hold them for interrogation. As we went back, there were ARVNs all over the place. The ARVN did not want to go into the jungle to check the area and capture VC. When the helicopters arrived one of the ARVN just took his automatic weapons and shot one of the wounded prisoners by emptying the magazine into him.

A day or two after the St. Valentine's Day massacre, a black trooper named White refused to go to the field, and he offered his refusal loud and clear out in the battalion street where he could be heard by one and all.

"You're going out, White, just like everybody else," I told him.

"Like hell I am, you son-of-a-bitch. I ain't fighting for no whities."

"Right, White, you're going to fight for your country or for the dollars or for anything else you can think of, but, by God, you're going."

"Like hell I am," he said, taking off his glasses and slamming them against the ground. They were unbroken. He stepped on them and ground them into tiny pieces. "Now, you bastard," he said, stepping back, "I ain't going because I can't see."

I shrugged and laughed at him. "So I'll have you put on a listening post. Guys with bad eyes always do better at night."

"You dumb son-of-a-bitch," he laughed. "You don't understand. You send me out there and I'll desert."

"No you won't, White, because out there, baby, ain't back here. You leave the guys out there and you're on your own." I tapped him on the chest. "But, listen, I'll tell you what I'll do. You go AWOL out there and make it back here and I'll give you a Bronze Star, and even if you don't, I'll see to it that you get a Purple Heart. Out there, baby, when you're on your own, you're anybody's and everybody's meat. If the VC or the NVA don't get you, the locals will. You are money and they're all bounty-hunters."

"I'll cut out as soon as I get back then."

"No you won't, because you either straighten out out there, or when the company returns, you'll be transferred to the unit that replaces them."

He reached into his shirt pocket and pulled out another pair of glasses. He was swaggering as he walked away toward the helicopter. "Big guy! Big, bad guy. You'll get yours, baby. We didn't miss Nicholson by much."

The best I could hope for would be that he would do a good job. It was his only chance. If he didn't cut it, he was going back out with the next unit just as I had promised. It was the only way: reward the right response and do everything you can to get it. Most of the time it worked. It didn't with White.

He performed poorly in the field, just as he had vowed he would, and I had him held at the gate when his unit came back. I had asked Childers to get the very best trooper he could find to guard White until the replacement unit he was going to join came out—someone who wouldn't scare—and he came up with PFC Schnelling.

"Don't take any crap from him," I told Schnelling. "And watch out. The unit coming out will pick him up."

That was it—except that Schnelling drilled him through the head and killed him right outside the gate. White had had some words and Schnelling had paid no attention. White had made a threat and then gone for his rifle. He got it to his shoulder before Schnelling squeezed his trigger, and the MP at the gate had seen and heard it all, thank God. It was that cut and dried. Schnelling had done his job. I brought in the Criminal Investigation Division people. They questioned every-one, took statements, and that was it—except that later in the day I had Schnelling into the office. A crowd of White's friends gathered outside chanting: "We want Schnelling. We want Schnelling. He killed a brother. He killed a brother. We want Schnelling. We want Schnel-ling."

I reached over and picked up my M–16. "Look, Schnelling, you are now a Spec Four—not because you killed a man but because you didn't fail to do it when it was your job. Now, about that out there, that's up to you. I'll tell you what I'd do. I'd walk out there and end it right now. I'd pick out the biggest mouth out there and walk up and explain the facts. Tell him you just made Corporal and if they don't clear out, you might take it into your mind to try for Sergeant." I jacked a round into the M–16 chamber. "I'll cover you from here and if anyone so much as raises a weapon, I'll drop him. That's the least I can do," I shrugged.

He stepped through the door and walked over to the group. I could not hear what he said, but they dispersed and I never heard White's name again—which is sad, too, sad that a man could die and, snap, just fade out of people's minds and disappear.

7

In the six months prior to my taking command of the 2d Battalion, well over $50,000 in American equipment had been lost, including more than $15,000 worth of M–16s, a few generators, and three 81-millimeter tubes. It cost about another $25,000 to replace this equipment, but nobody gave a damn because Uncle Sugar could afford the tariff. He was paying through the nose with the 2d Battalion, though we were probably no better or worse than any of the hundred other battalions scattered across Vietnam when it came to supply records. The worst part of our lack of accountability was the fact that so much of the stuff turned up in the hands of the VC.

Grenades were a case in point. Under Franklin's orders and against my better judgment, I turned over case after case of grenades to the ARVN battalion commanded by Colonel Nim and headquartered at English. Finally, Childers suggested that we mark the grenades we were donating by painting the fuses. At least we would know where they had originated if we captured any. So we marked them on a Monday and most of them were back by Friday. That's how much the ARVNs thought of us; they didn't even have the courtesy to wait a reasonable length of time. What was known as the Chieu Hoi program included not only surrender and good treatment, but rewards for equipment as well: so much for a rifle, more for a machine gun or a rocket, and $30 for a grenade. (There was also "solatium," as from "solace": payments for innocents killed, for the women and children the Vietnamese had the guts to bitch about and we couldn't cover up. We paid for them like meat—so much for a boy, so much for a girl, so much for a mama-san, until some bright soul at Brigade came up with what was thought a more equitable method of "by the pound." Weigh 'em in and pay for 'em right there—cash on the barrelhead.)

So we gave the grenades to Nim, he gave them to his troops, they divvied them up among their relatives and friends, and what didn't continue on to the VC their kids brought back to us for $30 apiece. John Q. Citizen had bought them twice.

I took the evidence to Franklin. He called me a liar and a troublemaker who was trying to cause friction between the Brigade and an ally. He and General Barnes were determined to get along with the ARVN people, despite what was going on right under their noses.

One day Nim's executive officer threatened to assault our positions because we had denied him the right to walk through them towing away one of our generators.

"Let the son-of-a-bitch come on," I told Bill Hill. "I know him and he hasn't got a shoestring for a gut. It would be the best thing that ever happened on the whole perimeter."

Hill agreed that it might be a good time to find out just who the hell was running English. We took the matter to Barnes, and on his orders we turned our backs while the ARVNs walked off with the generator.

I believed then that someday somebody would have to answer for the shortages, especially of weaponry, because the enemy was using our own guns on us.

I refused to sign the weapons report without an accounting, but it was a wasted protest, because Brigade just had us tear up the Property Book pages and presented us with new ones. We got new rifles with new serial numbers, and we got them without signing for them. It was "corrective action," I suppose—the kind of technique that was becoming standard operating procedure in the U.S. Army in Vietnam. Cover Your Ass. It was over my dumb head, because I was no great shakes as a supply officer and never claimed to be. All I really understood about supply was command responsibility: "Pecuniary liability may be delegated, but command responsibility may not," the book said—and that's the way I thought it was. It was all I had to understand.

I should never have had any problems in Vietnam, because it was an infantry war—infantry and helicopters. At Ft. Benning, they called it the Helicopter War and, I suppose, in time it became just that. Like all of our toys, we abused the chopper, using it for every-thing, transforming it into a crutch and a panacea for all our ailments. Instead of making the best use of it and having the common sense to recognize when it should not be used, we turned it into one more novelty. There was Barnes, for instance, using one as a "pizza chop-per" to ferry purchases from the Pizza Palace out to his commanders in the field. One time when I used it for evacuating two of my wounded, when there was no other bird available, he exploded and chewed my ass over the fact that I had gotten blood and vomit all over its floor, that I had "misused" it.

As a transport, however, the helicopter was unparalleled in the history of warfare. It could move troops rapidly and in concentration from one point to another over rugged terrain faster and better than they had ever been moved before. It was an absolute dream for getting there first with the most, and as a life-saver, it was unequalled. There are thousands of men breathing today who would have died out there had it not been for the Medevacs—the dust-offs. Moreover, there are a hell of a lot of people who owe their lives to the chopper's resupply capabilities—and the birds were the keystone of reconnaissance and artillery controls as well.

With a different quality of commanders, the helicopters could have played a very important role in command and control. The un-fortunate fact was that the commanders kept their butts glued to the seats in the birds. I don't think I can overemphasize the weaknesses inherent in this. From 1,500 feet up, war was simply a lot of little guys in green running here and there, shooting up the landscape. There were little straw huts burning, as though someone had set a match to the miniature village inside the circle of a child's electric-train set. The bodies were just bodies—neat and clean, like the holes in Fearless Fosdick's head. All you did was fly down, give the troops a little advice, say hello, pat them on the back, and lift off—not for-getting, of course, to have your radio operator register with head-quarters the fact that you "went in." You flew in and flew out and never spent a night in the field and never walked a patrol with your men and never humped through the bush with them. Why should you? It was Vietnam, the Helicopter War. Ten years ago, a commander who did not hack it down there with his troops would have been fired.

In November 1971, General Barnes was quoted by Morton Kondracke, a reporter for the Chicago *Sun-Times,* as saying he had never been able to understand my penchant for being down on the ground with my troops—as though I were caught up in some perverse deviation from the norm. I'll grant the General that my desire to be on the ground during an operation rather than observing from a chopper did represent a departure from the standard policies and practices of the Brigade, but then, of course, almost everything I believed to be proper and effective in fighting a war also seemed peculiar in that environment. Barnes did not understand war, he did not understand Vietnam, and he did not understand command.

The rule of thumb in the infantry had always been to be at the critical place at the critical time—to be where the action could best be influenced—and not up at 1,500 feet, giving directions to move men from Point A to Point B in fifteen minutes. With your ass in the grass, you knew there was no such thing as moving from Point A to Point B in fifteen minutes. There might be a dense wall of jungle, as well as other human beings who were determined not only to prevent your movement from Point A to Point B but to kick your ass off Point A if possible. From up there it was a snap; it wasn't necessary to get down and pick up the pieces with the guys and see the results of your handiwork. The bird-men may have been commanders in the technical sense of the word, but they weren't leaders, and the grunts knew it.

Down there was their world. It was a ground war, an infantry exercise, and as infantry we could have won it. Man for man, we were better, and we could have won it with less than half the people we had there. All we had to do was get rid of the wasted headquarters chaff, get rid of the PXs and the steakhouses and the clubs and the massage parlors and the pools and the pizza houses and the commissaries and get down to fighting an infantry war. We had the training and we had the men who could have done the job.

The problem was not only a lack of command leadership, but a distinct lack of mission. We didn't have one before I got there, we didn't have one while I was there, and we never had one after I left. But an army requires a mission; it desperately needs some direction toward a specific goal.

It was all charts and graphs for us, with machine technicians, like the West Point engineers, running the show.

I don't think we have to be conditioned to kill. We need no training to destroy; we're built for that. Killing comes easy. Establish no rules, and leave a vacuum, and what you come up with are My Lai and Cu Loi. The absence of policy and mission was a policy in itself.

Larry Pippen was a helicopter pilot, and a damned good one. It was rumored that he had killed over 200 enemy during his tenure in Vietnam. I believed it, after seeing him in action. He flew low—"down at gut level," he said—and he flew often, and he was my C and C pilot frequently because I damn well requested him. Allison and Larry Kahila were also good, and between the three of them, I was never handicapped for a pilot. But Pippen was ideal. He was just as aggressive as I, and I don't believe I had to correct him in flight even once.

We were heading up to a deep bamboo field where a recon patrol had flushed eight men. Pippen kept making passes up and down, hoping, looking, moving the grass with the wash of the blades, firing a burst here and there into a clump—and finally we flushed six of them. The door gunner knocked down four and Pippen got the other two with his .45, right out his window. It was equivalent to Custer riding at full gallop, leaning back over his shoulder and picking off Sitting Bull at 800 meters. I kept asking for Pippen and we kept ending up with each other because he was asking for me from his side. I witnessed more than a dozen more of his personal kills before I departed.

But most of the job was being done at night on the ground through ambushes set between the villages and the hills. It was what Harry Skeins had taught me that first day. We set up the ambushes on their communication and supply routes and they were working well.

Franklin and Barnes liked to call them "mini-ambushes" or "hawk teams," as though they had invented something new. In fact, they were the same kind of small, mobile ambushes that men have been laying ever since Cain whacked Abel out there in the grass. In fact, the Ranger Department at Ft. Benning and at Eglin, Florida, and Dahlonega, Georgia, had been advocating the light, flexible groups of from two to six men for seventeen years before Barnes and Franklin discovered the concept and gave it a tricky little name. That was the problem with ticket-punchers. They went to school to get their credits, not to learn.

Perhaps that was why the 2d Battalian had most of the starlight scopes in the Brigade. Nobody else knew their value; nobody else used them or wanted them, and they were never given much of a sales pitch by either Barnes or Franklin. The starlight was really something. It was a scope that magnified the minimum light available, regardless of whether it was from stars or the moon or a reflection or whatever. It turned night into day for our side. At night, a man could scan as well through it as he could through binoculars in the daylight. It was a bit delicate, true, and had to be handled as a separate scope until Grimshaw and Quirin came up with a way to mount them on rifles—and then everybody wanted one. We made damned fine use of them.

The ambush moved into position at dusk and stayed there until after the families had settled down. The mama-sans were finished crooning their lullabys, which carried all the way to the hills, the children were quiet, and the jungle was still. Then the ambush moved again, applying the principle I had explained to the company commanders soon after taking command: to move just a short distance—a hundred meters or so—and then bring out the starlights and begin scanning. Not every patrol used the method continuously, but at least one or two every night, night after night, first one patrol, and then another and another.

LeRay had one of the best nights in the history of the battalion. It was not a case of Congressional Medals or Silver Stars all around. It was simply the kind of infantry operation that warms the heart of an infantryman—the kind of operation to be remembered, except that when it was all over LeRay, a longshoreman from Louisiana, didn't even bat an eye and said very little. Oh, he did raise hell about the two that had got away and he praised Zin, the Kit Carson, and he swallowed down some other words about the two losses.

It had been an exceptionally cool night for Vietnam, and LeRay's patrol had moved inside an old broken-down hooch just inside the edge of an abandoned village. The walls kept some of the wind off, but by midnight the wind had died and the silence set in. "You know about spook shadows, sir?" LeRay asked later. "Well, spook shadows are what the Cajuns back home talk about—some kind of haunted stuff, I think—and that's what we had out there, sir, spook shadows from all the rubble and wreckage around." LeRay had posted the starlight man on the north side of the village, and about 1:30 that morning he focused in on a patrol of about fifty men, crossing the paddies to the north from west to east. It was too big a target for LeRay, his five men and Zin. At least, he said, that's what he thought at first. "I just sat right down in the middle of that old hooch, just sat there and tried to drive them out of my mind," he said. "But I couldn't do it. There had to be a way of intercepting them." Zin tapped him on the shoulder and guided him over to the west wall of the hooch. There was movement. He called the scope man and took a look. There were about thirty more coming straight at the building from the west. He still had time to move his people out, but he chose not to. He believed that if he cut it just right, he could take them. I would have felt the same way, I think. The aggressive ones are all like that. Tell them they haven't got a chance and they spit in your eye. Besides, if a man is aggressive enough, he always has more than a 50–50 chance. LeRay made his choice. He would stay and wait until they walked right in on him or were square abreast to him. No one would fire until he started. He crawled from man to man passing the word, and while they rearranged themselves as quietly as possible, he crept back to the west wall, laid the scope back to his eye, and watched them approach. The scouts were first, moving up and checking the north-south trail about twenty-five meters away. They came toward the hut with the main body about fifteen meters behind them. If they came up and knocked at LeRay's door, they would have to be dropped and adjustments made. He kept his scope on the lead scout, watching him move up, put his ear to the ground, then rise up and give a hand signal to the scout behind. LeRay dropped his hand behind his back, signaling his people to be ready, and then waited until the patrol was right up on them, its flank wide open, its scouts already some twenty meters or so past the hut. LeRay began firing. The others followed. "It went like clockwork, sir," he said. "We dropped damned near half the entire group on the first burst and that was it. They scattered every which way."

"So you got yourself surrounded, right?" I smiled.

"Who gives a shit, sir, we zapped them good, and besides, I knew help was coming along in a minute."

He had been right. The system we had put in was working. The reaction platoon was on its way—but LeRay couldn't wait. The survivors of the first blast and the group that the scope-man had spotted earlier crossing the paddy got together and brought in a machine gun. They dug it in near LeRay's hooch and poured it on. "It was the only tight part of the operation, sir," LeRay said. "That damned gun had to go and I couldn't wait for the help. First, we tried with a couple of grenades. No luck. Then, the next thing I knew, Zin and Marriot were headed right out through the door after the gun. Zin made it a couple of steps, but Marriot got the son-of-a-bitch even though he caught some rounds in the chest. That was it for those sorry bastards, because without that gun, they were nothing. And we cleaned their clocks."

That they had done. They were finished before Bill Hill and the reaction group arrived. I came in at first light. By that time they had made an entire sweep and found more than twenty-five dead. In addition, they had got the patrol leader himself by following one of the many blood trails into the bush. He was an officer whose leg had been mangled. LeRay handed his pistol to me and we sent him back as soon as we could get the dust-off back from its first trip of the morning—taking Sergeant Marriot and Zin's body back to English. I congratulated LeRay, said a couple of words to Hill, and left Donovan there with them to help in the follow-up of some of the other blood trails. I grabbed the C and C and followed the dust-off bird back. After we landed, I walked down to see if they had come up with anything from the wounded officer. I knew they were NVA, that was for sure, but what kind of unit had it been and where had they come from and where were they headed? I needed to know. Why had there been so many? I wanted to hear his side of the action, too. It might be important.

Military Intelligence interrogated him while they worked on his leg. MI had wanted the medical people to hold off so that they could use the saving of his leg as a reward for his cooperation, but the medics wouldn't hear of it. I was glad they took that stand, because it let me stay out of it. I wasn't particularly interested in hurting any more MI feelings and have them go running to Franklin so that I would have to go in and screw with him some more. All we ever learned from the NVA officer was that he was a lieutenant and commanded a headquarters-type supply unit, roughly similar to our Quartermaster Corps outfits. The other, smaller unit on the flank had been sappers on their way to Tam Quan District Headquarters to pay us back for the St. Valentine's Day Massacre, he said. He said he thought the ambush had been perfect, that they had no idea we were sending out such large groups. I felt great about that, but I kept my mouth shut. It was none of his business how large LeRay's ambush had been. Everybody in his group had been hit, he said. More than twenty were dead before he was hit himself. The rest was chaff. I stood up and touched the NVA lieutenant on the head.

"Take care," I said. I turned to the doc. "How about the leg?"

"It comes off."

I looked down at the guy. He was twenty-one, maybe a little older.

"But he'll live," the doc said.

I started to leave, but the lieutenant grabbed my hand. They had been questioning him through an interpreter, but he spoke to me in English.

"Thanks, Colonel," he said, still gripping my hand.

"It's okay," I said.

Outside the medical hooch, I stood for a moment and cleared my throat. I started back to the TOC wondering whether the kid had told us the truth. He may have been a quartermaster, but he had still been a soldier, and he damn well looked and acted like one even on that litter. But quartermasters moving cross-country at night on their own? I didn't think so. It didn't sound right.

There was a tall, skinny, stringbean of a platoon leader in Grimshaw's company named Miller. Nicholson thought he was one of the "most immature young officers" he had ever met—but beauty, as they say, is in the eye of the beholder, and for my money Miller was a winner.

He and a radio operator were on one of the roving patrols I had instituted—just the two of them and a starlight scope—and they were following the pattern well: moving a bit, holding in tight against the dike banks, scanning a bit, moving some more, waiting, scanning again. They went up and across an old bamboo foot bridge and then down onto the path atop the dike on the other side. Miller heard the bridge creak behind him. He led the radioman into brush beside the trail, left him and took a position on the other side. He brought the scope to his eye and caught them in its light less than thirty meters

273

away, coming straight up the path. He waited until they were right on top of them and then opened up. The radioman joined in and they both emptied their magazines. Then they turned and ran like hell up the trail, turning once more to toss a grenade. There was one scream after the explosion and then what Miller called "jibber-jabber." They eased themselves off the trail and onto the edge of the paddy. Miller began scanning with the scope again. There were bodies on the trail and some movement in the bamboo off to the other side. Two men came through the reeds and started dragging the bodies away, and there were voices and steps back on the bridge. Somebody was giving somebody hell, Miller reported. Then there was a short interval of silence and the group reformed and started walking up the trail again toward the two Americans. This time their scouts were out, and this time Miller slid back off the dike until the scouts had gone past and the main body was abreast of him. He squeezed off the entire load, slammed in another magazine, and stepped out onto the trail just in time to catch the two scouts on their way back. They got it along with the rest. The radioman shouted and a grenade exploded off in the bush. It was the last blast of the night. The two of them stayed in tight together until first light, just as they had been instructed, and then policed up the night's work: seventeen bodies, weapons, documents, grenades, a medical kit, and a radio. Two blood trails led off into the bush.

I submitted LeRay and Miller for Silver Stars. Both deserved more, given the standards for decorations prevalent in Vietnam. Marriot went in for the Distinguished Service Cross and Zin got the highest award we were permitted to give a Vietnamese: A lowly Bronze Star for Valor. I read in *The New York Times* later about a General who received a Silver Star simply as a matter of paperwork, and I wondered what LeRay and Miller thought that might have done to theirs, and what Marriot and Zin would have said.

Word spread pretty quickly about the success we were having with the ambushes and Barnes flew in to have a look for himself. Franklin asked me to report to Brigade, and congratulated me on the "luck" that the battalion was having; but, he said, he wanted to caution me that the war was being wound down.

"Tactics are only minor parts of the whole," he said. "At this point, administration is the key to success, and you're going to have to stand accountable for the administration of your battalion as well as for its tactical successes."

"Yes, sir, I understand."

"In fact, I don't think you ought to get too carried away just because you're having a little better luck than the other battalions—especially considering the administrative state of your battalion as compared to the others."

"I don't understand," I said, but I did.

"Well, there's going to be an IG of the 2d. I called Werner on it today. The others have had theirs and you're going to stand yours."

"But, sir, it was scheduled for late March."

"Well, goddamn it, I just moved it up. And another thing—I'm getting sick and tired of your swaggering around this area just because you've killed a few dinks. Understand?"

There was no point in argument. I think he would have been happier if LeRay and Miller had botched it. I nodded my head. "I understand, sir. We'll be ready for the IG." Hell, we already were. What did Franklin think we had been doing? The state of the battalion wasn't something to be prepared for an inspection. To me it was a way of life. The 2d was ready. I think Franklin must have believed otherwise, though. As he put it, I had "bled" my headquarters "to fill out my field strength." He apparently did not see that with one-fourth as many men in the rear, there was less than one-eighth of the previous work load. I wasn't worried, anyway. Werner was fair and so were Booth and Abbott. If the IG inspection date was designed to put me in a panic, it was wasted effort. If I didn't cut it administratively, I "would have to be relieved regardless of combat results," Franklin said. Did I understand his position, he asked. Who the hell was he kidding? Then he mentioned that he had noted that I had not yet replaced Grimshaw as the commander of D Company. He said he already had a senior captain in mind for the job.

"May I ask who, sir?"

"Captain Harvey. One of Colonel Angel's right-hand men." Harvey was the commander of the Administrative Company at An Khe. He worked for Major Crouch.

I was not particularly interested in having him command for me. "I like Grimshaw," I said.

"Well, I don't," Franklin snapped.

"I think he's the best company commander in the Brigade."

"Not in my opinion."

"I'm sorry, sir." It was no time to tick him off. "I'll keep my eye on it," I said. That seemed to satisfy him.

"Good, good. Keep me posted," he said, and then went back to the IG inspection. When I came out of his office, I felt drained. Only the Grimshaw thing bothered me, but that bothered the hell out of me. I didn't want to lose him or any of the rest of them. I just couldn't afford to lose them. After Harry Skeins was transferred, I had come to understand my position completely. There was little I could do. Harry had not wanted to serve under me, Franklin had said; that's why he was being moved—but Harry said he had never said that. If it could happen with Harry, it could happen with Grimshaw because he had been so goddamned successful. Maybe, as Franklin viewed it, success was all right as long as it didn't happen under my command. Moreover, Franklin had asked me to tell Grimshaw to get rid of his tiger suit. Just like Westmoreland: with all the ills in the U.S. Army, Chief of Staff Westy was all concerned about haircuts and the width of watchbands. Who the hell cared about the tiger suit Grimshaw liked to wear when he was the best damned commander anybody ever had? "Have him get rid of it today," Franklin had said.

"I understand, sir."

The striped suit was Grimshaw's mark. He had been wearing it when I joined the battalion, along with a hell of a lot of others in the Brigade. But I suppose Barnes had to make his mark, too, and he didn't like the tiger suits. He didn't wear one and so nobody would. The General had forced everyone in the Brigade, except the recon people, to get rid of them, and almost everybody had complied except Grimshaw and one or two guys in each of the other battalions. Nobody really gave a damn. If a man felt more comfortable wearing one or it inspired him to fight a little better, what the hell? Wear it. Now, all at once, it was important.

I called Grimshaw on the net and told him to get it off and wear something else before Franklin's next visit—which I knew would be within the next hour or so. It always was after he ordered me to comply with anything.

I never saw Grimshaw in his tiger suit again, and Franklin never mentioned it again. Months later, Grimshaw wrote me to say that

276

Franklin had claimed he had never asked me to tell him to stop wearing it. I was in Saigon when I got the letter, and its point seemed more extraordinary because of the presence there in the capital city of thousands of chairborne commandos running around all starched and wearing—you guessed it—tiger suits. Out in the grass, where it might have been of some value to fighting men because of its camouflage markings, it wasn't available. In Saigon, it was the uniform of the day. The same phenomenon applied to the bush hat. You couldn't get them, much less wear them, in the 173d, but in Saigon, even the typists at the Capitol Military Assistance Command Headquarters had them. They looked combat, you know, and even if you never had the opportunity or felt the need to fight, you at least could look the part.

In Korea, the same syndromes were visible. You could always tell the difference between the real troopers and the rear-area commandos in cities like Seoul, Pusan, Taegu, or Taejon. When the trooper had the chance for a day or two back in town, where he could get a scrub and a shave, he never missed the opportunity. Meanwhile, the "commandos" ran around as dirty and as unshaven as possible, trying to look like Willie and Joe, carrying burp guns or other "captured" weapons on slings around their necks. The real troopers wouldn't be caught dead with those weapons.

We had the weapons buffs in Vietnam, too. When they went home they mounted them on beautiful pieces of processed wood with engraved plates beneath them, citing the date and place of capture. In Vietnam, the men at the lower ranks carried them on slings, and in the offices of the higher brass you could see them on the walls.

As we continued to score every night, Franklin began to increase his visits to the field. Finally, he made it a point to be on hand to personally count the bodies, and I found myself as his constant escort, guiding him from one dead man to the next, and standing by while he snapped photos. It was another syndrome: the guys that didn't kill anybody were the ones who broke their asses to get a picture. What the hell? It would probably have been the same way with Indian scalps if we'd had cameras back then.

"How was he killed?" he would ask.

"How do you know for sure?" he'd press.

"Oh, he had a weapon? Where is it now? There? Oh, yes. Thanks."

Or: "Were there any documents?"—and on and on and on until I convinced myself that he was out to prove we were killing civilians or, worse, to come up with a situation in which I could not prove that we had not. I comforted myself with the knowledge that if that was the case, I had no sweat. My troops clearly understood my policy. There weren't going to be any civilians, so my suspicions just transformed themselves into a daily, dull pain in the ass. But occasionally, they dug deep. One day in Franklin's office, I put it to him directly. "I get the idea, sir, that it is being implied that I'm either lying or exaggerating about kills."

"Oh, that's not true, Tony," he said. "If you have any friend down here on this staff, it's me. All of these people are headquarters types and they find it damned near impossible to believe the fantastic results you've been having. They want irrefutable proof." He shook his head. "They hate you, Tony, more than any other guy I know." He raised his fist and shook it in my face. "You stick in their craw—every last one of them. The entire staff."

"The entire staff, sir? Angel, Bethea, Crouch, and Accousti are not the entire staff."

He ignored it. "But you can live with it, Tony," he said, "and by God"—he slammed his fist down lightly on the desk—"as long as I'm in command here you've got a friend." He stepped back from his desk, waiting for an answer. I could have told him that, as inconsequential a fact as it might have been, it was indeed a fact that he was not my commander. I could have told him also that I knew he was not my friend. But I kept my mouth shut. What the hell, I thought, it was his office. "Your friend, Tony, your only friend," he said, dropping into his chair. "You stick with me, tell me the truth, and the rest you can live with." I felt the blood rising in my neck. He seemed unable to accept the possibility that I was not lying or exaggerating. It was what I had come there to talk about in the first place. At least we were still on the same track.

"I always tell you the truth," I said.

"Okay, okay, don't bite my damned head off. No reason to get pissed," he said. He was smiling broadly.

"I'm not pissed," I said, sensing an opening, "but I just don't like being called a liar day after day."

He was still smiling. "No one called you a liar."

I started to answer, but I had learned my lesson. It was an old story to me by then: first him, then me, then an argument. I bit my tongue. "Yes, sir," I said. I was out in a couple of minutes instead of an hour later, and feeling a hell of a lot better. I was learning—but Jesus, it was an unreal situation. The troops had it all pegged. Vietnam was the "unreal world," they said, "Brown Disneyland" . . . "Six Flags Over Nothing."

I talked it over with Hank Boyer. "I don't think you ought to trust him very much, sir," he said. "In fact, I don't trust any of them down there."

"Like who, for instance?"

"Like the entire WPPA," he said. The West Point Protective Association.

"Come on, Hank. These guys are grown men."

"They don't change, sir. They don't ripen, they rot."

"And what about our Franklin?"

"Well, sir, since you asked, I think he hates your guts, and I think he's jealous of you. He didn't want you in as battalion commander and now you're the one that's really cutting the mustard. If the other battalion commanders were doing it, it would be all right because they're classmates—Point men. But you're not one of the fraternity brothers."

"Come off it, Hank."

"Listen, sir, if the fraternity people look good, Franklin looks good. If the Brigade looks good, he looks good. But don't you see that if only one battalion is cutting it, then he and Barnes look bad— or else why aren't the rest of the battalions cutting it, too?" He was still shaking his head. "It's you. The bastards can't stand you." He pointed a thick finger. "You!"

Whether he was right or wrong was beside the point. We had to get along with Brigade. "Come on, Hank, I have a lot of good friends down there, and even if I didn't, it wouldn't make any difference. That's Brigade. Piss them off and the entire battalion suffers, and I just can't afford it. So, we get along. We bend over backwards, and we maintain that policy. If you hear anyone else bitching about it, put a stop to it. From now on, Hank, that's a policy. At last," I laughed, "at last I has got me a policy."

Hank laughed. "You want me to write it up, sir?"

"Hell no. The bastards will get me for blue ink or something."

Then we both poured a cup of coffee and laughed about the whole damned thing.

In fact, it did become our policy. As long as it posed no hardship on anyone but members of our battalion staff, we bent over backwards to get along with Brigade. We called it Project Adversity and it wasn't really such a tremendous task. I only had to deal with Franklin and sometimes Accousti. With the rest of the staff there were no problems.

Bethea, Barnes's so-called chief of staff, occasionally entered the picture by simply overriding the personnel officer. As a result, the 2d Battalion ended up with the lowest assigned field strength—which didn't bother us at all because of our ass-in-the-grass emphasis. Besides, with Bethea, I was able to apply some of my reverse psychology on assignment problems. Generally, if I simply suggested that I didn't want a particular man under any circumstances, I got him, and thanks to that technique, I picked up Parrott, de Gyurky, Sergeant Jesse Ramil, Captain Ron Ray, and a lot of other good men.

I suppose one of the problems with Brigade was our physical proximity. It was just too close; we could almost hear each other breathe. It worked the other way, too, though, so there was no real complaint. It was a special asset in Intelligence because Donovan simply hounded Brigade Intelligence, and they were near enough so that he could. Everything seemed just around the corner: the Brigade Intelligence shop, the Military Intelligence compound, the POW cages and the enclosure for detainees. If information was available to Barnes and Franklin, then it was available to me, and I had a hell of a lot better man doing the interpretation. Donovan was good, and he didn't have to spend his time preparing for the evening briefings, the pony shows. Donovan worked his butt off. He was mission-oriented. Brigade MI "elicited" information from the enemy and Donovan in turn elicited it from MI, in most cases from David C. Smith, a young lieutenant down there who cared as much as Donovan about mission and didn't give a piddly damn for Beacham and the pony shows. He was the only real intelligence officer in the entire section, and we made good use of what he was feeding us and gave him credit when we could without getting his butt in a sling.

I was persuaded that the Intelligence shop at Brigade was operating on the premise that its most important job was the presentation at the evening briefings of such tidbits as "Last night, the VC held a major meeting in the village of Cu Loi," or "We have learned that on the day before yesterday, an NVA battalion bivouacked at coordinates such and such." It was so much eyewash, but it was put on as a real show. Those briefings at Brigade were on almost as grand a scale as those so lavishly staged at higher headquarters—which seems only natural, I suppose, for a Brigade commander who somehow managed to come up with a "chief of staff."

The briefings were held in a large room. Two large leather easy-chairs—one for Barnes, one for Franklin—faced a raised stage in the front of the room. Behind them were rows of metal folding chairs, all neatly aligned like recruits on parade. The side walls were covered with charts and graphs, a pattern broken occasionally to allow for an air-conditioner or a fan. The rear wall of the stage was hidden by giant maps and charts on sliding frames, waiting for the proper moment when they would be slid into full view. A lectern stood on the left side of the stage. It was impressive.

Every evening at 1700 hours—if you said five o'clock, you got "dinged" and had to buy the brandy—everybody who was anybody in the 173d gathered in the room to win the war.

In that room, we were doing better than any combat unit had ever done in the annals of the infantry, and if winning it at the pony show had been all there was to it, we would have been finished and out in 1966. The Brigade chaplain, the artillery battalion commander, the Brigade engineer, the Brigade chemical officer, the Brigade surgeon, the provost marshal, the Brigade S1, S2, S3, S4, and S5 were all there every evening. Unfortunately, because we were headquartered at English, Hank Boyer, as battalion executive officer, was also required to attend. One of the most important members of the pony show team was the sharpest sergeant they could find, a guy getting combat pay for supposedly being a leader in the field, who stood on the right side of the stage, across from the lectern, with a pointer in his hand, cracking the appointed spot on the maps at the appointed time. It was important to him, if he wanted to keep the job there and eat and sleep like the rest of the headquarters group, that he move the pointer sharply against the map at precisely the instant that the man doing the briefing, across the stage behind the lectern, spoke the words.

Major Beacham, the S2, or his representative always went on first with the "intelligence report," as he and the rest of them were bound and determined to call it:

"At zero-two hundred hours an enemy force was spotted in the vicinity of coordinates such and such; a recon of the area was run at first light; negative results. At zero-two-four-one hours, a Red Haze mission was flown in the vicinity of coordinates blankety blank northwest to coordinates blankety blank"—and whap! whap!—the sergeant would rap the map. "Negative results. Snoopy flew two missions: one at zero-four hundred, the other at zero-six hundred." Whap! Whap! "Negative results. At zero-seven-ten, a squad from the fourth batt drew fire from the vicinity of a hill at coordinates so and so. Returned fire immediately. Two friendlies wounded. Enemy casualties undetermined. A search of the area is presently underway. At fourteen-hundred hours, one lone individual enroute to base camp mess in the third batt was killed by a sniper. Fire was returned in the vicinity of coordinates such and such"—whap! whap! "Enemy casualties undetermined at this time. At fourteen-twenty hours, a patrol from C Company third batt, came upon what was estimated to be an enemy base camp of company size. During the conduct of the search, two men triggered booby traps and were killed. There were no enemy casualties. At fifteen-zero-five hours, a patrol from the first batt, operating in the vicinity of coordinates blank and blank"—whap! whap!— "triggered one booby trap. The point man lost both legs but is doing all right in the hospital."

They would all breathe a sigh of relief and turn and nod to each other. The guy was okay. He wasn't dead.

"Five minutes later, the patrol drew fire from a thicket in the vicinity of coordinates so and so, sustaining one dead. Fire was returned immediately. The patrol withdrew and called in eight rounds of one-oh-five high explosive. A search of the area has not been conducted as of this briefing."

On and on it went, right up until seventeen hundred, then the S1 would move to the lectern to tally up the counts, rattling off the dead, wounded, and evacuated, and listing the replacements and the total strengths. The S4 followed him and then the S5 reported on the civil affairs projects completed and partially completed. He never

282

had any unsuccessful projects. The doc would give the malaria and VD report by battalion, followed by the artillery commander, who took the stage and retraced the day's events in terms of tonnage first and then, by God, with a round-by-round description of every last shot fired by his people.

The S3, Major Accousti, came on last and wound it up with a bang. No matter how dark the actual situation, we were operationally cleaning their clocks. Casualties were all forgotten by the time he started, and what he had to say became the real meat of the briefing: operations conducted, operations in the process of being conducted, or plans for future operations. It was during his time at the lectern that we usually won the war. Barnes and Franklin would interrupt occasionally to instruct the S3 to move the operation up thirty minutes, or to try to get another ambush out in the same area, or to tell Henniger to report immediately after the search. God, the brilliance of those briefings. It glowed in there, just glowed. The strategy and tactics were so damned thick, they ran like molasses across the floor. Afterwards, everyone went to the General's cocktail porch, stopping first by the month's score sheet at the back of the room to see who was leading the league in kills. We included every last wound on both sides, every last body, every last blood trail, foamy or otherwise, every last case of malaria, falciparum or not, every last case of VD, every last bar of soap, every last straw "construction" burned, every last meter of ground "destroyed"—we called it "emplacements destroyed" —and occasionally we would even find out at the pony show that we had destroyed "fifty meters of holes or dug-outs." How the hell a B–52 "destroyed" a hole by blowing it into a bigger one was a mystery to me.

The entire briefing was a fiasco, a complete waste of valuable time. Barnes seldom said anything worth noting and Franklin liked to use the time to upgrade his own status. "That's not exactly how it occurred," he would say to a briefer. "I was there." Nobody ever dared say a word in response except Art Stang, the S2 under General Allen, who once warned Franklin never to "pull that shit again unless you're prepared to stand up and be counted."

Under Barnes, operations were geared to the pony show instead of the reverse. The staff worked and worried more about the agenda than about field results because they knew it was at the nightly pony show that their tickets were being punched.

One evening I wondered if the other side had pony shows and what perchance they might have been saying that night. Earlier in the day, Accousti had been out in one of the choppers and, while opening his maps and materials, everything had blown out the door—the map with his notes, the radio codes, everything. He did not report it. I imagined what their pony show might have sounded like:

"Comrades, we have two kilos of documents," the NVA briefer would begin.

"From where, comrade?" the commander would ask.

"From right out of the sky, comrades," would come the answer. "Yes, yes, from the sky."

"Ah so," the commander would remark. "Then Joan Baez is incorrect. God is on our side!"

Our pony shows emphasized what had happened: returning fire, breaking contact and calling in artillery, searches with negative results, blood trails and footprints. I was always reminded of what my father had told me one cold day when we were hunting deer in the mountains. I had pointed out deer tracks in the snow and was quite excited about finding them.

"What you got, son?" he asked.

"Deer tracks, Pap, deer tracks!"

"Take 'em home, son."

"What?"

"You take 'em home to Mum, 'cause I ain't never tasted no deer-track stew before."

I had first heard about the guy when I was IG. He was a black private, in the Support Battalion at An Khe, one of Jack Angel's commandos. He had a reputation for hard drugs and he was one hell of a problem for his immediate superior, Captain Harvey. The guy was a real mouth but short on courage, and he managed to fool quite a few people. He had beaten up a couple of people too drunk to defend themselves and had taken on a couple of other kids who probably had never been in a fight before. It all added to his stature, and when he began carrying a .38 Puma under his jungle suit, beneath his left armpit, he became an even bigger man. U.S. forces in Vietnam were forbidden to carry concealed weapons, and civilian weapons were not permitted at all except in special cases. The exceptions did not include privates in administration companies. Still, nobody ever relieved the guy of the pistol, and he continued to get away with his bluff against drunken soldiers, timid officers, and kids who didn't know what a fight was all about. Then one day he went too far and tangled with the administration company's first sergeant, a guy called "Machine Gun" Bryant in deference to some past exploit. The guy decided to take the sergeant out with a grenade. He lost not only the grenade but most of his teeth and not a little blood. But he still hadn't learned his lesson. One afternoon, while sitting in the latrine with a sergeant named Wolfe, he decided to try again. Unlike Bryant, Wolfe was a lean, almost frail man, but he was an expert with a .45. The guy gave Wolfe an ultimatum. He could either get the hell out of the latrine or draw. The guy made a grab beneath his jacket and Wolfe accepted the second alternative. He pulled his .45 and drilled the kid neatly and cleanly through the shoulder, knocking him off the toilet seat. His scream was terrifying, and Wolfe said he thought he had missed and "gut-shot the bastard by mistake." But he pulled himself together. "If he's dead, he's dead, I said to myself. He was crying and blubbering like a baby, so I got some help and we got him off to the hospital."

There the guy underwent a complete transformation. Instead of being a big-mouthed smart-ass who had challenged the wrong man on the wrong toilet-seat, he became the poor misunderstood black GI who had done his bit by fighting the VC and defending his country and who had wound up getting gunned down for no apparent reason by some rear-echelon son-of-a-bitch of a supply sergeant. It was Cover Your Ass time. Both Angel and Harvey began drawing up charges against Wolfe. He came to the IG office and we accepted his case. A short investigation produced a report that exonerated Wolfe. We proved in no time at all that the guy was known to carry a weapon beneath his jacket. We found pictures of him displaying the weapon and took statements from men who said they were well aware of his tendency to challenge people with the gun. The charges against Wolfe were dropped, and at the end of my report I recommended that he be promoted for being one of the few people in An Khe who hadn't been bluffed by the kid. A little later, Wolfe got his promotion.

Several months later, after I'd taken over the 2d Battalion, Barnes received a letter from the kid's father. Since I had handled much of the case, he asked for my recommendations on the proper response. The father wanted to know about the court-martial of the sergeant who had shot his son. I offered to write the reply myself.

"What would you say?" Barnes asked.

"I'd tell the man that the sergeant is not going to be court-martialed but that his son is—for trying to frag Bryant and for various other violations of directives, written policies, and regulations. I'd also tell him that his son was not really a misunderstood youth but a hoodlum who had never served his country well. I'd tell him that he shirked his duties completely and never even fired a shot in anger against the enemy and never took any fire from the enemy. I'd tell him his son was, in fact, a substandard soldier who was a disgrace to both his family and his country."

Barnes was aghast. "You can't say that," he said. "The boy was black."

"So was Machine Gun Bryant," I said.

But the General didn't buy my approach at all. There was *The Overseas Weekly* to contend with, he said, and there were other newspapers as well. "We have an image, Herbert. It has to be maintained. Colonel Angel and I talked this over this morning. It could go bad for us—I mean Sergeant Wolfe's promotion and all."

"I understand, sir," I said with a shrug.

I think I did. I didn't like what I understood, but I did grasp what he was saying. No waves were to be made and the fact that the kid was a criminal who had threatened lives was of no importance. It was all to be forgotten for one reason and one reason alone: the kid was black. We really hadn't come very far since the Emancipation Proclamation, and it was no wonder to me that many of the black soldiers in the Brigade felt no respect for their headquarters. They recognized bigotry and hypocrisy when they saw it.

I didn't write the letter to the kid's father. If one was written, I don't know who wrote it.

The sergeant up for the CMH didn't get it. Instead, he was told he would receive the Distinguished Service Cross. The Bummer was to receive the Soldiers Medal at the same formation, but he refused "for personal reasons." General Peers, commander of IFFORCEV, Barnes's boss himself, was coming to present the awards, so I insisted that Bumgarner be there. He insisted that he would not stand in the same formation with the hero-sergeant. I went to Bethea and explained the situation, suggesting that we level with General Peers on the Bummer's reasons for refusal or else send him out in the field that day. Bethea and the Brigade chose the latter, and so the formation was all the hero-sergeant's.

But he had become a problem. He seemed intent on getting back to An Khe as often as possible, using almost every reason in the book: pay, record, IG, orders, NCO meetings, Red Cross. At first I tried to chide him but finally had to bluntly refuse his requests. He could register his complaints and take care of his business by phone just like everyone else. It didn't please him. He said he wanted to see Jim Flannery, the Red Cross representative. His wife was having trouble with the kids, he said, and he wanted to go home to take care of it. The Red Cross, he said, had already taken care of it and it was deemed by them to be an emergency. I called Flannery, who told me that they had indeed checked into the hero's family situation and had judged that there were no domestic difficulties sufficient to require his presence.

"Sorry, Sarge, back to the grass," I said.

"I want to see the IG."

I handed him the phone. "Use the switchboard Paragon to Parachute."

"I want to see him in person."

"Not on your life, unless he says so." I offered him the phone again.

He became quite angry. I was trying to screw him, he said. After all, he argued, he had the DSC and he was entitled to more respect. He had fought his war, and he was becoming a nervous wreck.

"Sure, you've fought your war—back at An Khe at the NCO Motel, huh?" I leaned both elbows on the table top. "Look, Sarge, you can bullshit the others if you want to, but not me, huh? You signed up for a tour and, by God, you're going to pull it—all twelve months, just like everyone else. I'll tell you another thing. From experience, I know that getting medals is the easy part; proving you were man enough in the first place goes on for the rest of the career. You either cut it, or else you're a fake, so get hold of yourself, man. You've got some weeks to go yet, and, like I said, you're damn well going to pull them."

I felt sure he would. I didn't know how wrong I was.

He said he wanted to fight me for "calling me a coward."

"Sure, Sarge, if you insist, but I'll whip you."

Then he cried and said he had to get out.

"No soap."

He said he wanted to see either Franklin or the General, and I granted him permission to do either. The next thing I knew Franklin had called me in and I was getting my butt chewed.

"You called one of the heroes of this Brigade a coward," Franklin said.

"That's a damned lie. Get him in here and let me hear him say that to my face," I said, not knowing that my request would have been impossible to meet because Franklin had already let the hero go home. In the future, he said, all such cases would be referred directly to him and not to the Red Cross or any other civilian agency.

"Do you understand, Herbert?"

"Yes, sir, I understand."

"Good, Herbert, good."

So we lost the hero. Sergeant Cloud was next. He was getting an in-country, extra R and R at Red Beach, a resort center we had established and were maintaining for just such little vacations. It was remarkable how many guys were getting third and fourth and sometimes fifth R and Rs. Generally, they were the headquarters types who "could be spared." Once in a while, even the grunts were included—which didn't make it any more advisable as far as I was concerned.

When you considered that on every tour of duty the U.S. Army was giving one out-of-country R and R, one in-country R and R, plus one leave in or out of the country, and you added to that travel time, preparation time, in-processing and jungle school when they arrived and out-processing when they went home, the Vietnam tour was far, far shorter than one year. Then, if you threw in a couple more weeks for extra R and R at Red Beach, it didn't take long to understand what Westmoreland was talking about when he said that it took fifteen American soldiers to defeat one Viet Cong guerilla. Some of us were persuaded that it could have been done differently, but it didn't matter, because that was the way it was being done. So I was losing Sergeant Cloud, one extra fine infantry platoon sergeant. I had moved him back into the field soon after I took command; he was drawing combat pay, and he soon began to earn it. He was a bit older than the average sergeant, but he was certainly not out of the running physically. Nevertheless, Franklin and Bittorie agreed that he should go down to Red Beach for a rest.

"He needs a break, sir," Bittorie said. "He's been around a long time."

"Me, too, John. Three wars, same as you. So what do we do? Quit?"

"Okay, I get the picture, but how about for just a week?"

"How about not at all, John," I said. "Goddamn it, he's a platoon sergeant and a damned fine one at that, and he's got a job just like we do. His platoon needs him. Take him out and we end up with somebody else doing two jobs. What about that somebody else?"

Franklin came across from his office and interrupted. "Herbert, I'd like to see you a minute," he said. I followed him across to his hooch.

"Sir."

"I gave the R and R suggestion for Cloud to Sergeant Major Bittorie. Cloud's been in the field too long."

"No longer than Sergeant Welch and the rest of them, sir."

"He's a lot older, and he's seen a lot of war."

I started to say something smart, but I knew it was useless. Franklin was determined to take Cloud away from me, and I knew that no matter what I did or said, that was the way it was going to be. But I didn't have to agree. "He's no older than I am, sir, and he's seen a hell of a lot less war."

"Well," he said, "I'm not going to stand here and debate the point. I want him transferred to the Beach and I want it done today. And that's the end of it. Understand?"

"Yes, sir. I'll have him down here with his papers this afternoon."

"Papers?" Franklin arched an eyebrow.

"His transfer orders, sir."

"Nobody said anything about a transfer."

Now I was really getting pissed. I didn't mind what was happening to me personally so much, but when it affected combat efficiency, it had to be dealt with, if possible. "That's correct, sir. No one did. No one ever does. Just bleed them off, count them against field strength and let Brigade shove them into the Steak Houses and the swimming pools and Red Beach and anywhere, while some other guy carries their load and gets no credit for it."

I was steaming by now and it showed.

"Well, no more. Not from the 2d Battalion. From now on when they get pulled, it's going on paper, and if the Brigade won't put it down, then I will. I'm ordered to send Cloud to Red Beach. Okay, I'll send him—but with papers and all, plus a letter in his records explaining his duties and a skill-level digit change on the guy that has to do his job to ensure that he gets credit for it."

He interrupted. I was almost finished anyway. "Herbert, Herbert," he said, holding both hands in front of him and waving them back and forth, signaling me to stop. "If you feel that strongly about it, just forget it." He dropped his hands. "I only wanted to borrow him for a week."

Sure he did, I thought. "A week? Okay," I said. It was an acceptable compromise, and it let him off the hook honorably. That was fine with me. I was in no position to provide him with more ammunition than he could get himself. "When?"

"Well," he said, waving his hand. "Get with the sergeant major on that, okay?"

"Yes, sir. I understand now that it's for one week. Correct, sir?"

"More or less."

"I understand, sir."

I went back across to Bittorie. "Well, you've got him for one week, anyway, John."

"Franklin chew your ass?"

"A little."

"My fault?"

I shook my head. "Negative. When do you want Cloud?"

"How about Monday through Sunday?"

"He'll be there. I'll send him down to see you and you coordinate it, okay?"

"Sure, sir, and thanks," Bittorie said, holding out his hand.

I shook it. "John, you son-of-a-gun, if Cloud drowns down there at Red Beach, I'll come looking for you with an M–16."

"He'll be back in a week," he laughed—and, as always, we parted friends.

Captain Cording never came back and never talked to me again after the incident in the mess hall over his R and R. No, Franklin said, Cording would not be back. He was being transferred to the 1st Battalion of the 50th Mechanized Infantry. When I asked why, Franklin said Cording was just a crybaby and was "substandard anyway."

"But, sir, Nicholson always said he was one of the best."

"I don't give a damn what Nicholson always said. Cording was down here bitching about getting out of the 2d Battalion and going to the 1st, so I moved him. I moved him all right—right off jump status. Let him try it at one hundred and ten a month less for a while."

"So what do I do for a CO?" I asked and immediately bit my tongue. I could have kicked my own ass for asking it. I had Noriega until his tour was over, and then I had Captain Manschreck, who was assisting Webb in the S3 shop and had commanded the company before Cording. There was no sweat for a new commander. Why the hell had I asked.

"I have a guy in mind," Franklin said. I sagged inside. It would be Harvey again, Angel's sidekick. I was wrong. "It's a Captain Forepaugh," he said. "From up in the 1st Battalion. Can't seem to get along there, so I figured that since you're both so gung-ho airborne, maybe you can get along with him."

"I'd like the opportunity of talking to him, sir."

"That's not necessary, Herbert. He's a good man. I'll have him down next week." That was it. I wondered what was happening and it crossed my mind that perhaps I should have settled for Harvey. Maybe I was getting paranoid. Was Franklin doing me a favor or was I getting screwed again? Who the hell was Forepaugh and if he was any good, why was Franklin letting me have him?

Ernie had already heard about the transfer via the grapevine. "Franklin must be nuts and Major Woodall [the commander of the 1st Battalion] too. Vance Forepaugh is one of the finest officers I have ever served alongside and one of the best company commanders around."

Childers said the same and offered an explanation. "Forepaugh and Woodall don't get along," he said.

"Why?"

"Because Forepaugh is a fighter and he can't stand all the Mickey Mouse shit."

If they were right—and I had every reason to believe they were since they had both known the man and served with him—then Franklin, if he was trying to screw me by bleeding off the good and sending in the bad, had screwed himself again.

Our first major MEDCAP was in a plague-stricken village in the foothills of the Tiger Mountains, just off the beach. Although the 1st Battalion had been alerted to handle the operation, Henniger turned it down. The plague shots in his unit weren't up to date, he said. We were given the assignment, and took it gladly. Doc Tally and Larry Potter had wanted it right from the start and I liked it, too. Keeping people alive always leaves a better taste than killing them. While Ernie and I mapped out the tactical aspects of the operation, Doc and Larry ran a records check on the battalion's shots and caught up wherever it was necessary.

We went in with Company B in the late morning. LeRay's platoon, with Warden along as usual, was first on the ground with the rest of the company held on standby, just in case. We had flown over the village first, talking to the people on the loudspeaker, asking them to assemble on the beach so that no one would be injured accidentally. Through an interpreter, we told them to place anyone who couldn't move outside their homes on one of the pathways and the troops moving through the village would help them to the beach. No one would be harmed, we said. We repeated it several times, making long, noisy passes across the village in the C and C, before the platoon landed on the south side. We dropped the smoke out on the beach and followed LeRay and Warden down.

Ernie and the C and C went back to English, less than a five-minute flight away. LeRay already had his troops out in a skirmish line against the edge of the palms. I found him on one knee, leaning against one of the trees, talking on the radio to Bill Hill. I waited until he was finished.

"Anything?" I asked.

"No, sir. Just the people moving out onto the beach."

"Great. You can move in whenever you're ready."

"Roger."

Just then a helicopter streaked in from the seaward side, screaming low over the trees.

"It's Commando Jelly, sir," LeRay's radio man said.

"Huh?"

"Commando Jelly, sir. Speedster," he repeated.

For a moment I thought perhaps the entire call-sign schedule had been changed and I had not been told. "Commando Jelly?" I looked at Potter.

"It's a joke, sir," he explained, with just a trace of a smile.

"Oh," I said, rather dumbly. I didn't have time to go into it, though, because Franklin—Commando Jelly—was already on the ground about a hundred meters west of us. I nodded at LeRay.

"You got anybody over that far?"

"No, sir, I haven't."

"Then get somebody over there before he gets blasted off the grass."

"Yes, sir," LeRay responded, signaling Warden. "Take a patrol and go over and see what Colonel Franklin wants, Sergeant Warden." He waved his arm. "The rest of you guys into the village. Let's move."

I stood next to the tree with Potter and watched the platoon move toward the first huts, then turned and started in the direction of Warden and his two-man patrol. I could still see the tail-rotor of Franklin's bird through an opening in the brush that ran alongside a deep ditch. When Larry and I jumped the ditch, the helicopter lifted off and wheeled away toward English, leaving Warden and his two men standing in the field talking with Brigade Surgeon Winkler. When Warden spotted us approaching, he came over.

"There were three of them in here, sir," he said, pointing over my shoulder toward the ditch. "They were in the ditch facing this way, and we just walked up behind them. They didn't have no weapons except grenades. There was a couple of belts and some field gear," he said. "It's over here." He guided me to the pile near Winkler and Warden's two men. There were four or five grenades, a mess kit, two belts, a cooking outfit, three nylon hammocks, a ball-point pen clipped to some paper, and two wrist watches. I picked up the pen and paper, unclipped them and thumbed through the paper. It was blank. I clipped the material back together and dropped it back on the pile. "Okay, Wally, get it bundled up and out onto the beach. We'll take it back in the C and C when it gets here."

"Yes, sir," he said. "Sir, Colonel Franklin took the detainees before I had a chance to tag them."

I shook my head. "Not your fault, Wally. We'll get them when we get back. I'll take care of it." I turned to Winkler. "Any signs of plague on them?"

He shrugged. "How could I tell? Franklin had two in the chopper and one on the skids and was gone before anybody had a chance to say anything, let alone examine them for plague."

I shook my head again. "We'll check them out when we get back. Okay, Doc?"

"Sure," he said.

"And since you're here, you might as well come along." I turned and started down one of the paths toward the village. Doc Winkler and Larry Potter fell in behind. Wally and his two men were still kneeling on the grass behind us, rolling up the gear into three separate bundles.

We walked through the village and out onto the beach where the operation was moving well. The villagers were all organized, lined up in neat rows. Some were getting shots, some were receiving food, some were getting soap, and some were being rigged for evacuation. The troops were handling most of it. Doc Tally was joined by Larry in the inoculation line, and on Potter's suggestion a trooper began taking down names. There was a good reason. We handed out one day's medicine at a time, a practice based on the premise that the medicine could fall into the wrong hands and wind up curing some VC or NVA, as if these people would give away the stuff that could save their lives. If the VC took the stuff from them, then they lost their support, and either way we won. Still, the VC stressed to the locals that the only reason we were willing to give away anything was to get something in return. That's why, the VC would tell them, the Americans always bring in the Military Intelligence on MEDCAP missions. It was quid pro quo—something for something. So on this one, Potter had suggested that we leave Donovan and everybody else connected with MI behind, and he wanted the names taken so that we could come back every few days and check on progress. I liked the idea. I was learning to respect Potter more and more as each day passed. His father would have been very proud of him. As proud as I was even.

I turned to Doc Winkler. "Want to help out?" I asked.

"Why not?" he said, and he quickly rolled up his sleeves and began assisting Tally and Potter with the inoculations. I walked up the beach to where Bill Hill, the commander of B Company, had just arrived. We sat down on the sand and talked casually for a few minutes before we were interrupted by the interpreter, who came up leading an elderly Vietnamese man. The fellow's face had that quiet, calm appearance of a man deeply immersed in his religion for years and years. I jumped to my feet and nodded my respects to him.

"He wishes to speak with you, sir," the interpreter said.

"Tell him that I apologize for the inconvenience to his village today, but tell him that it was necessary because of the great sickness. Then ask him what I can do for him."

The interpreter spoke briefly with the old man. What he wanted, he said, was two small brass temple dogs someone had "mistakenly taken" from one of the shrines in the village. Whoever took them, the old man said, had surely "not understood the village customs."

I asked him to sit down. He refused. I turned to Bill. "I want them back, Bill. No ass chewings, no nothing. Just tell the guys that whoever took them return them."

In a matter of minutes, he came back with one of the dogs. The guy who'd had it said he had taken both but had lost one somewhere in the brush while helping carry an old woman to the beach. I nodded to Bill and turned back to the old man and the interpreter. "Tell him that I'm sorry but that one of the statues has been lost. Tell him I will get another to replace it. Tell him that at noon tomorrow there will be a helicopter down this way and that it will drop another statue just like this one tied to a smoke grenade." I gave the old man the single dog. The interpreter spoke to him, and the man bowed and left. I was sure that he was glad to get even one of them back, and I knew he never expected to see another one. With what he had probably experienced with the U.S. Army, why should he expect anything else? He had already done a pretty damned courageous thing from his own perspective; he had approached us and accused us of stealing something quite valuable to the village. He was probably thinking that he was fortunate not to have been butt-stroked across the forehead and sent running back to his meditations.

I asked the radio man to call for the C and C and suggested to Bill that he let his men have a swim as long as he had security out. It would help burn off some of the jungle rot.

When I arrived back at English, Ernie Webb was hopping mad

and intent on, as he put it, "going over and having it out with Franklin."

"You mean over the detainees?" I said. "Come on, Ern. Who the hell cares who gets credit for them?"

"No, goddamn it, not the detainees," he said. "His mouth. The bastard stood up in the mess and in front of every officer there he announced that we had been abusing detainees and all the rest."

Webb was funny, he was so worked up about it. "What rest?" I asked.

"He said our troops were looting the village and that they had taken some watches off the detainees."

I laughed at him. "Come on, forget about it. I'll go down and have a talk with him later. Let's have a cup of coffee." But I knew it wasn't funny. It was dangerous, talking about the abuse of prisoners. It had to be stopped. I didn't linger over the coffee. I headed straight for Franklin after stopping off at the MI compound to check on whether the two watches I had seen on the pile that morning had been turned in.

Franklin wasn't in his office. I caught up with him at the mess. "Say, sir," I called to him. "What's this I hear about an announcement on some wristwatch incident?"

He spun around. "You bet your ass I made an announcement, Herbert. You and your goddamned ways are finished. I saw that black bastard Warden strip a detainee right in front of me this morning and pocket the gear. Stole the guy's wrist watch right off his wrist. He—"

"That's a damned lie, sir, and you know it. Warden doesn't have to steal any watches."

That was a fact. Nobody did. Watches we had plenty of, courtesy of the NCO Club at An Khe. Using the troops' cash, the Club had ordered watches by the hundreds at $16.00 each from some clever rascal in Japan. A 173d patch was emblazoned on the watch face. The Club found out they were worth a couple of bucks apiece so it donated them to the battalions free. The troops called them Mickey Allen watches, and we had damned near a case of them still in the 2d Battalion. We couldn't even give them away because almost everybody was wearing either a Seiko or a Rolex. Warden, I knew, didn't need a lousy ten buck VC watch.

Franklin was shouting. "Herbert, I saw it."

I shook my head from side to side. "No, sir, you didn't. You didn't even see me, you were in such a hurry to get out of there."

"What the hell are you talking about?"

"Me, sir. You didn't see me coming across the ditch."

That seemed to catch him off guard, but only for an instant. "You're a goddamned liar," he shouted.

"No, sir, I'm not. Ask Winkler—and there were two watches on the pile of gear to be turned in."

"That's a goddamned lie."

"No, it's not, sir. I just came down by MI. I—"

He cut me off and screamed for Beacham, the MI man. Beacham trotted up in a hurry and Franklin ordered him to go straight to MI and get a list of the gear turned in and the names of those who had turned it in. Then he ordered me into the mess, told me to stay put, and left.

A half hour later, he returned and apologized. That was it. "But what about the announcement you made?"

"So what about it?" he said.

"Who tells them that it was a mistake?"

"That, Lieutenant Colonel, is none of your goddamned business."

I called it a day, thanked him and left. There was nothing else to do. Later that afternoon, I asked Sergeant Potter to go downtown and purchase two temple dogs and tie them to a smoke grenade. The next morning, one of the pilots dropped them down on the beach right outside the village.

"I think everybody in the village was out there waving, sir," the pilot told me. He paused a moment with a quizzical look on his face. "With one rocket, I could have creamed the whole bunch." I glanced at his face. I don't believe he realized what he had just said.

A couple of days later, we received our first assistance from the locals of the area. A patrol from our battalion was crossing a paddy when two of the villagers came out and guided them across, pointing out every last booby trap. I felt so good about it that I made certain it was entered on the log. Two days later, the Mike Strikes (Vietnamese) went in and burned part of the village to the ground.

"Why, sir?" I asked Franklin.

"None of your goddamned business," he said. "The Mike Strikes work for Brigade, not for you."

"But why that particular village?"

"Because, Herbert, maybe some of your guys were getting too attached to it. That's a VC village. The next thing I know, you'll be wanting to go in there and help organize their meetings."

It was the closest I ever came to hitting him.

"But it's a violation of the rules of land warfare," I argued.

"The Mike Strikes are Vietnamese."

"They're led by U.S. officers and NCOs, sir."

"So write your Congressman," he said, turning his back and walking away.

Franklin picked up another nickname besides Commando Jelly, and he was proud of the new one. The troops used it in front of him, unlike the other one, and he didn't mind at all. He had become the "Ice Cream Man." He wanted every trooper in the field to have ice cream at least once every three days. I passed it along to De Gyurky in our headquarters company.

"Once every three days, sir?" he said.

"Once every three days, Mike."

"Once every three days, sir? Really?"

"Once every three days."

"You've got to be joking."

"I'm not. You just miss one day and see if I'm joking."

"Once every three days, sir?"

"That's right. Once every three days."

Mike never missed a day, and often when he had it ready, Franklin loved to stop by and deliver it himself as a personal present to the troops. Most of the time, they laughed at him—at least those who had been there long enough. The humpers knew that ice cream in the jungle isn't the best present in the world. It makes you thirsty. Cokes are great. Beer is okay. But ice cream doesn't cut it as field rations.

Grimshaw always made a great fuss about Franklin delivering the ice cream. "Jesus, sir, that's big of you," he would say. "Absolutely marvelous of you to do this," he would add and Franklin would beam. After he left, Grimshaw would dump the ice cream out on the ground and send the cans back. Franklin remained convinced that nobody in the whole damned Brigade took more pleasure in his little project than Grimshaw and the Demons of Company D. He tried never to miss a delivery there.

Finally, Grimshaw had enough. He thanked Franklin for the ice cream, picked up two mermite canisters full of it, walked over to a tree, sat down, took the lids off the ice cream, pulled off his boots, and plunged a big foot down into each of the cans.

"Ahhhhhhhh," he crooned. "Great!"

That day I got one of the worst ass-chewings of my career. "Grimshaw went too far, Herbert," Franklin raged. "Too goddamned far, and I want that bastard relieved and I mean it."

There was absolutely nothing to be said in either his or my defense. All I could do was assure the Ice Cream Man that I would take care of it—and then laugh my ass off when he was gone.

Longshoreman Lieutenant LeRay and his platoon had flushed two of them in a rice paddy, but one escaped. As I came in on the C and C with Ernie and the radio man, I noticed Franklin's helicopter moving up and away from the paddy where the one who had been captured was being interrogated by personnel from Military Intelligence. I assumed it was interrogation, although I had not witnessed their particular technique before. Since there was no ground action, the three of us left the bird and walked over to the spot where an MI trooper was sitting astride the Vietnamese. A rag was clamped down over the prisoner's face. Another American was leaning over him holding an open canteen.

LeRay was standing nearby, along with Sergeant Carmody of MI. I sauntered over.

"What's going on?"

"They caught this one hiding in the cane, sir," the sergeant said, motioning to LeRay. "His buddy's still out there."

"Where's Warden?" I asked, turning to LeRay.

"He's looking for the other one," he answered.

"Any weapon on this one?"

"No, sir," the sergeant said. "They're still searching. He's a leaflet distributor for the village north of here."

"Any leaflets on him?" I asked.

"Two, sir," Carmody replied, handing them to me. They both included pictures of a VC squad zinging rockets into an American Armored Personnel Carrier from the 1st Battalion.

"So what's this?" I asked, pointing to the guy on the ground and the American astride him.

"It's a field interrogation, sir," Carmody said. "It's a legitimate technique."

"Sure, sure," I said. I reached out and grabbed the canteen from the soldier. "But not in this here AO."

His face flushed. He was a proud man. His neck veins bulged. "It's a legitimate technique, sir," he insisted. I really didn't know whether it was or not. All I knew was that I wouldn't have wanted a rag clamped over my face and water poured down my throat, and that was enough. If I didn't want it done to me if I were captured, I didn't do it to anyone else. "Maybe so, but not out here. What you people do in MI is your business, but out here, it's my business, and I say no soap. Get him on his feet. We're going back." While I was talking, I noticed Larry Pippen, my pilot, taking pictures through the windshield of the C and C.

"But, sir, I'm telling you it's a legitimate technique."

He was talking low, not wanting to create a scene, I suppose, so I followed the lead. "And like I said, Sergeant, maybe so. I honestly don't know anymore. I thought I did, but I don't know anymore. I cream my people's asses for a lot less than this, so how could I explain it to them? You tell me. Okay?"

"You going to report it?" he asked.

I glanced at the guy as they lifted him to his feet. He was a sack of oats. "If he dies, Sergeant, you've had the course," I said.

We loaded him on the C and C and headed for the Brigade. The closest the prisoner ever came to consciousness was when he heaved up his guts. I tried to pump out some of the water they had poured in, but without success. When we arrived at English, he was still unconscious. Carmody called for a jeep and they took the prisoner to the MI compound.

I was perplexed. I did not want to make problems for Carmody because he had a fine reputation in the Brigade, and when I had seen him before on the first day out with Cording and C Company, he had been quite impressive. He had, like the Bummer, been with the 1st Cavalry's recon units, and that meant a lot. It meant out front, for one thing—out front on his own, dealing with the VC and the NVA like nobody at the table in Paris could ever possibly understand. It meant lonely nights and lonely days and steep risks. Like the Bummer, Carmody was tough, and the two of them were remarkably similar in their passions. The story in the Brigade was that Carmody was not particularly fond of Vietnamese, especially Vietnamese women, since it was rumored that he had planned to marry one who had eloped with a Vietnamese man. He was an enigma, but his record was that of a damned fine soldier—and goddamn it, now I had found him applying water-torture to a prisoner.

I decided what I had to do. I went to see Franklin.

"What the hell did you expect, Herbert? Cigarettes? Candy? Flowers?" he said. "Goddamn it, man this is war. W-A-R! War. And if you can't stomach it, then get the hell out."

"I can stomach it, sir," I answered, "but it's not war. There's no legitimate reason for torture."

"What about information, Herbert? How about that? The kind of information that keeps those grunts you say you care so much about alive. How about that?"

Either way I answered, I would have lost. "Not in our AO," I said, finally.

He shook his head, disgustedly. "You know, Herbert, you are really something. You say you care, but you don't mean a word of it, and you're sure as hell getting soft." He looked up at me in disbelief. "Haven't you ever seen anything before?"

I tried to ignore him. "Just not in my AO, sir, not as long as I'm commander."

He laughed at that. "Which may not be for long, Herbert, unless there's a deep changing of the ways."

That, I assumed, was intended to frighten me. "That's the General's prerogative, sir," I said.

"Anything else, Herbert?" he said, still laughing.

"Just one thing, sir. I don't want any more field interrogation in my AO ever again."

"Anything else?"

"No, sir."

"Then, you're excused."

"Good evening, sir."

"Good night, Herbert."

Murder and torture were bad enough on their side, but especially reprehensible on ours. Franklin had not yet asked me for statements on Cu Loi or the young lieutenant accused of ordering the murder of a detainee. I was bothered. I had seen it before in Korea and even in the Dominican Republic. Hell, maybe I always had been soft. Maybe they just thought I was hard because I was tougher than they were. I dismissed it. There was no time to waste on the philosophy. I had a night operation going in a couple of hours with Company B and Company D.

Under Barnes, the only night operations the 173d pulled off were Cordon and Search missions. They involved a unit being lifted into position just before dawn. The village would be "surrounded" and after daylight it would be searched. Brigade remained mystified at the continuing negative results of such operations. They shouldn't have been. It was fairly simple. Did they think the VC were deaf or blind? You can't sneak a dozen helicopters into somebody's backyard at four o'clock in the morning, and you can't cordon off a village by deploying troops around it in the dark. At night the choppers generally were restricted to only one or two LZs. The VC certainly knew the village and the surrounding terrain at least as well as we did. They simply picked their apples before the wolf arrived, and it wasn't necessary for them to leave the village to do it. They had two or three hours before we moved in—ample time to get rid of the equipment, gear, and documents that marked them for what they were. They used the time to bury it all under fire-pits, carefully wiping away the traces, or they sank it beneath the mud of the pigsties, knowing full well that the fastidious Americans were not inclined to dig there unless a leader stood over them and damn well insisted. Sometimes they tunneled it under the buffalo manure right in the stall with the animal, where no American was particularly interested in searching. The Vietnamese buffalo didn't especially like the strange odor of carnivores from another world, and they raised a hell of a ruckus when an American was in their bailiwick. The fact of the matter was that, in Cordon and Search operations, the cordon was impotent and the search fruitless. Yet as long as I was in the 173d with Barnes, Franklin, and Accousti, the Cordon and Search along with the Search and Destroy was a favorite mission. Meanwhile, back in the States, we were teaching in our infantry schools that one of the major characteristics of VC-NVA operation was inflexibility—as opposed, of course, to our own ability to adjust and adapt with great speed.

Still, I was convinced that a real night operation would work—a night march across the paddies and through the bush, done with stealth, silence and surprise. We would come in from all angles and seal off the area suddenly. Then we would sit tight and quiet, and wait for the enemy to wake up, rather than doing it for them, as with the Cordon and Search operations. We would avoid the noise of the choppers and the stumbling around in the dark, and we would use the companies familiar with the terrain. If they had not been there as long as the VC, they at least had been there longer than most of the NVA around. With no pre-dawn noise to alarm them, there would be no digging, no tunneling, and no burying of gear beneath the buffalo manure and the pigsties. Then, with first light, we would move in, as the British say, "with great dispatch."

"It can't be done," Accousti had said. "Two entire rifle companies, moving quietly over jungle terrain at night? Not even Darby's Rangers would try it." Maybe he was right, but I wasn't Darby, and Grimshaw's people and Hill's men were not Darby's Rangers, not by a long shot. They were better trained and better conditioned than anything Darby ever dreamed of commanding in his day. "And what if you run into an ambush en route?" Accousti had asked.

"Then we change the name of the game and attack," I had answered. What the hell kind of size force did he figure they would field out there? There weren't going to be any ambushes en route from any size force that either company couldn't handle.

"Now, can I get the okay or do I have to go see Barnes myself?" I had asked.

"It's your battalion."

"Bingo, Ken—just keep it in mind." His face burned crimson.

I had already picked out the village and laid the plan. Bravo Company would cross the paddy and the bamboo thicket and come in from the south, taking responsibility for that area from three o'clock to nine o'clock. Delta Company would cross the paddy and the stream, moving in from the west and taking care of the area from nine o'clock to three o'clock. There would be small ambush groups set in on every escape route, I told Hill and Grimshaw, and they would be set in quietly. "It's got to be quiet, and I know I don't have to tell you guys that, but it would be a real waste to do it so well for so far and then have one guy blow it for everybody over some pissy little noise."

"No sweat, sir," they chorused.

I continued. No one was to move around or talk over the radio unless it was opened up for an emergency, or take up residence by smoking or feeding their faces. "You let me see one light out there and I'll have someone's ass," I warned. When the tie-ins were made at nine o'clock and three o'clock, Grimshaw would give me five cracks in the natural static of the radio. From then on, it would be a matter of the nearest commander playing it by ear. I would stay with Grimshaw and Delta, Ernie would be with Hill and Bravo. When we hit it, Bravo would sweep from south to north and the nets would be open for traffic. Ernie would carry a loudspeaker. I didn't want any civilians caught in this operation. I cautioned Hill and Grimshaw to be extra damned careful about their targets before squeezing the triggers. "Better a 'dink' gets away than we have to police-up some kid's body afterwards. You've all got long lives to live yet and the mind never forgets—so be careful, huh?"

"No sweat," came the responses.

And there wasn't.

Delta slipped the stream and the paddies like fog, and Bravo apparently did as well because there wasn't so much as a dog's bark from either side of the village as we slid into position. My radio man tapped me on the shoulder and pointed to the hand-set. Grimshaw had signaled. Everything was locked in tight. It was about three o'clock in the morning. I settled down on one knee and motioned the radio man to a seat up against one of the palm trunks. Now it was time to wait.

About an hour later, we had contact in the south sector. There was a single burst of fire, silence, and then all hell erupted. It was a substantial battle, from the sounds of it, and then there was silence again. Ernie came in on the radio. He reported that they had surprised about fifteen to twenty of them moving out of the village. A woman had been in front, guiding them. They had held their fire until she had passed and therefore had not been able to get all of them. They had about ten bodies in hand and perhaps a couple of possibles somewhere in the grass, and two seriously wounded VC. The woman was unhurt but in their custody, and they had policed-up five AK–47s, an SKS, some documents, and some other gear. Ernie asked for permission to move in and use the loudspeaker.

"It's your show," I said.

As he rang off, Grimshaw caught a large group trying to break out to the north. There were no weapons, he reported. "But these guys damned sure ain't farmers," he said.

One of our Kit Carsons dropped one trying to make it up a gully. He was toting an SKS.

I could hear Ernie on the loudspeaker, and he seemed much farther away than I had thought he was. The operation moved steadily, and we continued to find the people we had come there to find. Bravo Company killed six or seven more coming through the village, but had two of its people seriously wounded by grenades as they tried to go into bunkers. I could see the dust-offs going in from my position.

Ernie came in on the net again. He had another VC. "He's cut up pretty bad, sir. I don't think he's got a chance. He's crying like a baby and babbling to the Kit Carson about a cache of weapons down near the river in the bamboo. Over."

"How long before we get a dust-off back for him? Over."

"Too long," Ernie said. "He'll never make it. Over."

"Then tell the Kit to keep pushing him for directions. Over."

"Roger that, but he's going damned fast. Over."

"Can he read a map? Over."

"He's dead. Over."

"Give me your coordinates and stay fixed. I'll be right down. Out."

When Potter and I reached Webb, we discussed in detail every last word the Kit Carson had got from the dead VC. It wasn't easy. "Was anybody else around when you got him?" I finally asked, exasperated because our attempt to pinpoint the cache had yielded us almost nothing.

"A couple of kids and the woman."

"Where is she?"

"We turned her loose," he shrugged. "I guess I just can't get used to turning women and kids over to MI, sir."

I felt the same way. "Forget it."

We went north to where Hill and Grimshaw and their people had policed-up more than sixty males of military age. A new group from MI was already on the ground and at work. I had never met any of them before. "They've been in the country less than a week," Grimshaw told me. I guessed that was my reward for my complaint about the water-torture. What the hell? The new guys did the best they could, which wasn't much, and when they had finished, they had tagged most of the detainees for immediate release.

"Based on what?" I asked.

"They have ID cards," one of the MI people answered.

We let them go.

ID cards? Every last NVA, VC, and VCI could be guaranteed to have one, updated and in proper order. They were the only ones around who couldn't afford to have it otherwise, and they had the money to ensure it. But not the plain, innocent rice farmer. When he was issued a card, he carried it until it was lost, worn out, or outdated, and even then he would wait until someone forced him to come in and get another one. He did not keep it neat, clean, and unfolded, encased in plastic and ready for presentation at the first suspicious glance. Nope, that was the mark of the VC, the VCI, and in some cases, even the NVA. Every one we ever killed or captured had a legitimate, updated, correctly maintained ID card signed by the appropriate official, as well as a code-coin tucked down in one corner of his wallet: a 20-piaster note if he was VC; a 20-piaster note plus a 5-piaster Français coin if he was VCI. If he was hard-core NVA, he had the 20-piaster note and a 5-piaster Français coin dated 1954, the year they ran the French out of Vietnam. The notes had like mint numbers for individuals from like units. Almost everybody around seemed to understand all of this except our Intelligence people. They said it just hadn't come out as "hard intelligence" from higher headquarters yet and, therefore, it couldn't be true.

I eyed the two groups of men the MI people had. The group they had tagged for interrogation were obviously rice farmers. The ones they wanted to release were military age, with thick thighs and shoulders, clean fingernails, and rucksack burns on their shoulders. They were sharp-eyed and silent, and I knew they weren't farmers. I shook my head in disgust, but Grimshaw was stoical.

"So what, sir, just let them go. What the hell? If we run out of VC, we run out of a job," he chuckled. "Besides, we're going to get them sooner or later"—he turned to the group the MI didn't want—"and you bastards know it, don't you?"

We let them go.

Franklin flew in and wanted a body count. I gave him seven for Grimshaw and Delta and twenty-two for Hill and Bravo. He wanted to examine them, he said. Not up to it just then, I turned Franklin over to Grimshaw and asked him to take him around to the bodies. Grimshaw showed him only Delta's and the battalion later received credit for only nine kills. It didn't matter to me, because I realized that after Franklin's on-the-scene inspection, it was highly unlikely that we would ever again be bothered about the official score card. Dead was dead. Even Franklin could see that; or, as Grimshaw said:

"A dead VC is a dead VC and a dead NVA is a dead NVA and a dead VCI is a dead VCI, except, of course, when killed by the 2d Battalion. Then they're dead only if Franklin touches his toe to them—and they better be wearing a uniform and have a weapon."

I took Webb and a platoon from Bravo Company over to the riverbank and down into the thick bamboo. The prisoner had said the cache was about 500 meters away on the north bank of the stream. The entrance was beneath the surface of the water, he had said, and there were rifles, automatic weapons, ammunition, and rice. How many or how much? He had called it a large cache, but what was "large"? It proved the point I had been pushing. He was dead, and he wasn't worth a damn to us that way. Alive, he might have led us directly to the cache. It was strange; we had all lost when he died—he and his country and us and ours, and now without him we were all chest-deep in a goddamn creek, ducking under every meter or so on both sides, searching for that entrance.

We stayed until dark and came back for most of the next day with the same platoon, and we came up with nothing. When we finally found it a week or so later, everything was gone. The results of our efforts were practice for the platoon, a medal probably for the old woman or one of the kids, and a royal ass-chewing for the commander of the 2d Battalion—me.

What the hell was I trying to do, Franklin asked. I had to be an ass to move two rifle companies that distance in the dark. Why, they might have opened up on each other if either of them had become disoriented in the dark.

"And besides," he said, "it was one big waste. We could have taken them in on a Cordon and Search and saved all the inconvenience."

He apparently believed it. Perhaps he hadn't been kept posted on the negative results from past Cordon and Search missions—but Accousti had sure briefed him about our little tête-à-tête.

"Why the hell do you continue to refuse to get along with the staff and with MI?" Franklin asked. "It was damned embarrassing out there to have to placate that son-of-a-bitch of an intelligence captain when you just flat stated that if he didn't haul that bunch back that he'd already cleared, you'd do it yourself and turn them over to the 4th Division MI."

He opened the screen, spit out into Barnes's flower bed—inherited from General Allen along with that damned duck—and let the door swing closed again. He didn't mention a single word about the fact that of the group we had not handed over to the MI people, most had turned out to be confirmed VC.

"There'll be no more company-sized night operations without my specific permission, do you understand?" he said.

Why not? "Yes, sir," I answered.

8

Dorney, the commander of C Company, always produced in combat. Because he led his unit well and obeyed orders, the fact that he differed with my philosophy and my approach—he considered me a bit flamboyant for his tastes—was a minor point in our relationship. He was picked for a Brigade Search and Destroy operation, a label that meant Brigade expected bodies without any definite mission or specific target. I had only one bit of instruction for Chris before he left. "Search, yeah, but don't destroy anything unless it becomes absolutely necessary." I sent along Ernie Webb to make any spot decisions that came up.

The general area around a fishing village on the coast of the South China Sea was chosen, Brigade said, because it was listed as 98 per cent unpacified on the S3 charts. I figured it closer to 100 per cent, but that didn't make me any more willing to send Chris and his people in there without some cautions on indiscriminate destruction. The company was to land south of the village and sweep straight through to the north while Ernie was making passes with the loudspeaker, asking the villagers to move out onto the beach voluntarily. If some of them decided to board their sampans and put out to sea, we planned to fly across their course and order them back—with the loudspeaker. "You do that one time," I said. "Then place a trace of machine gun fire in the water and let them understand that any boat that crosses it will be sunk. You turn them back and get them back on the beach with the others." With Ernie and Chris in charge, I had no qualms at all about the mission. They were both excellent men with instinctively sound judgment.

Nevertheless, it was screwed up, not by us but by the same

ignorant Vietnamese outfit from Tam Quan District that had made such a hellish mess of things on St. Valentine's Day. Ernie called me late in the afternoon with the story.

Perhaps as many as 600 or 700 villagers were gathered on the beach, just as they had been ordered, and C Company had moved through their locale and out onto the beach with them. Behind C Company came the Vietnamese police, looting every last thing they could lay their hands on. This time the American lieutenant was gone and their advisor was an American captain. They brought it all out in big bags—chickens, ducks, household goods, temple statues, rice, everything that was portable—and carried it to the beach where the villagers could see it. The crowd of natives began to mill around a bit. Dorney walked over to the American captain and asked him to have his charges return the stolen property. He refused. Dorney gave him a direct order to do so, and he refused again, so Chris called in Ernie.

Webb settled the matter quickly and in language his mother never taught him. The loot was returned, Ernie reported to me. He came back to battalion headquarters with over eighty ARVN deserters and about a dozen VC. I asked Ernie to write up the log and started down to see Franklin to render my after-action report. This was standard operating procedure—between Franklin and me, anyway.

He was absolutely furious. Once again, I was a no-good, lying son-of-a-bitch. Once again, I was either exaggerating or simply not telling the truth. Once again, I had better start learning to get along with the Vietnamese people who were on our side.

"Or else, one of these days, you better be prepared to lose your ass," he said, throwing up his hands in disgust. "How in God's name you ever earned a direct commission, nobody at Brigade will ever understand."

I ignored all of it.

"Any of your darlings killed this time?" he asked, referring to the villagers.

"No one was killed, sir."

"Then, are you finished?"

"Yes, sir."

"Then, good night."

"Good evening, sir."

Two days later, he called me back in. The American captain who had been with the Vietnamese police at the village had written a letter of complaint to MAC-V with an information copy to General Barnes. It blasted Ernie for "insulting me in front of my Vietnamese counterpart."

"They had been looting and Ernie stopped him," I said.

"Maybe so," Franklin said, watching me carefully. It was quiet in his office, almost eerily so. He said he now had us both—Ernie and me—"so if you don't want to have me handle it personally, I expect to see a request for an Article 15 on Webb down here by this afternoon."

I told him I had no intention of requesting an Article 15 on Ernie. He had complied with orders and had done precisely what I would have done had I been there.

"Well, maybe a letter of reprimand will do."

"No. Not even a letter of reprimand, not even a verbal reprimand. Nothing."

"You will prepare that letter."

"The hell I will, sir. I want to see the General."

"That isn't necessary," he said. "The General is already shook up enough over this. You have Webb report to me directly. I'm sick and tired of you, Herbert, and now you've gone one step too far. Both of you are going to pay the price for your folly. If it's the last thing I ever do, I'm going to see this baby through to the bitter end—and right now, I want Webb in here immediately."

As soon as I returned to the battalion, I told Ernie to go down as ordered. When he came back, he sat down at his desk without a word and began writing.

"So?"

"So Franklin wants a written report on why I cussed out the captain and he wants it today."

"Good, Ernie, then get down in there the fact that this was the same unit that carried out the executions on the 14th—and get in everything about the looting and mention the fact that both Franklin and Accousti guaranteed both of us that that rag-tag bunch would never ever be in with us again—and if that doesn't do it, come back to me, and keep me posted."

The next morning, Franklin called me in again. Now, he said, he was *really* pissed.

"I'm going to have your ass, Herbert," he ranted. Both Ernie and I were liars, he argued, and this time he said he had the goods to prove it. "You and I are going up to MI. Bowers [Captain Norman L. Bowers, senior interrogator and executive officer of the 172d MI Detachment] is there getting some statements from some of the detainees, and then it's going to be your ass and Webb's, too. Your days are numbered, Herbert. Let's go."

We met Bowers coming out the door of the MI hooch.

"I have those statements you wanted, sir," he said.

"Good, good," Franklin answered.

"They substantiate not only the looting. . . ," Jesus H., I noticed he was talking to me, not Franklin . . . "but also the murders of the 14th. Some of them were there."

Apparently Bowers, being only a captain, had not been told what he was supposed to find. Or perhaps I was just being unfair to Franklin; maybe he had really believed that Webb and I were liars and had been trying to substantiate it. Either way, it didn't matter. He had played his ace and blown it.

I felt Franklin's hand on my shoulder. "I'm sorry," he said.

I pulled away. "Sure, sir, it's okay." I turned back to Bowers. "Thanks," I said, and then, speaking to Franklin again, I asked if I could assume that he would clarify the matter with General Barnes.

His antagonism returned. "Goddamn it, Herbert, you can assume nothing. I don't have to explain to you." Then, spinning around to Bowers: "And I want to see you and O'Kane later, Captain, understand?"

I glanced at Bowers. He was shaken. I saluted and walked off, leaving them standing there with each other.

The score sheet for February was posted and published at Brigade:

February 1969
MANEUVER BATTALIONS

INDICATOR	1/503	2/503	3/503	4/503	1/50
Enemy KIA					
Body Count	14	84	4	29	36
Enemy POWs	8	90	0	0	3
Contacts	60	66	34	27	37
Enemy Weapons					
Captured	15	57	11	3	17
AWOLS	24	8	14	24	26

Article 15s	39	24	56	57	52
Summary Courts	8	0	13	0	0
Delinquency Reports	17	5	9	11	10
Malaria	3	3	3	3	0
Special Courts	6	3	5	4	1
Reenlistments	0	53.3	0	40	0
Total Score					
Body Count	70	420	20	145	180

RECAP

1 2/503 = 420
2 1/50 = 180
3 4/503 = 145
4 1/503 = 70
5 3/503 = 20

I was glad to note that, unlike past score sheets, this one included plus marks for declared prisoners of war. They didn't count in the actual scores, but at least it was some progress.

Major Beacham called with an urgent note in his voice. He had a long-range reconnaissance patrol in the foothills of the Tiger Mountains, just south of the Hoi An River. They were in trouble and he wanted us to pull them out. If we could get there in a hurry, he said, he would clear it with Brigade, take care of the artillery, and get the helicopter gun ships on the way.

I ordered the alert-standby platoon at the Berm into the air, and Webb and I joined them and the gun ships enroute to Beacham's patrol. I studied the terrain while Ernie coordinated the communications between our birds and the gun ships and then initiated radio contact with Beacham's people, ordering them onto the same network as the rest of us.

A few minutes later, the patrol called in. "Dink patrol pressing us at about 100 meters to our southwest," the leader said. "Do you have visual contact?"

"Negative," I answered. "Drop a smoke. Over."

"Roger that. Out."

Beacham's patrol was moving at a trot in a northeasterly direction, scampering down a hill. A second later one of the door gunners tapped me on the shoulder and pointed down to a billowing cloud of yellow smoke. I spotted the patrol racing down a path about fifty or seventy-five meters northeast of the smoke and pointed them out to Ernie. "Get Star Blazer [the gun ships] in there southwest of the smoke," I told him. Pippen, our pilot, banked us out of the gun ships' path, and while we orbited twice, they went streaking in, northeast to southwest, screaming in low right over the patrol, peppering everything southwest of the smoke.

The patrol immediately came back on the network, trying to cancel the gun ships' runs. They insisted they were in the line of fire. They weren't and Ernie explained that the gun ships had them in sight and were restricting their fire to an area southwest of their smoke. Just in case, Ernie got the Star Blazers back on for a confirmation.

"This is Star Blazer One. Affirmative. Yellow smoke northeast edge of hill, southwest edge of clearing, vicinity of two structures. Keep all fire southwest of lemon smoke. Friendlies northeast. Over."

Ernie switched back to the patrol, patiently explaining again that all fire was on the other side of the smoke from their position. "Drop another smoke when you break out of the brush and are ready for extraction," he said. The LZ was selected just adjacent to a recently burned-off field slightly north of the trail the patrol was using in their escape. No one in our bird had yet observed the enemy patrol our people said was pressing them.

One of our birds was lost on touchdown because the pilot tried to land it exactly where he had been instructed not to land it—smack in the center of the burned-out patch. It happened while the other choppers were setting down in the grass area, as ordered. As the first one came down, it blew up a giant black cloud of ashes from the charred grass, robbing the pilot of his visibility. He clipped off his tail-rotor on a burned stump when he swung the ship around for a lift-off, and then the bird rolled down the hill. The crew was unhurt and we evacuated them along with the recon patrol.

Franklin called and said he wanted to see the pilot and his people immediately. I cut in and told Franklin we could lift the downed chopper out in a couple of minutes. He said it was no longer my concern and told me he would have a Chinook out for it later in the day. "Now get back here as you've been ordered," he said.

I glanced down at the chopper just sprawled there in the field, chock-full of gear. "If I were the dinks," Ernie said, "I'd have that son-of-a-bitch long before the Hook gets here."

I nodded my agreement, then turned my attention to the approach into English. For some reason Franklin did not get the Chinook.

Late that afternoon, Franklin flew the same patrol we had extracted back into the area to wire the downed chopper for detonation, but again he changed his mind and withdrew the patrol. The bird sat there through the night, unguarded and rigged, crammed with the original gear and a couple of Claymores Franklin had ordered the patrol to stash aboard. Apparently his intent was to lay a booby trap for the enemy. When we flew over the next day, it was still there, intact. I informed Accousti and he ordered the gun ships out to destroy it. I knew that if the VC had been in the area, they would have stripped and re-rigged it. But nobody knew for sure. We just flew in and blew it and gave up one bird for free.

When Ernie and I returned to Brigade later that day, Beacham told us he wanted to discuss our extraction of the patrol, so the three of us went over to the General's Mess and drew three cups of coffee.

"What's on your mind?" I asked.

He said he simply wanted to level with me so that I would not feel that he had gone behind my back. He was in the process of taking statements from the crews of the gun ships that had participated in the extraction of his recon patrol. Captain James, who was company commander of the Long Range Reconnaissance Patrols (LRRP), had reported that the leader of the patrol had complained that I had called in the gun ships right on top of his men before I took them out.

It was absurd. "For what reason would I have done that?" I asked, smiling.

"Well, Franklin figures it was because you were so anxious to kill the dinks pressing my people that you didn't much care about the patrol you were supposed to be saving," Beacham said.

I stopped smiling. "I'll tell you what, Beacham, you do that little chore—get your statements—and when you're finished, then come see me." I stood up. "Come on, Ernie, let's get some fresh air."

"Don't get pissed, sir," Beacham said. "This isn't personal."

Ernie was already at the door. I glanced back down at Beacham. "Yeah, I know. It never is. It's always just good clean innocent fun, right?"

"Well, Franklin says—"

"That's right, Beach," I interrupted, "you hang in there, and someday you, too, will be a big, strong colonel and then you can speak for yourself. Maybe you will, if we still have an Army by then." I picked up my cup. "Remember now, Beach, make it a good solid report and leave out Franklin's name."

He turned red and seemed to want to say something else. Ernie had the door open and we left and walked up the hill together. "Do you want a statement from me, sir?" Webb offered.

"What for, Ernie? Yours, like mine, wouldn't be worth the paper it's written on in this Brigade." I laughed and grabbed him by the shoulders. "Besides, who gives a shit? We've got a battalion that's cleaning up at every turn, and that's what it's all about, right?"

We stopped by Military Intelligence to check on their material. It was a zero, so we headed back to our area. Late that day, Beacham caught me outside Franklin's hooch and apologized. He said the whole thing had been cleared up. The gun runs had only seemed close because they were screaming right over the patrol's position. I felt myself trying to get a little satisfaction from him. "Position, my ass," I said. "Your recon patrol was running like rabbits."

"Well, I do want to apologize," he continued. The gun ships and the rest of the men in the patrol as well as Captain James had confirmed everything that I had said. Beacham then said he was sorry that it had gone as far as the General.

"I'll go in and clear it up, if necessary," he said.

"Necessary? What the hell does that mean? If I insist, huh?"

"Well, sir, it's not something one would ordinarily bother the CG with since it's already closed."

"But no one minded bothering him with the allegations in the first place, did they?"

"It wasn't me, sir, but if you insist that I go to see him, then I will."

He was right. He hadn't been the one, so if he went in now to see Barnes he wouldn't be able to clear it up either. Barnes would probably say the allegations could not be proved, which was akin to saying that everything was true but everybody was willing to lie on my account. "Forget it," I told him. We probably would have talked more about it, but Franklin called from his office and asked me to come in. Beacham walked off. Franklin said he just wanted me to know that when he had found out about Captain James and his allegations, he had been appalled and had gone right to work to get it cleared up. He had ordered each pilot to write a complete statement, he said.

"I ended it right there," he said, snapping his fingers. "Just like that."

"Thank you, sir," I said, trying to look humble, but laughing inside.

"And another thing," he continued. "You better keep a sharp eye out because that guy Beacham hates you like the plague."

The intelligence officer in the 1st Battalion, a close friend of our own man, Donovan, came up with some information about a VC headquarters unit loggering in two villages just south of our area of operations, in the northernmost sector of the 1st Battalion's area, Henniger's bailiwick. Donovan's friend explained that he had come to us with the information not out of any sense of disloyalty toward Henniger, but rather because nobody in the 1st Battalion was paying any attention to it. They would not give it any thought, he said, until it became "hard intel," which would be in a couple more days—too late for the information to be of any value to anyone. He said he was fairly confident that Henniger could be persuaded to give permission for us to operate in his area, since he seemed not to be particularly interested in it for himself. It was good intelligence, he said, and he had worked hard to get it. I had no doubt that he had, but getting permission to go into another battalion's area of operations was tricky business. Sweep into Henniger's AO and make a major contact? Nope, he'd never buy it, and since I'd be making the request, neither would Franklin. But I decided to try anyway. I owed at least that much to this guy for going out on a limb to bring us the information.

"What was Henniger's reason for not wanting to follow up?" I asked him.

"He just said he didn't have the people available for a commitment."

"Well, maybe there's a way," I said. "Thanks for coming over."

After he left, Ernie, Donovan, and I pulled out the map and matched the location against the information given to us. It all held water. The spot was ideal for a VC headquarters, with excellent access routes for supplies and evacuation routes for the couriers and wounded. It had been pinpointed from information that had come out of the marketplace, which was precisely the kind of source that caused Brigade to turn up its nose. Back home we would have called it barroom talk, and as far as I was concerned it was one of the most reliable repositories of hard intelligence in Vietnam. In fish markets and bars nobody holds back much of anything, because nobody is paying anybody for anything except fish and booze. It is people-to-people conversation, and when the pieces fit together, it can be damned reliable. This time the pieces all fit. The guy from the 1st Battalion had realized it, and now Donovan, Webb, and I knew it. All that remained was to persuade Franklin, Accousti, and Henniger that it was good stuff and convince them that something should be done about it.

Ernie and I met with Franklin and Accousti in the General's Mess. I laid out the intelligence and the tentative plan we had devised. Accousti wanted to know if the intelligence had come from Beacham or the Brigade MI, and I assured him that it had come from neither source but rather was rumor from the fish markets. He glanced at Franklin, who returned the look. I could count on their reactions by then. They had become highly predictable men.

"I suggest that I coordinate with Henniger this afternoon," I said. "I could place two of my units under his operational control."

"And what about you?" Franklin asked.

I told him that for the sake of the operation I was willing to be under Henniger, too. "This thing will need a split operation anyway, sir, because of the two villages in question. With Henniger's permission, I would like to control one portion of the operation."

"Which one?" Accousti asked.

"Either one. Whichever one he decides," I said and pressed ahead with our plan. It would be best to hit just after first light, I said, rather than going in on a Cordon and Search; the terrain just wasn't suitable for that approach. Accousti looked dubious. We had nothing to lose, I continued, and it would be good experience for the two battalions to work with each other and get in some "combined operations" experience. I realized that was my strongest point up to now. I could almost see Franklin and Accousti thinking about how it would look on the record. "Combined Operations"—damned impressive.

"Okay," Franklin said. "But there's no need for it to be under Henniger. It's your idea," he said, pointing at me, "you can run it."

"It's the 1st Batt's AO, sir," I said. "What about Henniger?"

"Screw Henniger," Franklin said. "He does what I tell him."

Webb shot me a glance. "Look, sir," I said to Franklin, "for the sake of just getting along with everybody, I really would like to have the 1st Battalion maintain operational control. It would be good experience."

Surprisingly enough, Accousti came to my aid. He liked the idea, too, and Ernie agreed as well.

"Well, it's stupid," Franklin said, finally. "But it's your battalion."

"Then we set it for tomorrow, sir?"

He glanced at Accousti. "Get him the choppers," he said, and turned to me. "That's good enough." He seemed pleased. He had done me a good turn, and I could never deny that he had. I dismissed it. The mission was the primary concern. For all practical purposes, I had quit paying attention to anything Franklin said except for tactical orders. I had a battalion to run and I was convinced by then that he was intent on doing whatever he could to screw it up.The only way to counteract that, I had decided, was to run the show as best I could, as I would have even if there had been no Lieutenant Colonel Joseph Ross Franklin. I went out of my way to avoid contact with him, except on tactical matters, and that's what we had there that day—a tactical matter.

Ernie started to say something, but I cut him off. "Let's get down to the 1st while we still have some weather," I said, and we both left and headed down, giving Henniger a call on the way and informing him that we would like to have a discussion with him about a joint operation. He was waiting in his battalion mess when we arrived.

I gave him what we had and told him we had Brigade's approval if he was willing.

"This way, we don't have to come in and go it alone if you can't handle it," Ernie added. I shot him a nasty glance. He was enjoying the hell out of the situation. He unrolled the map and began to outline the plan from the beginning. Henniger and I sat back with our coffee.

Our battalion would provide two rifle companies for the operation. Both would be under the 1st Batt's operational control. Henniger, Webb said, would be in overall command of the mission with all kills, captures, and weapons credited to his unit rather than ours. "We just appreciate the opportunity to come in and help out since your people are all so tied up in heavy operations," Ernie said with just the hint of a smile on his lips.

"We might be able to shake a company loose," Henniger said—

and then he bought the entire plan just as Ernie had presented it. Webb said he would come back later in the day and work out the details. We headed back to English.

Over the noise of the rotors, Ernie shouted that our offering to give Henniger the statistical credit was the thing that sold the plan.

"So who cares?" I shouted back. "A dead guy is a dead guy, and it all goes up on one board down there at Saigon. It's U.S. Army, Vietnam—and that's us, right?"

He shook his head and laughed. "Airborne, sir!"

As we clattered on, I reviewed the plan in my head. This time we would take along a national police unit of my own choosing. I had made friends with a squad from downtown Bong Son, and they were actually living out in our area by then, just like the Kit Carsons. Generally I had great respect for those police who had been police before we had come to the area. They knew the populace, if anybody did, and they understood the workings of the hamlets, villages, and towns.

In fact, I had a great deal of respect for the fighting capabilities of the Vietnamese troops. They were, as a rule, far better than most Americans realized, especially when they had a cause for which to fight, as did the NVA and VC. Most of the ARVN failures could be traced to one basic failure: lack of cause. It was something none of us seemed to understand, slow as we were to realize the lack of respect for the Saigon government in the provinces.

During my stay in Vietnam, I never once heard the South Vietnamese government referred to as legitimate by any Vietnamese who could be trusted. Nevertheless, many of them fought, not for one year each, as we were required to do, but for years and years, ever since the earliest stages of World War II and even before. First they fought the Japanese and then the French, and now some of them were fighting us, while others were fighting the VC and the NVA. Their losses had been staggering. In short, I liked the true Viets, and the squad of police from Bong Son were true Viets in every sense of the word. They weren't fighting for the Saigon government, but for survival. When it finally ended, they knew they would come out either winners or total losers. I decided to take the squad in with us on the combined operations. At least we wouldn't have another St. Valentine's Day.

It paid off handsomely. We grabbed a batch of legitimate prisoners of war, and sustained no friendly losses. Because it was a headquarters unit, just as the fish-market talk had indicated, they put up only a minimum of resistance. There were a couple of diehards, yes. There always were even in headquarters groups. But we just rounded up most of them like strays from a cattle herd. The leader of the national police squad pointed them out to us by name, one by one. He fingered the doctor and his assistant, two of the nurses, and the propaganda chief and his assistant, and finally he picked out the head man: the VCI chief of the area. This guy was the only one he really wanted to take care of personally, regardless of his promises to me, because four years ago the man had murdered his father, mother, and younger sister.

I waltzed the police-leader off to one side.

"A promise is a promise," I said, remembering Valentine's Day. "Besides, the guy is worth information alive. If he dies, it's the last of him—and if he dies, you'll never go with us again."

He was still in a rage and there was murder in his eye, but everything I had ever learned about the Vietnamese pointed to a deep sense of honor, particularly about man-to-man commitments.

"I not only have your promise, but I gave my own promise based on yours," I said.

He argued and told me of the horrors of that day four years before when the VCI chief had taken his family from him, but we finally came to an agreement. He did not like my decision to keep the man alive, but he had given his word and he would abide by it.

He continued picking out as many as he could. It was a hell of a good-sized group. We turned approximately eighty over to Brigade and they, along with the KIAs, the weapons, and the other gear we captured, were all credited to Henniger and the 1st. I had some difficulty explaining that little item to my own two companies, but that was the way we had set it up and they finally accepted it with a minimum of bitching.

The 1st Battalion had not come up with a single POW. They had a couple of detainees and had registered two kills, but no prisoners. I did not hear or see Henniger during the entire operation. The company he had sent had come in overland since helicopters were, he said, "too risky" under the circumstances. I couldn't quite grasp that.

When it was all over at the village, I flew back to English and then down to the Tam Quan District Headquarters to coordinate a night pick-up of some agents. I mentioned the incidents of the 14th and asked how the investigation was progressing. Nobody knew anything about an investigation.

Ernie decided that he should be allowed to accompany a night patrol.

"You mean tonight?" I asked. "Aren't you tired?"

"From what?" he said. "Flying in a chopper?"

He joined the patrol just before dusk after making all the preparations—the tie-downs, the camouflage, the muffling. He was going out as a private and it was to be a roving patrol, the type Lt. Miller had been leading when he hit the group at the foot-bridge.

At about 2 A.M., they were just inside a village. An elderly woman was out in front of her hooch, stoking the fire and singing in the night. It was a good cover, but Ernie and the patrol weren't buying. Singing? At this time of the morning? They moved in.

The old woman was covered, and as one of the patrol covered the back of the hut, Ernie and the leader went inside to search. At first glance they found nothing. They went through the rafters, the walls, and then turned to the floor. Still nothing. They walked to the fire and Ernie swept it aside with his boot. An iron plate was revealed. Webb lifted it, cracked off one round into the floor and shouted, "Chieu Hoi!" A set of hands appeared, followed by a man. The patrol leader went down into the hole and brought out an SKS and some documents. The old woman continued to sing as though nothing had happened.

"I just gave her hell and let her go," Ernie said later. "Maybe we're getting soft, huh, sir?"

Maybe so.

Maybe the old girl would do the same thing again. So what? It hadn't helped the man in the hole, had it? I didn't know if my logic was valid or not, but it was at least comforting, and it worked for me. As long as it continued to work, I was intent on maintaining its principles. A philosophy of war is a personal matter, to be dealt with by each individual. It has to be that way or you go bananas.

Bravo Company, under Bill Hill, Charlie Company, under Chris Dorney, and Delta Company, under Jim Grimshaw were all clicking along with regular contacts almost every night. It was the kind of steady leadership that makes the difference between killing and getting killed. The three units had been in the grass for ten days as I waited for Vance Forepaugh to show up and take over Company A, the unit Cording had left. Noriega was doing all right, but I had an idea he would do much better if I got him and his company off the Berm and back out where the action was. It was as good a time as any to find out if I was right, so I called in Bravo and got Noriega and Company A ready to go. Just to see how they would do, I decided to go along with them their first night out. I had selected a village just south of English across the Hoi An River. It was a place with a history of VC. Several incoming and outgoing flights had drawn sporadic small-arms fire from the area. Even in the dark, it was less than a three hour march.

I had Noriega and his men leave the Berm early in the morning to get resupplied. They spent until about noon cleaning their weapons and gear and laying it all out for inspection, then rested until dusk, when we moved out toward the village.

We reached the river bank just before midnight. Noriega handled the crossing flawlessly. Every last move was made silently, and I felt good about being there with Company A. With the entire force on the south bank, Noriega gave the word and they broke up into smaller units and disappeared into the night around the village. The unit I had joined slipped down along a deep drainage ditch, up into a paddy, and then locked in tight against a dike. I leaned back against the mud and thought about the difference in this group and those I had accompanied over the months I had served as the IG. This one was set in as well as any I had ever seen in Ranger training. Nobody talked. Nobody moved around. Nobody coughed. Nobody cleared his throat. Nobody removed one piece of gear. No one lit a match or struck a light. No one smoked. No one decided it was time for a snack. Half of them were awake all the time, and the men on guard were alert and ready. It was one damned fine ambush, and I was proud to be a part of it. If Vance Forepaugh didn't show up pretty soon, it wasn't going to make any difference—except that I might not have a place for him. Hell, I already had me a commander for Company A.

As the night passed, two of the ambushes had contacts, but nobody in my group ruffled a feather. They stayed off the radio and remained locked in behind the dike until morning, when Noriega called them in for the day-logger.

Ernie came in a bit later, and the two of us went over to the sites of the two ambushes that had made contact. Between them, they had six dead VC and one wounded, plus three SKSs and a stack of grenades. Wire-cutters and some fuse cord were found on one of the bodies. The wounded man said he had been with another young buddy who had been wounded, too, but had been helped away by his girlfriend, who had been guiding them out of the village.

"Where would they have gone?" I asked.

"He hasn't said," the patrol leader replied.

We talked with the wounded man some more and pointed out that we could certainly do his friend a lot more good than any village doctor. He considered that logic and finally told us that about 300 meters away there was a small cave hidden beneath thick brush. We asked if he was well enough to travel that distance for a friend, and he agreed. After patching him up as best we could—his wounds weren't really that serious—Webb, Potter (my radio man, not Larry), a sergeant from the platoon, and I headed south with the guy. He led us right to the place and I followed him, crawling in and under the dense thorns. There was nobody there. I decided to go in. It was really a tiny, tight hole rather than a cave—a place ideally suited for a kid who wanted to get away from it all with his girlfriend. It was clean, except for some foamy blood-spots on the clay floor, which spelled out that the wounded guy's friend had had the course. I backed out and flew back to English, well satisfied with Noriega and Company A.

That same morning I had a meeting scheduled with Colonel Nim, the commander of the Vietnamese battalion stationed at LZ English, and his American advisor, also a colonel. Nim said he wanted to discuss a deal on starlight scopes. What kind of deal, I asked. Well, the American advisor explained, since the 2d Battalion had so many of the scopes, Nim would like to get a couple.

"Not on your life," I said.

"What do you mean?" the American asked.

"I mean I'm not going to do that even if I'm ordered to by General Barnes himself. I don't have enough for my own patrols," I said, which wasn't precisely true but would have been my answer even if I'd been ass-deep in scopes. Nobody else seemed to have given a damn about where those one thousand grenades we had painted had gone, but I sure as hell did.

"Perhaps we could arrange something else, then," Nim suggested.

He said he was in a very compromising position, since our battalions were operating in the same general area and mine was destroying VC every night while his was having great difficulty even locating the enemy. His superiors were beginning to question his capabilities. "There must be some kind of arrangement," he said.

Sure there was, I said. It was the same proposal I had made the first day I took command of the battalion: combined operations between us and the Vietnamese. It would work this way: half a squad of Vietnamese from Nim's battalion and half a squad of GIs from mine out in each ambush site together. In his area, they would be commanded by his men and in ours they would be commanded by Americans. My teams would provide starlight scopes and radios.

"That should increase both of our potentials, don't you think?" I asked.

"Well, no," Nim answered. "My superiors would never permit Vietnamese troops to be under U.S. command."

"Then I'm sorry, Colonel. I just don't have any scopes to spare right now in any other way." I got up to leave.

"Wait, wait," Nim said, motioning me back down. "Perhaps it could be arranged."

"That would be good, sir," I said. We were of the same rank, but I had made my point. "We can begin at your discretion, Colonel Nim."

"Tomorrow night, Colonel Herbert?"

"Tomorrow night, sir. I'll have Major Webb come over and coordinate with your operations officer." I got up to leave again, and the American advisor asked to see me outside. He followed me out and walked with me toward the gate.

"That was very embarrassing to me, Colonel Herbert," the American said.

I stopped and turned. "Oh?"

"Colonel Nim is an excellent officer. General Barnes respects him a great deal, and counting on the General, I guaranteed Colonel Nim that I would get him the starlight scopes."

"You did?"

"Yes, I did."

"Well, then, Colonel, I'm afraid you're going to have to apologize because I ain't giving him any. I fucked up on the grenades—you remember the grenades, don't you, Colonel?—but I'm not about to screw up on the starlights. And I'll tell you another thing, Colonel.

I'll damage every last one of them if the General orders me to turn them over to Nim."

"That's disloyalty."

I reached up to his shirt and brushed some imaginary dust from his collar. "Yeah, that's me, Benedict Herbert. But I'm alive and, what's more, I intend to stay that way. Now you take care of yourself, Colonel, and advise well."

Heading back down the road, my driver mumbled something about the American colonel being an organization man.

"An organization man? What's that?"

"You know, sir, like in Whyte's book."

"Hell, man," I laughed. "I thought you guys were supposed to be reading comic books and skin books. Where do you get off telling me about William H. Whyte?"

He laughed, too. "But he is one, isn't he, sir?"

"I think you're right," I said, nodding. "Yep, he's one all right, and a piss-poor one at that."

But I didn't know what to make of Nim. Although he was much too immaculate for my combat tastes, he had an impeccable record with the French against the Viet Minh. Still, he was always decked out in those stiffly starched tiger suits, and I found it difficult not to equate him with the similar types I had seen by the busloads in the States, particularly at Ft. Benning and Ft. Bragg, where so many of them came for training. They were neat, clean, starched, French-educated, and like Nim, always immaculate. They were the silver-spoon-fed aristocracy of Saigon, the ones the French had believed in and educated into the power elite. In America, however, they failed to carry their share of the load on the training patrols. They didn't expect to have to participate in the hand-to-hand combat training or the bayonet schooling or the obstacle course. They loaded up on hi-fis, radios, other electronic gear, and most anything else they could lay their hands on before heading back to lead their Army to victory. All their aristocratic manners told me nothing of their loyalty or disloyalty. Colonel Nim? I just didn't have any reliable evidence either way—except for the fact that since he had been around the 173d, he had accomplished absolutely nothing. That he had accepted such a fat-assed advisor was one more strike against him as far as I was concerned. The American colonel was living in the past, constantly talking about Korea and World War II and maintaining maps almost as

326

elaborate as Barnes's and Franklin's. He served no useful purpose except as a body at the pony shows and a meal ticket for Colonel Nim. In fact, I think I had a lot more respect for Nim than for the advisor.

The advantage in my relationship with Nim was that he knew that I knew; he never pressed and never tried to go through Barnes or to Barnes through the American advisor. He began to spend more and more time in the 2d Battalion's area, and although he was pleasant company I kept my mouth shut when he was around. I had learned a long time before that, if you wanted to succeed in Vietnam, never mention your plans to Vietnamese. I had learned also that if you wanted to plant an idea, true or false, the best thing to do was to mention it around a Viet—the next day, the VC would have it. It wasn't always intentional, I knew. In fact, it was frequently a matter of necessity, because the Vietnamese had relatives, some of whom may have lived in the areas of the proposed operations. They had to be warned so that they could get out before it was too late, and so the word was passed.

With Nim, it was not a matter of distrust, but neither was it a case of trusting him. I just didn't know, so I kept silent.

I had called Chaplain Van Dyke at First Field Force Victor about Davis, and he came down to English to talk. He asked for an update on the young chaplain so that when he returned, he could offer some kind of report. When I had finished, he looked dubious. "Look, Padre," I said. "I know Davis is probably as busy as he states, but for Christ sake, and I mean that literally, how about explaining to him that his job is out there in the field and not in the base camps?"

Van Dyke laughed and slapped me on the back. "Tony, Tony, aren't you ever going to change?" he asked.

"I hope not, Padre," I replied. We settled down to business. I told him I needed Davis to go out into the grass with the troops because when a guy needed the last rites out there he should be able to have them.

"Besides, that's where religion is, isn't it, out there in the grass?" I said. "What do you think, Padre?"

"Well, yes," he agreed. "But there are other considerations, too. Davis has units besides the 2d Battalion, and he is supposed to regulate his time accordingly."

327

"Okay, then, can I have another priest when he's gone?"

"No, no, Tony, that's impossible, but don't worry about it. I'll have a chat with Davis and see what I can do. Now, you stop fretting, Tony. Davis is a fine chaplain."

"Oh, I'm not worried or fretting, Father," I said. *"Adeum qui le tificate yu ven tutem meum qui a tuix Deus for te tu pe meus"*— mumbling through the altar boy's portion of the mass as best I could remember it, which was half-assed at best, but Van Dyke was kind.

"Ah, Tony, you're a priest at heart," he laughed.

"Nope, Padre, just an ex-altar boy, a Father Kelley one."

"Okay, okay, now you forget all about this. Davis will go out with the troops just as you want him to."

"I hope so, Father, I really do hope so," I said. I dropped the subject. He had agreed to talk with Davis and that's what I had wanted in the first place. The next day, he and Davis went to field and said mass in every unit. I was happy and I was satisfied. Not that I was so religious anymore, but I was a Catholic and having served as an infantry private in Korea I knew how much it could mean. What the hell else did a private have out there? He had marijuana and heroin, or he had religion.

A letter of commendation from General Peers arrived.

I read it and filed it under S for Scrap. Who gave a damn what he thought? Just too damned much had happened. I had pushed the issue of the murders just as I had pushed everything else since I had been there, and I knew I was about the least liked son-of-a-bitch in the world as far as the Brigade "key staff" were concerned. I had made all the wrong enemies, and I had swaggered more than a little, and I hadn't given a damn about telling people what I thought. The letter may have been an attempt to soothe me and assuage the tensions. Maybe Franklin was right about me; maybe I was getting old, because letters and papers and commendations and medals just didn't mean very much anymore. Maybe they gave me too many too soon. Hell, I already had over forty decorations, and I didn't even know what some of them were for. I never wore them except when ordered to do so for a photo or a briefing or some other such junk.

Besides, there was something not quite right about my getting this letter. Peers was the commander of First Field Force Victor.

Generally when a commander at that level issued a letter of commendation, it was to his subordinate commander at the next level—in this case, Barnes—who if he chose to do so would then simply endorse it and pass it down the line to the unit or individual involved. But mine was a personal letter, addressed to me and signed by General Peers, saying I'd done a good job at Cu Loi and keep up the good work and all that. Why? I wondered.

"Here, Hank," I said, handing him Peers's letter. "Run off a copy for each individual in the platoon with the proper endorsement, okay?"

"Sure, sir." He looked it over. "Does 'total killed' include the ones the Tam Quan group murdered?"

"Yeah, I reckon," I nodded.

"By the way, sir, do you still want to go over the documents that Noriega brought in?"

"Yeah, sure, why not? With less than four months left, who the hell can afford to sleep?"

He brought them in, and I stayed up until nearly dawn reading. It was well worth the effort, and the next day I went out to move part of Noriega's company back in by helicopter. We took along a man Franklin described as a village chief from that area. He was going to finger any VC or VCI, should we find any suspects, and Franklin or no Franklin I was glad we had him.

He turned out to be a three-dollar bill, a phoney of the first rank. Not only did he not know anyone in the village, he got lost as soon as we stepped out of the choppers. The son-of-a-bitch had never even seen the area before, and he sure as hell had never been a village chief there. He tried to point out a few VC and went so far as to try to slap a few of them around. A sergeant stopped him, and we put him back on the bird for English. As it lifted off, the sergeant shouted to the sky: "Tell that dumb fucker Franklin we don't need no village chief. We can do it ourselves."

I ignored him. If I hadn't, I would have had to do something about his remark, and besides, I was beginning to feel the same way. The so-called village chief was a loser, like most of those to whom we paid a monthly stipend, who talked constantly about waiting for the right moment to return to their people. But he had fooled Brigade. Still, the operation wasn't a complete loss. We got two in a drainage ditch later in the day and captured four more. Then Franklin sent the so-called village chief back out, and this time the guy tried to make the most of it by kicking everybody's ass and taking names all over the place. He was really storming. I had to grab his wrist and talk pretty sternly to him. "No slapping and no torturing and no killing today. You understand?"

He did, but he seemed not to understand why. He had been buffaloing Americans for so long he was stymied by us. But I only had to tell him once, and the rest of the day he stood next to me as though we were cemented. He was not the first "exiled village chief" I had encountered. They were the robber barons of Vietnam, the scavengers of war. They lived off the blood of their brothers, and the only difference between them and their counterparts in previous wars was that we were paying them.

Operation Skyscope was General Peers's idea. A large and powerful telescope would be mounted on top of the most inaccessible peak in the south edge of the Tiger mountains, the General suggested. From that vantage point it would overlook the 1st Battalion's area of operation. But Henniger said he couldn't spare the troops to man it, so Franklin decided that his company and mine would share the load, alternating weeks. Henniger didn't buy that either. He said he just couldn't afford the personnel, so we ended up with the whole thing. I accepted it with great enthusiasm, because I believed the plan had real merits. One platoon could do the job well and there would be a minimum of resupply to the peak. From up there, one man could see for literally hundreds of square miles, and he could observe a long way seaward to boot, including the entire beachline for ten or fifteen miles. All he needed was average weather. Skyscope proved a fine idea, and once we had it locked in, either Ernie or I, or both of us, visited it for a few minutes almost every day. We dropped off mail, if there was any, or rations, beer, or soft drinks. It was near enough so that the platoon on duty at the peak could be kept in almost as fine a style as the ones on the Berm. We tried to make sure that they were.

Franklin visited it one time. Within an hour after his departure, I received word from Lieutenant Chris, the officer in charge up there, that Franklin had been trying to "push the troops" into making written statements suggesting that I was mishandling things and providing substandard leadership. "Franklin's tricky, sir," Hank Boyer cautioned. "You better get a statement from that lieutenant while the thing is hot." I took his advice and Chris delivered a statement later in the week.

I wrestled with the situation in my mind and finally concluded that, if what I thought was happening was really happening, a showdown with Franklin was inevitable. But I was unable to fathom his reasons. If he hated me, fine—but why? There had to be a reason. The evidence of his hatred was almost incontrovertible. Some of the troops expressed the frictions with nicknames. Franklin was Commando Jelly, and Barnes was Maxwell Smart. I asked once what they meant. A young lieutenant explained it:

"Come on, sir, you know. It's the bulldog mouth and the puppy-dog ass, and they're all over the place. The guys know, as you know, too."

"Okay, thanks," I said. "But you just get the word out not to use those names when I'm around. I don't like the position they put me in."

"Sure, sir," he smiled. "We understand."

As I had expected, after a while we had to alter our operations a bit. In some areas the VC and the NVA had begun to adjust to our night style and were moving their people at about the same times we were moving ours into or out of the ambush sites. Within a day or two we adjusted our timing and started picking them up again as regularly as clockwork.

One of the combined US/ARVN patrols came back in with a report that some prisoners they had taken had said their units were moving out because they no longer trusted the population in the area. They were losing too many troops, the prisoners said. If they were being truthful, it was probably the direct result of our night movements. Were we separating some of the fish from the sea already, I wondered. No, I cautioned myself, it was much too early for that grand a speculation. Perhaps the prisoners were moving out for replacements. We had been cutting them up pretty badly lately. Or perhaps they were moving out for resupply or a rest. It was, at least, interesting, and I had Donovan file it.

In the next couple of days I went out with more and more patrols. The pickings were getting slim. The enemy began to restrict his movements to the barest of minimums. He went even deeper underground and started operating further into the hills.

We tried to follow, striking at the NVA. Grimshaw began to work the caves more and more aggressively, while Hill and Dorney worked the coastline. They were having continuous contacts and frequent kills of two and three a night.

On March 14, I received a formal Letter of Reprimand in General Barnes's name from Bethea.

Not only was it the very first I had ever received, it was the most ridiculous piece of crap I'd ever read. There wasn't one thing in it that I could get my teeth into. What had prompted such a letter? What was it all about? If I was going to be reprimanded, I wanted to know what for—because I sure as hell intended to answer.

I went to see Franklin.

"What is this thing about?" I asked, shaking the letter.

"It's about your relationship with the staff."

"Just what does that mean?"

"Okay, Herbert," he said. "Okay, you bastard, if you want specifics, you'll get them, and"—he began to scream—"goddamn it, you'll be held accountable for your answers. Do you understand? You're going to get specifics, so get your goddamned ass out of here."

I think if he'd had a vase or a rolling pin handy, he would have thrown it. Jesus, I thought, walking back, if I ever do get my psychology doctorate, I'd give a thousand dollars for a copy of his records.

Two days later, on the 16th, I received my specifics:

SUBJECT: *Required Report on Military Police Blotter*

Commanding Officer
2d Battalion (Airborne), 503d Infantry
173d Airborne Brigade

1. At approximately 1900 hours 10 March 1969, Military Police Patrol 10 (SPRAGUE and JOHNSON) observed a small Vietnamese boy sitting on Bunker #41, LZ English. The patrol went over to clear the area but was refused entrance by the men in the bunker. When Sgt SPRAGUE asked the senior man of the bunker for his I.D. the senior man refused and ordered the patrol to leave.

2. The Commanding General's note from the Military Police blotter recording this incident is quoted for your information and compliance:

"I want a full explanation of this and report of action taken against responsible individuals."

3. Required report will be submitted to this headquarters, ATTN: AVBE-XO, not later than 20 March 1969.

JOHN D. BETHEA
LTC, INF
Brigade Executive Officer

It was crazy.

We weren't in the Russian Army and the provost marshal wasn't the NKVD, and Franklin and Barnes weren't czars. There were rules and regulations as well as customs in the military, and they could damn well abide by them. No provost marshal or MP or anyone else had the right to violate the chain of command upon which the entire system was predicated. Yet they had gone out there to the Berm without first checking through battalion headquarters. It would have been a simple act of military courtesy. Evidently, even big, bad Provost Marshals needed to learn the rules when they worked for Franklin. Major Meurrens, the PM, and I had spoken about it before. Meurrens had a habit of calling straight down to the companies and asking to see someone at a certain time. He very seldom came through the battalion headquarters, which would have been the regulation channel. He seemed not to appreciate the fact that individuals were first responsible to their squad leaders, platoon sergeants, and platoon leaders, who in turn were responsible to their company commanders, who in turn were accountable to the battalion commander, in this case me. I had talked to him at length about it. If he wanted to see Private Jones, all he had to do was call battalion headquarters, and we would get the man to the appointed place at the appointed time, if it was at all possible. I had asked Meurrens if he understood, and he had said he did.

Now there I was with the letter. I didn't know if the incident had occurred exactly as described, but if my people had run the MPs off, then they had acted exactly as I had ordered them. It had not been a vague command. "No one—do you all understand?—no one goes anywhere in this battalion and talks to anyone unless he checks in through this headquarters first," I had instructed them.

"How about when we're out on the Berm, sir?"

"I said anywhere, goddamn it. If they want to talk to somebody on the Berm, then they come through this headquarters and one of us will come on out with them. Any other way, you run them off, except for Franklin and the General, and even then I expect a call back in for clearance. Now, is there anyone who doesn't understand?"

As far as I knew, no MPs had come by for any permission to visit the Berm. I gave the letter to Hank Boyer and asked him to check into it and give me a written report. A couple of days later, he handed it in.

After questioning Hank lengthily, I endorsed his report and sent it down to General Barnes. A day or so later, he stopped me outside Brigade headquarters and said:

"Forget the reprimand. Tear it up. It's already out of your official records."

"Thanks, sir. I'd like to explain why I believe it occurred."

"Yes?"

It was then or never. "Well, sir, I believe it has to do with the atrocities."

"Atrocities?"

"Yes, sir. The murders of the 14th at Cu Loi, the water torture incident, and the looting incident I reported to Colonel Franklin. I think—"

His hand sprang up between us and his voice was cold. "Look, Tony, I've told you before and I'm telling you again. Anything of a tactical nature, you take up with Colonel Franklin. Do you understand?"

"Well, yes, sir, but—"

"Then, from this point on, you do it," he said, turning abruptly and walking off.

At first, I thought he was pissed because I had violated one of his pet rules. But eventually, it occurred to me that he was applying, whether intentionally or not, the Westmoreland Precept: see no evil, hear no evil, and you will avoid being contaminated by evil. It was the philosophy that kept the generals in Vietnam clear, their only defense to the Yamashita Doctrine.

I didn't court-martial my men for smoking marijuana. Nobody wins in a court-martial. If I knew or suspected a guy was using the stuff, I called him in for a talk. The first thing I told him was that I did not know for sure if marijuana was indeed the kind of drug the Army was saying it was. I suspected that it was not, and I knew that it was not habit-forming, both of which were, of course, beside the point. It was illegal. If the guy was caught with it, I told him, then he would damn well have to pay the price. Then I would take another tack with him. I would say, okay, let's agree that it's no more harmful than liquor. You wouldn't expect me to let you drink and then go on guard, would you? No, of course not, he'd answer, and I'd conclude by asking him why he should think that grass would be any different. Look, I'd say to him, you have a year to do here, and it's a piss-poor year at best, so why make it worse for you and me and your friends? What did his buddies have to do with it, he would ask, and I would explain that anytime he was stoned, he was risking their lives as well as his own.

"Whether you hit the weed or not is really none of my damned business except that the Army has made it my business—and the fact that you're here in this god-forsaken place with me where we could both get killed if we aren't careful makes it my business, too. So for Christ's sake, hold off a few months and give us both a chance, okay? Who knows? It might be legal next year, and we can all laugh about it. Until then, I'm asking for your cooperation."

I wasn't joking, either. I needed the guy's cooperation, and I cared about him and the others. I handled all the other "trouble-makers," as Brigade loved to call them, in the same way. If a guy was a bad-debt case for $2,000 or $3,000, I just didn't see how a court-martial and a fine would help the man back to his feet. If a guy was accused of something, then I figured the least a commander could do was run an investigation that would determine whether the accusation held any water. I felt very close to every man who ever worked for me, and I believed that in some way I was responsible for what each might turn out to be. I never felt that enlisted men were inferior to officers. I was a commander and they were drafted privates, yes, but only because of a different choice of professions. I even went so far as to make the men feel that, if there were no other way to handle our relationship, they could come pick on me rather than some poor innocent civilian. They all knew that if they wanted to fight me, I would always do my best to accommodate them. But we got along well and seldom disagreed. They called me "The Animal," and I did not resent the name. I lived on less than they did. My wants were basic, almost primeval. I could kill with my hands and do it better than the best of them, I could ferret out the enemy with what they called "animal instinct," and I zeroed in on a kill as if it were the only important scene in the world. It was my world, my animal world, and everybody we accounted for took from me, grabbed a part of my soul and whisked it off to wherever it was headed. Some of the men called me "The Cultured Animal," perhaps in deference to my education. I suppose that I was some part of both names and all of neither. What I was trying to be was simply a soldier—a doggie who had just happened to become a lieutenant colonel—doing the best I could in the job I knew best. My "animal instinct" was nothing more than the application of the basics in which I had become so well versed. I spent my time and energy applying the lessons I had learned over so damned many hours and days and weeks and months and years. My "animal instinct" also included a basic distrust of the men I recognized as the "New Army," the pseudo-leaders who helped turn Vietnam into a tragedy for our country and the world.

Franklin notified me that he had information about a VC-infested village that "was a regular R & R center for the bastards." Beacham, he said, had all the hard intelligence on the place. This one was no fly-by-night speculation, this one was really it, he said, and the only way to go in was loaded for bear.

"Plaster it with artillery and then go in and police it up," the deputy commander said.

"What about the innocents?"

"Tough, but that's the way war is. Besides, the place has already been okayed as a free-fire zone. You land your choppers out about 400 meters and go in behind a rolling barrage, and if there's anything left standing, then take care of it, too."

Ernie and I studied the map and then called in Donovan and asked if he thought Beacham's intelligence was hard.

"If it is, then I sure have been out of it lately," Donovan said.

"Look, site it the best you can, Donovan," I pressed. "VC or no VC."

He glanced down at his notes. "As close as I can, sir?"

336

"As close as you can," I said.

"Well, then, there's nothing there except maybe a few coconut farmers."

With that in hand, I sent Webb down to talk with Accousti. "Tell him we'll take in one company and hold one in reserve at English, and we don't want artillery except on call. I want it that way or else I want a written order. You tell them that, Ernie, in case they're not there like Beacham says they are."

After he left, I went over it all again. I had been to the village before, and as well as I could recall it was an almost totally destroyed coconut grove. Again, it was in the 1st Battalion's operational area, but since this was a Brigade operation the jurisdiction lines were irrelevant. It was already dusk, so there could be no fly-over that day; I had to settle for the recon I had and the map. It wasn't all that bad, really. I had discovered after so many years in the field that the Army's doctrines on reconnaissance were pretty flimsy. At every school I had ever attended—Infantry, Ranger, Airborne Infantry, Pathfinder, and all the rest—a man absolutely had to make a physical recon before every patrol, every attack, every withdrawal. He had to, that is, if he wanted to pass the course. Usually it was a complete waste of time. The man is given a patrol order. He then gives his patrol a warning order, and they begin drawing equipment. The patrol leader usually has an updated map, but he has his work cut out for him, and time is of the essence. Nevertheless, we insist that he make a recon, which usually means going up through the woods, glancing out a couple of hundred yards, walking back and continuing his preparation. That night he covers all of the territory he scouted in maybe 15 or 20 minutes, and then he's back on the map again—and maybe because of the recon time that afternoon, it's a map he doesn't fully understand. After a few such blunders myself, I concluded that, given the choice, I would prefer to use my time with a map. I realized that there might very well be changes on the ground, but if there were, I knew the map well enough to recognize them and take them into account on the spot—which is where decisions should be made anyway. Until you get to the spot, a plan is always tentative, changing continuously as more and more information is added. That's tactics: a constantly changing set of circumstances. For infantry, more than half the battle is the map. A thorough study of the map puts you, in effect, in your own ballpark, but not a ground recon at the expense of complete map familiarity. If you have the time, then you make both kinds of studies —ground and map—and you throw in an aerial survey, too. I could get that in the morning, I decided. Ernie and I stayed up most of the night studying the maps and making last minute preparations with Donovan.

At about 2 a.m., Franklin called. "What's this about no artillery, Herbert?" I tried to explain."Bullshit, Herbert, artillery is a part of the Brigade team, and it took a lot of convincing to get that town declared a free-fire zone." It was a village, I had noted, not a town. There was a difference, but I didn't say anything. "Now, damn it, you want to just scrub it, is that correct?"

I went over it all again and tried to explain my position more clearly. I told him I hadn't as yet had the opportunity to recon the area from the air, that I would like to hold off on the artillery at least until after that had been done and then bring it in on call, if necessary. "That way," I said, remembering the manual, "we can do as much damage as possible with as few rounds as necessary." Being a good cadet, he thought that made sense and hung up.

"What was that?" Ernie asked.

"Nothing," I said. "Franklin just let me know we could do it better with artillery."

"Do what better?"

"Kill."

Donovan opened one eye from his perch in a chair in the corner. "Kill who? Women and kids? There ain't no dinks in there."

I raised my hand and wagged my finger in his direction. "Tut, tut, my good man," I said. "We have hard intelligence."

"Bullshit," Donovan said, closing his eye and returning to his nap. When the birds came in and were ready, he joined us for the flight. He had maps and bags in his pockets and under his arms and stuffed down inside his shirt. He was S2 all the way.

"Looks just like Beacham, don't he?" Ernie shouted as we lifted off. Donovan gave him the finger and a laugh.

I took the C and C in about a half hour ahead of the company so that I could get that air recon before we landed. I would select the landing zone and then make the decision on the artillery as well as any necessary last-minute changes in the plan. We headed straight south through the Tigers and then slightly west down across the plains.

Ernie and I picked out the LZ simultaneously, each one pointing it out to the other.

As I looked down, I knew immediately it was not the village I recalled. Yet it was the village. It had been pounded to pieces by artillery and bombs since I had last been down that way. Vegetation was already growing up over some of the rubble, but the major damage was out in the orchards. Not a single coconut tree had been left standing. Suddenly I remembered what had happened. It had been about a week or so before—the first of what Barnes had called the Coconut Raids and what the classified documents had described as "environmental adjustment." Webb called it "one crummy fucking plan," and the rest of us in the battalion agreed. "Environmental adjustment" had no tactical value whatsoever. It served no practical purpose, except as punishment. It was, in fact, a punitive operation. You made the population pay the price for helping the guerrillas, and you made their kids pay, too, and in some cases their grandchildren and everybody else who might want to live in the area for the next twenty-five or thirty years. It was simple to accomplish: you destroyed the orchards, the coconut groves, the mango groves, and the paddy dikes on the hillsides as well as the villages. Coconut palms take about five to seven years from the time they are replanted before they bear their first fruit, and coconuts were the most important fruit-bearing tree in that part of the world and the very staff of life in Vietnam. It was more than just a fruit and a source of commercial copra or oil. The salt-water-resistant fiber taken from it was used to manufacture their nets, baskets, ropes, mats, and brooms. Its peat or dust was used for their crops. They used it for their beer, their wine, their salads, their furniture, and their huts. If you destroyed the coconut palms, you destroyed a way of life. If Carthage had been as dependent upon the coconut, there would have been no need for the Roman plow; they could merely have leveled the trees.

A mango or a mangosteen orchard takes about twenty-five years to mature, and the paddy dikes terraced up the steep mountain slopes were continuous projects, passed along from father to son for centuries, each succeeding generation building and adding its own. Destruction served absolutely no purpose except to make the area virtually uninhabitable for decades to come. To me, it seemed a policy far beneath our dignity as a nation—but it was a policy the technicians who were running the war understood completely. They were in a predicament—Westmoreland, Abrams, Barnes, and all of them—and revenge can be a handy outlet. I never met a single trooper in Vietnam who understood the "environmental adjustment" policy.

The LZ Ernie and I had selected was south of the village, as close to the trees as possible, and after orbiting we came in with the last chopper. We climbed out of the C and C and started through the village with the troops. Except for one old family, a couple of kids with what looked like typhus, and two ARVN troops on leave, it was completely abandoned.

The Vietnamese soldiers interested me. I checked out their story on the radio and they were telling the truth. They were from a mechanized unit that had located west of the village and were on their way to visit sick families. I asked if they had any knowledge of recent VC movements in the area. Not in about eight or nine months, they said, not since their unit had moved into the area.

"Further east maybe VC," one of them volunteered. "But too close here."

While I was speaking with them, Franklin and Accousti flew in. They joined us around the two ARVN soldiers as one of them said he had heard that there was to be a VC meeting that very evening at a village southeast of where we were. The village, he said, was close to a mountainous outcropping we called the Rockpile.

"How does he know?" I asked, and the interpreter relayed the question.

"Fisherman talk," the answer came back.

"Where did he hear it?" I asked the interpreter.

"In the fish market this morning."

"Is his unit doing anything about it?"

The interpreter asked the same question, and the ARVN soldier shrugged and smiled. He was only a private, he explained. He did not know what his unit's plans were—they did not tell him. I turned to Accousti and Franklin and told them what we had been told. "And you want to waste the afternoon over there, right, Herbert?" Franklin said sarcastically.

"Yes, sir," I said. "Maybe Major Beacham's information was sound except for which village." I thought he might grab that if there was a possibility that the mission could be credited to the Brigade.

"Well, if you want to waste your time and your troops' time, go ahead," Franklin said. "As far as Ken and I are concerned, I think

340

we'll just head back and have a little talk with our friend, Mr. Beacham. Suit you, Ken?"

Accousti tried to look tough, and I was reminded of the way Patton described Montgomery: a man about to spring out like a vicious rabbit. "That suits me fine, sir," Accousti answered.

As they lifted off, a fine drizzle began to fall. Webb looked at the sky and then at me. "Think it was Beacham or the rain, sir?"

"So who gives a shit as long as we don't have to entertain them all day?"

"Airborne, sir," Webb said, smiling broadly.

The radio man announced that the choppers would be back for us in half an hour, so Ernie and I began to study the area around the Rockpile. When the birds arrived, I told Bill Hill to take everyone back to English except one platoon and then let me know when he was in the air enroute behind us. I boarded the C and C with Ernie and "Bugs" Benny, our artillery liaison officer, and we headed southeast toward the Rockpile. The drizzle was setting in, heavier, harder, denser.

Larry Pippen was flying again that day, and a couple of miles from the Rockpile I asked him to change his course to due south, stay on it until we were five or six miles beyond the site, and then bank east and come north along the coastline. This was the standard helicopter route to the north and would give us a chance to take a look without creating any undue suspicions. "Just keep her on course, Pip, straight up along the coast until we're out of sight. Then we'll cut back west, pick up the platoon in the air and come back in straight south."

"Rodge," Pippen replied.

So we passed the Rockpile far to the west, headed south. It was one gray mass of boulders standing stark against the choppy whitecaps of the South China Sea. The rain was easing a bit. It faded from sight and about a minute later, I felt the chopper push up beneath me as Pippen swung it around to the east and then to the north. The coastline was now clearly defined out the left door. The gunner jacked back twice on the operating handle of the door gun. I reached back and thumbed his safety, shaking my head negatively.

"Rockpile coming up," Pippen's voice crackled over the headphones. "Jesus, sir, get a load of that bunch up against the palms about a hundred meters south."

There were perhaps a hundred of them. "Keep it north steady,

Pip," I answered, studying the group as long as I could through the binoculars. None of them was moving. They were tight and still up against the trees, utterly convinced that they had not been seen. Their weapons had been stacked in close against the trees. It was made to order if we could pull it off. They had a good hundred meters to the first hooch, and if we came in close and hard and fast in the east-west gulley between them and the Rockpile, we would have them cut off from the hill. There was open ground to the south and west and water to the east. It would work if they didn't panic and move out before we linked up with Hill's birds. If they'd wait just a few minutes, we'd have them cold.

About four kilometers north of the group, Pippen banked off to the northwest, and I was already straining out the door looking for the flight. Ernie was on the net and Potter was listening in on his handset. He kicked my foot. "They're down at Uplift, sir, refueling." I glanced at Ernie. About fifteen more minutes, he signalled with his fingers. I turned back to the door just in time to catch three sharp flashes from the edge of a pond to our left rear, then, a second later, the snap, snap, snap crackling by the open door.

"Dinks at seven," Pippen shouted over the headset. "Down near the paddy in tight against the bank." I kept my eye on the spot and ordered Pippen around in a sharp turn, keeping him far enough off for me to hold the site on the left side of the chopper.

"Drop her down, Pip, we have a couple of minutes." We came in close over the roofs on the south side of a village, up against a pond, just as one of them lofted a rifle out into the water and four others still carrying their weapons broke up along a thicket that bordered a path back into the village. There were four grown men and a kid. Three of the men were in uniform. The other adult was trying desperately to keep his rifle in tight against his left leg, and then just as desperately he was trying to get it up to fire at us. The left door gunner blew him up along the dust and into the thick thorns. The boy broke through the thicket and out the other side and raced along the path, carrying a bundle in his arms. He stopped for a moment and tossed it over a wall to an old woman who scuffed it up and raced inside one of the buildings. I held off both guns. We swung left as we lifted and then back to the right, swinging around in a close orbit, trying to keep our eye on the thicket. After still another orbit, I was convinced no one had left.

"Next go-round, Pip, swing down alongside that trail and let Potter and me take a look. You cover us from the air." But just as we flared away to make the turn, two men broke from the thicket and the right door gunner finished them. Potter and I climbed out and stripped the three bodies. We never found the boy or the other man. There were no documents, only two SKSs and some grenades.

Later, Accousti had this to say about our activities that day:

"Colonel Herbert, himself, told me that as he was returning from his engagement on the 16th, he indicated to me that he stopped enroute in his Command and Control aircraft and he engaged six enemy, killing them all, on the way from the village back to LZ English. I attempted to confirm this with various sources and was absolutely unable to do so."

Ernie Webb, who was in the chopper, cleared up the matter with his statement:

TO WHOM IT MAY CONCERN:
The following is an accounting, to the best of my memory, of the actions of the command and control group of the 2d Battalion 503d Airborne Infantry on 27 March, 1969. . . .

We were returning to Uplift to refuel when LTC Herbert and his RTO shouted "We're being shot at." As the pilot turned the plane around LTC Herbert and his RTO started firing. From my position on the other side of the helicopter I could see three men running, one was carrying a rifle. He was also attired in the greenish outfit the VC wore in that area. The VC were heading towards a wooded area which had one house on the edge. LTC Herbert had the pilot set the chopper down and he (Herbert), his RTO, and the Arty FO disembarked and advanced towards the area. . . .

When LTC Herbert's RTO called for us we landed appproximately 500 meters from where we had originally landed. At that point I saw the body of one of the men I had seen running. Some equipment was thrown on the chopper, including a VC belt with grenades. (I believe it was actually a web belt, G.I. type, but the grenades were fixed in the usual VC manner.) I do not recall exactly what LTC Herbert said had happened on the ground. I was concerned with getting refueled and back to see Delta company in the raid. I felt we could get all the details together on our return to base.

After refueling we returned to the hamlet area with the company. Just as the lift choppers were getting ready to go in we spotted one VC, in uniform, and holding an SKS. His location was several hundred meters from where the troops were going to land. As we came down close he attempted to hide, we called to him and he ran. The Arty FO and LTC

Herbert fired and killed him. They then went over to his body and picked up the rifle. As we were regaining altitude, the lift ships and the troops reported booby-traps, and several casualties. The supporting gun-ships also reported receiving fire and groups of armed men running for a wooded ravine. The ensuing operation took considerable time. . . .

Later on the evening of 27 March a report was rendered to Brigade concerning the operation on the coast. With the excitement of this operation, our casualties, and the problems with the platoon which remained overnight, I had forgotten about the earlier incident, and consequently did not report it. Later that evening, while discussing the day's activities I realized that I had forgotten to report it and told LTC Herbert. He said he would report it in the morning at the Bde Cmdrs. meeting. The following morning he told the Bde Opns officer, LTC Accousti.

ERNEST L. WEBB
Maj. Inf.

The Army ignored Ernie's testimony, and Potter, Pippen, the co-pilot, and the door gunners were left unquestioned.

The Army chose instead to ask radio man James L. Smith about it, who had not been with us at all, except later on in the day after we had finished at the Rockpile. Had he seen it take place, he was asked. No, he had not, he answered. What else could he say? It was the truth. If we had found Ho Chi Minh masturbating on the porch of one of the hooches, Smith wouldn't have been able to say yea or nay. He wasn't there.

We flew over to the paddy and tried to locate the rifle and the other guy, but with no results. The platoon was in the air, Potter said. We got back up, too, and headed southeast, coming in on the west side of the village, orbiting around once counterclockwise and finally coming into the gulley headed due west. The C and C made one more pass around, trying to draw fire. Then the Star Blazers came in on the net and asked for permission to "cream" the village, a legitimate request since we had been drawing fire. I said no and Ernie relayed it. I listened in on the net as he gave them the word: "No fire inside the hut area, everything ravine and north and then only at actual identified military personnel targets." One of the Star Blazer pilots was a little pissed, and I had to cut in on the net and clear it up.

"Ravine and north only," I said. "Got it?"

"Roger that," he finally answered.

It worked out all right for them, because no sooner had he acknowledged my transmission than a group of about twenty enemy

344

broke up the draw toward the west and the Star Blazers came streaking in on their gun runs, their skids right over the roofs of the hooches.

Just below us, a man ran out of a doorway and raised an AK–47. I squeezed off about six rounds and drove him up against the straw wall and down into the cement. Another man with a rifle ran out past him and into the next hut and began firing through the open doorway and then through the window. Someone in the C and C whipped out a grenade and heaved it out right smack onto the roof. It exploded just behind us as we passed over, and it was one ball of an eruption. A thick black column of fire and smoke climbed some 100 to 150 feet into the sky. If we had been a second or so later in our pass, it would have taken the ship apart. I never found out if it had been ammunition or demolitions in the hut. Lieutenant Sigholtz, the platoon leader, came in on the net. He was taking booby trap casualties in the ravine and would have to slow it down. Then Franklin broke in and began asking questions. I had Ernie tell him to get off the tactical net until after the operation.

We saw about five men break out of the ravine and start south through the village, their rifles in close along their legs. Star Blazer came back on the net. "Six, six, am drawing heavy small-arms fire from vicinity of hooches on the north edge of the village. Request permission to return fire."

I shook my head at Ernie.

"This is three," Webb answered. "Negative, negative. I say again: negative. Do you roger? Do not fire into that village. Over."

"This is Star Blazer. Roger. Out."

One of the five men spun around and raised his SKS. Three of them dropped to their knees in a small drainage ditch with their rifles up against the sides. The other one just kept right on moving down the trail, SKS tight up against his leg. Pippen wheeled the C and C around and Potter, the door gunner and I all opened up simultaneously, plastering the three in the ditch and the other one on the trail. We streaked in behind the last one just as he turned into a hooch yard and headed for the door. I squeezed off two rounds into the dirt in front of him, and he spun and whipped up the rifle. I kept right on squeezing, spinning him around and dropping him face down into the clay. A bag of documents went flying from beneath his arm. Ernie and Potter and I got out and retrieved them, jumped back in the bird, and started around again, up along the sea. Men were popping out of the hooches, firing a few rounds, and moving on to the next one. One man ran up and down the huts at the ravine's edge, putting a torch to them. The hut our grenade had exploded was already a ball of fire. I signaled to Pippen to drop down and take me in, pointing to a spot close to the burning hut.

"No place, sir," he said.

"Then drop it down as close to the beach as you can get and I'll take it from there."

"Roger that, sir," he said, flanking west and flaring the machine up. He went in as close as he could without hitting the seawall.

Ernie grabbed my shoulder. "Where are you going?"

"To earn my pay. You stay up and keep me posted."

I yanked my arm loose and jumped, hitting waist-deep water about two or three meters from the beach. Potter crashed in beside me, followed by Ernie and Bugs about a meter behind. I spun around to give Webb hell.

"If you think we're letting you go in alone, you're nuts, sir," he said.

It was too late to argue. "Take the right, Ernie, you and Bugs. Potter and I will go left." We crossed the sand and went over the seawall and into the first hooch. Potter went on along to the second hooch, where I had shot the man with the documents. When Potter came out, he said there were two dead children and a dead woman on a bed. I went in. They were laid out on a bed with no wounds that I could see, and they looked as though they had died in their sleep. I checked the roof for holes. There were none. Outside again, I policed up the AK–47 and the two SKSs out of the sand and threw them into a pile on the path. Potter checked the bodies in the ditch. They were young guys, all between eighteen and twenty. One had an SKS, one had a U.S. carbine (M–2), and the other had a revolver and some documents. I raced over to the ditch and helped Potter strip the bodies. There were two other SKSs jammed up against the ditch, and I kicked them out into the clear with the rest.

The Star Blazer streaked in above us and started pounding the Rockpile itself. Behind us, Sigholtz and his platoon were making it up out of the ditch. Ernie and Bugs started drawing fire, so Potter and I went to help. A man bounced out through a window and Potter dropped him in his tracks. Ernie and Bugs had a guy slammed up against a building next to a bunker, with a gaping hole in his thigh.

346

A girl was rocking back and forth in the doorway, crying and moaning.

Bugs had his rifle down inside the bunker doorway. I stepped into the doorway behind the wounded guy. Inside were a pistol and a camera. I kicked them out into the open. Ernie was talking to the woman. "There's a dink inside, sir," he said, pointing into the bunker Bugs was covering. "She says he has her kid."

"Tell her to call for him to come out and hand out the kid," I said. I turned to Bugs. "Watch out for the kid," I yelled.

All at once the woman began crying even louder, and Ernie moved over to the doorway and shouted something in Vietnamese. The next thing I knew, a gray cloth came fluttering out the doorway. Benny grabbed it and discovered he had the baby in his arms. He handed it to the girl and the wounded guy behind us shouted something. A second later, a shot rang out in the bunker, followed by an explosion down inside.

"Watch it, Ernie," I said, moving over to help cover. It was a damned small hole, and I started stripping off my gear to go in. I had my pistol in my hand as Ernie came up.

"My turn, sir," he said, taking the pistol from me and handing me his M–16. "Loaded?" he asked.

"Eight rounds."

He went past me and down into the hole. Bugs and Potter had taken positions on the far side. I stepped aside to get a better view. "Wham! Wham!" came the reports from inside and Ernie came diving out like a rabbit breaking from cover. "Grenade! Grenade!" he screamed, scrambling past me up against the hooch. Nothing exploded and a second or so later he asked sheepishly if my pistol had been loaded with tracers.

"All eight, Ernie."

We both burst out laughing. "I thought the glow was a grenade primer," he said.

"What else did you see?"

"A body. He's dead."

"Want me to go in and get him?"

"Not necessary, sir," he said, getting up and brushing himself.

By the time Ernie had retrieved the body, Sigholtz's platoon was in and around us, moving from hut to hut—professionally, just like in the manual. I recalled a bitch-session I had had with the young lieutenant. He had said he was going to give up the Army when he got back to the States, and I had called him every name under the sun—not because I disliked him, but because the Army needed him and it was the only way to talk to him. His father had commanded the 2d Battalion prior to Nicholson, and he was one hell of a lieutenant. We needed his kind, and I intended to make every effort to ensure that he made the Army a career. As I watched him move the platoon that day, I knew why. He was better than just good for a lieutenant; he was great.

I had the C and C come in as close as possible to the beach and pick up Ernie and Bugs while I went along with Sigholtz and helped clear the rest of the village, rounding up the inhabitants and getting them out onto the beach.

When we had finished, I stood back to see what we had. I ordered Sigholtz and some of his crew to put out the fire still blowing from the hooch that had exploded and from others that had been set ablaze. These were grass enclosures north of the ditch that appeared to be sleeping lean-tos and storage sheds, all of them temporary shelters. None of the regular village hooches was on fire except the one that had gone up in the big bang. We had about three to four hundred people out on the beach. Most were sullen and silent. A couple were crying. Franklin and Accousti flew in, joining the approximately fifty Americans already on the ground.

"Fine job, Herbert, fine job," Franklin congratulated me. "Beacham was right." He shook my hand and left. He had to make his report, he said, as well as get some MI people down to the village for interrogations. "All you have to do is provide security," he said. "I'll see you later back at English."

After he left, we began to sort out what we had. We separated the people into groups of about fifty each and had them sit down on the sand. Then we went through each group, separating the military-aged males, most of whom were young studs with big, broad, straw coolie hats pulled down low over their faces. Many of them held children tight against them, and the children were invariably screaming for their real parents. There was always a woman nearby, waiting to get her baby back but unable to keep her terror-filled eyes away from the child as she had been ordered. There were approximately thirty young studs in the whole group, and a female agent in the village fingered twenty-six of them as being VC. Then she went on to pick out eight others we had passed over when we were separating the people. One of those she fingered was her own brother. He had, she said, killed her husband a few weeks before. It was quite a haul. The MI people flew in and we turned the suspects over to them. Some of Sigholtz's people were still closing out the fires. I left some instructions and called in the C and C which had just returned from dropping Ernie and Bugs off at English. Three Vietnamese were aboard already when I hopped on: an elderly man who had turned in an old rusty revolver and surrendered; a younger fellow with a minor leg wound; and a child who was ill rather than wounded. The kid had come in with the old man. By the time we landed at Medevac, it was already night and Ernie was waiting at the pad with the jeep.

"We've got to get over to Brigade, sir," he said excitedly. "Franklin has reported to higher that we put the village to the torch and massacred women and children."

A month or so before, it would have shocked hell out of me. Now I was just nauseated. "Okay," I said, "as soon as we get these Vietnamese inside." I helped carry the old man and the wounded guy inside, then came back out and climbed in for the ride to Brigade TOC.

Franklin had already made his report. He said that he had told higher headquarters that we had "littered the beach with women and children," had razed the village and had killed innocent civilians. He made no bones about telling me what he had reported in front of Webb.

"Your ass has really had it this time, Herbert," he said. "You burned that village right down to the sand—"

"That's a goddamned lie."

"Right down to the sand, women and kids all over the beach, a hundred and four, a hundred and four, we counted them, gun runs on the village—"

I glanced at Ernie and settled down to listen. I wanted Ernie to see what was happening. I knew that it would be important at a later date. When Franklin finished, I began.

"That's just not true, sir. The only fires set in that village were by the Viet putting the torch to the straw enclosures, and the only women and kids dead were the ones I already reported—the ones Potter found—and there were no women's and children's bodies littering the beach."

He took up the challenge. Tomorrow, he said, he would send in an "entire medical team under Brigade control to save as many of the wounded civilians as they can." He would also dispatch four Chinooks loaded with rebuilding materials under Major Laurence, the Brigade S5, "to rebuild the village and pray for the people to forgive us." His eyes were shining, his lips were wet, and his voice was high and tense.

"You do that sir," I said. "You take care of the wounded civilians and rebuild the village and then render another report, and this time" —I touched his desk with my hand—"I'm going to demand a formal apology." I pulled my hand back and saluted. "Good evening, sir." I turned to Webb. "Let's get out of here, Ernie."

Outside, a sense of calm set in, as it almost always did at such moments. I knew he had gone much too far this time. It was really his problem, not mine, except that he didn't realize how deep he was in.

"That filthy son-of-a-bitch," Ernie ranted as we walked away.

"Cool it, Ern," I said. "Tomorrow's another day, old man, another day completely."

Ernie went on up the road, back to the battalion, and I leaned against the wooden wall of Franklin's office, sucking in a couple of deep breaths. The sense of calm began to drain out of me. The bastard, I thought, anything goes as long as it's get Herbert. Well, screw him, Herbert wasn't about to be got. And Barnes, what about him, with his goddamned flower bed, watered by enlisted men two or three times a day. I reached down and plucked a posy and crushed it in my fist. Screw him too, I thought, and stepped forward, starting towards the road—footprints through the posies. Then suddenly there he was before me: Colonel Gander, the whole kit and kaboodle. I remembered how the General, as a joke, had suggested that certain of his men salute the little fellow. One squawk and I had him by the neck and wrung it right there in the middle of the posies.

I got out on the road, then realized the enormity of the deed. Colonel Gander, the General's very own ducky, dead, and with my hands around his neck. And crushed posies behind me. If I had been seen, it was all up. I stood rock still for a second. Silence. Finally I tucked the evidence under my shirt and headed up the road to a four a.m. duck dinner at "Paragon Mess."

The team Franklin sent out came back after treating one kid for a laceration and rebuilding nothing. They brought the four loads of materials back to the Brigade. They had tried to rebuild the shelters

350

on the edge of the village—the ones the Viet had set the torch to—but the province chief had forbidden it, explaining that they were not part of the village at all but rather had been constructed by the VC for storage. I waited until the teams were back before I returned to the village to find out how much MI had elicited from the detainees. When I arrived, both the MI and the detainees were gone.

"Where?" I asked Sigholtz.

"They sneaked off early this morning, sir."

"All of them?"

"Yes, sir."

"And where the hell were you and your platoon?"

"Searching, sir."

"Searching for what?"

"For dead civilians in the village."

"Why? What the hell possessed you to do that?"

"Colonel Franklin's orders, sir."

I bit my tongue. What the hell? It wasn't Sigholtz's fault, and at least he hadn't lied or tried to put the blame on someone else. I cleared my throat. "Find any?"

"Any what, sir?"

"Civilians."

"No, sir. Just the same woman and the two kids."

I shook my head. "Okay, get your people in a skirmish up at the south edge of the village and get ready for another search. This time we're looking for gear."

"Yes, sir."

"Every last nook and every last cranny, Sigholtz. Under the fireplaces, the hay piles, the holes, the buffalo stalls, the pigsties, the rice barrels—the works. Right?"

"How long, sir?"

"As long as necessary, plus the time we've stood here bullshitting, right?" I was trying to let him know that as far as I was concerned the detainees and their escape was a dead issue. I smiled and he laughed and turned, calling for his platoon sergeant. I walked along the beach toward the south edge of the village and then fell in behind the searching platoon, with Potter and Childers alongside. It was a damned fine job, and Sigholtz was responsible for the platoon's excellence. He was a fine leader and a hell of a man. He was killed less than a month later, soon after I left the battalion.

Childers came up and asked to see me alone.

"What's up?" I asked.

"One of the MI sergeants, sir. He's down there," pointing to the hut where we had found the two kids and the woman. "He's rearranging their bodies up against the wall, talking about getting a photograph for *Life*."

"Who is it?"

"I didn't get to see, but I believe it was Carmody."

"Okay, thanks," I said. "Get down there and have them place the bodies back where they were and I'll take care of it later."

"Got it," Childers said and left. I pulled out my canteen and leaned up against a palm for a moment. I needed to think. I had had my warning as far as Carmody went. Better I get back to English, report it to Franklin, and let him decide. It was the Brigade's ass, not mine, if he faked a photo and sold it. I left Ernie in charge and flew back to Brigade and reported it to Franklin. He called O'Kane from MI and ordered him to go back with me and confiscate any film and destroy it.

O'Kane rode back with me to the village, where Carmody denied having taken any pictures. He did turn a roll of film over to O'Kane, which he promptly exposed in front of me. "Satisfied, sir?" he asked, looking at me.

"You're stupid, O'Kane," I said. "I don't give a damn about the photo except that I knew Franklin would. Besides, if that was the roll of film with the picture on it, then Carmody's not smart enough to be a sergeant in the first place."

"Well, I'm satisfied," he said.

"Good. Convince Franklin, not me."

At that point, Carmody interrupted by saying that one of my sergeants, a Sergeant Cherry, he said, had just "creamed a civilian."

"A civilian? A civilian?" O'Kane repeated it, urgently.

"Just who the hell is Sergeant Cherry?" I said. I knew we had no Sergeant Cherry in the 2d.

"Not Sergeant Cherry," one of the men volunteered. "I said a cherry sergeant," referring to a sergeant new to his rank and to Vietnam.

"And where is the guy?" I asked.

"Right here, sir," he said, stepping out of the group. "I was nervous. The old guy reached under his shirt and I thought he was going for a grenade."

"How many times did you hit him?"

"Once."

"Where?"

"Over there, sir," he said, and both he and Sigholtz, who had just walked up, pointed simultaneously.

"No, I mean where did the round strike the old man?"

"In the chest, sir."

"Let's take a look," I said and started toward the brush.

On the way, Sigholtz explained what had happened. "They had been guarding some of the villagers, sir," he said, "and searching a hooch when this guy went with his hand under his jacket, and the sergeant, being sort of new and nervous, dropped him."

O'Kane and Carmody were right behind us when Sigholtz leaned over and parted the brush. The man was still sprawled where the Sergeant's round had splattered him, and his right hand was still hidden beneath his shirt. He looks like a village elder, I thought, as I stepped in and dragged his body out into the clearing. I yanked off four buttons from the front of his shirt. Underneath was an old MI bandolier with four grenades attached. I dropped him in front of O'Kane and Carmody. "Civilian, my ass," I said. I walked over to the sergeant. "Okay, but next time, how about taking it a little easy on the trigger, man? It takes several seconds for a grenade to go off, if there is one, and you'd hate like hell to really cream an innocent by mistake, right?"

"Yes, sir, I know."

O'Kane, Childers, and I walked back to the beach to board the C and C while behind us Carmody started clicking off pictures. I glanced over at O'Kane and shook my head. All the way back to English, he sat silent in his rig.

9

The IG team came down to my battalion, just as Franklin had predicted. If their report turned out poor, he had warned me, it would signal my relief because "a commander, Herbert, is as responsible for administration as he is for tactical successes." I had thought about asking him if the reverse were also true—that if a commander couldn't cut it tactically, would he be relieved too? Since we were fighting a war, I assumed that that would be the case, so I didn't bother him with the question. I don't think he would have caught it anyway, and besides, by that time, I'm sure, he was looking for some way to nail me. The IG report just might have been it—but it wasn't. Its conclusions? Outstanding In All Areas. The 2d was the only battalion in the whole Brigade with no unsatisfactories, no major deficiencies to be corrected, and no minor irregularities to be answered for.

Franklin seemed stunned for a moment before extending his hand. "Congratulations, Herbert, the General will be very pleased," he said.

I was in the TOC the next day when a call from a Wildcat team came in. They had spotted a patrol headed straight toward their position and were going to have to blow their cover. They asked for standby extraction, so I laid on the C and C in case they should need it. The enemy patrol was made up of three men, three women, and a child of about six or seven years. Two of the women and one of the men were armed, while the others were carrying rucksacks. I asked if the Wildcat team could fire without hitting the kid. They said that would have been impossible from their position at the moment but perhaps not when the patrol was closer.

"Okay, then, wait, but don't hit the kid," I said. "We'll have the C and C up and we'll be in with the first shot to help out. Got it? Over."

"That is correct. Out."

As Potter, the radio man, and I headed up to the pad where the C and C was waiting, the enemy patrol stopped for a rest break about 150 meters from the Wildcat position, but once we were in the air, the seven moved on again, inching ever closer to the Americans. Ernie instructed Larry Pippen to keep the bird out of sight until the first shots. About eighty meters from the Wildcat position, one of the men in the patrol dropped down to one knee and checked the path. The Americans concluded it was then or never and opened fire. Ernie heard the firing on the radio and gave a thumbs-up sign to Pippen. I felt the chopper buck beneath me in its climb as we headed up and over a ridge separating us from the action. We arrived in time only for the results. The three men were dead, their two AK–47s beside them in the grass, and the American was chasing the three women down the trail. I signaled Pippen and he dropped the helicopter down into the women's path and flared it up. Potter and I were both covering the one woman who had not gotten rid of her rifle and probably would have dropped her had she fired, but she chose instead to toss it out into a nearby stream. The little boy was cutting across a paddy behind us, high-tailing it for a village 200 meters away. I signaled to Pippen to forget the kid as the radio man and I climbed out to lend a hand to the three Wildcats. We gathered up the weapons, some documents, the three women, and the Americans, and got the hell out of there. It was no place for one C and C load of headquarters types to be hanging around without gun ship protection.

I studied the women on the way back. One was about thirty, while the other two were in their late teens or early twenties, and they were all fine looking women. They were Honeys. That was more than a personal judgment. It was the name we had given to the girl-friends in the NVA and VC cadres. The Honey was usually the cream of the local crop, and since the VC and the NVA were the local heroes, their attracting these girls was not remarkable—especially since a Honey did not have to work in the field, pay taxes, or get her ass kicked around by GIs on Search and Destroy missions. One of the younger girls pulled a sheaf of papers from beneath her blouse and tried to throw them out the open door of the chopper. I stopped her by clamping my boot down on her fist. As I picked up the material I noticed that it seemed to be poetry wrapped around an embroidered handkerchief. I put it all in my pocket and waggled my finger at the girl. At the Military Intelligence compound, we turned her and the other two over to the MI people, along with the material, and answered questions as best we could. Had they been carrying any weapons? One had, we said, and pointed her out. How about the others? Rucksacks, we answered, handing them over. Had they talked? Nobody's asked them to yet, we replied. Before we left, we told the MI folks that we would like a rundown on anything they gleaned from the women, and we would like it as soon as possible. We were interested, we said, in the answers to such questions as where they had been heading, where they had come from, and what had made them suspicious on the trail.

"I'll stop by later in the afternoon and see what you get," I said. "Okay?"

"Right, sir," one of them answered.

Ernie and I left and began debriefing the Wildcat team. Debriefing was important because in combat little things remembered could sometimes be of great importance in planning or training for the next mission. We wanted the answers to such questions as how and where they had first spotted the patrol, what it had been doing at the time, whether anyone in the Wildcat team had moved, how long had they been in position, and what the weather and the light conditions were. The answers could be inconsequential or significant; you never knew until you asked the questions, and it was one more difference between a good unit and a bad one. Military Intelligence should have been providing the same kind of information to field units, but they weren't, and that was only one aspect of MI's failures in the Brigade. They were no worse and no better than most intelligence units in Vietnam. They were just part of the sickness. Perhaps their weaknesses were partly caused by the reluctance of anyone to capitalize on their information. It had been a long, long time since anyone had used intelligence intelligently, and if the MI people were frustrated and stale, it was understandable.

That afternoon I went back to the MI compound, an enclosure less than 100 meters from General Barnes's air-conditioned sixty-foot trailer. The interrogation of the women was still in progress in the back room, I was told, and they had not yet found anything either incriminating or significant. I asked about the material the girl had tried to chuck out the helicopter door and was told that it had not yet been read.

"Can you read Vietnamese?" I asked the sergeant on duty in the outer office.

"No, sir, but Nguyen here can," he said, pointing across the room to a young Vietnamese.

"How about having him take a look at the stuff, okay?" I asked, picking up the material and handing them to the young man.

"Sure, sir."

His reading took less than ten minutes. The stuff turned out to be not poetry but VC propaganda, calling for everyone in the villages to band together and work together day and night to remove the yoke of the U.S. imperialist aggressors. There were also some directions for understanding what he believed to be code words, but he said he could not be sure without some further study.

"Sure, Nguyen, take your time," I said. "Everyone else around here does."

As he pored over the documents, I walked to the rooms in the back and knocked lightly on the door of the one on the right.

"Who's there?"

"Herbert."

"Just a moment, sir," someone answered, and a second later the door swung inward. Sergeant Carmody greeted me.

"Come in, sir."

I squeezed past him and he closed the door behind me. Inside, in addition to Carmody, were Captain Bowers, a Vietnamese man, and one of the Honeys the Wildcats had captured that morning. She was seated to my left, in a chair against the wall and just off the corner. Carmody was standing to her right, my left, and the Vietnamese man was sitting just off my right foot, facing the girl in the chair, their knees only a couple of inches apart. Captain Bowers was just behind the Vietnamese man, sitting in a chair and leaning over the Viet's shoulder.

The girl was moaning and trembling.

"Find out anything?" I asked turning to Carmody.

"She claims she was out picking waterbugs, sir," he said and laughed.

"What about the patrol? Where was it headed?"

Carmody turned to her and asked something in Vietnamese. She shook her head. He hit her with the back of his hand, raking it down along her face. "You're a fucking liar," he shouted. The blood began to rush into the long abrasion on her cheek.

It began to happen in a rush. I turned to Bowers, thinking he would say something. Carmody said something in Vietnamese. Bowers nodded to the Vietnamese man in front of him and touched his shoulder with his hand. The girl screamed. I glanced down and saw for the first time that there were wires from her body to a telephone between the Viet's knees. He was cranking it. I grabbed the wires and yanked, damned near lifting the Viet up with them before the wires separated from the phone. It clattered to the floor.

"Are you crazy, Bowers?" I yelled.

"Sir, I—"

"What the hell kind of crap are you pulling here?"

"Sir, I—"

"Go get O'Kane."

"Sir, Major O'Kane says—"

"I don't give a damn what he says, you go get him," I said. I turned to Carmody. "And knock this off until this thing is settled."

Bowers left, and Carmody, the Viet, and I followed him out into the hall, leaving the girl alone in the little room. In a moment, Bowers returned.

"Major O'Kane isn't here," he said.

"Where the hell is he?"

"He's gone down to Brigade, sir," he said—and behind him, through the open doorway, I saw the major getting into a jeep.

I left, too, and walked down to Franklin's office, where, not surprisingly, O'Kane was still deep in conversation with the deputy commander. Franklin signaled me to hold up until he was finished. When O'Kane left, Franklin called me in and immediately began screaming. We were right back where we had left off.

"You son-of-a-bitch," he ranted. "You dirty, rotten son-of-a-bitch. How many times have I warned you to stay the hell away from MI or have your tap cut off?"

It seemed the time for accuracy. "Four times, sir," I said.

"And did you understand?"

"Yes, sir, but I understand torture, too."

"I don't give a shit about that, I—"

"Sir—"

"Goddamn it, Herbert, don't 'sir' me. I gave you a direct order. Did you understand it?"

"Yes, sir, but they were torturing a Vietnamese—"

"Did you personally see them torturing this girl?"

At least, he knew it had been a girl. "Yes, sir, they—"

"U.S. soldiers?"

"No, sir, this Vietnamese—"

"Goddamn it, Herbert, how many times must I explain the rules of land warfare to you? Over here, what the Vietnamese do is none of our damned business."

"But, sir, this guy was cranking this phone generator while Bowers was—"

"Who was cranking the generator?"

"This interpreter, I guess, and—"

"Was he Vietnamese?"

"Yes, sir, but—"

"And was Bowers cranking?"

"No, sir, but—"

"Then, goddamn it, that's the end of it. O'Kane said all that there was to know." He lifted his hand and shook his finger. "One more goddamned interference, Herbert, and you're all washed up at MI. Understand?"

"No, sir, I don't. Carmody was—"

"Did you see Carmody crank the phone?"

"No, sir."

"Did you see any U.S. crank that phone?"

"No, sir."

"Then what's your bitch?"

It was the first chance I'd had to really complete a sentence. For one thing, I told him, it was a violation of U.S. Army directives, as well as the Geneva Accords and the Rules of Land Warfare. "And for another," I finished, "it just isn't Army."

"Oh, you son-of-a-bitch," he said. "You're so goddamned righteous. You never did anything like that, right?"

"No, sir, I haven't. He slapped the girl and—"

"And you never have, huh, Herbert, is that correct?"

"That is correct, sir, I—"

"But you saw Carmody slap her, huh?"

"Yes, sir, I did, I—"

"And so all at once you're the judge, the jury and the executioner. Is that correct, Herbert?"

"No, sir, I—"

"No, sir, I. No, sir, I. No, sir, I. I'll tell you what you are, Herbert. You're disloyal and you're maybe getting kind of old. You just can't stomach it anymore. What the hell is the matter with you? Look," he said, with relative benevolence in his voice, "let me explain. These are the enemy. Even you must be able to understand that. Right? These are the guys who killed your buddies."

"Whom did she kill, sir?"

"Goddamn it, I'm talking about the enemy in general," he said, raising his hand. "Let me put it this way: they're VC."

I decided there was no sense in carrying out the farce further. "And we are supposed to be soldiers, sir, American soldiers. I want to make a charge. I'd like to—"

"Charge? Charge, my ass. You've already made a charge and now it's an investigation—and I'll take care of that, not you. You just be able to back your mouth with sworn, verified testimony."

"Sure, sir," I said. "Anytime." The only thing that worried me as I walked out was his use of the word "verified."

The next day, I cost an American soldier his life.

I had promised Hank Boyer, my executive officer, a day out of the office. It was against my better judgment, but policies—even mine—were made to be violated, and besides, Hank had been doing an excellent job. Once in a while, even an XO deserved a day away. So I took him along in the C and C with Ernie, Potter and me on what would have been a fairly routine day had it not been for the Phu My District Headquarters Advisory Team, a group of American advisors out of Bong Son, and six or seven young Viet Cong. We were on our way back toward English when Ernie spotted the VC moving south along a path, trying to blend in with the woodwork. They were carrying bundles of sticks on their shoulders. We dropped down for a look and hovered about ten feet off the paddy alongside the path. At that point, we did not know for certain that they were VC, but I should have known or at least suspected it. Their rifles could have been inside the bundles; all I had to do was make them strip them apart, which I could have accomplished by a mere signal from the air. But I didn't. We just left them walking along the trail toward a wooden bridge, and wheeled away with me taking some call on the radio. Soon afterward, we were zipping along the Hoi An River when we received a call from Brigade about an ambush at a bridge. An advisory team out of Phu My District Headquarters at Bong Son had been caught by the VC. An American major and his men had escaped, all except one sergeant who had been "separated from the group," Brigade reported, asking if we could lend a hand. While Ernie got the coordinates, I ordered Pippen to bank the bird around and head back toward the bridge we had left shortly before. I didn't need Ernie's damned coordinates. I knew it was that bridge, and I kicked myself in the ass a hundred times as we clattered toward it. Those blasted stick-bundles were a nightmare in my mind.

The sergeant was sprawled on the west side of the ravine spanned by the bridge. He was dead. A jeep seat lay broken and sprung on the road nearby, and another body was lying face down on the opposite side of the bridge. Pippen banked around once before Hank, Potter, and I left the bird and started for the GI's body. Hank was the first one to reach it and the only one among us who had known the man. He was a redheaded sergeant who had been the advisory major's righthand man and had attended several of the pony shows at Brigade. As our XO, Hank had attended the same meetings. He tried to lift the body up and the head fell apart. There was no skull. Apparently, they had forced him to kneel, placed an M–16 or an AK–47 to his head and literally blown it apart. I glanced around. The evidence wasn't hard to piece together. The jeep seat, the eighteen empty magazines scattered around him, his weapon missing—it all added up. Whoever had been in the jeep with him had bugged out and left him, while he had either jumped out or fallen out. The sergeant had fought until he had depleted his ammunition, and then he had surrendered. They had crossed the bridge, put him on his knees, and blown away his skull. His face was a sloppy red rubber mask. We crossed the bridge to the other side. The six or seven bundles of sticks were there, torn apart, along with spent casing from an M–16.

I called in the C and C and we loaded him onboard. Ernie called for the alert standby platoon to come in, and I gave them instructions on the radio. I wanted those VC guys bad, and I would have stayed and worked with the incoming platoon except that Brigade called again to tell us that Captain Striker had upset his helicopter in a rice paddy and needed help immediately.

"Brigade says it will be an hour or so before they can get anything else to him, sir," Ernie said from his spot by the radio. "They want to know if you'll help."

I looked down at the redheaded sergeant's body, and shook my head. "Tell them no, Ernie. Tell them I don't want to be late for dindin," I said. Those people were incredible. Would I help? For Christ's sake, of course I would. I leaned forward, gave Pip some directions and then leaned out the door to look for Striker's lame duck. We finally found them. Strike and his co-pilot were standing there in the paddy, their faces muddy, the flipped-over bird behind them. Pippen was low on gas, so after he deposited Ernie, Potter, Hank, and me, he flew back to refuel. With Striker and his man, and the four of us from the 2d Battalion, we set up a sort of perimeter around the helicopter and awaited the extraction bird. It arrived about half an hour after dark. We helped get things rigged and then flew out with it.

It had been a long day, a miserable, long day—especially for that redheaded sergeant—and maybe for the bastards who had run off and left him. If only I had checked. No matter how old the dog, there's always one more new trick—and I had blown it. I stayed awake most of the night going over it again and again.

The redheaded sergeant was dead because I had failed to follow my instincts when we observed the Viets with the stick-bundles—and God, it hurt. It hurt that night and every night since. Yet there was more to his death than my own failure. He had been left behind. It was no guess. Hank, Ernie, and Potter had seen the evidence: the deep tire marks, indicating the abrupt halt and the pivot, the seat that had gone out with the sergeant when he had tumbled out to fight—and not because he was already dead as it had been reported. He had fought long after they had left him. The evidence for that was plentiful: the empty magazines, the bullet scars around his position, and the footprints where he had come out to surrender. They had flat left his ass there. If they had stayed and fought, not only would they probably all have made it, but they would have had a good chance to cream the VC in the process. We were that close to them, and so was English. There was no way in hell they could have lost if they had stayed and fought with the sergeant. Maybe someday, whoever left him there—his officer, his driver, and whoever else—

would sit down and figure it out the way I had, and then maybe they would share some of the pain in my gut. But not the Army. The Army would obfuscate the issues with an award, the hallmark of the new system. Once something was on paper, it was a fact, and the award could always be referred to later as the official proof of what had really happened.

The Bumgarner incident came a couple of days later.

The Bummer was drawing his equipment for a routine patrol, one of the Wildcat teams of three men with which he had chalked up some remarkable success. They were tying down gear, packing, checking radio batteries, checking calibrations, testing out the contingencies, laying on "on call" concentrations of artillery. I stopped by late in the morning after Bumgarner had wound up most of the preparations and was putting the finishing touches on his own gear. He sat on the hooch floor, bullshitting with me as I sat on one of the footlockers his team maintained in his bunk area. The lockers were for "sensitive items," he said. My foot touched up against the M–16 riflebag in which he always carried his weapon and the scope for which he was famous. He turned to his rucksack and began stuffing in rations, a sweater, and some other items. I nudged the tightly packed canvas rifle bag and felt what I knew was a bottle inside. "Is that one of the sensitive items?" I asked.

He glanced up and laughed. "Want a snort?" he asked.

"Any good?"

"The best," he said, turning from the rucksack to unzip the canvas from around the rifle. He took out everything to get to the bottle, pulled the cork, and handed it to me.

"Brandy," he said.

I didn't recognize the bottle but the taste was familiar. It was Courvoisier. I drank deep, wiped my mouth and handed it back. "Thanks," I said.

"No sweat," he said, replacing the cork without taking a taste himself. He stuffed the bottle back inside the case and replaced the other gear. After he zipped up the bag, he went back to his rucksack while we continued talking. When he was finished, I lifted the rifle case and walked beside him out to the TOC, where he stashed the gear before going to lunch. I had watched him pack every last item he was taking on the patrol. It would be a critical point later. I saw them off, wishing them good hunting, and went about my chores until late in the afternoon, when Hank caught up with me near the TOC as I was coming in from out on the Berm. He was huffing and puffing.

"Sir," he panted. "Sir, I've got to talk to you right away."

I had better get right down to the Bong Son town gate, he said. Franklin and some of the others—Paul Ray and Doc Winkler—were already there along with a large crowd of Vietnamese. There were three bodies, and Franklin was saying that the Bummer had killed three civilians and then mutilated the bodies.

"That's a bunch of crap," I said. "Goddamnit, he knows damned well they're VC."

The Bummer had called in earlier and reported the kill, listed the equipment, and requested a chopper to come out and get the bodies. Franklin had refused to release the bird and for very standard reasons. If there were no documents and no rifles, the bodies were just pulled out in the clear and left.

"Yeah, maybe he does know, sir," Hank said, "but right now he's down there at the gate claiming they were innocent civilians and saying they've been mutilated—and Major Ray is there calling it a war crime, conducting an investigation right now."

"So, okay, if they're already investigating, what do you want me to do?" I started taking off my harness and hanging it on a peg inside the TOC.

"Just be there, sir," Boyer said. "You know Ray and you know Franklin. And what about the Bummer?"

"Forget it, Hank, the Bummer's okay. He reported the action and he's got the gear that came off the bodies, and he reported that, too. Forget it," I said, shaking my head. "He's in the clear."

"And what about the crowd down at the gate? What about the VCI in town making the most of it? What do we do then?"

That, I agreed, was another matter. I decided to go, lifting my harness back off the peg and turning toward the doorway as I put it on. "Okay, so let's go," I said. "What the hell are you dragging your ass for? Get the jeep." I reached up by the door and picked my M–16 off the wall. Just outside the gate at dusk was no place to be without a weapon. Hank jumped in back and I rode in front down the dusty road to the gate of English, through it and past the guard and then on down the road another 300 meters. We pulled up behind Franklin's vehicle, the last one in a line of eight, all parked bumper to bumper, pointing toward the town. We got out and I turned back to my driver. "Turn it around and move back up the road about fifty meters or so and sit ready with your weapon. Cover the rest of these idiots who were too damned involved, I guess, to obey their own parking rules." He spun it around in the center of the road and headed it back. Hank and I turned and walked past two MP vehicles and one MI vehicle and came up behind the crowd. Everyone was looking at three bodies stretched on a poncho. There were murmurs and mumblings. Paul Ray was doing most of the talking. He turned as we came up.

"Colonel Herbert, sir," he said, "have you ever seen anything like this?" He pointed to the three dead VC. I studied their bodies for a couple of seconds. They had been blown to hell, there was no doubt about that. I could feel Franklin hanging on every word I would say. "Not since a week ago," I replied, remembering the Rockpile.

"With their penises cut off?" Ray asked incredulously. "Castrated?"

I looked more carefully at the bodies. "Damn it, Paul, they haven't been castrated." They were chewed up around the area of the groin the same as they were everywhere else. That was the way M–16s and grenades were; they just didn't respect any part of the anatomy. "They're not any more chewed up than a hell of a lot of others I've seen lately, including some of our own people."

Some MI and CID interpreters were off to one side near a hut, questioning the townsfolk.

"My God, sir," Ray said, and I turned toward him. His face was ashen. Franklin still hadn't said a word.

"They're dead, Paul. What the hell do you expect? Neat little plugs between the eyes?" It was the same with every rear-area commando I'd ever met. They seemed as bloodthirsty as the most ferocious out-front soldier until they had to stare at the results. These three on the poncho had been hit by grenades and M–16 fire. No worse, no less than a hell of a lot of others from both sides. I had dragged some of them into choppers or picked them up in bags. "Did you ever see what an M–16 round does when it goes through the head, Paul?" I asked.

"They weren't even VC, sir," he said.

"Who says they weren't?"

"I said it, Herbert," Franklin finally broke in.

I turned toward him. "Based on what?" I asked. "Intuition?"

"These poor kids were farmers."

"Yeah, I know, sir, and Uncle Ho is a gardener and Mao is a poet and Giap is a schoolteacher, and they say Hitler was a paper-hanger when he wasn't burning Jews."

I glanced again at the bodies. They were young, all right, between sixteen and twenty-five. They had thick thighs and thick shoulders, but their hands were clean and so were their fingernails. "Yeah, sir, just innocent farmers."

"I want Bumgarner back in immediately," Franklin said.

"Yes, sir," I said.

"I think we should demand an autopsy," Ray said, playing Perry Mason.

"Sure, Paul. You want me to do it?" I said.

Ray turned to Doc Winkler. "What do you think?" he said.

"There's no need for one," Winkler said. "They're dead if that's what you need to know."

"But how, Doc, how? An autopsy would clear all that up and prove the mutilation," Ray persisted. "I think we should have one and prove just how they died."

"You want it written, Paul?" Winkler asked.

"If possible, yes."

"Good," Winkler said. "Anybody have a scrap of paper?"

Hank handed him one and Doc scribbled on it in the palm of his hand and handed it to Paul. I glanced over to read it as he did. It said: "No traces of poison."

Paul folded up the paper and shoved it in his pocket. "I still think we should have an autopsy," he argued.

Franklin was talking again. "This is a real tragedy, Herbert." The crowd was starting to mill around a little bit too much for my own comfort. The dust was deeper now, and with the dark coming on we could easily get a grenade. I pointed out that possibility to Franklin. He began rounding everyone up and got ready to go. Winkler was over talking to one of the villagers. Ray was still staring down at the bodies. Hank and I went back to meet the Bummer and his patrol at the back gate of English and arrived a couple of minutes before they did. It was almost dark.

"Look," I told him, "Franklin and the provost marshal will be up to pick you up in a couple of minutes. Do you know your rights under Article 31?"

"Yes, sir, I do," Bumgarner answered.

"Don't open your packs or anything until he arrives. You have all the captured gear?"

"Yes, sir. Wire-cutters, demo, cord, fuses, and a couple of B40 rockets."

"Good, hang on to them."

Major Meurrens and two military policemen approached. They read the patrol their rights and then asked me if it would be okay for them to take them in. I nodded an affirmative.

"And eight grenades and six caps," the Bummer said as they led him away. Hank and I followed up the road for about a hundred meters. When they cut off toward the provost marshal's office, we went the other way to the battalion. I called Franklin on the phone and reported that the patrol was in and in the custody of the PM. I also listed the equipment.

"Did you see it?" he asked.

"No, sir, not yet."

"We'll see," he said and hung up.

I went to the PM's office where they were laying the equipment out on the floor in front of the desk sergeant. I counted it myself, and it matched the Bummer's own inventory. Then I went down to see if I could talk to Barnes or Franklin, or both if possible. The two of them were on the General's porch having a drink. They came to the edge of the porch and I told them about the equipment found on the three dead VC.

"Good," Barnes said. "Then that's that."

"They might have carried it out with them as an excuse," Franklin said.

"Thanks, sir," I said to the General, ignoring Franklin. "Bumgarner's a good soldier." I saluted and started to go.

"Have time for a cocktail?" the General asked.

"No thanks, sir, not tonight if you don't mind," I answered and walked away. On my way back to the battalion, I stopped back by the Provost Marshal's office to check on my men and see if they needed anything. They were in good spirits. I asked the Bummer if they had been questioned yet and he said that they had. I asked him if he had been made aware of his right to legal counsel. "No, Major

Meurrens said it wasn't necessary because this is all routine. He said we weren't going to be charged with anything so it wasn't really necessary."

"Look, Bummer," I said. "Let me give it to you straight. They've got you people in here for murder, one, and they're trying to prove a war crime, mutilation, against you as well. You ask for a goddamned lawyer right now while I'm here to witness your request."

I called Meurrens over and told him that Bumgarner wanted a lawyer. He said it wouldn't be necessary. I asked him if he intended to release them that night, and he said he had not planned to.

"All right, then, goddamn it, he wants a lawyer tonight," I said. "And I recommend that you not question any of them anymore until we talk to Paul Ray."

I left immediately and went to get Ray. I brought him back to the PM's office where he asked a couple of questions, had some hard words for Meurrens, and finally flatly informed him that there would be no further questioning until all of the men had lawyers.

The next two days were incredible. We were accused of all kinds of things, of causing havoc in the provost marshal's office, of interfering with justice, of smuggling goodies and cigarettes as well as clean clothes to Bummer and his guys, as well as a host of other accusations.

No one mentioned or seemed to give a damn about the fact that Bumgarner and his men had not been charged with anything, had not been tried, and certainly had not been convicted; or the fact that every last right to which they were entitled had been violated; or the fact that, since they were in the 2d Battalion, they were still my responsibility.

A couple of days later, I signed the charges sheet against Bumgarner—not because I believed him to be guilty but because I felt he deserved the chance to get it over with in court right then. They hauled him off to a stockade in Nha Trang and I went back to running the battalion.

The next night was fun, too. We were having a farewell over in the Recon section for some of the guys who had decided, after the Bummer incident, that perhaps they'd rather go home than extend as he had done. We drank to it and I told them that the Bummer wasn't out of it yet, but that I would see the matter through personally all the way to the top if necessary. After that, we broke it up. Some of them were still there finishing up the last few cans of beer, some headed off to the movies, and a couple more just gave up and headed for the sack. I went back to my own bunk. About an hour later, Meurrens came in. I felt honored. It wasn't often that he was seen out after dark. "It wasn't my idea," he allowed. "I'd much rather have waited until morning, but Colonel Franklin said he felt we should strike while the iron was still hot."

"What iron?" I asked.

"There's been a murder," he said. There was never a doubt with these guys. It wasn't manslaughter—whatever the hell he was talking about—and it wasn't an accident. It was already murder. He said a prostitute had been murdered in Bong Son. It wasn't the first one that had bought the farm there, but it was the first one that Brigade had ever shown any concern for.

"So what can I do to help?" I asked.

"It was one of your men," he said. "The big, blond guy in the Recon who carries the big Bowie strapped on his right leg."

"You have anything else?"

"Yes, he had on a tiger suit."

"And what exactly did he do?"

"He ran that knife into the girl and ripped her straight up the middle from her vagina to her chin," he said. "There was rice and guts all over the floor."

"How do you know it was him?" I asked.

They had a description from one of the other girls, he said, and Franklin had recalled that the guy was one of my men. "He said he'd seen him with the knife," Meurrens said.

I, too, recalled that a kid named Oliver in Recon—a big, blond kid—carried a black-handled Randall Model 14 attack knife on his left leg. "The guy's supposedly down at the movies," I said. Meurrens thanked me and ordered a patrol to go down to the movies to get Oliver. They met him coming back. He said he was "returning from the movies." They read him his rights and locked him up. I went to see Paul Ray about getting counsel for the guy, but Ray was at An Khe. As I was about to leave his office, Hank called to tell me that Meurrens had just been over to Battalion and wanted to apologize.

"What for, Hank?"

"He said he just got a confession from a guy in one of his long-range recon patrols," Boyer said. "The guy said he killed her for love."

"What about Oliver?"

"He's back, sir."

"Good," I said. "Look, Hank, apologize for us all."

"He's already in the sack, sir."

That was the end of it. Franklin and Meurrens never mentioned it again. And as far as I know, the guy who confessed was never tried.

"Too bad it wasn't Oliver who did it," Boyer said later. "They could have hung his ass and then showed the Viets what honorable men we are."

The next morning we buried our dead—not literally, but in a symbolic service customarily held for every battalion member who got it. It was a service which should have been held within days of the death. I didn't even know the man we were "burying" that day. He had been killed weeks before my taking over the battalion. Boyer had come to me with the matter because both Nicholson and Chaplain Davis had apparently neglected to hold the required services. The battalion was required to reply by endorsement that such a service had in fact been held.

"There were lay services," Hank said.

"But why not the other?" I asked.

"You know Davis," he shrugged. "He just wasn't available."

I nodded. "Okay, get me all the information you can on the guy. I'd at least like to know a little bit about him."

Five minutes after Boyer left, Davis came in and recommended that we "have a ceremony for one of my boys who was killed a while back."

"Who's that?" I asked.

"One of the guys from the company," he shot back.

"Which company?"

"Uh, I can't recall which one right offhand, sir."

"What was his name?"

He was getting angry. It showed in his voice when he spoke. "Well, I, uh, don't have his name handy either right now, but I have it listed over in my book." His face was turning crimson.

"Sure, Padre, sure. We'll have the ceremony. You see Major

Boyer, right?" I shuffled some papers around on my table while he saluted and left. I didn't want to embarrass him any more than he already was.

"Thanks," he said as he went out the door.

"Sir," I said.

"Thanks, sir," he said. As he left, he passed Hank, who was on his way back to tell me he could find out nothing about the dead man. The guys in his unit who had been his friends had long since returned to the States, and none of the others had known him well enough to provide any information. The company commander was still checking, Hank said, but by the time the service was to be held, we still knew nothing. Franklin came in for the service as the "CG's rep," he said. He seemed proud of that designation, but he declined to speak at the service either for himself or in behalf of Barnes. "What can you say about a man nobody even remembers, Herbert?" he asked. I was inclined to agree. So Davis presided over a brief service and then it was my turn to speak. There were about 200 men present. I stepped to the microphone, took off my helmet and placed it under my arm. I wasn't sure what I would say, but I knew damned well that a U.S. trooper had died and somebody should say something.

"I'd like to explain that I didn't know the man we're honoring here today," I told the men. "It's the same with many of you, too. I haven't been here long enough to recognize all of you and remember your names yet. So why talk, you could ask, if I didn't know him and don't know you either? Well, for one reason, I want to talk because I think somebody should, and for another, I think I probably did know this dead sergeant and I think I probably really do know you—because you and he are grunts, infantry, parachute infantry—and I know all of you."

They were listening courteously. I continued, telling them Ernie Pyle's theory about picking out a real infantryman by the way he wears his mud and insisting that none of them there, including the dead sergeant who wasn't there, were average Americans.

"I wonder at what some of you have gone through and that you're still alive and sane. Some, like the sergeant, won't come through that way—but some guys back in the States are going to get run over crossing the road at night with a bucket of paint in their hand headed for a brick wall—and that is precisely the difference between you and the guy on his way to paint four-letter words on the wall. He's the average American. You're not. Neither was the sergeant, and I hope that when he died he knew that he wasn't.

"That's what I want all of you to know and understand before you go back out there tonight."

I had no idea if I'd made an impression on them, but I knew I'd said something that I'd wanted to say for a long time.

Franklin stopped me as we broke up and said something about it being a fine speech and something else about what he would have said had he talked. I didn't have time for a long talk. I had an appointment with Beacham and Accousti down at the Brigade. They had come up with a brainstorm and wanted to discuss it with me.

Killer Fire Base, they called their big idea. It was more Beacham's creation than Accousti's, but they both liked the words. Killer Fire Base. It had a really malevolent ring to it, and they used it as frequently as they could work it into our discussions. This was another mark of the war: the further up you went in the chain of command, the more violent the label for an idea. Up front, leaders called their operations Mary Ann or Jenny or Cherry or Apple or Orange, but back there, you always ran into Killer and Search and Destroy and Blitz and Bloodlet. The Killer Fire Base was a lousy name, but it wasn't a bad idea, at least in part. Besides, they only wanted a security platoon from me, since it was mainly an artillery operation. They planned to put in a battery of 105s at night on top of a mountain up in the An Lao Valley, bad NVA country. They would provide security for the battery and long-range scopes and paste the hell out of any opportune targets for the next couple of days or so, and then move out before the Viets could get together any type of large-scale operation against them. After a day or so, they would repeat it elsewhere.

"We can reach out and plaster those spots presently out of range," Beacham said.

"And we can make use of some of the long-range recon patrols and maybe a couple of your Wildcat teams, okay, sir?" said Accousti.

"And then the 2d Batt will have to provide a platoon to go in and pick up the pieces, okay?" Beacham asked.

No, I said, it wasn't okay. The An Lao Valley was a hell of a long way off. It was deep and treacherous and definitely NVA. A rifle company, maybe, but a platoon, no. Once we got a platoon in on the ground, there would be no way to reinforce it quickly over that distance or provide it with adequate fire support or air support. Moreover, the NVA was quite capable of mounting battalion-sized operations in that area on short notice. "There's no way," I said.

"But we'll provide the air," Beacham argued.

"With napalm," Accousti added.

"In triple canopy?" I asked. "You can't get enough on the grass to heat up a platoon's C rations. Besides, why the hell do they have to be counted? A dead guy's a dead guy, isn't he? Why risk a platoon just to count dead people?"

They glanced at each other but I was firm. It was an unrealistic concept. If you commit a platoon, you must be able to commit the remainder of the battalion if necessary, and the same applies for a brigade, an army, and a country. There was no way to commit my people and provide for either reinforcement or extracting at that distance.

"Nope, not on your life," I said.

"I thought the 2d Batt liked combat," Beacham chided.

"The battalion's not voting," I said. "I am. But if it's body count, why not use your long-range recon patrols to go in and tally up the score? A couple of those people can add, I've heard, and one or two can even multiply."

Franklin came in and they repeated their idea for him. When they were finished, I reiterated my objections, but he flatly stated that I would provide the platoon both for the security of the artillery and a second one for the search and count. It was the end of the argument. "Herbert, you provide those platoons starting tomorrow," he said, which meant that I had some work to do that afternoon. The two platoons, especially the one that would be on standby for the count, would have to be briefed carefully. I told the standby leader that I did not want him to lose physical contact with whatever LZ he was placed down on, and I didn't want him taking any chances or risking anybody just to count dead or pick up a few lousy dollars worth of equipment and weapons. "And don't get tied up in contact," I added. "This time play it like you're the VC in our area, because that's exactly what you're going to be: the guerrilla in his backyard. Play it very cool and smart. Get in, get the job done, no dilly-dallying, and then get the hell back out. Understand?"

"Yes, sir," he said.

The next day's action was termed by the Brigade as a "smashing victory." I didn't see it quite that way. The artillery indeed had a field day. From its vantage point atop a crest overlooking the valley, it had zeroed in on a company-sized NVA operation and, for once, the dead did not include any civilians. All of the people they plastered—and they really did one hell of a good job—were in uniform. If it had been left there, perhaps it would have been a smashing victory, but they had to have that goddamned body count, and my standby platoon was ordered in late in the afternoon, less than three or four hours before dark.

There was no LZ site worthy of being called that. There was no decent air cover available, and even the artillery battery that had done the initial job on the NVA was already moving out. The selected site was on the side of a steep hill rising from a narrow draw. There was room for only one helicopter at a time, and each bird had to come down the draw with its left flank completely exposed to the high side of the hill, hover for the unloading, and then bank off suddenly to the right around and back down the draw, climbing as fast as possible to make room for the next in line. A bird-dog spotter plane was buzzing in the area, and Franklin was orbiting around in his bird. Since it was a Brigade operation, Ernie and I were there in the C and C, although not really participating.

It was a Brigade operation—that is, until they knocked down one of the choppers. Suddenly it became a 2d Battalion operation. "Get those men out of there, Six," Franklin ordered on the radio, and I got the operation as quick as that. It was our third bird in. They dropped it as it was lifting away from the LZ, before it had begun its steep right-hand bank. Its oil lines were ruptured by the NVA fire, so it auto-gyroed in rather than crashed, and no one in it was injured. The crew began working feverishly to get the door guns off and out into the bush where they could be better used. The other ships in the platoon flight continued to unload men, and they were already in contact with NVA forces between the LZ and the downed helicopter.

"How large a force?" I asked the leader.

"Maybe ten to fifteen. We can take them. Over."

"How far are you from the bird? Over."

"Less than a hundred meters. Over."

"Keep the smoke out in front for the gun ships. Over."

374

"Roger that. Our lead element just overran their lead positions. Dinks headed every which way through the bush. Over."

"Stay with it, and stay in touch. Over."

"Roger that. Out."

I helped Ernie coordinate the two gun ships' runs, and they strafed as closely as possible around the downed crew while my platoon was working its way toward them. Pippen tried to get the C and C down for a closer look, but it was useless. The smoke-cans spewed up a dense canopy. I asked Ernie to get the downed crew's estimation on whether their ship could be saved. "Hell, yes," they answered. "Just get us a Hook." I called Franklin and requested a Chinook, knowing there was one on the pad at English.

"Hook on the way," he replied, and I went back to the platoon. They were moving through the NVA positions rapidly by then, and there were about thirty bodies scattered around. Most had been there when they put down, a result of the devastating work of the artillery. The platoon was going after the last ones between them and the crippled helicopter.

Suddenly, Franklin came back on the net. "Get every one in, destroy that ship, and then get everyone out. The bird-dog has gone down in the valley south of here. Over."

"Is the Hook on the way? Over."

"Roger that. Over."

"Then let's save the bird. Over."

"Negative. Negative. Get everyone out ASAP. Do you roger? Over."

"Roger. Out," I said and then, turning to Ernie, I asked him to inform the crew of Franklin's decision. "Tell them to blow it, get back to the LZ and start extracting."

"That's a rodge," Ernie said. I got on the intercom to Pippen.

"Let's get up over that ridge to the south there and see if we can pick up that bird-dog."

"Roger that," he answered and banked so suddenly south that I almost went out the north door. We flew low up along a stream that came down through the next draw into an open, flat area. The little L19, the plane used for forward observation, had crashed on the north bank. We called in one of the gun ships and made the extraction of the bird-dog pilot and his observer with no hitches. Both were unharmed.

We ran gun-passes on the plane until it burst into flames and then went back up over the ridge to help with the extraction of the platoon. It was over before we got back. Six enemy weapons had been confiscated; the rest were destroyed because of the haste and lack of personnel; there were no documents in the haul, but they had policed up two NVA prisoners. If it was a smashing victory, you couldn't prove it by me. We had four seriously wounded men, we had lost the chopper and the L19 spotter plane, and they wouldn't have been wounded or lost except to satisfy the numbers game fixation. The body count was a sickness that had infected the whole Army. It produced score sheets that amounted to nothing more than playthings for so-called soldiers who were nothing more than technicians. The statistics were the motivating force, not a tool. I felt fortunate that the day hadn't turned out much worse. We had been lucky, damned lucky.

The next brainstorm originated with Barnes. It was a dilly. The idea was to first have your planes saturate an area with tear gas and other chemicals and then come in with napalm and blockbusters. Following that, you called in strafing runs and then summoned up the choppers with rockets and gun runs. Last came the troops.

"The men will pick up the pieces and do the counting," Barnes said. "You want the mission, Tony?"

"No, thank you, sir."

"Then it'll go to the 1st Batt and the 1st of the 50th and they'll get credit for the body count."

"And be held responsible for the civilians, too, sir?" I added.

Franklin chimed in. "Herbert's kind of old-fashioned, sir. He'd prefer to do it with bayonets and rifles at the cost of his troops." It was a stupid thing for him to say. The 2d Battalion, by that time, had the largest body count in the entire Brigade. It was, in fact, over half of the Brigade's total and amounted to more than the other five battalions combined. Yet the 2d Battalion had the lowest casualty rate in the entire theater of operations, not just the Brigade. Since I had taken over the Battalion, we had lost only one U.S. soldier to enemy action.

"I guess that means the 1st Batt and the 1st of the 50th will pass you up this month, Tony," Barnes said.

"Good luck, sir. They're all friendly forces," I laughed. "As far

376

as I'm concerned, a dead enemy is a dead enemy regardless of who gets credit for killing him. Besides, sir, maybe on judgment day that will be a few less I'll have to explain." It seemed clear that Barnes believed it was one big game with the A team competing with the B team. Franklin caught me outside later.

"I didn't like the way you talked to the General in there," he said.

"He didn't seem to mind, sir," I said.

"Well, goddamn it, I did."

I shrugged. "I'm sorry."

"Not nearly as sorry as you're going to be after this operation. When they turn in their counts, you, Great Hero, will have to eat crow in front of everyone."

I shrugged again and spoke to him as sincerely as I could. "Sir, I really do wish them well. It's just not my type of operation. I had a choice and I made it, right or wrong, but I really do wish them both the best."

"Just keep pushing, Herbert," he said. "Just keep pushing until you really get your ass in the wringer." He turned and stalked off, leaving me there, standing in the path.

The next day, the 2d Battalion went north to the An Lao Valley while the 1st Batt and the 1st of the 50th ran the operation, which wasn't any great shakes for us as operations go. We got two NVA. But it must have been one hell of a grand day for the other two units. They fired up over $700,000 worth of ordnance and wound up with two dead wild pigs and four civilian woodcutters. The next day, inspired by their stunning achievement, they ran the operation again and killed fourteen monkeys and two roebucks.

When I remember the folly of it all now, I rationalize a bit and tell myself that there wasn't time enough to be fully sensitive to the finality of death. For instance, to say that it had not been a very important day because the 2d Battalion had but two NVA kills now seems ludicrous; it was a damned important day for those two dead men. When even just one man died or got his fingers blown off or his leg shattered or his hearing impaired or his eyes bloodied and blinded, it was one hell of a costly battle—especially if you happened to be the guy who got it that day. It's something generals and presidents can never understand—only mothers, fathers, brothers, sons and daughters, and wives. Maybe if I were a general or a president who never went to war with his men and who never risked paying the same price, maybe I'd want to convert the whole damned show into a statistical table to be read solemnly by some broadcaster every Thursday night. Generals and presidents are fine for explaining to all of us those things that we ought to be willing to die for, but when the war is over, all that's left are the statistics, and the generals and the presidents are always among the living. If anything has happened to our country as a result of the Vietnam war, it is our national infection with the sickness of the numbers game. We reduced the blood and the suffering and the death and destruction to mere ciphers, and in so doing we reduced our own souls. Numbers don't die; people do. Columns of figures don't disintegrate in the explosion of a bomb; human beings do. Statistics don't bleed, and if you can make your war a war of numbers, you have no trouble sleeping. Most generals and presidents sleep well.

It was late in the evening and Ernie and I were just outside the battalion's TOC, leaning up against a sandbag wall, discussing some proposed operation and watching Colonel Nim's ARVN troops dropping mortar flares around Bong Son, the pearl of Phu My province.

"Look at those dumb bastards, sir," Ernie said. "With this wind, it won't be long before they set the whole city on fire."

"How's that?" I asked, glancing toward the nearby town.

"They're dropping those flares upwind, sir," he explained. "See? They're just popping them in like they're trying to burn up the place."

Even as he was talking, one of the straw-roofed huts on the edge of the residential area caught fire. Ernie rushed inside to notify Brigade, and I remained and watched the fire spread across the rooftops. By the time he came back outside, one entire section of Bong Son was ablaze.

He stared at the fire. "Well," he laughed, "maybe they'll give us a MAC-Ver," referring to MAC-V Directive 20–4 which required the reporting of war crimes, alleged war crimes and atrocities, crimes against the people, and mutilations—whether by U.S. or Vietnamese or anyone else. "They're going to put Beacham on the fire right away as some kind of fire marshal or something. . . . Major Meurrens is going to help, too," he added just as the radio man came out of the TOC and told us that Franklin had called and asked for our alert platoon from the Berm.

"Meurrens and Beacham will be by to pick them up, sir," Potter said.

"When and where?"

"Right here, sir, at the TOC in about ten or fifteen minutes."

"Okay, Ernie, alert the platoon and get them up here," I said. I nodded to the radio man. "Tell Brigade okay." We were only 200 meters from the Brigade. They'd be there pretty quickly, I thought, and a good thing, too, because the fire in the town was spreading rapidly. I could see the silhouettes of the villagers against the flames. They were fighting a losing battle. The alert platoon from the Berm showed up at our TOC in ten minutes, followed twenty minutes later by the two fire marshals. Beacham roared up first in a quarter-ton jeep with Meurrens right behind, leading two water tankers and a pair of gun jeeps, the little scout-cars on which M–16s were mounted. MPs were standing braced in the back seats, ready for action. It was stunning, absolutely stunning. They were going to the field. Everyone was in combat gear. Their jaws were squared and the muscles in their necks were firm with courage and devotion. Their eyes were steely. In the glow of the burning town, it was a glorious scene.

Meurrens ran over to me. "Sir, sir?"

"Yes, Major?"

"Can we borrow some M–60 ammo?"

I was splitting inside, and Webb braced himself against the sandbags to keep from laughing. I was asking the radio man to bring the major four boxes when the leader of the alert platoon rapped his rifle against the water tanks.

"Hey, sir," he yelled. "Both these fucking trailers are empty."

Beacham jumped down and hit the road running. "Oh, Christ!" he was saying. "Oh, Christ!" He bounced off toward the trucks and rapped them with his knuckles, confirming the platoon leader's estimation. Then he came trotting back toward his jeep, still muttering "Oh, Christ! Oh, Christ!"

One of the grunts in the waiting platoon couldn't contain himself. He burst out laughing. "While he's Oh, Christing," the kid chortled, "Bong Son is burning to the ground."

Beacham ran up to the TOC. "Major Meurrens, you take the task force down to the English gate and I'll meet you there with the water," he said.

They both ran back to their vehicles. Beacham jumped in and stood up in the front seat, grabbing the windshield with his left hand, à la Rommel. Waving his right arm above his head he sang out like John Wayne to the cavalry. "Truckers," he shouted, "follow me!" His driver jerked his foot from the clutch-pedal and Beacham was slammed down into the seat as they went lurching down the road with the two empty water trucks rumbling behind.

Meurrens moved up to the front of the platoon convoy as the smoke and ashes from Bong Son began to drift into our area. "Let's go," he shouted and off they went—down the wrong road.

Webb was hysterical. "The only goddamned use for water down there now is for drinking," he said, nearly doubled up with laughter.

The radio man came outside. "Brigade is on the line, sir," he said. "They say we forgot to call in a clearance time at the gate."

"Well, tell them that the patrol or the convoy or the task force or whatever the hell they're calling it has not yet cleared the gate and that Beacham is down getting some water, we think."

The next day we found out that the water-mission hadn't gone well for Beacham. He ran into a Specialist Fourth Class at the pump who refused to hand over the key. The conversation, passed around the next day, reportedly went:

SPEC/4: What you want it for?

BEACHAM: The fire downtown, you goddamned idiot.

SPEC/4: Don't you call me no idiot.

BEACHAM: Then give me the key to the pump.

SPEC/4: The General says nobody gets water except to drink.

The General had indeed made that order and the Spec/4 did indeed obey it. We also found out the next day that Meurrens was left at the gate waiting for someone with a key to let him out of English.

But that night we knew only that the two of them and their task force had set off for the water pump and Bong Son on a mission of mercy. We were still watching the town burn down when Franklin called the TOC again and ordered us to try to get through to the leader of the alert platoon and scratch the mission.

"Scratch it?" the radio man asked.

"Yes," Franklin said.

"Why, sir?"

"Because the fire is over, that's why."

The next afternoon, Brigade put out the official version of the Great Bong Son Fire. The VC had torched the town, it said. Colonel Nim's ARVN troops had engaged the enemy in the streets and had successfully defended the town, backed up by U.S. forces in a "ready standby posture," led by Major Beacham, the Brigade S2, and "his Task Force Deputy," Major Meurrens, the Brigade Provost Marshal. To ensure its officialness, I suppose, the version was written up in the Brigade newssheet, *The Sky Soldier.*

The caves in Delta Company's AO provided a marvelous haven and refuge for the Viet Cong; they were a virtual way station on their main north-south route of travel. The VC used them extensively, crawling back in them for a day or so of rest and then moving on. It was a large complex of nooks and crannies winding up and down from the top of the mountain all the way to the plain, and it was possible for a VC to enter at the top or the bottom and come out at the opposite level without ever exposing himself. Everybody had tried to clean up the caves and everybody had met with the same lack of success. Chemicals had been used, but they failed. Napalm was tried with the same result. Foot troops had been used occasionally on a small scale—here a VC, there a VC—but the caves remained a virtual fortress, unassailable and sticking in our throats. I had planned one day to take the whole damned battalion in and see if that might be an effective means—but that was for some future date. In the meantime, Grimshaw and Delta Company were trying it their way.

They moved in, quietly and smoothly, checking every last crack and crevice, working their way from the top to the bottom of the rock formations. It was tedious, tiring work. One man covered while his companion searched. The sun beat down fiercely on the surface of the rocks and the heat was blinding.

Finally, a small group of the enemy was panicked by the search as it got nearer and nearer to their hole. They broke out into the open and tried to run. One of the scouts ripped off a burst of fire and drove them back into the cave. It was a deep one. Grimshaw approached it with a grenade in his hand. A sergeant stood at the other side of the entrance and shouted for its occupants to surrender. A child's cry was heard from inside along with some excited chatter, and suddenly two young women came out with their hands locked behind their heads. Everyone relaxed. Abruptly, a grenade sailed out of the cave, over the women's heads, and the Americans scrambled for cover up against the rocks. The women made a dive back into the cave. The grenade injured only one man and his was a superficial wound, but the women had played rough and, by the rules of the game, they were then fair game. That was the way it could have been played, at least, but it wasn't the way Grimshaw and Delta Company chose to play it. All of us were learning, I suppose. Grimshaw bounced up from the rocks, the grenade still ready in his hand. The sergeant took his position again on the other side of the mouth of the cave. It grew quiet on the mountain-side. Grimshaw suddenly dropped down to his knees and crawled into the cave, whispering softly in Vietnamese. A couple of minutes later, as his men watched open-mouthed, he emerged from the cave carrying a baby in his arms. The three Viet Cong soldiers and the two women followed closely behind. It was cool. Nobody asked him why he did it. He never explained. I submitted him for the Silver Star, the country's third highest combat decoration. He more than deserved it, but he never received it.

Franklin was confusing me. I was getting the distinct impression that the quality of our relationship was due in great part to the success of my battalion. We were doing much too well to suit him. A lot of it was luck, I knew. We had the highest kill count in the Brigade, the highest prisoner count, the fewest court-martials, the smallest number of accidents, the lowest drug report, the lowest AWOL report, the highest IG inspection report, and the lowest casualty rate. We had lost two men in action since I'd taken command of the battalion, and not a single civilian had died of causes directly attributable to my troops. That was phenomenal—and, of course, it was the result of one hell of a lot of sheer good fortune. Even the most cautious and careful commanders in Vietnam eventually caught civilians in a cross fire or an artillery strike or an air call. I realized that the bubble of luck protecting the 2d from that kind of grief was a fragile one and could burst any day. As it so happened, though, I wasn't destined to be around that much longer. Perhaps that was a good thing, too. If I'd ever been inadvertently involved in the death of noncombatants, no matter how remotely, Franklin and Barnes would have had a field day.

As it was, however, the deputy commander seemed satisfied to operate with charges of exaggeration and lies. He seemed intent on getting rid of me for the good of the Brigade, not to mention the good it could possibly do some of the people whose rhythms I had upset as the IG. He never let up. The next hassle came when Franklin asked me to assign two people to a restructured version of the Green Line Force back in An Khe. At least something was being done about that shoddy element. The Line was getting a new title and was about to be transferred out of Angel's hands to the control of the 1st of the 50th. Each battalion was asked to provide two additional troops for the new unit, and Franklin asked me personally for a "better class" of troop. "Don't send down any dogs," he said. I told him I'd never sent scrap to anybody anywhere, even though the Brigade policy had always been to try to get rid of the troublemakers as quickly and as quietly as possible by making them someone else's problem. I notified Boyer and Captain Parrott of the need for two transfers and explained that the Brigade had requested that the men provided have good combat records and not have more than one Article 15 or any other type of company punishment on their file. We finally selected two fellows, one whose record was completely clean and another, a Sergeant Hill, who had picked up one Article 15, but on his previous hitch. At least, that was the only one on our records.

A day or so later, Major Crouch called from An Khe to tell me that Hill did not meet his requirements because he had two rather than one Article 15.

"Could you read them off to me?" I asked.

"I don't have the second one, sir," he said.

"Then how do you know he had a second one?"

Crouch said one of his sergeants had seemed to recall it. I decided to send Hill anyway.

"How about Colonel Franklin, sir?" Crouch asked.

"Look, if there's a gripe, put it on paper and send it on down to the General," I suggested. "The General will call me if there's a problem and we can iron it out. I'm not going to stand here and debate the issue with you. If the CG or Franklin has reason to turn Hill down, then that's that. Have either one of them turned thumbs down?"

"Well, no sir."

"Have I violated any of the instructions for the transfer of men to the Green Line?"

"Well, not officially, sir, since we really can't locate the second Article 15," Crouch said.

"Then he does meet the criteria, right?"

"Yes, sir."

"Good, then he's one of our two transfers."

Almost before I could hang up the phone, I was called in to Franklin's office where he berated me and accused me of swearing and cursing at Crouch and of being abusive in my attitude toward him. "All of that is grounds for an Article 133 charge," he said. "But what's worse is that you violated my trust in you and my very specific orders by sending a dog down to the Green Line."

I denied his accusations and he responded by asking if I was calling Crouch a liar. "I want a written statement from you—and if what you say is the truth then Crouch has had it."

I shook my head. "I'm not writing out any statement accusing a major of telling lies when I have not heard him tell the lie," I said.

"Goddamn it," he roared. "Now, you're calling me a liar. I'm saying Crouch said it."

"Well, then sir, if he lied to you then you write out the statement," I said. I had seen too many others go that route with the ticket-punchers. Everybody wrote a little essay and the guy who wrote the best one didn't have to go to jail. "Besides, Colonel, I had witnesses to that conversation with Crouch," I added.

"Witnesses?" he said. "Who?"

I told him that Boyer and Parrott had been present while Crouch and I talked.

"And you refuse to make a statement, is that correct?" he said.

"That is correct, sir."

We both sat there in silence for a moment. Finally he called Captain Parrott and ordered him to write a statement and to get one from Boyer and to bring both to his office within an hour. I sat by his desk for the next forty minutes or so, glancing at a magazine, until Parrott came in with the statements and handed them to Franklin. He read them and his face turned red. "I want you to take these two state-ments back and have them rewritten in the proper format," he said finally. "Doesn't anybody in that damned battalion of yours know how to do anything right?" He handed them back and without another word dismissed me. Later in the day he called for the originals again and I heard nothing further on the matter until the day I was relieved.

Sergeant Brewer, the Bummer's right-hand man, came in to ask if there was anything he could do to help with the case against his boss.

They were very close friends. The Bummer had handled the field work for the recon patrols and Brewer had taken care of the back-home chores. I told him that about the only thing he could do to help the Bummer was to take over the recon patrol and go back out into the grass.

"I can't do it, sir," he said. "I'm just not the Bummer."

"Then, I'll have to give the platoon to someone else," I said.

"But it belongs to the Bummer," he argued.

"But there is no Bummer around and the battalion still has to function and we've got to have that recon platoon at work," I said. "You're just going to have to take it over."

"I can't sir," he said. "They'd kill me."

"What?"

"They'll kill me."

"Who'll kill you? What the hell are you talking about?"

Then Brewer told me about his fear that he would be killed by the same two men he said had killed the young lieutenant we all thought had been killed accidentally when he told his men to open fire in his direction.

"He was murdered, sir," Brewer said.

"Murdered?"

"Yes, by a couple of potheads he had caught smoking grass a couple of hours before. He had threatened to turn them in the next day."

I told him I was skeptical of his account but he insisted it was true.

"They shot him down in cold blood. Hell, he wasn't out in front of the ambush like they said. He was in back of it up on the high ground and the bullet that killed him went up through him," he said, jabbing a finger upwards into his hip. "Hell, sir, he was still alive even then, but they finished him off before the dust-off came in."

I was incredulous. "Why the hell didn't you report it when you came in, Brewer?"

"We did, sir. We reported it to the captain but nothing ever came of it because he walked into the helicopter blades and we decided not to ever mention it again."

The captain he mentioned, I remembered, had been the company commander at the time, and the story was that he had been killed when he walked into the rotors of a helicopter. I had wondered about it the first time I heard it. It sounded pretty stupid for a man who had been around the birds for as long as he had to just walk in and get his head whapped off. The story of how the young lieutenant had died had also seemed a bit illogical to me. Now, both seemed to have met their deaths in a related way. At least, a link was implied between the two deaths if Brewer was telling the truth. I read him his rights under Article 31 and asked him to tell me the story of the lieutenant again. I was even more fascinated the second time around.

"You know I'll have to report it, don't you?" I said.

"If it'll help the Bummer, sir, I'm ready."

I didn't quite understand what he meant by that, but his relationship with the Bummer was close enough that perhaps he thought anything he did for me would in turn be of benefit to the Bummer.

"In the meantime, Sergeant Brewer, keep this to yourself."

He left and I called in Boyer and discussed the story with him. It was his opinion that the sergeant was not telling the truth. He raised the point that the dead captain had not been the type of man who would have covered up anything. I pointed out that there was at least a possibility that he had not been covering up anything but had been working on the matter when he fell into the blades. I emphasized the verb "fell." Then I mentioned the names of the two men Brewer had accused of killing the lieutenant. Boyer said they were known potheads and that both had been on the patrol the night the lieutenant was killed. But Brewer, as he recalled, had not been on the patrol, and it was Boyer's personal judgment that it was simply a bunch of crap.

"It has to be reported anyway," I reminded him.

"To MAC-V, sir?"

"To Brigade."

"Want me to call it in."

386

"Forget it, man. I'll go down and see Franklin after din-din. Right now, let me buy you a free drink."

But I skipped dinner because I wanted to make sure I got to Franklin before he and the General went off to the movies. They were both regular first-nighters.

Again, as had happened time and time before, Franklin accused me of lying and bringing more trouble and shame to the Brigade. Moreover, he said, I was bringing charges that assassinated the character of a good officer. I pointed out that I was making no charges and was not impugning anyone's reputation but was rather rendering a duly required report. I asked if he had rather I'd ignore the UCMJ.

"No, damn it, I wouldn't like that," he said. "I'll take care of this." Then, as I had instructed Brewer, he instructed me not to talk about the matter until it was over.

"Do you want to see Brewer, sir?" I asked.

"No, not right now," he snapped. "I'll get around to him later."

"Yes, sir," I said, looking for a dismissal.

"And I'll get around to you too, Herbert."

"Will that be all, sir?"

"That will be all, Herbert."

"Good evening, sir."

"Good evening, Herbert."

I went back to the battalion. Colonel Franklin went to the movies.

The next morning, Ernie and I flew up to Skyscope and arrived just as the man on the glass began reporting a great deal of activity going on in the beach area of a village north of the Rockpile. It wasn't the same village we had hit before, but was about a mile by sea further north. I got down on one knee and began scanning through the scope. He was right. The little harbor was filled with boats and a large crowd of people was unloading them and then walking up a long trail to the first hill. The people working the boats were not in uniform, but the men walking the trail were—and they were armed. They were transporting supplies direct from the Rockpile to that beach and then carrying them up into the Tiger mountains, and they were doing it in broad daylight. They were making no attempt whatever to conceal their weapons or their uniforms, which gives you some idea of the respect they had for the mighty Sky Soldier Brigade. The whole affair was taking place in Henniger's Area of Operations. I counted about 35 sampans and perhaps 200 people involved with at least 50 or 60 of them armed.

I asked Webb to get Accousti on the net and give him a rundown on what we'd seen. "Then, lay on the choppers, alert the platoon and have the rest of the company stand by for a back-up," I said. "And tell Accousti we'll be in in a couple of minutes to give him the details and a plan."

General Barnes was in Nha Trang that day, no doubt telling his superiors how well he was bringing about the pacification of his Area of Operations. One of Barnes's favorite phrases, Bittorie told me later, was that it was "almost completely under control." Two years later, Barnes would be traveling around to Army posts for Secretary of Defense Melvin Laird, handing out the same kind of nonsense, while in Vietnam General Abrams would still be officially calling the area one of the least pacified in the country.

Hell, I guess it was a good thing Barnes was off preaching his pacification successes. Otherwise, it would have taken three days for the sampan convoy to become hard intelligence—the kind on which the General would have okayed an assault.

Accousti didn't like the idea of going in there after them. There were only enough birds to take in one platoon, he said, and if there were as many as I said there were, one platoon couldn't do the job.

"Why not use an air strike?" he suggested.

"An air strike? What about the civilians?"

"We'll get it declared a free-fire zone."

"And you'll get nothing except the women, the old men and the kids," I said.

"Okay, okay," he relented. "It's your platoon and Franklin and Barnes aren't here, so if you want to go the birds are available. I just want you to remember what my advice was. I say no to the whole thing."

The leader of the ready platoon was a young lieutenant named Thomas McCaan. I had met him the first week after taking over the battalion and had told him at the time that I was going to send him back out into the grass with the rest of the "homesteaders" from the rear area. He had argued that he'd already spent his time out in the field and that Colonel Nicholson had moved him back to cool it until he was ready to be processed out and head back home. That would be in about ten more weeks, he had said. Boyer had supported his position, which surprised me. McCaan was going to get married soon and that's what moved Hank, or so he said. I didn't buy it at all. I told him that he was being paid as an infantry officer for infantry duty and getting credit for it on his records and that he was headed back to the field the next day. Both McCaan and Hank responded by telling me that he had already earned a Bronze Star for Valor.

"Good," I said. "In ten more weeks out there you'll have time to pick up another one and maybe get a Purple Heart, too."

That had been weeks ago, and now here we were going into action together. "If Accousti's right," I said to Ernie, "McCaan may just get his Purple Heart today."

I got McCaan on the command channel and told him there would be no artillery and only two loches (Light Observation Helicopters). There would be no gun ships but the Navy would have Rice Twix, a swift boat, in the area on station as soon as it could. The platoon would cover the beach, the security elements, and the village, I told the lieutenant. The hills would be handled by the C and C and the loches. If possible, we would go right straight in on top of them.

"There'll be smoke on the LZ and I want the lead bird right on the can. Un-ass immediately and get in tight in contact—and then play it by ear and stay in touch," I said. "Don't use full automatic fire. There are people down there who won't be fighting, and I don't want a single hooch up in flames. I'll be on the ground as soon as I can."

"Roger that," McCaan's voice came back on the radio.

"And listen," I added. "Be ready when you come out the door. They're there."

"How long a flight time?"

"About fifteen. Anything else?"

"No, sir. Airborne, sir."

"Okay, just stay in close, be aggressive and drive."

"Yes, sir."

"Don't sweat it. You can cut it or I wouldn't have picked you."

"Yes, sir."

"See you on the LZ. Take care. Out."

It was one hell of an afternoon. I marked the LZ myself after we had killed some of the VC from the bird. The Rice Twix came steaming up from the south and the birds banked in low from the same direction. The ship's fire was directed into one of the hills. I cautioned them about hitting our own choppers and told them to keep their fire out of the village. Then, dropping to one knee, I waited for the first bird. It came in close enough for me to reach up and hit the left skid. The door gunner dropped two enemy off to my right as they were racing along the sea wall, trying to get away. Potter, the radio man, killed another who was up on one knee against the side of a hooch firing at me. Two rounds smacked into the sand in front of me. Sergeant Hubbard jumped from the first bird and I shouted to him: "Into the village! Into the village! Up over the sea wall." I waved an arm. "They're there—" and no sooner had I made that observation than one of them jumped up on the sea wall and opened up on the helicopters. One of the door gunners knocked him back down and he disappeared from sight on the other side of the wall. The two loches were coming in overhead with their mini-guns going full blast against the hill. I turned and rapped Potter on the shoulder and then jumped over the sea wall. Some of McCaan's platoon was off to my left, already out in front. A couple of NVA in uniform sprawled face down on the concrete patio just off to my right. I jumped to the side of a small bunker and shouted for its occupants to surrender. An old woman and two military-age men in their shorts came out with their hands behind their heads. Potter jumped down into the bunker and brought out two pistols and a rifle. He threw them into the sand. Someone from the platoon came over and we turned over the trio of Vietnamese. I told him to get them out against the sea wall and set up a collection point for prisoners or detainees. Another trooper came around the back of a hut off to my right dragging two dead men. He dropped them in the sand. Hubbard ran up, and breathlessly informed me that Lieutenant McCaan had cornered about twenty in the other end of the village.

"To hell with the other end," I shouted. "Let's clear this side." Without waiting, I leaped into the next hooch and caught a guy just as he heaved a grenade that bounced off my shoulder and into the street. I drove him down against the straw with a round through the chest, and hit the floor myself—hard. With the explosion, I bounced up and ran back outside just as another grenade hit the sand beside me. Hubbard swept it aside with his foot down inside the bunker, and there was a hell of a scramble inside as two men leaped out and fell into the sand just as the grenade exploded behind them. A third guy didn't make it all the way out of the bunker. He was smashed up against the straw wall of a nearby hut, leaving a trail of blood and intestines behind him. I turned to Hubbard and pointed to the bunker. "Clean it out," I ordered, and one of his brand new sergeants came trotting up with a grenade in his hand. I saw the pistol and the face appear in the doorway between his legs. I squeezed the trigger of the M–16 and damn near blew the sergeant's crotch away. My round hit the little face in the door square in the center. "Jesus," the young sergeant moaned. "Thanks, sir. Thanks a lot."

"We clean out a hole with .45s, Sarge," I said, handing him mine. "Out in front of us, ready to fire."

Hubbard moved up beside the hole and gave the sergeant some cover as he went down on his gut and crawled in, the .45 out in front of his face. I turned to Potter. "Get the C and C in. I want to get a look from the air." I started off back toward the beach, passing the collection point for prisoners and detainees and wounded. "Any documents?" I asked.

"Yes, sir," the sergeant in charge said, handing me four or five bundles.

The C and C came in to a hover and Potter and I threw on the document bags, two captured AK–47s and two pistols, and leaped aboard. Ernie signaled me a thumb-up and I nodded. The bird lifted, then banked to the right and started back in against the hill. One of the loches was coming up on our left rear. The left door gunner in the C and C came on the intercom. "Dink woman with a kid in against the rock."

"Fire, damn it," someone shouted. He started to turn his muzzle around just as I spotted the woman. She was crouched in a crack between two boulders with her eyes closed and an AK–47 pressed in against her belly. I grabbed the door gun barrel as it swung around and pushed it off.

"Let her go," I said over the intercom. "She's out of it." I was too hasty. Too damned hasty. No sooner had I shoved the barrel away than she stepped out of her cover, raised the AK out in front of her and fanned the air around us and behind us, and then disappeared down the hill out of sight, leaving the baby behind.

The next thing I heard was someone on the loche behind us signaling a MayDay over the net. Pippen banked to the right and followed the loche into the sand. Potter and Ernie and I jumped out and began pulling out its crew with me continually apologizing. "Sorry about that, guys, but she had a kid and her eyes were closed."

"It's a damned good thing they weren't open," one of the crew cracked as he brushed the sand from him. "A goddamned good thing."

"A woman?" the other crew-man asked.

"Yea," I said, "and she wasn't even pretty."

Potter called in a Huey. The downed bird was picked up and we went back to the C and C. I had Pip fly a long pass so that I could get an idea of just how much progress we had made. Then he set me back down on the beach just in time to help count the bodies. Lieutenant McCaan, Hubbard, and the others were just about finished. Hubbard came in first and reported eighteen dead up on the hillside, according to one of the loches, and thirty-three dead on the ground. There were thirty-four weapons, mostly pistols and revolvers, with a couple more AK–47s and a few SKSs, and one or two carbines. There were approximately seventy-five pounds of documents and hundreds of grenades, but not a single one of the bundles we had seen them taking off the sampans and toting into the underbrush. The little boats were still there up against the beach, empty.

We had eight wounded and nobody dead. One of those wounded was Lieutenant McCaan himself. He had picked it up on the south side of the village in hand-to-hand combat. An NVA with a grenade in his hand had broken from one of the huts and run directly down the path toward the lieutenant, flinging the grenade right at his feet. McCaan let the guy have it with a vertical butt-stroke just as the grenade exploded. They were both peppered with fragments. McCaan went on to kill two others in close combat, and then he was standing in front of me on the beach, bloody, a bit angry, and proud.

"Everything is secure, sir," he said. "I'm hit and Hubbard's in charge."

I looked him over closely. He had superficial cuts in his face and upper body. "You got any other holes, Mac?" I asked.

"No sir."

"You too sick to go on?"

"No, sir, not if necessary."

"It's necessary," I said. "Get a patrol up the hill and lay out the bodies and check for documents and then get going back through the village, hut by hut, as thoroughly as you know how."

Magically, Franklin showed up with Accousti on the beach. Wherever he'd been, he'd returned just in time to count the bodies—and he wanted to see every last one of the fifty-one we had called in to Brigade. I took him around personally to look at the thirty-three we had killed near the beach and the village, and every time I showed him some bodies he asked a battery of questions. How had they been killed? Who killed them? Where was the equipment? How had we been sure they were enemy? We finally finished the tour of the village.

"But that's only thirty-three," he said. "You gave a report of fifty-one."

"There's eighteen more up on the hill, sir," I replied, pointing up with my rifle.

"Then let's go."

"Okay, sir, but watch your step and keep your eyes out for mines and booby traps. We haven't cleared this place yet," I said. I jerked a round out of the chamber of my M–16, just out of habit, and reseated a new one. "And there may be one or two of them still around that we missed," I added.

I stepped out in front and started walking along the trail between the huts, headed toward the hill. We had walked about forty meters or so when he stopped me and asked how long the body inspection would take. He glanced at his watch as he spoke.

"Not long, sir," I said. "They're laid out in a string up in an open spot."

"Well, then, goddamn it," he said. "Why didn't you tell me. No need to walk. We can see them from the air and save a lot of precious time."

"It's up to you, sir," I said. "We have Hubbard up on the hill. I can give him a call and he'll have them laid out for you proper."

"Proper?"

"Side by side, sir, so you can count them, face-up."

He glanced down at his watch again. "Yes, that'll be fine," he said. He held out his hand and we shook. "Fine job, Herbert. I'm going to see to it that you get a DSC for this. Anything else I can do before I go back?"

"Well, yes sir, there is. Rice Twix did one hell of a job for us and I'd like to give them some of the weapons if you don't mind. Sort of their share of the credit," I said. We were back on the beach by that time and Childers handed me the sack of pistols. I passed them to Franklin and stood watching while he opened the sack and counted them.

"All of these?" he asked.

"Yes sir. Why not? They did a fine job."

"Well," he said. "You've got to realize that if they get the weapons, your battalion cannot be credited with them."

"I understand, sir."

"Then it's up to you."

"Thanks, sir." I handed the bag back to Childers and turned to Potter. "Call Rice Twix and tell them I appreciate their work and ask if they can send in a boat for the two of us."

Franklin and Accousti flew out and a few minutes later the boat from the Rice Twix came in. Just as Childers and I were about to board, Franklin came in on the net. "One thing I forgot," he said. "Scuttle the sampans."

"All of them, sir?"

"Every last one of them."

"Will do, sir."

Then while the platoon extracted its wounded, tagged and extracted the detainees, and conducted another search, Childers, Potter and I went out to have a Coke on board the Rice Twix.

I gave the young commander the bag of weapons. He was elated. "Did we really do that well?"

"Probably better, but it's all you get credit for. Just fourteen."

"Nobody else ever gave us credit for anything before," the Navy man said.

"Well, maybe they just didn't have the time before," I replied.

"We actually killed fourteen?"

"There were eighteen up on the hillside alone, already policed up before I came out here. Who knows? There may be more that we'll turn up in a search."

"Damn, sir, my guys are sure going to feel great about this," he said. He called his crew together and had a chat with them while we sat there with our soft drinks. When we left the boat, the entire crew stood on the starboard side and waved us off with big, broad grins on their faces.

We returned almost a hundred detainees. "That's too many for MI to handle alone," Franklin said and called in the same sons-of-bitches from the Vietnamese National Police who had been on hand for the Cu Loi murders on February 14, the same bunch that had tried to loot the village two weeks later. Franklin brought them right into the MI compound at English under American jurisdiction and American control, under the direct command of General John W. Barnes and the direct supervision of his deputy commander, Lieutenant Colonel Joseph Ross Franklin. He brought them into an area less than 150 meters from their offices and quarters and placed an American officer and a senior sergeant in charge. The interrogation began.

That evening, I was called to Franklin's office. He told me that the General, having heard the story of the previous day's action at the beach from "the officers of the battalion and the pilots and troops who had been there," had directed that my name be submitted for the Distinguished Service Cross for gallantry in action. I was surprised —and concerned. If there was anything I didn't need right now it was a medal for me. Hell, I had been the one preaching the fact that it was troops who did the job, not commanders—and now, just like the rest of the ticket punchers, I was to receive mine. Franklin could tell. He looked at me curiously.

On the way back to the battalion, I heard a man crying and spotted a sergeant from Military Intelligence sitting against a dirt bank with his head in his hands. My first thought was that he was on drugs. "Can I help?" I asked, approaching him.

When he looked up he seemed relieved. "I didn't see you, Colonel," he said.

"What's the matter?"

"You've got to help, sir," he said. He pushed himself up off the bank and came so close to me that our noses almost touched. There were still tears shining on his cheeks. "They're torturing the girls, the old women, everyone," he blurted. "You've got to help."

I didn't have to ask who, but I did anyway.

"It's the interrogators, sir," he said. "Up in the cages," pointing toward the MI compound. "It's the VNPs and our own."

"Is Bowers there?"

"Yes, sir."

"O'Kane?"

"Yes, sir."

"Well, then we better go and see what I can do," I said. We trotted toward the compound and went around the building and back behind to the wire enclosures we called the cages. Inside were three open Conex containers, the kind the officers had been taking to the field for quarters. The entire area was brilliantly lit by floodlights. In each of the containers was one chair and one table. Two of the three Conexes were occupied. One young girl was sobbing in one and another girl, a bit older, was crying in the other. Each of them was seated with her hands on the table palms down. A Vietnamese was strutting back and forth in each of the containers, shouting questions into the girls' faces. Another Viet policeman was standing off to the side handling a long, springy rod of bamboo split into dozens of tight, thin flails at one end. It was a murderous weapon. I had seen this thing take the hide off a buffalo. When it was struck down hard, the flails splayed out like a fan, but an instant after impact they returned to their order, pinching whatever was beneath.

They were lovely girls who were giving the wrong answers. The first wrong answer brought the flail on the hand. The next one brought the flail smack across the face. Then across the breast, taking off skin, nipples—and the screams were hideous. But as for information, nothing.

I reported it. Nothing ever happened.

Everybody seems tired of hearing about war crimes. Even when Seymour M. Hersh, now working for *The New York Times,* got a copy of the Peers report, kept secret until it came into his possession, and told us that something happened at another village very near My Lai on the same day the massacre occurred there—something equally ugly—nobody raised an eybrow. The country had heard enough of such things. That's a luxury our country can ill afford. We have to listen. We have to hear. We have to do something about it.

On April 2, 1969, Barnes gave me a letter of commendation from General Conners, who had replaced General Peers as the Commander of First Field Force Victor. He also handed me a letter from Peers which had come all the way over from the States. Peers was quite complimentary, and Barnes added that the 2d Battalion was the best in the Brigade and that I was the "best battalion commander" he had personally ever known. Then he handed me his own letter of commendation, the score sheet for the Brigade, which again listed the 2d as the top battalion, and the official IG report which listed the 2d battalion as the tops in the Brigade. He also assured me that I would very soon begin reaping the rewards for my efforts, as he called them. He said the DSC was being prepared by Boyer and he, the General, already had a verbal assurance that it would be approved.

I went back to the battalion and sat down with a warm, iceless bourbon. My God. What was happening? Two months of nothing but crap from English and now all this in one day. Maybe things were really going to be different. Maybe the Brigade was really going to shape up. With less than two and a half months to go, sweetness and light were in the air, and there were signs that everything was going to be okay.

But something gnawed at me. I had reported eight atrocities, or war crimes or whatever the hell they wanted to call them: the abuse of the detainees in the compound at An Khe, the three torture incidents, the murders at Cu Loi, the looting, the alleged murder of the young lieutenant, and the alleged execution of the detainee in the custody of the hero-lieutenant.

If I could get those things cleared up, I'd really be up to date, and I knew I'd better get my statements down soon or I would have to be writing them from back in the States, taking time out from the Command and General Staff College at Leavenworth. And I didn't expect to have that kind of time.

I went down on the morning of April 3 to talk with Franklin about them. "Sir," I said jokingly when I entered. "Your best battalion commander of yesterday would like to have a talk with you today, okay?"

"Sure, Herbert, come in," he said. "Have a seat."

I sat down where he indicated. It was the only chair in the room.

"What's on your mind?"

"The eight allegations, sir. The atrocities I reported. I want—"

"Atrocities?" he interrupted. "What the hell are you talking about? Atrocities?"

"Eight, sir," I said, and ticked them off one by one, counting them on my fingers as I went. "Sir, I'm going home in less than ten weeks and most of the other witnesses have gone already. I'd like to get my part wound up now while I have the time and things are going kind of slow!"

He looked at me sternly. "Are you on grass, Herbert?"

"Sir, I don't even smoke tobacco."

"Then, you must be crazy," he said—and it was just one damned time too many for me. I didn't want to be called crazy or a liar or stupid or anything else again—not by him.

"No, sir, I'm not crazy. And I'm not any of the rest of the things you've called me. I made eight reports in accordance with the rules of land warfare, the Geneva Accords, and MAC-V Directive 20–4, and now I want a statement in writing saying that I did."

"For killing guerrillas?"

"For committing war crimes, sir."

"You must be nuts or drunk. Go back and sleep it off and we'll talk about it tomorrow."

"No, sir. We won't. Because this time if I don't get an answer from down here I'm going to Nha Trang tomorrow and report it there."

"You do that, Herbert," he screamed as he stood up. "You do that and I'll tell you where you'll go. You'll go to LBJ." He was referring to the Long Bin jail, the Lyndon Baines Johnson ranch as the troops called it. "You'll end up in LBJ for a hell of a long time," he said.

That didn't scare me. I made up my mind to let it alone with Franklin forever. I stood up and started to salute.

"Goddamn it, Tony," he said, his mood suddenly changed. "The investigations are going on. What more can I do?"

"Just let me make my statements, sir."

"Okay, okay," he said and sat down again. "Maybe I have been a little negligent, but I've been damned busy too."

"I understand, sir."

"No, you don't understand—completely, that is. Barnes is one hard man to work for," he said. "I sort of forgot about you going back so soon, too, I guess." He shook his head, indicating his understanding of my problem. "It's got to be done soon, that's for sure, if for no other reason than to settle that queasy stomach of yours, huh?"

"Yes, sir."

"Okay, stand by tomorrow and hold off on that trip of yours to Nha Trang."

"Yes, sir."

"And I'll get to you some time in the afternoon, okay?"

"Okay, sir."

That was it.

Late that afternoon, Boyer came from the pony show and told me that General Barnes wanted to see me at eight o'clock the next morning. I wondered what the hell that could be all about and finally figured he wanted to have a talk with me about his pacification plan for the AO. He knew I didn't like it. In fact he'd overheard me saying just that in no uncertain terms.

The next morning when I reported, Barnes was behind his desk and Franklin was in a chair to his right.

It was quick.

"Colonel Herbert," the General said. "I'm going to replace you as commander of the 2d battalion." I felt the blood drain from my head.

"Replace, sir? You mean relieve?"

"Not relieve, Tony, replace. I'm giving you a maximum efficiency report and sending you to Saigon."

It hit me like a ton of rocks. "Is it over the allegations I've made, sir?" I asked.

Franklin leaped to his feet screaming. "That's right, you son-of-a-bitch—that and your goddamn lies about Beacham and Crouch and all the rest—that poor lieutenant from Tam Quan and every other one of your damn lies and exaggerations."

I felt cold and empty—and then a wave of relief swept over me and calm set in. I stared at Franklin as though he were an insect and tried to speak as deliberately and as coolly as I could. "I'm not talking to you, sir," I said. "I'm trying to speak to my commander, General Barnes." It stopped Franklin's ranting and gave me a chance to turn back to Barnes. "Sir," I said, "the very least you owe me is a complete investigation to see just who really is telling lies and exaggerating."

The General had his head down over his desk, scribbling on a piece of notepaper. "Colonel Franklin has already investigated all of your charges and I'm satisfied," he said, reaching out and handing me the note. "You'll be out of LZ English in one hour. There are two planes leaving An Khe for Saigon today. Be on one of them. Your records will be ready for you in An Khe when you get there. You report to Colonel Lew Ashley in Le Van Duyet in Saigon. It's on the note."

"Sir," I said, "I have a battalion. I'm signed for over a million dollars' worth of material and equipment. I just can't clear out in one hour."

Franklin broke in. "One hour, Herbert. One hour or you'll be picked up under arrest and taken out by the provost marshal."

"One hour," Barnes said again.

I saluted. "Don't do me any favors with the efficiency report," I said. "I intend to see you all again."

The General returned the salute and glanced over at Franklin. It seemed to be a nervous look.

An aide in the outer office watched me as I walked toward the outer door. "I'm sorry, sir," he said. I told him it didn't matter anyway. "What the hell," I said. "I'm alive and I'm going home." I didn't mean a word of it.

I walked down the steps and into the open and took my first deep breath of fresh air since I'd entered the office. I looked at my watch. "Damn," I said to myself. "Sixty minutes." I turned to take one more look at the General's area and spotted his imported flower bed. I walked over to it and stood there for a few seconds, remembering the night I had tramped through it, the night I had wrung Colonel Gander's neck after which Bittorie and I had cooked the bird—the symbol of all the silly crap we had seen around there—and made four duck sandwiches and eaten them. We had damned near choked, trying to eat and laugh at the same time.

Franklin came out past the flowers and hailed me.

"Herbert," he shouted.

"Sir."

"I don't want you to go off half-cocked and do something rash which you'll regret later. You have an excellent record and you can live this down. And especially with the max efficiency report the General's giving you. You've got a bright career ahead of you."

I stared at him. "Are you crazy?" I asked. "I don't intend to have to live anything down. I intend to go straight to General Abrams and get it cleared up properly. I haven't lied and I haven't exaggerated. I neither deserve to be relieved nor replaced nor anything else."

"Look, Tony," he said. I interrupted him.

400

"Why, sir? For another classmate?"

"Goddamn you, Herbert, I—"

"Sir, I only have fifty-three minutes left and I'd like to spend them with my friends. If you'll excuse me." I saluted and walked away. It was the last time I ever saw the man.

As I walked by the TOC, they were posting the March score sheet:

March 1969
MANEUVER BATTALIONS

INDICATOR	1/503	2/503	3/503	4/503	1/50
Contacts	157	710	148	338	56
Percent 1st Term Reenlistments	107	80	111	0	100
	264	790	259	338	156
AWOL	66	9	30	42	6
DR	56	32	28	112	6
Accident	27	9	3	9	12
Malaria	35	15	70	85	10
Narcotics	30	30	90	30	5
Art 15	50	3	41	35	21
Sum Ct	4	0	2	0	2
Spec Ct	30	12	9	15	0
Gen Ct	0	0	0	0	0
	298	110	273	328	62

RECAP

1	2/503	790 − 110 =	+ 680
2	1/50	156 − 62 =	+ 94
3	4/503	338 − 328 =	+ 10
4	3/503	259 − 273 =	− 14
5	1/503	264 − 298 =	− 34

As I walked back toward the battalion, I told myself it was important to remain calm, cool, and collected. I knew I had them both— just as long as I didn't blow it. They had gone far beyond their authority in moving me out without any grounds for relief. I was convinced by then that it had to be something more than any allegations of atrocities. Hell, everybody knew about them anyway. Somebody else would be bringing them up again, and soon. If they thought that by getting rid of me, they were also getting rid of the shame of what had occurred—that they had got it under the rug—they neither understood me nor the Army. At that point I still had faith in the system.

I crossed the road and thought about the battalion. What should I tell them? Ask the officers to go down in mass protest and quit—like the West Pointers in Ranger school? Not hardly, Franklin and Barnes or no Franklin and Barnes. It was still the United States Army and I was still me.

I called Ernie and told him to get as many of the officers as possible over to the TOC in thirty minutes. Then as Childers came up, I told them both that I'd been relieved.

"You're joking," Ernie said. "We'll all quit."

"You're damned right," said Childers.

"Cut the crap," I said. "Get the officers and get them now." I walked into my hooch and began shoving things into a bag. I called Captain Parrott and had him gather up some of the documents I thought I would need. I finished packing the bag and took it outside and dropped it beside the sign which said:

COMMANDING OFFICER: LTC ANTHONY B. HERBERT
SERGEANT MAJOR: MASTER SERGEANT RICHARD CHILDERS

I walked over to the TOC. Ernie had most of the officers gathered in the briefing room. He had already told them. "Look," I began. "There's no time to screw around. You know I've been given the boot. That's why I wanted to talk to you right away. I've only got about fifteen more minutes before I have to be out of here, but I wanted to take some of the time to thank you and to get the chance to shake as many of your hands as I could before I have to go."

There were some protests and a few remarks about quitting. I stifled that quickly. "The Army has a system of military justice and rules and regs, so none of you needs to go off half-cocked and try to take things into his own hands. And nobody quits either. Just keep thinking about the battalion. That's what important. Not me. If you quit you're letting down not only me but every last one of those grunts out there. They have to stay. They can't quit. You can, but they need you, and the guy who replaces me is going to need you. It's not going to be his fault what happened to me. So stick with the battalion and stick with him and stick with them," I said, waving toward the boonies. I started shaking hands.

"We're going to quit," someone shouted.

I stopped. "Like shit you are," I said. "You're going to stay and do the best you can." I waved my arm to include them all. "Every last one of you—or else I've failed and Franklin was right."

"We'll stay," Doc Tally said, "but we don't have to like it."

"Thanks, Doc," I said and shook his hand again.

I went back to the hooch, picked up my bag, and had Smitty drive down to King pad where the bird was waiting. Webb was standing by the skids. I stepped inside. Potter and Childers were there waiting. "What the hell is this?" I asked.

"I got permission from Bittorie," Childers said. "I'm going down to Saigon to look for a new job. They're going to fire me anyway and Potter decided he didn't want to stay any longer. It's okay."

I could have hugged them. "Dumb bastards," I said.

"Me, too, then," Ernie said, grabbing my hand at the door of the bird. "I can't stay either. I'm going to quit tomorrow, but quietly."

"They need you, Ernie," I said.

"Not me," he said, shaking his head. He stepped back and waved as the bird lifted off in a clatter. I looked down at the sandbags on the floor to hide the tears in my eyes. The craft swung into a wide turn around English. Childers punched me and pointed down through the open left door.

In the Caspar area, men all along the ground were lined up, pulling off smoke canisters of every color in the rainbow. There were maybe a hundred men out there, a hundred smokes. It was their honors. Smoke. When the troops were coming back after a kill, they buzzed the field with a smoke lit on each skid, and when one of their own left, they lit from one to five depending on how well he was liked plus his reputation as a fighter. And I was looking down on at least a hundred of them, knowing all the time that nobody was that good, but choked with appreciation nevertheless. I waved and they waved back. The pilot banked the ship again and I sat back against the rigging and wiped my eyes.

10

We landed in Saigon a bit before 9:00 that evening, and although I should have been feeling like a bastard on Father's Day, I didn't. I was relieved—in more ways than one, I suppose. I reasoned that if Barnes and Franklin had hated me that much, I was better off out of the outfit. I had the marbles in my pocket. They had nothing to fall back on but their own lies and falsifications. I knew I had been lucky. I could have had accidental kills of women and children or other noncombatants, and then they would have had the marbles in their pockets. I could have ranked second or third on the IG inspection. I could have had a high court-martial rate or accident rate or a large number of Article 15s or delinquency reports from the military police, or any one of a number of other things that could have been used against me. But I'd been lucky. Franklin, I mused, had let his personal dislike for me get the best of him. It had forced him into a premature confrontation that I was bound to win. The battalion had been doing great. Both Franklin and Barnes had said that, and the records showed it. Getting rid of me couldn't have been their response to my opposing the new pacification plan. Hell, I'd just said I didn't like it; I had every intention of following orders related to it. That left me only with the enemies I'd made as IG and my allegations about war crimes and atrocities.

I kept hearing both of them talk about "the good of the Brigade." I had smeared the Brigade, and neither of them could live with that, however stupid their reaction. Perhaps, given the premise on which they had built their Army careers, they had had no choice but to act against anyone whose own actions were a threat to their unit's image. They had had only three other choices. They could have sent me to jail on some ruse, and discredited me; they could have arranged to lower the odds for my survival in combat; or they could have tried to buy me off—which it occurred to me they had done with the mention of the efficiency report. But they had doped it wrong. I wasn't buying. In fact, I was going to General Abrams the next day and the waves would begin.

I caught a ride downtown with Childers, found a room and slept like a log for the second night in a row. Maybe I really was cracking up if I could relax like that when my world was crumbling around me.

The next morning I said goodbye to him. He had his own business to take care of. He started walking away. "If you need me," I said, "give me a ring out at Le Van Duyet."

"I'll stay in touch," he said.

"Take care, man," I said. "Try to stay out of trouble, huh?"

"That goes double for you, you crazy bastard," he said.

"Not this time, guy, not this time," I said. "This time, I may have to stay in trouble the rest of my life."

I let go of his hand, picked up my bag, and left for Le Van Duyet, where I reported immediately to Lieutenant Colonel John Green, the personnel officer of the Capitol Military Assistance Command, the organization responsible for the defense of Saigon. Here was one more extraneous, wasted, tail-on-the-dog command to give a general and his staff something to do, to create more slots for more promotions. In fact, it was so bad that at one time there were twenty-one generals and their staffs working out of Saigon, few of them in command of actual troops. It was, for all practical purposes, a briefing headquarters, a bigger, better stage for the pony shows.

"I'm to report to a Colonel Lew Ashley," I said to Green. "Then I'd like to see General Abrams as soon as possible."

"That would have to be cleared with Ashley," he said. "But let me tell you this much before you ask. The onus is already on you, Tony. Barnes has called down and said you were a liar and could not be trusted."

I felt my face turn red. "Isn't that kind of against regulations, to put a stigma on a man in his next unit?" I asked. "Oh, hell. Not that it matters—but it figures because it shows he's pretty scared at this point, and I can tell you this, he has every right to be scared."

Green looked puzzled. "The General? Scared?"

"It's too long a story for right now, John, but I can tell you it has to do with bodies in the sand and murder winning out. I'll tell it to you later," I said. "But right now I'd like to see Ashley."

"Sure enough," he said, dropping the questions. He picked up his hat, whistled for a driver, and followed me outside. The jeep arrived and we drove to Ashley's office, where John went in first, talked a couple of minutes and then signaled for me to come in.

Ashley shook hands and offered me a seat before launching into a spiel about the water having passed under the bridge and how what was past was past. He referred to Franklin as "Ross." When he was finished, I asked for four or five days off and permission to go to Long Binh, the headquarters of the U.S. Army in the Republic of Vietnam (USARV), for the purpose of seeing General Abrams.

"Why do you want to do that, Herbert?" Ashley asked.

"I want to talk to him about some allegations of war crimes that I've made and about my relief from command of the battalion," I said.

"You really ought to think that over a day or so before you rush into it," he said. "It could hurt."

"It already has, sir," I said. "And I've already thought it over. I need four days, even if it's leave time."

"No, no, no, that won't be necessary," he said. "Take the four days and then if you absolutely need more, let me know. By the way, do you have transportation?"

"No, sir, but I'll get there."

"Take the sedan," he said, calling in his sergeant major to make arrangements for the car. "Now, let's talk about what you're going to be doing here," he said. I explained that my time in-country was short, and he told me that his was, too. "So, us short-timers will just stay together," he said. "You can be my deputy and you can start right now."

"Deputy? Deputy what?" I said.

"You're going to be the Deputy Chief of Staff of the Capitol Military Assistance Command," he said. "You'll do studies and stuff like that. You'll be a writer. Okay?"

"Anything."

"Didn't you write a book or something once?"

"Yeah, once."

"Well, then, you'll do fine," he said. He took me to the sweltering hall outside his air-conditioned office, where he assigned me a desk next to the sergeant major, the Vietnamese maids, and the drivers. I sat down at the blank, bare desk, and Ashley went back into his office.

"What the hell did you do, sir?" the sergeant major asked.

"I got relieved of my command," I said. "You?"

"I shot my mouth off," he said, waving his arm. "Welcome to limbo, sir."

"Better than hell, Sarge," I said. "One hell of a lot better than hell."

The next morning I drove to Long Binh, which was not only USARV headquarters but the site of the LBJ ranch to which Franklin had threatened to send me if I didn't mend my ways. Instead of seeing General Abrams, I was permitted to talk with the Staff Judge Advocate, the top lawyer and judge in the country, a Colonel Douglas. He listened to my story patiently, hardly raising an eyebrow when I related the war crimes, and when I was finished he said very quietly that he wanted nothing to do with it.

"Against a general? Not on your life," he said. "I wouldn't touch it with a ten-foot pole."

I protested, but that was it. I argued that, under the provisions of the Uniform Code of Military Justice, I was entitled to make allegations and to file charges just like anybody else—even if they might involve a general. I told him there were witnesses. I told him it involved not only my career but other careers, as well as the integrity of the U.S. Army. When I was finished with my argument, he politely dismissed me. I left his office without having "formally" filed my complaint. In Army use, the word simply means that it was not receipted for in writing. I had presented it, by God, but not "formally" filed it because nobody signed for it. Hell, nobody would. This would be the first in a long series of refusals to sign a receipt for my complaint. Without the receipt, it was just one guy's word against that of a superior officer who, it was always said, "had no reason to lie." So I was out, out of Douglas's office at least. But there were alternatives, and the first was in the very same building.

I went upstairs to the office of the USARV Inspector General, who not only received me kindly but turned me over to a member of his staff who read me my rights and then heard my story, including the part about the rebuff downstairs in the SJA's office. His advice was to write out my side of the story—he emphasized that the story just might have more than one side—but to omit the war crimes issue or, at least, not raise it directly. "Sort of sneak it in," he said, so that they would think I was just out to get myself exonerated. "They'll understand that," he said. "But I don't think they'll ever go for an investigation of a war crimes cover-up by the command." His strategy sounded fine to me: to try to right a wrong by having the circumstances of my relief from command investigated and, during the course of that inquiry, bring into the case the allegations I'd made. "That way, you can get them into the official record," he said. It made sense and I agreed. He provided me with a desk, a yellow legal pad, pens and pencils, and the services of a typist, as well as a place to bunk until I finished. So I sat down and, as hastily as I could, prepared my initial statement, avoiding the issues of the war crimes just as I'd been advised. I filed it "formally" in the office of the IG and then went back to my desk and my "duties" at Le Van Duyet—I was, after all, the Deputy Chief of Staff of the Capitol Military Assistance Command —to await some action.

What I had legally done was request an "investigation for erroneous relief of command" under provisions of Article 138 in the Uniform Code of Military Justice. On April 22, I received notification that Major General Joseph Russ, an old friend of Abrams and Westmoreland from West Point days, had been assigned to investigate and report on my case. The general reiterated what the IG aide had told me. He said war crimes charges were out of the question under the provisions of Article 138, and he told me he was not authorized to even discuss them. But he said that when we got to the hearing on the Article 138, I would be able to raise them in the cross-examination of witnesses.

I went out looking for a lawyer. Major Ted Voorhies, a long-time acquaintance of mine I had run into accidentally at Long Binh, had given me the name of an Air Force attorney who, he said, would do a good job of representing me. I put in my request. It was turned down. The man was not available, USARV said, urging me to "use one of our attorneys," and finally appointing a Major Peter Kane to serve. It was really an advantageous choice, they assured me. I met with him once prior to our appearance before General Russ in Nha Trang, and we discussed the case for about ten or fifteen minutes. His counsel to me was to present my case in a positive manner, avoid attacking the characters of either General Barnes or Colonel Franklin, and try at all costs to avoid antagonizing General Russ. "We'll get our chance in the cross-examination," he said, and according to Army regulations, he was precisely right. I believed him because I still believed in the Army.

At Nha Trang, I presented my initial statement to General Russ and the "court" or "board" appointed to serve with him on the investigation and hearing. I told them exactly what had happened, but not being an attorney I forgot my own counsel's advice and twice started to bring in the issue of the war crimes. On both occasions, General Russ stopped the proceedings, called a "recess," and told me that if I wanted to talk about crimes, the board would have to be adjourned and my allegations would have to be made under a different article of the UCMJ back at USARV. But, again, he assured me that I could bring up anything I wanted during the cross-examination of witnesses later in the hearing. Again I bought it. The board continued.

With the plane waiting on the apron, its engines warming up for the trip up north to LZ English and the witness phase of the hearing, General Russ came up with the clincher. There was no room on the plane for me, he said. I exploded, but he convinced me that I could hurriedly write down the points on which I wished cross-examination to take place and that he would then take care of it himself. My lawyer agreed that it was a bitch of a way to handle the case, but that this wasn't the time to antagonize anyone. "Let's just see what he does with it," he said. So I acquiesced and they all went to English without either me or my attorney. We sat in Nha Trang and drank beer until they came back. Then we sat down to read the record of the hearing up there.

General Barnes had been the first witness.

> I gave LTC Herbert his battalion against the recommendation of my staff who had dealt with him as a staff officer previous to my arrival. However, Colonel Franklin interceded for him and recommended that I give him the battalion because he was an Infantry lieutenant colonel and because he had sufficient time to put six months of command in, because the IG for the Brigade does not call for a lieutenant colonel, and because he was on the list to go to the Command and General Staff College. And I felt that I was morally obligated to give him the battalion so that he could have his chance.

There had been no cross-examination. Had I been there I would have tried to point out that there were several inaccuracies even in that opening statement. First, I did not have sufficient time in-country for a full command tour. I had only four months left before I was scheduled to return to the States, and General Barnes knew that, being aware of the fact that I was scheduled to attend the Command and General Staff College at Leavenworth; moreover, the two of us had discussed my short time on several occasions. Secondly, it was not true that the IG slot in the Brigade did not call for a lieutenant colonel. The Brigade had in fact received approval for just that and, besides, my rank and its relationship to the job of IG hadn't bothered anyone in the Brigade for the previous six months.

The General went on to deny that any commitment of a combat command for me had ever been made by General Allen. He said that if Colonel Franklin had ever wanted to have a friend of his assigned as commander of the 2d Battalion, he had never mentioned it to him. It would have been good at that point to have heard from Sergeant Bittorie, who overheard the conversations that would have substantiated both points, but since there was no cross-examination and Bittorie was already back in the States, that little point was missed.

General Barnes also said during his testimony that I had "developed small unit tactics into something really exemplary. But I felt that he was doing it as a result of my instructions." I wondered why, if that was the case, the other battalions under his command, all presumably getting the same kind of "instructions" from the General, did not respond as readily as mine. He also denied that he'd given me an hour to clear out of English and that I'd asked for redress of any form in his office when he relieved me. The latter was true. I had only asked for an investigation. General Barnes, during his testimony, said, "I did not even know that there was an Article 138, UCMJ, until about ten days afterwards when I was so informed by Brigadier General Bowers from Saigon that this whole thing was on the way." I don't doubt this point at all, but I must say I cringed a bit to learn that a general in the U.S. Army did not know of the existence of one of the basic means of justice within the military—Article 138.

It was General Bowers, he said, whom he had called in Saigon about me. He told him, he said, that I wasn't to be believed, according to the rating officer on my efficiency report. The rating officer, of course, was none other than Joseph Ross Franklin. He also told the board that I had told him that I had completed work on a doctor of philosophy degree in psychology. He said he was "surprised to see" the mention in my own statement that I was "making preparation for

410

completing the Ph.D." In the first place, I had never told him any such thing—of course, that would be his word against mine—and in the second place, my education record was on my personnel file, which he stated under oath he had studied. Why was he surprised to learn that I only had a master's degree if he'd actually read the file? Among other things, he said that I had not been recommended for the DSC, though he did admit telling me that he would inform the men that I was being transferred to some other responsibility in Saigon rather than "broadcast to the world" that I had been relieved.

Then the General concluded:

> I would like to enter into the record that during Lieutenant Colonel Herbert's two months in command there were five general courts-martial that are pending in his battalion. These are the first general courts-martial this Brigade has had since last fall, when they had one. Two of these general courts-martial are for murder, one murder in the first degree. The other three are for rape. The three for rape, the Article 32 investigation has already gone forward to IFFV and the two cases of murder are now being prepared for general court-martial. It is my personal feeling that these general courts-martial were a direct result of Lieutenant Colonel Herbert's mercilessness and his view of killing which he pursued almost blindly during his tenure of command to the extent that he personally led squads and killed VC, civilians and so on.

There were five courts-martial pending. Four of the defendants were found innocent of the charges. But what was more important in this testimony, General Barnes laid himself open to being charged with a serious violation of the regulations. He stated under oath that I had personally led squads and killed Viet Cong and civilians. Wasn't that supposed to be a crime, to kill civilians? And if he knew that I had, why had he not seen to it that justice was done? Why had he not ordered an investigation that would have produced grounds for formal charges against me and ultimately a general court-martial for the murder of civilian Vietnamese, as was done with Lieutenant Calley? Was he trying to cover something up? Was that the way he operated? Or had I really killed civilians? It was a fascinating question, there in black and white. If General Barnes knew I'd killed civilians, he had never filed charge one, he had not started even the first investigation.

Finally, the General read into the record the comments he had written on my efficiency report—the very first adverse report I'd ever received as an officer in the U.S. Army. All the rest had been outstanding. But in General Barnes's view I was incapable of commanding a battalion:

> I concur completely with the comments of the rating officer. Colonel Franklin kept me informed of all the incidents to which he refers. The Brigade Executive Officer kept me informed of the increasingly intolerable friction between Lieutenant Colonel Herbert and the Brigade Staff as it developed. On 14 March 1969, I wrote Lieutenant Colonel Herbert a letter of reprimand whose last two paragraphs were as follows:
> "2. You have created unnecessary and unjustified friction between yourself and several of my principal staff officers, the Support Battalion Commander, my Executive Officer, and the supporting Aviation commander. You have, in effect, pitted your battalion against the Brigade. This situation cannot continue.
> "3. Your battalion has performed its tactical mission in a superior manner. However, you are responsible for its administration and its relations with other elements of the Brigade. Repetition of incidents of the type described above will be cause for your immediate relief."
> This letter resulted in no significant improvement in the areas cited; in fact, the relations between him and the staff worsened. Lieutenant Colonel Herbert is a brilliant small-unit tactician in the sense that he can inspire, lead and teach a squad or platoon to excel in precision killing with minimum casualties. However, he was incapable of commanding a battalion in the sense of being a part of the Brigade team, considering the needs of others, sharing available assets and being responsive to the Brigade staff. In my opinion, Lieutenant Colonel Herbert should never be allowed to command again and, consequently, his orders assigning him to attend Command and General Staff College should be revoked.
> That's it, sir.

The next witness was Franklin and he hadn't so much as warmed up the chair before General Russ explained to him the nature of the proceedings in a way that, according to Army regulations, might be considered a little curious.

"This is an informal investigation," the General said. "I'm conducting it at various places at various times. All testimony will be taken verbatim and there will be no presentation of witnesses with respondent and counsel present. This method has been adopted because of the diversity of location of witnesses and the critical, sensitive combat mission of the unit involved, which precludes a formal board hearing."

It was a key point. It meant that no matter what, my lawyer wasn't going to get a crack at them. His only usefulness to me would be to point out on which line on which form I should sign my name.

Franklin told the board that I was totally lacking in honesty, integrity, and loyalty and "totally unfit to be an Army officer."

> Related to this is his tendency for character assassination, of which I have asked witnesses to come forth and testify before you. I have heard him call the Support Battalion Commander, the Adjutant General, the S2, company commanders, DSC winners, he has called cowards, Goddamn liars, stupid shits, totally corrupt—all of these things. All of which will be given in sworn testimony to you.

For some reason, though, that testimony was never presented.

It is important, I think, to keep in mind that the reason General Barnes assigned me to a battalion command, as both he and Franklin remembered it, was in part because Franklin recommended me. Whether that is true, I can't say, but the following story, given under oath, was supposed to have occurred before my assignment:

> Reference jumping to my feet and stating that I had more university degrees and higher military decorations, this was after listening to about ten minutes of him going over his past record and how honest he was and all the integrity he had, and he had all these decorations. And I just got sick of it and I was angry. And I told him that I didn't care to hear that. I had higher decorations than he did and more university degrees—which apparently he felt was laughable.

Nevertheless, Franklin went to Barnes, he said, and asked that I be given a combat command. That is what you call magnanimity. Like Barnes, he said that the tactical changes I initiated in the battalion were not my idea, but rather emanated down from the Brigade. "I'd like to say in Herbert's defense, he executed them better than anybody else," Franklin added.

Then the hearing got as close to the war crimes as it ever did. Franklin testified:

> OK, sir, on 14 February, this action here. I won't go into that. He was the only one that got a decoration for this. I talked to four people in that platoon about another thing I was directed to talk to them about. The body count they gave was half of what Herbert reported. Colonel Bethea and the S1 were present at this conversation. It was about a 21 body count reported. On this action of 14 February, Colonel Herbert was the only one who got an award. The body count reported by Colonel

Herbert was about twice that reported by the platoon with which I spoke. Colonel Bethea and Major Durbin, the S1, heard that and they're coming in as witnesses.

Was he talking about Cu Loi? I guess we'll never know, except that the only action for which I received an award for gallantry on February 14 was Cu Loi. And what other thing was Franklin directed to talk to the platoon about? Who reported that other thing to him or how did he find out about it? Is it possible that someone came to him and told him that people had been murdered at Cu Loi?

Moreover, if I was suspected of inflating body counts, why wasn't something done about it? After all, Franklin said he had the witnesses to prove it, or at least to cast a doubt on the body counts I reported. Throughout his testimony, Franklin repeatedly referred to my "continued misrepresentation and exaggeration," but he was never specific about what I supposedly misrepresented or exaggerated. Perhaps it was my allegations of war crimes—but that couldn't be it because Franklin later told the Army's Criminal Investigation Division that he had never heard of any of the things I was saying I had reported to him.

It's also important, I think, to note that the body count I reported for the Cu Loi action on February 14 was later included in the citation for the Bronze Star I received for action that day—a Bronze Star that Colonel Joseph Ross Franklin recommended I be awarded. The same is true of Franklin's later dispute of what happened at the Rockpile. He claimed in his testimony that I had again exaggerated the body count by reporting an agent's figures of twenty-nine dead and seventeen wounded. "To give this as fact in an official report is misleading, to say the least," Franklin testified. Yet, in the Bronze Star I got for the Rockpile action and in General Barnes's letter of commendation, those are precisely the figures used.

The transcript of the testimony went on and on and on. Reading it was like reliving the entire period of my service in the 173d Brigade. For a while, it was quite discouraging. After Barnes and Franklin, the testimony came from Bethea, Accousti, O'Kane, and Bowers, and it looked as though the board was getting nothing but inflated body counts and killing of civilians. Then came Warrant Officer Larry Pippen, my C and C helicopter pilot. His testimony refuted several major points that Franklin had made—among them, that the village near the Rockpile had been burned. But then along came Chaplain Davis, who told the board that in my first briefing with my battalion staff I had said I had no integrity; and Captain Cording, who also presented a very dim view of my command. It was the same story from Meurrens and Beacham and Angel and Crouch. By then, I wasn't surprised. I could hardly have expected them to say otherwise. Yet every one of their major contentions—that I was disloyal, that I was cruel and merciless, that I caused dissension in the Brigade, that I exaggerated or misrepresented, that I could not be believed on anything—all of them were once again refuted by the testimony of others, including Paul Ray and several men from my own battalion, especially Jim Grimshaw, Lieutenant Sigholtz, Dick Childers, and Ernie Webb.

All in all, I wasn't really worried after reading the transcript— except that I complained to General Russ that I hadn't noticed any of the cross-examination he'd promised on the points I'd outlined. I also noticed that even the overt contradictions in testimony were never pursued by members of the board. For instance, Franklin said that when he gave me the General's letter of reprimand, I just laughed and began talking about how I papered my walls with those things. Then, General Barnes testified that when Franklin gave me the letter, I said nothing.

I told Russ I was angry about not having had the opportunity to cross-examine. It was my right and he had promised to do it for me. He said it hadn't been necessary since "there seems to already be enough evidence to clear this matter up."

"But what about the investigations of the crimes?" I asked. He said they were "probably" being conducted and, if not, they could be brought up at a later date. He assured me that this case was not over. "Not by a long shot," he said. His advice was to immediately file a rebuttal to those points already on paper. Anything else would have to be covered "under a separate heading," he said.

I was stupid. I thought it was moving well. I did as I was advised to do. I filed a letter of rebuttal, answering only those points I'd noticed in the transcript. I was ordered back to Saigon from Nha Trang by General Russ and was promised a record copy of all the board's proceedings, including its conclusions. "They'll certainly be an eye-opener to a lot of generals," Russ said. I left for Saigon.

Although I learned on May 6 that the board had reached a conclusion on the hearing, I was refused a copy. Major Kane, my lawyer, finally demanded one and got it the next day. In the way it began, it was comforting to read. Under the section headed "Findings," I read:

The investigating officer (the board), having carefully considered the evidence of record, finds—

Based upon the testimony received in this investigation and after reviewing the facts and circumstances thereof, I believe substantial evidence has been adduced to reach the following findings which I now make:

1. That LTC Herbert is a strong, aggressive, outspoken personality who was respected and admired by most of his subordinates and who had great confidence in his leadership and tactical ability.

2. That there is no question as to LTC Herbert's personal bravery or leadership quality.

3. That no positive evidence was presented which would reflect on LTC Herbert's loyalty.

I was relieved to read that. I felt a surge of gratitude for the Army's provisions for justice and some chagrin at being angry at General Russ about the lack of cross-examination. I remembered what I'd told my officers the day I'd been relieved of the battalion command. "Don't quit," I'd said. "I'll take care of this. The Army has ways of taking care of things and that's why I'm going down to Saigon. It's going to work out. Don't worry."

And I'd been right. It was working out. I turned the page to continue reading the findings.

4. That the letter of reprimand of 14 March 1969 from the Brigade Commander was only partially based on facts and that some of the observations presented were those of Brigade Executive Officer and Brigade Deputy Commander which related to LTC Herbert's performance of duty as an IG.

5. That there was friction between LTC Herbert and certain members of the Brigade staff, stemming mostly from LTC Herbert's IG assignment.

6. That there is a dispute in the evidence as to whether LTC Herbert received the letter of 14 March 1969 from the Brigade Commander concerning action taken on delinquency reports.

7. That LTC Herbert is a strong individual with an insatiable desire to excel, often utilizing unconventional means to obtain results, thus creating tension and strained relationships with some for whom he works.

8. That LTC Herbert did on a number of occasions conflict with the Deputy Brigade Commander, another strong, aggressive individual, which led to a collision course between these two strong-willed personalities. The proximity of these two personalities aggravated an already strained relationship which would probably not have existed had they been separated.

9. That certain testimony presented indicates that LTC Herbert, either knowingly or unknowingly, did exaggerate the situation or equivocate with the truth.

10. That the Deputy Brigade Commander and former Executive Officer, LTC Bethea, were prone to reach judgments regarding LTC Herbert's performance of duty, loyalty and integrity and render opinions thereon to the Brigade Commanding General without in all cases determining all the facts, pro and con.

11. That the Brigade Commanding General formed his evaluation of LTC Herbert's performance based on information primarily received from the Deputy Commander and Executive Officer as well as his own feelings, observation and intuitions. Some of these specific incidents that were related to the Brigade Commanding General concerning LTC Herbert's loyalty, integrity and performance of duty have not been substantiated by evidence adduced in this investigation.

12. That the events of March and April were cause for extreme worry and concern on the part of the Brigade Commander who felt that the series of incidents relative to LTC Herbert's battalion were reaching a crescendo and some action had to be taken. Based on his personal observation, best judgment and the incidents which occurred during this period, the Brigade Commander lost faith and confidence in LTC Herbert's ability to perform as a battalion commander in support of the Brigade mission.

Well, it wasn't bad, I concluded. They had said that, for one reason or another, I might have exaggerated or equivocated with the truth, but all in all I felt the findings were in the general area of the truth. I turned then to read the recommendation made by General Russ. It was short and not so sweet.

In view of the above findings, the investigation officer recommends:
That Brigadier General Barnes, as Brigade Commander, acted on the facts as he knew them, his judgment of LTC Herbert's character and his lack of confidence to entrust the lives of others in him when he relieved LTC Herbert for the good of the Brigade; and that no redress be granted concerning LTC Herbert's relief from command.

I couldn't believe it. I read it over and over again, and again, and I still couldn't grasp the relationship between the findings and the recommendation. The findings said that, sure, I'd been aggressive and maybe a bastard here and there, but that any of the friction that existed had its origin in my IG work and that the General's conclusions were based on what he was told by Franklin and Bethea, who often drew conclusions without evidence. But "for the good of the Brigade"—there were those words again—no redress of my grievance. The efficiency report, which described me in no uncertain terms as a piss-poor officer, and General Barnes's recommendation that I never be allowed to command again were still on my record. I could not believe it. I had spent half my life in the Army, but I could not believe it. I still can't.

I left Vietnam later that month. On the plane home I read a letter from Jim Grimshaw, who was still up in the area with his Delta Demons.

Sir:

1SG Ramil and I are sitting here in a lighted bunker at the Bong Son bridge, fully participating in the new pacification mission. I saw Childers today and he says he goes to a security company in Qui Nhon in a few days. He tried to get D Co. and let Ramil go to the Brigade LRPs but evidently the Brigade SJM did not go along with that.

I'm sure that nothing I could say would relieve your personal hurt and the pride you lost because of the situation, but the officers, NCOs and troops of this battalion all know what happened and are extremely bitter. Since you left, we've lost our fighting spirit and many of us our faith in the Army. Capt. Dorney submitted his resignation, which probably won't be allowed to go through, but that's how strongly he felt about his membership in the West Point Protective Association.

Dorney, Hill and I were at a meeting yesterday reference the pacification and we all agreed that we're unfortunately in a state of Limbo and will not probably benefit as much as we thought we might have under your command. We can't help but get the feeling that with your departure we lost out on the usual rewards one usually receives if he hacks it as a company commander.

Colonel Franklin buzzed in to our location the afternoon you left and asked Ramil and I what we thought, but knowing that my shit was still weak from the tiger suit business, I didn't say much. The day after you flew out to tell me about the uniform business, Franklin flew out and the first thing he asked me was why I didn't have my tiger suit on. I told him that I had received word through you to wear the regular uniform because the CG and him had put the word out to you. He then

418

told me that he had told you no such thing and that I could wear it. No sweat, I didn't believe him.

Major Webb will leave today or tomorrow for IFFV as LTG Cochrane's aide. His words to me yesterday were "Be careful!"

Aircraft support has been cut again and with this pacification bit, we're not going to be able to react and run up the body count.

Sir, if there's any additional paper-work or items you need for your investigation, Dorney, Hill and I will be more than glad to assist with it. It's the least we can do—we'll be more than happy to make statements or testify if it will help. You backed us, particularly me, and I'd like to repay in any way possible.

Well, we all wish you the best in the world and want you to know it was a privilege and honor to serve under you. If at any time in the future I could serve under you again, I'd jump at the chance.

Best wishes,
JIM GRIMSHAW

The letter kept me company all the way back to the States.

11

I don't know what I expected from General Russ. His alternatives were really rather limited. After all, if he had followed the logic dictated by his own findings and granted me redress from my command relief, it would have been a mark on General Barnes. Given a choice between a lieutenant colonel and a fellow general, what the hell could he do. But the handwriting was there. The findings had exonerated me, I thought, but the recommendation left General Barnes with some face. I'm convinced now that Barnes and Russ, not to mention Franklin, firmly believed that that would be the end of the matter. They had no idea how wrong they were.

The first thing I did when I reported to Leavenworth was to contact the lawyers there and inform them of my intention to press for an investigation of the allegations of war crimes, and for the removal of the adverse efficiency report from my file.

I had told my wife of my plans to continue to try to get something done and she had agreed that I should. But, with the savvy that an Army wife has, she predicted it would be a rough go.

The next Saturday afternoon—it was now July, 1969—Marygrace, Toni-Junell and I were entertaining an old friend of mine in our new quarters at Leavenworth. Dr. Yancy Beamer was a neurosurgeon I had met during my tour in the Middle East. When he heard I was at Leavenworth he flew out from Virginia for a visit. We were sitting around, talking old times, when the phone rang. It was Colonel Buck Newman of the Army's Officer Personnel Section calling from Washington. He said, "If you're going to get involved with war crimes, you're not going to have time to go to school." His meaning was clear, but so were my intentions. I told him I meant to go through with it and he said that perhaps I ought to talk it over with my family. I left the phone for a moment and walked over to Marygrace.

"Colonel Newman says I ought to talk it over with my family, so that's what I'm doing," I said.

Dr. Beamer interrupted. "Talk over what?"

I explained my dilemma. He shook his head. "I'm glad that's your problem and not mine," he said.

Marygrace said, "You know I want you to do what you want to do." The whole discussion took less than a minute or so. I returned to the telephone and told the Colonel that after discussing it with my family, the decision was the same. I was, as he put it, "going to be involved in war crimes." His response was clear enough. There would be no Command and General Staff College.

I can't say I was overjoyed at being deprived of what is actually a signal opportunity in the Army. The CGSC is one of the places where future generals' tickets are punched on the way to the top. I wanted that and I wanted it badly. I had always mouthed around about not ever wanting to be a general, but deep down I knew better. Hell, I wanted to be the best in the Army. That had always been the way I'd operated. General Russ had been exactly right in his findings. I was aggressive and I was ambitious and I did have an insatiable desire to excel—and damn it, I wanted to go to CGSC.

But not at the expense of my integrity, the integrity my efficiency report from Franklin and Bethea and Barnes said I didn't have. I made my decision. I've always been proud that I did. I haven't always been happy since that day, but I've never been ashamed.

The first thing the Army lawyers at Leavenworth told me was that I had presented evidence that was insufficient for charges. I saw their reluctance only as another stall in the game. I already had the names and the dates and the places. The lawyers were the ones who were supposed to go out and gather the statements. They said that would not be how it would work. I would have to provide the statements myself, and then they would see if there was enough evidence to warrant charges. So I set out on that course, but when I began using Army facilities there at Leavenworth, the commander of the post, Major General John Hay, personally told me that I would not be able to use the Army telephone system for my investigation. So I fell back on my last resort. I began using my own funds to put together the investigation. The phone bills were enormous, and when I started to fly around the country gathering statements from the people involved in the allegations, the air travel costs were staggering. At least, they were staggering to me. I ended up finally shelling out most of my family's savings trying to get the damned thing going. It was about $8,000 altogether, but I don't regret a single dime of it, and Mary-grace was never one to complain about money. Not many girls from Herminie, Pa., do. As for Toni-Junell, well, we planned to send her to West Point anyway, and that's free.

I was operating on two fronts, trying to get the investigation of the crimes together and at the same time pressing for a removal of the adverse efficiency report from my files. I wrote to the Department of the Army about it on September 11, 1969. My request was refused.

While I was at Leavenworth, I was assigned as the G2 or intelligence officer for the post. In mid-October, 1969, the operations officer, Colonel Jenkins, was sent to the hospital for surgery, which left me with both jobs. Right after his departure I was called up by the post commander, General Hay himself. "We've found out," he said, "that there's going to be a general uprising of dissidents both inside and outside the Army." The plan, as he understood it from reports from Washington, was that inside the Army they were planning a mass sick-call. Outside, in our area at least, they were planning at the same time on the same day a march on Leavenworth Prison, an entire city that existed within walls forty feet high and in some cases forty feet thick. A battalion of artillery couldn't have breached those walls in a week of firing.

"Well, Herbert, what do we do?" he asked, and I gave him what I felt was a reasonable suggestion.

"Let them storm the walls," I said. "The best they can do is paint a few four-letter words on the walls and maybe beat their heads against the stone. When it's all over, all we need to do is go out and wash off the paint. That way there's no damage and no confrontation and nobody gets hurt."

"You must be stupid, Herbert," he said. "This is big, really big. I think it's them or us." I understood his frustrations at being shelved in Leavenworth after having served as a combat commander in Vietnam. Now he had nothing to command but a prison and a few garrison troops. "We are going to meet them and defeat them," he said. "I want every last thread of intelligence kept up to date."

That wasn't really such a big task since I had twenty-two agents out working the countryside around Leavenworth, including one in the governor's office. By late October, we found out that there would be no massive sick-call and that we could expect a maximum of twenty-five marchers to "storm the prison." The General called and asked that I go with him, his chief of staff, and a couple of other staff members down to Leavenworth's City Hall for a meeting with members of the governor's staff, the head of the Kansas Bureau of Investigation, one of the wheels from the Kansas State Police, the Sheriff of Leavenworth County, and a bunch of other lesser officials.

As we walked down the hall toward the mayor's office, the General asked how many dissidents we could expect. I told him about twenty-five at most. I sat in the back of the room daydreaming while the others took turns talking—and talking and talking and talking—until finally one of the governor's aides turned to the General and asked how many dissidents could be expected.

"Five thousand plus," the General said without batting an eye. I damn near fell out of my chair. My God, what had I said to the man in the hall? Had it been a slip of the tongue—my tongue? Five thousand? Where in hell did he get that figure?

"What would you say, Chief?" he said, turning to his chief of staff.

"More than ten thousand, sir," he said.

"Do we have any hard intelligence?" the governor's man asked, and the General turned to me.

"Give it to him, G2," he said.

It was my turn. A smart, level-headed young officer would have replied "At least, sir." But I was a dumb-ass lieutenant colonel who was out of school working on war crimes charges against my superiors. "I'd prefer to brief you back at camp, sir," I said.

The chief of staff looked furious. "Goddamn, man, spit it out."

"Twenty-five, sir," I said.

Someone snickered. The chief of staff came right up over the chair, towering over me.

"Goddamn it, man," he said. "You must be the dumbest goddamn lieutenant colonel in the Army or else you're one of them," referring to the dissidents.

423

I tried to laugh it off. "More than likely I'm the dumbest lieutenant colonel, sir, because I'm sure not one of them."

The meeting broke up and as we went down the hall toward the cars, the General asked me how many troops we had available. I told him we had two MP companies and a headquarters company, which was enough to handle more than 10,000 rioters. "Get me another company," he said. "And how many chemical grenades and mines?"

"Five thousand, sir."

"Get me five thousand more from Fort Riley," he said.

"Yes, sir."

"How many agents available?"

"Twenty-two, sir, counting the one in the governor's office."

He stopped in his tracks. "Get me all of them in for this operation. I want everybody working."

"Sir, if the one in the governor's office is recognized, it'll be blown."

"Recognized? Among 10,000 faces?"

"Yes, sir."

"Now, Herbert, get me up a plan."

"Yes, sir."

"What do you intend to call it?"

"I hadn't given any thought to that, sir."

The General looked wisely at his Chief of Staff. "Well," he said. "They're demons, all of them, and they're going to be struck down like demons and it will be in November. So, we'll name it OPLAN NOVEMBER DEMON."

The chief of staff nodded and smiled. "That's good, sir," he said.

"Yes," the General beamed. "Operation November Demon. I like that. What about you, Herbert? You like that?"

"Yes, sir," I said grinning. "I like that a lot."

I called in the agents and ordered the extra chemical grenades and the extra troops. We all went into intensive training, awaiting the day when the army of dissidents would storm Leavenworth Prison.

The day came. The information available said that they would form up at St. Mary's College, and the plan we had hit on called for the county and city police to pick them up there and accompany them along with forty-two state police cars to a point just short of the gate where we had laid out some strong, double-strand concertina barbed wire. It was the same kind we had used to keep the VC out of our installations around LZ English and Bong Son. Behind that wire, we stationed a company of MPs at the ready with gas masks and fully loaded weapons. Behind them, serving as back-up, were two more companies, hiding behind the hill. The General, the Chief of Staff, and I planned to be, in the General's words, "at the forward command post," about 100 yards back from the gate. All twenty-two agents would be out in the crowd, taking pictures for later identification and evidence.

Confrontation day was a Sunday, a very cold, very clear Sunday with the temperature just below freezing. When I got up that morning, Marygrace asked what I planned to wear to the wars. My usual greens, I said. They were what I wore to the office every other day. I saw no reason to change. But when I arrived at the forward command post, the General and his entire staff were in full combat regalia, binoculars and all. The General and his chief of staff also had on long green overcoats in the Rommel tradition. We had even opened up the Emergency Operations Center, that little room with all the radio equipment which is supposed to be operational in the event of nuclear attack or similar catastrophe. In order to keep our EOC open, it meant that the one in Chicago at the 5th Army Headquarters also had to be opened—and on a Sunday, too.

We started making our calls. Nobody in town could find anybody, and as time passed the state police seemed to be getting more and more irritated. Finally someone reported that a crowd of about fifty people, with a few signs, had begun a march from the vicinity of St. Mary's College. The Chief of Staff seemed relieved. "It's them," he said. "It's started." The General nodded grimly.

Suddenly, a 1951 Chevrolet broke through the gate area and went sailing past at a pretty high speed. We only got a glimpse of its occupants. They were in green fatigues, Castro beards, and Che Guevara hats. "It's them," the General shouted. "Get them!" Unfortunately he did not specify who or how many should get them, and every last MP sedan we had screamed after them in pursuit. It left us with no vehicles at all. But they got their suspects. They were five Special Forces reserve officers in from Kansas City for a parachute jump. Two of the MPs were laughing outright and the Provost Marshal took their names down in a book and said something to them before turning away with a chuckle himself.

Then, there they were. There were forty-six of them, if you

counted the twenty-two agents who were trying to hide their faces from the newspaper photographers on hand to record the event. It was just a bunch of kids who marched by the prison, sang a few stanzas of "We Shall Overcome," and then went on down to the park where they roasted a few hot dogs, drank some coffee served to them by a woman the Chief of Staff called a "damned Communist," and then went home.

The General watched it all through his binoculars. "An undetermined number," he said.

"They see our show of force and they are disbanding," said the Chief of Staff.

"Forty-six," I said. The Chief of Staff bumped me with his elbow and gave me a dirty look. The General kept the binoculars to his eyes.

"Call it off," he finally said. "Call it off, Herbert. That's it."

But, unfortunately, that wasn't it. We had opened the EOC. "What about the EOC, sir?" I asked.

"Tell General Mock at 5th Army that we were opposed by an indeterminate number who upon seeing our show of force dispersed without a confrontation or injury to anyone on either side."

"He's going to ask me how many, sir," I said. "I know General Barsanti who's with him and he knows me, and he's going to say that if I couldn't count heads then I should have counted the feet and divided by two. They're going to want to know how many."

"If he asks, give him an estimation," he said, and with that both the General and the Chief of Staff walked off. The Provost Marshal followed. Most of the nearby troops barely held their laughter until they were gone. I went back and closed the EOC. Then, Major Dick Sharpe and I sat there laughing until our stomachs were sore. There were tears streaming down our faces as we told and retold the story again, laughing harder and harder with each retelling. Finally, we had to call the Chicago EOC.

"How many?" General Barsanti asked.

"An undetermined number, sir," I replied, grinning at Dick.

"Goddamn it, Herbert," the General said. "If you couldn't count heads then you should have counted feet and divided by two. How many were there?"

"An estimated forty-six, sir."

"Plus the agents?"

"Including the agents, sir, all twenty-two of them."

"I'll be down to see your boss in the morning," he said and hung up.

Dick and I went to the officers' club and had a beer and laughed some more until it got dark and we finally went home. When I walked in, the phone was ringing. It was the General. He wanted me to report to his quarters. "In old clothes," he added.

"Maybe he wants to beat me up," I said to Marygrace as I changed.

I was ushered into the General's house by a white-coated black man.

"Uh, Herbert, you're on demolitions pay, is that correct?" the General asked.

"No, sir, not for some time."

"But you are a demolitions man, correct?"

"Yes, sir."

"Good," he said. "Well, Herbert, we have these chemical mines out there in the ground yet and with the wind shifting and all if some drunk triggers one it's going to drift right back into downtown Leavenworth. Know what I mean?"

"Sir?"

"Herbert, I want you to go out and defuse those mines."

"Sir," I complained. "That's pick-and-shovel work. I'm a lieutenant colonel. We have privates who—"

"We have no one else," he interrupted.

"I'll need some help, sir."

"We couldn't get a volunteer."

"Just to hold the flashlight."

"Uh, look Tony," he said. It was the first time he'd ever called me by my first name. It was also the last time. "Maybe you could get someone, huh?"

I looked at him standing there on a huge Persian rug in the center of his grand dining room. He seemed a little less than a general to me.

"I guess I can find someone, sir," I finally said. "May I have the safety pins for the mines?"

"The aide lost them," he said, looking as though he had just been caught urinating on himself.

"Oh, well, that's alright. I'll use commo wire, sir." I said. I wanted only to get out of there quick before I started laughing again. I couldn't wait to tell Sharpe.

At first, I thought of my wife as the flashlight holder, but finally ended up with the young son of a neighbor to whom I paid a few bucks for the great privilege of shining a light on the fuses.

OPLAN NOVEMBER DEMON had ended.

As Operations Officer, the job I'd inherited from the ailing Colonel Jenkins, I was exposed to one of the more interesting facets of the vast workings of the U.S. Army. It was OPLAN MISSOURI. The first and perhaps most essential part of the plan was a telephone call every single morning from the post to Independence, Missouri to determine the health and disposition of former President Harry S Truman. If the call ascertained that he was in good health and spirits, then the hundreds of people involved in OPLAN MISSOURI relaxed for the rest of the day, because the plan was essentially the master blueprint for Mr. Truman's funeral.

All over Kansas, Nebraska, Oklahoma, and Missouri, scores and scores of lieutenant colonels and majors had been on a steady standby for several months—and for all I know are probably still on standby. Moreover, every automobile dealer within a hundred miles was committed to providing scores and scores of shining new sedans. The officers were on tap as escorts to Congressmen who would be expected to come to the old man's funeral, and the cars, of course, were to be their transportation. It was one hell of a job keeping track of the men and the vehicles, not to mention the ever-changing roster of scores and scores of enlisted men as drivers. Every once in a while, one of the Congressmen would call on us to complain that according to information provided to him by his friends in the military, the car being reserved for him was not commensurate with his standing as a servant of the people and a member of that august body. "You've got me down for a Chrysler and I hear that you've got Congressman Witherspoon in a Lincoln," they would say. Or sometimes the gripe would be that the aide assigned to them was not befitting their own importance. "I've got a major and you've given Congressman So-and-So a colonel," they would say. "Do you think that's fair?"

Day after day, the plans were always changing. Once a week,

428

the manifest of automobiles had to be reconfirmed as well as the availability of the drivers. If anyone went on leave, he was automatically and immediately replaced, and if one of the dealers happened to sell one of the cars on reserve—they had all agreed not to do that, but you know how car dealers are—then we had to make those changes too.

But by far the most critical part of the plan was the route of the funeral through downtown Kansas City. That precise part of the plan came from Mr. Truman himself. He said he wanted it to go down this street and up that one and pause here and end up there. It was so intricate and Mr. Truman was so adamant on the route that the city fathers, after considerable argument and no little consternation, finally agreed to remove one complete traffic island from one of the downtown thoroughfares. It seemed that since the caisson bearing the body would be pulled by Army horses, and the entire rig was so unwieldy, the parade would have to be as straight and direct as possible. At first it was suggested that a small wooden bridge be constructed over the traffic island, but since there would be such short notice before it would be needed, and because horses have a habit of shying away from walking on wood, that was abandoned. As a last resort, the traffic island was simply removed.

In December, 1969, I received word that my request for the removal of Barnes's and Franklin's efficiency report from my files had been denied. I was still running up the phone bills and the airlines were getting rich from me, but the lawyers at Leavenworth were still telling me that I didn't have enough as yet. When the time for regular Army promotions came up, I was told that because of the efficiency report and because I was dealing in war crimes, I could not be promoted. That didn't bother me. I hadn't expected to be promoted. Nor did it bother me when they transferred me back to Georgia again, this time to Ft. McPherson where the commanding officer, Lieutenant General Albert Connor, an old friend of Westmoreland from West Point, could keep an eye on me. Connor, who has since retired, was commander of the 3d Army. My job at McPherson would be in the recruiting program for the 3d Army, with special emphasis on re-enlistments. Marygrace and I were really happy to get back to the South. We'd always liked it ever since our days in Columbus, Dahlonega, and

Athens. We bought a house with a pool in an Atlanta suburb and settled down, as much as we could.

Having been back in the States for more than a year and still not seen any progress on the war crimes investigations, I went to see a civilian lawyer. Charles L. Weltner, a former Congressman who was handling one of the My Lai cases, told me I could file charges in federal court. Before I did that, I told him, I wanted to let my superiors at Ft. McPherson known what we were planning. I was intent on being as open with the thing as possible. General Connor's Adjutant General, Colonel Fred Hansard, asked me not to go the Federal court route but to stay inside the Army as long as I could so that it would be handled properly and privately.

I told Weltner about his advice and he said it wouldn't hurt to give it one more try. I'd already been to the legal people in Saigon and Long Binh and Leavenworth and hadn't gotten anywhere, but I was willing to make one more effort. I reported to the Inspector General at Ft. McPherson and, to my surprise, he turned the problem over to the Department of the Army's Criminal Investigation Division. More than a year after coming home from Vietnam, more than a year after having been relieved of my command, more than a year after having reported war crimes to my superior officers—after losing a promotion to regular army major and the subsequent reserve promotion to colonel, after spending $8,000 of my family's money, after getting cheated out of a slot at the Command and General Staff College, and finally, after threatening to go to federal court with my problem—the United States Army responded.

I know now that it wasn't just the Army. It was General Westmoreland in particular. He tried to do everything he possibly could to keep my case covered up and out of the public's attention because of the heat then being placed on the Army from the My Lai cases. The Army itself had already discovered that there had been a systematic cover-up of the massacre by Calley and the others at My Lai. Westmoreland certainly could not afford to have similar charges coming up in public right on the heels of My Lai.

Moreover, my case had some special embarrassments connected with it. In the first place, General Barnes's immediate superior during the period when I reported the crimes was Lieutenant General William Peers, and it was General Peers who was selected to head the Army's board of inquiry into the question of whether or not there had been a cover-up at My Lai. That raised an interesting possibility: if my charges ever really got out into the open and General Barnes were asked if he had reported to General Peers what I had reported to him, and Barnes said yes, where the hell would the Army be then? But there was another aspect that must have had Westmoreland worried. Colonel J. Ross Franklin was one of the members of the Peers Commission. General Peers had hand-picked him, and had gone before Congress especially to ask that he be approved as a member because of his special expertise in airborne fighting and his familiarity with that particular part of Vietnam. My God! Of all people to serve on a board instructed to investigate war crimes and to judge whether or not the Army had handled them well. The report of the Peers Commission had been kept secret since it was written—or most of it had, anyway—but Seymour M. Hersh somehow got a copy, and that's how we found out what else the commission discovered besides the My Lai cover-up.

During the My Lai investigation, according to the Peers report, one witness was recalling how a woman was shot after she had ignored an order to halt. Franklin interrupted by saying, "Well, can you think of a better way to stop people that are running than doing that?"

In short, what the Army faced was my insistence that I had reported war crimes to the direct subordinate of the man who was investigating the cover-up. Westmoreland's first move was to appoint Major Carl Hensley to conduct the Department of the Army Criminal Investigation Division Agency (DACIDA) investigation. The very first time I met Hensley he said he was out to prove that I was a liar. I wasn't particularly shocked. Having served under Franklin was perfect training for that sort of thing. In fact, there were moments during that period in my life when I considered suspect almost anyone who seemed to believe me or to indicate that he trusted me. I told Hensley that whatever he had in mind was all right with me. I was questioned by the investigators in November, 1970, and then heard nothing for several weeks. Finally, I was told the thing would be finished by Christmas, but then January passed, and February, and still nothing. I was getting a bit edgy. On March 10, 1971, I flew to Washington from Atlanta to talk with Major Hensley again. Surprisingly enough, as the investigation had gone on, with my being called back to Washington again and again to make statements before the CID, the Major and I had become fairly friendly. He was a quiet, introspective man, always courteous and always with a rather quizzical expression on his face. But my patience was wearing thin that day, and I rather exploded when I saw him.

"When are you going to finish this damned thing?" I said. "Give me a date."

Hensley stared at me, quizzically as usual. "You think we're stalling to let the statute of limitations run out against the general and the colonel, don't you," he said.

"You said it, Carl, not me, but it's exactly what I think. And what I'll prevent, by filing formal charges, then you can take as long as you want, okay?"

I returned to Atlanta, went to the Judge Advocate General's office, and after several delays—they couldn't find a typist, they couldn't stay after four-thirty on a Friday afternoon, they couldn't do this or they couldn't do that—I filed the following charges against General Barnes:

Specification One: In that Major General John W. Barnes did, at LZ English, Bong Son, Republic of Vietnam, on or about the month of January, 1969, violate a lawful general regulation, to wit: Paragraph 5, MACV Directive 20–4, dated 27 April, 1967, by failing to report to his commanding general and to Headquarters, Military Assistance Command, Vietnam, incidents and other acts thought or alleged to be war crimes and probable war crimes, to wit: the intentional physical abuse upon Vietnamese detainees by U.S. personnel at An Khe, Republic of Vietnam, on or about the month of January, 1969.

Specification Two: In that . . . Barnes . . . did violate a lawful general regulation . . . by failing to report incidents and other acts thought or alleged to be war crimes and probable war crimes, to wit: the intentional infliction of death and/or injury upon Vietnamese detainees by ARVN troops under the direction and control of U.S. personnel in Cu Loi, Republic of Vietnam, on or about February 14, 1969.

Specification Three: In that . . . Barnes . . . did violate a lawful general regulation . . . by failing to report incidents and other acts thought or alleged to be war crimes and probable war crimes, to wit: the intentional looting and pilfering by ARVN personnel, under the control and direction of U.S. personnel at a hamlet in the vicinity of Cu Loi, Republic of Vietnam, on or about early March, 1969.

The other three specifications charged the General with dereliction of duty in failing to ensure a proper, thorough, and impartial investigation for each of the allegations I'd made: the abuse of detainees at An Khe, the killings at Cu Loi, and the looting of the hamlet.

On the same day, March 15, 1971, I charged Franklin with fourteen separate specifications. They included a failure to report to his commanding general and to Headquarters, Military Assistance Command, Vietnam, the following incidents: the intentional mutilation of a Vietnamese corpse by U.S. personnel at Bong Son (this was the Christmas card incident) during or about the month of December, 1968; the intentional murder of a Vietnamese detainee by U.S. personnel near Bong Son (this was the execution ordered on the phone by the lieutenant); the St. Valentine's Day murders at Cu Loi; the water torture by U.S. personnel; the looting by the ARVN troops; the electrical torture of the girl by the Military Intelligence people at Bong Son; and the torture of the detainees by ARVN people with bamboo flails at Bong Son.

The other seven specifications, as in my specifications against the General, charged a dereliction of duty in Franklin's failure to ensure that an investigation be conducted into each of the incidents reported.

When a letter from Captain Sisler arrived in Atlanta, I recalled General Peers's letter of commendation to me and at last figured out what had been puzzling me about it. Mason Sisler was an Army careerist. He had worked in the 173d in 1969 and a part of his tour had overlapped my own. I had met him since we had both returned and we had discussed casually and briefly some of our common experiences, as well as the problems I was having getting anything done about my allegations. His letter was brief.

Dear Sir:

My wife and I would have been honored to have stayed at your home last September. The only excuse for not writing a letter of regrets is basically a series of military complications as I know you will understand. My wife constantly asks if I have written you. I continually answer the same: I haven't had time. (That is the truth, sir.) I heard a news report tonight on AFVN reference your preferral of charges against M/G Barnes and Franklin. It is my thought, off 15 months in the 173d, that I wish to remind you of my past positions in the capacities I occupied in that time. They are as follows:

1. Situation Report Writer (SITREP) to IFFV. A report used to brief Lt. Gen. Peers at that time.

2. My function required me to consolidate all spot reports over the period of each day from June 1968–March, 69. If I can be of any assistance to you, please don't hesitate to ask me.

Loyally yours,
Mason B. Sisler
CPT, In

I told Hensley about Sisler and he said they'd talk to him. More than a year later, when a television producer was researching my case and attempted to find Sisler, he was told by the Army that he had deserted from Vietnam and gone to Canada, leaving his wife and child behind in the United States.

I couldn't believe it. Sisler was a professional. I simply couldn't believe that a man of his caliber would deal with any kind of problem in that way. Desertion was not within his personality—not the desertion of the Army and not the desertion of his wife and child—unless there were extraordinary cause.

My charges got a lot of publicity, some of it national, and on March 20, 1971, the Army "flagged" my records and told me that they just might possibly charge me with a war crime myself. I was relieved to hear that. I knew I had done nothing, and I also knew that if it had been possible for the Army to pull off some trumped-up charge, they would have tried to do it long before now. But it was uncomfortable. Once, they talked to me about throwing Vietnamese detainees out of helicopters. No, I said, I'd never done that. I had talked about a suggested plan with Ernie Webb one day to try to frighten detainees into talking by throwing out a dummy, but I'd turned thumbs down on it and we'd never discussed it again. None of the people the CID was talking to—those who would have been in a position to verify it had I ever thrown anyone out of a bird—ever saw it happen. That's what they told the CID, and that was the end of that gambit.

Then they came to me with the incident at Ft. Bragg, the night I'd cancelled the parachute jump and had had a little set-to with Bowden. Fine, I said. It was all in the records at Bragg. Apparently they checked them, because that was the last I heard about it.

The next one was laughable. They said they had a fellow named Mike Amiorri who would testify that I had physically assaulted him and administered a severe beating. I couldn't quite place him, but the name was familiar. I sat there in a Pentagon office, looking at this guy who was looking very sternly at me—that's the way CID people always look—and trying very hard to pull back Mike Amiorri from my past. Suddenly I remembered, and I almost fell out of the chair laughing. It happened almost twenty years ago, during my first tour in the Army, at Ft. Lewis, Washington.

I was a pretty healthy kid. I weighed around 170 pounds and I had been in some pretty good scrapes back in Herminie. In those days, a boxer in the Army was given fifteen dollars for a win and five dollars for a loss. I decided that might be a good way to earn a little spending money and I went out for the boxing team. I finally learned the difference between a cross and a jab and started fighting three-rounders within the company. I won fourteen in a row, all by technical knockouts and decisions. I was moving right along when I stepped into the ring for my fifteenth fight. In the first round, the guy decked me eight times. I went down five more times in the second round and six more in the third. Once the guy hit me in the arm and knocked me down, he was so damned strong. It seemed that he was training for a crack at the 1948 Olympics. His name was Mike Amiorri. I never saw him again after that night. I did not want to ever see him again after that night.

"Okay guys," I told the CID people, "I think I'll just admit that I did beat up Mike Amiorri if you can guarantee that it gets some publicity."

Then I told them who he was and what had happened. They even got a laugh out of it, but not very much of a laugh. I think when you become a CID man, you sign a statement in which you waive your rights to laugh with much gusto.

They kept coming back at me with allegation after allegation—corporal punishment of people I commanded, war crimes, lying, stealing—but none of it was the kind of stuff I could even raise an eyebrow over. None of it was true.

In early April, the Undersecretary of the Army, Kenneth Belieu, summoned me to Washington for "just a little chat," as the invitation said, and so once again I headed north. Belieu and I were old friends. We had met in 1951. He had lost his legs in Korea and I had dedicated my book to him. It occurred to me on the plane between Atlanta and Washington that perhaps things were looking up for me with Ken Belieu in my corner. He was, after all, the kind of man who made the kind of soldier who made the kind of Army I believed in. When I walked into his office in the Pentagon that day, it was like a college reunion, all smiles and how's your family and how've you been and do-you-remember-old-what's-his-name. But when he began his discussion of my case I quickly discovered that even Ken had been touched by the disease. "Tony," he said. "I know you're telling the truth, but you've just got to let up a little for the good of the Army. We're cleaning our own linen, don't you see. We're going to take care of it. It's not going to do anybody any good for the thing to get splashed all over the country."

I wondered then if I'd made a mistake about Ken so long ago. I decided I hadn't. He was and is a good man caught up in a corrupted system. Inexplicably, I began to think about Franklin in the same way. I had never had any basic dislike toward him other than on those specific occasions when we had clashed. I had come to believe then and I do now that we were simply two totally different men. He had all of his yesterdays and I had all of mine. There was no explaining specifically why one man is the way he is; he simply is. I had always accepted Franklin as one of those Army officers who happened to be eccentric and who happened to want to be a certain way that I didn't want to be. I had seen plenty of them and I had served under them and over them and they hadn't ever worried me—even Franklin, even during those weeks when I was having frequent words with him over my allegations of atrocities. He had said he was investigating. He had said he was taking care of them. I had believed. Beyond that, I had developed a kind of confidence in the order of things that allowed me to believe that sooner or later Franklin would be taken off by General Barnes. That had always been the way it had worked out for me. When I ran into problems with a man whose eccentricities made it hard to work with him, sooner or later the Army handled him—transferred him, censured him, dealt with him in some way. I believed Barnes would do just that. I believed it until the day I was relieved, until the moment I walked into that trailer. I believed it until the second the General declined to look me in the eye and turned his face to the papers on his desk. That's when I stopped believing that Ross Franklin would be taken care of by John Barnes. I didn't know why just then, though I knew for a fact that for some reason Franklin was winning. It was with the same kind of faith that I had gone to

Ken Belieu's Pentagon office, knowing that Ken was the kind of man from whom I could expect some right responses. But Ken's Army wasn't my Army, apparently, and I left knowing there'd have to be some other way.

Shortly after I saw Belieu, Major Hensley called me and told me something very important. He said they had determined as a result of their investigation that the crimes had occurred the way I said they had. He also said he intended to get some results. He would see his immediate superior, the chief of the Criminal Investigation Division, Colonel Henry H. Tufts, and would lay it right on the line.

"You think he'll listen to you?" I asked.

"He better or—I'll get back in touch with you," Hensley said.

I have no idea what occurred when Hensley talked with Colonel Tufts. I do know that Tufts sent him to the hospital for a psychiatric evaluation. The psychiatrist who examined him asked him to come back on April 17.

On April 16, Major Hensley went into the bedroom of his home, put a shotgun to his head, pulled the trigger with his toe, and blew his head off. The Army immediately issued a statement saying that his suicide had absolutely nothing to do with the investigation he was conducting on the charges I had made. Since Hensley left nothing in the way of an explanation, determining precisely why he took his own life would seem fairly tenuous. Nevertheless the Army, while not stating why it happened, was quick to say why it had not happened. Later the Army's people in Washington suggested that Hensley was mentally unbalanced. I wonder. Wouldn't people have noticed that before in a man serving in such a sensitive, pressure-packed job, the man Westmoreland had chosen above everyone else to conduct the investigation of my allegations? How quickly the Army concluded that anyone who went against the stream was crazy. If you didn't follow the party line of the moment, you were instantly mentally unbalanced. I don't know what really happened with Carl. No one ever will. But there is a rational explanation. With that label on him— the label the Army immediately tagged him with once he started making the wrong kind of noises—he would have inevitably been passed over for promotion and eventually kicked out of the service. He would have had no retirement pay to fall back on, and with six children he would have been in one hell of a pickle. Remember, most of the time it's only the generals who walk out of the service into those corporation jobs or into the commandant slot of the military schools. Carl would have been forced back into civilian life without the means to survive economically. With no money, the children would have suffered. So I think Carl Hensley did what he believed was the most honorable thing he could do: he put himself into a position in which he could provide for his family. I think it was a choice that took strength, not weakness. I think it emanated from integrity, not mental unbalance. Alive, he was economically insolvent at a period when money was of critical importance to his family. Dead, he was worth survivors' benefits that amounted to more than $900 a month. I think his concern for the future welfare of his family tilted Carl and pushed him past the last barrier. No one will ever persuade me that the Army was not primarily responsible. I know the Army hasn't answered yet for the death of Carl Hensley, and I doubt that it ever will.

Still they kept pressing me, and the journalists who kept coming to talk to me continued to write about my charges. Suddenly General Barnes, by that time back in the country and serving in a Pentagon desk job, became available to the news people. Up until that time he had been inaccessible, except on one occasion when he told a reporter from *The New York Times* that he had never heard of any of the crimes I said I'd told him about. (That's what Yamashita, the Japanese admiral, said just before we executed him in the Philippines.) When the General finally granted a formal interview, it was with the *Arizona Republican*, Sen. Barry Goldwater's favorite newspaper. Instead of a news story, the paper chose to handle the interview with the General in a column. Among the several things that he said, according to the columnist, was that he simply could not understand a man like me who got down on the ground with his troops and went into an attack just like a trooper. The General said you had to be a killer to do that.

All of that is no doubt true. First, Barnes really didn't understand a man like me. Second, you did have to be a killer to do that. Generals aren't killers, I suppose—at least it's been my experience that they are not the kind of people who go out and actually bring direct death to people they see. All the generals see are body counts. It is not their responsibility to actually count the bodies, though. They don't have to actually go into the grass and gather together the pieces of what were once human beings.

It's easy to forget what war can be, even if you've seen it several times. I know that the horrors I saw in Korea are less horrible to me now than a few months after I saw them. Time is the marvelous healer, and the generals who were once lieutenants and captains and who once had that kind of thing in their hearts have forgotten about it by the time they get their first star. When you stay on the ground and out of those damned helicopters, you not only know the problems of your men but you recognize the basic, rather unchangeable misery of war. The General can call in a barrage of artillery fire that obliterates hundreds of men, women, and children, all without ever stepping out of his air-conditioned trailer. I never had that luxury. I have picked up the guts and the legs and the arms of people, including infants just beginning to breathe. I have smelled the stink as I gathered up the remnants of human life and deposited them in rubber bags. That is the part of war the General cannot know from the little sheet of paper that comes sliding across his desk every morning.

General Barnes called me a murderer during that interview. The columnist asked about my victims and the General said, "I can't identify."

Next they trotted out McCaan, the young lieutenant who had done so well on the sampan raid. He had made captain before leaving the Army but he surfaced again to write a letter to the Secretary of the Army stating that he was a former company commander of mine and that he had personal knowledge that I lied about body counts and beat up my enlisted men. (McCaan, although a good soldier once I got him into the field, had never been a company commander.) My only answer to McCaan's allegations was and is that if they were true—which they weren't—the Army would have had my ass for them a long, long time ago.

Back at home, it was getting harder and harder to remain one of the bunch at Ft. McPherson. Once, when I left town for an inspection trip down to Augusta, Ga., I was under surveillance the entire time.

439

I noticed it almost immediately and asked the young captain if indeed he were doing what it certainly looked like he was doing, namely keeping an eye on me? Yes, he said, and he was on orders. From whom, I asked. He wouldn't say. I didn't blame him.

In late March, a general I had known for several years called me at my home and asked that I meet him at the Ft. McPherson officers' club that evening so that we could talk. When I arrived at the club, the General was not there. I sat at the bar, drank a couple of beers, and then just waited around until the other people there began to leave. He wasn't going to show, I decided. I started out the door and ran into a visiting lieutenant colonel whose brother I had known in Germany. I asked him to stay with us at our home, but he declined and said he'd already made arrangements to spend the night at the BOQ. We shook hands and I started out the door.

"Where are you going?" he asked.

"Home."

"How? You walking?"

"Nope, my car's out here."

"There aren't any cars out there. I just came in that way," he said. "There's only one car, a Volkswagen, and some people are working on it."

"That's mine," I said, wheeling toward the door.

We walked to the car. It looked just as it had when I had parked it a couple of hours before and gone into the club. I opened the lid on the back to look at the motor, thinking perhaps that someone had removed the distributor cap as a prank. Inside I found four half-sticks of dynamite attached to twelve inches of time fuse. The fuse was attached to a match head which, in turn, was on top of the exhaust. Had I started the engine, the charges would not have detonated until I was well off the post.

I removed the dynamite and took it to the desk sergeant at the provost marshal's office on the post. He logged it in and told me that I could get a copy of the log the next morning when it was complete. When I went back the next day, I was greeted by a civilian Criminal Intelligence Division employee who acted as though I had gone crazy. "Are you sure you brought some dynamite to this office, sir," he said condescendingly. "Well, there's certainly no record of it on the log. Here, you can see for yourself." There wasn't. "Maybe you just had a bad dream, Colonel," the man said.

"Goddamn it, I didn't dream it," I said. "I'll prove it to you."
I left and went to the BOQ to get my witness from the night before.
He was gone. He does not wish now to get involved. "I have a career,
you know," he told me when I finally located him and talked with
him about it.

I found out that when the CID interviewed Franklin in connec-
tion with my charges—the interview took place in Manila, where he
was on leave from Vietnam—they had spent the bulk of their time
asking him about possible war crimes I might have committed. Franklin had been transferred out of the 173d Brigade to a combat command
of his own after I left Vietnam. He was relieved of that command soon
afterwards and wound up in the Mekong Delta, working in the
Delta Regional Assistance Command.

On July 15, 1971, Major General John H. Cushman, commander
of the Delta Regional Assistance Command, decided that based upon
the CID's investigation of my charges against Franklin, there was no
substantiation for them and dismissed them. I wasn't surprised. I
wasn't surprised by anything after Hensley's suicide and the dynamite
in my car. I wasn't surprised that an Army investigation of an Army
officer charged with a cover-up—an officer who had himself been on
the Peers commission—would produce nothing.

The dismissal of the charges came only a week after a story in
Life magazine called "Confessions of 'The Winter Soldiers.'" It contained a long interview with me in which I was highly critical of
atrocities in Vietnam committed by U.S. troops and by ARVN people
under U.S. control and direction. I told the reporter that much of what
had happened over there could be traced directly to the "failure of
command responsibility" and I also said that some of "this stuff would
stop if we'd hang a couple of senior commanders." Of course, the
Army tried to make it sound as if I was advocating that we actually
execute a couple of senior commanders, whereas I was simply making
the observation that if the Army were to get rid of them, some of the
stuff would stop—on the condition of course that the late, lamented
senior commanders were replaced by people who knew what they were
doing and who understood what command responsibility was all
about.

But that really blew it at Ft. McPherson. The phone lines from the Pentagon were red-hot, and because of the *Life* interview I became the subject of another investigation, this one headed by the Inspector General of the 3d Army. On July 27, I was called by Colonel C. W. Guelker, the chief of the investigative branch of the 3d Army's Inspector General's office, and told to report to his office in the afternoon. I asked if I might bring along a tape recorder or a secretary. He said nothing doing. I asked about the possibility of being accompanied by an attorney. That wouldn't be necessary, he said.

By that time I had made contact with Charles Morgan, Jr., the director of the southeastern office of the American Civil Liberties Union. The repeated attempts by the Army CID to question me about the war crimes they suggested I had committed had moved me to begin thinking about some legal protection outside the Army system. I called Mr. Morgan and told him about Colonel Guelker's orders to report to his office. He assigned Morris Brown, one of his staff attorneys, to the case, but a military lawyer, Captain Dick Heintz, also in touch with Mr. Morgan, went to Guelker's office with me. The colonel did not make an issue of Dick's presence.

Guelker advised me of my rights under Article 31 and then, right out of the blue, he calmly told me that he was under orders from General Westmoreland to investigate the remarks attributed to me in the *Life* story. He said he had a series of questions to ask me, to see if "any unusual actions are warranted against you." I stopped the thing right there and told him I wanted first to confer with my attorney. He said for us to come back the next day, which we did, and he again said he was going to put a series of questions to me. Under Heintz's advice, I said I chose to remain silent and would make no statement. We figured that anything that had to be said had already been said at the three previous investigations and were on the record for Guelker's use. I requested permission to leave. Guelker pressed the issue but finally granted me leave. Three hours later, he called again and asked me to come back. Again, he pressed the questions, but I told him nothing doing and was finally permitted to leave.

I got my efficiency report for my Ft. McPherson work in recruiting and re-enlistment in early August. The total number of personnel re-enlisted in fiscal 1971 came within twenty-six of the all-time high achieved in 1964, when the 3d Army strength was more than one-third greater. My rater had this to say about me:

> Although this was his first assignment as a re-enlistment officer and a position which he did not seek, he applied himself vigorously and quickly mastered that important re-enlistment program. Lt. Col. Herbert is an experienced and highly competent officer. His background has provided a practical approach to superior supervision and guidance of administrative action. He is a sheer hardworking officer. He has an adaptable disposition and is completely cooperative which enables him to operate very efficiently. He is enterprising and energetic, gets things done quickly, a versatile thinker who achieves positive results. His superb educational background is utilized to the fullest in the practical solution of daily problems. He is a very personable officer who gets along well with his subordinates and his superiors. He and his wife gracefully enter the activities of the community.

Once again, I was rated in the top 5 per cent of all the officers in the Army, but I got a very low score on tact and selflessness because of all my trips to Washington. Selflessness is defined on the efficiency report as that trait in a man which allows him to "subordinate his personal welfare to that of the organization."

On Labor Day, a story written by Jim Wooten appeared in *The New York Times Magazine*, and the next night Wooten appeared on the Dick Cavett Show in New York City and discussed my case. A couple of weeks later, I accepted an invitation to appear on the same show. On the program, I talked to Mr. Cavett simply about what I'd seen and knew to be facts. At Mr. Morgan's advice, I stayed away from rumor and hearsay. The Army flipped. More strange things began to happen, including my transfer from the re-enlistment program to the glorious job of assistant director of industrial operations for Ft. McPherson. Like the Deputy Chief of Staff of the Capitol Military Assistance Command, it was a shelf-job, a pretend slot. Even what little work I did was make-do, except for the first day. One of the duties of the industrial operations department is to supervise the mortuary, and there hadn't been a death on post in ages. The night I took the new job, a WAC committed suicide, and I spent the next day making funeral arrangements. But most of the time, I did nothing except make the short drive from my house to the post and the office, sign in, take a seat at my desk and a book from the drawer, and spend the day catching up on my reading. It was a luxury I had not been able to afford for several months, but thanks to Connor and Hansard, I was knocking off about a book a day. There were several more trips to Washington, including one on which I spoke with some members of Congress. That one was duly noted by the Army. The people on the Hill that I spoke with were immediately contacted by the Army's congressional liaison officer and asked the nature and content of our conversations.

In August, my Army attorney was asked by Colonel Felix Millhouse, the chief investigating officer for the Military District of Washington, if I would submit to a lie detector examination that would focus on two questions: whether I reported the murders at Cu Loi to Franklin and whether I subsequently asked Barnes to initiate an investigation into those murders. Morgan and my military lawyer, Captain Heintz, agreed to the polygraph and then got together with the Army people on the man who would administer the test. The expert chosen was Benjamin F. Malinowski, a retired Army Chief Warrant Officer who had served as a senior instructor at the U.S. Army Military Police Polygraph School at Ft. Gordon, Georgia, for four years. He had graduated from the same school in the early 1960s, had taken additional training and graduated from the National Training Center of Lie Detection, as well as completing the Polygraph Transition Course and the Polygraph Personnel Screening Course conducted by the Army. In short, he was an Army polygraph expert, recognized as such by the Army and in civilian life as well.

A date was set for my test. The only point remaining was my lawyer's request that Barnes and Franklin be given similar tests. At first the Army agreed, but two days later they told us that Franklin and Barnes had refused to be tested. I agreed to take the test regardless. Arrangements were made to fly us up to Washington, but the day before we were due to go the Army called the whole thing off for the second time. My lawyers then simply hired Malinowski, the same man the Army had agreed upon, to give me the test anyway and submitted a copy of his report to the Army.

444

Lt. Col. Herbert voluntarily submitted to polygraph testing. His voluntariness was accomplished in writing.

Instrument utilized during the testing was a Stoelting Four Pen Polygraph Model #601.

The Polygraph test question technique utilized was the Zone of Comparison Technique.

The following relevant questions, answered with a "Yes" by Lt. Col. Herbert, were asked:

(1) Did you on or about February 14, 1969 advise Col. Franklin of the killing of Vietnamese detainees? Answer: Yes.

(2) On or about April 4, 1969 did you personally request Gen. Barnes to conduct an investigation? Answer: Yes.

Lt. Col. Herbert did not exhibit any specific responses indicative of deception when he answered the aforementioned relevant questions. It is the opinion of this examiner that Lt. Col. Herbert was truthful when he answered the relevant questions with a "Yes."

The tempo was increasing. They began harassing me like a West Point plebe. Colonel John Reid called me in one morning and gave me a lesson in saluting. I had just turned to leave his office, after snapping off what I thought was a sufficiently sharp salute. He called me back and asked where I'd learned to salute like that. "In the United States Army, sir," I said. He then had me salute over and over again, giving me instructions each time. "Tilt your hand, Colonel," he said, and I tilted my hand. "A little higher, Colonel," he said. It went on like that for several minutes. I came out of his office as one of the best damned saluters in the Army.

In early October, I discovered that a sergeant in my office, at the request of Lieutenant Colonel Paulk, the Director of Industrial Operations and my immediate superior, had been keeping a detailed log on my comings and goings. The paper on which he kept the record was taped to the sliding panel in his desk. I peeled the tape away, took it to the sergeant, and asked him why he was doing it. He confirmed that Paulk had directed him to do so. I then took the paper to my military attorney, Captain Heintz, and he immediately xeroxed it. Later in the day, we had a confrontation in the office of the post commander, Colonel Hawley. There were some heated exchanges, including one in which Colonel Oliver, the acting Staff Judge Advocate, suggested that I had no need for Heintz, even though he had been serving as my lawyer for the previous six months. I mentioned the possibility that I might file charges against Paulk for spying on me under Article 138, and the matter of the lawyer was not mentioned again.

The next day, Heintz talked with Mrs. Ruby Jones, a civilian worker in the office of industrial operations, and learned that she had overheard Paulk giving the sergeant his instructions on how to monitor my activities. According to her, Paulk had told the sergeant that he wanted him to keep track of every time I left the office, where I went, and how long I was gone. Heintz asked her if she had received the impression that Paulk was interested in recording my leave time, which was the explanation Paulk had given to Colonel Hawley. No, she said, it did not pertain to leave. Later that day, Heintz asked Mrs. Jones to come up to his office and talk about the matter and a few minutes later Colonel Reid, the deputy post commander and the same fellow from whom I had received my saluting lesson, called Heintz and told him that Mrs. Jones did not wish to speak with him at all. Heintz called Mrs. Jones again, but Paulk was eavesdropping on the telephone line and told him that Mrs. Jones could not speak with him, a point repeated even more sternly to Heintz that afternoon by Colonel Reid. Mrs. Jones was present then and Heintz asked her if it was indeed true that she did not want to talk with him. Yes, she said.

Eavesdropping on my telephone lines was not uncommon at Ft. McPherson. Neither was the unauthorized opening of my personal mail, including letters from members of Congress who had taken an interest in my case. Some of the mail was inconsequential, of course, but I was getting dozens of letters every day as a result of the story in *The New York Times Magazine* and my appearance on the Dick Cavett Show, and I was pretty ticked off about the fact that these people couldn't write to me with any assurance of privacy in their communications. I expressed that complaint to Paulk, to Hawley, and to Reid. They did not seem to consider it important.

What they did consider important at Ft. McPherson was keeping me busy with such monumentally important tasks as counting the tombstones in the army cemeteries. There were other little inconveniences. I would arrive home in the afternoon, change from my uniform into civilian clothes, and the telephone would ring and I would be asked to report back to the post in a hurry. I would reverse the dressing process, drive back to the post and report in, only to be asked what I had done with a particular document. That happened several times. I finally talked with Mr. Morgan, my civilian lawyer, about it. He decided that every time I was called back to the post from my home, I should have an attorney with me. He placed two of his staff lawyers on a twenty-four-hour alert for that task.

But there was nothing Morgan could do about my new neighbor. He was a CID man who moved in during the height of my problems with the Army. Every time I had a visitor that spring and summer and fall, he began to mow his lawn. Rain or wet grass, he was out in his yard, always humming along my property line. One afternoon when Dr. and Mrs. Yancey Beamer were visiting us, he removed a camera from beneath his jacket and began photographing their car, as he had done when other visitors had parked in front of our house. Mrs. Beamer came in the house, took a camera from their bags, and went outside to photograph him.

On September 15, the Army dismissed my charges against General Barnes on the grounds that there was insufficient evidence to continue the investigation or to recommend a court-martial. Throughout the affair, the Army had acted in secret. Barnes and Franklin had been investigated by the Army to determine if there was enough evidence to bring them to an Army trial, and the Army decided there was not. This was no great surprise to me, but what did seem extraordinary was that after repeated interrogations by the CID and after the Army refused to prosecute Barnes and Franklin on the charges I swore were true, I was not charged with making a single false statement. There were a lot of inconsistencies in their testimony—including cases which I was able to document as perjury—but the Army let them pass. When I pointed them out and filed an official allegation, I was told by Army people in Washington that there was indeed proof of false swearing. "But," they said, "we're not going to do anything about this, Herbert, because these men are going to be tried for war crimes anyway. If you charge them with false swearing it would be like having someone already convicted of rape charged with indecent exposure." When the war crimes cases were dismissed against them, I asked again about the cases of false swearing. "Well, the statute of limitations has expired on those," they said. "Sorry."

It was over.

In mid-October, the Army notified me that my request for the deletion of the adverse efficiency report given me by Barnes and Franklin had been "reviewed comprehensively again" and that the Secretary of the Army had decided to remove the report and all related correspondence from my official records. The period of December 13, 1968 to April 4, 1969 would be, they said, non-rated and "since the removal of the efficiency report constitutes a material change in your official records, they have been referred for whatever promotion reconsideration is appropriate."

Just like that—no official battalion command, no official controversy, no official records. That whole period in my life had been declared officially nonexistent and the embarrassment to the Army of ever having to explain it was eliminated. Perhaps I was to be rewarded with a promotion. It was like Father Kelley's magic ink again. He had made me three years older; the army had simply taken a few months from my life, classified them as "non-rated," and consequently removed them from any official record.

The Army explained it this way in a fact sheet issued on November 5, 1971, which said in part:

> While this review centered on Herbert's relief from command and one particular efficiency report, the Secretary also considered the matter within the broader framework of LTC Herbert's many years of service; and he bore in mind that this efficiency report, covering only fifty-eight days of duty, might have reflected an unfortunate exception to the record of otherwise effective service. As a result of this review and with the recommendation of the Chief of Staff, Secretary Froehlke directed that the efficiency report in question be removed from LTC Herbert's file. Secretary Froehlke was able to make this decision without reference to the war crimes and atrocity allegations and charges leveled by LTC Herbert since these allegations and charges were not mentioned anywhere in the voluminous file of material associated with LTC Herbert's relief nor with his efficiency report.

On October 22, Secretary Froehlke concurred with a promotion board's recommendation that I be promoted to Regular Army major, the President made the nomination to the U.S. Senate—and presto, the whole matter was resolved. Without the promotion, I would have been forced out of the Army. With it, I would have been able, under a Federal law, to remain on active duty.

I took comfort in that little fact sheet, despite its being crammed full of misstatements, factual errors and plain untruths. It contained the Army's first public admission that what I had said I had told Barnes and Franklin—and some of the other allegations I had made—were true.

With regard to the allegation that ARVN people had looted a village, the Army had this to say:

> Two American officers stated that they witnessed the looting by Republic of Vietnam (RVN) Regional Forces from Tam Quan District during March, 1969. There was contemporaneous inquiry by the 173d Brigade into this incident. The inquiry made clear that as a result of an American officer's actions, the looted items were returned to the Vietnamese villages at that time.

The American officer was Ernie Webb, who happened to be flying over the village at the time of the incident, landed, and made sure the stuff was returned after a near altercation with the American captain who was with the ARVNs as an advisor. I reported the incident to Franklin, exactly as the regulations said I should. Franklin told me to submit Ernie Webb for a court-martial or some other kind of discipline. The fact sheet says that American officers took care of the situation and that, I suppose, is meant to imply that everything was handled satisfactorily. But the truth of the matter is that the officers were mine, and I was told to punish them for their actions.

Moreover, the Army's fact sheet explained that the American captain on hand that day as an advisor did not have command authority over the Vietnamese unit. This is pure nonsense. Anybody who has ever served in Vietnam realizes that although the American may be called an advisor, what he actually is is the boss. He commands. He is told to command by his own superiors. If he doesn't command, he gets his ass chewed. Nevertheless, all of that is really rather moot because the Geneva Conventions, to which the United States is a signatory, require that we deal with war crimes committed not only by soldiers wearing the uniform of our country but by allied personnel as well. We are bound by the Conventions to apprehend the offenders and turn them over to their government for trial—or as a last resort, prosecute and try them ourselves. But in its fact sheet the Army neatly sidesteps that entire point by simply stating that "since all offenders were Vietnamese nationals, the results of the USACIDA investigation were transferred to the U.S. Military Assistance Command, Vietnam, for forwarding to appropriate RVN officials." What the hell good could that possibly do now, years after the fact and the event? There's another question here, too: who knows whether the U.S. Military Assistance Command, Vietnam, actually did turn the matter over to the Vietnamese officials? I've never seen anything that would document that transfer and neither has anybody else who was involved in this case and requested official permission to read such documents.

With regard to the St. Valentine's Day murders at Cu Loi, the Army told the American public that it had determined on the basis of its investigation that:

> Four individuals were located who claim witnessing the execution of detainees by the Vietnamese police on 14 February, 1969, but no one could substantiate the execution of the female detainee. The lieutenant advisor who accompanied the Vietnamese unit denies seeing or hearing about any detainee killings.

Right there is one of the larger surprises of the Vietnam war. The American lieutenant says he didn't see or hear anything that day. Did the Army expect that he would sit down and write out a confession for them? What the Army is saying in essence is that a lieutenant colonel and four other eyewitnesses are wrong about the four murders and the lieutenant who was implicated in the deaths was right. Their contention that "no one can substantiate the execution" of the woman is more of the same kind of hogwash. I can. I saw it with my own eyes. I saw that guy pull that knife across her throat, I saw the blood spurt, and I saw her crumple to the sand. I saw it, and two American helicopter pilots and one of my sergeants have made sworn statements that they saw it. What does the Army want? A videotape? Why not go to court and prosecute either the young lieutenant or me and find out the truth once and for all?

The Army contends in its fact sheet that I could not possibly have reported the St. Valentine's Day killings to Franklin because he was on his way back from R and R in Hawaii at the time. "A check of hotel records in Honolulu confirms that Colonel Franklin was registered until 7:30 p.m. on 14 February, 1969, or 3:30 p.m., 15 February, Vietnam time. Because of this distance between Vietnam and Hawaii, Colonel Franklin could not have returned to brigade headquarters before 16 February 1969." Which is for the birds. Franklin was in Vietnam. Eyewitnesses can substantiate that, including Ernie Webb, my pilot Larry Pippen, and several others. The receipt he produced from the Ilikai Hotel was signed by his wife. Did Franklin, an airborne colonel, just stand by while his wife handled the payment of their hotel bill? It doesn't add up. You're on R and R, and the wife joins you. Five days later you head back to Vietnam and your unit, and your wife, as many of them do, stays on for a day or two. But Franklin was damned well in Vietnam that day, and he was telling me to forget about the murder of defenseless Vietnamese detainees.

The Army dismissed the matter in this way: "The American advisor did not have command authority over the South Vietnamese unit. Since all alleged offenders were Vietnamese nationals . . ." etc., etc., etc.

But there was no passing the buck possible on my allegations that American personnel had tortured the girl in the MI room with their hands and electricity, and my charges that Vietnamese had used bamboo flails on Vietnamese girls while in the American military intelligence compound at Bong Son. The Army says these investigations are still pending, but no one has explained why, if those investigations are still in the works, the charges against Barnes and Franklin were dropped. If the thing is still going on, how could they promote Barnes from Brigadier General to Major General? Those crimes took place within sight of his trailer. I told Franklin about them. He and Barnes both deny any knowledge of them.

On the water-torture in the field, the Army's fact-sheet reported that it had located witnesses to the event—two men who admitted that they had used the water-torture—but both had returned to civilian life. The important fact, though, is that they weren't in civilian life when I made the allegations. They were still in the Army, and one of them was a career soldier, a sergeant first class. I believe the Army let those men out to prevent having to charge them. I can assure you that in my case, if the Army could have found anything, even the slightest little thing, to charge me with, I never would have been allowed to say goodbye.

I finally agreed to let my allegations on the Christmas card drop, but the Army's fact sheet said that indeed such a card had been prepared but that it was merely a thoughtless act and not a violation of the law of war. The captain responsible for the card was reprimanded, the Army said—and that was that.

The last allegation I made was the abuse of the detainees in An Khe that occurred when I was IG. The Army said the Brigade had run an investigation on that and had determined that there was not enough evidence to substantiate my allegations, and that they had been unable to make any positive identification of the people I'd accused. The Army decided in its later inquiry that there wasn't enough evidence to impugn the findings of the original investigation—conducted, incidentally, by a major whose efficiency report was written by the lieutenant colonel who would have been charged if that investigation had been conducted honestly. But interestingly enough, Colonel Felix Millhouse, who was handling the later inquiry for the Army, showed me and Captain Heintz, my military lawyer, the statements of the witnesses. Their statements, of course, included denials that they had beaten the detainees. They said they merely "tapped them in the mouth too hard with our fists." They admitted they "kept them on their feet all night" and "abused them to prime them for interrogation in the morning." The detainees did require medical attention, the statements said, but they did not receive any because, as the interrogators put it, "They didn't ask."

The score was impressive—at least I thought so. I had made eight allegations and all of them had been proved, including the one I later dropped. The Army's fact sheet said I had made a total of twenty-one allegations. I suppose they thought that if they inflated the number and then proved that a lot of them were unsubstantiated it would look better for them. The fourteen other incidents were merely included in the investigation as a result of the CID's interviews with me. They would ask me questions about this incident or that incident and I would tell them whether I had ever heard anything about it and, if I had, exactly what I had heard.

The harassment continued. The Dick Cavett Show asked me to appear again and I agreed. I had over seventy days' leave time accumulated and I saw no problem in taking off a few days to press my case. On the day I was to appear, the Army abruptly cancelled my leave and issued an ultimatum that I would have to clear any contacts with the media in advance. I started all over again, reacting to a new order cut for my benefit which forbade frequent short-term leaves. Throughout that day I applied for leaves of varying durations: five days, two weeks, three weeks, thirty days, sixty days, and finally all of it. All my requests were turned down.

At the same time, I was talking with the Cavett people, not knowing whether or not I was going to be able to make an afternoon flight to New York City, where the show was taped at 6:30 p.m. Finally, they decided that if it came to that, they could produce the show with me in an Atlanta television studio and Mr. Cavett in the New York City theater where the show originates. Fine, I said, except for one little problem. I still did not have permission to appear on the show.

I received a call from the post a half hour or so before I was to have been at the Atlanta studio to appear on a split-screen hook-up. I was told to come to the post in about twenty minutes to pick up the Army's final decision. What was it, I asked, thinking perhaps that if it were yes, then I could inform the television people and save a little time. They couldn't tell me, I was told. Just come to the base and pick up the piece of paper. I did, but I was kept waiting when I got there. The paper gave me the permission to appear on the Cavett show on that date only. The show is broadcast in the eastern time zone from 11:30 p.m. until 1 a.m. the next morning. I wasn't about to get my ass in a bigger sling because of time zones. I called the Cavett people and told them that it just wasn't going to be possible. Even if I had decided to go on the show that night, I wouldn't have been able to make it across town to the studio in time for the taping.

Later the Army said there had been no such special order on frequent short-term leaves, but sure enough on March 1, 1972, the day after I left the Army, Paragraph K of Army Regulations 630–5, as amended by General Connor a couple of days before I was scheduled to appear on the Cavett show for the second time, was rescinded. It read:

> Leave-approving authorities will insure that personnel do not abuse leave entitlements. Repetitive leaves of four days' duration in a calendar week (Monday through Thursday) or frequent one-day leaves commencing on Monday or Thursday are considered abuses of the intent of leave policies and will not be permitted. An occasional leave of this type or duration used as a means to resolve personal problems is considered proper and may be allowed.

It became known at Ft. McPherson as the Herbert Paragraph. I guess I should have been honored. I wasn't. Nothing was very funny in those days. The pressure was building on the Army, and they relieved a bit of it by harassing my family.

Once Colonel Paulk called the house at 6:30 a.m. My daughter answered. He asked if I were at home. She replied that I was not but was expected later in the morning. "That's strange," the good colonel said, "because he got on a plane for Atlanta hours ago."

She was upset. So was my wife. Later in the morning, he called again. I still wasn't home. "Have him call if he gets home," Colonel Paulk said. "He's AWOL."

On another day, Colonel Reid, my saluting instructor, called my home while Captain Heintz, my military lawyer, was there. Marygrace answered the phone. He asked if I was there. By now it had gone on too long. No, she fibbed. "Well, have him call as soon as he arrives," Colonel Reid said. I called immediately. "No, Herbert, I didn't call you," he said. "Maybe your wife's cracking up."

I told him she wasn't cracking up and I said that if there were any harassment to be handed out the Army should focus its venom on me and not Marygrace and Toni. Reid said, "If you'd just forget about Dick Cavett and *Life* magazine and all the rest, you wouldn't have to worry about your wife and kid."

I still thought I could withstand anything they wanted to dish out, but I wasn't sure my family could, nor did I have any intention of subjecting them to such trash. On November 7, 1971, a beautiful winter Sunday in Atlanta, I announced through my ACLU attorneys that I had decided to retire from the Army. This was the statement I dictated:

> On the field of battle, both as an enlisted man and as an officer, I have served to the best of my ability. In that service, I have been shot five times and bayoneted three times, none of which was as painful to me as the decision I must now announce.
>
> For two and a half years I have struggled to help the Army eliminate the stigma of the concealment of war crimes I personally saw or had knowledge of.
>
> Due to the recent actions of the President and the Secretary of the Army which have eliminated those blots which others have attempted to place upon my record, I am now eligible for retention and continued service.
>
> During the last twenty years, I have served my country in every one

of its military crises. During each tour of duty, my wife, Marygrace and our 12-year-old daughter, Toni-Junell, have accepted the uncertainties of combat and a military career.

The strain of the last two years and the pressures placed upon our family during the last week have proved intolerable.

I have been advised this weekend by Marygrace's personal physician, an old and dear friend, that the stress placed upon us can no longer safely be borne by my family.

Additionally, the actions taken by certain members of the Army at both the local and the Pentagon level have convinced me that to continue seeking correction within the military would be useless.

Tomorrow, November 8, 1971, I intend to:

(1) Advise the Army of my intention to retire on February 29, 1972.

(2) Apply for leave status so that I may remove my wife and daughter from the strain to which they have been subjected through me. Additionally, I must plan for adjustment to civilian life and the beginning of a new career.

(3) Advise the Army that while I am still in its services I have no present intention of violating those restrictions which have been placed on me, which forbid me to state my views to the media, although I do believe the public has every right to know what is happening in the Army. I have therefore instructed my attorney to advise the media (both Army-approved and -disapproved) that under the present circumstances I cannot see them.

I have much to be thankful for.

I have received support from old and new friends inside the Armed Forces.

I have found a willingness on the part of the media, from Dick Cavett to local news reporters, to fight for my rights as well as their own.

And the American people and many of their representatives in Congress have come to my assistance.

But most of all I have my wife Marygrace and my daughter Toni-Junell to thank for their continued support over the years and now.

Thus, I end a career.

Nearly four months later, I stood in that office with Lieutenant Colonel Schneider and watched the spring from the broken ball-point pen fly across the room. I looked up from the pile of retirement papers and noticed that Schneider was grinning. It was a wary, nervous grin, but a nice one nevertheless.

"Guess what?" he said.

"What?"

"They're going to blame that on me," he said. "Whatever goes wrong with this entire operation of your retirement, they're going to blame it on me."

"Don't sweat it," I said. "If you get in trouble, call me. I know some good lawyers."

He laughed and I joined him. Then the little room was quiet and we both just stood there for a moment, our hands down at our sides. Finally, he reached into his shirt and pulled out another pen and handed it to me.

I leaned over the desk and signed my name, again and again until the lines were all filled. I straightened up and turned to Schneider. He saluted sharply, and then extended his hand.

"Good luck, Tony."

"Thanks," I said. "I'm going to need it. It's been a long time since I was a civilian."

"You can make it," he said.

"Yeah," I said. "But who wants to make it as a civilian?"

I walked down the hall, through the door and out into the brisk morning. The flag was still snapping in the breeze. I drove away.

Appendix

Statements and Testimony Related to the Service of LTC Anthony B. Herbert with the 173d Airborne Brigade in Vietnam.

A. Statement by Colonel B. F. Delamater (Activities of LTC Herbert as IG, 173d Airborne Brigade).

B. Testimony of Colonel Ross Franklin at the hearing of the board of officers convened under Article 138, UCMJ to investigate LTC Herbert's relief from command of the 2d Battalion, 503d Infantry, 173d Airborne Brigade.

C. Two statements by Sergeant Major Henry Bittorie, Headquarters, 173d Airborne Brigade.

D. Statements by staff officers and NCOs, 2d Battalion, 173d Airborne Brigade.
    1) LTC Henry Boyer Jr.
    2) MSG R. L. Childers (hearing of the board of officers, Article 138 investigation)
    3) Captain Jack R. Donovan
    4) Major Francis P. Tally
    5) Captain Laurence A. Potter III

E. Statements by company commanders, 2d Battalion, 173d Airborne Brigade.
    1) Headquarters Company: Captain Szabolcs M. de Gyurky
    2) Company A: Captain L. P. Forepaugh
    3) Company B: Captain William Hill
    4) Company C: Captain Christopher J. Dorney
    5) Company D: Captain James M. Grimshaw

F. Statement by Major Leonard H. Dancheck (Conversation with Major Paul Ray regarding army policy on investigations of war crimes charges).

Appendix A. *Statement by Colonel B. F. Delamater (Activities of LTC Herbert as IG, 173d Airborne Brigade).*

1. During approximately two-thirds of the period July-December 1968, while serving as Deputy Commander of the 173d Airborne Brigade at the forward CP near Bong Son, Vietnam, I came to know LTC Anthony B. Herbert fairly well. By assignment of the Brigade Commander, Brigadier General Richard Allen, LTC Herbert worked briefly on some special projects at/near Bong Son, then became the Brigade IG with duty station at ANKHE where the Brigade's Support Battalion and numerous non-Brigade elements were located.

2. Once or twice a week COL Herbert would come to Bong Son to talk with the CG, as well as the Deputy or Executive Officer and other staff members and to handle local IG matters. On several occasions in October-November '68, GEN Allen directed fairly extensive investigations concerning alleged illegal drug usage, AWOL problems, and even activities which were closely allied to consequences of tactical operations at a fire base.

3. The nature of some of his IG official duties undoubtedly caused subsurface resentment because of the information obtained and the high standards of behavior demanded by GEN Allen, whose views were made clear by frequent discussions and memos and by staff verification. Insofar as the IG was concerned, most of the time I was available to read the draft reports or at least discuss these matters with COL Herbert before he talked with GEN Allen. The truth was not always good news but the CG quite correctly reserved for himself the authority to exercise compassion and consider the extenuating circumstances. Sooner or later, I probably knew what was reported, but on perhaps 30% of the occasions it was the Executive Officer, LTC David L. Buckner (now in USAREUR Hqs), who first discussed matters with the IG. With no questions to my knowledge, all members of the staff understood the official status of COL Herbert. I do believe a few officers considered COL Herbert somewhat aloof and brusque in his unofficial activities, but equally as many voiced admiration for his great energy and devotion to doing the job—fighting a guerrilla war all day and every day.

4. It is my opinion that GEN Allen had a very high regard for the careful, thorough, extremely vigorous and prompt actions accomplished by COL Herbert. Undoubtedly, he gave him guidance privately as was his custom with all. As I remember, it was long before mid-December when GEN Allen planned to "give" a Battalion Commanding Officer job to COL Herbert when a vacancy occurred, either upon completion of someone's normal six months command tour in this, the only US tactical airborne unit, or when combat operations might create a vacancy. Prior to that contingency occurring, to the best of my memory, it was at the request of LTC Herbert that GEN Allen did not send him to fill the first uncommitted vacancy as battalion commander. I do remember feeling relieved that the fine IG work would not be interrupted for a while. Before another command vacancy actually occurred, the General left on normal rotation, but tentative plans for COL Herbert to command a Battalion were still

planned, I think. I, too, left the unit but remained in the same geographical area where the "Brigade rear" was located (ANKHE). I continued to see LTC Herbert briefly from time to time on an unofficial basis.

5. The next Brigade Commander was another outstanding officer, Brigadier General John Barnes, but I never had reason (that I remember) to discuss with him the professional or personal qualities of LTC Herbert. Nor to my remembrance did I have reason to discuss these factors with GEN Barnes's Deputy, a COL Ross Franklin, except during an initial orientation when I undoubtedly discussed each of the main staff officers with COL Franklin a few days before GEN Barnes arrived. Both COL Franklin and LTC Herbert were very strong, outspoken individuals and both, oddly enough, were geared to a GIs viewpoint most of the time. It so happened the new Executive Officer for GEN Barnes had been around the 173d approximately a month and the S1 longer than I had. It is my guess that each of them shared my high regard for the outstanding duty performance by COL Herbert as Inspector General. If their personal opinions differed, I was unaware of it.

6. In summary, I believe LTC Herbert performed as Brigade IG exactly as his commander, Brigadier General Allen, directed; that he rapidly and tirelessly accomplished investigations which helped the Brigade far more than most people recognized; that his cases were generally well documented and did cause some officers and some EM to be punished by prescribed procedures; that the CG fully intended to put him in a battalion command position because of his demonstrated characteristics and because of awareness (in part through letters, I believe) of the previous tactical experiences of LTC Herbert as well as his current familiarity with the operational area(s) in which the 4–6 battalions operated.

Appendix B. *Testimony of Colonel Ross Franklin at the hearing of the board of officers convened under Article 138 UCMJ to investigate LTC Herbert's relief from command of the 2d Battalion, 503d Infantry, 173d Airborne Brigade.*

COL ROSS FRANKLIN *was called as a witness and testified as follows:*

RCDR: Do you swear or affirm that the evidence you shall give in this case now in hearing shall be the truth, the whole truth, and nothing but the truth? So help you God.

COL FRANKLIN: I do.

PRES: Sit down, please. The general nature of these proceedings is to investigate the complaint of Lieutenant Colonel Anthony B. Herbert, filed under the provisions of Article 138, UCMJ, alleging that he was relieved from command of the 2d Battalion, 503d Infantry, 173d Airborne Brigade by the commander without justification. These proceedings will determine the validity of that complaint and recommend redress, if appropriate, to the CG, I Field Force Vietnam who is the officer exercising general court-martial authority over the Commanding General, 173d Airborne Brigade.

In addition, because of the nature of these proceedings, the provisions of paragraph 14, AR 15–6, are applicable to you. Accordingly, as you were informed in my letter, you are entitled to have counsel present, and or consult with counsel if you so desire. Counsel may be civilian at your own expense, or military counsel of your choosing. If you desire military counsel he can be either certified under the provisions of Article 27b, Uniform Code of Military Justice, or not. Any military counsel you may request will be appointed, if reasonably available.

This is an informal investigation. I'm conducting it at various places at various times. All testimony will be taken verbatim and there will be no presentation of witnesses with respondent and counsel present. This method has been adopted because of the diversity of location of witnesses and the critical, sensitive combat mission of the unit involved, which precludes a formal board hearing.

You've read this letter. Would you like to make a statement or reply to certain questions I ask?

COL FRANKLIN: I would like to make an initial statement, which will be made rather at length, sir.

One of the bases for this is the fact that I cast aspersions upon his honesty, integrity, and loyalty. I'd like to make it a little stronger, that he's totally lacking in these virtues and in my opinion, which will be backed up by the evidence you will hear, totally unfit to be an Army officer. Related to this is his tendency for character assassination, of which I have asked witnesses to come forth and testify before you. I have heard him call the Support Battalion Commander, the

Adjutant General, the S2, company commanders, DSC winners, he has called cowards, Goddamn liars, stupid shits, totally corrupt—all of these things. All of which will be given in sworn testimony to you.

I'm also particularly concerned about the picture of me presented in this allegation. If this were true, I would not be a very good Army Officer. Because of this I would request that you would ask the witnesses coming in, most of which are Colonel Herbert's, about my reputation in the Brigade. I think it's improper for me to speak of it and if there is anything that means something to me, it is this reputation. And I would like to feel that part of the admiration, pride and affection I feel for the troops reciprocates, and I think we should call these people.

If I may just follow the format of the allegation, the request for investigation, and just make certain comments and then recommend witnesses to you. I'm trying to do this because I am the most implicated. I have attempted to get other witnesses to do most of the talking.

On page 2, reference paragraph sub 2 and sub 2 . . . Well, even before that, paragraph sub 1. Major Crouch and Colonel Angel will give testimony on these things. I have no personal knowledge of it. I would only like to say that Colonel Angel is the finest technical service officer I've ever known, and an outstanding battalion commander.

Now reference paragraph 4, the part concerning the Executive Officer . . . There were extremely strong feelings between the Executive Officer and Colonel Herbert, to the point that Colonel Bethea finally slammed down the phone and told Herbert he could not work with him. He repeatedly came to me and stated to me, "I fear if anyone gives Colonel Herbert a battalion, I fear for what will happen to this Brigade." He finally came to me, as will come out later, and said, "Colonel Herbert should not get a battalion. Because of the fact that one time I was programmed for the 2d Battalion, I ask you not to recommend me for the 2d Battalion in the event Colonel Herbert is not given a battalion." There was no question of Bethea's integrity, but he was so concerned it might be misconstrued.

Despite the fact that Herbert had been continuously involved with the staff, as future testimony will show, and despite the fact that the Executive Officer strongly recommended not giving him a battalion, I went to the Commanding General when he asked me if Herbert should get a battalion, and I said, "Yes." So despite the recommendation from the Executive Officer, other battalion commanders, I recommended to the Commanding General that Herbert be given a chance and be given a battalion. I feel that I am more responsible than any officer in the Brigade for Herbert getting a battalion. The Staff Judge Advocate will come later. He happened to be sitting out on the porch. I have a loud voice. And he will give testimony to the effect that it appeared that I was trying to convince the General to give Herbert a battalion.

Now I bring this out because on the following page in the allegations, paragraph d, he makes the statement: "There was some dickerings going on for a friend of the DCO by the DCO in order to get the friend assigned as the 2/503d CO." I have never recommended any officer to the Commanding General or to the Executive Officer since I've been in this Brigade. And contrary to the allegation, I more than any other officer am responsible for Herbert getting that battalion. And I resent that statement and it is totally false.

Reference paragraph e, this was an incident in which I was . . .

PRES: This is the so-called "General Allen investigation."

COL FRANKLIN: Yes, sir. Without exception the battalion commanders mistrusted Herbert when he was the IG. Colonel Wyand will be down here tomorrow, sir. You may talk to him. He's coming down for the Housing Conference. I talked to him long before Herbert got . . .

PRES: What was Colonel Wyand?

COL FRANKLIN: He was the battalion commander of the 4th Battalion, sir. Colonel Burke, now present Executive Officer, told me this. Basically what it was, Herbert would come down to a battalion and tell the battalion commander that nothing would be reported, that there was nothing to worry about, and this letter would come down all filled with all sorts of allegations. There will be subsequent examples of one of his IG investigations. The 1st Battalion Commander had received a very strong letter from General Barnes based on one of these IG inspections. So without exception there was very little confidence in Colonel Herbert and strong animosity generally across the board. The Artillery battalion commander, I never recall hearing say one thing or another about the IG.

When I was seated in Colonel Angel's office in the month—Whenever this was, I guess January—General Allen called Colonel Angel, the Support Battalion Commander, and he stated he had been called by his former Aide, a Lieutenant Northington, that a sergeant had made allegations that General Allen's disciplinary policies were all screwed up, and that Woodall had agreed with this and that he wanted certain documents sent to him. And he told Colonel Angel at this time: "You can tell Woodall I don't care what he thinks about my disciplinary policies." This upset me. I was wondering why Northington was calling General Allen on a confidential IG investigation. This was a confidential investigation. It was between your IG and our IG. It was not General Allen's Aide as reported in this. He was a Special Services officer and a former Aide. And Herbert got a hold of this rather immature lieutenant and had him call a general officer and give him such information that reflected improperly and unfavorably on an outstanding battalion commander, Woodall. And that's why I called Herbert up. And I told him he had exercised extremely poor judgment in doing what he had done, and that he wasn't going to screw up my battalion commanders as he had done. I used the expression, "My battalion commanders" because I have an obligation to them. But he had gotten Woodall in an awfully lot of trouble that was very unfair. And he had disclosed confidential information. And at this time he began to give me this business and he did everytime I talked to him where he was always on the side of right and justice and everybody else was wrong. And he started talking about my loyalty to General Allen and all the rest of this business, and I told him at that time, "Then you should have called General Allen." And on the report where he says . . . You have this on file up in your IG office up at IFFV, Colonel Wilson made a statement as I recall—this is by memory—that Colonel Herbert generally agreed with the allegations, with the caveat that Herbert did add that certain battalion commanders used this as a crutch for their own weaknesses. But Colonel Wilson made the statement that Colonel Herbert generally agreed with the allegation, which is a little different than the loyalty expressed here by Herbert to his former commander. The statement that I said that, "I owed General Allen nothing and to consider such loyalty necessarily foolish as I already had my efficiency report" is totally and completely false.

Reference jumping to my feet and stating that I had more university degrees and higher military decorations, this was after listening to about ten minutes of him going over his past record and how honest he was and all the integrity he had, and he had all these decorations. And I just got sick of it and I was angry. And I told him that I didn't care to hear that. I had higher decorations than he did and more university degrees—which apparently he felt was laughable.

And this thing finishes up that the Sergeant Major told him it was professional jealousy and to be aware of it. The Sergeant Major is not here. I feel the Sergeant Major had a pretty high opinion of me, sir. I don't believe it but I have no evidence to offer in contradiction.

PRES: Has Sergeant Major Bittorie gone back to the states?

COL FRANKLIN: Yes, sir, back to the states. The only thing that I will say, that Bittorie told me when Herbert was relieved, "I'm not a bit surprised. I've known him since he's been a second lieutenant. He's been in trouble his whole Army career." As to paragraph f, sir, I wish you would speak to a Captain Cording who was a company commander on this operation. Captain Cording was rated best out of four rifle company commanders by previous battalion commanders. He came to me and said he could not work for Herbert, that he had taken him to task, that he was called a coward by Colonel Herbert, and he was moved.

PRES: Is Captain Cording here?

COL FRANKLIN: He's available and standing by. He will give testimony on Colonel Herbert's conduct on this particular operation where he had antagonized a village to the extent . . . Well, he'll just speak on this brilliant action, sir. And he will give evidence Colonel Herbert, some of his manners of dealing with subordinate officers. To my knowledge, every company commander has been humiliated in that battalion by Colonel Herbert.

And I would like to add another witness, sir, who is standing by, Father Davis. Father Davis will give sworn testimony that at Colonel Herbert's opening address to his officers and staff he stated, "I have no integrity." He will give examples of a DSC winner crying because he was called a coward. And he will give testimony that a dead company commander was accused of taking pot. And he will give testimony along the lines of Colonel Herbert's comments on his loyalty to his subordinate officers. Chaplain Davis incidentally—Colonel

Herbert told your Assistant Chaplain, Van Dyke, that Davis had a drinking problem and was not liked by anyone in the Brigade and that he never went out in the field. Chaplain McCloy, our Chaplain, is here to give evidence that this is totally false, sir. And this again is typical of the viciousness of this man. Your own Chaplain investigated it and it was found not to be so. But I'd like to emphasize Herbert's opening remark in his first speech, "I don't have any integrity; I get the job done."

Paragraph g, on changing these concepts of operation after he assumed command, on fire maneuver and the rest of that stuff. These concepts were certainly not Colonel Herbert's.

PRES: General Barnes testified to that, so unless you have something else to add I don't see any real reason to go into it.

COL FRANKLIN: OK, sir, I'd like to say in Herbert's defense, he executed them better than anybody else.

OK, sir, on 14 February, this action here. I won't go into that. He was the only one that got a decoration for this. I talked to four people in that platoon about another thing I was directed to talk to them about. The body count they gave was half of what Herbert reported. Colonel Bethea and the S1 were present at this conversation. It was about a 21 body count reported. On this action of 14 February, Colonel Herbert was the only one who got an award. The body count reported by Colonel Herbert was about twice that reported by the platoon with whom I spoke. Colonel Bethea and Major Durbin, the S1, heard that and they're coming in as witnesses.

On these awards, sir. Despite the allegation of my professional jealousy, I personally directed the Battalion Executive Officer to submit Herbert for three of them. Now one of these, the General told me to go ahead and do it. Major Boyer, the Executive Officer, will give testimony to this, that I'm the one who directed that he get the awards. In fact his Executive Officer made the statement, "I wish I had thought of this with my past battalion commander, that someone had done as you did. He should have been awarded and was not."

Paragraph i, sir, "On three or four occasions after this I was called in by Colonel Franklin and told I was a superior battalion commander." That is correct, but each of these times I talked to him about the dissension that he was creating in the staff and that his continual misrepresentation and exaggeration made my job very difficult. Next to him I wanted him to succeed more than anybody else, but I could not do my job and support him if what he told me was either misrepresented or totally false. And he would always laugh and say, "Well, I don't lie to you, sir." As far as telling him he was my friend, I never used this word. He makes the statement, "I came to expect these chats after each successful action and they became a joke in the battalion." I bitterly resent this remark. It is totally false and anybody that comes in here—and you can talk with Major Boyer, the Exec,—you can ask them about my reputation in that battalion. And I don't think there is anything to substantiate this.

As far as talking to him about the AGI, that he would be relieved if he didn't do well in the IG inspection, I didn't mention this. I am charged with tactical operations. I have a certain interest but I don't even know the schedule of these. I get the results. They come from the XO to the General. They just pass by my desk. I know we are in good shape on these things. This is totally false. I talked with him about his relations with the Brigade Staff and his apparent inability to tell the truth.

Paragraph j, sir. This is considerably exaggerated and false. In this action I landed with the assault elements of one of his platoons. I had the Brigade Surgeon with me. And Herbert, who states he was there, was not there. Colonel Winkler, the Brigade Surgeon will give testimony on this. While talking to a machine gunner who happened to be from Denver, Colorado, about ten feet away two VC were in a hole and were dragged out. When they were discovered they jumped out or were pulled out. Immediately all of their personal belongings and other stuff was taken and put in a plastic bag. The platoon sergeant of this platoon in one motion drew back this watch as it came off and it went into the pocket. I didn't say a word. Herbert was not there, contrary to what he says here. Winkler will testify to this. And when I left I told the Platoon Leader, "We're airborne soldiers. We can do better than that. Get that wrist watch back to the individual." Subsequent to this . . . I never said anything to Herbert because Herbert wasn't there. Subsequent to this the General came to me and said Herbert was quite upset because I had accused his people of taking wrist watches and that he said that subsequent investigation had proved that said watch had tagged and turned in at the IPW cage as per SOP. This really burned me up. I had the XO make a check. That battalion has never turned in a wrist watch in the memory of the oldest living man in the MI. Major O'Kane will make further testimony on several things that Herbert did along this line. And as to the fact that certain equipment that should have been turned-in was not turned-in, he will also give testimony to the effect that Colonel Herbert could not be trusted at all, sir. But as to that watch, it was turned-in because I told the platoon leader to get it back after I had seen it. Colonel Winkler was there and he can verify this, and there was no question in my mind and no question in Colonel Winkler's mind that watch went off an arm into a pocket, sir, and there was no intention of turning it in.

Also, I would like Major Ray, the staff Judge Advocate, and Colonel Bethea, the XO—he has the sequence of events on this—and Major Meurrens, the Provost Marshal, to talk to this. Basically Colonel Herbert gives the impression that one of his men was being investigated. He went down to the Provost Marshal to see the man was advised of his rights and properly taken care of. This is totally false. He was there repeatedly. There was pandemonium in the Provost Marshal's Office. The Sergeant Major came to me with the Provost Marshal and Staff Judge Advocate and said, "I'm afraid the 2d Battalion is going to claymore the MPs." Major Meurrens would come to me at midnight and said he could not do his job with Herbert in there. Herbert's officers were in there. One was given a direct order to leave by Major Ray and he did not leave and stuck around and came back. And I told Herbert I wanted some disciplinary action taken against this man and Herbert laughed. I called Herbert on the phone and told him to stay away from the MPs, that I was the investigating officer and I resented the fact that he thought that he was the only one capable of protecting their rights, that they would be protected. But Herbert was repeatedly in there. His officers were in there. The Provost Marshal, the JAG and the XO came to me on about four occasions and stated that Herbert was interfering with the investigation. But basically on this investigation, sir, feelings were running high. I was concerned about relations with the 2d Battalion and the Provost Marshal. Considering the seriousness of the subject alleged murder and considering the fact that on at least four occasions people had come to me who were thwarted in the performance of their duties by Colonel Herbert or his people, considering that I had called him and talked to him about staying away, finally after it was reported to me that Herbert was up there making inquiries amongst the MPs themselves, I went up there with him and I told the MPs if he comes in here any more you lock him up and release him only to me. I said this half seriously and half kidding, but he didn't go there anymore.

Herbert came to see me one night when the General was gone and he was very upset about four men being called murderers, riflemen. I was also extremely upset. I delayed the supper—I was in command—and I sent for the four men. I listened to them. Herbert had gotten them all excited. I told them it was not my policy to call our riflemen murderers. If this were being done it would be stopped and I subsequently told the XO to knock it off, regardless of whether it was accepted practice or not. Until four people were found guilty, they would not be called murderers. And I subsequently sought these people out in the field to tell them that I regretted this incident. Herbert made the statement, "I think they're going to write their Congressmen." He was stirring them up and Major Boyer will give testimony that heard Colonel Herbert tell them to write their Congressman. I do not consider this a loyal act, sir, or what's expected of a battalion commander. And one has since written his Congressman, a very fine soldier named Vickers. I request you ask Major Boyer if he heard words to that effect.

Reference paragraph m, sir, I suggested to the General that I give these two letters of reprimand, or the letter of reprimand to Colonel Herbert. He didn't seem too fazed by them. He requested no clarification. He said, "I take these for what they are. You know that everybody is against me. You're getting bad information." He said, "In fact I paper my walls with these things." Sort of a joke. I was rather embarrassed by his lack of becoming upset. But as to requesting clarification and this thing on Major Boyer, I think the General discussed that. He requested nothing. He just stated, "The XO, Crouch, and the Support Battalion commanders are against me." And they were liars and cowards, and the rest of these things, but he would accept it because he was very honest, himself and had great integrity—the normal standard reaction he had to all counseling.

Again, sir, about d, I consider this the most serious, the most flagrant lie and the most easily disproved. I was with the S3, airborne, when I was notified that second battalion was making a CA. I observe or accompany most of the CAs in this Brigade, sir. I flew over there. I found most of the village in flames and the troops were hitting booby traps as they landed. They had taken nine casualties but I don't recall any specific fire on the rifle company. I tried to land and was yelled off "Mines or booby traps." I finally landed on the beach, hundreds of people on the beach, at least 50 per cent of the village in flames. The doctor was holding a bloody baby in his arms. There was a dead man on the beach and his wife came to me and showed me the ID card and everything. She was saying, "Is this what you do?" The company commander and the platoon leader and the people I've talked to were not too aware of what was going on. They had taken casualties. They were getting all of their information from the C and C.

PRES: Information from who?

COL FRANKLIN: From the Command and Control helicopter. The execution was very good on this mission. They landed right where they should have landed. Colonel Herbert was extremely aggressive as C and C and his attempting to block with his command group was very heroic and well conceived. I have no quarrel with this. This was done well. But when I arrived over this village and saw it smoking and burning and all of these people on that beach I was greatly concerned in trying to find out what was going on. Herbert never told me to get off his net. Most of my transmissions on the net were to get help for him to pick up a helicopter that was shot down, and the other to take out all those detainees and these people on the beach that had been rounded up and were on the beach in a group, and women and children were crying and the flames were blowing around and things were blowing up. I'd never quite seen anything like it, sir. So when I finally left I heard on the Battalion push the instruction given to pull all the troops out and leave, and here the town is in flames. And at that time I directed that they will not leave. There will be some troops left there and I want Colonel Herbert to report to me. Colonel Herbert came in and in the presence of the S3 and the S2. . . .

PRES: Battalion S2 and S3?

COL FRANKLIN: Brigade S2 and S3 and described the action. He stated that gunships had never fired in the village. This is totally false, his own witness who will come here, saw the gunships fire. A Spec Four Smith saw the gunships fire on the village. To my knowledge at no time were they receiving any kind of heavy fire from the village, sir. They had a chopper shot down from outside the village. We have some pictures that will be introduced into evidence. But the rules of engagement are very specific around here. Unless you are in imminent danger or taking heavy casualties, you do not fire into villages. Herbert states that he saw a man with a torch running around setting the fires and he landed and tried to put the fires out himself. Major Webb, who you can see later, did not observe this. The pilots did not observe this and Specialist Four Smith on the C and C did not observe this. This fire was set on fire by gunships, sir, which Herbert in the presence of the Brigade S2 said they did not fire.

PRES: He states that upon returning to LZ English, "I reported to the Deputy Commander who then accused me of burning a village to the ground and littering the beaches with hundreds of dead women and children."

COL FRANKLIN: Totally false. I wanted to know, "Why in the hell did you burn the Goddamn village, Herbert?" That was the question. OK. "The next day the Brigade S5 was sent in to rebuild the village and a medical team to treat civilians still alive." I don't know who these quotes are from, sir, but they're sure not me. "As a result of their inspection no village had to be rebuilt as only a few straw huts had burned in a known VC area and only three civilians received treatment, none for gunshot wounds. One woman and three children were found dead. These were present in the village the day before and were reported officially by both myself and Major Webb." Sir, here is the Province Report on this which states: "On 16 March the 2/503d Infantry combat assaulted a company into the area around Tan Phu [phonetic] Hamlet, My Tho Village. Fights were scattered throughout the day with 29 VC killed and 17 wounded. U.S. casualties reported light. During the fighting approximately 50 per cent of the hamlet was destroyed by gunships leaving 40 families homeless. The district and 173d Airborne Brigade have provided emergency rations and some shelter for the families." And he states, "A few huts were burned up." So I think at least half the village was burned down, sir. He says three civilians received treatment, none for gunshot wounds. In his own C&C, with him in it, four were evacuated for gunshot wounds, at least two children. SP4 Smith will testify to that. We'll produce a picture of that guy with his stomach shot out, sir. And the pregnant woman and two children killed, we'll give you a picture of her. And his statement that this was reported the day before is a bunch of crap. It is not true. They were killed in this incident. So half the village or approximately half—I can't tell you how much—was burned down. Four civilians were evacuated or five. The pilot thinks five that he evacuated—he'll give the testimony—for gunshot wounds. There was at least one dead plus the women and two children.

PRES: Who was the pilot on this?

COL FRANKLIN: Mr. Pippen, sir. Now, sir, the final count on this is given as 29 VC killed and 17 wounded. This is a C3 report from an agent. Herbert's reported 29 bodies. Nobody, to my knowledge saw any more than 15. That was the pilot. The only report is Colonel Herbert's figure, sir, and again he exaggerated as he normally did. And I would like to make it very clear. This Brigade is very proud, sir. General Barnes said, "We put our foot on his chest or he's not claimed." And this is done throughout the Brigade, Colonel Herbert being the exception. But the fact he says that 29 were killed and 17 wounded, this is an agent's report which is a C3, sometimes reliable and possibly true. And to give this as fact in an official report is misleading, to say the least.

Major O'Kane and Colonel Accousti, sir, will confirm this and give more detail. Major O'Kane will also give testimony to the effect that Herbert stated he had some 10 or 11 year old kids and thought they were VC. He will also give other testimony.

Coming back to this operation, Herbert made the statement that on the way back he had dropped down in his chopper and killed six, but he didn't want to report it because every time he reported something it got him in trouble. This is not remembered by three people in the airplane whom I've talked to, two of which you can talk to here and Major Webb whom you can speak with back at IFFV, General Corcoran's Aide. I think you should talk to Webb on these things. In fairness to Herbert, Webb was extremely close to Herbert and had great admiration for him. In fairness to Herbert, Webb should be talked to, sir.

I have no comment to make on q, sir, except that on this operation I was down there and I sure as hell didn't see 50 bodies. But that was a good action. That was an excellent action and Colonel Herbert is to be commended for his aggressiveness and flexibility to react to the situation. His XO was directed by me to put him in for a medal. I said it may be a DSC, but just get the evidence and let's see what it is. [Inaudible portion—estimated approximate ten words.]

I believe that's the Silver Star for the action in which the village was burned. I haven't seen this, sir. I haven't seen this recommendation and I'm on the board. You must have gotten this from somebody else. Incidentally, on the Silver Star . . .

PRES: Who signed these things? Does it say?

COL FRANKLIN: The S1 and the XO, sir. Now on the Silver Star recommendation, sir . . .

PRES: Now this is a recommendation for the Distinguished Service Cross. Did Boyer do these?

COL FRANKLIN: He was the XO and acting battalion commander. He's available for testimony.

PRES: But this was actually a recommendation for the DSC submitted by an individual, but which has not reached the board. Is that correct?

COL FRANKLIN: That's correct, sir. The Silver Star is the same way, sir. And we have a policy in the Brigade that for one action, all the awards for the action are submitted together. For this action where the village was burned no one in the rifle companies were submitted for anything. And for the C and C ship there was five recommended for Silver Stars and three for Distinguished Flying Crosses. When these things hit, they were very poorly written and there was considerable contradiction and I gave them back to Major Boyer and said, "You all couldn't have killed the same three guys. As to whether they were killed from the chopper or killed on the ground, you'd better get them together and redo these statements if we're going to get these things through. They'll have to be redone." So that's where they stand right now. They are still being redone, the five Silver Star recommendations and three DSCs, all for the members of the C and C helicopter for this action.

On these AGI reports and that action with 50 people—he did darn good, sir. I said so in his efficiency report. Tactically, Colonel Herbert is a fine battalion commander, but I can tell you he has no integrity. He's dishonest and he's disloyal.

On t, sir, basically this entails the forming of a provisional rifle company for attachment to the 1/50th Infantry at An Khe. I talked to the battalion commander of the 1/50th and he said he didn't want to get a bunch of duds—because they're mech and not airborne and this is a very sensitive thing. We have to watch that we don't dump our guys. I spoke to Colonel Herbert in the presence of Colonel Accousti and said, "Herbert, I want you to send good men, three good men to Woodall." He said, "I never send bad men. I send nothing but good men and I got three men with no Articles 15s." I complimented him. I said I really appreciated his attitude. The next thing I know I get a note from the AO that he had called the AG and wanted to know why this guy with two Article 15s, for sleeping on guard, is unacceptable. The AG has about four documents, sir, he's going to give this event here. But this time I wrote a letter to Herbert. I was fed up with his constantly misleading and lying to me. And I called him to give him this letter. Now Herbert claimed he didn't know these people had Article 15s. The statement by his own Adjutant, sir, he was called by a Mr. Northe and told that this guy had two Article 15s. The Adjutant states he went to Colonel Herbert and informed him of this. Colonel Herbert had told me he was sending men with no Article 15s. And Colonel Herbert called the AG and wanted to know why the guy was unacceptable. And I considered this typical of his performance. I called him in to show him this letter and I read it to him. He stated, "Major Crouch is a liar. He told me he was acceptable." Major Crouch was not available. He was on a trip somewhere so I made the statement. "Well, one of you guys is flat lying and when Crouch gets back we're going to find out who and we're going to take all the action necessary." During this talk he went into a long thing. Herbert again reviewed how honest he was, his character, courage, and the rest of this business.

He told me that we had released a very high ranking VCI, that Beacham had told him they classified this guy as an innocent civilian. And he told me a long story which is included in his statement here about Beacham here. . . . He told me this story on Beacham, basically to the effect that after an investigation was made of an alleged action some gunships under Herbert's control and some Rangers, that Herbert was told by Beacham, "I'm going to investigate this and if you did all these things I'll take it to the General." Herbert's telling this story. Well, it turned out the allegations were false. Herbert says he told Beacham, "Are you going to take the fact that now that your captain screwed up, are you going to take that to the General?" And he said, "No, I'm going to drop it." And Herbert gave this as an example about how everybody's out to get him. If he screwed up it would go to the General, but for somebody else it was not done. Major Beacham will testify that he offered Herbert, "I'll go see Colonel Franklin or we'll go see the General. I apologize for these allegations. I'll do whatever you want." So I found out that the VCI in question, we still had in our custody.

And when I talked to Beacham on this specific incident I realized that we were long overdue in relieving Herbert. And at that time I went to the Brigade Commander and I said, "This guy has got to go, sir." And that's about it.

But I hope in your testimony that comes before you on these incidents, I think you'll get the fact that he cannot be relied upon by the staff. I think a lot of them will tell you they couldn't believe anything he said. And also this tendency to make the most violent accusations against someone he didn't like or didn't agree with. I also hope, sir, that you'll pose questions as to my reputation here, as my reputation here is not very favorably portrayed in that letter.

PRES: This first question, did you tell Herbert that he was a superior battalion commander, that he was hated by the staff and in fact he was the most hated man in the Brigade?

COL FRANKLIN: Not in those words, but generally the thought. I never mentioned "the most hated man in the Brigade." I told him this, "You're the best battalion command that we've got in this Brigade. If you never opened your mouth you could run circles around the rest of the battalion commanders that we've got because of your background and your knowledge and your ability to react to a tactical situation. I don't understand, therefore, why you have to continually misrepresent even the most inconsequential things. You are highly disliked by the staff. You are constantly embroiled with these people. But if you could just learn to tell the truth I think you could live with it and we could still get along." But not "The most hated man," no, sir. I would say he was, but I didn't tell him that.

PRES: Did you announce at mess after a 2/503d operation that personnel of that battalion had stolen personal effects belonging to detainees?

COL FRANKLIN: I discussed this with the Commanding General at the mess, I think, sir, at the table. I mentioned the fact that I saw a watch, not personal effects, just the watch that was taken that I had directed the Platoon leader to get the watch turned back in.

PRES: Did subsequent investigation develop that in fact this watch had not been taken?

COL FRANKLIN: No, sir. You should ask Colonel Winkler the same question, sir. Subsequent investigation showed that a watch had never been turned-in, according to Colonel Bethea, to the MI, sir. This particular watch may have been turned-in. I mean previous to this a watch hadn't been turned-in.

PRES: This letter of reprimand . . . Strike that. Did you hand Colonel Herbert a letter of reprimand on the 14th of March? That's this letter (indicating).

COL FRANKLIN: I'm not sure of the date, sir. I handed him the letter of reprimand. . . .

PRES: This one (indicating).

COL FRANKLIN: Yes, sir, I did.

PRES: Did Colonel Herbert request it be written in more specific terms?

COL FRANKLIN: He did not, sir. He seemed to be really not too impressed by it.

PRES: Was this letter withdrawn or not placed in Herbert's field 201 file?

COL FRANKLIN: I have no knowledge of that, sir. I assume it would be placed in his file. I don't know, sir.

PRES: On the 2d of April you wrote this letter to Colonel Herbert, a letter of counsel. Was this given to him?

COL FRANKLIN: It was not, sir. I read it to him and I was going to give it to him, and then when he said, "Major Crouch is flat lying," and I couldn't get a hold of Major Crouch . . . First, this was a rather unexpected development. So I said, "I'm going to wait on this letter until I get Crouch and then one of you two is lying."

PRES: Did you ever get a hold of Crouch on this?·

COL FRANKLIN: Yes, sir, and Crouch will give testimony that he wasn't lying, that what he told me was true and he'll give you a bunch of documents.

PRES: Did you accuse Colonel Herbert of using abusive language to Major Crouch, the AG?

COL FRANKLIN: Sir, the word that I used is "irate," speaking in an "irate" manner.

PRES: Was this refuted?

COL FRANKLIN: Major Boyer and Captain Parrott made sworn statements that he at no time was abusive and cursed Major Crouch. And Major Crouch basically stated that having dealt with Herbert before he just listened "Yes, sir; yes, sir" and Herbert did all the talking and finally Crouch just hung up. I did not tell Herbert it was abusive. I said "In an irate manner." And it's written in that letter, sir. It was refuted that he did not. I believe that he did not curse or use abusive language, but I didn't accuse him of it.

PRES: Was your efficiency report on Lieutenant Colonel Herbert covering this period of such a nature that it should be referred to him?

COL FRANKLIN: Without question, sir, I think he should be dismissed from the service.

PRES: Has this been referred to him?

COL FRANKLIN: It's been forwarded. I believe it goes to DA and then

472

DA forwards it to him. I don't know how that's handled. It was written after he had left, sir.

PRES: Did you call up anyone in Saigon relative to his relief and relative to his character?

COL FRANKLIN: I did not, sir.

PRES: In specific terms will you tell me why you recommended Herbert to be relieved.

COL FRANKLIN: He was incapable of telling the truth, sir, even on inconsequential matters. He was constantly creating turmoil within the staff. The staff officers were coming to me and saying he created friction. And after the events of 16 March I realized the man was extremely dangerous. I had doubts even as to his sanity and I was fearful for what he might do in the future.

PRES: Thank you. This hearing is recessed and will be reconvened at a later time to be determined by me.

COL Ross Franklin was recalled as a witness and testified as follows:

PRES: You are reminded that you are still under oath. Colonel Herbert in his letter has attached a recommendation for a Silver Star, and one that he did not attach but he produced a copy of the Distinguished Service Cross. Where are these now? What has been the action on these.

COL FRANKLIN: Sir, these things are forwarded to the battalion to a promotion board. The promotion board does not meet as such. It's the Adjutant General, the S1, the Executive Officer, and myself.

PRES: You said, "forwarded to battalion."

COL FRANKLIN: To Brigade, sir. And each of us makes recommendation, either recommend approval or disapproval. It goes to the General and he makes . . . We don't have authority to approve or disapprove these decorations.

PRES: You don't have authority either to approve or disapprove?

COL FRANKLIN: We can disapprove. I believe we can disapprove.

PRES: You better check that out.

COL FRANKLIN: To my knowledge, I cannot remember seeing a request being disapproved yet.

PRES: Where are these two now?

COL FRANKLIN: I'd have to check and find out where they are.

PRES: Could you find that out. In the meantime we'll just finish up. You referred to this Beacham incident as "the straw that broke the camel's back." Could you relate that again. I went over it and as I understood it, he supposedly had fired gunships into a LRP patrol and there had been no coordination between the pilot and the people on the ground. Yet the investigation revealed that there had been coordination and that the matter was apparently dropped, according to the S2. Yet how did this thing come up again?

COL FRANKLIN: All right, sir, while I was talking to Colonel Herbert reference to the sending of this sergeant, or attempting to send a man with two Article 15s to the Provisional Company, we had a rather lengthy discussion. And during this discussion Herbert made two statements to me. One, as an example of of how screwed up our military intelligence was, we had released a prisoner who was a high ranking man in the National Liberation Front, very high ranking. We had control of this man and we released him. This was shocking to me, naturally. I told him I'd check it out.

A second point he made was the point concerning this thing with Beacham. It was suggested that anything that Herbert did would immediately go to the General. And he related it. It was the first time I'd heard this story. Now the story as Herbert relates it and the way Beacham had related it to me is generally about the same, except Herbert when he tells it ends it completely different than Beacham which puts an entirely different light on it. That is to say, after the allegation of Beacham, or Captain James, the LRP Commander, were made and proven to be false, according to Herbert he said, "What are you going to do about it? Are you going to take it to the General now?" And Beacham said, "No, I'm not going to do it. I'm going to drop it." Herbert implied, in fact Herbert said, that if Herbert had been guilty it would have gone to the General, but because it was the Ranger Company Commander who works for Beacham it was let to be dropped. I questioned Beacham on both of these things I'm relating. Beacham said it's a flat lie. The National Liberation Front member is still under our custody; that he offered to go to the General after the results of this investigation or go to Colonel Franklin or do anything he wanted. "I apologized to him." So at that time I realized—Colonel Herbert had lied to me twice or Beacham was lying. Well, it wasn't too hard to check on the National Liberation Front guy. That's easy to find out. We've still got him under custody. And I realized at that time that it was just a waste of time to continue on this thing and that Herbert had to be relieved.

PRES: Did you prepare this letter of 14 March, this letter of reprimand?

COL FRANKLIN: No, sir, I did not. I didn't see it until it was written, sir.

PRES: Do you know who wrote it?

COL FRANKLIN: Colonel Bethea, I would guess. And then General Barnes had a lot he put in there himself. I would say perhaps a draft was made that was initially written by Colonel Bethea.

PRES: Were you present when General Barnes relieved Colonel Herbert?

COL FRANKLIN: Yes, sir.

PRES: Did Colonel Herbert ask for more specifics on the relief and did he ask for an Article 138, Uniform Code of Military Justice investigation?

474

COL FRANKLIN: No, sir, he never asked for the 138. It was sort of a shock. He said something about "Would you reconsider?" and then there was some conversation, as I recall, it came up where he said, "I do tell the truth," or words to that effect. At which time I did stand up and referenced these Beacham incidents. I know General Barnes remembers the example of the prisoner.

PRES: Now what was the prisoner?

COL FRANKLIN: The story I just related.

PRES: I see, I see.

COL FRANKLIN: But I did stand up and tell Herbert in the General's presence that, "You don't tell the truth. You've lied, and as an example you lied just yesterday." And then I related these stories here.

PRES: Would you check and see what the disposition of these is?

COL FRANKLIN: Yes, sir, I should have that to you in about 15 minutes.

PRES: Thank you very much.

(COL FRANKLIN withdrew from the room.)

COL ROSS FRANKLIN was recalled as a witness and testified as follows:

COL FRANKLIN: Sir, reference to those awards, the DSC and the Silver Star. In the last couple of days they were sent to the AG. They were sent back to the 2d Battalion and are presently with the 2d Battalion to be put with the other awards for same action, and then all of them forwarded back to Brigade. Our Adjutant just called the 2d Battalion Adjutant. He stated that he thought he would have the package of awards for both recommendations up to Brigade tomorrow.

PRES: This is a Brigade policy that they all come in together?

COL FRANKLIN: For the same action. This precludes that several people don't get. . . . Well, it makes it so you have it all in one package, sir. And then this goes through the different staff offices. There is not a formal meeting. We make recommendations to the Commanding. Basically it's recommended for approval or disapproval and goes to the Commanding General. He signs the letter personally forwarding it to IFFV where the decision of Silver Star is made; and it goes further than that for a DSC.

PRES: Referring back to the incident of the sergeant taking the watch. Yesterday in his testimony the S2 said that the watch was turned-in.

COL FRANKLIN: Yes, sir.

PRES: I gathered from your testimony that it was not turned-in.

COL FRANKLIN: No, sir, I testified that when I had the Executive Officer check with MI that there had never been a watch turned-in—in Colonel Bethea's words: "In the memory of the oldest living MI guy." This was the first time a watch had been turned-in. And it was turned-in because they knew that I knew they had taken it. I told the Platoon Leader, "Just get the watch back."

PRES: Thank you very much.

(COL FRANKLIN withdrew from the room.)

Appendix C. *Two statements by Sergeant Major Henry Bittorie, Head-quarters, 173d Airborne Brigade.*

On the evening of 3 April 1969 while in the office of General Barnes, Commanding General, 173d Infantry Brigade (Airborne), introducing my recently arrived replacement, General Barnes stated that he was being forced to relieve his "best battalion commander," Lieutenant Colonel Herbert, and the Battalion Sergeant Major, Master Sergeant Childers, the next day because Lieutenant Colonel Herbert could not get along with the brigade staff. While still under the blow of this statement I exited the office of General Barnes and met Colonel Franklin, the Brigade Deputy Commander, to whom I introduced my replacement, stating that now however he, my replacement, would probably have to go to the 2nd of the 503d, Lieutenant Colonel Herbert's and Master Sergeant Childers' battalion. Colonel Franklin appeared shocked I knew this and asked just how I did know this, to which I replied that the CG, General Barnes, had just told me. I then made a comment to the effect that it was a shame that Colonel Herbert was "in trouble again" over a couple of knuckle heads with petty gripes, that for no other reason than because he was an individualist and not a clique member he had to be relieved. The next morning I departed the brigade for purpose of DEROS. I had in no way by word or manner stated or implied that the relief was expected or deserved but exactly the opposite, that Colonel Herbert was an excellent commander and a strong soldier who was being relieved by virtue of his not being a clique member refusing to participate in military politics. In no way could my words or actions be construed honestly to mean otherwise. Lieutenant Colonel Herbert and I were on excellent terms. It was I in fact who recommended to the previous Brigade CG, General Allen, that he could best utilize Colonel Herbert as a battalion commander. And though due to other necessary requirements Lieutenant Colonel Herbert was not assigned as such immediately under General Allen, it was common knowledge in the brigade that it was General Allen who recommended to General Barnes that Lieutenant Colonel Herbert be so assigned.

I was assigned as Brigade Sergeant Major of 173d Airborne Brigade (Sep) APO San Francisco, 96250, from May 1968 to April 1969. I have known LTC Anthony Herbert since he was a Platoon Leader. I was the Battle Group Sergeant Major of the 505th Airborne Infantry, Mainz, Germany, from 1959 to 1962. At that time, he was the Platoon Leader of the Ranger Platoon, and also the Company Commander of Company B.

Due to his strong leadership, these units were considered the best in the Battle Group. Company B, which CPT Herbert commanded, at the time, won the Best Company Award month after month for approximately a year. In February, 1969, as a LTC, he was Commanding 2d Battalion, 503d Airborne Infantry, APO San Francisco, 96250.

In my opinion, the 2d Battalion, under LTC Herbert's Command and leadership, was the most efficient Combat Unit in the Brigade. The morale of the men was high, and they had the record of having the highest enemy body count and the least friendly casualties. I attributed this to the strong, aggressive leadership of LTC Anthony Herbert. The Senior NCOs of the Battalion, who I have talked to, have a high professional regard for LTC Herbert as a Commander. I personally considered him as one of the best Combat Commanders that I have known in my 27 years in the service.

Appendix D. *Statements by staff officers and NCOs, 2d Battalion, 173d Airborne Brigade.*

1) LTC Henry Boyer, Jr.

During the period 5 Feb 69 to 5 Apr 69, I served as the Executive Officer of the 2d Battalion (Airborne) 503d Infantry, 173d Airborne Brigade, APO San Francisco 96250. During this period the Battalion Commander was LTC Anthony B. Herbert.

During the last week of March 1969, the Brigade Provost Marshal informed me that a Vietnamese woman had filed a complaint that she had been raped by some American soldiers. The alleged rape took place in a village just north of the operational area of the 2d Battalion. The unit nearest the location of the alleged rape was Co. C 2d Battalion (Airborne), 503d Infantry. I immediately informed LTC Herbert of the allegations and he directed that I go to the field immediately and visit the Company Commander to determine whether or not the rape could have taken place. The following day, I went to Company C and talked with CPT Christopher Dorney, the Commanding Officer of Company C. CPT Dorney told me that the rape could have occurred because one of his platoons was operating just south of the village where the rape was alleged to have taken place, but he was sure that it hadn't. Upon my return to the battalion rear area, I informed LTC Herbert of the result of my conversation with CPT Dorney and he and I immediately went to the office of the Brigade Provost Marshal, Major Bernard Meurrens. LTC Herbert reported what he knew about the alleged rape and offered to assist the military police in their investigation. On his own, to my knowledge, the following day LTC Herbert brought the platoon under suspicion back to the battalion rear area to facilitate the CID investigation, which was an unusual practice. It was standard that the investigators shift for themselves before this and visit best they could in the field. The investigation resulted in three men from Company C being charged with rape. LTC Herbert then had charges drawn up. LTC Herbert left the battalion on the 5th of April and that was the reason that he did not sign the charge sheets though it was he that insisted the investigation be continued and did everything within his power to see that it was completed satisfactorily. The three men were tried by General Court Martial in late June and all were acquitted.

While he served as the Commanding Officer of the 2d Battalion, LTC Herbert was recommended for an Army Commendation Medal with "V," a Bronze Star with "V," a Silver Star, and a Distinguished Service Cross. I initiated all the awards and personally wrote the recommendations for the Silver Star and the DSC. LTC Herbert continually emphasized awards for his men while deemphasizing awards for himself and refusing to even permit himself to be considered for an award. On one occasion he inadvertently saw the awards for the ARCOM and BSM and tore up the paperwork. I had them rewritten and resubmitted without his knowledge.

LTC Herbert insisted that Chaplain Charles Davis, as well as all of us and himself, spend the majority of his time and effort with the men of the battalion in the rifle companies in the field. I concurred wholeheartedly with LTC Herbert in this matter. Father Davis was extremely reluctant to spend time, particularly nights, in the field with the troops. Of the four Battalion Chaplains that I supervised in my years in Vietnam, Father Davis spent less time in the field than any of the others, and not sufficient time in my estimation expected of a Chaplain with Infantry. In my opinion, he was the least liked of all the Chaplains of the Brigade.

2) MSG R. L. Childers. *Hearing of the board of officers, Article 138 investigation.*

> *MSG RICHARD L. CHILDERS was called as a witness*
> *and testified as follows:*

RCDR: Do you swear or affirm that the evidence you are about to give in the case now in hearing shall be the truth, the whole truth and nothing but the truth? So help you God.

MSG CHILDERS: I do.

RCDR: Would you give your name, grade, organization and duty assignment.

MSG CHILDERS: Richard L. Childers, Master Sergeant, Headquarters and Headquarters Company, 2d Battalion, 503d Infantry, 173d Airborne Brigade. My job is Battalion Sergeant Major, sir.

PRES: You were Battalion Sergeant Major when Lieutenant Colonel Herbert was Battalion Commander?

MSG CHILDERS: Yes, sir.

PRES: What did you think of Lieutuenant Colonel Herbert as a battalion commander?

MSG CHILDERS: Sir, without a doubt I think he's the best commander I've ever had in 22 years of my association with the Army.

PRES: You have implicit trust in him?

MSG CHILDERS: Yes, sir.

PRES: Do you know of any occasion when he has wrongfully accused his officers or men of being cowards?

MSG CHILDERS: No, sir, I don't.

PRES: Were you present when Colonel Herbert took over the Battalion?

MSG CHILDERS: No, sir, I was on R&R. I came in about three days after he took over.

PRES: Were you present when he departed?

MSG CHILDERS: Yes, sir.

PRES: Would you relate what happened when he said that he was leaving.

MSG CHILDERS: Sir, we got up early that morning. We were supposed to make an air assault. We had bad weather. We sat around until about 7:00 and then they called it off. He told me to go ahead and lay down, that he had to go see General Barnes and he'd see me after he'd seen General Barnes. So I went down to my room to lay down on the bed. He came in and he woke me up and he said, "I've just been relieved, Childers." I said, "I don't believe that, sir." He said, "Well, it's true. I've got an hour to pack my bags and get out of the area."

He asked me if I wanted to go with him, that he'd try to get me a job down where he was going. The Brigade Sergeant Major, Sergeant Major Bittorie came up and told me they had received an E9 in and he would be coming up here as Battalion Sergeant Major and it would be effective today. This is the 5th of April. So I told Sergeant Major Bittorie that I'd like to go with Colonel Herbert and see if I could get another job. It was related to me that I could have any job in the Brigade. General Barnes didn't particularly want to see me leave the Brigade, and any job I wanted in the Brigade I could have, other than the Sergeant Major because they were all filled up with Sergeants Major. And at that time I thought it was best that I move out of the Brigade. I did move down to CMAC with Colonel Herbert.

PRES: Are you down there with him now?

MSG CHILDERS: No, sir, I'm still in the 2d Battalion.

PRES: Are you familiar with the case where some individuals of Company A, that Colonel Herbert felt their rights were being violated by improper accusations by the Provost Marshal?

MSG CHILDERS: Yes, sir. It had been reported to us that these people were suspected of murdering innocent civilians. We asked them what grounds. They said, well, the individual that had been killed was the father of an RVN soldier. This was the story that was related to me. And then we brought these people in out of the field. There was an investigation run on it. And they were accused as murderers and told they had to make statements. Myself and Colonel Herbert went down to talk to these people. They was told they had to make statements. They was given an order to make statements. And they came over and asked us what to do. We told them that under the provisions of the Uniform Code of Military Justice they didn't have to make any statement. If they wanted, they would make an unsworn statement, or they could make a sworn statement. If they wanted, they must be provided a counsel before they made any statement. And our advice to these people, if they did make a statement, we recommended that they have a counsel or qualified lawyer before they made a statement. This dragged on for approximately two weeks so the people were left in from the field. And the reason behind this I think was because one man was on R&R. After they were cleared—there was no accusations made against them—we didn't get the clearance to send them back to the field for approximately five days after it was all over. Finally the Brigade Sergeant Major called the Provost Marshal and got them cleared to go to the field.

PRES: Are you familiar with the Bumgarner case?

MSG CHILDERS: I am somewhat, sir, but I was told to stay out of the Provost Marshal's Office; it was not of my business to be over there; I was not to talk to those people.

PRES: Do you think that Colonel Herbert looked after his men?

MSG CHILDERS: I think he did so in an outstanding manner, sir. As a commander it's his job, I feel, to look after his men as well as the Army's interests. And I think he did this in both cases.

PRES: You think he did both?

MSG CHILDERS: Yes, sir.

PRES: As far as you know he was loyal to his men as well as to his commander.

MSG CHILDERS: Yes, sir.

PRES: Thank you very much.

(MSG Childers withdrew from the room.)

3) Captain Jack R. Donovan

This statement is made in response to certain allegations made by members of the 173d Airborne Brigade Staff covering firstly the chain of events and conditions in the PMO the evening of my removal from the PMO by the PM, and secondly the relationship of the 2d Battalion to the 172d MID.

When I entered the PMO on 26 Feb. 69 to obtain permission to speak with SFC Bumgarner and SP4 Rodarte, the office could hardly be described as chaotic. As a matter of fact I was the only member of the 2d Battalion in the office. After obtaining permission from the PM to talk with SFC Bumgarner, I proceeded to the building behind the PMO where SFC Bumgarner was being detained and after conversing with him for five minutes, returned to the PMO, obtained permission from Mr. MacDonald, a CID Agent, to speak with SP4 Rodarte and was in the middle of a conversation when it was interrupted by Major Ray, the Brigade SJA.

I informed Major Ray that SP4 Rodarte had requested counsel. Major Ray then in an extremely loud, rapid manner asked Rodarte, Do you want counsel? Who do you want? and Do you want Capt. Donovan? Major Ray obtained a reply to the third question only—which was a shake of the head indicating "no." The PM then called me into his office and stated that I was interfering with his investigation and I was asked to leave. This I subsequently did and did not return. I was at the time, once again, the only 2d Battalion member present and there existed no chaos. These factors only increased my surprise at such abrupt and abusive treatment by Major Ray and towards myself and SP4 Rodarte.

On the question of frequent visits to Lt. Col. Herbert and myself to the IPW section of the 172d MID, I can say they were allowed and even encouraged by the Brigade S2. I conducted personal liaison with the Brigade S2 on an almost daily basis and this frequently referred to the results of Battalion Staff visits to the IPW Section. As a whole, IPW was very receptive to our visits for not only were we able to supplement capture data, but information of value to the troops still in contact was made immediately available and forwarded with substantial results in a number of instances. Our frequent visits were necessitated in large part by not infrequent time lapses of up to forty-eight hours before intelligence was provided 2d Battalion. The 2d Battalion established a reputation in the Brigade intelligence community of rapid response to intelligence of reasonable reliability and was appreciated by collection agencies because the agency was not condemned for reports that did not pan out. Col. Herbert's often repeated philosophy was: the one time in ten that the information proved accurate more than made up for the nine dry runs. In the year I was with the Brigade . . . Col. Herbert was the first Battalion CO to adopt this constructive attitude and the results speak for themselves.

As an intelligence officer, I can easily state Col. Herbert was an outstanding Battalion CO. Intelligence was not fed back from a contact as regularly as most intelligence people prefer, but this is because he concentrated all efforts toward closing with and killing the enemy and at the conclusion of the contact returned with a consolidated report. I can think of no instance in which valuable information was lost because of this practice.

4) Major Francis P. Tally

TO WHOM IT MAY CONCERN:

I, Francis Patrick Tally, Maj. M.C., 036-26-0367, am writing in behalf of Lt. C. Anthony Herbert. I was the Battalion Surgeon of 2/503 Inf. in 173 Airborne Brigade while Lt. C. Herbert was Commanding Officer. I found Lt. C. Herbert to be very compassionate and humane towards his men and the people of the Republic of South Viet Nam. He was very helpful to me as the Battalion Surgeon in dealing with emotional stress in the men. His training in psychology enabled him to give me greater support with troops with psychiatric disorders. His compassion for the Vietnamese people is best exemplified by his planning and execution of a C.A. of "B" Comp. into a V.C. controlled village on the coast of R.V.N. near Bong Son River so that a Medcap could be carried out. The village was reported to have Bubonic Plague, and I was able to treat four Vietnamese people who had plague and then immunize the rest of the Village against plague. This operation went off so well that not one person, American or Vietnamese, was injured or wounded.

Because of the above stated reasons, I believe that Lt. C. Anthony Herbert is a compassionate, understanding and just soldier whom the U.S. Army and the people of the U.S. can be proud of.

5) Captain Laurence A. Potter III

This certificate is written to attest my personal respect for LTC Anthony B. Herbert as a Commander and an individual and to give evidence as to his honor and integrity, the high regard in which he was held by the officers and men of the Battalion, and the exceptional manner in which he performed his duties as Commanding Officer of the 2d Battalion Airborne 503d Infantry, 173d Airborne Brigade.

Every fact given and opinion derived from the facts is based on personal observations and experience during the period 6 February 1969 to 4 April 1969. This certificate is written from the point of view of a man who received orders from LTC Herbert and was called upon to carry them out. I served as S5, Asst S5 for civic action, Medical Operations Assistant and Medical Platoon Leader. I had served in these positions in the 2d Bn 6 months prior to his taking command. I served under two Battalion Commanders prior to LTC Herbert and one after he was relieved. Prior to my serving in Vietnam I had been assigned to the 82d Airborne Division.

I was a dependent of an Army officer and have been associated with the military my entire life. My father retired October 1969 as a Major General in the Medical Corps after 30 years of service. I am a Regular Army career officer in the Medical Service Corps. I give these facts to indicate my lifetime commitment to the military as well as my prior experience and potential awareness of the setting about which I am giving evidence.

My record will reflect that LTC Nicholson, the Commander immediately preceding LTC Herbert, indorsed a 99 OER. I request that whoever reviews this certificate contact BG Manley Morrison, the Chief of my corps for confirmation of my record and my credibility in giving evidence.

I have never been rated by LTC Herbert nor is it likely that I will ever serve with him again, though I would willingly do so anywhere, anytime and in whatever capacity required. My short contact with LTC Herbert was a significant factor in my deciding to make the Army a career in spite of attractive civilian offers.

It should be made clear at this time that no statements made are intended to be taken as derogatory toward my former 2d Battalion Commanders. They were excellent commanders in their own rights and well liked by their officers and men. The accomplishments of LTC Herbert are over and above this and in their brilliance tend to make prior accomplishments seen pale by comparison.

LTC Herbert in his short time in command instilled in the officers and men an esprit, a pride and a willingness to fight the enemy which is truly incredible. He did this not by coercion or threats but by realistic and effective tactical plans, dynamic personal leadership, a willingness to listen to and adopt

484

valid ideas, and unswerving impartiality in his dealings with everyone in his command.

The initial reaction to his operational concepts was that of wariness and in some cases anger as a result of that wariness. In less than three weeks it was difficult to staff positions in the rear area. Cooks, drivers, clerks—everyone wanted to go to the field and fight with LTC Herbert. Those who were forced to stay in the rear areas worked day and night willingly, and without supervision in most cases. Projects that no one had been able to get to before now were accomplished with half the people to do the work. Sick call was down to nothing. People with major injuries and limiting conditions had to be ordered to quarters or they would be back out into the field.

LTC Herbert would allow no abuse of civilians or prisoners. On one operation in the Bong Son plains, northeast of Bong Son, I saw LTC Herbert prevent national police field force troops from assassinating prisoners. They were intending to make them talk by going down the line shooting them.

I accompanied most "Skysweep" and "Skytrap" operations conducted by the battalion. I went as an extra aid man in the initial assaults and provided MEDCAP capability for the civilians afterwards. It was LTC Herbert's desire that a MEDCAP be conducted after every operation.

There was so much activity compressed into that short period of time that I will only mention two of the major operations. The first operation evolved around the "Rockpile." The "Rockpile" is a peninsula on the coast south of the Bong Son River. It has a large rock hill on it and a large expanse of sand separates it from the inland tree line. Delta Company air assaulted to the village and moved into it on line. Numerous gunship runs were made on the village since they were receiving fire from it.

I don't recall the actual number of VC dead reported for the operation (approximately 25) but my count and the official count were the same. I know this because I was questioned about this fact specifically at the time.

Tracer rounds from gunships started fires in some of the hooches. A strong breeze that day spread the fire. It was impossible to contain it until after all the VC had either been killed, captured or fled from the village up into the rockpile. It has come to my attention that claims were made that numerous civilians were seriously wounded. I treated all civilians wounded. There were less than six, only one seriously. Two civilians were killed.

I remember the DCO, COL Franklin, coming up and talking to me while I was carrying an eleven year old child who had received some shrapnel wounds and had a lot of blood on him—though he was not seriously wounded. The child had a laceration on the foot and was in mild neurogenic shock which was why he had to be carried. He was not in danger of losing life or limb. One woman had been killed in a hooch that had received gunship fire. A machine gun was firing at the gunship. I remember this clearly because a soldier who was part of the prisoner interrogation team from Brigade was taking pictures of the dead woman and mumbling that *LIFE* would like to get this one. An old man had been killed also but I have no knowledge of the circumstances.

The other operation was also along the coast. I don't know the name of the village. The Battalion had made an amphibious assault on it earlier in the year. In this operation no civilians were wounded and a large number (approximately 36) of VC were killed. There was close contact fighting, in some cases, hand to hand.

These two operations were typical of those conducted by LTC Herbert: minimum US and civilian casualties; no destructions of civilian property if possible; maximum enemy casualties.

LTC Herbert never abused his officers. He treated them as men. He would give praise when it was due but made us face up to our mistakes. He counseled his commanders aside, not in front of his men.

My one regret from my tour in Vietnam was that LTC Herbert did not finish his full tour with the 2d Battalion.

Appendix E. *Statements by company commanders, 2d Battalion, 173d Airborne Brigade.*

1) Headquarters Company: Captain Szabolcs M. de Gyurky

I, CPT Szabolcs M. de Gyurky, 233-60-1331, during the period March, April and May 1968 was commanding officer of HHC, Battalion 503 Infantry 173d Airborne Brigade, located at LZ English, Bong Son, Vietnam. The 2d Battalion, 503d Infantry, of the 173d Airborne Brigade at this time was commanded by LTC Anthony B. Herbert, until he was relieved of command for reasons I am not completely familiar with.

As HHC Commander, I was almost always in a position to observe him, and my frequent trips to the field on combat operations as well as administrative matters made me very familiar with LTC Herbert, from a personal point of view, as well as how the troops in general felt about him, by talking with my colleagues and fellow officers and NCOs of our battalion.

My observations from the daily contact with LTC Herbert at the nightly staff conferences, as well as constant personal and official conferences were as follows:

LTC Herbert is an absolutely hard task master, very demanding of his subordinates, accepting only the most professional performance, rejecting all others. From a personal point of view, I was pleased with this situation, because there was never a doubt in my mind about what I did right and what I did wrong. This drive of LTC Herbert's for perfection, I believe, comes from an intense love of country and pride in the Army especially the infantry and airborne. It is the kind of pride which makes him stand out from all other officers I know. His loyalty and devotion to his men was not a show but a practical thing resulting in a low casualty count of our troops, and achievement of great tactical success. Only discipline in its finest form will permit "Esprit de Corps" and only a unit with pride in itself will conduct itself in battle with honor, utter bravery and humanity. We were such a battalion. LTC Herbert, when speaking to the troops, could make the lowest (reg) recruits chest grow two inches bigger, in the pride of being a United States Infantry Soldier. I witnessed this many times.

I know of not one officer, or enlisted man who did not respect and trust him. During the period he commanded the 2d Battalion 503d Infantry there was a general remark about our battalion in the Brigade, as "2d Battalion (Separate) 503d Infantry." It may have been a jest, but it was true the battalion was proud, honorable, military and American to the core.

Never during a briefing as I recall, was a stress made on *large body counts*. If we discussed combat operations it was to gain contact with the enemy and destroy (of) or capture him. This we did, because it was in our character as American Airborne Soldiers, to love a good fight. Company commanders who turned in the battle results were accepted at their word. I must stress this point, LTC Herbert, by being an honorable and brave leader gained my loyalty, and that of the rest of our battalion. He certainly did have our loyalty out of respect because he was extremely exacting in all his demands and we worked twenty-four hours a day to do his bidding. When LTC Herbert was relieved it came as a shock, no one had expected it, and my feelings and those around me were, "that it hurt." At first most of us wanted to leave the Brigade by submitting 1049s. Colonel called us together for a staff conference and told us, that he would not accept such talk. That we had to remain in the battalion because the next battalion commander needed us, so most of us remained.

It was known to me, although of course I had no proof, that there were differences between the Brigade Deputy Commander and Colonel Herbert. I personally attributed this to the fact that both were tough leaders and that therefore a personality conflict arose. As a company commander I only knew that Colonel Herbert, during our staff conferences demanded of us complete adherence to Brigade policy and obedience to the desires of the DCO. I am completely aware of this personally down to detail. For example as HHC CO I did not take seriously a policy of the DCO on maximum emphasis placed on ice cream for the combat units. Up to this time, if we (nee) had ice cream it was always nice, if we did not, it was nothing to worry about. I was mistaken, and suffered for it somewhat. When helicopters were available they were standing by for ice cream runs, and I was responsible for the ice cream not melting. In combat this does not seem to be very important, but it was adhered to to the letter. We, especially I, were aware of the personality conflict between the DCO and Colonel Herbert. Never in my presence did Colonel Herbert say or speak in any but good naturedly manner about our DCO, his loyalty as an officer and gentleman did not permit it. If he would have we would never have felt toward him the way we did. Our battalion did not go for the body count racket, not from what I am familiar with. The mission of the U.S. Infantry as stated, is what we pursued. On one occasion, I recall the Colonel, LTC Herbert giving the credit for enemy killed by us, to the Navy and Air Force, this included the war trophies we captured. We wanted the pistols and rifles, and during the briefing he told us that, we really did not need the body count tally, and the Navy and Air Force would be real proud if we told them of the fine support and gave them credit for it.

Perhaps to me personally it was too important, to be serving under a commander in whom I could place absolute confidence. I am an individual who still believes that an officer must lead by example in everything. I have, in twelve years of service met only four officers senior to me who met all the ideals I placed in the service. LTC Anthony B. Herbert is one of these. His strength to me, as seen through the eyes of a company commander was his integrity and love of truth, which he always told bluntly, and never backed down from it or apologized for it, his love of country and unshaken confidence in the American Soldier, his devotion to duty and his loyalty to his superiors and subordinates.

Finally he is a brave soldier, braver I have not known, with a quality which makes men, who are not panicky at the thought of dying follow him into hell if he wants to go there. This is my opinion, sacred to me as a servant and officer of my country, and sworn before God to be true.

Company A: 2) Captain L. P. Forepaugh. *Hearing of the board of officers, Article 138 investigation.*

> *CPT LAWRENCE P. FOREPAUGH was called as a witness and testified as follows:*

RCDR: Do you swear or affirm that the evidence you are about to give in the case now in hearing shall be the truth, the whole truth, and nothing but the truth. So help you God?

CPT FOREPAUGH: I do.

RCDR: Would you state your name, grade, organization, and duty assignment.

CPT FOREPAUGH: Lawrence P. Forepaugh, Captain, Infantry, Command Officer, Alpha Company, 2/503d.

PRES: Were you Commanding Officer of Alpha Company, 2/503d, when Colonel Herbert was battalion commander?

CPT FOREPAUGH: Yes, sir.

PRES: What did you think of him as a battalion commander?

CPT FOREPAUGH: Fine, sir, as far as I was concerned.

PRES: Was he a better battalion commander than most of them that you've served under?

CPT FOREPAUGH: Well, he was a different type of individual, but he was fine for me. I thought he was fine, no problems with me.

PRES: Which way was he different?

CPT FOREPAUGH: Well, he was very aggressive, sir, very aggressive—which was fine—more so than many people.

PRES: Was he over-aggressive in pushing people into doing things?

CPT FOREPAUGH: No, sir, he was very realistic.

PRES: Was he unduly abrasive to any of you officers or enlisted men, or noncommissioned officers?

CPT FOREPAUGH: I have heard stories of that, sir, but it was not in the time frame that I was there. Anything I would say, I know it would be pure hearsay.

PRES: You heard it from men in your company?

CPT FOREPAUGH: Well, actually, sir, the first time I heard it was from the person who originally had the company. The reason I took over the company was because this former company commander did not get along.

489

PRES: Was this Captain Cording?

CPT FOREPAUGH: Yes, sir.

PRES: Were you present when Colonel Herbert took over the battalion and made some remarks to the battalion?

CPT FOREPAUGH: No, sir, I've only been in the battalion a month and two days. I came on the 28th of last month. He wasn't there very long.

PRES: 28th of March.

CPT FOREPAUGH: Yes, sir.

PRES: So you were only with him a week or so.

CPT FOREPAUGH: Yes, sir.

PRES: But during that time you grew to respect him as a battalion commander.

CPT FOREPAUGH: Yes, sir, there were several recommendations I made to the man and he said, "Fine, get it done." Just like that. He treated me with respect in that time frame.

RCDR: Do you think he was a team player in terms of supporting the Brigade Commander's policies?

CPT FOREPAUGH: Again, sir, the time period that I was here was so short with Colonel Herbert that anything I would say on that would be pure hearsay. Let me tell you this. I came here on the 27th. I flew in from An Khe on a helicopter. I walked over and put my pack down and he said, "Come on, we're going out." We went out and killed a bunch of VC. And the next day I went up to my company. And that was the last close contact we had, or I had with Colonel Herbert—just an afternoon and an evening in the battalion area. So I went up to the company on the following day and I guess I saw Colonel Herbert two, three, maybe four times when he'd come out to visit. So I didn't know what was going on at Brigade and whether or not we were countering it, or what.

PRES: From your point of view as a company commander you felt that he was a good man and a good battalion commander.

CPT. FOREPAUGH: Yes, sir, but I think it has to be stated that I was only there about a week, a rather short period of time to judge any man. Just as long as that's part of it.

PRES: All right. Thank you very much.

(*CPT. FOREPAUGH withdrew from the room.*)

3) Company B: Captain William Hill

Author's Note: At the time of the investigation, Captain Hill, having been wounded in combat and consequently evacuated, was not available for a statement.

Since then, however, Captain Hill has made a supportive statement under oath which has subsequently been classified by the U.S. Army. Since Captain Hill is still on active duty as a member of the Army in good standing, his request to not publish his statement at this time is honored.

AJH

4) Company C: Captain Christopher J. Dorney

Lt. Colonel Anthony Herbert was my battalion commander in 2/503d Infantry (ABN), 173d Airborne Brigade, APO San Francisco, 96250. During this period I served as company commander of C Company.

My personal opinion was that the battalion increased in tactical proficiency and that the morale and efficiency of the men was outstanding, due to his personal leadership.

As the commander of C Company I was never issued an illegal order by him or by any member of his staff. All reports rendered by me concerning enemy Killed In Action or Wounded In Action were accurate and were reported to Brigade by the battalion accurately.

On several occasions I witnessed Lt. Col Herbert's actions on search and clear operations. I found him to be demanding in the accomplishment of the mission. In all these operations I did not witness nor hear of any illegal actions by him. On the contrary, I was constantly being reminded by him to watch out for the safety of the civilian populace and to avoid the destruction of their "hooches," unnecessarily.

I feel that the battalion killed more V.C. during this period because of aggressive leadership and the application of tactical techniques. Lt. Colonel Herbert increased ambush patrols, forced us to carry less weight and reacted swiftly to all contacts and intelligence. The mood of the battalion during this time was that of trying to make contact with the enemy. There was never an undercurrent, however, of killing or destroying for the sake of death and destruction. The only undercurrent was that we were better than the V.C. and that we could move and fight on his terms. I personally attribute this to Lt. Colonel Herbert. His personal leadership and actions influenced every man in his battalion. I feel that every man who served under him during this period would be proud to do so again.

5) Company D: Captain James M. Grimshaw

I, James M. Grimshaw, Captain, Infantry, United States Army, SSN 162-34-7950, was Commanding Officer of Co. D, 3d Battalion (ABN), 503d Infantry, 173d Airborne Brigade in the Republic of South Vietnam during the period 10 December 1968 thru 29 June 1969. I served under LTC Anthony B. Herbert during the time he was my Battalion Commander, which was the period from on or about 11 February 1969 to on or about 10 April 1969. At no time during his tenure as Battalion Commander was he abusive to me or the other officers and men of my Company. Under his command, the Battalion led the Brigade in the number of enemy soldiers killed and, during the month of February 1969, my Company accounted for the most enemy killed in the Battalion. I never reported to LTC Herbert any enemy casualties unless a body could be produced as evidence. This was according to LTC Herbert's instructions to me when he assumed command of the unit. He reiterated this order several times during his command. On several occasions when I returned to the Battalion rear area at LZ English, Bong Son, Republic of Vietnam, I checked the enemy killed or wounded figures which were posted on a chart in the Battalion Briefing Room. Each time I checked, the only figures shown for my Company were exactly as I had reported them. Because I had worked on the Brigade Staff before assuming command of my Company, I knew several officers who still worked on the staff. Usually when I visited these officers on my return to the rear area, I saw them at their place of duty. One of these places was the Brigade S3 where a "Body Count" Chart was maintained by the Brigade for all the Battalions. I never saw any discrepancies in the figures which would indicate a gross inflation of the 2d Battalion's report. It should be noted that at this time all Battalions were under a Brigade rating system and one of the methods of measuring a Battalion's success was by the number of enemy soldiers it killed, captured, or wounded. On an operation during the night of 4 March 1969, LTC Herbert accompanied my Company on our mission to link up with Company B of our Battalion and encircle a village complex in Tam Quan District, Binh Dinh Province. When the enemy discovered our presence, they tried to escape through our cordon. One of my platoons received fire and killed one enemy soldier. This was determined by actual body count. My platoon leader had initially reported three enemy killed because he had seen three enemy soldiers fall during the exchange of small arms fire in the predawn darkness. When it was light enough to search for the bodies, they could not be found. Later that morning when Colonel Joseph Franklin, Deputy Brigade Commander, talked with LTC Herbert at my location, LTC Herbert mentioned the three bodies that we thought my Company had killed, but he further stated that we only had proof of one body and, therefore, would officially report the same. Only one body was reported. LTC Herbert is the finest officer and Battalion Commander for whom I ever worked. His integrity is unquestionable. During his command, the morale and esprit-de-corps of my Company and the Battalion was the highest it ever was during my entire tour. His personal bravery and outstanding leadership inspired the officers and men to put forth a greater effort. LTC Herbert never interfered in my job. He let me command my Company my way. He offered me advice and counseling only when it was necessary. He demanded that we did our jobs properly and rewarded us justly. While he was the Battalion Commander, our unit was a well-oiled fighting machine—a close knit unit that accomplished more than the other Battalions in the Brigade.

Appendix F. *Statement by Major Leonard H. Dancheck (Conversation with Major Paul Ray regarding army policy on investigations of war crime charges).*

On 7 May 1970 I was in Charlottesville, Virginia at the Army JAGC School interviewing a potential witness for the case that I was defending, This case was being prosecuted by the Army JAGC Office at Headquarters, First United States Army, Fort Meade, Maryland and arose out of the charges preferred at the direction of the LTG Peers' Investigating Group. This witness had been spotted for me by Major Paul Ray. Before and after the witness interview, I had the occasion to talk with Major Ray who was assigned to the JAGC School and who was also a counsel in the Fort Meade My Lai cases. Major Ray and I discussed several topics but our conversation eventually turned to war crimes—their incidence in Viet Nam and the problems and dilemmas they posed for Army commanders and lawyers. Major Ray related his own experiences as Brigade Judge Advocate of the 173d Airborne Brigade, working for a BG Barnes. Major Ray stated that his commander predicted a witchhunt on the subject of war crimes coming out of the Vietnamese War. BG Barnes recalled Senator McCarthy's witchhunt into the Malmedy Massacre interrogations sometime after the conclusion of World War II. As a protective measure, BG Barnes placed emphasis on the investigation of any incident that smacked of being a war crime. To the best of my knowledge and recollection, Major Ray intimated that there were times when these investigations were conducted in such a fashion so as to satisfy the requirements of existing regulations but in a way as to not jeopardize the personnel and commanders involved and the combat effectiveness of the brigade. Major Ray did not identify the author of the policy of muting war crimes investigations in the brigade when circumstances dictated.

Index

Abbott, Sgt. Major Charles T., 124, 144–146

Accousti, Major Kenneth W., 247, 248, 318–319

Airborne initiation rite, 81–83

Allen, Gen. Richard, 120–121, 148–151, 154–155, 159, 164–165, 458, 459, 462–463

ambush techniques, 133–134, 269–270

Amiorri, Mike, 434–45

An Khe (Vietnam), 115 ff.

Angel, Lt. Col. Jack, 113, 115, 119–120, 144–146, 147–148

artillery, usage of, in Vietnam, 208–210

ARVN (South Vietnamese Army), 265–266, 320

ASCOM City (Korea), 41–42

Ashley, Col. Lew, 406

atrocities, in Vietnam, 299–302, 357–360, 395–396; see also Cu Loi incident; U.S. Army, handling of atrocities by

Barnes, Gen. John W., 165, 167, 169–172, 191, 201–202, 266, 267–268, 388, 399–400, 409–412, 430–431, 432, 436, 438–439, 444, 447, 448, 449, 451, 459

Basic Infantry Officer's Course (BIOC), 67–70

basic training, 25 ff.

Beacham, Major, 313–317, 379–381, 470–471, 474

Beamer, Dr. Yancy, 420, 421, 447

Belieu, Kenneth, 435–437

Berry, Gen. Sid, 208

Bethea, Lt. Col. John D., 184–188, 202, 461

Bittorie, Sgt. Major John, 154–156, 163, 170–171, 178–180, 226–227, 289–290, 477–478

black marketing, 144, 265–266

body count, 376, 377, 378, 468–469

Bowers, Capt. Norman L., 312, 357–358

Boyer, Major Henry, Jr., 213–214, 224, 225, 279–280, 386–387, 479–480

Brigade Operations in Vietnam (Berry), 208

Bumgarner, Sgt. Roy E., Jr., 225–229, 363–368

Capitol Military Assistance Command (Saigon), 406, 408
Carmody, Sgt., 299–301, 352–353, 357–358
casualty rate, 178–179
Cavett, Dick, 443, 452–453, 454, 455
Childers, Master Sgt. R. L., 196–197, 480–482
childhood, 5 ff.
Chinese Army, in Korean War, 43 ff.
CIA (Central Intelligence Agency), 101–102, 105–106
coal mining, 6 ff.
Command and General Staff College (CGSC), 421
Congo, mission to, 93–95
Connor, Gen. Albert, 429
Conquest to Nowhere (Herbert), 66
Cording, Capt. Louis K., 206–208, 213, 291, 463
Cordon and Search missions, 302–303, 307–308
Crouch, Major James E., 122, 123–124, 139, 176–177, 184–188
Cu Loi incident, 246 ff.; see also atrocities
Cuba, plans for invasion of, 90–91
Cushman, Gen. John H., 441

Dahlonega camp, 70 ff.
Dancheck, Major Leonard H., 493
Davis, Chaplain, 214–216, 327–328, 463–464, 479–480
Delamater, Col. B. F., 458–459
"dinging," 171–172
Dominican Republic, U.S. intervention in, 99 ff.
Donovan, Capt. Jack R., 482–483
Doolittle Commission, 25–26
Dorney, Capt. Christopher J., 236–237, 491

"environmental adjustment," in Vietnam, 339–340
Ethiopia, 109
European tour, 61–62
Expert Infantryman's Badge (EIB), 80–81

1st Infantry Regt., transfer to, 81
fixed defense, fallacy of, 117
Forepaugh, Capt. L. P., 291, 489–490
Ft. Benning, 30–32, 67–70, 90–91
Ft. Dix, basic training at, 25 ff.
Ft. Leavenworth, 422 ff.
Ft. Lewis Ranger Creek Camp, 32–33
Ft. McPherson, 3–4, 429
Ft. Monmouth, 39–40
fragging, 153–154
Franklin, Lt. Col. Joseph Ross, 160–162, 167–172, 191–193, 197, 212–213, 224–225, 259–261, 274–275, 278–279, 289–290, 291, 297–299, 302, 310–312, 316, 318–319, 330–331, 349, 358–360, 393–394, 397–398, 399–401, 412–416, 431, 433, 436, 441, 444, 447, 448, 449, 450–451, 459, 460 ff.

Green, Lt. Col. John, 405–406
Green Berets, 91
Green Line, 116–117
Grimshaw, Capt. Jim, 192–194, 237, 275–276, 305–307, 418–419, 491–492
Guelker, Col. C. W., 442
Gyurky, Capt. Szabolcs de, 237–238, 487–488

Hansard, Col. Fred, 430
Hay, Gen. John, 421, 422, 423–427
Heintz, Capt. Dick, 442, 444, 445, 446, 452, 454
helicopters, misuse of, in Vietnam, 266–268
Henniger, Lt. Col., 317–321
Hensley, Major Carl, 431–432, 437–438
Herbert, Marygrace Natale, 36–39, 64–65, 67, 79, 180–184, 420–421, 454, 455
Herbert family, 1, 5 ff., 21
Herminie, Pa., 6 ff., 37–39
high school, completion of, 36–38
Hill, Capt. William, 236, 237, 490–491
Hill 868, battle for, 57–60
hunting, 5–8

Indian-Pakistani War (1966), 107–108
intelligence assignments, 63–64, 103 ff., 422 ff.
intelligence briefings, 281–283

Jones, Ruby, 446

Kane, Major Peter, 408
Kelley, Father Bernard, 14–16, 17
Kennedy, John F., 90–91
Killer Fire Base, 372–376
Korean Army (ROKs), 42
Korean War, 40, 42 ff.

Latimer, Doc, 16–17
Leopoldville, Congo, 93–95
LeRay, Lt., 270–273

McCaan, Lt. Thomas H., 388–390, 392, 439

Malinowski, Benjamin F., 444–445
marijuana, use of, in Vietnam, 157–160, 335
Mataxis, Col. Theodore, 84, 85, 88
Meurrens, Major, 367, 368, 369
Middle East, mission to, 102 ff.
Military Intelligence (MI), failures of, in Vietnam, 356
Millhouse, Col. Felix, 444, 452
Mobutu, Col. Joseph, 93–95
Morgan, Charles, Jr., 442, 444, 447
Mountain Ranger Training Camp, 70 ff.
My Lai cases, 430–431

Newman, Col. Buck, 420–421
Nicholson, Col. 193–196, 201–202
Nim, Col., 324–327
Noriega, Capt., 236, 323–324

173d Airborne Brigade, 112, 127–128, 131–132, 136–137
Operation Missouri, 428–429
Operation November Demon, 424–428
Operation Phoenix, 105–106
Operation Skyscope, 330–331

Pakistan; see Indian-Pakistani War
paratrooper training, 30–32, 86–87
Pathfinder training, 77
Paulk, Lt. Col., 445, 446, 454
Peers, Gen. William, 162, 163, 328–329, 430–431
Pennsylvania National Guard, 67
Pentomic concept, 78, 88–89
Pippen, Larry, 269, 341–343
plague, inoculation against, 292–294
Potter, Lt. Larry, III., 195–196, 239, 484–486
PX, abuses of, 118–119

497

radio school, 39–40

Ranger Creek Camp. Ft. Lewis, 32–33

Rangers, 83–84; *see also* Mountain Ranger Training Camp

Ray, Major Paul H., 130–132, 154, 186, 188–189

redress proceedings, 408 ff., 460 ff.

Reid, Col. John, 445, 446, 454

Ricci, Joe, 19–20

ROKs; *see* Korean Army

Roosevelt, Eleanor, 62

Russ, Gen. Joseph, 408, 409, 412, 415, 417, 420, 421

St. Edward's R. C. Church, 14–16

Schneider, Lt. Col. Robert, 4, 455–456

scuba-diving training, 77

Shearer, Uncle Joe, 13–14

Shotwell, Lt., 194–195

Sisler, Capt. Mason B., 433–444

16th Infantry Regt., 8th Div., 77, 79 ff.

Skeins, Major Harry, 202–203, 204–205, 211

Skorzeny, Otto, 84–86

Solkinus family, 8 ff.

Special Forces, 91 ff.

Spizzali, Tony, 22

Stanton, Jay, 194–195

Street Without Joy (Fall), 92

STRIKE command, 102, 103

Stryker, Lt. Emil J., 33–35

Tally, Major Francis P., 239, 483–484

Theibert family, 9 ff.

Triangular concept, 77–78, 88–89

Truman, Harry S, 61, 428–429

Tufts, Col. Henry H., 437

Turkish soldiers, in Korean War, 45–48

University of Pittsburgh, 66

U.S. Army; direct commission from, 70; discharge from, 36, 64–65; enlistment in, 22–23; handling of atrocities in Vietnam by, 397 ff., 407 ff., 430 ff., 448 ff.; officers' corps in, 240–242; postwar changes in, 25–27; re-enlistment in, 39; retirement from 2–5; *see also* Vietnam

Vietnam: Operation Phoenix, 105–106; service in, 112 ff., 198 ff., 408 ff.; *see also* U.S. Army

war crimes, 408 ff., 493; *see also* atrocities; Cu Loi incident

Warden, Sgt. Wallace A., 217–219, 243–244, 261

Weltner, Charles L., 430

Werner, Major Walter J., 151–152, 165–166, 176, 184, 187–188

West Germany, service in, 77 ff.

West Pointers, 74–75, 279

Westmoreland, Gen. William, 240, 241, 430

winter survival training, 32–35

Wooten, James T., 443

Yalu River, retreat from, 43 ff.